Tammy Woodman

On Her Own Ground

The Life and Times of Madam C. J. Walker

—⟡—

A'Lelia Bundles

A LISA DREW BOOK

SCRIBNER

NEW YORK LONDON TORONTO SYDNEY SINGAPORE

SCRIBNER
1230 Avenue of the Americas
New York, NY 10020

SCRIBNER and design are trademarks of Macmillan Library Reference USA, Inc.,
used under license by Simon & Schuster, the publisher of this work.

Designed by Colin Joh
Text set in Goudy Old Style

Manufactured in the United States of America

1 3 5 7 9 10 8 6 4 2

Permissions are on page 387.

Note: The dustjacket is a composite of two photographs. The foreground photograph
of Madam Walker at the wheel of her Model T was taken in Indianapolis in 1912.
The background photograph of Villa Lewaro was taken after its construction in 1918.

Library of Congress Cataloging-in-Publication Data
Bundles, A'Lelia Perry.
On her own ground: the life and times of Madam C. J. Walker/A'Lelia Bundles.
p. cm.
"A Lisa Drew Book."
Includes bibliographical references and index.
1. Walker, C. J., Madam. 1867–1919. 2. Afro-American women executives—
Biography. 3. Cosmetics industry—United States—History. I. Title.

HD9970.5.C672 W3533 2001
338.7'66855'092—dc21
[B]
00–057372

ISBN 0-684-82582-1

In memory of my mother,
A'Lelia Mae Perry Bundles,
who knew this was my story to tell

Contents

Biological Ancestors of Fairy Mae Bryant (Mae Walker)

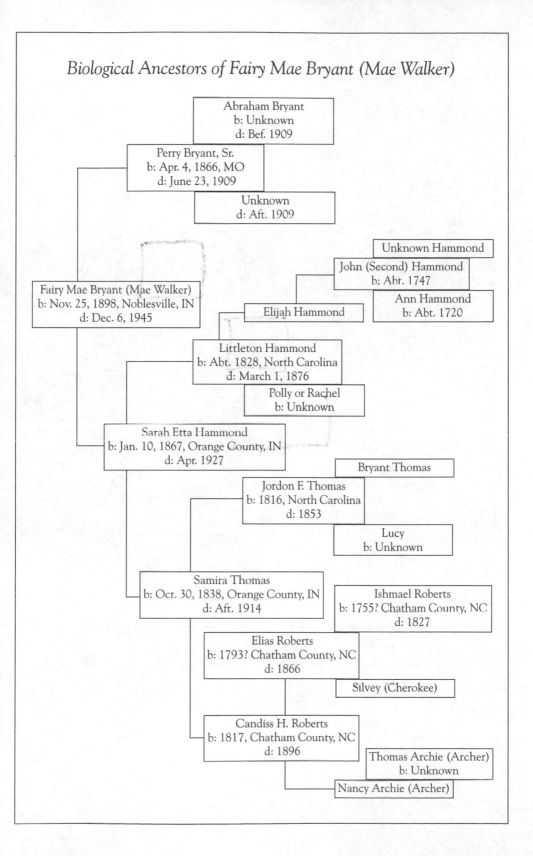

Abraham Bryant
b: Unknown
d: Bef. 1909

Perry Bryant, Sr.
b: Apr. 4, 1866, MO
d: June 23, 1909

Unknown
d: Aft. 1909

Fairy Mae Bryant (Mae Walker)
b: Nov. 25, 1898, Noblesville, IN
d: Dec. 6, 1945

Unknown Hammond

John (Second) Hammond
b: Abt. 1747

Ann Hammond
b: Abt. 1720

Elijah Hammond

Littleton Hammond
b: Abt. 1828, North Carolina
d: March 1, 1876

Polly or Rachel
b: Unknown

Sarah Etta Hammond
b: Jan. 10, 1867, Orange County, IN
d: Apr. 1927

Bryant Thomas

Jordon F. Thomas
b: 1816, North Carolina
d: 1853

Lucy
b: Unknown

Samira Thomas
b: Oct. 30, 1838, Orange County, IN
d: Aft. 1914

Ishmael Roberts
b: 1755? Chatham County, NC
d: 1827

Elias Roberts
b: 1793? Chatham County, NC
d: 1866

Silvey (Cherokee)

Candiss H. Roberts
b: 1817, Chatham County, NC
d: 1896

Thomas Archie (Archer)
b: Unknown

Nancy Archie (Archer)

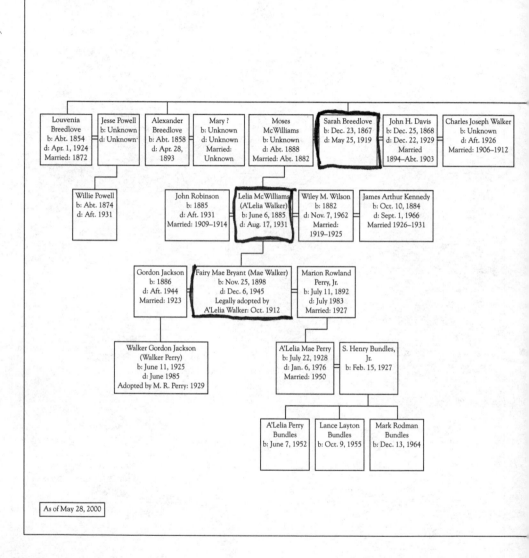

| Louvenia Breedlove
b: Abt. 1854
d: Apr. 1, 1924
Married: 1872 | Jesse Powell
b: Unknown
d: Unknown | Alexander Breedlove
b: Abt. 1858
d: Apr. 28, 1893 | Mary ?
b: Unknown
d: Unknown
Married: Unknown | Moses McWilliams
b: Unknown
d: Abt. 1888
Married: Abt. 1882 | Sarah Breedlove
b: Dec. 23, 1867
d: May 25, 1919 | John H. Davis
b: Dec. 25, 1868
d: Dec. 22, 1929
Married 1894–Abt. 1903 | Charles Joseph Walker
b: Unknown
d: Aft. 1926
Married: 1906–1912 |

Willie Powell
b: Abt. 1874
d: Aft. 1931

John Robinson
b: 1885
d: Aft. 1931
Married: 1909–1914

Lelia McWilliams
(A'Lelia Walker)
b: June 6, 1885
d: Aug. 17, 1931

Wiley M. Wilson
b: 1882
d: Nov. 7, 1962
Married: 1919–1925

James Arthur Kennedy
b: Oct. 10, 1884
d: Sept. 1, 1966
Married 1926–1931

Gordon Jackson
b: 1886
d: Aft. 1944
Married: 1923

Fairy Mae Bryant (Mae Walker)
b: Nov. 25, 1898
d: Dec. 6, 1945
Legally adopted by
A'Lelia Walker: Oct. 1912

Marion Rowland
Perry, Jr.
b: July 11, 1892
d: July 1983
Married: 1927

Walker Gordon Jackson
(Walker Perry)
b: June 11, 1925
d: June 1985
Adopted by M. R. Perry: 1929

A'Lelia Mae Perry
b: July 22, 1928
d: Jan. 6, 1976
Married: 1950

S. Henry Bundles,
Jr.
b: Feb. 15, 1927

A'Lelia Perry
Bundles
b: June 7, 1952

Lance Layton
Bundles
b: Oct. 9, 1955

Mark Rodman
Bundles
b: Dec. 13, 1964

As of May 28, 2000

Descendants of Owen Breedlove, Sr.

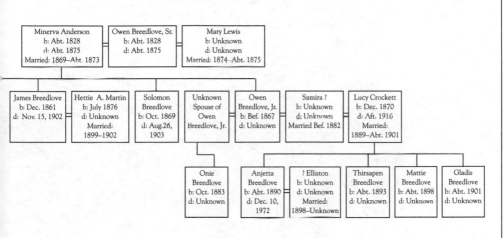

On Her Own Ground

Prologue

Madam C. J. Walker's story has always deserved an expansive loom on which to weave the threads of her legendary life with the broad themes and major events of American history. As my great-great-grandmother's biographer—and as a journalist who loves a well-told story—I consider it to be my good fortune both that she was born in 1867 on the plantation where General Ulysses S. Grant staged the 1863 Siege of Vicksburg and that one of her brothers joined other former slaves in the 1879 mass exodus to the North from Louisiana and Mississippi. I could not have fabricated a more perfect scenario than her confrontation with Booker T. Washington at his 1912 National Negro Business League convention or her 1916 arrival in Harlem on the eve of America's entry into World War I. I could not have invented her 1917 visit to the White House to protest lynching or her decision to build a mansion near the Westchester County estates of John D. Rockefeller and Jay Gould. Certainly when I learned that she had been considered a "Negro subversive" in 1918 and had been put under surveillance by a black War Department spy, I was convinced that reality indeed was more interesting than most fiction.

It has surely been a bonus for me that Madam Walker knew so many of the other African American luminaries of her time because the work of their biographers has provided invaluable guidance. From the correspondence, papers and books of antilynching activist Ida B. Wells-Barnett, educators Mary McLeod Bethune and Booker T. Washington, National Association for the Advancement of Colored People executive secretary James Weldon Johnson, *Crisis* editor W.E.B. Du Bois, labor leader A. Philip Randolph and others, I have been able to resurrect long-forgotten relationships.

As a pioneer of the modern cosmetics industry and the founder of the Madam C. J. Walker Manufacturing Company, Madam Walker created marketing schemes, training opportunities and distribution strategies as innovative as those of any entrepreneur of her time. As an early advocate of women's economic independence, she provided lucrative incomes for thousands of African American women who otherwise would have been consigned to jobs as farm laborers, washerwomen and maids. As a philanthropist, she reconfigured the philosophy of charitable giving in the black community with her unprecedented contributions to the YMCA and the NAACP. As a political activist, she dreamed of organizing her sales agents to use their economic clout to protest lynching and racial injustice. As much as any woman of the twentieth century, Madam Walker paved the way for the profound social changes that altered women's place in American society.

My personal journey to write *On Her Own Ground*, the first comprehensive biography of my great-great-grandmother really began before I could read. The Walker women—Madam, her daughter A'Lelia Walker and my grandmother Mae Walker—were already beckoning me at an early age, sometimes whispering, sometimes clamoring with the message that I must tell their story. In a faint childhood memory, their spirits envelop me in filtered gray light beneath a tall window inside my grandfather's apartment. On a nearby dresser, just beyond my reach, I can see their sepia faces inside hand-carved frames.

Even as a little girl I sensed that these grandmothers belonged not only to me but to the world and to those who would claim them for their own dreams and fantasies. Black history books had long recited the outlines of Madam Walker's classic American rags-to-riches rise from uneducated washerwoman to international entrepreneur and social activist, from daughter of slaves to hair care industry pioneer and philanthropist. Poet Langston Hughes crowned A'Lelia Walker the "joy-goddess of Harlem's 1920s." The Negro press fancied Mae—A'Lelia's adopted daughter and only legal heir—a tan Cinderella. By the time I discovered the Walker women's public mythology, they had already begun to draw me into the world of their private truths.

My grandfather, Marion Rowland Perry, Jr., first met Mae during the summer of 1927 at Villa Lewaro, Madam Walker's lavish Irvington-on-Hudson, New York, mansion. A handsome young attorney and World War I army officer, he was quite proud of a lineage that included college-educated parents. Mae was a recent divorcée and the future Walker heiress, whose thick, waist-length hair had helped sell thousands of tins of Madam C. J. Walker's Wonderful Hair Grower. That weekend, A'Lelia Walker invited Marion to the Cotton Club with *her* friends—and without Mae—to take the measure of the man she considered a potential son-in-law. She discreetly slipped him a hundred-dollar bill to gauge his comfort with paying large tabs.

Apparently he passed her test, for a few weeks later, on August 27, he and Mae drove to Port Chester, New York, in his green Pierce-Arrow to be married by a justice of the peace. The following July, my mother, A'Lelia Mae Perry, was born.

In 1955, when my mother, my father, S. Henry Bundles, and I moved to Indianapolis, I was three years old and Mae had been dead for nearly a decade. For a few weeks while we waited to move into our house, I slept in a bedroom of my grandfather's apartment surrounded by Mae's personal treasures. I remember that, in the months afterward, whenever "Pa Pa" opened his front door to greet us, the gluey aroma of roast lamb, Lucky Strikes and old-man musk coated my nostrils. In the entryway, as my mother knelt to adjust my hair bow and smooth my three long braids, my eyes always fixed upon a tall, moss-green Chinese lacquer secretary. Letters, keys, stamps and paper clips tumbled from its tiny gold-trimmed drawers and secret cubbyholes. A serene Ming Dynasty maiden stood guard on the door of its locked upper cabinet. Even before I learned it had belonged to Madam and the first A'Lelia, I was tempted by its mysteries.

Beyond the foyer, the apartment rambled down a long, hushed hall. At one end, Pa Pa's sleeping alcove opened onto a sitting room crammed with the Walker women's belongings—A'Lelia's first editions of Jean Toomer's *Cane* and Countee Cullen's *Color*, Mae's gold harp and Madam's crystal Tiffany vases. At the other end, toward the rear of the apartment, two shadowy bedrooms—one of them Mae's—and a rarely used dining room led to a bright, white-tiled kitchen where a dented porcelain pot always simmered with soup bones and stock, and where Pa Pa held court at his knife-scarred oak table.

While Pa Pa and my mother talked, I escaped into Mae's room, drawn time and again by a mauve moiré silk vanity. Even now I can feel a quiet enchantment as I recall grasping cool ivory mah-jongg tiles and miniature enameled King Tut mummy charms. I remember a fluffy ostrich fan in one drawer and mother-of-pearl opera glasses in another. The more I stirred Mae's belongings, the more the scent of her Shalimar dusting powder emerged, masking the familiar grandfather mustiness that clung to all the other rooms. Each piece of clothing, each photograph, each bejeweled mirror and monogrammed napkin became a genie's lamp waiting to be rubbed.

Three blocks from Pa Pa's apartment, my mother worked as vice president of the Madam C. J. Walker Manufacturing Company, the hair care products firm her great-grandmother had founded in 1906. Often when we arrived at the block-long flatiron building in Momma's 1955 black Mercury, Whitfield, the janitor, would be waving at us from beneath the marquee of the Walker Theatre. His official job title notwithstanding, I still think of him as the ambassador of the Walker Building, full of news about the boiler, the freight elevator and whoever had just gone into the Walker Beauty Shop. Opened in 1927, the brick-and-terra-cotta structure housed an elaborately decorated, African-themed theater that offered first-run movies and live jazz. Generations of the city's African Americans had danced under the rotating mirrored globe in the upstairs Casino ballroom, met for Sunday afternoon dinner in the Coffee Pot or walked past the third-floor law offices of attorneys Mercer Mance and Rufus Kuykendall on their way to see Dr. Lewis or Dr. Cox.

For me, riding the elevator was always an adventure. Once inside, I fixated on Mary Martin's shiny, finger-waved tresses and cherry-rouged cheeks as she snapped shut the accordion brass gate with one fluid flick of her wrist, then lifted us four floors toward my mother's office. Another glissade of Mary's manicured hands and the door clanked open. The percussive clickety-clack of my mother's spike heels led me across a cayenne-flecked terrazzo lobby. With each step the sweet fragrance of bergamot and Glossine from the factory downstairs made me wish for candy. First we passed Marie Overstreet (the bookkeeper, who would have been a CPA had she been born sixty years later), then Mary Pendegraph (the tall, dignified beauty who speedily processed hundreds of orders each week), then Edith Shanklin (the efficient Addressograph operator who always had a gossip morsel for my mother). In Momma's office, I must have imagined myself a businesswoman as I played with her hand-cranked adding machine and manual typewriter, sure that my random keystrokes had meaning. No visit was complete without a trip to the second floor, where Myrtis Griffin and Russell White, the ladies of the factory, still mixed some of the Walker ointments by hand in large vats.

At home, there were more reminders of my famous grandmothers. In our living room, I learned to read music on A'Lelia Walker's Chickering baby grand. We ate Thanksgiving turkey on Madam's hand-painted Limoges china and ladled Christmas eggnog—made with A'Lelia's secret recipe— from her sterling silver punch bowl.

Our all-black suburb was filled with doctors, teachers, entrepreneurs, musicians and attorneys, many with connections to the Walker Company or the Walker Building. Our next-door neighbor was the son of F. E. DeFrantz, a former trustee of Madam Walker's estate and longtime secretary of Indianapolis's black YMCA. The son of Freeman B. Ransom, Madam Walker's attorney and general manager, lived two doors away on Grandview Drive. Ransom's granddaughter, Judy, was one of my closest childhood friends. On the next corner was the daughter of Robert Lee Brokenburr, the lawyer who had filed the papers of incorporation for the Madam C. J. Walker Manufacturing Company in 1911. Farther up Grandview was Violet Davis Reynolds, the secretary who had joined the Walker Company in 1915 when she was seventeen years old. A few blocks from her was Mrs. Pendegraph, who would retire as corporate treasurer—and the last employee—when the original Madam C. J. Walker Manufacturing Company closed its doors in the mid-1980s.

Surrounded as I was by so many accomplished people, it would be several years before I fully understood my extraordinary family heritage. Fortunately my mother had taken great care, I now realize, to keep the legacy of the Walker women in manageable perspective so that I could discover its power in my own time, on my own terms. While she had been expected to assume her role as a fourth-generation executive at the Walker Company—and had studied chemistry at Howard University in preparation to do so—she wanted me, her only daughter, to be free to follow my own interests in journalism. But she had also given me the name A'Lelia because she wanted me to value the connection and to respect its origins. Neither of us could have predicted that my love of words and my passion for history would eventually return me to the inheritance I had seemed to be abandoning.

For many years I was more attracted to A'Lelia Walker's story than to Madam's. My heart raced each time I saw "our" name on the pages of the dusty books that were stashed in our attic. I was thrilled to discover that our birthdays were so close: hers on June 6 and mine on June 7. But most important, the original A'Lelia intrigued me because she provided a link to the Harlem Renaissance. For a teenager who loved to read—but who had always gone to predominantly white schools where little black literature was assigned—knowing that she had hosted Langston Hughes and Countee Cullen at The Dark Tower, her celebrated Harlem salon, affirmed my dreams of becoming a writer.

While I was embracing A'Lelia, however, I was growing ambivalent about Madam. A'Lelia represented the fun, flamboyance and glamour of the Roaring Twenties. Madam, on the other hand, was associated with more serious matters: business, philanthropy and the politics of hair. And, during the late 1960s and early 1970s, hair was as much a battleground as Vietnam. Whether it was hippies with ponytails or brothers and sisters with Afros, the scalps of baby boomers had become the symbolic stage on which to express racial pride, political militancy and personal liberation. Because many people believed that Madam Walker's products were designed primarily to straighten hair, she became an easy target for accusations and complicated emotions in an era when black pride was measured by the length of one's "natural." The woman who had been among the pioneers of the modern cosmetics industry—and who had fostered self-esteem, glamour and power among several generations of African American women—temporarily fell out of favor.

During those years, I was hungry for information about the history of black Americans, reading every book and article I could find, earnestly taking the messages to heart. When E. Franklin Frazier, the venerable Howard University sociologist, accused Madam Walker of running advertisements that "tell how the Negro can rid himself of his black or dark complexion, or how he can straighten his hair," I flushed with embarrassment. Without my own research, how was I to know that while Madam Walker was alive the Walker Company never sold skin bleaches and the words "hair straightener" never appeared in her ads? It would be years before I would learn that her Walker System was intended to treat the scalp disease that was so rampant in the early 1900s, when many women washed their hair only once a month. "Right here let me correct the erroneous impression held by some that I claim to straighten hair," she told a reporter in 1918 after she had been called the "de-kink queen" by a white newspaper. "I deplore such an impression because I have always held myself out as a hair culturist. I grow hair."

Equally persistent was the widely circulated and incorrect belief that Madam Walker had invented the straightening comb. In fact, this metal hair care implement probably had been sold at least as early as the 1870s, when Parisian Marcel Grateau created his famous Marcel Wave, and was advertised in Bloomingdale's and Sears's catalogues during the 1880s and 1890s, presumably for the thousands of white women who also had kinky hair. Years later I would learn that the claim probably originated in 1922—three years after Madam Walker's death—when the Walker Company purchased the rights to a patent from the widow of a man who had manufactured combs for Madam Walker.

Certainly in 1970 most people who recognized Madam Walker's name associated her with the hot comb. And so did I, even as I sat in the Walker Beauty School watching the cosmetology students transform my chemically straightened flip into an Angela Davis–sized Afro. During college I remained self-conscious about my connection to Madam Walker until one winter afternoon when I discovered W.E.B. Du Bois's laudatory obituary of her in the August 1919 issue of *The Crisis.* From deep in the stacks of Harvard's Widener Library, Du Bois, whom I considered my intellectual hero, had armed me with a strong retort. Madam Walker, he wrote, did not intend "to imitate white folk." Whereas Frazier had criticized her "conspicuous consumption" in *The Black Bourgeoisie,* Du Bois praised her philanthropy and credited her with "revolutionizing the personal habits and appearance of millions of human beings" by educating them about hygiene and grooming. Even to this day, the complex issues surrounding African American women and beauty continue to be debated.

A few days before my mother died in January 1976, I sat in the middle of her hospital bed and talked about the research I was doing on the women in our family. The previous fall, when Phyl Garland, my adviser at Columbia University's Graduate School of Journalism, learned that I was related to Madam Walker, she gently refused to let me even consider another topic for my master's paper. Of course, I had long ago memorized the legend and its litany: *Born Sarah Breedlove in Delta, Louisiana, in 1867, Madam Walker was orphaned at seven, married at fourteen, a mother at seventeen, widowed at twenty. While working as a washerwoman, she began to go bald. Miraculously, she claimed, the formula for the scalp treatment that had restored her hair was revealed to her in a dream. When she died at fifty-one in 1919, she was one of America's wealthiest self-made businesswomen.* That was the story that every-one—or at least most African American women born before 1950—knew. But now that I was mining new biographical territory, I had begun to dis-cover flaws and occasional lapses of truth mixed in with the victories and accomplishments. There were difficult divorces as well as business suc-cesses, legal feuds as well as large charitable contributions. Just when I needed my mother the most to help me make sense of what I was learning, she was too weary from months of chemotherapy to focus on memories.

"What should I do about these things?" I asked, knowing that I would not have her much longer. "Should I include *this* part? And what about *that*?"

Mustering just enough energy to leave no doubt about her wishes, she leaned forward, looked into my eyes and said, without hesitation, "Tell the truth, baby. It's all right to tell the truth."

Her words were a powerful final gift and a charge that I have tried to honor.

During the two decades after my mother's death, I worked as a network television producer for ABC News and NBC News, traipsing from coast to coast telling other people's stories, all the while yearning to resurrect my own family saga. Each year I managed to spend at least part of my week-ends, vacations and holidays excavating the details of the Walker women's lives, learning that for every fabrication others had created, there was a more profound and interesting reality. Occasionally I found myself at the end of cold trails, but more often I was blessed with serendipitous little mir-acles that revealed a person or document or place, exactly the clue I needed for the next step of my search. Fortunately, Madam Walker, A'Lelia Walker and my mother had known so many people that the usual six degrees of separation were reduced to two or three. One phone call, maybe two, almost always opened the door that I needed. Few people refused to help.

An innovator and visionary, Madam sped through the final decade of her life too busy to reflect and ruminate. Where others of her generation had penned memoirs and autobiographies, she left only the flimsiest clues about her early life. Fortunately for me she understood the power of the press, and had actively cultivated relationships with black newspaper reporters who chronicled her activities on a weekly basis. As well, hundreds of her personal letters and business records, faithfully preserved by her secretary, Violet Reynolds—and now archived at the Indiana Historical Society in Indianapolis—provided my original road map to her travels between 1913 and 1919.

The same sense of adventure and anticipation that had led me to the dresser in my grandmother's room accompanied me through the libraries, archives, courthouses and historical societies of more than a dozen United States cities between 1975 and 2000. In the St. Louis Public Library, as I scrolled through thousands of feet of microfilm, I discovered three brothers Madam Walker had never mentioned in her official company biography. In Savannah, Georgia, I felt an unspoken healing as I hugged R. Burney Long, whose family still owned the land where Madam Walker was born and where her parents had been slaves. Through the years I followed Madam Walker's path from Delta, Louisiana, to Vicksburg to St. Louis, from Denver to Pittsburgh to Indianapolis, then to Harlem and Irvington-on-Hudson, New York.

During the summer of 1982—with the last of the Walker friends and employees still alive—I was welcomed into the parlors and living rooms of a fascinating array of men and women in their eighties and nineties, all eager to entrust me with the legacy we shared. In New York, Gerri Major, long known as *Jet*'s "Society World" columnist, spun stories of A'Lelia's weekend soirees and afternoon poker parties. Confined to her bed with vertigo, Major was still glamorous in a white satin lounging jacket as she described typesetting the *Inter-State Tattler*, the tabloid she had edited under the name Geraldyn Dismond during the 1920s and 1930s. Blues singer Alberta Hunter, who was then performing at the Cookery in Greenwich Village, described her visits to Villa Lewaro and told me that A'Lelia had a "beautiful singing voice." Over a mimosa-filled brunch across the Hudson River in Hoboken, writer and artist Bruce Nugent recalled the crowded October 1927 opening of The Dark Tower as well as spaghetti dinners in A'Lelia's hideaway on Edgecombe Avenue. In Chicago, Marjorie Stewart Joyner, the former principal of the national chain of Walker Beauty Schools, sparkled as she recounted her first meeting with Madam Walker in 1916.

For my grandfather's ninetieth birthday, I traveled to Pine Bluff, Arkansas, his childhood home, to which he had returned in the early 1960s. On the second day of my visit, I asked him about a large steamer trunk that I remembered from his Indianapolis apartment. "Try the closet in the front bedroom," he suggested. And there it was, behind a stack of newspapers and boxes. After I dragged it into the living room, where he was sitting, we unsuccessfully tried every key in the house. Finally we called a locksmith, who in no time was there popping the lock. To my delighted astonishment, the treasures of my childhood—the ostrich fan, the King Tut charms, the opera glasses—all appeared magically before me. For the rest of the day Pa Pa and I explored. In one drawer we found the license for A'Lelia's second marriage with a spray of baby's breath still pressed into the folds. Beneath that document was Madam's last letter to A'Lelia, written just nine days before she died. Folded in another compartment was Mae's hand-embroidered wedding dress from her 1923 marriage to Dr. Gordon Jackson. Throughout the afternoon and into the evening, Pa Pa—still seated in his straight-backed chair—was ready with an explanation for each item I retrieved. Too excited to eat, too charged to sleep, we continued past midnight. As soon as Pa Pa's head fell to his chest, he was awake again, mesmerizing me with family stories until the sun peeked through the window blinds.

Six years earlier, my mother had granted me permission to present the Walker women's lives as I found them. On this hot July night, Pa Pa passed the baton of family griot.

Certainly whatever teenage reservations I may have had about Madam Walker are long gone. My original childhood curiosity has remained my most reliable guide. And now that I am the same age as Madam Walker when she experienced her greatest achievements, I fully understand why many consider her an American icon. It is a privilege to tell her story.

A'Lelia Bundles
Alexandria, Virginia

A word about A'Lelia Walker: During the early 1920s Lelia Walker changed her name to A'Lelia Walker. Because her mother had originally named her Lelia and because that was the name she used during the years of Madam Walker's life, she is called Lelia throughout the remainder of this text, except in the afterword.

For ease of reading, research source citations have been placed at the end of the book.

CHAPTER 1

Freedom Baby

— ≈≈≈ —

Into a time of destitution and aspiration, of mayhem and promise, Sarah Breedlove was born two days before Christmas 1867. It was a Yuletide that offered her parents, Owen and Minerva, no other gifts. Their sloped-roof cypress cabin possessed as its primary source of warmth and light an open-hearth fireplace. No official document recorded Sarah's birth. No newspaper notice heralded her arrival. No lacy gown enveloped her tiny cocoa body.

To the world beyond her family's rented plot of ground in Delta, Louisiana, Sarah was just another black baby destined for drudgery and ignorance. But to her parents, she surely must have symbolized hope. Unlike her slave-born siblings—Louvenia, Owen, Jr., Alexander and James—Sarah had been born free just a few days shy of the Emancipation Proclamation's fifth anniversary. Still, her parents' lives were unlikely to change anytime soon. For the Breedloves, even hope had its limits.

Tethered to this space for more than two decades—first as slaves, then as free people—they knew what to expect from its seasonal patterns. Spring rains almost always split the levees, transforming land to sea until the floods receded from their grassless yard to reveal a soppy stew, flush with annual deposits of soil from the northern banks of the Mississippi River. Summer dry spells sucked the moist dirt until it turned to dust. Steamy autumns filled creamy-white cotton fields with swarms of sweating ebony backs, blistered feet and bloody, cracked cuticles. On a predictable cycle, wind, water and heat, then flies, mosquitoes and gnats, streamed through the slits and gaps of their rickety home.

Beyond the nearby levee, the syrupy mile-wide river formed a liquid highway, bringing news and commerce like blood transfusions from New Orleans and Natchez to the south, St. Louis and Memphis to the north. Three miles upstream and a half-hour ferry ride away in Vicksburg, black stevedores unloaded farm tools and timepieces, china and chifforobes from steamboats, then stacked their decks with honeycombs of cotton bales just hauled in from Jackson and Clinton and Yazoo City.

During the Civil War the river had also become an avenue of invasion, so central to the Confederacy's east-west supply trains and north-south riverboats that President Abraham Lincoln declared it the "key" to winning the war. Confederate President Jefferson Davis, whose family plantation was located barely thirty river miles south of the city at Davis Bend, was equally aware of its strategic position. From atop Vicksburg's two-hundred-foot red-clay bluffs, Confederate cannons glowered at Union gunboats and controlled this patch of the Mississippi Valley, frustrating the federal navy for more than two years until the Confederates' decisive July 4, 1863, surrender.

Having been reduced to eating mule meat and living in caves during a forty-seven-day bombardment and siege, Vicksburg residents, and their Louisiana neighbors on the western side of the river, found their mauling hard to forget or forgive. As General Ulysses S. Grant's blue-uniformed columns streamed triumphantly toward Vicksburg's stalwart courthouse, thousands of freedmen cheered. But for many generations after the troops had left, the former slaves and their descendants would suffer from the federal army's vindictive pillaging and the retaliation inflicted upon them by their former masters.

Life and living arrangements were so scrambled after the war that Owen and Minerva, both born around 1828, may have been squatters on the plantation where they had lived as Robert W. Burney's slaves since at least 1847. Their African family origins, as well as their faces and voices, are lost to time, silenced by their illiteracy. Because the importation of slaves had been illegal since January 1, 1808—though the law was flouted for years—it is likely that they were born in the United States. Whether Burney purchased them from an auction block in Vicksburg, New Orleans or Mobile—places he frequented—probably will never be known.

Before the war, Owen and Minerva's labor had helped make their owner a wealthy man. In 1860, a banner year for cotton in Louisiana, Burney's "real property"—including his land and his sixty slaves—was valued at $125,000, his personal property at $15,000. Such holdings secured his place in the top 10 percent of slave-owning Southern planters, and put him among the 30 percent who owned more than 1,000 acres.

But now, with the South defeated, the Burney fields were "growing up with weeds," their house and farm buildings—like those of most of their neighbors—destroyed as they fled with their slaves during the first campaign against Vicksburg in 1862. Hoping never to see Union soldiers again, they had found themselves in a rented home in Morton, Mississippi, and squarely in the path of General William Tecumseh Sherman's destructive 1864 march across that state, a prelude to his more famous 1865 swath through Georgia.

By the spring of 1865, when the Burneys, and probably the Breedloves, returned to the peninsula where their plantation sat, the Union commanders at Vicksburg had confiscated the land for a refugee camp filled with several thousand newly freed men, women and children. "The scenes were appalling," wrote one Freedmen's Bureau official. "The refugees were crowded together, sickly, disheartened, dying on the streets, not a family of them all either well sheltered, clad, or fed."

The Burney farm had also become a burial ground pocked with mass graves for hundreds of the 3,200 Union soldiers who had died of dysentery, typhoid and malaria as they kept watch over Vicksburg during the scorching summer of 1862 and the soggy winter of 1863. The troops, along with 1,200 slaves confiscated from nearby plantations, had followed a Union general's order to excavate a canal—a kind of jugular slash through the base of the peninsula's long neck—intended to circumvent the impenetrable hills of Vicksburg.

By late 1867, as the Breedloves awaited Sarah's birth, all that remained of a once grand plantation were "one or two little houses or shanties near the river" and a large ditch marking the failed bypass.

Robert W. Burney was only twenty-two years old in August 1842 when he arrived with his oxen and farm implements on 167 acres of rented land in Madison Parish, Louisiana, near the Mississippi River north of Vicksburg. By the following February, when he purchased the land for a mere $1.25 an acre, he already had a small group of slaves at work preparing 65 acres for corn and cotton.

His personal good fortune was the result of a nationwide economic crisis that had financially strapped the previous owners. For a young man as ambitious as Burney, the uncultivated soil of the Louisiana frontier held more lucrative promise than the depleted farmland of the more heavily populated eastern United States. Overextended land speculators, ruined in the Panic of 1837, were forced to sell to men like Burney, who, unsaddled by debt, could dictate advantageous deals for modest amounts of cash. A native of Maury County, Tennessee—home of President James Knox Polk—Burney became the recipient of some of the country's most fertile farmland, its alluvial soil so suited for long-staple cotton that it would soon become one of Louisiana's wealthiest parishes.

In April 1846 he nearly doubled his holdings with the $300 cash purchase of 160 acres just three and a half miles south of Vicksburg, one of the busiest cotton-trading ports between St. Louis and New Orleans. This time his land abutted the water, providing direct access to passing steamboats. It was situated on a mile-and-a half-wide peninsula that jutted northeastward toward Vicksburg like a finger poised to make a point, and its picturesque panoramas earned it the name Grand View. What Burney did not plant with cotton and vegetables in this dark, fertile turf remained a virgin forest of moss-draped oak, elm and cypress. Eventually a railroad designed to link trade on the Mississippi River with the Atlantic and Pacific oceans would pierce the center of his cotton fields.

With prime property and favorable future prospects, Burney's relative affluence made him a most eligible bachelor. In October 1846, he chose for his bride Mary Fredonia Williamson, the educated seventeen-year-old daughter of the late Russell McCord Williamson, a wealthy Mississippi landowner and delegate to the second Mississippi Constitutional Convention of 1832. Williamson, who like Burney had grown up in Maury County, had been a childhood friend of the Polk boys, their families so close that one of the Williamson slaves had assisted in the funeral of the President's father.

Williamson also had ties to another President, Andrew Jackson, under whom he had fought as a teenager in the 1815 Battle of New Orleans. In 1834, during the first year of his second term, Jackson appointed Williamson surveyor general of all public lands south of Tennessee amid the feverish Mississippi land rush for the confiscated ancestral territory of the Choctaws and Chickasaws. At least a second-generation slave owner, Williamson had no reason or incentive to quarrel with the views of President Jackson, one of the South's largest slaveholders, on the topic of chattel labor. "Ownership," Jackson's biographer Robert Remini wrote, "was as American to these Jacksonians as capitalism, nationalism, or democracy." What property Williamson possessed, he passed on to his offspring. To Mary Fredonia he bequeathed at least a dozen slaves, nearly doubling her husband's holdings of human assets.

Independent of his wife's inheritance, Burney had prospered well enough to attract the attention of Oliver O. Woodman, a Vicksburg investor who owned several businesses, including a pharmacy and a bookstore. In 1848, the two men agreed to combine their "negroes, Oxen, Corn, Farming Utensils, horses, etc. . . . into a copartnership." Among the slaves Burney brought to the deal were nineteen-year-old Owen, valued at $700, and nineteen-year-old Minerva, valued at $600. At the time of the January 1, 1848, inventory, Minerva was not yet Owen's wife and neither of them had any children.

In exchange for co-ownership of 524 additional acres, which Woodman had purchased next to Burney's existing property, Burney agreed to manage the plantation, the goal being "to clear up and cultivate the land as fast as the timber is taken off." The partnership found a ready market for the timber's by-products, especially the cordwood needed by the ravenous wood-burning boilers of the steamboats and packet boats that lumbered all day and night around the corkscrew twists of the Mississippi and Louisiana shorelines.

All the profits from the enterprise were to "be invested in negroes" who were to be "kept on the place during the copartnership." In a relatively more humane gesture than that expected of other, more ruthless slave owners, Burney and Woodman agreed that, "should there be any negro women with children, which are joint property, at the expiration of the copartnership, either party getting them are to take them at valuation, as children under ten years old should not be separated from the mother." For that, at least, the Breedloves could be grateful.

Whether Minerva, who was a year older than Mary Fredonia, worked primarily in the fields or in the house eludes historians. But with a growing family, eventually numbering six daughters, the mistress of the house surely needed Minerva's help. Despite having her own children, who were roughly the same age, Minerva was expected to come to Mary Fredonia's aid whenever she was called.

By 1850, seven years after Burney's arrival in Madison Parish, his property was valued at $10,000, a reflection of the increasing wealth of the nation's 350,000 slaveholding families. As the slave population burgeoned, especially in Madison Parish, where blacks would come to eclipse whites nine to one, planters grew more paranoid, advocating hard-nosed control over their human property. The prospect of a literate slave population was so frightening to some that an 1830 state law had forbidden "teaching them to read and write on pain of imprisonment for one to twelve months."

"There is among the slave population throughout the states far too much information for their own happiness and subordination," the nearby *Richmond Compiler* editorialized. "Without rigid regulations and strict subordination, there is no safety."

As late as 1860, Delta was an unincorporated village with only ten households of fewer than sixty whites as well as hundreds of slaves who were scattered over a few thousand acres. By then the Burneys, who had prospered splendidly during the previous decade, had every reason to believe their good fortune would continue. The Breedloves, who had never known freedom, had no reason to believe their luck would ever change. But by the end of the war in April 1865, nothing about their parallel worlds remained a certainty. A year later Robert Burney was dead of a stroke, perhaps overwhelmed by the daunting struggle to regain his land and his lost wealth. That November, Mary Fredonia, still nursing an infant, succumbed to cholera. Their six young daughters would spend decades untangling legal disputes over their father's property.

For Owen, Minerva and their growing family, freedom constructed new hurdles. The scant 1866 cotton harvest was followed by an even more disastrous yield in 1867, when Madison Parish was decimated first by the worst flood in its history, then by army worms that left the cotton fields "blackened like fire had swept over them." By winter, thousands of Louisiana farm families, stunned at their meager earnings, were starving and homeless, "having no place to go and no clothing but rags." With the Burney family in too much disarray to monitor their balance books, at least the Breedloves had their shack. Like thousands of other indigent black families, they may have placed some faith in the intangible hope of full citizenship for themselves and education for their children that had come with the overthrow of the Confederacy.

During the rainy spring before Sarah Breedlove's birth, Congress had overridden President Andrew Johnson's veto and adopted the Reconstruction Act, dividing the postwar South into five military districts and enfranchising more than 700,000 black men—most of them newly freed slaves—throughout the eleven states of the former Confederacy. This Radical Reconstruction would last until 1877, when the Democrats orchestrated the demise of the last Southern Republican government and claimed "redemption" for all they had lost. But in August 1867 almost two-thirds of Louisiana's 127,639 registered voters were black, and still hopeful that their first efforts at participatory democracy would deliver the dignity and political rights they craved. With emancipation, Madison Parish's overwhelmingly black workforce also had become an overwhelmingly black electorate.

Owen, now thirty-nine, was eligible to cast the first vote of his life in an election calling for a Louisiana constitutional convention to rewrite state laws. In late September, when the votes were tallied, exactly half the delegates were black and half were white. Only two were not Republicans. When the conferees met in New Orleans in late November, a month before Sarah's birth, the *New Orleans Times* derisively labeled their assembly the "Congo Convention." President Johnson, Lincoln's successor, delivered a similar indictment, accusing Radical Republicans of trying to "Africanize . . . half of our country" and calling blacks "utterly so ignorant of public affairs that their voting can consist in nothing more than carrying a ballot to the place where they are directed to deposit it."

While most of the new voters were, in fact, illiterate, most of the black delegates had as much or more education than their white counterparts, and in some instances more than President Johnson, a tailor who had taught himself to read. Some were former slaves; most were freeborn.

Among the large property owners, a few had owned slaves. At least one, Fortune Riard of Lafayette, had been educated in France, where he served as a naval officer.

During the final weeks of Minerva's pregnancy Curtis Pollard—the Breedloves' family minister and a newly elected delegate to the constitutional convention—talked optimistically of guaranteed suffrage for black adult males and statewide public education for the newly freed slaves. On December 31, eight days after Sarah's birth, Pinckney B. S. Pinchback, another black delegate who later would serve as acting lieutenant governor of the state, introduced civil rights legislation outlawing segregation on trains, on ferries and in public places.

The Democrats were outraged, holding fast to a platform advocating "a government of white people" in which there could, "in no event nor under any circumstance, be any equality between the whites and other races." Without the votes required to ensure this outcome, the party faithful struck back with terror and intimidation. During the next several months, the vigilante Knights of the White Camellia, who had organized in southern Louisiana in May 1867, began to gather members and sympathizers from other parts of the state. For a while, at least, Madison's black population was not subjected to the more flagrant violence, in large part due to its numbers, as well as to the presence of federal troops in nearby Vicksburg. But any sense of personal safety would prove to be illusory and temporary.

CHAPTER 2

Motherless Child

— ⟨⟨⟩⟩ —

N ight riders and vigilantes bloodied Louisiana's back roads during the score-settling campaign of 1868. Still an infant, Sarah was sheltered from knowing about the year's one thousand politically motivated murders, many of them sanctioned by the Democratic leadership in its efforts to vanquish Republican rule and cower black elected officials. But soon enough she would understand the fearful midnight whispers of her elders and the courageous tales of those who escaped the wrath and the rope of the Knights of the White Camellia. Later in life, she would crusade against such outrages with both her wealth and her passion.

Throughout the late 1860s, Owen and Minerva did their best to protect their children from the turmoil around them. White conservatives and Confederate sympathizers made no secret of their resentment at being governed not only by a racially mixed, Republican dominated legislature but by Governor Henry C. Warmouth, a corrupt carpetbagger, and Lieutenant Governor Oscar James Dunn, a man of ethical reputation whose primary flaw in their eyes was his African ancestry. He was "as black as the ace of spades, but a grander man from principles never trod God's earth," said Pinckney B. S. Pinchback, his successor as lieutenant governor.

The Democratic offensive to regain power was so exacting and pervasive that by November most of the parishes that had supported Republican candidates in the April gubernatorial election had flip-flopped to the Democratic column as a result of ballot tampering and a petrified, stay-at-home electorate. Once again, however, Madison Parish's proximity to the Freedmen's Bureau regional headquarters in Vicksburg had spared it the more blatant bullying that prevailed elsewhere in the state. Consequently, Republican presidential candidate Ulysses S. Grant received 90 percent of its votes, his widest margin anywhere in the state, over Democrat Horatio Seymour, a man whose platform declared "This Is a White Man's Government."

No doubt Curtis Pollard, the Breedloves' minister and a Louisiana state senator, had played some role in keeping the night riders at bay. Often called bulldozers, these self-appointed vigilantes earned their name for plowing down defenseless blacks. Twenty years Owen's senior, Pollard was a man Owen could admire, because of his success as a farmer and grocer, as well as for his outspoken advocacy of the freedmen's interests. That summer *The Daily Picayune* called this former slave "a black man, uncompromisingly so, and a Republican equally uncompromising." During his first year in the state senate, and two years before the ratification of the Fifteenth Amendment, Pollard had championed Louisiana legislation that protected farm laborers from employers who threatened to fire them for supporting Republican candidates.

Fortunately for the Breedloves, the abundant 1868 cotton harvest ushered in the first of the two most productive growing cycles since before the war. Owen's skills as a blacksmith also made him a likely candidate for extra work rebuilding the railroad that ran through the Burney property. Its tracks destroyed during the war, the North Louisiana and Texas Railroad Company decided that year to construct its eastern terminus at Delta.

The crop of 1869 was called "so unmanageably large" that laborers, for once, had some bargaining power for their wages. The penny a pound the Breedloves and others earned probably meant sufficient food for their families and brought such "improvements in dress and appearance" that an official in the nearby Freedmen's Bureau headquarters took note. The family's relative prosperity may have provided the catalyst and the confidence for Owen and Minerva to pledge the $100 marriage bond that allowed them to wed on December 16, 1869, legalizing the union they had formed nearly twenty years earlier during slavery. Senator Pollard conducted the modest ceremony, which included the almost two-year-old Sarah, her two-month-old baby brother Solomon, and the four other Breedlove children, whose ages now ranged from seven to fifteen.

Years later Sarah's childhood friend Celeste Hawkins remembered her as an "ordinary person, an open-faced good gal" with no remarkable traits to predict her future achievements. "We played together an' cotch craw-fish in de bayous," she told an interviewer who attempted to capture her dialect. "We went to fish-frys an' picnics; we sot side by side in the ol' Pollard Church on a Sunday." They also worked alongside their parents in the fields, the suffocating Louisiana heat blasting against their chests. Using a nickname that

Sarah had long ago discarded, Hawkins recalled a glimmer of the competitive woman she was to become. "Twasn't nobody could beat me an' 'Winnie' a-choppin' cotton an' a-pickin' dem bolls clean," she proudly said.

Hawkins also remembered their look-alike hairstyles. As with many black girls, their hair, said Hawkins, was "twisted and wropped with strings" in an ancient African grooming custom guaranteed to make them wince in the process. After their mothers had pulled the strands and sections tautly at the roots, their temples and scalps smarted for days.

Their world was insular, circumscribed by the peonage of their parents. During 1874, when Sarah was old enough to enter first grade, public schools in Louisiana—where they had existed at all—were shuttered when the state legislature declined to fund them. By then the Freedmen's Bureau had disbanded its education division. Throughout the region, "the hostility to schools for the Negro," noted one traveler, "is . . . often very bitter and dangerous." In some parts of the state, schools were torched, teachers harassed, even killed. The freed men and women fervently sought education for their children and themselves. Just as during slavery, planters feared a literate workforce, especially one that could choose to keep its children in class during harvesttime or learn enough to challenge the political and economic status quo.

Sarah later told a reporter that she had had only three months of formal education, its quality undoubtedly inferior. If the Pollard Church helped her learn her ABCs and other rudimentary literacy lessons in Sunday school, she was more fortunate than most children in her parish. At least she was surrounded by the stimulation of commerce, especially around the time of her third birthday, when the trains returned to Madison Parish. Arriving every morning at eleven o'clock not far from her family's cabin, the whistling locomotive roused the village into a busy hive. Certainly the passengers—whether in finery or rags—would have stirred a young girl's imagination as she watched them embark upon journeys far beyond the dusty roads of Delta.

Without warning, whatever carefree moments Sarah enjoyed as a child ceased with the death of her mother, Minerva, probably in 1873. Within a year, perhaps less, her father remarried. By late 1875, he, too, was dead.

Decades later, after Sarah had become the well-known entrepreneur Madam C. J. Walker, she reminded audiences that she had had to fend for herself since childhood. "I had little or no opportunity when I started out in life, having been left an orphan and being without mother or father since I was seven years of age," she often recounted in stoic acknowledgment of her loss.

Publicly, at least, she did not elaborate with details, dates or causes of death. The particulars remain unknown but the possibilities are many. Disease stalked the swamps and bayous of the Mississippi Valley, often in the form of epidemics poised to activate at deadly, unpredictable intervals. Cholera, once in motion, lurked in drinking water contaminated by open privies and raw sewage. In the absence of a death certificate, there is no way to know how Minerva died, but she was vulnerable to the 1873 cholera epidemic that claimed thirty-four Madison Parish victims. Without vaccines or medical treatment, pneumonia, smallpox, measles, typhoid, tuberculosis and a half dozen other highly infectious diseases went unchecked. Less likely as a cause of the Breedloves' deaths was yellow fever, a disease usually more fatal to whites than blacks because of its West African origins and the immunity many blacks carried as a result.

If Sarah witnessed her mother's and father's final breaths, she left no clue about the bewildering heartache a young child experiences at the loss of a parent. But the painful aftermath shaped her attitudes for the rest of her life. Dependent upon her older and now married sister, Louvenia Breedlove Powell, she was forced to live in the household of her brother-in-law, Jesse Powell. Years later she would describe him as "cruel," suggesting, but never fully revealing, the extent of his threats, taunts and abuses.

Rather than be destroyed, Sarah learned to turn her vulnerability into resolve and resilience. Her determination to escape was her most reliable asset.

If Sarah was personally at risk, her entire community's safety was subject to the statewide political turmoil that had only grown more intense since the murders of 1868. The gains blacks had realized during the early days of Reconstruction were being snatched systematically from them throughout the early 1870s. By the spring of 1874, Louisiana had become "an armed camp." Determined to oust the Republicans, many conservatives—including a number of former Confederate military officers established the White League, heir to the Knights of the White Camellia. Emboldened by the Democratic Congress in Washington, the League frequently carried out its assaults in broad daylight, vowing that "there will be no security, no peace and no prosperity for Louisiana . . . until the superiority of the Caucasian over the African in all affairs pertaining to government, is acknowledged and established."

With the country's economy teetering from the lingering effects of the Panic of 1873, and the House of Representatives no longer under Republican control, President Grant and his party had few resources and even less will to devote to black enfranchisement or civil rights. In 1876, with both parties claiming victory for local races in Louisiana and for the presidency in Washington, the contested outcome placed the Republicans in a tenuous position. In order to seat Republican Rutherford B. Hayes, the national party struck the Bargain of 1877, a compromise that secured a sufficient number of Democratic electoral college votes to install Hayes in the White House in exchange for his agreement to end federal intervention in the South. In short order, Senator Pollard and most of the state's black representatives were stripped of their posts in Baton Rouge. With the removal of federal troops from Louisiana in April 1877, Radical Reconstruction collapsed resoundingly.

The next year, during statewide elections, the violence that had long bombarded Madison Parish's neighbors edged ever closer to its borders. If any members of Sarah's immediate family were beaten or threatened, she did not discuss it as an adult. But there were many opportunities for her to witness the results of such intimidation in her parish, whether in the form of whip marks and bruises on the living or on corpses as they were retrieved from nearby bayous.

Three weeks before the 1878 election, a black Republican candidate for Congress escaped a band of "bulldozers" less than forty miles from Delta in Waterproof, Louisiana. After hiding overnight in a moss-covered hollow log, the politician dressed as a woman to gain passage on a New Orleans–bound riverboat. The story was so well publicized in the Northern press and so widely told among local blacks for its defiant conclusion that Sarah and her friends almost surely heard it. By December, close to seventy-five people had been murdered in neighboring Tensas and Concordia parishes. The remaining black state representative from Madison, William Murrell, later recalled seeing a man with a companion, "hanging in the swamp . . . with a brand-new grass rope around him."

"This of course excited the colored people in my parish at the time," Representative Murrell later testified before a congressional committee. "They proved to be good prophets. They said it was only the question of another election, and they would reach Madison, too."

That terror—and the economic disaster brought on by yet another bad cotton year and one of the worst yellow fever epidemics in the nation's history—pushed Sarah and her sister and brother-in-law off the farm and across the river to Vicksburg. In mid-November 1878, the Hinds County *Gazette* predicted that as many as four thousand of the area's black laborers would be "homeless, breadless and in rags in January next." With no cotton to pick, there would be no work.

Jesse and Louvenia, like many others, were forced to look for jobs in Vicksburg. Both illiterate, their prospects were limited, and Jesse's violent temper in all likelihood only added to their problems. For Sarah, however, the move meant more opportunities to see Alexander, her eldest brother, with whom she had remained close. Already living in Vicksburg for at least a year, he worked as a porter at C. L. Chambers Grocery on busy Washington Street and lived on Crawford Street near the crowded waterfront, where rents were cheapest.

Despite Sarah's wretched surroundings, a magazine reporter who interviewed her in her richly furnished Harlem town house years later wrote that "as a child she craved for the beautiful. She had an inordinate desire to move among the things of culture and refinement." Such longings would not have been unusual for a curious adolescent who frequently walked past the manicured gardens of Vicksburg's grand antebellum homes. Near the grocery where Alexander worked, shopwindows displayed bolts of taffeta and dotted swiss, pastel hats and supple leather shoes. Waistcoated dandies on steamboat layovers always drew attention as they strolled to Vicksburg's saloons. Even in Delta, Sarah had been inside the well-furnished home of Lillie Burney Felt, one of the six daughters who had returned to the Burney plantation in the late 1860s. Around 1875, with the help of her new husband, Lillie had carefully re-created part of the floor plan and façade of the home her parents had lost during the war. It seems certain that luxury was not an alien concept to young Sarah. It seems equally certain that she had no reason to expect she would ever possess it.

Because Jesse Powell viewed Sarah as a burden, he expected her to contribute to the household income. Even for girls as young as ten, and sometimes younger, there was always work tending to the needs of white children or helping with housework behind the walls of the town's mansions. Sarah was just old enough to work as a laundress, "the province of black women exclusively," according to historian Jacqueline Jones. The work, in fact, was so "onerous" that it was the main chore nineteenth-century white women "would hire someone else to perform whenever the slightest bit of discretionary income was available."

While Sarah may have felt safer in town with Alexander nearby, Vicksburg was no haven of security. After the 1874 election, a group of whites had ambushed a meeting of black men at ten o'clock in the morning. "The whites came with the 16 shooters and just shot and killed every Negro they saw," a man who witnessed the attack later told a congressional committee. "I think they killed about a dozen or so; they killed them because they were Republicans. Nothing was ever done to them for the killing." Again in 1876 whites shot and killed two black men in full view of the courthouse.

The freedmen were alarmed at the continued brazenness of the assaults. They were also panic-stricken over a proposal in Louisiana's legislature that was designed to abridge their rights in ways that closely resembled slavery. Those fears, along with their inability to turn a profit after thirteen years of sharecropping, made thousands in the Mississippi River valley ripe for flight from debt and oppression.

In early 1879, just as black farmers were receiving the now perennial news that they owed more than they had earned, Benjamin "Pap" Singleton, a charismatic black Tennessean, visited several river communities touting the solution for which many had prayed. Cheap land, the right to vote and freedom from harassment awaited them in Kansas, he promised with evangelical enthusiasm. "Now is the time to go," he declared. "Ho for Sunny Kansas," announced fliers trumpeting Singleton Settlement's prime location on the Missouri, Kansas & Texas Railway. Like the railroad company circulars that had lured French, German, Norwegian, Swedish and Welsh immigrants to the unsettled West, Singleton's pamphlets guaranteed "plenty of coal, water and wood" on "one of the finest lands for a poor man in the World."

Having lost faith and patience, thousands of black men, women and children spontaneously journeyed to the riverbanks laden "with their poor, battered and tattered household goods." Within weeks they had clotted together at Vicksburg, Delta and two dozen other Louisiana and Mississippi levees from Greenville to Natchez, convinced that steamboats were en route to convey them north to Kansas-bound trains. During late February, when sixty Madison Parish residents boarded a steamer for St. Louis, eleven-year-old Sarah undoubtedly watched family friends depart. Within days, when another large group headed up the river toward Missouri, the *Vicksburg Herald* sarcastically reported that "the African hegira continues."

From the pulpit and in public places, Curtis Pollard preached deliverance and urged the emigrants on. Having seen the evil intentions of the Democrats from inside the state senate chambers, he harbored no illusions about the freedmen's immediate future in Louisiana. Pollard actively aided two Richland Parish men who had tried to migrate against their employers' will in mid-February. "One of them [was] cut very bad . . . [T]hey said the bulldozers had got a hold of them for wanting to go to Kansas, and had pretty nearly killed them," he later said.

When former Lieutenant Governor Pinchback visited the Delta levee in early March 1879, the promised exodus had drawn nearly 700 refugees to that site alone. He found "every road leading to the river filled with wagons loaded with plunder and families who seem to think anywhere is better than here." Pollard, who had led a rally in Delta on the day of Pinchback's visit, was forced to flee his home and abandon his family three days later when a white Madison Parish doctor threatened to kill him. "I was accused of teaching the people to immigrate to Kansas [and was told] my neck would be broke," he later testified. Because Sarah had known Pollard all her life, word of his escape must have frightened her. More significant, however, was the departure of twenty-one-year old Alexander, who was old enough to understand the political implications of the movement. His job in a downtown store must have made him more aware than most of the dangers a young black man faced. If he missed the 1879 wave, Alexander was part of the second surge in March and April 1880, his own departure possibly triggered by the election-eve murder of Madison Parish's black Republican Club president. In the end, nearly 20,000 black Mississippians and Louisianans joined the migration. Madison Parish, with 1,600 Exodusters, lost more than any other district.

Like many of the migrants, Alexander never reached Kansas, settling instead in St. Louis, where the African Methodist Episcopal and black Baptist churches welcomed the refugees with housing, food and advice. His first job as a porter quickly led to another as a barber. Such rapid progress was more than enough encouragement for Owen Jr. and James to trail him up the river before the end of 1882. With all three of her older brothers gone, Sarah was fully at the mercy of Jesse Powell.

CHAPTER 3

Wife, Mother, Widow

—⟨❦⟩—

"I married at the age of fourteen in order to get a home of my own," Sarah always said of the day she ran off with Moses McWilliams. Nothing more. Nothing less. But clearly she believed her survival was at stake.

Did Moses court her with thoughtful gifts and affectionate gestures? Did their eyes first meet at a picnic, in church, at a Sunday social? Or was the marriage merely a desperate effort to escape an unbearable situation? All the details of Moses's life—his age, birthplace, physical bearing and occupation—remain matters of conjecture.

The union was very possibly a common-law arrangement since neither bride nor groom could have afforded to pledge the $200 Mississippi marriage bond. At any rate, no marriage license has yet been found in Madison Parish or Warren County. In later years, Sarah's memory of the relationship would become strikingly devoid of romantic sentiment. Her intent, she consistently said, was pragmatic, her approach unhesitant.

A photograph taken a few years afterward shows that she was a physically attractive young woman. While any clothing she owned surely was worn, even shabby, her waist had begun to contour between a full bosom and rounded hips. Her chestnut-brown body was firm from field work, her forearm muscles thickened and defined from the washboard. A heart-shaped face framed alert ebony eyes, slightly flared nostrils and purposeful lips. As with so many other black women who had long forgotten the elaborate grooming rituals of their African ancestors, her crudely braided hair was usually covered with a patterned head wrap.

In 1885, during the spring between Sarah's seventeenth and eighteenth birthdays, her daughter, Lelia, was born on June 6. If she and Moses lost other children before or after, she kept the painful knowledge to herself in later years. But there is no doubt that Lelia's arrival gave Sarah's life new meaning and made her determined to protect this sparkly eyed baby girl from the cruelty, hunger and hardship she had endured as a child. So long deprived of her own mother's touch, Sarah had had little exposure to the overwhelming, all-consuming maternal protectiveness that Lelia stirred in her. For the rest of her life, Lelia remained the center of her affection, the source of her motivation.

Though their lives were still difficult, the new family was in a position to benefit from the increased wages that came from two exceptionally good back-to-back cotton crops. Despite the periodic flare-ups of political violence, Vicksburg remained a magnet for blacks from rural Mississippi and northern Louisiana, spawning churches and benevolent societies, separate from and parallel to those in the white community. The Negro Masons, the Grand United Order of Odd Fellows and the Order of Colored Knights of Pythias attracted the more prominent African American men to their ranks, their wives to their auxiliaries. Moses and Sarah's lowly social standing would have excluded them from membership, but nothing would have prevented them from viewing the groups' colorful annual parades and enjoying country picnics with Lelia.

Finally, when it seemed Sarah had pieced together all the elements of the family she had lost, Moses died, probably sometime during 1888. Rather than lead her out of poverty into the promised land as his biblical namesake had done for the children of Egypt, Sarah's Moses abandoned her in the wilderness. The circumstances of his death have long been fodder for speculation. In the absence of Sarah's own words on the topic, the temptation to fill the void has been great. At least three different writers have fashioned plausible accounts of a violent demise. But considering her passionate commitment to the antilynching movement in later years, it is hard to imagine that Sarah—who was to become the outspoken, politically astute Madam Walker—would not have used a personal experience as poignant as a husband's murder to punctuate the horrors of mob violence.

Curiously, all the articles claiming his tragic end were written years after Sarah's death. While she was alive and could either refute or confirm the accounts, no reporter who had personally interviewed her—including antilynching activists Ida B. Wells, W.E.B. Du Bois and James Weldon Johnson—ever mentioned an alleged lynching. Nevertheless the story continues to resurface.

Konrad Bercovici, a prolific social historian, created the first known version of the lynching story after an interview with Lelia in her Harlem home during the 1920s. "Her father having been killed in a riot, she is anything but passive on the subject," he wrote in *Harper's Monthly*. "Rising from her chair as she talked to me, she looked more like an African empress than the offspring of a former slave. Speaking about negroes whose relatives and parents have been killed in riots or in lynchings, her frame trembled, her lips quivered and her eyes filled with tears. She looked like an avenging nemesis." This melodramatic episode loses credibility when Bercovici incorrectly identifies Sarah as "Mrs. Lillie C. Walker . . . a speaker and singer . . . a former slave," as if he had jumbled his notes into a composite character of several notable black women of the era. A little exaggeration may have pleased his editors and titillated the magazine's subscribers at a time when many white American and European writers craved the exoticism and primitivism they believed Harlemites possessed. But the hyperbole resulted in bad journalism and worse history. After reading the article, Lelia wrote to a friend, "I don't think he has been quite truthful . . . He drew a colorful description, but not truthful."

Twenty years later Marjorie Stewart Joyner, a longtime Walker Company employee and loyal family friend, wove a less sensational, though probably no more accurate, story. In her version, Moses was named "Jeff" and was "reported killed in a race riot in Greenwood, Mississippi." Yet another account, by another writer, placed the supposed uprising in Greenville, Mississippi.

Harry B. Webber's 1952 series about Madam Walker in the popular *Pittsburgh Courier* further embellished Joyner's tale. In his made-for-Hollywood scene, a plaintive young Lelia asks, "Is Daddy coming back?" as the now-named "Johnson" gallops away on a horse "to take a new job on a big cotton plantation up near Vicksburg." After the requisite crescendo, Webber unveiled the crushing news. "The details came slowly—a race riot in Vicksburg the night of the day her husband vanished, the deaths of Negroes in violence, their bodies thrown into the river," Webber waxed. "It indeed had been farewell that hot morning on the levee. For one of the bodies was that of hopeful Johnson, who rode on his horse to Vicksburg seeking a new life but perished a few hours later in unsought death."

With no death certificate and no dependable oral history from Sarah herself, it is unlikely that anyone will ever know whether Moses McWilliams was one of the ninety-five people whose lynchings were documented in 1888. Two years earlier, on March 16, 1886, more than twenty black men had indeed been massacred in Carrollton, Mississippi, not far from Greenwood, but Sarah consistently said she "was left a widow" when she was twenty years old.

It is certainly possible that Joyner's Greenwood race riot and Webber's Vicksburg incident went unreported. Mississippi historian Vernon Lane Wharton believed it "impossible to make any estimate of the number of individual Negroes lynched or murdered by whites during the period . . . When reported at all, they were generally given a line or two in very small type in the 'Mississippi Brevities' or 'Miscellaneous Items' columns of the papers."

The Madison *Times-Democrat*, in Sarah's home parish, carried just such an item in July 1889. "There have been several lynchings in the past eighteen months, none of which have found their way into print heretofore." Contemporaneous courthouse records provide no answers, since such murders were rarely prosecuted. In fact, in Mississippi "there seems to have been no single instance throughout the period in which a white man was hanged for killing a Negro."

But thousands of lynching articles did make their way into the pages of the black press as a matter of record, and even into some Southern white newspapers as a form of editorial and social intimidation. Using data from those stories and other sources, E. M. Beck's detailed listing of nineteenth-century Mississippi lynching victims includes no men named McWilliams between 1882 and 1889, all the possible years Sarah was married to Moses. Likewise, Ralph Ginzburg's painstakingly documented inventory of "5,000 Negroes Lynched in the United States since 1859" lists not a single McWilliams in Louisiana or Mississippi. And aside from murder, Moses could have died from any number of illnesses or accidents. Even desertion was not impossible or implausible.

Many years later, Sarah's memories of her husband's death were characteristically spare and emotionally unrevealing: "I was left a widow at the age of twenty with a little girl to raise." But at the time she must have confronted a hauntingly familiar abyss of emptiness, uncertainty and utter panic as she examined her options.

She refused to return to the Powells' home. And Vicksburg would never offer her more than the field, the washtub and a weekly fistful of Indian-head pennies. So just as she had fled Jesse Powell, Sarah knew she would have to flee Mississippi. With little more to encourage her than raw determination, she began plotting her trip to St. Louis. Her decision to leave was not easy, but it was not unusual. Hundreds of young, single and widowed black women left the South each year during the last quarter of the nineteenth century, seeking jobs, bolting from abusive relationships, searching for better lives. And a decade earlier, many of the most eager Exodusters had been women. Now with 200,000 unmarried working black women, most of whom lived in the South, the pool of potential migrants was large.

During early 1889 Sarah and three-year-old Lelia headed north, maybe on a train, but probably on a New Orleans–St. Louis Anchor Line steamboat. Far from the luxury of the boat's upper promenades, they would have been invisible, lower-deck passengers on the weeklong journey. Their three- or four-dollar fare would have bought the equivalent of steerage, a cramped space somewhere among the cargo, the smelly livestock and the deafening, vibrating engine.

* * *

When Sarah and Lelia reached St. Louis, the Breedlove brothers were already familiar figures in the neighborhood around St. Paul African Methodist Episcopal Church where their barbershop had been located for six years. Alexander, James and Solomon all lived near the family business, clustered within eight blocks of each other. Owen had left St. Louis around 1883, moving to Albuquerque, New Mexico, and deserting his wife, Samira.

As self-employed barbers, they had joined a trade with a long and lucrative tradition among St. Louis blacks. Even before the Civil War, a handful of freemen, who considered themselves the "colored aristocracy" of the city, had become wealthy shaving and cutting the hair of a predominantly white clientele. Their successes were duplicated in several cities across the country.

By 1860 one of their group claimed $20,000 worth of St. Louis real estate. A little more than a decade later James Thomas, a former riverboat barber, owned nearly two blocks of downtown property and a twelve-chair, marble, lace and chandeliered tonsorial palace in one of the city's most exclusive hotels. Thomas also had had the good fortune of marrying Antoinette Rutgers, the daughter of Pelagie Rutgers, a mulatto whose estate had been estimated at a half million dollars at the time of her death in 1867.

Such accomplishments among African Americans must have stunned Alexander and his brothers when they first arrived. Black men controlled no businesses of consequence in Vicksburg. But in St. Louis many of the nearly 300 black barbers were considered the best in the city. They were also the largest group of black entrepreneurs. While most did not become wealthy, they enjoyed more independence than laborers, servants, teamsters, messengers and porters—the jobs held by most black men. Even so, the business was changing around them. In Philadelphia, where blacks had dominated the trade since 1838, they had lost their foothold by 1889. Soon afterward, the Breedlove brothers faced a similar crisis, brought on by a racist backlash against black barbers, then later made worse by King Gillette's introduction of the easy-to-use safety razor.

By 1891 Alexander had sold or lost his shop, though he continued to be listed as a barber in the St. Louis city directory. In 1896 the *St. Louis Republic* reported, "The colored barber in St. Louis is about to become a thing of the past." In less than a year, the paper predicted, "the darky barber . . . who shaves a white client will be an oddity."

Sarah surely was awed by the riverfront metropolis. Only a church spire and the courthouse jutted above Vicksburg's roofline. Delta had few buildings taller than one story. But St. Louis's granite-and-limestone insurance companies, department stores and commodities exchanges loomed above her. Instead of streets that muddied with every rain, boulevards were surfaced with macadam and paved with bricks. Where two railroad lines serviced Vicksburg, tracks for more than a dozen freight and passenger companies radiated from St. Louis's massive Union Depot. Where Vicksburg could claim a respectably busy cotton trade, St. Louis was the nation's largest inland cotton market. It was also home to Anheuser-Busch, the world's largest brewery, and Liggett & Myers, the world's largest manufacturer of plug tobacco.

Even the air was different. Sarah was accustomed to the thick, wet humidity of the lower Mississippi. But in St. Louis the steaminess churned into a grimy roux of soot and smoke from the iron ore foundries and industrial furnaces along the river. Ashes and cinders from the cheap, soft, sulfur-rich coal glommed on to her skin and clung to her hair. So polluted was the air in 1906 that certain trees and shrubs had died off within the city limits. "We can no longer grow the evergreen conifers, with the exception of the Dwarf Junipers and the Austrian Pine," complained the director of the Missouri Botanical Gardens. "While we grow a good many roses, it is only the hardiest that stand the present smoke."

To escape the pollution, St. Louis's wealthiest residents pushed the city limits westward, fanning away from the river like a peacock spreading its feathers. At its far reaches were the mansions of Grand Avenue and gated enclaves like Vandeventer Place, heavily populated with prosperous German immigrants. With the advent of the nickel trolley into the far suburbs, the abandonment of downtown by those who could afford to leave escalated in 1890. Some members of the small black middle class settled on the nicer, near-in blocks that whites had relinquished. But the Italian, Jewish and black poor, like Sarah, were wedged into tenements between the business district and the eastern end of the more desirable residential areas.

Sarah's first place—probably more a room than an apartment—was at 1316 Wash Street, a street well known on the police blotter for its stabbings and murders. It also was not far from the dance halls of Twelfth Street and the saloons and brothels of the infamous Chestnut Valley near Union Station. To support herself and Lelia, she worked as a laundress, "washing for families in St. Louis," she told a *St. Louis Post-Dispatch* reporter years later.

Jennie Lias and Ida Winchester met her shortly after she arrived, offering advice, friendship and leads about jobs. Like more than half the employed black women in St. Louis, they were washerwomen, filling slots that were shunned by immigrant and first-generation American working women who dominated the other domestic service jobs there. Sarah and her friends preferred laundry chores, at least in part because they could watch their children while they worked. On Mondays they were among the army of washerwomen who returned to their homes, customarily toting a week's dirty laundry from two or three white families. Another laundress remembered carrying "ten to twelve sheets . . . twenty to thirty towels, twenty-four pillowcases, three and four tablecloths, and no end of shirts and other clothes and things" from each family.

The work, all done by hand in wooden washtubs and iron pots of boiling water, was steamy, strenuous and laborious. Wet sheets and tablecloths doubled in weight. Lye soap irritated hands and arms. Heated flatirons were heavy, cumbersome and dangerous. Sarah, however, took pride in her work, often ironing late into the night to meet Saturday's delivery deadline. She knew that a broken dress button or a scorched shirttail meant a cut in pay, a reduction of a washerwoman's weekly $4 to $12 wages.

By Sunday, her only day off, Sarah welcomed the release that church services always brought her, for she had long embraced the power of prayer. As a newcomer to a fast city and as a recent widow, she needed the solace it brought. Although she had attended the Pollard Church in Delta, she would later say that she had been "converted" at St. Paul AME, the church one block from her brothers' barbershop and six blocks from her first St. Louis home. That conversion to a deeper religious faith may have taken several months, or it may have occurred shortly after she arrived.

In September 1889, St. Paul's new pastor, Reverend Ezekiel T. Cottman, began an aggressive outreach, bringing more than two hundred new parishioners into the church during Sarah's first year in the city. Sarah herself was a likely prospect for membership, especially among the middle-class women of the church who made it their business to know the needy among them. The concern of this small educated elite, with their interlocking familial and friendship ties, would continue to help Sarah for years to come. Not long before she moved to town, the St. Louis Colored Orphans' Home—located less than a block from her brother Alexander's house—had been founded by Sarah Newton, a black Oberlin College graduate and former public school teacher. It would have been quite characteristic for Newton, herself a widow, to have personally reached out to Sarah, persuading her that the facility was interested in providing education, religious instruction and "a reverence and love for God's word," not just for orphans but for "half-orphans" like Lelia.

As much as Sarah doted on Lelia, she apparently agreed to accept the help offered by the women of the orphans' home, arranging for her daughter to live there at least part of every week. In March 1890, Maggie Rector, the home's matron and one of the founders, escorted Lelia to Dessalines Elementary School with the other thirty or so young residents, and enrolled her in first grade. As she was tall for her age, perhaps like her father's family, Lelia's school registration listed her as six years old, though she was still three months shy of her fifth birthday. Already her big smile had begun to work its charm. Sarah would never forget the "kindnesses that were shown her daughter there" by Rector and the others.

CHAPTER 4

St. Louis Woman

———— ✑✒ ————

"I was at my washtubs one morning with a heavy wash before me," Sarah later recalled. "As I bent over the washboard, and looked at my arms buried in soapsuds, I said to myself: 'What are you going to do when you grow old and your back gets stiff? Who is going to take care of your little girl?' This set me to thinking, but with all my thinking I couldn't see how I, a poor washerwoman, was going to better my condition."

For most of the next decade, Sarah pivoted between the cauldron of the streets and the haven of the church, praying for answers. She was desperate to **deliver** herself from drudgery, determined to free Lelia from a similar fate. Daily she struggled to resist the undertow of the dismal life she knew in favor of the prosperous life she coveted. Straddling two worlds, it was as if she carried dual identities. To her neighbors she was "Sallie" McWilliams, a struggling laundress just like them. In her other vision, she was "Sarah," a woman with dreams beyond anything they could imagine.

Always at the mercy of others, she and Lelia moved frequently, often twice or more in one year. For months at a time, she lived with one of her brothers. At other times she and Lelia were scarcely steps ahead of homelessness, squeezed into whatever room they could beg or afford. Because nothing in Mississippi had prepared Sarah for the riptide of the city, she was sucked under again and again by family tragedies, an abusive marriage, a dangerous neighborhood. Finally the resilience she had first mustered after her parents' deaths reemerged. As she set about to reinvent herself, she began to erase relationships and events too painful and shameful to acknowledge.

St. Louis's neighborhood churches battled for the hearts, minds and especially the souls of newcomers like Sarah. In the Deep South, their labor had been essential. Here, the factories preferred to hire equally poor European immigrants over people with darker skins. Here, when life trampled them, they lashed out at each other. Here, corner honky-tonks and beer eased the sting of hopelessness.

St. Paul AME, the Central Baptist Church and the other large black congregations in St. Louis positioned themselves as straitlaced alternatives to vice and immorality. Inside their sanctuaries, Jesus was the antidote to failure, and temperance saved all sinners. Their middle-class members considered themselves the "right kind of Negroes," whose steadfast strategy for racial progress required thrift, self-help, charity and education. Their weekly services, Bible classes, recitals and revivals competed fervently with alley crap games and all-night dives.

When St. Paul moved to a new building a mile west of the central business district in March 1891, Sarah's neighborhood lost its most powerful spiritual anchor. But the women of the church, already linked to Sarah through Lelia's stay at the orphans' home, continued to reach out, encouraging her involvement. Founded in 1841, St. Paul was the second-oldest black Protestant church in St. Louis and the oldest African Methodist Episcopal congregation west of the Mississippi. Steeped in the AME Church's long tradition of political militancy and self-reliance, its ministers had advocated abolition, conducted clandestine schools during slavery and harbored emigrants like Sarah's brother Alexander.

Inside St. Paul's granite-and-stone edifice, Sarah tracked the mannerisms and conversations of local dignitaries and prominent members, especially its doctors, teachers, lawyers and clubwomen. Just as important, she was surrounded by the tangible evidence of their economic clout. Reverend Ezekiel Cottman was proud to remind his flock that they occupied the only church in St. Louis "constructed by and for Negroes." The largest organ in the city, built by the renowned German designer Kilgen, soared above their altar. Their tithes and offerings had made it possible for them to savor Mozart anthems, soothing hymns and sedately rendered Negro spirituals each Sunday.

It was no small joy on a frosty winter morning for Sarah to nestle into a pew and feel the warmth she could never generate in her unheated flat. If she occasionally longed for the rousing, toe-tapping music of Delta's Pollard Church, she certainly did not miss the raucous noises and sour odors she had momentarily left behind on her block. As sunbeams warmed through the stained-glass windows and chandeliers twinkled above the carpeted aisles of the amphitheater sanctuary, Sarah and the 900-member congregation heard religious as well as political messages. In 1892 Reverend Cottman joined several prominent black Missourians to declare "Lamentation Day," a gathering that drew 1,500 blacks to St. Louis to protest lynching through fasting and prayer. Visiting bishops and church officials often discussed global issues, from the church's missionary work in Africa to the persecution of Russian Jews and Turkish Christians.

Around the time St. Paul moved to Lawton and Leffingwell, a still predominantly white area, Sarah joined her younger brother Solomon at 1407 Linden Street, near the church's former location. Having the rest of her family—James, Alexander and his wife, Mary, and Owen's estranged wife, Samira—within walking distance was a welcome bonus for her and her daughter. Dumas Elementary, the school Lelia probably attended at the time, was a straight shot through their yard to the next block over on Lucas Street. Between 1891 and 1896 Sarah and Lelia remained in the same area, switching from rooming house to rooming house along Linden, an overcrowded alleyway where stoops served as parlors and windowsills as terraces.

In April 1893, Sarah had to have been devastated when Alexander died from an intestinal ailment. With their eldest brother gone, the family in St. Louis now included two widows (Sarah and Mary), one abandoned wife (Samira) and brothers James and Solomon. Owen, the brother they probably had not seen since his 1883 move to New Mexico, now ran a saloon and "gaming table" in Albuquerque. With his new wife, Lucy Crockett Breedlove, he had started a new family, now numbering two daughters. In March 1892 he had been elected chairman pro tem of the Albuquerque Colored Republicans, no doubt aided by his brother-in-law, C. C. Crockett, an already established member of the town's black community. Sarah's sister Louvenia remained in Mississippi, with problems of her own: her son Willie Powell would soon be convicted of manslaughter in Natchez, Mississippi, and sent to Mississippi's notorious Parchman Prison.

With her family grieving and in disarray, Sarah drifted into a relationship with a man named John Davis, who had recently arrived from De Soto, Missouri, a town twenty-five miles south of St. Louis. Because he had no home of his own to offer, he moved in with Sarah and nine-year-old Lelia during the spring of 1894.

A few months later, on Saturday, August 11, they married before a justice of the peace in a stuffy City Hall chamber. Outside, despite a light breeze, the city baked at a suffocating 100 degrees in the midst of a weeklong Midwestern heat wave. That night a brief shower roused the humidity along the dank brick sidewalks. The sweltering weather was a fitting launch to a troubled marriage. Almost from the start, Sarah regretted her decision. A decade later she would begin the process of jettisoning all mention of Davis from her scrupulously crafted life story. But at the time she must have believed it was the best that she could do.

On her own for so long, Sarah no doubt welcomed the presence of a man, perhaps convincing herself that Lelia needed a stepfather. Surely she wanted companionship and the respectability that seemed to accompany marriage. But Davis was a poor choice, unable to deliver on any of her expectations. Something as simple as the signatures on their marriage license told part of the tale. His name was scrawled so haphazardly that "John" was barely decipherable, "Davis" only relatively more legible. "Miss Sallie McWilliams," on the line below, lacked flourish, but was deliberate and clear.

Sarah could not have had any illusions that marrying Davis would allow her to put away her washtubs. As with most unskilled, urban black men, his options were limited to low-paying, temporary and seasonal jobs. St. Louis's German workers controlled the trade unions and had no qualms about reserving positions in carpentry, bricklaying and plumbing for themselves. Despite thousands of jobs in the city's foundries and plants, blacks made up only 2 percent of factory workers. Those few who passed through industry's gates were relegated to menial chores in the clay mines, brickyards and tobacco factories. Washerwomen like Sarah often were their families' primary breadwinners, not because their husbands did not want to work, but because recent European immigrants were crowding them out of the market. In 1900, with decent-paying employment off-limits to large numbers of black men, 26 percent of all married black women in America worked—most as domestics or farmworkers—while only 3 percent of married white women were employed. An overwhelming 65 percent of the nation's washerwomen at the turn of the century were black.

Whatever legitimate difficulties Davis may have had finding work, Sarah soon learned that he was a shirker. "He was never a man to work and provide for his family as a man ought," her friend Jennie Gully Lias said, remembering that he and Sarah "were constantly in quarrels because she failed to get a reasonable portion of his wages." They also fought about his girlfriend and his drinking. "The general rumor of the community was that he was dividing his wages with a woman by the name of Susie," said Lias. "He was addicted to the habit of drinking and would come home in a drunken condition and upon being questioned, would strike, beat and maltreat Sallie."

Sarah's longtime friend Ida Winchester called him "fussy, mean and dangerous." Another acquaintance said he had been "before the courts many times," causing Sarah much humiliation and disappointment. But she remained locked in this volatile dance, trapped just as she had been in her brother-in-law's house. To survive, she developed an iron exterior, but she also knew that she was subjecting her daughter to Davis's belligerence. Just as a young Sarah had been able to run to her brothers from Jesse Powell, Lelia may have found safety a block away with her uncle

James. Whatever misdeeds Davis inflicted upon Lelia, she and Sarah buried it in their pasts.

As the black population began to shift westward into the areas that whites had abandoned, Sarah's central city district deteriorated into the "toughest neighborhood in St. Louis," so dangerous the police called it the Bad Lands. In 1894 and 1895, when local murders nearly doubled from twenty-five to forty-seven, the police chief pronounced Eleventh Street—four blocks from Sarah's Linden Street apartment—"the most prolific murder center in the city." Nearly every drinking establishment—the White Lion, William Curtis's Elite Saloon, Dutch Diegel's and Stark's—along that corridor could be linked, if not to a murder, at least to a bloody brawl.

Sarah had every reason to be concerned about what Lelia saw and heard when she passed the dives near Twelfth and Linden, where "female denizens, clad in diaphanous wrappers, constantly congregate on the street ... filling the air with the plaint of barefaced solicitation and the revolting sounds of lewd profanity." One block north of their apartment, dingy yellow awnings shaded busy Morgan Street's secondhand clothing stores, cafes and barbershops. From morning until night, brothels and ten-cent bathhouses hosted a stream of unsavory patrons.

A few of the bars along Morgan fancied themselves a cut above the gut-bucket hangouts—among them, the headquarters of the Four Hundred Social Club, which had given "entertainments that were the admiration of the colored race, the envy of all competitors and the terror of the police," a reporter wrote at the time. On November 19, 1895, the group's Grand Cake Walk Contest was the talk of the neighborhood. Staged a few blocks from Sarah's home at Stolle's Hall, a respectable gathering place, its judges included B. J. Owens, a family friend and partner in Alexander's first barbershop. The promise of festivities spiked with ragtime's syncopated rhythms guaranteed a crowd. A dance competition, regardless of the church's admonition against such evils, delighted nearly everyone in a part of town where few affordable pleasures flourished.

Apparently the evening unfolded without incident. But later that night, the first of a spate of nasty murders that spilled over into the new year began near Sarah's street. All it took was a bottle, a gun and a jealous boyfriend to leave another man dead on the floor of an apartment at 1245 Gay Street, the building where Sarah's brother James had lived just a year earlier. Less than a week later, on the day after Thanksgiving, three blocks from Sarah in the 1200 block of Linden, a ruffian named Alexander Royal slashed his girlfriend, Jessie Sims, ten times with the butcher knife they had used to carve their holiday turkey. The couple was so well known in the neighborhood that the details of Sims's cuts—including "two stab wounds in the chest, one penetrating the lung"—quickly spread from house to house. Two hours afterward another domestic dispute left a woman near death from multiple lacerations at 1207 Wash Street, close to Sarah's first St. Louis rooming house. Not two weeks later, in a fight related to the Sims murder, one neighbor fatally shot another at 1902 Linden.

On Christmas morning, two days after Sarah's twenty-eighth birthday, Shelton Lee, better known as "Stack" Lee, fatally shot William Lyons at Curtis's Elite Saloon at Eleventh and Morgan, just four blocks from where Sarah and John Davis lived. The fight, as a popular song later recounted, began when Lee accused Lyons of stealing his "magic Stetson" hat.

> Stackalee shot Billy once; his body fell to the floor.
> He cried out, Oh, please, Stack, please don't shoot me no more.

"Stackalee," as he came to be known, was so outrageous that he bribed his way out of jail for a five-hour Sunday afternoon saloon cruise six weeks after his arrest. Accompanied by two generously bribed deputy sheriffs, he drew crowds and headlines as he visited his girlfriend near Twelfth and Wash, then bought a round of drinks for everyone at the bar where he had murdered Lyons. By then the shooting had sparked a turf battle between Stackalee's friends, who were members of "The 400," and Lyons's friends, who belonged to a rival social club. "There is continual warfare between the two divisions," wrote the *St. Louis Republic*. "Excitement over the crime is, and has been, ever since it occurred, at white heat among the colored people."

While official St. Louis prepared for the June 1896 Republican convention, the Bad Lands murders continued. By the end of the year all the Breedloves had fled the neighborhood, moving west to the still notorious, but somewhat less lethal, Mill Creek Valley, where blacks had lived since the 1850s. Bordered by Twentieth Street on the east and Grand Avenue on the west, the area derived its name from a dammed creek that had powered a flour mill earlier in the century. A web of train tracks formed its southern edge behind the magnificent, two-year-old Union Station, then the largest passenger terminal in America. Within its boundaries was Chestnut Valley, a stretch of saloons, bordellos and pool halls that clustered along Chestnut and Market streets across from the depot and catered to residents and layover passengers alike. Musician W. C. Handy, composer of "St. Louis Blues," recalled nearby Targee Street during the early 1890s. "I don't think I'd want to forget the highroller Stetson hats of the men or the diamonds the girls wore in their ears," he said, adding a description of the area's prostitutes. "There were those who sat for company in little plush parlors under gaslights."

In 1898, Sarah, John and thirteen-year-old Lelia shared a home with James Breedlove at 2142 Walnut Street, one block west of Union Station and only a few blocks from St. Paul Church. Following their pattern on Linden Street, Sarah and John lived in at least four homes on Walnut Street between 1896 and 1902. Twice they shared an address with James until he married in September 1899.

Although the trains squealed through the night, and the Market Street revelers stumbled along their alley until daybreak, Sarah likely preferred the mix of new neighbors. Here, forced together by segregation, both laborers and middle-class blacks mingled on the same block. Among them was Maria Harrison, a board member of the orphans' home and founder of the Missouri Federation of Colored Women, who lived across the street.

At nearby L'Ouverture Elementary School, Lelia was surrounded by other black children from a variety of backgrounds. Her classmates' parents included a journalist, a doctor, a music teacher and a railroad porter, though 95 percent were unskilled laborers, washerwomen or domestic servants. Girls with neatly parted hair and pinafores sat side by side at double wooden desks with boys in heavy woolen suits. Some children, recently arrived from the South, had never attended school. Though their classrooms were cramped and their supplies inadequate, the proportion of black students enrolled in St. Louis's public schools exceeded that of white students during the last twenty years of the nineteenth century.

Davis's disruptive behavior made Sarah all the more determined to create stability in Lelia's life. She was so insistent that her daughter attend school regularly that Lelia missed only six days of class between September 1898 and June 1899. But her 1899 school year was tumultuous. Sarah, rather than John Davis—who previously had been listed as Lelia's guardian—was now named as Lelia's parent on the September enrollment record, suggesting that they had separated. And while Lelia's attendance remained excellent during the first quarter, the rest of the year was disastrous. She attended only twenty-three days of school between November and June, missing the entire third quarter. By the end of her seventh-grade year, she had been readmitted a startling six times.

Was Sarah hiding from Davis during this time? Did she move away to protect herself and Lelia? Was Lelia ill? The answers lie in the part of her life story she wished to keep hidden. But clearly the consistency she had tried so hard to establish for her child crumbled that year. When Lelia reenrolled in September 1900, John Davis was once again listed as her guardian, perhaps because he and Sarah had reconciled. That year Lelia missed only thirteen days of school.

Lelia's June 1901 graduation was a ceremony L'Ouverture's teachers took great care to fill with poetry, music and orations. But Sarah may also have felt that even on this day of triumph, she had failed Lelia. Unlike many of her classmates, Lelia had not been admitted to Sumner High School, perhaps because the months of school she had missed had prevented her from passing the entrance exam. It was a disappointment, to be sure, because Oscar Minor Waring, the city's first black principal, was well known for inspiring his students with missionary zeal. An Oberlin graduate who spoke five languages, Waring had helped establish the curriculum for the first generation of black teachers in St. Louis.

Because class and color lines were sharply drawn in St. Louis's black community, Lelia—the dark-skinned daughter of a laundress—was excluded from the parties, teas and charity events hosted by the Twentieth Century Girls' Club. A social group that included some of her schoolmates, the club accepted members only from those families it deemed prominent and worthy.

But Lelia, with her flashing brown eyes and easy smile, surely did not go unnoticed among her peers. At sixteen she probably was near her adult height of close to six feet. And though her stepfather may have embarrassed her, Lelia was always well groomed, her clothes at least as well laundered, pressed and starched as those of Sarah's best customers. But with no clear plans for Lelia's schooling, Sarah fretted about her daughter's future. As an adult, Lelia was passionate about music and dancing, so it is not hard to imagine that Chestnut Valley's honky-tonks would have held a strong lure for a curious young woman.

Tom Turpin's Rosebud Cafe, headquarters for the city's best ragtime pianists, was "open all day and all night" and shared an alley with the Davis/McWilliams household. For at least the first few months Turpin was open, James Breedlove and his wife, Hettie, lived across the street at 2213 Market. Turpin, "the uncrowned master of American syncopated music," had penned "Harlem Rag" in 1892, just as the new music form was emerging. While Scott Joplin's name and compositions have endured, it was Turpin whose piano playing first ignited a generation of St. Louis musicians.

Whatever aspirations Sarah had for herself, her hopes for Lelia were even greater. The possibility that her daughter might spend her life either frequenting bars or leaning over a washboard motivated Sarah to work harder. "I did washing for families in St. Louis, and saved enough . . . to put my little girl in a school in Knoxville, Tennessee," Sarah proudly told a reporter years later. To keep Lelia from the delicious distractions of Market Street, she gladly sent $7.85 to Knoxville College for the first month's room and board during the fall of 1902. She very likely welcomed the news that Sunday chapel was mandatory and that permits to visit the city were only "sparingly granted, and at night never without safe escort."

Founded by the United Presbyterian Church in 1875, Knoxville College—whose curriculum included high school and college-level courses—focused both on practical, "industrial" education for the descendants of former slaves and on "normal school" instruction to train teachers. Atop a hill shaded by oak, maple and cedar trees, the school looked down upon a sleepy town of only 50,000 residents, one-tenth the population of St. Louis, and with hardly any of the temptations.

When seventeen-year-old Lelia arrived on the twenty-two-acre campus in September 1902, she was admitted as a seventh-grade student, a reflection of the lessons she had missed during her sporadic 1899 school year. As one of twenty-four students in her class, she studied handwriting, elocution, English grammar, arithmetic, geography, physiology and sewing. Like the school's three hundred other students, she dressed in an intentionally unremarkable uniform: a $6 navy-blue serge Norfolk jacket and plain gored skirt in winter, a $1.75 navy chambray shirtwaist in spring. In Elnathan Hall, the girls' dormitory, she and the other students were expected to help with laundry and dining-room chores.

While Lelia was away, two of her mother's three remaining brothers died within eight months of each other. First, in November 1902, forty-year-old James died of heart disease after a monthlong illness. Less than a year later, in August 1903, Solomon succumbed to tubercular meningitis, one of the contagious respiratory ailments that accounted for 16 percent of St. Louis's African American deaths at the turn of the century. Now only Sarah, Louvenia and Owen remained of the original Breedlove siblings. But once again Owen had dropped out of sight, abandoning Lucy and their four daughters—Anjetta, Thirsapen, Mattie and Gladis—who had moved from Albuquerque to Denver in 1901.

In November 1903, just weeks before Sarah's thirty-sixth birthday, John Davis claimed that she had deserted him. Certainly it was a long-overdue decision, and may actually have happened even earlier than he recalled. To no one's surprise, Davis wasted no time moving in with Susie.

Because Sarah so rigorously tried to obliterate any memory of Davis, the details of their final separation are skimpy and contradictory, pieced together from faulty memories almost twenty years after the fact. Their failure to legally divorce was an unfortunate oversight that eventually would cause trouble for both Sarah and Lelia. But during the final months when they lived together—while Davis continued to flaunt his relationship with Susie—Sarah had begun quietly seeing a man named Charles Joseph Walker, possibly as early as the fall of 1902, when Lelia left for Knoxville. Conveniently, he lived at 1519 Clark Street, just east of Union Station and within easy walking distance of Sarah's home.

Listed in the 1900 St. Louis city directory as a newsman, Walker likely sold subscriptions and advertising and may have done some reporting for one of St. Louis's three black newspapers, possibly *The Clarion*. He may also have worked for a time as a barber and in a saloon, the kinds of jobs that helped hone his skills of persuasion. Walker, who had just enough formal education to impress Sarah, struck her as a man with the right amount of ambition to match her own. In turn, he admired her drive and desire to succeed. He was a mix of boaster, charmer and self-promoter, fancying himself a natural-born salesman. Of medium build, he loved fine suits and considered well-shined shoes a necessity. He was "what you would call yellow," an acquaintance later remembered, referring to his light complexion. C. J. Walker, Sarah believed, was someone with whom she could build a future.

One of the friends who may have encouraged Sarah to leave John Davis was Jessie Batts Robinson, a member of St. Paul AME Church, who was to become a lifelong confidante. An 1889 graduate of Sumner High School, Jessie had taught at Banneker Elementary School during the early 1890s. In a class photograph during that period, her serene and pleasant face is framed by smoothly twisted French knots at the nape of her neck and atop her head. If she and Sarah did not meet during the year or two that Lelia attended Banneker, they most certainly became acquainted in the fellowship hall at St. Paul. And although their experiences were vastly different, Jessie early recognized Sarah's eagerness to improve her life. As one of the privileged few who had benefited from Oscar Minor Waring's tutelage, Jessie felt duty-bound to assist women like Sarah. At some point, she opened her home to mother and daughter, exposing them to a world of culture, etiquette and letters far removed from the drunken outbursts of John Davis.

Once Jessie married, she became an active member of the Court of Calanthe, the women's auxiliary of the Knights of Pythias. Modeled on the white Knights of Pythias, which had been founded in Washington, D.C., in 1864, the fraternal organization was one of the many secret societies developed by blacks during the nineteenth century for the health and social welfare of their communities. Eventually Jessie would persuade Sarah to join the Court. Her husband, Christopher K. Robinson, held leadership positions in the group, serving as Grand Chancellor of the order of Missouri during 1895 and later as Supreme Grand Secretary of the national body. A slim, brown-skinned man, whose oval face was distinguished by a neatly trimmed mustache and a receding hairline, "C.K." was publisher of *The Clarion*. In that role, he often interacted with the mayor and other prominent St. Louis citizens.

* * *

With Lelia enrolled in school at Knoxville, Sarah had accomplished more than she had ever believed possible. Now it was time to work on herself. During that period she was "educated in night school in St. Louis," according to one source. Although no public school records exist to verify the dates of her enrollment, it was not unusual for adult black women to attend school, as did sixty-three washerwomen who studied bookkeeping, English, reading, arithmetic and geography in night school at Dumas and L'Ouverture in the fall of 1900. In 1903 students older than twenty paid twenty cents per week for a five-week course at Dumas, Delaney and L'Ouverture. There were also free evening schools during the fall of 1904, including one at L'Ouverture from seven to nine o'clock three nights a week and one offered by George Vashon, who was "forming female classes for instruction in language and belles-lettres, mathematics and penmanship . . . three evenings of each week."

St. Paul's Mite Missionary Society also allowed Sarah to develop social skills while doing good deeds. By helping those who were now as needy as she had been when she first arrived in St. Louis, she gained confidence. As fellow members of the church and the missionary society, Jessie Robinson and Sarah worked together on community projects. "Membership within church clubs blurred, somewhat, the economic, educational, occupational and social distinctions between the women," historian Darlene Clark Hine has written. "To be sure, the better educated and more socially prominent women generally dominated the presidencies of the more prestigious church clubs. With rare exceptions, however, what counted was the amount of time, energy, willingness to work, fund raising ability and leadership qualities which individual women exhibited."

Sarah quickly took the initiative to create leadership roles for herself. Touched by a *Post-Dispatch* story about an elderly man struggling to support his blind sister and invalid wife, Sarah collected money for the family from her friends. "She felt it was her duty to do even more [so] she arranged for a pound party through which means groceries in abundance were given, also a purse of $7.50," a St. Louis newspaper reported many years later. No longer the recipient of charity, she had become, in her own small way, a benefactor.

Around this time, her relationship with C.J., a more self-assured attitude and an improved status seem to have merged to make Sarah wish for a more smartly groomed appearance. Especially self-conscious about her hair, she was no longer content to cover it with the head wraps that now seemed to her more suitable for plantation cotton fields than city life.

In the mid-1890s, shortly after Sarah married John Davis, her hair had begun to fall out. The complaint was a common one for women of the era, due usually to a combination of infrequent washing, illness, high fever, scalp disease, low-protein diets and damaging hair treatments. Stress triggered by Davis's mercurial behavior may also have aggravated her hair loss.

In a photograph taken around the time of her marriage, Sarah's gaze was determined and focused. Primly dressed, she wore a single piece of jewelry—a simple silver brooch—below the piping of her high-necked collar. But, in an era when long tresses dominated newspaper illustrations and the covers of ladies' magazines, she was less than satisfied with her look. Though she had likely fussed over her hair for the sitting, the best she could do was to smooth her short, stubbly sides and fashion a dry, fuzzy puff of bangs above her forehead.

When her hair had begun "breaking off and falling out," Sarah later said, "I tried everything mentioned to me without any result."

Her experimentation soon would lead to a solution, not just for her hair but for her life.

CHAPTER 5

Answered Prayers

— *ev_{no}* —

"I was on the verge of becoming entirely bald," Sarah often told other women. Ashamed of the "frightful" appearance of her hair and desperate for a solution, she "prayed to the Lord" for guidance. "He answered my prayer," she vouched. "For one night I had a dream, and in that dream a big black man appeared to me and told me what to mix for my hair. Some of the remedy was from Africa, but I sent for it, mixed it, put it on my scalp and in a few weeks my hair was coming in faster than it had ever fallen out." After obtaining the same results on her daughter and her neighbors, she later told a reporter, "I made up my mind I would begin to sell it."

But going into business had not been her original goal. "When I made my discovery, I had no idea of placing it on the market for the benefit of others; I was simply in search of something that would save or restore my own hair." This miraculous concoction, she believed, was nothing less than "an inspiration from God," a heaven-sent gift for her to "place in the reach of those who appreciate beautiful hair and healthy scalps, which is the glory of woman."

Sarah's account of her discovery, embellished with claims of divine providence and intervention, proved to be an ingenious marketing device. By also invoking Africa, she invested her potion with the magical power of herbal medicine still practiced by some of her potential customers. Her secret ingredient, she maintained, came not from the sources known to the white-owned hair-preparations manufacturers whose ads regularly caricatured black women in St. Louis's Negro weeklies, but from "a big black man" and the land of her ancestors. Her efforts to portray herself as a healer with a direct link to Africa were not unique. Among others, a Dr. W. D. Deshay regularly advertised his "Hair Feeder" as being "well recommended by the leading hair dressers in Biblis, Egypt and Gondar City, Abyssinia."

Although nothing in Sarah's scalp ointment appears to have been available exclusively from Africa, she well may have been referring to her use of coconut oil, an ingredient that *could* have come from West Africa's tropical coast. The impression that her salve contained rare and difficult-to-secure substances only enhanced her dramatic dream scenario. At any rate, all the other items—thick petrolatum for her oil base; beeswax as a stabilizer; copper sulfate and precipitated sulfur as sanitizing and healing agents; violet extract perfume to mask the sulfur; and the disinfectant carbolic acid for a separate treatment—were easily obtainable in St. Louis, because at the time only New York rivaled that city in the number of wholesale pharmaceutical houses and drug and chemical suppliers.

When skeptics found Sarah's story more apocryphal than verifiable, she acknowledged that "part of my story may sound strange, but it is the absolute truth." In one ongoing dispute, however, her account would serve as a virtually unchallengeable defense to fend off a rival who claimed noticeable similarities between the hair care products they both manufactured.

Sarah's personal struggle with scalp disease and baldness had made her excruciatingly aware of the importance others placed on hair. Even her Bible offered no comfort. "Judge in yourselves: is it comely that a woman pray unto God uncovered? . . . If a woman have long hair, it is a glory to her; for her hair is given her for a covering," read I Corinthians. So woe be unto those women like Sarah who failed to measure up to their more generously tressed sisters. "And it shall come to pass, that . . . instead of well-set hair, baldness . . . and burning instead of beauty," read an Old Testament passage.

Growing up in the postbellum South, Sarah had been bombarded with messages that she was unattractive, that her frizzy, brittle hair was ugly and unsightly, that her skin color rendered her powerless. If her grandmother or mother had learned ancient African beautifying hair care techniques, those traditions were not transmitted to Sarah or her sister, Louvenia. On some plantations during slavery, such visible Africanisms—along with tribal names, drums and religious practices—were prohibited lest slaves be emboldened to plot some clandestine insurrection. Even had they been allowed, antebellum life left little chance for intricate, time-consuming braids and elaborate cornrows. And slave masters tended to mock any efforts at personal adornment as "putting on airs." Though Sarah's transplanted foremothers may have fashioned special garments and accessories from their limited slave-era wardrobes for Sunday worship and holiday celebrations, daily grooming, by necessity, had become utilitarian and perfunctory for all but a few black women.

Like most late-nineteenth-century rural Americans whose crude homes lacked indoor plumbing, Sarah was ignorant of the most basic hair care hygiene. She later recalled the care she had given to laundering her clothes and those of her customers, but old wives' tales had convinced many women—black and white—that monthly hair shampoos were more than sufficient. Some washed their hair even less frequently during the winter because they feared catching colds or pneumonia in unheated tenements and shacks. The result was rampant scalp disease: dandruff, lice, eczema, fungal infections, alopecia and tetter, a particularly pesky form of psoriasis.

Even as a child Sarah noticed the value that was placed on hair texture and skin color. As a woman with African features, she frequently was reminded that white skin and shiny, straight hair were more prized than black skin and coiled, kinky hair.

During slavery these obvious physical traits had effectively distinguished slave from freeman and been used to maintain social, economic and legal control over the bondsmen. By comparing blacks' hair to that of sheep's wool, some whites used pseudoscience as "proof" that people of African descent were more animal than human, and therefore inherently inferior. And it was not only whites who enforced a social hierarchy based on skin color. Those slaves and free people of color who could claim white ancestry—especially those whose slave-owning fathers had provided for their education in America and abroad—formed the core of an antebellum elite that clustered in Washington, Philadelphia, Charleston, New Orleans, Atlanta and a handful of other cities. Well into the twentieth century some of their descendants continued to distance themselves from their darker brethren to protect their own tenuous social standing.

By the early 1900s, upward mobility among some formally educated and ambitious darker-skinned African Americans had begun to blur the class lines in some communities, but the merit bestowed upon long, straight hair remained. Among the women around Sarah—in her church, in her neighborhood, throughout the city—appearance correlated with prosperity. Well-groomed hair among the black elite meant hair that was not matted and scraggly like Sarah's. For most African American women the desired look depended upon a mix of European or Native American genes, and frequently both. As Sarah continued to lose her hair, she was susceptible to the trends that were set, not just by the unattainable standards of the well-coiffed mannequins in St. Louis's department store windows, but by those of her friend Jessie Robinson and some of the stylish middle-class women of St. Paul AME Church.

Black men's opinions on the subject—and their criteria for selecting marriage partners—fueled a contentious debate within the black community that Sarah herself observed. "It is generally the case that those Black men who clamor most loudly and persistently for the purity of Negro blood have taken themselves mulatto wives," wrote T. Thomas Fortune, editor of the *New York Age*, one of the nation's most widely read black newspapers. Fortune, himself a former slave, was descended from Africans, Native Americans and Europeans, including an Irish grandfather.

Fannie Barrier Williams, an activist and social reformer, blasted those black men who, she charged, were "apt to look to other races for their types of beauty and character . . . What our girls and women have a right to demand from our best men is that they cease to imitate the artificial standards of other people and create a race standard of their own," she wrote. Rather than choose "the most royal queen in ebony," alleged Nannie Helen Burroughs, an eloquent orator and masterful organizer, "there are men right in our own race, and they are legion, who would rather marry a woman for her color than her character."

In a society that denied legal rights and economic opportunities on the basis of race and gender, Sarah and other women endured daily emotional and psychological pressure to assimilate by minimizing the physical reminders of slavery. No matter how beautiful, how well groomed, how stylish she may have managed to make herself, Sarah would never meet America's standard of beauty. At the turn of the twentieth century that standard was the Gibson Girl.

"You can always tell when a girl is taking the Gibson Cure by the way she fixes her hair," said one observer of the wasp-waisted young white women created by magazine illustrator Charles Dana Gibson in 1890. All the rage for nearly two decades, this "ideal American girl," with her "chic, haughty and graceful" pose, was in part distinguished by the long, silky tresses artfully arranged beneath the brim of her beribboned hat. The faultless Gibson Look, when attempted by women of any race or class, seemed most easily attained with the artist's ink pen. Most black women, and certainly Sarah, were hard-pressed to twist their full lips into a dainty Cupid's bow. That the tightly nipped Gibson torso was physically impossible to sustain for any woman who needed to exhale did not prevent American women from attempting the impossible.

In America and in Europe, long, lustrous locks were prized for their beauty as well as for their commercial value. "Fashionable Paris alone, and London as much more," wrote Dr. C. Henri Leonard in 1880, "consumes annually over one hundred thousand pounds of human hair in the manufacture of her chignons and wigs." Blond hair was favored over brunet or black, bringing as much as two dollars per ounce, "if of fine quality."

Hair care—or the lack of it—was a carefully calibrated indicator of class, no more so than among middle-class blacks, who warily watched the steady flow of Deep South newcomers, most of them unsophisticated, uneducated and haphazardly groomed as Sarah had been when she first arrived. Newspaper editors frequently commented on the migrants coarse and country ways. "With the approach of summer comes the annual appearance of heads out of windows," ranted a *St. Louis Palladium* editorial. "On Lawton, Market, Morgan, Johnson streets . . . can be seen: HEADS. NAPPY HEADS! WOOLLY HEADS! COMBED HEADS! UNCOMBED HEADS! Heads of all descriptions, especially when a band is near by or the congregation of a church is being dismissed." While some black newspapers in other cities refused to accept ads for face bleaches and hair straighteners, St. Louis's three black weeklies—presumably in need of the money—were filled with such promotions.

Eager to cure her baldness, Sarah likely tried some of those concoctions, including the ones that claimed the ability to simultaneously grow and straighten hair. Had she already had healthy hair, she may have been satisfied to style it into her own black version of the proper Victorian-era coif. But because her hair was too abused and damaged to display whatever natural beauty it possessed, she was vulnerable to the patent medicine industry's fraudulent advertising, unchecked in the heyday of cure-alls and elixirs. Not until popular magazines such as *The Ladies' Home Journal* and *Collier's Weekly* exposed these firms' misleading claims during 1904 and 1905 did Congress take steps to pass the Pure Food and Drugs Act of 1906, requiring the manufacturers to deliver the results they promised.

"During my many years of research endeavoring to find something to improve my own hair, in preparations manufactured by others, I was always unsuccessful," Sarah often said of her predream experiments. But another St. Louis woman charged that Sarah's late-night revelation was entirely fabricated, that her "research" was filched. In fact, Annie Minerva Turnbo asserted that it was *she* who had "personally" restored Sarah's hair.

When Turnbo arrived in St. Louis in 1902 from Lovejoy, Illinois, she set up shop on bustling Market Street directly across from Tom Turpin's always open Rosebud Cafe. An ambitious woman, whose childhood fascination with her sisters' hair had led her into the hairdressing business, Turnbo moved to Missouri to capitalize on the hoopla surrounding preparations for the 1904 World's Fair. Inside her four-room flat at 2223 Market Street, she specialized in scalp treatments and hair growing. After a very brief marriage to a Mr. Pope, she adopted the name Pope-Turnbo for her products.

Exactly how Sarah Breedlove McWilliams Davis met Pope-Turnbo is unknown. After hearing of her reputation for hair restoration, Sarah may have sought her out. They could also have become acquainted through Sarah's widowed sister-in-law, Hettie Martin Breedlove, whose family, like Pope-Turnbo's, was from tiny Metropolis, Illinois. And just as easily, their first meeting could have been the result of a fortuitous knock on Sarah's door. Pope-Turnbo, after opening her modest workspace, conducted a "diligent house-to-house canvass" to introduce her preparations to the women of Chestnut Valley. In order to attract potential customers, she persuaded neighborhood mothers and daughters to accept free scalp treatments.

Some years later Pope-Turnbo would declare that she had treated Sarah on "South 16th Street," a possible reference to 1519 Clark, the apartment near Sixteenth Street where C. J. Walker lived from 1900 to 1905. What is not in dispute is that Sarah was one of Pope-Turnbo's earliest sales agents, probably joining her sometime during 1903.

Pope-Turnbo claimed that, in the process of teaching Sarah her hair growing method, she also had successfully treated the scalp ailments which had caused her hair loss. The two most likely problems—seborrhea, commonly called dandruff, and psoriasis, then known as tetter—had plagued humans for centuries. Tetter's tiny scales itched intensely, inflaming scalps and creating sores. Dandruff—which was sometimes severe enough to cause baldness—had been likened to the mealy consistency of bran by Hippocrates, the father of Western medicine, more than two thousand years ago. In chronic cases such as Sarah's, dirt, lint and sebum—the fatty secretion from the scalp's sebaceous glands—clogged pores, inhibited circulation and destroyed hair follicles. If Sarah used the widely distributed patent medicines that were heavily laced with alcohol and other harsh chemicals, she only made the malady worse by stripping her hair of its natural oils. From Pope-Turnbo, she may have learned to shampoo her hair more often. "Clean scalps mean clean bodies," Pope-Turnbo preached to her clients. "Better appearance means greater business opportunities, higher social standing, cleaner living and beautiful homes," her company literature later said. It was a self-improvement strategy that Sarah already had observed among her church sisters.

Sarah and Pope-Turnbo had much in common. Both now in their midthirties, they had been orphaned as young girls and reared by older sisters, though Pope-Turnbo's childhood seems to have been free from the physical abuse and material deprivation that Sarah endured. Her father, described as a Civil War veteran, had owned a farm in southern Illinois. Unlike Sarah, Pope-Turnbo, the tenth of eleven children, attended elementary school and at least a few months of high school until an unidentified illness caused her to end her formal studies. To distinguish her from other hairdressers, Pope-Turnbo's official biography claimed that "with the return of her health, she turned to the study of chemistry for the scientific background which she realized was necessary to make her proficient in the art of hair culture." In other versions of her story she said she had had "a natural gift from childhood for growing hair."

In 1900, when Pope-Turnbo was thirty-one years old, she moved from her sister's home in Peoria, Illinois, to Lovejoy, where she set up a crude laboratory, developed a liquid shampoo and began her "business of beauty culture and hair dressing" in a rented "weather-beaten building." After much trial and error, she said, she also developed her Wonderful Hair Grower. "I went around in the buggy and made speeches, demonstrated the shampoo on myself, and talked about cleanliness and hygiene until they realized I was right," Pope-Turnbo said of her efforts to convince naysayers.

Pope-Turnbo—and later Sarah—made much of their proprietary mixtures, but the real secret was a regimen of regular shampoos, scalp massage, nutritious food and an easily duplicated, sulfur-based formula that neither of them had originated. Home remedies and medicinal compounds with similar ingredients had been prescribed at least since the sixteenth century. Later in 1842 British surgeon Sir John E. Erichsen favored "stimulating washes, ointments [and] lotions," including solutions with copper sulfate, cayenne pepper and Spanish fly. "Beauty Notes," a syndicated column originally written in 1904 for the *Washington Star*'s predominantly white readership, advised twice-daily applications of sulfate quinine, glycerin and other ominous-sounding ingredients to remedy baldness. "Shampoo with tar soap once a month and brush dandruff from the scalp every week," the writer advised. With aspirin available for less than a decade, and penicillin's discovery more than twenty years away, the state of American medicine, especially in regard to nonfatal skin diseases, was rudimentary at best.

By the time Pope-Turnbo met Sarah, there were scores of packaged products—some effective, some bogus—available in pharmacies and via mail order to fill the medical void. Even Sears, Roebuck and Company advertised "Princess Tonic Hair Restorer" in its 1897 catalogue.

In early 1880 the drug firm of Weeks & Potter began a national promotion for Cuticura—"the purest, sweetest, most effective remedies for skin, scalp and hair"—for the same ailments that troubled Sarah. "Bathe the affected parts with hot water and Cuticura Soap . . . and apply Cuticura Ointment freely, to allay itching, irritation and inflammation," read one advertisement. Cuticura's high-quality products attracted both white and black customers. But many other white-owned businesses openly exploited the insecurity many African Americans had developed about their distinctive hair texture. Knowing that tightly curled hair would automatically appear as much as several inches longer when straightened, these companies advertised their hair straighteners as hair "growers." In the process they equated naturally kinky hair with inferiority and homeliness. Companies with products like Kinkilla, Kink-No-More and Straightine all presented themselves as manufacturers of the "only" and "most wonderful" products of their kind. The Boston Chemical Company claimed to have marketed its hair tonic and straightener, Ozono, to "members of the colored race" since 1875. "Ozono will take the Kinks out of Knotty, Kinky,

Harsh, Curly, Refractory, Troublesome Hair," heralded its ad. "It will make short, harsh hair long and straight" and keep hair "straight forever."

The Original Ozonized Ox Marrow Company, proclaiming its product since the 1860s as "the first preparation ever sold for straightening kinky hair," contrasted a pen-and-ink drawing of an unkempt, wiry-haired black woman with her well-groomed mirror image to illustrate the "results" of its product. The Richmond, Virginia–based Crane and Company's pitch for its Wonderful Face Bleach—guaranteed to create a "peach-like complexion"—was equally insulting. Their cream, they promised, would "turn the skin of a black or brown person four or five shades lighter, and a mulatto person perfectly white." Although the St. Louis Palladium ran such ads each week—possibly because its publisher, J. W. Wheeler, happened to be the local distribution agent for Ozono—many black newspapers refused the revenue because they objected to the content.

In 1905 Fred Moore, editor and part owner of the Colored American Magazine, informed the Continental Chemical Company, "I am determined that no such advertisement shall appear in this magazine that promises to make kinky hair straight; for it is one of the things I have little confidence in, and I do not believe that such can be brought about through artificial means." At the bottom of a copy of the same letter, which he had forwarded to powerful Tuskegee Institute principal Booker T. Washington, he wrote, "Don't you think I am right in refusing such? It will, I am sure, pay in the long run." Moore, no doubt, knew that Washington, his magazine's secret financial benefactor, also opposed the sale of hair straighteners and complexion lighteners.

But the New York Age's T. Thomas Fortune, another Washington associate, readily accepted these ads despite his own indisputably militant politics and editorial positions. Fortune's compromise, most likely driven by dwindling finances and waning health, left him vulnerable to ridicule from The New York Times. Ironically the paper accused him of lacking "race pride." Still routinely using the term "negress" to refer to black women, The Times hardly could stand in judgment of the Age, which "uncompromisingly demanded equality" for African Americans. And although the black Yonkers Standard agreed that "such advertisements are improper in Negro journals because they give the impression that Negroes are ashamed of their features," it blasted The Times for its hypocrisy in devoting "all of its energy to stirring up sentiment against the Negro throughout the country."

Scalp specialists like Sarah and Pope-Turnbo considered their work separate and apart from the much criticized hair straighteners. What distinguished them and their motivations was their race. The Johnson Manufacturing Company's Hair and Scalp Preparations were "not the so-called hair straightening goods; but Preparations scientifically and carefully prepared for the proper treatment of the Scalp and Hair," insisted its founders, a black husband-and-wife team who had studied dermatology and beauty culture before the turn of the century. Mrs. J. W. Thomas, an attractive, thick-maned black woman who advertised her Magic Hair Grower in several cities, assured customers: "If your hair needs attention try it and be the happy owner of a beautiful head of hair. It is NOT a STRAIGHTENER." Like Mrs. Thomas, the Johnsons distanced themselves from those white-owned companies that pushed hair straighteners. Yet their own ambivalence about Negro features was displayed in their artwork of a mulatto woman with long wavy hair. Significantly absent from their ads, however, were the wild-haired caricatures used to sell Ozono and Kink-No-More.

Even then the controversy around whether African Americans should straighten their hair—and what the decision meant psychologically and politically—was not new. An 1859 *New York Times* article derisively recounted the mishaps of a Mr. Hodgson, "the Great African Hair Unkinker," who had rented a hall in downtown Manhattan to demonstrate a new hair straightening process. After Hodgson applied his heated concoction to "one side of a woolly head," the paper reported, "what had been tight curls was suddenly 'straight as a coon's leg; as glossy as a wet beaver's back; and several inches in length.'" The assembly turned to mayhem as a woman in the audience protested that "she wouldn't desert her race to get straight hair."

In 1903, as Sarah looked at the bald spots on her scalp, straight hair was not her primary goal. Regardless of the debates among news editors, power brokers and race leaders, wanting to have hair had nothing to do with mimicking whites. Her main concern was better employment and financial opportunity, and Pope-Turnbo was looking for agents.

"When I was a washerwoman, I was considered a good washerwoman and laundress," Sarah often recalled. "I am proud of that fact. At times I also did cooking, but, work as I would, I seldom could make more than $1.50 a day. I got my start by giving myself a start." She knew that without a formal education, self-improvement and self-promotion were the only ways to change her life. It was clear that only the most well-educated black women—graduates of schools like Oberlin, Spelman, Fisk, Howard and Atlanta University—could aspire to be teachers or nurses. Another handful who had developed skills and social connections could become seamstresses, milliners and caterers. With few employment choices open to her, hairdressing offered Sarah an alternative to the washtub and a chance to make at least twice as much money each week as she had as a laundress.

Whether she knew it or not, beauty culture was a long-established tradition in the African American community. Since at least the eighteenth century, black women—both slave and freeborn—had found work as hairdressers for white women. Eliza Potter, a black hairdresser who had served wealthy white customers in Cincinnati and New Orleans in the mid-nineteenth century, traveled from plantation to plantation training other slave women in the trade. Some, like New York's Mahan Sisters, called "the crème de la crème of sable artists," owned their own shops. Others, like Harriet Wilson, the author of *Our Nig*, the first published novel by an African American woman, may have visited their Manchester, New Hampshire, clients in the privacy of their boudoirs during the 1870s. Mme. L. C. Parrish established a wig-making and hair-weaving trade for black women in Boston around 1889. Others also offered manicuring and chiropody services to their clientele.

Compared with sharecropping and domestic chores, as Katherine Tillman observed in 1907, "hair-work seems to be pleasant and profitable and those running first-class shops and those doing 'satchel trade' from house to house earn good salaries and wages and form valuable acquaintances among the wealthy class of white people." As well, they had begun to discover a lucrative trade among black women. "Some colored hair dressers earn a good living by giving scalp treatments to colored women's heads," Tillman said. "Splendid results often come from these treatments and a nice growth of soft healthy hair replaces the short, harsh hair of former days."

For an emergent early-twentieth-century urban black population, whose rising social and political expectations were accompanied by a desire for a more sophisticated appearance, black beauty culturists had begun to create an amalgamated aesthetic, an African American look that borrowed, adapted and reconfigured the fashions of both cultures. Sarah would not be the first to conceive the idea, but, in time, she would catapult it to unprecedented horizons.

CHAPTER 6

World's Fair

—ℰ❦ᴐ—

Just as St. Louis was glossing its image for the 1904 Louisiana Purchase Exposition, muckraker Lincoln Steffens was branding its outrageously corrupt elected officials with the charge that they ran "the worst governed city in the land." But by the Fair's April opening, civic leaders were headlong into a crusade to create a "New St. Louis" with less graft, less bribery and better municipal services. The city's boosters hoped to transform the town into a place worthy of its new international aspirations and pretensions.

Nudged in part by *St. Louis Mirror* publisher William Marion Reed, and swept up in the reform spirit of Mayor Rolla Wells, the nation's fourth-largest city appropriated millions of dollars to install gas streetlights, construct sewers, and engineer a purification system to eliminate the notoriously cloudy drinking water. Because Sarah's Market Street neighborhood happened to surround Union Station, the transportation hub for Fair visitors and dignitaries, its most visible streets received at least a superficial sprucing-up.

In addition to the evidence of the Fair's impending arrival just beyond her doorstep, Sarah could easily have read about the preparations in the *Palladium,* the paper owned by fellow St. Paul member J. W. Wheeler. But nothing could have prepared her for the daily procession of Fair-goers who flowed from the train depot by the thousands en route to the fairgrounds in the city's far western suburbs. By the close of the Louisiana Purchase centennial in December, nearly twenty million people had traveled by trolley, buggy, foot, horseback and the still rare automobile to enjoy the sights. Although no official attendance records were kept by race, an estimated 100,000 African Americans entered the gates of the largest exhibition the world had ever seen.

Electricity was still enough of a novelty in most American homes that Fair-goers were enraptured each night as the lightbulb-lined façades of the

Beaux Arts exhibition halls flashed on to create an incandescent paradise. With the evening sky darkening from copper to charcoal, reflections glittered upon the terraced waterfall that tumbled from the steps of the domed Festival Hall into a lake filled with boaters.

The Fair was a magnet for highbrow and lowbrow alike, and an opportunity Sarah would not have missed. Not far from the plazas and expansive gardens of the Ivory City, families strolled along the mile-long cobblestone Pike, a carnival midway that was geared to less lofty tastes. Engulfed in the blended aroma of hot dogs, cotton candy and sawdust, children and adults savored the latest confection: a thin, baked waffle ingeniously funneled around a single scoop of ice cream. International in its reach, the Fair attracted both foreign and domestic visitors, from President Theodore Roosevelt to German sociologist Max Weber, from American "Wild West" cowboys to South African Boer War reenactors.

Unofficially and inadvertently the Fair also provided a parallel showcase for African Americans. During the on-site Third International Olympiad, George Coleman Poage won twin bronze medals for the 200-meter and 400-meter hurdle events, making him the first person of his race to be so honored. In the large Filipino village, Lieutenant Walter H. Loving directed the disciplined and precise Philippines Constabulary Band, a group Philippines Governor-General (and future United States President) William Howard Taft had commissioned him to organize in 1901.

The Fair also attracted black orators, authors and entertainers, who displayed their talents in halls, theaters and churches within easy walking distance of Sarah and C.J.'s Clark Avenue flat. A few blocks away pianist Joe Jordan bested other ragtime legends to win Tom Turpin's national competition at Douglass Hall in late February. Three weeks later poet Paul Laurence Dunbar performed a grand recital at the Central Baptist Church. The Colored Knights of Pythias, arrayed in gold-roped regalia, proudly hosted brethren from other cities at their local headquarters. Small-time hustlers sported Stetsons and sparkling paste stickpins in pool halls along Market Street, an all-day, all-night amusement zone auxiliary to the Fair.

Scholar W.E.B. Du Bois and Tuskegee Institute founder Booker T. Washington, embroiled in an increasingly contentious public debate over Washington's more conservative, more accommodating approach to civil rights, both drew large crowds in separate St. Louis appearances. Washington, speaking on the fairgrounds in late June, was a veteran of World's Fair orations, having reassured whites at Atlanta's 1895 Cotton States and International Exposition that "the wisest among my race understand that the agitation of questions of social equality is the extremest folly, and that progress in the enjoyment of all the privileges that will come to us must be the result of severe and constant struggle rather than of artificial forcing."

Du Bois, who recently had helped launch the politically militant Niagara Movement that was to test Washington's preeminence, filled Douglass Hall with "the most intelligent people of the community," reported the *Palladium* in early October.

Much of St. Louis's black community welcomed the exposition festivities with optimism. Like other visitors, they were awed by the young century's newfangled inventions. Like other Americans, they wanted to see the 160 automobiles that were on display and to view the Missouri countryside from the magnificent Ferris wheel, whose trolley-sized cars comfortably seated more than four dozen passengers.

In frequent updates on fairgrounds construction, the *Palladium* encouraged readers like Sarah to visit early and often. Faithfully predicting that "no discrimination will be made," the weekly was enthusiastic about the prospects for exhibiting African American contributions to the development of the Louisiana Territory. "The representation of the Negro race at the Fair will, it is anticipated, be a highly commendable one," editor Wheeler assured.

For Wheeler and many other middle-class blacks, the Fair presented a forum in which to challenge Jim Crow segregation. Since 1896, when the Supreme Court of the United States had given its blessing to the disingenuous "separate but equal" doctrine in its *Plessy v. Ferguson* ruling, discrimination in public places had become entrenched. With global attention focused on St. Louis, the World's Fair Committee on Negro Day hoped to present "the true status of the Negro Question" and believed that "the coming together of so many thoughtful men and women of the race can not fail to make a favorable impression on the assembled multitude."

For hundreds of African Americans the Fair also meant jobs. While a few black musicians performed on the Pike, most black Fair workers were relegated to unskilled service jobs. Those with entrepreneurial instincts cashed in on off-site services to black visitors, providing lodging, food and drink in their own establishments. With the segregated white hotels filled to capacity for the run of the Fair, hundreds of black St. Louisans and job seekers from bordering states filled positions as maids, cooks, porters, janitors and butlers. More work meant unprecedented disposable income for a community that had always found itself at the mercy of a racially circumscribed job market. Some of those extra quarters and dollars found their way to hairdressers like Sarah, whose services appealed to women with rising personal expectations and a growing acceptance of cosmetics. Increased wages were also channeled into more substantive investments. According to the *American Eagle,* African Americans in St. Louis bought real estate valued at more than half a million dollars during 1903 and 1904.

"Ragtime Millionaire," a tune heard often during the Fair, characterized the mood:

> I'm a ragtime millionaire,
> I've got nothing but money to spend;
> Automobiles floating in the breeze,
> I'm afraid I may die of money disease.
> Don't bother a minute about what those white folks care:
> I'm a ragtime millionaire.

At the time Sarah certainly was not prosperous enough to suffer from "money disease," but she, like most of St. Louis, was engulfed by an over-whelming infusion of ideas, people and possibilities. From time to time, though, the African American enthusiasm for the Fair wavered, especially when rumors surfaced in April that the exposition was falling short on its promise to showcase their community. In response to an invitation from the chairman of the proposed August 1 Negro Day, Booker T. Washington suggested that his decision to speak would be influenced by the treatment blacks received on the fairgrounds in the coming weeks. "The impression is fast spreading through the country among the colored people that they are to receive nothing in the way of accommodations in restaurants, etc., on the Exposition grounds and this report is causing a rather bitter feeling among the race," he informed William Farmer, chairman of the event.

In fact, Washington's fears were confirmed: few eating establishments were willing to serve African Americans. "The black man who desires refreshment on the Exposition ground," wrote one Fair-goer, "had better carry his knapsack and canteen with him." When the freshwater concessionaire worried that whites would not patronize his fountain if blacks used the same glasses, he designated "distinctively marked goblets" and "special tanks of water . . . for colored people."

Long gone were the early, official promises that blacks—"now an element of such great importance in the industrial, political and social life of the Union"—would be included in the exhibits just as they had been at the Atlanta and Nashville fairs in the 1890s. Instead of an opportunity to display their achievements since Emancipation, they were largely omitted from the fair's exhibits. The Old Plantation, a Pike concession "showing Negro life before the War of the Rebellion," lamented Emmett Scott, Booker T. Washington's private secretary, "is all there is to let the world know we are in existence, aside from a small exhibit of a Mississippi College, and one or two other exhibits of no very particular moment."

If Sarah and other local black visitors were proud to see themselves reflected at all in the Missouri State exhibit, it was small consolation that an area set aside for a lone photograph of Sumner High School's faculty and the *Palladium*'s 1903 press run was all their presence in the state merited.

But a dismissal of African American contributions was only part of the Fair's overarching racial and cultural agenda. In the quarter century between 1876 and 1901, civic leaders across America—from Charleston to New Orleans, Chicago to Nashville, Philadelphia to Atlanta—had competed for the honor to host world expositions. Designed above all to boost commerce and promote innovative technology, the financially lucrative events also reinforced Anglo-Saxon cultural supremacy and provided a justification for the racial discrimination that Sarah and other African Americans frequently faced. While comprehensive exhibits at the St. Louis World's Fair traced a century's evolution in the fields of electricity, machinery, transportation, agriculture and education, W. J. McGee, head of the Fair's Department of Anthropology, aimed also "to represent human progress . . . from savagery to civic organization" in living "museums" throughout the fairgrounds. "It is a matter of common observation that the white man can do more than the yellow, the yellow man more and better than the red or black," McGee had written five years earlier.

If Sarah and C.J. ventured to McGee's exhibits, they saw that he had stratified the world's nationalities into re-created village "laboratories" where nearly 2,000 mostly people of color had been imported like curios from their native countries. The Japanese were considered the most highly evolved Asians, elevated not only by their exquisite art and architecture but by their recent victories in the Russo-Japanese War. Beneath them McGee placed groups of Patagonians from Argentina, Pygmies and Zulus from Africa and Native Americans from the Western U.S. territories. But the anthropologists' most ambitious undertaking was a United States government-sponsored forty-seven-acre reservation of more than a thousand Filipinos, ranging from Manila-based paramilitary troops to tribes that Fair planners described as Babogo "savages" and "monkey-like" Negritos. Tourists who visited the Filipino reservation were left with a skewed view both of the Philippines and of world civilization, and with a clear sense that "white and strong," in McGee's words, were "synonymous." It was the same message Sarah had heard all her life.

By the time the National Association of Colored Women—a group of the most prominent black women in the country—arrived at Sarah's church for its fourth biennial convention in mid-July, the stage was set for a highly charged showdown over the Fair and the "race question." Although Exposition president David R. Francis, a former Missouri governor and U.S. Secretary of the Interior, had issued a "general directive that discrimination had to cease," the planned August 1 Negro Day was in jeopardy. Just a few days earlier, members of the 8th Illinois Regiment of Chicago had rejected an invitation to march at the Fair when they learned that white Georgia troops had objected to their presence among other American military men. Now the 200 NACW delegates also were debating whether to cancel their own daylong excursion to the fairgrounds.

Assembled in St. Paul's sanctuary for their opening ceremony, the handsomely dressed women enjoyed a recital of classical and religious music performed by the L'Ouverture Elementary School children's chorus and the St. Paul and Central Baptist Church choirs. "Future success commensurate with that of the past is ours, if we hew to the line in teaching our sons and daughters to love virtue," NACW president Silone Yates of Kansas City advised the members in her convention charge. Yates and the others saw themselves as "progressive colored women," whose motto—"Lifting As We Climb"—served as a promise to their "neglected and unprogressive sisters," especially those in need of "uplifting influences of freedom and education."

For Sarah and the other members of St. Paul, these well-educated, well-traveled visitors—representing 15,000 women from thirty-one states—created a vision of black elite propriety. The St. Louis delegation, whose members belonged to the community's church circles, benevolent societies, literary clubs and the colored Women's Christian Temperance Union chapter, included many women Sarah had come to know at St. Paul. Among them were Lavinia Carter, an early board member of the St. Louis Colored Orphans' Home, and St. Louis Federation president Maria Harrison, Sarah's former neighbor and president of the orphans' home.

With the field of social work still in its infancy, these women had already founded orphanages and retirement homes for aging freedmen and freedwomen, opened kindergartens and tuberculosis recovery camps, and crusaded against alcoholism and prostitution. Fifteen years earlier Sarah and Lelia had been beneficiaries of their early initiatives. And while the women may have pointed during the conference to Sarah's accomplishments with some sense of pride, most of them were not yet ready to bring a former washerwoman into their inner social circle. Eventually, however, she would become one of their most valued members.

In 1896, six years after the founding of the white General Federation of Women's Clubs, the NACW held its first meeting, consolidating two smaller national black women's organizations. The impetus to launch the group had arisen in part because of the GFWC's refusal to grant their membership request, in part as a response to a slanderous insult regarding the morality of black women.

After Ida B. Wells-Barnett, the pioneering journalist and antilynching advocate, blasted America's tolerance for lynching during a well-received speaking tour in Great Britain, James W. Jacks, president of the Missouri Press Association, fired off a letter to an officer of the newly formed British antilynching society. "The Negroes in this country [are] wholly devoid of morality," he indicted. "The women [are] prostitutes and all [are] natural thieves and liars." Unable to tolerate the affront, black Bostonian and suffragette Josephine St. Pierre Ruffin sent out the call that assembled the National Federation of Afro-American Women, the predecessor to the NACW.

With protest so much a part of the association's short history, many of the St. Louis conventioneers vowed to voice their objections when they learned that Hallie Quinn Brown, a world-renowned elocutionist and NACW member in excellent standing, had been denied an opportunity to apply for a job on the fairgrounds. Led by a "vehement" Margaret Murray Washington, the wife of Booker T. Washington, the women passed a resolution "to withdraw the decision to hold a session at the World's Fair grounds." Although the local committee opposed the boycott, Margaret Washington charged the exposition directors with discrimination "against Colored women in the matter of securing employment on the grounds and against the race in general."

The Missourians were sorely disappointed because they had planned a festive day, including a motorcade along the boulevards of the Ivory City with hopes of making a conspicuous and symbolic statement. Their planned spectacle of several hundred well-dressed and dignified Negro women, they believed, would counter the Pike's portrayal of the world's people of color as primitive and savage. Instead, the group canceled its outing and reconvened at St. Paul to continue the assembly's more substantive business proceedings.

Lynching, a topic that would concern Sarah in the years to come, was high on their agenda. Troubled by the escalation of racially motivated murders since the Civil War—nearly 700 blacks had been killed by whites in the South just in the decade leading to the World's Fair—the women approved a resolution condemning mob violence. "We the representatives of Negro womanhood do heartily deplore and condemn this barbarous taking of human life," they asserted, aware of the irony that their race had been labeled "barbaric" by the Fair organizers. Mindful that many of them would soon be returning home on filthy, poorly ventilated Jim Crow train cars, they also urged a boycott of segregated transportation systems in "Southern cities, states and towns that discriminated against blacks."

Two other contentious issues—more cultural and moral than legal—had surfaced during the convention. Ida Joyce Jackson, president of the Colorado State Federation, urged the delegates to support her condemnation of ragtime music. With equal fervor, Cornelia Bowen, founder of Alabama's Mt. Meigs School, denounced "hair-wrapping" because she considered the practice imitative of whites. Jackson, a classically trained musician, viewed the increasingly popular "rag time, coon songs, and cake walks as disgraceful, vulgar and destructive of good taste and self respect [for] all Colored people, who indulged in or tolerated them." In language reminiscent of the late-twentieth-century furor over gangster rap, temperance activist and future NACW president Lucy Thurman bemoaned the fact "that the musical taste and talent of the race is being destroyed by this so-called 'music.'"

This collision of art and ethnicity, of cultural expression and morals, created tension among African Americans, especially across class lines. Sarah's thoughts on the debate are not known, though years later she enjoyed ragtime and jazz, unlike Du Bois, who considered ragtime and cakewalk dances "the chief amusements of 'fourth and third grade Negroes.'" Yet Du Bois sensitively articulated the "double-consciousness" and "sense of always looking at oneself through the eyes of others" that were reflected in ragtime and accounted for much of the emotional and psychological conflict African Americans experienced. "One ever feels his two-ness,—an American, a Negro; two souls, two thoughts, two unreconciled strivings; two warring ideals in one dark body."

The dichotomy he described was never more apt than in the conundrum of Negro hair, a subject about which Sarah had given a great deal of thought. And just as race, morality and music had collided at the NACW convention, so too did racial identity, class and hair.

Cornelia Bowen, a former slave and member of Tuskegee's first graduating class in 1885, told her NACW sisters about Mt. Meigs's Anti-Hair-Wrapping Clubs, whose members had vowed "not to wrap their hair in an effort to straighten it." A Booker T. Washington protégée, Bowen likely was aware of her mentor's disdain for such practices. "It is foolish to try [to] make hair straight," she scolded, "when God saw fit to make it kinky."

Baptist organizer and NACW member Nannie Helen Burroughs agreed wholeheartedly with Bowen. "What every woman who bleaches and straightens out needs, is not her appearance changed, but her mind changed," she wrote in "Not Color but Character," a *Voice of the Negro* article published that very month. "If Negro women would use half the time they spend on trying to get white, to get better, the race would move forward apace," she admonished. Burroughs had a point. And such strong emotions confronted Sarah as she continued her work as a sales agent for

Annie Pope-Turnbo. But her customers' happiness, once their hair began to grow, was all the proof she needed that she was performing a useful service. She was convinced that she was helping her clients feel more attractive and confident.

Just as Sarah's scalp treatment skills had boosted both her income and her personal vision of herself, the World's Fair activities around her painted unexplored vistas. In the most American of impulses, she sensed opportunity and the chance to reinvent herself. Not yet divorced from John Davis, but living with C. J. Walker, she had grown increasingly anxious about remaining in St. Louis. In plotting her next move, she chose Denver, where her sister-in-law, Lucy Breedlove Crockett, still lived with her four daughters. Three states and nearly a thousand miles west of St. Louis, the Colorado capital was a place where Sarah believed she could make an unfettered start. And with twenty-year-old Lelia not yet willing to relocate, her nieces—Anjetta, Thirsapen, Mattie and Gladis—would provide a ready-made workforce.

On Wednesday, July 19, 1905, with the temperature passing ninety degrees, Sarah boarded a hot, sooty westbound train, her bag filled with Pope-Turnbo's Wonderful Hair Grower, her mind racing with anticipation.

CHAPTER 7

Westward

—⟨✦⟩—

As the Burlington Railroad locomotive steamed across Missouri's flattened plains, then skirted north along the Missouri River through
Kansas's eastern edge, Sarah and the other passengers could feel
the sticky July heat give way to cooler breezes outside their opened windows. In Nebraska spring rains had turned prairie grass as green as pea
pods. Tassel-crowned, emerald cornstalks, a few inches shorter than usual,
stood at attention, alternating with fields lined with harvested shocks of
wheat. Just north of the Nebraska-Kansas border—past Table Rock, Endi-
cott, Red Cloud and McCook—silos and farmhouses spiked the horizon
and stray cows grazed within spitting distance of the tracks. With each
passing mile, the limitations of Sarah's past vanished, and the possibilities
of her future materialized.

Why C.J. had stayed behind is unclear. Perhaps one ticket was all they
could afford. Perhaps this trip had been planned more as a trial run than a
permanent relocation. Perhaps C.J. had not sufficiently shared Sarah's
vision and she had elected to go ahead despite his reservations.

When she reached Denver the next day on July 20, 1905, temperatures
lingered in the pleasant mid-seventies, an agreeable relief from the stifling
mid-nineties of her final week in St. Louis. Outside Union Depot, the eastern edge of the snowcapped Rocky Mountains resembled a napping Gul-
liver sprawled lazily along the skyline. No World's Fair tourist brochures or
moving pictures could have prepared Sarah for the vastness of the view.
Always having lived in the embrace of Mississippi River humidity, she was
unaccustomed to the West's crisp, dry air. Despite its acrid ore smelters,
Denver's sun-sprayed skies were pristine compared with St. Louis's sun-
blocking murkiness.

An isolated outpost until 1859, when gold was discovered along Cherry
Creek, Denver had capitalized on its location at the foothills of the regal
Rockies to mold itself into a railway hub and tourist destination. Blessed

with access to Colorado's mining communities, the city had shared in the $850 million bounty yielded by the state's silver, lead, copper, tin, coal and gold deposits since the Civil War. The local Chamber of Commerce touted it as "the healthiest city in the United States," a haven for convalescing tuberculosis patients, and the gateway to the spas of Colorado Springs, its more sophisticated resort neighbor to the south. With the aid of irrigation, the area's farms served up apples, melons, strawberries, peaches and grain for local consumption and regional distribution.

Denver's unspoiled vistas facilitated escape and fostered recovery from troubled lives and cumbersome identities. In a place where fortunes literally waited to be unearthed in the next creek bed, discarding failed marriages and adopting fresh personas seemed entirely acceptable.

Migrants like Sarah from crowded urban areas marveled at the wide boulevards and absence of tenements. In 1900 Colorado's entire population of nearly 540,000 were less than the 575,000 souls jammed into St. Louis's city limits. Denver was home to a quarter of all Coloradans, close to 134,000 people, mostly of Irish, German and English descent, with a smattering of Italians, Chinese, Native Americans and Hispanics. In contrast to St. Louis's more than 35,000 African Americans, fewer than 4,000 Denverites were black, about half of them women.

Anheuser, Mallinckrodt and Danforth—names that symbolized wealth in St. Louis—were replaced in Denver by Tabor, Guggenheim, Cheesman and Witter, men who had made their fortunes in mining, smelting, real estate and finance. The state had its own notable black frontier legends, including adventurer Barney Ford, whose once elegant Inter-Ocean Hotel had been called "the best appointed hotel west of St. Louis" when it opened in 1873. There was also "Aunt" Clara Brown, a former slave and laundress who had padded her shirt-washing prices to meet the inflated boom-time incomes of gold prospectors, then used her nest egg to bring family and friends to Colorado after the Civil War. Jeremiah Lee, one of the black miners who followed gold fever to the peaks of the Rockies, had built a mansion in downtown Central City, Colorado, with part of the $100,000 he and his partners had extracted from their stake in an 1880 mine.

Throughout Denver, there were stories to fuel Sarah's own fantasies of prosperity, tales of women like Baby Doe Tabor and Margaret Tobin Brown who spent and behaved as they pleased, redefining upper-crust Denver with the spoils of their husbands' mining wealth. Horace Tabor, who had made his $5 million fortune in the Leadville silver bonanza, lavished upon Baby Doe, his second wife, a $7,000 wedding dress and a $75,000 diamond necklace. Before they lost everything in the 1893 silver crash, she had fulfilled her civic duty by donating office space to the Colorado Equal Suffrage Association in her husband's impressive Tabor Grand Opera House.

Margaret Brown, another woman whose husband cashed in on Leadville's mother lode, became an outspoken globe-trotter, best known as the *Titanic* survivor fictionalized in *The Unsinkable Molly Brown*. But she was also a philanthropist, popular among Denver's black Catholics for including them in her 1906 Carnival of Nations, a festival to raise money for a new cathedral. Known for her dramatic hats and Paris ball gowns, Brown was just as comfortable with silver miners as she was with British royalty. Because her activities were well covered in Denver newspapers and because she lived on fashionable Capitol Hill just four blocks from Lucy Brcedlove's modest home, Sarah certainly had many opportunities to learn about this independent, flamboyant woman. Both women had little formal education and both had been born in 1867 in shacks near the Mississippi River, though Brown had spent her childhood farther north in Hannibal, Missouri.

Like Brown, Tabor and Barney Ford, Sarah had set out for Denver with every intention of finding her own fortune. Although she had arrived with only "$1.50 in my pocket," Sarah later said of her plan to sell hair care products, "I was convinced it would be a success." Because she had heard that Denver's soil contained "alkali that was bad for hair," she believed a receptive market awaited her. In fact, the alkali-laden earth, whose salt content also affected agricultural output, leached nutrients from the hair, though probably not to the extent that Sarah had been led to believe. For the many black women whose curly hair structure inhibited the distribution of moisture, it was the low humidity as much as anything else that caused their hair to feel brittle in the mountain climate.

When Sarah first arrived in Denver, she probably roomed with Lucy. But she quickly found a job, in part to help with her sister-in-law's daughters— fifteen-year-old Anjetta, twelve-year-old Thirsapen, seven-year-old Mattie and four-year-old Gladis. "I got a job as a cook in a boarding house at $30 a month," she said. And although she gave no details about her employer or location, there is an intriguing oral history that provides possible clues about her early months in Colorado. Zenobia Fisher, whose mother had befriended Sarah, claimed that Sarah "was working for Scholtz . . . a wholesale druggist." Although by late 1905 Edmund L. Scholtz had moved into a home at 1351 Grant on Denver's "Millionaire's Row," at least for a short time in 1905 he was listed as a "roomer" at 1201 Humboldt along elite Cheesman Park.

Neither Scholtz nor Sarah left any public statements to confirm Fisher's contention, but the story is a plausible, if now unverifiable, one. Because Sarah needed soaps and medicinal supplies to supplement the products Pope-Turnbo shipped to her, she easily would have gravitated to the Scholtz Drug Company at the bustling Sixteenth and Curtis Street intersection. Often billed as the largest pharmacy west of the Mississippi River, the company claimed to carry "the most comprehensive line of goods known to the drug trade." Scholtz, one of the founders of the Colorado Pharmaceutical Society, had trained his druggists to give "special attention to the compounding of physicians' prescriptions and family recipes."

Speculation is required to tie the threads together at this point. But if Sarah indeed worked as a cook in the rooming house where Scholtz temporarily lived, or even if she only shopped at his store, Fisher's scenario seems entirely possible. "She was making extra money on the side selling Madam Poro's work," said Fisher, referring to the company name that Annie Pope-Turnbo later adopted. "He saw it one day and asked her what it was. And she told him. And he says, 'I can analyze this for you. And you can leave out some or put in more and you can make the money yourself.'" If Scholtz had made such a suggestion, or if Sarah herself had initiated the product analysis, she was not prepared to stop selling Pope-Turnbo's products immediately. At least for several more months she would call herself an agent for Roberts and Pope, the company name that Pope-Turnbo used during early 1906. But the seed of independence already had begun to germinate.

While Sarah continued her work as a cook, she would later tell a reporter that "in her spare time she mixed tubfuls of a hair restorer." As time went by, she would more frequently insert various versions of her divine intervention narrative, in one instance saying that she had dreamed of her formula "for three nights." And perhaps she had. But she had also intentionally chosen to omit Pope-Turnbo's role. Having saved enough money to resign her kitchen job, she later said, "I hired a little attic, which was my first laboratory," probably at 1923 Clarkson, where she was living in late November 1905.

With "two days a week doing washing" and five days giving hair treatments, her workload was reversed. At the same time she apparently had begun experimenting with ingredients for her own formula. "I began of course in a most modest way," she recalled. "I made house-to-house canvasses among people of my race, and after a while I got going pretty well." Her door-to-door solicitations were made all the easier because of the compactness of Denver's black community. Around 1904, African Americans had begun to spread north and east of the downtown neighborhood between Fifteenth and Twentieth streets, where they had settled in the 1880s and 1890s. But their shift was less than seismic during the next decade as they migrated a block at a time toward the Five Points area that emanated from Twenty-seventh and Washington streets a mere half mile away.

Just as Sarah had been drawn to the congregation at St. Paul in St. Louis, she joined Shorter Chapel AME Church. Like her sister-in-law Lucy she soon became a member of the Mite Missionary Society. Located only four blocks from her Clarkson Street apartment, Shorter had been founded in 1868 as Colorado's second black church. Along with connections Sarah would soon make in the local Columbine Chapter of the Court of Calanthe, Shorter offered spiritual support and a place to get her bearings. The church's annual Sunday-school picnic, always a highly anticipated and well-publicized event, was held at a nearby lake within a week of her arrival. As Sarah sought to promote her business, she certainly had everything to gain by attending.

During this time she discussed her business ideas with fellow Shorter parishioner George Ross, a recent Howard University Law School graduate who was operating a small printing business while he prepared for the Colorado state bar examination. "I sold her her first batch of cards advertising Pope-Turnbo articles," he proudly wrote years later. Sarah, who recalled using a portion of her initial $1.50 capital, confirmed the transaction. "I spent 25 cents of this to have some cards printed," she said of the neatly lettered bristol board calling cards announcing "Mrs. Sarah McWilliams."

As well as his printing services, Ross also solicited advertising for The Statesman, a Denver-based publication owned by his close family friend Chester A. Franklin. Aware of Sarah's eagerness to build her reputation, he also may have encouraged her to consider promoting her work in the paper, which claimed readership in Colorado, Wyoming, Montana, Utah and New Mexico. On December 1, for the going rate of a nickel per line, she placed a small announcement for her Clarkson Street "hairdressing parlor" in The Statesman. "Mrs. McWilliams, formerly of St. Louis, has special rates for a month to demonstrate her ability to grow hair," her first ad notified potential clients. A decade later Sarah would develop a reputation as a major advertiser in the nation's black newspapers. But for now she was intent upon convincing clients of the worth of her scalp treatments. As the Kansas City Star was to note: "As fast as she earned a little money, she spent it on advertising . . . spending more on printers' ink in the beginning than she spent on bread and butter."

In these early months, Sarah remembered, she rarely rested, so determined was she to succeed. Customers gravitated to her because of her "splendid personality." A charisma and conviction forged from her own difficult journey now shone through as a sincere desire to give excellent service and to assist other women.

No correspondence between Sarah and C. J. Walker exists from this era, but Sarah's messages about her progress clearly were persuasive enough for him to join her in Denver. By the time he arrived in late November or early

December, she knew the community well. Nineteenth and Arapahoe streets formed a crossroads for the several dozen black businesses, professional offices and meeting halls that spread out to Larimer Street on the north and Champa Street on the south. Along Arapahoe the shops ranged from Charles Call's Boot Parlor, C. A. Holly's Drum Repair and Henry Pinn's Ping Pong Parlor to W. J. Foster's Tailor Shop, Richard Evans's Mining Supplies and Frank Jones's Carpentry Shop. Miller's Bicycle Livery, Fountain's Barber Shop and the Odd Fellows' Hall clustered together on the northern end of the neighborhood. Within walking distance of their apartment the couple found eight black churches, a funeral home, two dentists and three physicians, including Dr. Justina Ford, Denver's first black woman doctor.

Accustomed to the fast-paced, fast-buck mind-set of Chestnut Valley, C.J.'s imagination raced with plans. He wasted no time in publicizing his presence, and with the aid of Sarah's friend George Ross, he was listed in *The Statesman*'s December 8 "Denver Doings" column as one of the "newcomers to Denver."

With C.J.'s holiday season appearance, he and Sarah had their choice of an array of parties at nearby Manitou Hall and East Turner Hall, the two most popular sites for black fraternal group gatherings. Throughout December the J. C. Harris Orchestra performed several nights a week for Denver's many black lodges, including the True Reformers, the Masons and the bewitchingly named Sisters of the Mysterious Ten, the women's auxiliary to the United Brotherhood of Friendship.

Two days before Christmas, Sarah celebrated her thirty-eighth birthday with C.J. Soon after the new year, on January 4, 1906, Reverend William Dyett, Shorter's pastor, performed a quiet marriage ceremony for them in the parlor of Sarah's friends Delilah and B. F. Givens. The Givenses, who lived in the 2200 block of Arapahoe, had been among the striving, working-class African Americans who, during the first decade of the 1900s, had begun to integrate Curtis Park, one of Denver's first near-in suburbs. Created in 1871 with the advent of the city's first horsecar trolley, the area's detached brick homes, with their charming parapets, fish-scale shingles and oriel windows, provided just the setting that Sarah relished for her third marriage and first real wedding.

The matrimonial trappings could not have been more perfect, except for a rather large, dangling piece of unfinished business: Sarah had neglected to sever her ties with John Davis. "There is no divorce record here by them," an attorney concluded after a thorough search of St. Louis legal documents several years later. And though Delilah Givens would later sign an affidavit attesting to Sarah's nuptials, a Denver attorney swore that he was "positively unable to find any trace of a marriage license issued to either C.J. or Charles J. Walker" after combing all relevant Arapahoe County records between 1867 and 1915. Sarah and C.J. apparently gambled that this vexing oversight would have no consequence, that Davis would exact no price. And for a very long time it seemed they were right.

Less than two weeks after Sarah had become Mrs. Charles Joseph Walker, she had a chance to try on her new name among friends at any one of several social events during Margaret Murray Washington's three-day swing through Denver. Elected NACW vice-president-at-large during the St. Louis convention, Washington had been invited by antiragtime crusader Ida Joyce Jackson to meet with black clubwomen in Colorado Springs, Pueblo and Denver. More than five hundred guests, "white and colored . . . filled every inch of space long before Mrs. Washington put in an appearance" in Shorter Chapel's sanctuary for her Monday night lecture. The "elaborately arranged" Tuesday afternoon reception was hosted by Mrs. Irving Williams, Delilah Givens's next-door neighbor. Williams, the widow of one of Shorter Chapel's earliest trustees, ran an embroidery and Battenberg lace business. News of her teas, suppers and musicales frequently merited attention in *The Statesman*'s society column.

In Denver, Sarah found class lines for such soirees less rigidly drawn than in St. Louis's black community, where some descendants of the pre–Civil War elite jealously guarded their positions. With so few blacks in Colorado, they could ill afford such attitudes. And in a town where striking it rich trumped all, personal drive and ambition, with which Sarah Walker was well endowed, more often than not determined one's social standing.

A month or so after their marriage ceremony, Sarah and C.J. moved to a well-kept rooming house at 2410 Champa on the southern edge of the Curtis Park area. Their landlady, Callie Fugitt, who catered "fifteen cents and up" dinners from her home every Saturday night, must have been pleased to have tenants as industrious as the Walkers.

In March 1906, perhaps with C.J.'s help, Sarah revised her newspaper ads to reflect her changed marital status. Now calling herself "Mrs. C. J. Walker," she notified customers of both her social engagements and business activities while on sales trips to Boulder and other nearby communities.

While Mrs. Walker developed her hair and scalp work, C.J. was busy with his own endeavors. He and a partner named B. W. Fields opened the Industrial Real Estate Loans and Rental Company at 212 Fifteenth Street in the shadow of the state capitol, where they offered "a number of houses to rent or sell in all parts of the city," as well as "homestead land for farming and grazing."

In a community eager for public events, C.J. seized economic opportunities both in real estate and in entertainment. Unlike St. Louis with its all-night music scene and constant influx of out-of-town lecturers and performers, Denver offered few cultural choices for African Americans beyond its local orchestras and small string quartets. When they attended events at the Tabor Grand Opera House, they were consigned to a segregated section.

On May 3, when nationally renowned vaudevillians Bert Williams and George Walker filled Manitou Hall, C.J. undoubtedly leaped at the chance to work the crowd to promote his upcoming "Grand May Festival and Popularity Contest," which was scheduled in the same hall a week later. As chairman of the True Reformers' arrangement committee, he was determined to make a splash with his first high-profile production in Denver. Along with strategic advertising in *The Statesman*, his scheme was to have the affair pay for itself by raising funds through pre-event ticket and raffle sales. "The lady receiving the largest number of votes at 10 cents a vote, will be declared the most popular in Denver, and will also win a handsome gold watch," his ad declared. In a stroke of marketing savvy, he had arranged to have the prize displayed in the window of the Boyd Parks Jewelry Company, the most prestigious jeweler in the city, known for "high class trade in high class goods."

The Walker husband-and-wife partnership appeared to be flourishing, with one's individual pursuits reinforcing the other's. Certainly any popularity-contest hopeful in need of a hairstyle for the special occasion would have been referred by C. J. Walker to the skilled hands of Mrs. Walker. And any of Mrs. Walker's attractive clients, especially those with outgoing personalities, might have been encouraged to enter the competition. Just in time to attract the business of the contestants and their guests, Sarah Walker's first eye-catching photograph was published in the April 20 *Statesman*. Below the headline "Mrs. Walker's Offer," her oval portrait presented her as the personification of dignity, posed with hair neatly pompadoured into soft, upswept rolls around her face. Her gaze was firm, though her eyes focused away from the camera. The corners of her mouth formed a small crescent just shy of a smile. Her high-necked dress, with its puffed sleeves and smocking, conveyed sensible neatness rather than frilly opulence.

With both Walkers drumming up business, Pink 592, the party-line phone at 2410 Champa, hummed throughout the spring with requests for tickets and hair appointments. Even before C.J. had staged his early May Festival, he was completing arrangements for a May 30 Decoration Day train excursion to Colorado Springs for residents of Denver, Pueblo and Trinidad. "A grand old-fashioned time is expected at the Springs on that day," promised his promotional materials. Seventy miles south of Denver, Colorado Springs had been established in 1871 by Colonel William Jackson Palmer, founder of the Denver & Rio Grande Railway, the north-south line that transported people and goods along the eastern base of the Rockies. His Antlers Hotel, built in 1883, was long considered "the only first-class hotel between Chicago and San Francisco."

In the May 25, 1906, *Statesman* on the Friday before the all-day outing, C.J. announced not once, not twice, but three times that he had secured the crowd-pleasing J. C. Harris Orchestra. "WHERE ARE YOU GOING on Decoration Day?" inquired his ad. "'I am going to Colorado Springs on the big Decoration Day excursion over the Rio Grande,' is the cry of all."

A week earlier Sarah had updated and strengthened her own announcements with an edgier, more direct message and layout. She had exchanged her previous pose—one of poise, but not force—for one with a more commanding demeanor. Now she stared openly into the camera, her hair cascading and full-bodied rather than pinned, tucked and restrained. In a second view from the back of her head, her shoulder-length mane, though slightly uneven, was healthy, bushy and abundant. "Two years ago her hair was less than a finger's length," the ad boasted, claiming that the growth was "the result of only two years' treatment."

To say that C.J. was a mere huckster would be too simplistic, but he clearly fancied himself a showman and a promoter. It was as if the gears required for wheeling and dealing ground audibly within his head. Sarah Walker had approved of enough of his speculative ventures to marry him. And because she had grand expectations for herself, perhaps his schemes did not strike her as impractical. For now, his ambition seemed to match hers.

Probably through their alliance with *Statesman* editor Chester Franklin, C.J. had managed to attract, as the Decoration Day keynote speaker, William T. Vernon, a graduate of Wilberforce College's schools of law and divinity, and president of the AME Church's Western University in Quindaro, Kansas. Celebrated as "a pulpiteer, platform lecturer and commencement orator," Vernon had recently been nominated by President Theodore Roosevelt to be Register of the U.S. Treasury. Blacks took particular pride in this appointment—which had already been held by two African Americans during the Garfield and Arthur administrations—because the occupant's signature appeared on all government bonds and U.S. currency. Vernon's personal history would have appealed to Sarah Walker. Born around 1871 in a log cabin, he had risen to "the highest place held by the race in America."

C.J.'s Decoration Day excursion, which drew a crowd from Colorado's four largest communities, boosted Sarah's business. As her own best walking advertisement for scalp treatments, she had impressed so many visitors that she began to receive invitations to demonstrate her products in the state's smaller cities.

In mid-May she paid to reprint a letter from Pope-Turnbo clarifying the difference between Roberts and Pope products and a competitor's ointment that Pope-Turnbo considered inferior. The correspondence appeared in both black newspapers, *The Statesman* of Denver and the similarly named, *Colorado Statesman*, which was owned by Joseph D. D. Rivers, a Booker T. Washington disciple. "Now as to the oil that woman has," Pope-Turnbo wrote, "it is nothing but vaseline with sulpher, quinine and ox marrow."

"Shops are failing every day simply from the fact that vaseline is too strong for the hair," she warned. "And no one has my preparation." No one in Denver, of course, except for her agent Sarah Walker, whose companion letter to the editor that week openly challenged another local hair culturist named Dora Scott. "I wish to say to my customers to not be led into buying of her and think you are buying the grower I represent, Roberts and Pope," Sarah, writing as "Mrs. C. J. Walker," warned. "I represent the preparation bearing the label of Roberts and Pope and it can be secured only from me."

But shortly after that exchange, Sarah Walker began to distance herself from Annie Pope-Turnbo. Abruptly Walker's ads ceased. For someone who had appeared in the local papers almost weekly for six months, the silence was uncharacteristic. The hiatus seems to have signaled both turmoil with Pope-Turnbo and Sarah's decision to market her own products under her own name. Perhaps the realization that she could thrive without Pope-Turnbo had come in Colorado Springs when so many people clamored to learn her beauty secrets. Whatever the impetus, by late July, when Sarah finally appeared again in *The Statesman,* she had emerged as "Madam C. J. Walker," adopting a title long used by modistes and hairdressers. While some may have considered the use of a French form of address to be at least a bit of an affectation, "Madam" Walker hoped to signal to her clients that she and her products were of the highest quality.

That month, armed with a supply of Madam Walker's Wonderful Hair Grower, she "spent two successful weeks in Pueblo," a town 112 miles south of Denver, where she had "many good things to say of the hearty support given her by the ladies of Pueblo." No sooner had she returned to Denver than she was off again to answer "an urgent appeal from Trinidad" to conduct her scalp treatment course. Noting that she had trained forty-five eager students in ten days, *The Statesman's* Trinidad reporter announced in his weekly dispatch that "Mrs. C. J. Walker . . . was very successful in her business" while there. Those completing her course could "secure a letter of instruction teaching them how to grow their own hair." Mrs. Walker offered her classes "at a very reasonable price," she said, "so that the very poorest may be benefited, and that those who have already been benefited will not suffer in my absence." While in Trinidad she was entertained at a card party and "one of the prettiest receptions" the small black community had ever arranged. Her hostesses clearly delighted in the pampering and grooming she offered. As well, they welcomed her moneymaking message.

From Trinidad she traveled north on the D&RG Railway for a brief stopover in Colorado Springs, but she cut short her planned week's visit in order to greet Lelia, who was scheduled to arrive in Denver on August 23. To aid Sarah's plan to broaden her market beyond Colorado's sparsely populated borders, Lelia had taken a hair-growing course in St. Louis in order to prepare herself to "take charge of her mother's business." Like her mother, she may well have first learned her skills from Pope-Turnbo.

As Madam Walker made arrangements to move Lelia into a house and office a few blocks away at 2317 Lawrence, the women could barely complete their packing as anxious customers streamed into their modest salon from early morning until late at night. "After locating in her new quarters," an ad announced, Madam Walker "will positively receive no customers after 4:30 p.m. Business hours will be from 7 a.m. to 4:30 p.m."

During her final two weeks in the city, Madam Walker took advantage of every chance to introduce Lelia. Statuesque, gregarious and beautifully dressed—in no small part due to her mother's indulgence—Lelia always made a lasting impression.

With Lelia now "in charge of the business," Madam Walker and C.J. "began to travel and work up a mail order business," leaving on September 15, 1906, "to place their goods on the market through the southern and eastern states." By the time of their departure, Madam Walker had dissociated herself entirely from Annie Pope-Turnbo, who had become angry enough to denounce her publicly. "The proof of the value of our work is that we are being imitated and largely by persons whose own hair we have actually grown," Pope-Turnbo accused in a letter to *The Statesman*. "They have very frequently mentioned us when trying to sell their goods (saying that 'theirs is the same' or 'just as good') . . . BEWARE OF IMITATIONS."

Now that Madam Walker had her own formula, the rivalry that would poison the two women's relationship had commenced. In reply to Pope-Turnbo's accusations about Madam Walker, eight satisfied Pueblo customers asserted that Madam Walker had "never claimed her preparation was the same or as good as yours; but she does claim her preparation is the best on the market." As long as they could secure Madam Walker's goods, they vowed that it was their intention never to use Pope-Turnbo's products.

"Until Mme. Walker came here we never heard of any hair grower . . . You are in St. Louis, and as far as you were concerned, we could have been bald-headed until now, so we consider your efforts purely spite work and see by your letter of a few months ago to the ladies of the West, how highly you recommended her." Sarah undoubtedly appreciated the endorsement, but she was more than capable of engaging Pope-Turnbo herself. "Mme. Walker's Wonderful Hair Grower has proven beyond question to be the most wonderful hair preparation yet discovered," her latest ad trumpeted. "It is soothing to the scalp and brings quicker results than any other."

Years later, in what surely was a fit of wishful revisionism, C. J. Walker would claim credit for advising his wife to develop her own line. "It is somewhat trying to me when I look back to the beginning of the first establishment of this business, and the hard struggles that the Mme. & I had in those days," he lamented. "I alone am responsible for the successful beginning of this business. Otherwise the Mme. would have taken the road for the Poro people." In fact, it was C.J. who "could see nothing ahead but failure" as they embarked upon their southern sales trip. "She was discouraged by her husband and many patrons who said she would not be able to make her expenses from one town to another," her authorized company biography later asserted. "However she was determined and inspired to do so."

Lelia, not nearly as thick-skinned as her mother, had been left with a hornet's nest of controversy over the Pope-Turnbo matter. Initially, however, she approached her work with enthusiasm, giving scalp treatments and pressing her customers' hair with the heated metal irons she had learned to use in St. Louis. In the evenings she cooked and stirred the product by hand, then packaged the "pressing oil, soap and hair grower" for shipments to her mother and to the mail-order customers who sent their dimes and quarters and dollars to Denver.

Right away her local ads were revised to display a cleaner, less cluttered layout with bolder fonts. "If you want long and beautiful hair . . . If you want your hair to stop falling at once, if you want your hair to look natural and fluffy, if you want your scalp cured of all diseases go to Mme. Walker's Parlors, 2317 Lawrence St., Mrs. Lelia McWilliams, Successor."

By the following May, however, Pope-Turnbo had dispatched a replacement agent to a parlor at 2118 Arapahoe, just two blocks from Lelia's office. "LADIES ATTENTION: Mrs. M. A. Holley, who has spent some time in St. Louis perfecting herself in the scalp and hair treatment of Mrs. A. M. Pope, has come. She is now prepared to do the same work as is done in the originator's parlors. She is the sole agent for the famed preparation, 'Poro.'"

That same week, *The Statesman* carried the following announcement:

"Madam C. J. Walker and Miss McWilliams, her successor, wish to announce to their customers, old and new, that they have decided to open up business elsewhere and close up their business in Denver." While the rift with Pope-Turnbo had been uncomfortable for Lelia, ultimately the Walkers' decision to leave Denver had more to do with Colorado's tiny black population and the limited potential for financial growth. Madam Walker's travels had quickly convinced her that her most lucrative future markets existed in the heavily black South and the expanding cities of the North. She had also discovered that she was a natural teacher, a leader with a gift for drawing crowds and persuading skeptics. The key to her success would not be just her "secret" formula, but her deep understanding that women wanted to be attractive, as well as her fervent conviction that they needed to be financially independent. Her determination and decisiveness soon would create unimaginable opportunities for herself *and* for her agents.

CHAPTER 8

On the Road

—⊘⁓⊘—

Within only a few months of leaving Denver, Madam Walker could boast of an income greater than all but the most highly paid American corporate executives. During 1907, her first full year on the road, she took in $3,652, nearly triple her total 1906 earnings. Clearly she had defied her friends' predictions that she would fail to cover her traveling expenses.

For a woman whose wages had rarely reached $300 a year, this two-year accumulation may have amounted to as much money as she had made during her entire lifetime. In an era when most working black women made only $8 to $20 per month as domestic servants, and white male factory workers had monthly incomes of $40 to $60, Madam Walker's business was averaging upward of $300 each month, a more than respectable sum by any measure.

C.J., initially quite skeptical about his wife's plans to build a national business, had begun to understand her vision. His attitude had been changed in no small part because he had created his own moneymaking venture. Inspired by the popularity of Madam Walker's products, he now offered a pair of dollar-a-bottle remedies: Walker's Sore Wash, "for sores of any description," and Walker's Sure Cure Blood and Rheumatic Cure, which he claimed would cleanse "impure" blood and end "eczema, tetter and falling hair." But unlike his wife's scalp ointments, his product formulas sounded suspiciously similar to the alcohol-laden concoctions the 1906 Food and Drugs Act had intended to ban.

For eighteen months the Walkers traveled throughout the southern United States, systematically canvassing the region where 90 percent of the nation's African Americans still lived in 1907. Throughout Oklahoma, Texas, Kansas, Arkansas, Louisiana, Mississippi and Alabama, they followed what had become an effective routine: contact the Baptist or AME church or both, find the best rooming house they could afford, introduce themselves to the officers of the local black fraternal organizations, arrange a demonstration at a church or a lodge, hold classes to train agents, take orders for Madam Walker's Wonderful Hair Grower, move on to the next place.

From Muskogee, El Reno and Okmulgee, Oklahoma, they sped on to Tyler, Houston, then Galveston, Texas, leaving behind dozens of satisfied customers. A few months after their trip to Dallas, Madam Walker received a letter from Julia Coldwell, a woman who, thanks to Walker's Wonderful Hair Grower, no longer needed the hairpieces—the "false braid or bangs"—she had become accustomed to wearing. "My hair was the talk of the town," she gushed. "All the people who know me are just wild about my hair . . . I have to take it down to let them see and feel it for themselves. I tell you I am quite an advertisement here for your goods."

In Helena, Arkansas, a preacher's wife who had learned the Walker Hair Culture Method in order to supplement her family income now had a long list of happy clients. "Do you remember the old bald-headed lady whom you treated while you were here, whom they all laughed at and said she should know better than to bring that head to anybody?" Mrs. O. L. Moody asked Madam Walker about a customer she had continued to treat. After missing a few weekly sessions during the fall harvest season, the woman had returned with gleeful news. "When she uncovered her head I liked to have dropped. I was utterly surprised to find her head entirely covered with hair, and she is tickled to death and said you were a God-send to humanity."

Without a doubt, Madam Walker had tapped a rich reservoir of desire with her scalp cure. The letters, as well as the steady mail-order requests, reflected a strong yearning for the personal care and attention she and her newly trained agents provided. With queries from places as far afield as California, Utah, Montana, Maryland and Kansas, she had succeeded in developing a national demand for her products in less than two years.

For at least part of 1906 and early 1907, after closing her Denver office, the mail-order operation may have been coordinated from Louisville by Walker agent Agnes "Peggie" Prosser, who was also C.J.'s sister. While Lelia probably accompanied her mother and C.J. for at least a part of this period, exact details of their peripatetic itinerary remain unknown.

After visits to New York and Pennsylvania during the summer of 1907, the Walkers realized that their business was expanding too quickly to handle their mail-order sales from the road. Because Pittsburgh's sixteen rail lines offered convenient and accessible shipping arrangements, they chose the western Pennsylvania town as their temporary headquarters, arriving sometime between August 1907 and March 1908.

Pittsburgh was so covered with the soot that rose geyserlike from its factory smokestacks that nineteenth-century author Charles Dickens had once described its skies as "Hell with the lid off." Rich in natural resources from nearby coalfields and iron-ore mines, the hilly city had grown from an early-eighteenth-century wilderness village into one of America's most profitable early-twentieth-century industrial centers. Home to glass foundries and iron-processing factories, it was the country's unquestionable leader in the production of structural, crucible and Bessemer steel.

Strategically located where the confluence of the Allegheny and Monongahela rivers formed the headwaters of the Ohio River–Mississippi River system, Pittsburgh's nine shipping lines transported nearly eleven million tons of freight to and from docks along its riverbanks during 1900. In the triangular wedge of land where the British Fort Pitt had once dominated the merging point of the city's three rivers, a cavernous business district now stood with a score of banks and investment houses, dozens of government and corporate offices and the Pittsburgh Stock Exchange. By 1906 the area's narrow streets were so crowded that a British visitor complained that "the congestion is greater than in New York, Philadelphia or Boston and is only surpassed by London."

As a depot on the Underground Railroad, Pittsburgh had attracted African Americans long before the Civil War. Between 1900 and 1910 the city's black community grew from 20,355 to 25,623. And although its black population ranked fifth among Northern cities, African Americans made up less than 5 percent of the city's total. At the time of the 1910 Census, New York was first, with 91,709 blacks, having bumped Baltimore to second since the turn of the century. Philadelphia, with 84,459, was positioned third, and Chicago, with 44,103 black inhabitants, placed fourth.

During the autumn of 1907, close to the time of Madam Walker's arrival, the outlook for Pittsburgh's steel industry had been highly optimistic. But by late October the city was suffering the effects of a national banking crisis. Foreshadowed by a record stock market decline in March, the collapse of copper prices in October plunged Pittsburgh into the nexus of the Panic of 1907. New York's Knickerbocker Bank, rumored to have been heavily invested in the metal, was stripped of all its reserves in just two days as thousands of customers squeezed into its imposing lobby demanding their deposits. Because Pittsburgh's steel industry and banks were so intertwined with powerful New York banking interests, the city and its industries were especially vulnerable. "Hardly another city in the country was hit as hard or stunned as long by the panic as was Pittsburgh," wrote two observers at the time. "From every type and class of labor came the report of a year with only half, or three-fourths, or even one-third of the time employed. The overwork in 1907 was out-of-work in 1908." By April 1908 there were breadlines in some sections of town. Short-lived though this depression was, it was significant enough to have led to the creation of the Federal Reserve Board as a means to stabilize U.S. financial markets. Nevertheless, it seemed not to have prevented Madam Walker from expanding her business.

In the midst of the economic crisis, she opened a "well-equipped" hair parlor at 2518 Wylie Avenue, a bumpy cobblestone street that stretched steeply above the financial district. In the Hill District, as in St. Louis's Market Street area, the façades of the brick row houses were flush with the sidewalks, leaving barely a breath between street life and home life. Once a favored residential area for German and Irish physicians, attorneys and bank presidents in the late 1880s because of its proximity to their downtown offices, the district had begun to change during the 1890s as recently immigrated Poles and Italians, as well as other blue-collar workers, moved into the older, mostly brick homes. Between 1890 and 1900 the area's black population quadrupled from just under 700 to more than 3,000. During the next decade Hill District residents became less affluent and more ethnically diverse. Blacks, who would come to comprise a quarter of the area's 46,000 people, remained too scattered to create a concentrated enclave, sharing blocks on either side of Wylie Avenue with Russian Jews, Hungarians, Italians, Syrians and the handful of German and Irish families who remained. Unlike in Denver and St. Louis, where black businesses formed a distinguishable commercial section, their enterprises were sprinkled not only in the Hill District and other neighborhoods farther to the east in Pittsburgh, but also in the town of Allegheny, a smaller community on the north side of the Allegheny River.

Given the era, however, there were an impressive number of black professionals, including five lawyers and twenty-two physicians. In addition to a "manufactory of hair-growing preparations"—no doubt Madam Walker's—a 1908 neighborhood survey listed an insurance company with twenty-eight agents and an asphalt-paving contractor who regularly employed more than a hundred men. But with no weekly black newspaper, Madam Walker and the others lacked a forum in which to advertise their products and services. Perhaps in 1909, when C. J. Walker listed himself as an "editor" in the *Pittsburgh City Directory*, he had hopes of filling that void.

While the Walker Hair Parlor was located in the Hill District to attract the largest number of customers, Madam Walker, like many prominent blacks, lived in Pittsburgh's East End, a relatively more affluent, predominantly white section removed from the "speak easies, cocaine joints, and disorderly houses" that dotted the rough alleys off Wylie Avenue. From her home at 139 Highland, she also treated customers.

Buoyed by her successful travels, Madam Walker immediately set about gathering endorsements from the city's black leadership, working the community just as diligently as she had worked a row of cotton. Employing her church connections and the national network of the Court of Calanthe, she sought influential preachers and fraternal officers, tapping into the web of social clubs and organizations, including many of the twenty-five chapters of the Pennsylvania State Federation of Colored Women's Clubs.

As Madam Walker made new acquaintances, she persuaded a group of respected church and civic leaders to sign a letter endorsing her work, with the intention of enhancing her standing in the community. "We, the undersigned, highly recommend Mme. C. J. Walker's work and worth," the petition read. "As a hair grower she has no equal . . . We found her to be a strictly honest, thorough-going business woman. Until her advent into this city . . . we did not believe in such a thing as a hair grower."

As 1908 closed, Madam Walker had earned $6,672—nearly doubling her 1907 tally—and had trained or treated several hundred Walker agents and customers since leaving Denver. The next year her earnings increased by 25 percent to $8,782, or just over $150,000 in today's dollars. She also landed a coveted feature article in the *Pennsylvania Negro Business Directory*, which called her "one of the most successful business women of the race in this community."

In her full-length directory photograph Madam Walker struck a more refined pose than she had in her 1906 Denver newspaper ad. Reflecting her increased income and newly acquired status, she wore a dress with a delicate ivory lace bodice. A thin fabric belt cinched her waist, accentuating her full-figured, well-proportioned body. With her hands clasped behind her back, the only sign of her former life as a farmworker and washerwoman was the stumpy shape of her forearms, their muscles enlarged from years of twisting and squeezing soap through waterlogged sheets and tablecloths. But of course it was her hair that she wished to emphasize. Madam Walker had pinned her now healthy tresses into a carefully coiffed crown, styled so that it gracefully swooped away from her face.

When women saw her photo and heard her life story, they clamored to take her course and sit for her treatments. The twin promises of enhanced beauty and financial gain—not to mention Madam Walker's own phenomenal personal example—served as a magnet to women who had always believed they would never be more than maids and laundresses. Except for only a dozen or so clerks and stenographers who worked in the city's small black businesses, and about a hundred dressmakers and seamstresses, more than 90 percent of Pittsburgh's employed black women were domestic servants.

Their husbands, sons and brothers had relatively more choices, but because the men's wages were rarely sufficient to support a family, the women had little choice but to work. Although half of the city's teamsters

Madam Walker before and after her wonderful discovery.

Earliest known photograph of Madam C. J. Walker (center), probably taken during the 1890s, shows her before the discovery of her hair care products. In one of her earliest advertisements, circa 1906, she proudly displays the effects of her Wonderful Hair Grower in these before and after shots. (A'Lelia Bundles/Walker Family Collection)

Cabin on the Burney plantation in Delta, Louisiana, where Sarah Breedlove was born on December 23, 1867. (A'Lelia Bundles/Walker Family Collection)

Wonderful Hair Grower, the Madam C. J. Walker
Manufacturing Company's most popular product.
(A'Lelia Bundles/Walker Family Collection)

An essential step in the Walker System of hair care was proper
cleansing of the scalp with Madam Walker's Vegetable Shampoo.
(A'Lelia Bundles/Walker Family Collection)

Madam Walker circa 1910, around the time she moved to Indianapolis. (A'Lelia Bundles/Walker Family Collection)

Madam Walker circa 1909, around the time she opened the first Lelia College in Pittsburgh. (Library of Congress)

Madam Walker portrait taken by Addison Scurlock circa 1914 and used extensively in her advertisements and company literature. This photograph appeared on a 1998 U.S. commemorative postage stamp honoring Walker. (A'Lelia Bundles/Walker Family Collection)

Madam Walker at the wheel of her Model T Ford in front of her Indianapolis home in 1912, with niece Anjetta Breedlove, book-keeper Lucy Flint and factory forelady Alice Kelly. (A'Lelia Bundles/Walker Family Collection)

Madam Walker and her daughter, A'Lelia Walker, in Indianapolis circa 1914 with unidenti-fied chauffeur. (A'Lelia Bundles/Walker Family Collection and Indiana Historical Society)

Madam Walker standing in front of her Indianapolis home circa 1912. (A'Lelia Bundles/Walker Family Collection and Indiana Historical Society)

Madam Walker's Indianapolis factory built in 1911 within a year of her arrival. (A'Lelia Bundles/Walker Family Collection and Indiana Historical Society)

Madam Walker in her Waverly electric car, which she preferred for afternoon trips to the movies and for shopping. (A'Lelia Bundles/Walker Family Collection)

Madam Walker in her Hudson seal fur circa 1915 (A'Lelia Bundles/Walker Family Collection)

Freeman B. Ransom, attorney and general manager of the Madam C. J. Walker Manufacturing Company, in his office. (A'Lelia Bundles/Walker Family Collection and Indiana Historical Society)

Madam Walker and Booker T. Washington (to the right of Walker) at the dedication of the Senate Avenue YMCA, with (left to right) *Indianapolis Freeman* publisher George Knox, Walker Company attorney F. B. Ransom, *Indianapolis World* publisher A. E. Manning, Dr. Joseph H. Ward, Louisville YMCA secretary R. W. Bullock and Senate Avenue YMCA secretary Thomas Taylor. (A'Lelia Bundles/Walker Family Collection and Indiana Historical Society)

The Walker Salon and home at 108-110 West 136th Street was designed by Vertner Woodson Tandy, one of the first licensed New York black architects. (Byron Collection/The Museum of the City of New York)

The Walker Salon in Harlem was opened in January 1916 with a lavish reception featuring the music of James Reese Europe. (Byron Collection/The Museum of the City of New York)

The parlor at 108 West 136th Street was one of two music rooms in the Walkers' Harlem home. (Byron Collection/The Museum of the City of New York)

MEMBER

NATIONAL CONVENTION OF MADAM C.J. WALKER'S AGENTS

Badge worn by delegates at the annual conventions of Madam Walker agents. (A'Lelia Bundles/Walker Family Collection)

First National Convention -1917- Philadelphia, Pa.

Madam Walker (center), flanked by attorney F. B. Ransom and factory forelady Alice Kelly, at the first convention of the Madam Walker Hair Culturists' Union at Philadelphia's Union Baptist Church in 1917. The agents protested the East St. Louis riots with a telegram to President Woodrow Wilson. (A'Lelia Bundles/Walker Family Collection)

Madam Walker with Ohio sales agents circa 1918. Madam Walker traveled extensively throughout the United States and the Caribbean training an army of Walker beauty culturists. (Sylvia Jones)

Walker Company advertisement appeared in A. Philip Randolph's *Messenger* in 1917. (New York Public Library/The Schomburg Center for Research in Black Culture)

Madam Walker meets with Japanese publisher S. Kuriowa, a member of the Japanese delegation to the Paris Peace Conference, at the Waldorf-Astoria Hotel in New York in January 1919 to discuss representation of people of color at the post-World War I proceedings. The meeting called by the executive committee of the International League of Darker Peoples included *Messenger* publisher A. Philip Randolph, R. D. Jonas, Thomas Wallace Swann, C. T. McGill and Louis George. (A'Lelia Bundles/Walker Family Collection)

Walker agents and beauty culturists assemble at Villa Lewaro, Madam Walker's Irvington-on-Hudson, New York, home in 1924 after her death. (A'Lelia Bundles/Walker Family Collection)

Walker agents on the back terraces of Villa Lewaro during the 1924 convention. (A'Lelia Bundles/Walker Family Collection)

Jessie Robinson (front row center with ruffled blouse), longtime friend of Madam Walker's, with 1939 graduates of the St. Louis Walker Beauty School, where she was principal for several years. (A'Lelia Bundles/Walker Family Collection and Indiana Historical Society)

The stylish A'Lelia Walker became known for her trademark, custom-designed turbans. (A'Lelia Bundles/Walker Family Collection)

A'Lelia Walker, circa 1913, around the time she persuaded her mother to open a New York office and salon. (A'Lelia Bundles/Walker Family Collection)

A'Lelia Walker, the inspiration for much of her mother's early entrepreneurial efforts, was once described as "royal with royal instincts." (A'Lelia Bundles/Walker Family Collection)

A'Lelia Walker in the music room of Villa Lewaro seated at the gold-trimmed Aeolian grand piano purchased by her mother circa 1913. Mother and daughter both loved music and furnished their homes with expensive musical instruments so that their friends could perform when they visited. (A'Lelia Bundles/Walker Family Collection)

Langston Hughes called A'Lelia Walker "the joy goddess of Harlem's 1920s," in part because of the lavish parties she hosted for racially mixed groups of the era's most well-known artists, writers and musicians. (A'Lelia Bundles/Walker Family Collection)

A'Lelia Walker (third from left) became president of the Walker Company after her mother's death. She is pictured here in the 1920s with attorney F. B. Ransom, factory fore-lady Alice Kelly, advertising manager Harry Evans, attorney Robert Lee Brokenburr, Esther Heidelberg, Violet Davis Reynolds and others. (Indiana Historical Society)

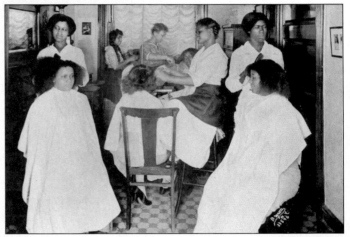

In the New York branch of Lelia College, A'Lelia Walker (seated on left) receives a scalp treatment while Mae Walker (standing, third from left), her adopted daughter, treats a customer. (Byron Collection/The Museum of the City of New York)

Mae Walker was adopted by A'Lelia Walker in 1912 and sometimes traveled with Madam Walker as a model for Walker Company hair care products. Her long braids reflected her Native American ancestry. (A'Lelia Bundles/Walker Family Collection)

Mae Walker married Dr. Gordon Henry Jackson in November 1923 in an elaborate $40,000 wedding at Harlem's St. Philip's Episcopal Church orchestrated by A'Lelia Walker. (A'Lelia Bundles/Walker Family Collection)

Mae Walker with bridesmaids at her wedding reception at Villa Lewaro. Many of her attendants had been members of the debutante club A'Lelia Walker founded in New York. Front row (left to right): Katherine Farnum Williams, Betty Payton and A'Lelia Ransom Nelson (daughter of F. B. Ransom). Back row (left to right): Mildred Randolph Fisher, Louise Jackson Gaither, Consuelo Street Smith, Marion Moore Day (daughter of *New York Age* editor Fred Moore), Kate Wilson Harris, Eunice Hunton Carter and Anita Thompson Reynolds. (A'Lelia Bundles/Walker Family Collection)

Mae Walker during the late 1920s. (A'Lelia Bundles/Walker Family Collection)

Marion R. Perry, Jr., Mae Walker's second husband and grandfather of the author, around the time of his marriage to Mae in August 1927. (A'Lelia Bundles/Walker Family Collection)

A'Lelia Mae Perry Bundles, the author's mother, as a student at Howard University in the late 1940s. (A'Lelia Bundles/Walker Family Collection)

First Lieutenant Marion R. Perry, Jr., in France during World War I. (A'Lelia Bundles/Walker Family Collection)

A'Lelia Mae Perry Bundles at her Indianapolis home circa 1959. (A'Lelia Bundles/Walker Family Collection)

A'Lelia Mae Perry Bundles, A'Lelia Perry Bundles and S. Henry Bundles in 1955, around the time the author first discovered her grandmother's treasures. (A'Lelia Bundles/Walker Family Collection)

The author with her parents, S. Henry Bundles and A'Lelia Mae Perry Bundles, and her brothers Lance and Mark circa 1968. (A'Lelia Bundles/Walker Family Collection)

The author with her mother in May 1975 in Indianapolis.
(A'Lelia Bundles/Walker Family Collection)

A'Lelia Bundles (to right of stamp) at the first-day-of-issue ceremony for the
Madam C. J. Walker commemorative stamp in January 1998. Bundles spear-
headed the national campaign which led to the stamp. Also pictured: ABC
News anchor Carole Simpson, U.S. Postal Service governor LeGree S.
Daniels and Madam Walker Theatre Center chair Karen Lloyd.
(Walt Thomas)

were black during the first few years of the twentieth century, and a fortunate few occupied municipal jobs as policemen, firefighters and postal workers, Pittsburgh's black men made up the large army of unskilled, poorly paid, underemployed laborers as they did in other cities.

By 1909, the financial crisis of 1907 had faded into a temporary and minor setback to Pittsburgh's growth. Its U.S. Steel Corporation remained the nation's most profitable company, with assets of $1,804,000,000. John D. Rockefeller's Standard Oil of New Jersey was second with $800,000,000, and American Tobacco was a distant though unquestionably substantial powerhouse valued at $286,000,000.

Industrialists like Andrew Carnegie, the founder of the company that became U.S. Steel, had engineered the transformation of the city into an industrial force and become an American legend in the process. A native of Scotland, Carnegie was born in 1835, the son of a weaver who had immigrated to the United States in 1848. With little formal education, he moved from a $1.20-a-week cotton mill job as a bobbin boy to clerical positions at Western Union and the Pennsylvania Railroad. After the Civil War, he established a bridge-building business, then leveraged his profits to construct the first of many steel mills. An antebellum-era abolitionist, Carnegie was viewed favorably by many black Pittsburghers, especially because his mills had hired blacks as early as the 1880s, then brought them in as replacements for striking workers during the union-busting Homestead Strike of 1892. In 1907 nearly 350 black men held jobs in Carnegie mills, though in most instances they were clustered in the least-skilled, lowest-paying jobs.

Having become the world's wealthiest man when he sold his Carnegie Steel Company to banker J. P. Morgan for $400 million in 1901, Carnegie set about to disperse the funds to an astonishing range of causes and organizations. Especially after contributing $600,000 to Booker T. Washington's Tuskegee Institute in 1903, Carnegie gained even more recognition among African Americans. That unprecedented gift to Tuskegee was widely discussed for years in the black community and would have been known to Madam Walker, who had already begun to develop her own approach to giving through her church missionary society and other organizations. But Carnegie's largesse, on full display throughout Pittsburgh, was on a scale beyond imagination, an outgrowth of the philanthropic philosophy he expressed in his famous 1889 essay, "The Gospel of Wealth." "The man who dies leaving behind him millions of available wealth . . . will pass away 'unwept, unhonored, and unsung,'" he admonished those who were miserly. "Surplus wealth which a man accumulates in a community is only a sacred trust to be administered for the good of the community in which it was accumulated." As Madam Walker became more prosperous, she would adopt a similar outlook.

During her travels Madam Walker perfected her sales pitch by using compelling, commonsense lessons. Because many of her students had only recently left the farms of the South, she found that agricultural analogies were particularly effective teaching tools. "Do you realize that it is as necessary to cultivate the scalp to grow hair as it is to cultivate the soil to grow a garden?" she inquired. Just as a farmer turned the soil around plants, she advised her students to loosen and remove the dandruff that blocked the flow of air and blood to the scalp. "Soil that will grow grass will grow a plant," she taught. "If the grass is removed and the soil cultivated, the plant will be a very healthy one. The same applies to the scalp."

No case was too difficult to solve, she assured potential agents, telling them that her "years of experience and personal contact with thousands of persons with scalps in all conditions" had proven to her that "every woman who wants hair can have it, no matter how short, how stubby, or what the condition of the scalp may be."

Having trained dozens of agents in Pittsburgh, she charged Lelia with keeping them supplied with goods as she went on the road again to expand her sales to women in nearby states. In Wilberforce, Ohio, during the late summer of 1909, she personally treated fifty-one women and girls, including Ada Parks, who informed her that "every one of them tells me that their hair is growing, and they are well pleased." Another Ohio woman, Mrs. W. A. Snead of Columbus, was also ecstatic about her new appearance. "I have not the knowledge or words to express my gratitude for what you have done for me," she wrote. "My hair is about 7 inches in the front and 6 in the back, and as thick as a woven rug." Like so many others who had put away their wigs and hairpieces, she was pleased to report, "The hair I wore when you first treated me I have on a doll now. I haven't worn it since before Xmas."

Hoping to groom twenty-three-year-old Lelia to eventually run the company, Madam Walker dispatched her daughter to untapped markets along the East Coast. Lelia dutifully complied, but sometimes chafed at the control her mother's wishes exercised over her life. At the end of October 1908, Lelia was in Bluefield, West Virginia, near the state's southern border, teaching the course and "making" agents. Madam Walker, no doubt, was focused on the possible business prospects of the community, aware that blacks had had a strong presence in the area since the coal boom of the late nineteenth century. As well, they had been lured by the jobs that came from the town's role as a terminus for the Norfolk & Western Railroad. As

Bluefield grew, a small black middle class developed around Bluefield Colored Institute, founded in 1895 to prepare black teachers for the segregated schools in communities around the coal mines.

A year after Lelia's trip to Bluefield, she married John Robinson, about whom little is known. Born in Columbus, Ohio, in 1885, he was described years later by a newspaper reporter as a "hotel telephone operator" who "had a nice figure and looked like somebody in his uniform." But a city directory published shortly after the marriage described him as a laborer, and many of the reporter's details—including the name of a nonexistent Pittsburgh hotel—appear to be inaccurate.

How long the bride and groom had known each other is uncertain, though it is possible that they met through a mutual friend, Grant White, who had known Lelia since her childhood in St. Louis. What *is* certain is that the marriage ceremony—performed by a justice of the peace in Washinton, Pennsylvania's Italian Renaissance courthouse—took place a twenty-seven-mile train ride away from Pittsburgh without Lelia's mother. If the two women disagreed about Robinson, they left no record of their feelings.

The newlyweds moved into Lelia's well-furnished home in Pittsburgh's East Liberty section at 5707 Mignonette, where Lelia continued operating a supply station for Walker agents. By the end of the year, Madam Walker had left her daughter in charge of the Pittsburgh office and was traveling again, looking for another city with a more vital black business presence in which to base her growing enterprise.

CHAPTER 9

Bold Moves

—⸎⸎—

During early 1910, as Madam Walker scouted a new city for her permanent headquarters, she seized every social and business occasion to engage potential investors. Each meeting, each introduction, each chance encounter, furnished an opportunity to advance her commercial dreams.

In January during an extended stay in Louisville, Madam Walker unveiled plans for a Walker Manufacturing Company stock offering to Reverend Charles H. Parrish, president of the Eckstein-Norton Institute, and Alice Kelly, one of the most accomplished faculty members at this Kentucky training school for black teachers. They were so impressed with Madam Walker's spunk and presentation that they urged her to solicit the support of Booker T. Washington, the founder of both the Tuskegee Institute and the ten-year-old National Negro Business League. Parrish, whose international travels on behalf of the black National Baptist Convention had made him well known among African Americans, allowed Madam Walker to mention his name in her letter of appeal to Washington. Parrish's gesture supplied just the opening she needed to capture the attention of the most powerful black man in America.

"Now what I would like to do, is to establish a factory and advertise it properly," she wrote enthusiastically of her "remedy that will grow hair of any kind" and of her plan to raise $50,000 from one hundred men and women. "We could form a stock company . . . and make this one of the largest factories of its kind in the United States." Just as important, she said, was her plan to "give employment to many of our boys and girls." She had come to him specifically, she wrote, because "I know I can not do any thing alone, so I have decided to make an appeal to the leaders of the race . . . I feel no hesitancy in presenting my case to you, as I know you know what it is to struggle alone with the ability to do, but no money to back it."

Madam Walker also was concerned, she confided, about bids from "white firms" that "want me to sell out my right[s] to them, which I refuse to do as I prefer to keep it in the race if possible." Washington's quick reply was reserved and noncommittal. "My dear Madam," he wrote, thanking her for her "kindly" suggestion. "My time and attention are almost wholly occupied with the work of this institution and I do not feel that I can possibly undertake other responsibilities. I hope very much you may be successful in organizing the stock company and that you may be successful in placing upon the market your preparation." While she surely recognized his artful dismissal, she could now feel certain that he knew her name and her objectives. In time, she would persuade him that those objectives were consistent with the self-help message he so ardently preached.

The more Madam Walker's horizons expanded, the less C.J. seemed able to keep up. While a guest at the Louisville home of C.J.'s sister, Peggie Prosser, Madam Walker began to learn more about the man she had married four years earlier. "My heart went out to her then," Prosser said. "I knew she was a good woman struggling to make a name for herself. And I know what a hard fight she had."

Prosser was particularly attuned to her brother's shortcomings, having been disappointed by him as a young girl. After their mother's death, he vanished from her life, leaving her with a grandmother. When she finally tracked him down sixteen years later, he agreed to a reunion at her home, but apparently with no intention of making amends for abandoning her. While enjoying her hospitality, he had the audacity—though likely in his characteristically charming manner—to request train fare for his return trip to St. Louis.

Prosser could not help being sympathetic to her sister-in-law's frustration with C.J.'s irresponsible ways. Even in early 1910, Prosser felt sure that he was squandering company funds. He was, Prosser said, "meeting the postman, getting the mail, not filling orders." Disillusioned as Madam Walker was, she continued to tolerate his behavior, likely hoping he would manage to make his own significant contribution to what had always been more her business than his.

Corpulent slate clouds glowered over central Indiana's snow-carpeted farmland as the train carrying Madam Walker and C.J. approached Indianapolis on Thursday, February 10, 1910. Outside the city's granite-trimmed Romanesque Union Station, street-cleaning crews, in one of their "worst battles of the winter," chipped away the ice chunks that had clogged trolley switch points since Tuesday night's storm. More freezing precipitation was expected on Friday.

Despite the bone-chilling high of twenty-eight degrees, the Walkers found themselves "so favorably impressed with Indianapolis" that they decided to move their operation to the Hoosier capital.

Their warm and "cordial" reception was substantially enhanced by their gracious host, Dr. Joseph Ward, the first president of the Indiana Association of Negro Physicians, Dentists and Pharmacists. A native of Wilson, North Carolina, and an early vice president of the National Medical Association, he had established Ward's Sanitarium, the city's primary black hospital, in 1910. Located on Indiana Avenue—the African American community's main commercial thoroughfare—the facility also served as a training school for black nurses. Ward, like Jessie Robinson's husband, C. K. Robinson, had been a state and national officer of the Knights of Pythias, the common tie that may have enabled Madam Walker, a member of the group's women's auxiliary, to approach him for lodging.

Two days after the Walkers' arrived, the *Indianapolis Recorder* announced, "Mme. C. J. Walker of Pittsburgh, Pa., THE NOTED HAIR CULTURIST, is in this city at the residence of Dr. J. H. Ward at 722 Indiana Avenue, where she will demonstrate the art of growing hair." She hoped her photograph—the same one that had appeared earlier that year in the *Pennsylvania Negro Business Directory*—would attract the black women of Indianapolis to her temporary salon.

It was Madam Walker's good fortune to have arrived during a particularly lively social season, one that, despite the raw, icy weather, displayed the community's vitality. February—the birth month of President Abraham Lincoln and the adopted birth month of abolitionist Frederick Douglass—had become a time of celebration among African Americans. With the fiftieth anniversary of the Emancipation Proclamation only three years away, the annual observances consistently drew sizable crowds.

The Walkers' host, Joseph Ward, rarely missed a Sunday at Bethel AME, one of the oldest and most prestigious black churches in the city, where he was a leading member. That week the sanctuary was busier than usual as Reverend Theodore Smythe led "soul-stirring" revival services. On Sunday afternoon another local church hosted an Abraham Lincoln celebration featuring reminiscences from black residents who had heard the President-elect's 1861 preinaugural address from the balcony of Indianapolis's Bates Hotel. That Monday, Joseph and Zella Ward—and their intriguing, out-of-town visitors—were quite likely on the guest list for the Valentine's Day tenth wedding anniversary celebration of Mr. and Mrs. Virgil Wallace, who lived directly across the street from the Ward home. Reveling continued into the night as the black waiters of the Columbia Club—an all-white Republican downtown men's club—hosted a masked ball for their friends at the Odd Fellows' Hall. Then, three days before the February 20 Douglass Memorial parade and celebration, elocutionist Hallie Quinn Brown, a pivotal player in the NACW's 1904 boycott of the World's Fair, performed dramatic readings and orations. But perhaps most important to Madam Walker was Friday's meeting of the local chapter of the National Negro Business League, the organization founded in 1900 by Booker T. Washington to encourage entrepreneurship among African Americans. Having just elected a slate of officers, the group was seeking new members. Madam Walker, still angling for its founder's support, was eager to join.

As much as she loved to socialize, Madam Walker focused almost entirely on her work after her first few days in Indianapolis. "Don't fail to call and see Mme. Walker," her ad invited. "Persons calling for treatment will kindly bring comb, brush and 2 towels," she advised. While she charged nothing for "consultation," her scalp treatments were a relatively expensive $1. Tins of her Wonderful Hair Grower sold for 50 cents. A month later, however, she had lowered the price of scalp treatments to 50 cents and added a 25-cent shampoo and a 35-cent manicure with hopes of gaining "the patronage of every woman of pride, who is in need of her services."

From time to time, Madam Walker offered incentives, including free treatments and cash awards, to build her client base. Through an early form of multilevel marketing, she challenged customers to compete with each other, offering "3 months treatment to the first one bringing or sending 10 customers." The strategies were so effective that by late March Wonderful Hair Grower sales had reached such levels that Madam Walker and C.J. were able to move around the corner from the Wards' home into a $10-a-month, five-room rental flat at 638 North West Street.

By mid-April she had also increased her advertising budget, allotting relatively more for the *Indianapolis Freeman,* by far the best known of the three local newspapers. Published by George Knox, a former slave who had purchased the paper with profits from his elegant downtown barbershop, the weekly's extensive coverage of traveling black theater companies and musicians, as well as its national circulation, had made it one of the most widely read and influential African American newspapers of its day.

As Madam Walker focused on the manufacturing operation, C.J. staked out a more autonomous niche for himself, traveling to small towns throughout Indiana to promote the products. Soon he would attempt to specialize in developing the company's out-of-state sales. The market was theirs to claim. "Before the entrance of Mme Walker," remembered long-time Indianapolis resident Ida Webb Bryant, "there were no beauty parlors as such, [though] there were a few women who would come to your home and give you a shampoo." Downtown hair parlors "catered mostly to people of the stage and to the wealthy whites," she said, though Sallie Brown, a black hairdresser with a largely white clientele, "would accommodate you if you wanted a 'braid' or 'switch' or other 'hair piece.'"

Home to more than 233,000 people in 1910, Indianapolis offered the ideal location for the kind of mail-order business Madam Walker envisioned. Known as the Crossroads of America, it was situated within thirty-five miles of the center of the nation's population and was the largest inland manufacturing city in the country without a major waterway. A daily convergence point for thousands of freight cars and nearly 500 steam and 100 electric passenger trains, the city also was intersected by a nascent national highway system.

Unlike Pittsburgh's, the Indianapolis economy was not dominated by any one industry. Surrounded by rich farmland, it was home to meatpacking plants, granaries, flour mills and two large starch companies. The city's foundries and machine shops produced steam engines, hardware products and household appliances. At the turn of the nineteenth century, local buggy and bicycle manufacturers reacted quickly to the automobile craze, converting their operations to produce electric cars and luxury vehicles with names like Cole, Waverly and later Stutz. Auto-parts producers, including the Prest-O-Lite Company, supported the emerging industry with headlights, batteries and other motorcar apparatuses. By 1913 it ranked second only to Detroit in auto production.

In the carefully laid-out city streets, platted by a surveyor who had helped map Washington, D.C., the domed state capitol, with its Indiana-limestone façade, was one of downtown's most imposing buildings. Diagonal avenues radiated from the Soldiers and Sailors Monument, a circular park located at the center of the city's precisely designed Mile Square.

Most of Indianapolis's black population, numbering 21,816 in 1910, clustered in small sections of the city's near east side and far south side, as well as around the northwestern edge of the Mile Square between the Central Canal and the White River along Indiana Avenue. After an 1821 malaria outbreak had decimated many of the early white settlers, the swampy area between the two waterways was deemed undesirable real estate and left to blacks and Irish immigrants. By 1900, the Indiana Avenue area, known as Bucktown, was home to thirty churches, as well as "many saloons and gambling dens." While its black population remained much smaller in absolute numbers than that of many other cities, African Americans comprised 9 percent of the city's total, putting them well above New York's and Chicago's 2 percent and giving them the highest percentage of any city north of the Ohio River.

At the turn of the century, Indianapolis's small black middle class—defined primarily as those who held professional, service or entrepreneurial positions—included eight physicians and ten attorneys, forty teachers, several postal workers and a few dozen shop owners. A decade later there were so many black-owned businesses along Indiana Avenue that Ralph Waldo Tyler, the National Negro Business League's national organizer, claimed that "Indianapolis had more Negro business establishments than any other Northern city."

One of its most notable entrepreneurs—whom Madam Walker would soon meet—was Henry L. Sanders, a former hotel waiter who had developed a competitive regional business selling uniforms and fraternal regalia. With her own dreams of building a factory, Madam Walker could not help admiring his soon-to-be-completed three-story office and manufacturing facility on Indiana Avenue.

Well on her way to another record-breaking sales year, Madam Walker purchased a $10,000 two-story brick home at 640 North West Street next door to the house she and C.J. had been renting. By December she was overseeing construction of two additional rooms and a bath and had purchased an investment property a few blocks away at 841 Camp Street. That month she reviewed final plans for a factory, laboratory and salon at the rear of the North West Street property.

To supplement her income, she took in boarders, a common custom during an era when few American hotels accepted black guests. "Room to Let," read her December announcement on the *Recorder*'s society page. "Mme. C. J. Walker has now thrown open her beautifully furnished home to the up-to-date traveling public. Her home is modern, including heat. Best board served in family style." Without hesitation, she funneled every dollar back into the business. "You understand she was struggling then to get a foundation," a close acquaintance observed of her activities during the fall of 1910. "At the time she was taking in roomers, cooking for them, manufacturing her own preparations in a back room, then doing heads in another room for the rest of the day." And as if that weren't enough, the friend said, "she did her [own] washing at night."

Convinced that personal contact was the key to accelerating her sales and raising her profile, Madam Walker spent the summer of 1910 canvassing several African American conventions. During July, she joined a large Indianapolis delegation at the NACW's seventh biennial conference in Louisville. While she had been on the sidelines just six years earlier at its 1904 St. Louis meeting, she was, without question, the most successful businesswoman among the delegates in Kentucky. Within the next few weeks she swept across the East from Indiana to New York, dropping in at fraternal and religious meetings, and surveying events where she was sure to encounter customers and investors.

In the United States, with more than 3.6 million black females older than ten years of age—and more than half of them employed—her potential market seemed enormous. Three million women multiplied by 50 cents for a tin of Madam Walker's Wonderful Hair Grower equaled $1.5 million! And that didn't include purchases of her vegetable shampoo, scalp treatments, manicures, repeat customers or any of the other products and services she planned to offer.

Just as Madam Walker had written Booker Washington seeking assistance from him to help finance her company, she was acutely aware that she also needed competent advisers and employees to shore up her own lack of formal education. Two young black attorneys, Freeman Briley Ransom and Robert Lee Brokenburr, quickly grabbed her attention in the Hoosier capital.

Ransom, born in Grenada, Mississippi, in 1882, was one of sixteen children who worked on his father's farm. Upon graduation from Grenada's black high school, he entered Nashville's Walden College, where he completed teacher's training. In 1908, he was graduated from the school's law and divinity departments as valedictorian of both classes. Before moving to Indianapolis in the spring of 1910, he "read law for nearly two years" at Columbia University in New York City.

"It was in the Fall of that year that I first met Madam Walker and represented her in a small way," Ransom later wrote. "I was a young lawyer then [and] had had my shingle out about six months." At other times Ransom told his family that he and Madam Walker had first crossed paths during his student days while he worked as a Pullman porter and dining-car waiter. "He always said [they met] on the train," remembered his daughter, A'Lelia Ransom Nelson, who had been named for Madam Walker's daughter. "And they got to be friends. And [he said that Madam Walker] always said, 'The day you finish law school, you come see me.'" Whatever the particulars of their initial conversations, it is clear that Madam Walker immediately recognized his talents. "He was very disciplined," his daughter recalled. "Probably rigid, I suppose you would say, in some ways." But his attention to detail and his high moral standards were precisely what Madam Walker believed she needed to systematize the operation of her business. As a young man, Ransom had taken an oath of sobriety upon joining the YMCA, probably at Walden, where the third black YMCA college chapter had been founded in 1877. "In those days you had to pledge that you'd never drink, dance or gamble. And he never drank, nor danced, nor gambled," said Nelson.

Brokenburr, a slim, handsome man with a deep brown complexion, had opened an office in Indianapolis in the spring of 1909 after graduating from

Howard University's School of Law when he was only twenty-two years old. A native of Phoebus, Virginia, he completed Hampton Institute—Booker T. Washington's alma mater—in 1906. The *Recorder*, praising him for his "honesty and efficiency," pronounced him a "real high class lawyer," who was "already known, not only in the city of Indianapolis, but throughout the length and breadth of Indiana and other surrounding states as well." Madam Walker particularly valued his discreet behavior. "He will not tell one incident of his many clients' affairs, not even for newspaper notoriety," the *Recorder* observed. "He holds the confidence that they have placed in him as sacred, more sacred than his own personal affairs."

At least for a short period, Ransom and Brokenburr roomed with Madam Walker at her North West Street home. Both men, who were close to Lelia's age, would continue to play significant roles in Madam Walker's life and in her company, becoming not just her legal advisers but her close and loyal friends. Each would go on to fashion exemplary careers, Brokenburr as the first black state senator in Indiana, Ransom as a highly regarded state and local civic leader.

As 1910 ended, once again Madam Walker's income had exceeded expectations, this time reaching $10,989, the equivalent of almost $200,000 in today's dollars. But as her fifth wedding anniversary approached, her marriage was fraying. C.J. had been traveling in the South for several months and she was not particularly eager to see him. The more clearly she plotted her future, the more disconnected their lives had become.

Lelia was struggling with her own personal problems as she prepared to join her mother for the Christmas holidays. During the summer, John Robinson had abruptly left her after less than a year of marriage. "We had a quarrel" was all she would say. "He left, and said he was not coming back." Her attempts at reconciliation failed. "We had a talk, but he didn't make any offer to come back." Two Pittsburgh Walker agents who knew Lelia well, and Grant White—her boarder and the friend who probably had introduced the couple—all surmised that, because "she supports herself by her business" and because Robinson had been unable to make any contribution to her support, he had grown to resent her independence. As the two women celebrated Madam Walker's forty-third birthday and looked forward to the new year, they realized once again how much they had always depended upon each other.

In August 1911, Lelia returned to Indianapolis for an extended visit with plans to enjoy the festivities of the sixteenth biennial Knights of Pythias convention later that month. Throughout the summer her mother's home remained filled with guests. Among them was Alice Kelly, the Eckstein-Norton teacher with whom Madam Walker had become friendly and whom she hoped to persuade to join the Walker Company.

Madam Walker was especially pleased to welcome her St. Louis friends the Robinsons: Jessie, who now held the Court of Calanthe's highest elected national office of Supreme Worthy Inspectrix, and C.K., who managed the organization's finances as Supreme Keeper of Records and Seals. The return of C.J., who had spent the first three weeks of August on a sales trip to Illinois, Missouri, Nebraska, Kansas, Oklahoma and Colorado, may have been greeted as another matter. Nevertheless, he was expected to reach the city just in time for the conference plenary on August 21.

Indianapolis's black community bustled expectantly in preparation for the event. The Knights were eager to show off their spanking-new $30,000 headquarters, touting their Pythian Temple at Senate and Walnut avenues as "the finest building owned by colored people in the central states." With equal anticipation, Madam Walker looked forward to providing tours of her recently completed factory to the many out-of-town visitors, especially Booker T. Washington, to whom she continued to write despite his earlier rebuff. Having learned through the conference planners—including her friend Joseph Ward, the group's national Supreme Medical Register and chair of the local publicity and decorations committee—that Washington was slated to deliver a keynote address, Madam Walker contacted the Tuskegee principal exactly one month prior to the meeting. "I thought to again remind you of your promise to visit and inspect our home and factory," she "respectfully" wrote with hopes that he could "make it convenient to do so."

"I hope to have the privilege of inspecting your plant when I visit Indianapolis," he replied, albeit with a caveat that allowed him to maintain his distance. "Of course, however, I shall be in the hands of Mr. Stewart's committee and shall be compelled to be guided by whatever program they may arrange for me." As one of *Recorder* publisher George Stewart's best advertising customers, Madam Walker likely felt no reluctance about approaching him to become part of "whatever program" his committee arranged for the Tuskegee visitor. Although there is no document to verify contact between Madam Walker and Washington during the conference, he could not have missed seeing her home and factory since both were conspicuously visible from the corner of Indiana Avenue and North West Street. As determined as she clearly was to speak with him, he also could not have avoided her at the Wonderland Park reception toasting him on Tuesday afternoon had she wished to approach him.

That same evening several thousand black and white Indianapolis residents crowded the cavernous Coliseum at the Indiana State Fair Grounds to hear Washington. With much of his message focused on his trademark themes of thrift, hard work and personal responsibility, he exhorted the audience, "No man of any race, whatever his color, who knows something that is of value to the world or can do something that is of value to his community can be held back.

"Through such an organization as this," he continued, "teach the youth of our race that they must not be ashamed to begin at the bottom, must not be ashamed to begin with little things and gradually grow to the point where they deal with larger things." It was a philosophy Madam Walker wholeheartedly embraced, and one that she had shared in her first letter to Washington nearly two years earlier.

Throughout the week, convention delegates enjoyed an array of social activities from nightly balls and receptions at Tomlinson Hall and the Pythian Temple to the elaborately costumed "operatic kaleidoscope" of the Black Patti Musical Comedy Company at the Park Theatre, Indianapolis's most popular vaudeville house. Led by the classically trained black diva Mme. Sissieretta Jones, the fifty-member traveling show performed an eclectic fare of minstrel routines, ragtime numbers, musical comedy tunes and an extravagant finale of arias from *Carmen, La Bohème* and numerous other operas.

After evenings filled with entertainment, the several hundred Knights of Pythias delegates—with the men in one hall, the women in another—assembled each morning to present financial and business reports about their insurance and burial programs. High on the agenda was the selection of new officers. Upon her reelection as Supreme Worthy Inspectrix, Jessie Robinson delighted the group with the news that, during her travels since the last biennial meeting, she had helped establish chapters in several cities, including New York. "When women get together that means something for the people they represent," she told the delegates, reminding them of their collective power on behalf of the organization's 52,000 members. Her friend Madam Walker, who now claimed 950 Walker sales agents and several thousand customers, shared the vision of harnessing women's influence. Each convention such as this and each conversation with someone like Jessie Robinson only fueled Madam Walker's imagination.

A few weeks later Madam Walker called upon Robert Brokenburr to formally draw up the articles of incorporation for the Madam C. J. Walker Manufacturing Company of Indiana, a firm created to "sell a hairgrowing, beautifying and scalp disease-curing preparation and clean scalps the same." Apparently unable to attract the investors she had envisioned in her 1910 letter to Washington, Madam Walker may have put her home up for collateral to create the corporation's capital stock of $10,000. She named herself, her husband and her daughter as the sole members of the board of directors.

That fall, C.J. departed on another extended trip, this time visiting Missouri, Kansas, Arkansas, Oklahoma, Tennessee, Mississippi, Alabama and Georgia. After trips to Boley, Oklahoma, and Mound Bayou, Mississippi, the *Freeman* reported, he described "the two Negro towns as the only two towns in the South where a Negro can breathe the breath of freedom." His sense of liberation also may have applied to the state of his marriage, a union that by now had become more business arrangement than affectionate alliance. Inevitably, in C.J.'s lengthy absences, his eye had begun to wander. Inevitably as well, during those absences, Madam Walker continued to reevaluate the purpose of the relationship. At the time, however, she was too wrapped up in her business affairs to make any final decisions about troublesome private matters. Soon, however, she knew she would have to address the issue.

CHAPTER 10

"The Salvation of Your Boys and Girls"

—— ❧ ——

J ust as Madam Walker had set about making the acquaintance of Indianapolis's notable citizens, she was also drawn to the families whose shotgun houses lined the alley behind her home and factory. Believing that "the Lord prospers her because of her giving," she quietly, and often, helped the poorest of her neighbors with rent and groceries. In her factory and office, she employed nearly three dozen people from the area. Throughout the year, she slipped nickels and dimes into the hands of children who ran errands for her beauty parlor. At Christmas she distributed turkeys and food baskets.

But she knew that her well-intentioned gestures could not solve the much larger problems that confronted her neighbors. Adequate housing and steady jobs remained their most pressing needs. In 1910, African Americans lived on blocks with the working-class Germans, Italians and Irish who remained in the increasingly black residential area that extended east and west from Indiana Avenue. All but the most well-off still had outhouses, coal and wood stoves and coal-oil lamps in their neatly kept homes, a mix of Victorian cottages, two-family doubles, two-story wood-frame flats and long rows of cheap one-story frame tenements.

"Quite a number own their own homes, and a few [have] small sums 'laid by,'" observed a 1900 visitor, referring to the thriftiness of some of the black residents he had met. "People had a lot of pride in those days," remembered Frances Stout, whose grandparents owned a vegetable stand in the City Market. "They were determined to try to get ahead." Although few had any substantial material wealth, most were strivers who took pains to beautify their surroundings. "Practically everybody had flowers," said Stout. "Marigolds. Petunias. Sunflowers. Hollyhocks. They were all in wooden buckets on their front steps and around their yards."

While Indiana Avenue was a far cry from St. Louis's notorious Chestnut Valley, its twenty-nine saloons and fifteen poolrooms—many of them "nothing but gambling places"—enticed the idle and underemployed young men who congregated along its busy corridor. For the majority who resisted the temptations of the streets, the Young Men's Christian Association at 443 Indiana Avenue provided a much-needed haven. Despite its cramped and poorly equipped facility, the converted storefront was filled seven days a week with scores of boys and men enrolled in Bible studies, physical education classes and reading groups. The first-floor gymnasium— one-third the size of a regulation basketball floor—was so small that the number of team players had been reduced from five to three. The upstairs meeting room stayed in such demand that there often were as many as three organizations in line every night to use it. Jerry-rigged showers and battered lockers occupied an adjacent coal shed. "It is utterly impossible," pronounced the *Freeman,* "to do the work that [needs to] be done in the present inadequate quarters."

In August 1911, as the Knights of Pythias convention was closing, Indianapolis's black civic leaders began focusing in earnest on plans to replace the run-down YMCA. Since that January, they had monitored the progress of Jesse Moorland, one of two black international secretaries of the Y's Colored Men's Department, as he led fund-raising campaigns for $100,000 buildings in Chicago, Washington and Philadelphia. Now Indianapolis was eager to have its own facility.

"We must get busy. We need the building," *Freeman* publisher George Knox implored in a September editorial. "Others have done the thing, and what others can do, we can do and we must do." As president of the colored YMCA board, Knox, along with several ministers, had already gained the tentative endorsement of Arthur H. Godard, the General Secretary of the all-white Central YMCA. Having recently helped to raise nearly $275,000 for his own newly constructed downtown Indianapolis Y building, Godard had agreed to approach members of his board of directors on behalf of their black YMCA brethren.

Knox, whom Godard probably had known for nearly a decade, had gained influence among prominent men in the city during the 1890s as proprietor of several barbershops catering to a white clientele. His best-known customer was Republican President Benjamin Harrison, whose policies he had trumpeted in the pages of the *Freeman.* In addition to his shop in the old Central Y building, where he had become familiar with the association's work, Knox had also managed the Bates House barbershop. Located in the city's most exclusive late-nineteenth-century hotel, it was then "likened to the elegant 'harem of an Eastern caliph'" with its ten chairs and fifteen baths. Through his personal alliances with state elected officials, Knox had been named an alternate delegate to the 1892 and 1896 Republican National Conventions. For many years, he remained the most powerful black politician in the state.

Madam Walker probably had become acquainted with Knox through their mutual friend Joseph Ward. Over time she had grown to admire his rise from illiterate slave to influential publisher. Coincidentally, he also had made his mark in the hair care business, even marketing for a time a "hair restorative" to rid the scalp of "dandruff and other impurities."

In the fall of 1911, Madam Walker supported Knox's call for a new Y because she believed it would help solve many of the neighborhood's problems and because she considered it her civic responsibility and Christian duty. But as a woman, she could neither join the YMCA nor serve on its executive planning committee, which included Joseph Ward, Henry L. Sanders and Sumner Furniss, a well-established physician whose brother, Dr. Henry Furniss, had been named U.S. Minister to Haiti. Nevertheless, Madam Walker was prepared to make a financial contribution to the cause.

Chicago's enormously successful fund-raising campaign was due largely to the zeal and organizational talents of Jesse Moorland, a Howard University Divinity School graduate, who had been charged with developing black Y's in the nation's cities. Spurred by two conditional $25,000 contributions from businessman J. W. Harris and Sears, Roebuck and Company president Julius Rosenwald, Moorland had helped the Windy City's black community raise $67,000 in just ten days, an astonishing feat for a largely working-class donor base with no truly wealthy prospects. Gifts from white YMCA donors pushed the building fund total to $150,000.

In December 1910, just before Chicago's whirlwind fund drive began, Moorland had been invited to lunch with Rosenwald. During the meal, he persuaded the mail-order magnate to extend his largesse beyond Illinois "to the Negro citizens of America." Moorland's proposition: donate $25,000 to any city willing to raise its own $75,000 to construct a Y in its black community. Because Rosenwald was "so favorably impressed" with Moorland, he agreed "then and there" to back the proposal.

With Moorland's blessing, Indianapolis became a candidate for the Rosenwald funds. The conditions of the pledge required that whites and blacks work together, something Rosenwald believed "would eventually help reduce prejudice." It was also the most pragmatic strategy for an African American community with little ability to construct its own building.

Moorland had become acquainted with Indianapolis's black community in February 1900, when board members of the Central Y invited him to assess the feasibility of "establishing an Association among colored men."

His six-day on-site survey revealed "four to five thousand young colored men" whose condition was "very sad and deplorable." By the time of Moorland's visit, the city's black population had grown to 15,931, comprising nearly a quarter of all blacks in the state. Most had migrated since 1880 from rural Indiana and the upper Southern states, including a particularly large number from Kentucky.

While Moorland found several thriving churches and fraternal organizations among working-class blacks, he was still alarmed by the conditions that some of the young male migrants faced. "Vice is on the increase among them and . . . there is nothing to counteract the downward tendency," he noted, with faith that a YMCA branch would provide an effective antidote to the lure of liquor and dice. "It is apparent to all that a definite work for colored men is needed here."

Upon Moorland's recommendation, two young physicians organized a "Young Men's Prayer Band" to lay the groundwork for a colored association. After the 1905 arrival of YMCA Secretary Thomas E. Taylor, membership grew to 400 boys and men, making it one of the largest Y's in the country by 1910.

The circumstances that Moorland had found in 1900 had only grown worse with a swelling black migrant population. Taylor's own survey of the city revealed hundreds of young men living in lodging houses where "several men sleep in the same room." The overcrowding, he lamented, had made tuberculosis and other communicable diseases "rampant."

Such living conditions, and the scarcity of decent-paying jobs for African Americans, Taylor believed, caused many young men to break the law. His investigation of 1910 police records revealed that of the 8,840 men arrested that year, 1,974—or more than 20 percent—were black, although African Americans made up less than 10 percent of the city's population. There was little consolation that most of the crimes were petty thefts, minor offenses and misdemeanors.

Marion County Police Court Judge James A. Collins had commended Taylor's "encouraging" rehabilitation of the young men Collins had put in his care. Taylor's work, the judge noted, deserved to be rewarded with a new facility. "What the young negro of today wants is an opportunity," Judge Collins wrote. "Give him the same chance the white boy has and you'll have better negro citizens."

Concern for public safety also was uppermost in the minds of the *Indianapolis Star* editorial board, who urged community leaders to overcome "race prejudice" and to support the new Y. "The presence in any city of an idle and lawless negro element is a problem and a danger," it concluded, then added, "It would be an almost inconceivably narrow and superficial soul who would object to such an enterprise on race grounds."

But the *Star* had reason to anticipate opposition in this ethnically circumscribed Northern town. From time to time, when Samuel Lewis "Lew" Shank, the city's folksy and flamboyant Republican mayor, rode in parades and made friendly speeches—as he had done during the Knights of Pythias convention—African Americans could temporarily enjoy a display of racial harmony. But after such ephemeral flirtations with brotherhood— quite often and quite transparently pegged to election seasons—the city's influential and affluent whites, who had crossed the social barriers seeking votes, returned to their own neighborhoods. For the most part, the city's white businessmen and professionals lived in impressive homes along and near the North Meridian Street corridor, while most blacks were prevented from moving beyond the boundaries of the Indiana Avenue area both by custom and by the refusal of Realtors to rent or sell them homes. Except in their jobs as servants, chauffeurs, laundresses and deliverymen, they were unwelcome in the city's fashionable enclaves.

With this in mind, Thomas Taylor had been careful to soft-pedal his objectives for the colored Y when speaking with the city's white civic leaders. In the kind of charade that many blacks felt obligated to adopt during an era of overt racism, he downplayed his community's desires. The Indianapolis association, he insisted, was content to provide education of a "practical kind" for young black men who, he implied, had no intentions of competing with their white counterparts. His aim, he said, was to "teach him how to become a better janitor, a better waiter or teach him some trade." Such an approach was quite acceptable to members of the larger community, who preferred to exist quite separate and apart from African Americans.

From Madam Walker's perspective, Indianapolis was no better and no worse on the matter of race than any other American city of the era. Despite the unmasked discrimination that periodically emerged, she still valued its location and transportation options. Nevertheless she must also have been aware that the white civic leadership liked to portray Indianapolis as a "100 percent American town." And in 1910 the notion of "real Americans" excluded blacks as well as most first-generation Europeans.

While nearby Chicago had become a magnet for thousands of Irish, Polish, Italian and German immigrants—who now composed 36 percent of that city's population—fewer than 9 percent of Indianapolis's residents were immigrants. Such numbers caused the Commercial Club of Indianapolis, the forerunner of the Chamber of Commerce, to boast of "almost a total absence" of what it derisively termed "the foreign floating element." With such sentiments so openly voiced, Indianapolis remained a racially segregated, economically divided city.

Still there were whites who wished to help the YMCA effort and who chipped away at the barriers. Former U.S. Senator Charles W. Fairbanks, who had served as Theodore Roosevelt's vice president from 1905 to 1909, had earlier urged the Central Y to pass a resolution to draw up plans to replace the Indiana Avenue branch. "It is to our selfish interest that this, the city of our residence, should be made the best city possible," he waxed, with high-flown sentiment, before his fellow board members. "And the greatest things are not those which merely build up the physical city, but those which tend to build up character and to elevate the people morally and spiritually."

But it had taken Chicagoan Julius Rosenwald's singular generosity to push Fairbanks and his Indianapolis colleagues beyond rhetoric. Now with Godard and the others on board, the leadership of the Central Y "agreed to bear the greater burden, knowing the colored men's inability to rear up such a building." Accepting Rosenwald's conditions, Godard's board proposed to collect $60,000, four times more than the $15,000 the Indiana Avenue Y was expected to raise. In response, Knox's committee vowed, on behalf of "the entire Negro population," to "put our shoulders together" for the appeal. "It is the responsibility of every Negro citizen, and only can it be accomplished by the united effort of us all . . . The cry is 'Unity!' The slogan is 'Get Together.'"

In anticipation of the ten-day Indianapolis fund-raising blitz, Moorland employed the winning formula that had cinched the Chicago appeal. With his high-level committees already in place—and racial pride and civic responsibility for both whites and blacks at stake—he scheduled "monster rallies" and lectures illustrated with glass stereopticon slides during the week leading up to the door-to-door canvassing. "A new building for your association is the salvation of your boys and girls. It will make better sons, fathers and husbands, and indirectly better girls and mothers in this city," he proclaimed at a mass meeting at the Pythian Temple. "You are belittled when it is said you will raise only $15,000 for such a building," he scolded the black Hoosiers. Apparently Madam Walker took his words to heart when he said, "I shall be surprised if you good people don't go way ahead of that."

On the day before the Monday, October 23, kickoff, two of the city's most prosperous white businessmen dramatically set the tone with leadership gifts that electrified the volunteers of this highly watched crusade. Arthur Jordan, a stalwart local YMCA supporter who had pioneered refrigerated railroad cars for transporting poultry between the Midwest and the East Coast, announced a very generous $5,000 pledge. Carl Fisher, a co-founder of the Indianapolis Motor Speedway, who had become wealthy manufacturing automobile headlamp batteries, bested Jordan with an even more striking $10,000 commitment.

That afternoon, the Indiana Avenue Y committee launched its campaign a few blocks away at the Pythian Temple with a few surprises of its own. To the grateful applause of 300 foot-stomping African Americans, Madam Walker confidently pledged $1,000. "If the association can save our boys, our girls will be saved, and that's what I am interested in," she said, echoing Moorland's earlier words. Characteristically, she also used the occasion to voice her own particular concerns. "Some day I would like to see a colored girls' association started." Her contribution, she told the audience, was tendered in order to spur more generosity and responsibility among the city's African Americans. "The Young Men's Christian Association is one of the greatest institutions there is . . . I am much interested in its work," she told the crowd. "And I think every colored person ought to contribute to the campaign."

By the end of the evening an additional $1,900 had been contributed, including $500 from Mrs. L. E. McNairdee, a clairvoyant who operated a well-kept boardinghouse. By coincidence, the two largest gifts from Indianapolis's African American community had come that day from black businesswomen.

The *Freeman*, which called Madam Walker "the first colored woman in the United States to give $1000 to a colored Y.M.C.A. building," showcased her photograph in an article that was read all over the country. At the time she claimed "an income of $1,000 per month," making the pledge a near tithe of her annual earnings. Skeptics wondered whether she could honor what seemed to be an "unthinkable" amount "coming from a colored woman." Of course, Madam Walker ignored their accusations, confident that she could deliver on her promise.

On Monday, the campaign opened at full throttle with 450 canvassers— including twelve Central Y teams and seventeen Indiana Avenue teams— who fanned out across the city in more than two dozen cars. Madam Walker's Auburn automobile was likely part of the fleet. But even in collaboration on behalf of the community's welfare, the line of racial demarcation prevailed. "By the rules of the campaign," blacks were required to "confine their solicitations to the people of their own race." Likewise, no member of the Central team was allowed to solicit subscriptions from blacks.

The *Indianapolis Star* and the *Indianapolis News*, the city's largest dailies, covered the campaign like a horse race, tallying the funds in morning and evening headlines, then reporting on the Central Y's lunchtime assemblies, as well as the Indiana Avenue Y's supper-hour meetings. On the second day of the campaign—with a third of their goal already secured—the black canvassers were buoyed by a congratulatory telegram from Rosenwald. "I am greatly delighted with your message, stating that $5,430 was reported from the colored people the first day," he had wired Moorland. "Your absolute faith in the integrity of the colored man, and his willingness to make a sacrifice, has been justified once more."

By Wednesday night, the black teams had filled another set of pledge cards, bringing their aggregate to $8,019.64 and putting them more than halfway toward their $15,000 goal. That evening after Madam Walker paid the first $250 installment on her pledge, General Secretary Godard placed the campaign's total at more than $64,000. In front of the Indiana Avenue Y, Secretary Taylor jubilantly displayed the day's total by adjusting the hands of an oversized wooden clock decorated with electric lights. "The men," an ecstatic Jesse Moorland predicted, "are just getting warmed up."

By Friday, in a city infused with the momentum of the contest, several more $1,000 pledges had arrived. Among them were promises from banker John Holliday, founder of the *Indianapolis News,* and his wife, Evaline Holliday, as well as James A. Allison, Carl Fisher's Motor Speedway and Prest-O-Lite partner. And there were other, smaller, but no less noteworthy gifts. Poet James Whitcomb Riley, who had known George Knox since his childhood in Greenfield, Indiana, contributed $100. The colored porters of the Eli Lilly Company, the growing pharmaceutical concern, also had taken up a collection to help the cause.

On Saturday the Indiana Avenue teams collected more than $2,000, pushing their total above $13,000. By the end of the day, with only four days left, the city was less than $19,000 shy of its objective. But Godard had grown anxious that the teams might fail to raise the $75,000 stipulated by Rosenwald's offer. "Unless there is a more generous response on the part of citizens from whom we have a right to expect support during these next few days, this enterprise will be in a precarious condition," he warned.

To motivate the Indiana Avenue canvassers, a large rally featuring a rousing 200-voice male chorus was arranged for Sunday afternoon at the Pythian Temple. "We're going to build that building," Godard told the audience of several hundred black men and women, "because we have faith in you . . . But, men!" he exhorted the team captains, "we want you . . . to roll up the biggest list of subscriptions ever made by colored people." The campaign, asserted one of the visiting white team leaders, was not only the "hardest ever undertaken" in Indianapolis, "it is the greatest thing ever undertaken for the city . . . We're going to put it through. We have eliminated failure."

On Monday, however, the Central Y canvassers hit a snag, bringing in only $2,912.50 on their only day without a single $1,000 subscription. "A chain is no stronger than its weakest link," said banker John Holliday, challenging his teams to push harder for the sake of civic and personal pride. "If our city is to be built up and grow strong in every way, we must take care of the colored people." And while his plea dripped with paternalism, it was consistent with the prevailing belief that African Americans would forever occupy a place beneath whites in the social hierarchy of the nation. As if in reply to Holliday, the black team leaders seemed determined to demonstrate their ability to "take care" of *themselves*. While the white teams had slumped that day, the black canvassers, sparked by their Sunday pep talk, reported a new daily record of $3,138.49. Not only had they inched past the Central Y's same day total by $225, they had exceeded their $15,000 goal by more than $1,000. "Here's our opportunity," Secretary Taylor said proudly. "We raised our $15,000 and more. From now on we will help the Central teams 'put the thing over.'"

On Halloween afternoon at the Central Y's daily check-in, the overall total topped $93,000, including Rosenwald's pledge. That evening when the Indiana Avenue Y's figures went over $17,000, its members discovered that the hour hand on their giant clock was stuck, preventing them from advancing it to the next $1,000 marker on the dial. Undaunted, the volunteers gathered around the timepiece and "gave three cheers for '$17,000.'"

The next morning, the *Indianapolis Star* headlines blared: "Effort Ends Today; $4,458.66 Is Needed." At lunch, the Central Y teams received marching orders to mount a "supreme effort." Electric railway entrepreneur Hugh J. McGowan's $2,000 pledge and former Vice President Fairbanks's $1,000 gift pushed them more than halfway toward the day's target. "This movement for a colored Young Men's Christian Association has made it possible for the colored and white citizens to join together in fellowship," said Fairbanks later that evening at a second Central Y gathering. "It will make better and more splendid our common citizenship."

At 7:30 P.M. the white team leaders—accompanied by Knox, Taylor, Ward, Moorland and, most likely, Madam Walker and dozens of others—moved en masse from the Central Y to 443 Indiana Avenue for "the biggest and most enthusiastic gathering" of the campaign. With the announcement of nearly $2,000 more in pledges from the black community, the final tally was an unexpected $104,000. In the end, more than 1,500 African American donors—from janitors to doctors—had contributed $20,610.73. The Central YMCA gave its final numbers as $59,126.15, almost triple that collected by the black fund-raisers.

"The colored people," wrote Knox's *Freeman*, "had their first experience in doing something in a big way—for a common cause. All elements were blended; sectarian and factional lines disappeared in the interest of the much-needed institution." It was, said Knox, "a sign of the best possible condition between the races."

Madam Walker's contribution, though smaller than that of Arthur Jordan or Carl Fisher, had put her on equal footing with other $1,000 givers in the city. And although the white dailies always relegated her to the *last* line of the $1,000 donors—despite the fact that she made the *first* $1,000 pledge—the *amount* of her donation matched that of former Vice President Fairbanks. It equaled those of industrialist James Allison and banker Stoughton Fletcher. It was, in fact, no different from the pledges of much wealthier white men.

The contribution also solidified her relationship with campaign chair George Knox, a man who, like Madam Walker, had succeeded beyond his wildest expectations. A "skilled debater and perennial master of ceremonies," he now wielded the kind of influence she hoped to acquire. In stepping forward she had helped her community, while also propelling herself to a higher level of visibility. Headlines in black publications across the country heralded her philanthropic generosity, allowing her to claim the title of "Best Known Hair Culturist in America," no doubt to the chagrin of her rival, Annie Pope-Turnbo. And no paper did more for her national profile and reputation than Knox's *Freeman*. "Hurrah for the $100,000 YMCA building! Hurrah for the white folks! Hurrah for the colored folks! Hurrah for Julius Rosenwald and Carl Fisher, Arthur Jordan, Madams Walker and McNairdee! Hurrah for the widow's mite also!"

"Mr. Rosenwald's gift challenged colored people to self-respect through self-support," Jesse Moorland observed years later. Madam Walker had been one of the first to grasp the significance of the movement. Certainly the symbolism of her gift challenged all conventional wisdom about black women and wealth in early-twentieth-century America. At a time when it was widely believed that women were neither emotionally nor physically suited to be involved in the world of commerce, she had long ago stepped beyond the circumscribed "natural role" of wife and mother. During an era when African Americans were believed to be incapable of developing their own communities, she had refuted the stereotype that blacks could not be successful in business.

CHAPTER 11

"I Promoted Myself . . ."

— ᴄ◌ᴢ◌ —

A s soon as she learned of Booker T. Washington's forthcoming January
1912 Negro Farmers' Conference, Madam Walker began planning
not just a trip but a pilgrimage to his school in Tuskegee, Alabama.
Two years after her first letter to Washington, she was still struggling to
convince him of the "merits" of her work. Even at the Knights of Pythias
gathering the previous summer, when he learned of her busy factory, he
remained reserved. Aware that an endorsement from Washington, the
nation's most well-known advocate for black entrepreneurs, would elevate
her business and her personal stature, she resolved to win him over.

Madam Walker had no doubt that Washington was aware of her YMCA
pledge, especially since Knox's *Freeman* was a paper he and his secretary,
Emmett Scott, frequently read. With hopes that he might view her more
favorably as a result of her $1,000 donation, Madam Walker wrote to him
in early December "to ask if you will allow me to introduce my work and
give me the privilege of selling my goods on the grounds." Enclosing an
attractive sixteen-page booklet, "which will give you an idea of the business
in which I am engaged," she felt sure her brief biography and the photographs of her home, salon, factory and employees would remind him that
she too had overcome an early life of hardship. Because advance publicity
for the assembly promised that participants would be "entertained as the
guests of the school" and given "a warm welcome in person" by Washington
himself, she anticipated an opportunity to interact with him more closely
than she had been able to in the past.

Basking from another prosperous year, Madam Walker sincerely believed
her story could inspire the 2,000 farmers who were expected to gather at
Washington's twentieth annual agricultural conference. Earlier that year,
almost as soon as the factory behind her house was completed, she had purchased a second building next door at 644 North West Street. Her annual

earnings continued their steady climb, reaching more than $13,000, a tenfold increase after just five years in business. But like the farmers, she had started out on a plantation. Surely Washington would see the value in including her on his program. His reply to her letter was prompt, in keeping with his mandate that all mail to his office be answered on the day it arrived, even "if it is necessary to remain at the office until twelve o'clock at night to do it." But it was also searingly curt. "My dear Mme. Walker," he began patronizingly, "I fear you misunderstand the kind of meeting our Tuskegee Negro Conference will be." And although Washington himself had earlier said that "the Negro farmer often passes from agriculture to business," he saw no place for her at "a meeting of poor farmers who come here for instruction and guidance, and who have very little or no money." With no compliments for the impressive prospectus she had mailed, he informed her that he was "well acquainted" with her business, "but somehow I do not feel that a visit to our Conference would offer the opportunity which you seem to desire."

The letter was vintage Washington, but it appears that Emmett Scott, and not Washington himself, composed it. After examining the correspondence, Scott's biographer Maceo C. Dailey, Jr., recognized the handwriting as that of Scott, who often served as Washington's authorized ghostwriter. But Madam Walker would not have known that at the time, so she would have accepted the sentiment as Washington's own. Familiar as Scott was with Washington's discomfort with the hair products advertisements that so often appeared in black newspapers, he may or may not have consulted Washington before dictating his discouraging reply. Once called Washington's Iago, Scott was so in sync with his superior's sensibilities and opinions that at times "it was almost impossible to tell which of Washington's communications was written by him and which by Scott," according to Washington biographer Louis R. Harlan.

Washington "first opposed membership in the National Negro Business League for . . . cosmetics manufacturers on the ground that they fostered imitation of white beauty standards, but he later relented," Harlan also noted. In taking such a stance, perhaps Washington was under the lingering influence of his straitlaced, Victorian-era education at Hampton Institute, where Mary Armstrong, wife of principal Samuel Chapman Armstrong, had reminded the black and Native American female students that "paint and powder" were undesirable artifice, "always unclean, false, unwholesome." While Washington included barbers in his 1907 book, *The Negro in Business*, he "deliberately left out" hair care products manufacturers. The two black women hairdressers who were permitted to address the annual National Negro Business League convention in 1901 and 1905 may have been acceptable to Washington because they catered to a white clientele and did not service black women.

Less than two weeks after the Washington/Scott letter to Madam Walker, Washington wrote *New York Age* editor Fred Moore that he had come to "view with alarm" the "considerable amount" of "clairvoyant advertising . . . hair straightening advertising, and fake religious advertising" that appeared in his newspaper. Such advertising, he admonished Moore—who had once vowed never to accept such fare—does not "add to the prestige of your newspaper" and "is of that character which subjects us to the ridicule of even our best white friends." Because Washington had "subsidized *The Age* for several years" and had "clandestinely advanced money to Moore" to purchase the paper, his words carried inordinate weight. "You ought to very seriously consider this matter and I hope you will," Washington warned not at all subtly.

In seeking to banish hair care ads from the newspapers he controlled, Washington had failed to grasp a changing trend affecting American women and their relationship with the nation's marketplace. Stubbornly old-fashioned on the issue, he seemed not at all attuned to a growing beauty products industry that was responding to increasingly urbanized women eager to move from homemade creams and pharmaceutical compounds to mass-marketed cosmetics and hair care aids. There had been "no identifiable 'cosmetics industry' in the nineteenth century, no large and distinct sector of the economy devoted to beauty products," according to historian Kathy Peiss. But by the early 1900s "an emergent class of managers and professionals were developing new methods that would come to dominate American business." Madam Walker was among those in the forefront who "devised a national system of mass production, distribution, marketing, and advertising that transformed local patterns of buying and selling" and made "cosmetics affordable and indispensable to all women."

The brusque letter from Tuskegee only made Madam Walker more determined to visit the campus in January. But in early December while she waited, she switched her attention to Lelia's forthcoming Christmas visit to Indianapolis. "It is pleasant to note with what joyous expectations Madam looks forward [to] your coming," F. B. Ransom, the young attorney and now family friend, wrote to Lelia.

To clarify her relationship to the Walker Manufacturing Company and its founder, Lelia had begun calling herself "Mrs. Lelia Walker Robinson" in advertisements and announcements. While adding "Walker" to her professional name may have made it clear that she was the daughter of Madam Walker, it was becoming less clear how much longer C.J. would remain her stepfather.

As the new year approached, the Walker marriage still was problematic. Unresolved, but not yet dissolved, the union slowly continued to unravel.

C.J., who had spent little time in Indianapolis since the fall, remained on an extended trip throughout the South and Midwest during January. And he was not spending all of his nights alone. In Kansas City, Missouri, where he had stopped the previous August, he arranged a rendezvous with a woman named Louise during December or early January. In mid-January when Louise answered his recent "sweet and kind letter," she professed her love and called him a "big, sensible, strong, businessman." While his wife had probably not flattered him so in a long time, Louise vowed that she was "content to wait for [him]," with hopes that they would be together by April. Less than a week later, Madam Walker, who seems to have known nothing about Louise, was joined by C.J. in Tuskegee for the Farmers' Conference. Of course, he volunteered no information about his tryst. But soon enough his actions would betray him.

Uninvited, but undaunted, Madam Walker traveled to Alabama armed with a letter of introduction from Thomas Taylor, the highly respected executive secretary of Indianapolis's colored YMCA. Shortly after reaching the 2,000-acre Tuskegee campus, she appeared unannounced on Washington's front porch. "She came knocking on his door at his private home," Louis Harlan recalled from a conversation with a Washington family member. Whether he saw her or whether an aide greeted her that morning is not known, but Madam Walker had come too far to be turned away. "He tried to discourage her," said Harlan, "but she insisted."

In her own hand-delivered letter, she entreated Washington to "be kind enough to introduce me" to the conference and "not deny me this one opportunity." Now instead of wanting to sell her goods, she wrote, she simply wished to tell the farmers how she had overcome some of the same obstacles they faced. "I want them to know that I am in the business world, not for myself alone, but to do all the good I can for the uplift of my race, which you well know by the great sacrifice I made in the interest of the Y.M.C.A. of Indianapolis," she reminded Washington. Hoping to lessen whatever irritation her brash behavior may have created, she signed her letter "Obeidently yours," a well-intentioned though misspelled closing line, exposing the spottiness of her formal education. Declining to address her directly, Washington once again dispatched Scott to respond to her.

"It is possible Scott may have taken some liberties of his own in saying 'no'" to Madam Walker's initial request to visit the campus, speculates Scott's biographer Dailey. "But when faced with [her] persistence [he] had to bring the matter to Washington for the follow-up decision." Whether it was Madam Walker's persistence or the letter from Taylor that ultimately made the difference, Scott's subsequent answer was the one she had long awaited. "I have talked with Mr. Washington and he agrees to arrange for you to speak for 10 minutes tonight in the Chapel," Scott wrote. But even in his invitation, he added a not so thinly veiled dig. "We will have a very full audience there at that time and it will be more proper we think to speak tonight instead of in the regular Conference."

That evening in chapel Madam Walker told the conferees of her "great struggle from the age of seven years without any parents to assist me" and how she had "succeeded in . . . the business arena . . . to where my income is now more than $1,000 per month." She urged them to keep at their work so that they could "do likewise."

The campus newspaper, which reported extensively on the school's activities, was surprisingly silent on her presentation, perhaps because Scott was its editor. But Madam Walker made few public appearances where she was not well received. And the reaction was sufficiently positive that she extended her stay *and* managed to persuade Washington to allow her to market her products.

"The folklore," according to Washington biographer Harlan, "is [that] she came to Tuskegee and demonstrated her method on [Washington's] family. Once he saw the results . . . he changed his mind." In fact Madam Walker claimed to have given "84 demonstrative treatments" of her hair care method, "among which number she has the honor of including Dr. Washington and his family." With Portia Washington Pittman, Booker T. Washington's daughter, married and gone from the campus, Margaret Murray Washington and her niece, Laura Murray Washington, may have been the family members whose hair Madam treated. If so, Margaret Washington, whom Madam Walker had met previously at NACW events, had proven to be more sympathetic to the concept of hair culture than her husband. As president of the Mothers' Council, Tuskegee's "lady principal" often encountered "barefooted" rural Alabama women with "hair uncombed," who attended her classes on hygiene, housekeeping, proper dress and child care. The treatments that Madam Walker offered could only have helped these uneducated, ill-groomed farmworkers. By the end of her ten-day visit, Madam Walker had "no end to her praises for the hospitality and courtesies shown her at the school," despite her testy start. Afterward she expressed her gratitude to both Washingtons for the kindness "shown both myself and my agent in Tuskegee. I shall always remember very pleasantly the inspiration I received from the sights at Tuskegee Institute."

A month later, while billing her for $40 worth of printing work, Booker T. Washington felt no hesitation in soliciting a donation for his school from the woman he at first had insulted. Her $5 contribution was small, but it was meant to cover a semester's worth of books for a deserving Tuskegee student. Washington thanked her "heartily" for her gift, though he may have been disappointed in the amount.

With her Tuskegee visit, Madam Walker had accomplished exactly what she had intended: recognition from Washington and a chance to promote her company. From a business standpoint, the trip had been so satisfactory that she had opened a "permanent agency" near the campus. For her local representative she chose Dora Larrie, an Indianapolis woman whom she personally had trained in the Walker Method. Pleased with Larrie's ambition and energy, Madam Walker felt confident that her operation was in good hands. But soon she would have reason to regret her decision.

After a brief return to Indianapolis to replenish their supplies, Madam Walker and C.J. headed south again, dividing the territory by branching out to different states. In late March they reunited in Jackson, Mississippi, but the time apart had not made their hearts grow fonder. Instead the relationship had become pricklier. The more they were together, especially in the company of others, the clearer it became that Madam Walker was the more impressive member of the couple and the more effective entrepreneur. While C.J. had the ability to be a charming companion and an effective salesman, he continued to squander and mismanage their money. Madam Walker was increasingly concerned with current events and political affairs, but C.J. seemed content to focus on cars, clothes and, unbeknown to his wife, other women.

To soothe his suffering ego, C.J. began another affair, this time with Dora Larrie. While Madam Walker remained in Mississippi instructing new agents, C.J. and Larrie met at the Dunbar Hotel in Birmingham, Alabama, and, as C.J. remembered, "laid our plans." He later admitted in a public letter that Larrie had prevailed upon him to leave his wife, having convinced him that he "was being badly treated by Madam Walker because she did not let me handle all the money." Instead, Larrie persuaded C.J. that as her business partner—with his "knowledge of making the goods, and her ability to do the work, and talk"—they could "make thousands of dollars." Most important, she promised a gullible C.J. that he would "be master of the situation."

The enterprising ambition that had persuaded Madam Walker to name Larrie as her agent had translated into a self-serving ambition that finally undermined what was left of an already unsalvageable marriage. Larrie "closed her work at Tuskegee" and joined C.J. in Atlanta, where, according to Madam Walker's secretary—in an impossible-to-verify oral history— Madam Walker discovered them together. The third-hand scenario may be more plausible fiction than fact. But Madam Walker is said to have made her way to their hotel, heard them talking through a keyhole, reached into her handbag for her revolver, gripped the trigger, then froze. "She realized that everything she had worked for would be destroyed," her secretary Violet Reynolds later recalled. "And she knew C.J. was not worth it. So she walked away."

Immediately Madam Walker returned to Indianapolis and met with attorney Ransom. A few days later, C.J. followed her there, his trip "cut short in the South," according to the *Freeman*, "as pressing business demanded his attention at home." The urgent matters, no doubt, were his wife's anger and humiliation and, most important, her decision to divorce him.

During the summer, while Ransom sorted out the legal details for the divorce, Madam Walker resumed her Southern sojourn. Newspaper articles about her trip—probably self-authored with Ransom's careful editing—reported not just on her business but on her interest in "the moral and social questions affecting her race." By mid-July she had joined forces with Mary Lynch, president of North Carolina's colored Women's Christian Temperance Union, who helped her navigate the state and provided introductions to ministers and clubwomen in each town they visited.

Fearless as Madam Walker was, the indignities and dangers of the Jim Crow South had made traveling alone an unwise and unsafe proposition. The "Negro coach," invariably a portion of a baggage bin or smoking car, was "poorly ventilated, poorly lighted, and, above all, rarely kept clean." More often than not the makeshift compartment was "a vantage point for all the engine smoke and cinders." And while white women were provided with separate, well-tended parlor cars, black women were relegated to messy, uncomfortable coaches. "No matter how many colored women may be in the colored end of the car, nor how clean or how well-educated these colored women may be, [their] car is made the headquarters for the newsboy" and for cigar-smoking white men, complained Booker T. Washington in a 1912 *Century* magazine article. Fortunately for Madam Walker, many of the Pullman porters—especially those who read and distributed the *Freeman*—knew of her. She, in turn, cultivated the friendship of these often college-educated young men, who went out of their way to provide her with the best possible accommodations under the circumstances.

From North Carolina, Madam Walker and Mary Lynch headed north to Virginia for the National Association of Colored Women's eighth biennial convention in Hampton in late July 1912. The sight of more than 400 purposeful black women on Hampton Institute's Chesapeake Bay campus must have been a balm to the traveling companions. Just two years earlier, when Madam Walker arrived at the NACW conference in Louisville, she had been largely unknown to most of the original members of the organization. After the 1912 meeting, that would no longer be the case as she set about to make herself an integral part of some of their most visible initiatives.

During the opening session, after hearing Mary McLeod Bethune describe her Daytona Normal and Industrial Institute for Negro Girls, Madam Walker volunteered to spearhead a fund-raising campaign for the eight-year-old school. In Bethune, who was making her first appearance at an NACW conference, Madam Walker could see another woman who shared her vision for educating black girls. Originally trained as a missionary, Bethune had managed to attract 250 students within two years of founding her Florida school. By 1912, when Madam Walker first met Bethune, the forceful and charismatic woman had already garnered the support of James N. Gamble, a founder of Procter and Gamble. Both of them daughters of the plantation South, Bethune and Madam Walker refused to bow in the face of rejection and insult. "No matter how deep my hurt, I always smiled," Bethune once said. "I refused to be discouraged, for neither God nor man could use a discouraged soul." It was exactly the kind of inner perseverance upon which Madam Walker continued to rely.

As always, the NACW gatherings were a mix of social welfare, culture and politics, producing resolutions denouncing the "uncomfortable and inferior accommodations" of Jim Crow cars, calling for an end to segregated housing codes and deploring lynching and mob violence. At the behest of Adella Hunt Logan, an outspoken suffragette and wife of Tuskegee treasurer Warren Logan, the group "declared in favor of full woman suffrage and advocated the formation of political study clubs to stir up" activism in their communities. But what most aroused the delegates' interest was a plea to help seventeen-year-old Virginia Christian, a young black washerwoman who awaited a mid-August electrocution in Richmond for murdering her white employer, a Mrs. Belote. Several weeks earlier, after Belote had accused her of stealing a skirt, the two women argued violently. When Christian continued to deny the theft, Belote attacked her with a heavy cuspidor. "In a blind rage" Christian retaliated, striking Belote across her forehead with a broken broomstick and "felling her instantly." To stop Belote's screams, Christian "thrust a towel down her throat," then walked off with jewelry and money from Belote's purse.

Christian certainly was no model of virtue. And the NACW had admitted as much, calling her an "irresponsible being." Nevertheless, they abhorred the death penalty for a minor and hoped to have her declared mentally incompetent in order to commute her sentence to life imprisonment. Mary Church Terrell, the founding president of the NACW, was appointed as head of a special committee charged with visiting Virginia governor William Hodges Mann. At dawn that Thursday she traveled to Richmond with a petition requesting leniency. "Owing to all the circumstances of the case we feel that the electrocution of this young girl would be repugnant to the Christian womanhood and manhood not only of the United States but of the whole civilized world," read the NACW appeal. At 10 A.M. Terrell presented the document to the governor and made her plea. But while he granted Terrell permission to visit Christian in jail, he declined to "show clemency on account of age for Virginia Christian." Late that afternoon, as Terrell returned to Hampton, she delivered the disappointing news to her colleagues.

In the evening, as Madam Walker was formally introduced to the group, she opened her remarks with the announcement of her donation to cover all travel costs for Terrell and the two other committee members who had ventured to Richmond. The woman the NACW delegates had scarcely known two years earlier now received a "rising vote of thanks" and was praised not only for doing "a great deal to improve the appearance of our women" but for the "interest [she has shown] in race progress by contributing one thousand dollars to the YMCA fund." Her speech was said to have "captivated the vast audience."

That Saturday morning, as the group was serenaded by the Hampton Institute Brass Band, Madam Walker and the other delegates sailed aboard the steamer *Hampton Roads* on an excursion through the lower Chesapeake Bay. At noon they docked at the Newport News Navy Yard for a lunchtime speech by Booker T. Washington, husband of the group's newly installed president, Margaret Murray Washington.

Once again Madam Walker found herself in the company of her reluctant Tuskegee host. In this setting he could not help but hear of her support for the Christian case and the Bethune scholarship. Money was a language she knew he understood, master that he was of drawing it to his school and his pet causes. And because she intended to keep using hers "in the interest of the race," she knew he would not be able to ignore her. In just a few weeks, in fact, she expected to see him again on his own turf while attending her first National Negro Business League convention.

Emboldened by the accolades she had received all summer, Madam Walker arrived in Chicago for the thirteenth annual NNBL meeting confident that Washington would not deny her request to address the delegates. Since the organization's first conference in 1900, the annual gathering had remained the premier showcase for black enterprise, a congratulatory three-day demonstration of personal triumph and race pride. Washington, the group's founder, also considered it an essential "instrument" for achieving "what he envisioned as a new emancipation" of economic independence for African Americans.

Along with Emmett Scott, Washington controlled the conference agenda, parceling out leadership roles and preferred speaking slots to friends, as well as to those newcomers he wished to spotlight and endorse. This year Madam Walker believed she had earned the privilege to be among those featured speakers. But, as usual, Washington remained non-committal when she approached him.

The seeds for the NNBL first sprouted in May 1899 during a discussion of the topic "The Negro in Business" at Atlanta University when conference planner W.E.B. Du Bois recommended "the organization in every town and hamlet where the colored people dwell, of Negro Business Men's Leagues, and the gradual federation from these of state and national organizations." By 1912, of course, Du Bois and Washington had become bitter ideological enemies differing over educational and political matters in the black community. But at the turn of the century—and even in 1912—they differed little on their belief that a key strategy for black "economic salvation" lay in the development of commercial enterprise.

Atlanta Baptist College instructor John Hope, a keynote speaker at the Atlanta University conference, similarly had advocated a brand of black economic nationalism as a defense against racial discrimination. "Business seems to be not only simply the raw material of Anglo-Saxon civilization, but almost the civilization itself," the militant and highly accomplished future president of Morehouse College had declared in his speech, "The Meaning of Business." Calling whites—and specifically Anglo-Saxons—"a conquering people who turn their conquests into their pockets," he insisted that blacks could no longer occupy the sidelines in matters of commerce. "The policy of avoiding entrance in the world's business would be suicide to the Negro," he warned. "Yet as a matter of great account, we ought to note that as good a showing as we have made, that showing is but as pebbles on the shore of business enterprise."

In fact, almost no blacks held stakes in mining, railroads, banking, steel or oil, unquestionably the true wealth builders of the late-nineteenth and early-twentieth centuries. "During America's greatest industrial and business expansion, there were few black manufacturing enterprises that reflected industrial America," according to business historian Juliet E. K. Walker. At the time of the first NNBL convention "the total wealth of black America, $700 million, amounted to less than that of the nation's first billion-dollar corporation, United States Steel," which had been organized just a few months later.

Du Bois's postconference study, "The Negro in Business," provided "the first careful documentation" of the nation's estimated 5,000 black entrepreneurs, in fact "a blueprint of the segregated black world's economic infrastructure." While completing the report, Du Bois was named director of the Business Bureau of the National Afro-American Council, a short-lived but visible civil rights organization that had become a battleground for the factions of conservative and militant blacks. Charged with organizing local business league chapters, Du Bois was forced to abandon his effort even before he began when the council's executive committee—led by a loyal Washington supporter—eliminated his meager postage budget. Not long afterward, Washington, with whom Du Bois still had a relatively cordial relationship, asked to see Du Bois's list of potential members. Roster in hand, Washington set about contacting the businessmen Du Bois had identified, then did nothing to include Du Bois in the founding of the NNBL or the planning of its first convention. Some observers suspected intentional sabotage on the part of the executive committee in an effort to wrest the organization from Du Bois's control. Antilynching crusader and National Afro-American Council member Ida B. Wells publicly accused Washington of stealing Du Bois's concept. And so, although "the business league idea was born in the brain of W.E.B. Du Bois," it was Washington who used it to most advantage.

By 1912 the NNBL had grown to nearly 3,000 members, but as E. Franklin Frazier noted in his cynical appraisal of what he called "the myth of Negro business," most of those on the rolls were not really businessmen, but a combination of professionals and clergy, as well as some entrepreneurs and bankers. Nevertheless the organization served Washington's purposes well. Through a national network of local chapters, he had created "an organized body of loyal, conservative followers in every city with a substantial black population, North or South." With an emphasis on self-help, thrift and hard work, members were encouraged not to grouse about the very real "racial discriminations" they faced, but to turn them into assets. "These discriminations are only blessings in disguise," one delegate said sanguinely at an early NNBL gathering. "They stimulate and encourage rather than cower and humiliate the true, ambitious, self-determined Negro."

The organization advocated a "buy black" policy—something Du Bois had also fostered—as a way to develop a kind of capitalism based on racial solidarity in which African American consumers would purchase most of their goods and services from other African Americans. To some degree this seemed a logical response, as the refusal of many white banks, funeral homes and insurance companies to do business with blacks had forced the growth of small but prosperous parallel, and segregated, enterprises in the increasingly urbanized black communities of the North and South.

At the same time Washington counseled that whites would patronize black entrepreneurs in the open marketplace regardless of race, if only they offered sufficiently valuable products. As early as his 1895 Atlanta Cotton States

Exposition speech he had said, "No race that has anything to contribute to the markets of the world is long in any degree ostracized." And in some instances this was true for those whites who did do business with blacks. Of course, in an era when large banks refused to extend credit to blacks and, on a smaller scale, when whites had all but abandoned the black barbers whose shops they had previously frequented, this approach may have been overly optimistic. But these annual events were so full of applause, praise and celebration that analysis of the obstacles was usually glossed over and not particularly welcomed by Washington.

Like the other delegates, Madam Walker had come to Chicago in late August to hear the motivational stories and to interact with Washington. But in contrast to the NACW convention—where civil rights issues had been freely discussed—the NNBL was strictly concerned with commerce. Even during an election year, noted the Chicago *Broad Ax*, a frequent critic of Washington's, he had chosen to ignore politics and the contest among President William Howard Taft, former President Theodore Roosevelt and Democratic challenger Woodrow Wilson.

Nearly 2,000 visitors and delegates packed the auditorium of South Side Chicago's Institutional Church for the opening session as temperatures rose to a warm but not oppressive low eighties. In addition to NNBL members, several other black organizations were represented, among them the National Bankers Association, the National Association of Funeral Directors and the National Bar Association, as well as National Negro Press Association reporters and publishers from more than fifty black newspapers. Traveling in her convertible Model T touring car, Madam Walker was probably one of the few delegates to arrive in a chauffeur-driven automobile. For such public occasions, she tended toward formal attire—worsted wool suits and dresses, corsets, long sleeves, plumed hats and buttoned shoes, even in summer.

A steady succession of inspirational narratives began immediately after the opening exercises. Among them, that of thirty-year-old Watt Terry, a Washington favorite, whose keen eye for real estate had transformed him from a $7-a-week shoe factory worker into a Realtor, whose $500,000 holdings in Brockton, Massachusetts, provided him with a monthly income in excess of $6,000.

But it was NNBL founder Booker T. Washington's annual address that evening that the delegates greeted with prolonged, enthusiastic ovations. Despite the increasing criticisms of his moderate approach to civil rights—especially from elite, educated African Americans—Washington was revered among the NNBL delegates. And while Madam Walker was frustrated with his lukewarm attitude toward her and her work, she respected both his power and his near-mythological metamorphosis from slave to race leader to presidential adviser. Having now seen the more than eighty buildings on his Tuskegee campus, she marveled at his ability to create an endowment fund of more than $1.2 million. In 1901, when Madam Walker was still a St. Louis washerwoman, Washington was dining with President Roosevelt at the White House. By the summer of 1906, in the early months of her business, Washington's Tuskegee Institute was celebrating its twenty-fifth anniversary.

Madam Walker admired him, but she did not fear him and she did not agree with everything he said. Yet she fully embraced his self-help, up-from-slavery philosophy and his faith in entrepreneurship as an underpinning of African American progress. "If we do not do our duty now in laying [the] proper foundation for economic and commercial growth, our children and our children's children will suffer because of our inactivity or shortness of vision," he said that first evening as handkerchiefs were waved in approval throughout the audience. "This is in an especial sense true of the Negro business man and woman."

Madam Walker certainly believed she was doing her part. And she believed Washington knew that too. Yet he continued to snub her. By the time his speech ended, she knew that at least three manufacturers of hair care products were scheduled as speakers before the close of the convention. That evening Mrs. Julia H. P. Coleman, a licensed pharmacist from Washington, D.C., discussed the success of "Hair Vim," a product that sounded quite similar to Madam Walker's Wonderful Hair Grower. "Every year the styles for hair dressing demand more and more hair," Coleman said, drawing laughter as she described the cause for the increasing popularity of her product. "By force of circumstance, birth, or misfortune, we represent a race whose head adornment does not . . . come up to the standard of beauty," she continued, with no apparent disagreement from the audience. "Where the standard calls for straight lines, those of the Negro's hair are rather crooked . . . Where it requires fluffiness, ours has stubborn-ness. To overcome these conditions, as well as to conform with, and keep up with the latest styles of hair dressing, it is very necessary to use the things that will assist nature." Her product, as well as others "manufactured by our colored women," she declared, are "some of the best hair preparations now on the market." The only gesture that could have pleased Madam Walker more than Coleman's indirect acknowledgment would have been an invitation from Washington to come to the podium. Instead Washington complimented Coleman as "the first woman of our race to open a drug store in the United States," then called upon the next speaker.

On Thursday morning Washington introduced Anthony Overton, whose Overton Hygienic Manufacturing Company, Washington noted, was "the largest Colored manufacturing enterprise in the United States." With more than twenty full-time workers, five traveling salesmen and 400 commission agents, he had sold $117,000 worth of goods in the last year. Having founded his company in 1898 with "less than $2,000," he now carried his original Hygienic Pet Baking Powder as well as more than fifty other items. Overton attributed his success to a unique promotional campaign targeting black consumers. "When we added our line of toilet articles, we placed colored girls' pictures on our Talcum Powder, Hair Pomades, and other toilet articles," he said of a marketing move guaranteed to evoke praise from his fellow NNBL members. His "High-Brown" face powder, one of the first mass-produced facial cosmetics for black women, had become his company's most well-known product. Each box contained a circular space that was reserved, he said humorously, "for the most beautiful colored woman in the United States, which we propose to put on the box later as soon as we find her."

With everyone in good spirits after Overton's uplifting presentation, Washington—as was his custom during the conference proceedings—requested comments from the audience. *Freeman* publisher George Knox, a longtime NNBL member and friend to both Madam Walker and Washington, stood to be recognized. "I arise to ask this convention for a few minutes of its time to hear a remarkable woman. It is enough said when I say she hails from Indianapolis, Indiana," he began, eliciting chuckling from those who annually heard him boost his fellow Hoosiers. "She is the woman who gave $1,000 to the Young Men's Christian Association of Indianapolis. Madam Walker, the lady I refer to, is the manufacturer of hair goods and preparations." Once Knox mentioned Madam Walker's contribution to the YMCA, Washington could have been expected to be more receptive. Having spoken in 1909 in Indianapolis on behalf of the YMCA—and having raised only $100 at the time—he was well aware of the significance of her gift. He also had more than passing interest in the movement to build colored Y's because his architect son-in-law, Sidney Pittman, had designed the Washington, D.C., branch. Instead Washington's reply was noticeably icy, especially when delivered to such a loyal associate as the *Freeman* publisher. "But, Mr. Knox, we are taking up the question of life membership," he said in a matter-of-fact manner. And then—in what would have been an anxious moment for most people—Washington, without appearing in the least bit ruffled, called upon an Oklahoma man, whose question was not about life membership but about Overton's business.

Knox and Madam Walker must have been stunned. Knox certainly knew Washington well enough not to have requested something inappropriate. And both he and Madam Walker knew that Washington could have altered the program had he wished. Instead he brought to the podium H. L.

Sanders, the Indianapolis uniform manufacturer, whose factory was a few blocks from Madam Walker's. Comparing oneself to others, especially in matters of charity, was a risky proposition. But Madam Walker must have noted that Sanders, the treasurer of the Indiana Avenue YMCA, had contributed only $250 to the building fund. And then, in an action that was even more insulting, Washington—who had seen Madam Walker's home and factory—went out of his way to praise Sanders's plant as "a creditable manufacturing enterprise" and "a pleasure" to visit. Madam Walker managed to maintain her composure, but she was fully aware of the differences in their businesses. Whereas Sanders employed twenty-two men and women, she knew her products provided jobs and commission opportunities for almost a thousand sales agents. Whereas Sanders's apparel items were distributed primarily in Ohio, Illinois, Indiana and Michigan, her Wonderful Hair Grower was marketed from California to New York, from Illinois to Texas. Why, then, had Washington used a neighbor to put her in her place?

By Friday, the final day of the convention, Madam Walker had lost all patience. Because Washington clearly was not going to *grant* her an opportunity to speak, she realized it had become necessary for her to *seize* the opportunity. After the morning's first speaker—a Little Rock building contractor who described his current projects—the presentations that followed were a blur of reports from members of the National Bankers Association. Then, as Washington thanked Reverend E. M. Griggs, president of the Farmers and Citizens Savings Bank of Palestine, Texas, for his "splendid address," Madam Walker could wait no longer. Rising from her seat, she fixed her eyes upon Washington. "Surely you are not going to shut the door in my face," she demanded, as heads began to turn in her direction. "I feel that I am in a business that is a credit to the womanhood of our race," she said defiantly, knowing of Washington's ambivalence about her products. "I went into a business that is despised, that is criticized and talked about by everybody—the business of growing hair. They did not believe such a thing could be done, but I have proven beyond the question of a doubt that I do grow hair!" she said to laughter and applause.

"I have been trying to get before you business people and tell you what I am doing," she continued, unable to hide her frustration and resentment. "I am a woman that came from the cotton fields of the South. I was promoted from there to the wash-tub," she announced proudly, causing nervous snickering among the delegates. "Then I was promoted to the cook kitchen, and from there I promoted myself into the business of manufacturing hair goods and preparations."

"I am not ashamed of my past," she added forcefully. "I am not ashamed of my humble beginning. Don't think because you have to go down in the wash-tub that you are any less a lady!" Fully wound up, and bolstered by the crowd's reaction, she had no intention of taking her seat. "Everybody told me I was making a mistake by going into this business, but I know how to grow hair as well as I know how to grow cotton."

After chronicling her annual earnings and real estate holdings, she proclaimed, "I have built my own factory on my own ground, 38 by 208 feet. I employ in that factory seven people, including a bookkeeper, a stenographer, a cook and a house girl." As the clapping mounted, she allowed herself to boast, "I own my own automobile and runabout." And then, as if sensing that she had little time left to convey the most important part of her statement, she commanded, "Please don't applaud—just let me talk!

"Now my object in life is not simply to make money for myself or to spend it on myself in dressing or running around in an automobile," she announced. "But I love to use a part of what I make in trying to help others.

"Perhaps many of you have heard of the real ambition of my life, the all-absorbing idea which I hope to accomplish," she said passionately. "My ambition is to build an industrial school in Africa. By the help of God and the cooperation of my people in this country, I am going to build a Tuskegee Institute in Africa!"

Although Madam Walker had clearly captured the crowd's attention, Washington still showed no sign that he was moved. Quickly, George Knox stood to endorse her remarks. "I arise to attest all that this good woman has said concerning her business in the progressive city of Indianapolis. You have heard only a part; the half has not been told of what she has accomplished," he said.

Although the NNBL's meticulously recorded transcripts reflected most details of that day's proceedings, they did not reveal Booker T. Washington's personal, unspoken reaction to Madam Walker's speech. Without missing a beat, or acknowledging her presence, Washington moved on. "The next banker to address us is Mr. W. W. Hadnott, of the Prudential Savings Bank of Birmingham, Alabama," Washington said, as if Madam Walker had not uttered a word.

A few weeks later the *Freeman* called her presentation one of the "big hits" of the conference and praised her "striking personality." She "at once impresses an audience with the fact that she stands for concrete achievements rather than brilliance of oratory," the paper reported.

It would take Booker T. Washington a while longer to come around. But a year later, he would willingly find a place for Madam Walker on the program of the NNBL's fourteenth annual meeting in Philadelphia.

CHAPTER 12

Breaking Ties, Making Ties

—⁓—

L ess than two weeks after Madam Walker returned home from Chicago,
F. B. Ransom filed papers for her divorce from C. J. Walker. As one of
Indiana's few black attorneys, Ransom—nattily dressed in his three-
piece suits—was easily noticed in the halls of the courthouse. Working for
the city's most prominent black entrepreneur had only enhanced his reputation. Now in *Sarah Walker v. Charles J. Walker*, Ransom discreetly set
about to terminate a union for which no marriage license existed. The possibility that a financially strapped C.J. might claim rights under a common-
law marriage—or as a member of the Madam C. J. Walker Manufacturing
Company board of directors—surely occurred to the meticulous young
attorney. A clean, legally recognized severance was the most prudent strategy for a client with the resources Ransom now realized Madam Walker
was capable of generating.

With an undisputed case of adultery involving Dora Larrie—as well as
Louise's letter as further evidence—Ransom had no difficulty extricating
Madam Walker from a potentially costly and embarrassing situation. On
October 5, after C.J. had failed to appear in the judge's chambers, the
divorce was made final. According to the docket, "no money" was paid to
either party.

Banished from 640 North West Street, C.J. retreated to Louisville to the
home of his sister, Peggie, and her husband, Calvin Prosser. Desperate for
money—and cocky enough to believe that he could compete with Madam
Walker on her own turf—C.J. placed two advertisements for his "Walker-
Prosser Wonderful Hair Grower" in the September 14, 1912, *Freeman*. The
larger of the ads was nearly identical to Madam Walker's three-panel
before-and-after layout, one that C.J. may have helped design.

By year's end, Larrie, herself not yet divorced, had joined C.J. in business. "We did not do so well under the name of The Walker-Larrie Company," C.J. later wrote, "so she planned to get a divorce that we might

marry." But soon after their March 1913 marriage, C.J. realized that he had been duped. "We were not married long before I discovered she did not love me, but that she only wanted the title Mme., and the formula," he lamented, calling his life "hell" since Larrie had had him arrested for "interfering with her business." The woman who had promised to make him "master of the situation" had instead "tied up what little mail there was coming in, so I could not get a cent," C.J. later complained in a letter to the editor of the *Freeman*. "All I got was ten cents on Sunday for a paper and shoe shine."

Madam Walker would publicly maintain that her third marriage had failed because of "business disagreements," and perhaps in the larger sense that was true. C.J. himself conceded that they "could not agree along business lines."

"When we began to make ten dollars a day, he thought that amount was enough and that I should be satisfied," Madam Walker later told a reporter. "But I was convinced that my hair preparations would fill a long-felt want, and when we found it impossible to agree, due to his narrowness of vision, I embarked in business for myself."

But of course their philosophical differences were only part of the problem. By his own admission, C.J. had "let drink and this designing evil woman come between" him and Madam Walker. In a public apology in a March 1914 issue of the *Freeman*, he denounced Larrie as "the cause of all my sorrow." In truth, C.J. himself had been responsible for his predicament. Now no amount of flattery could budge Madam Walker, the woman he unconvincingly claimed to "still love better than life." A few months later, when C.J. wrote begging for money and work, Ransom sent him $35 and some advice. "Madam does not understand why you do not go to Key West, Cuba, and other places which afford splendid fields, and in which she has few if any agents," he wrote. Ever the teetotaler, Ransom also suggested that C.J. "keep sober and build up a big business."

Not long afterward, Peggie Prosser warned Madam Walker not to send an additional $100 that C.J. had requested. His plan, Peggie wrote, was to use the money to start yet another company, this time with a Mrs. Barksdale, a woman she called "worse than" Dora Larrie. Perennially down on his luck, C.J. continued to appeal to his former wife, his pestering approaches ranging from breezy and conciliatory to pathetic. "Say Mme, How would you like to give me employment as one of your traveling agents?" he blithely queried a couple of years after their divorce. "I am sure I could be of much service to you . . . There is no one that knows the work better than I." Understandably, she remained unmoved.

At times C.J.'s entreaties were pitifully melodramatic. "My heart is changed," he vowed, doubtless when his wallet was empty. "I am tired of

Louisville and am writing these lines with tears dripping from my eyes." In another letter he whined about his rheumatism and accused her of ignoring his pleas. But Madam Walker had long since lost any sympathy for the man Ransom had accused of selling her formula to others and of teaching it to "some three or four women." As Madam Walker's buffer, Ransom warned C.J. against any "unwarranted" legal actions he might try to mount. Madam Walker, he threatened, "would spend every penny that she ever had in court before she would agree to give you one penny." For the rest of his life C. J. Walker would try, but fail, to maneuver his way back into the company that was to make his name a household word.

Neither Madam Walker nor Lelia could claim much luck when it came to matters of the heart. By the fall of 1912 John Robinson had been gone for more than two years, though Lelia had not yet filed for divorce. Without any existing correspondence between mother and daughter during the early 1910s, there is no reliable way to discern their thoughts and feelings on the subject of men and marriage. But one thing is clear: they discussed the absence of a family heir.

With no prospective groom in place, twenty-seven-year-old Lelia legally adopted thirteen-year-old Fairy Mae Bryant less than three weeks after her mother's divorce had been granted. Exactly how and when Lelia and Fairy Mae met remains unknown, though Lelia likely saw her while in Indianapolis for the Knights of Pythias convention in August 1911 as well as during the Christmas holidays later that year. Family oral history suggests that Madam Walker first encountered Fairy Mae as she ran errands for Walker hair parlor employees and customers. One of the better-educated neighborhood children, she easily would have qualified for the "secure position" as a "young girl solicitor" for which Madam Walker advertised in the *Recorder*. Certainly Fairy Mae's widowed mother, Sarah Etta Hammond Bryant, would have welcomed the "good commission" Madam Walker promised the youthful employees who distributed fliers and delivered Walker products. But it was Fairy Mae's braids—long, thick ropes that reached below her waist—that had caused Madam Walker to notice her. What more perfect walking advertisement for her bestselling hair grower than a young girl with hair so healthy and abundant that it captivated strangers? What more dramatic illustration of her hair care system than the transformation of Fairy Mae's bushy, cascading mane into soft, pliable plaits, something that Madam Walker could achieve with just a light touch of the heated metal comb she now marketed with her products?

Fairy Mae was petite, barely five feet tall, and well mannered. Approaching graduation from the eighth grade, at a time when most Americans had considerably less formal education, she was a bright and curious student.

But her family could not afford to send her to high school. With Madam Walker's interest, however, it seemed that her hair—an inky version of Rapunzel's locks—would provide a path from poverty.

"Mae had beautiful hair, and that's the thing that they wanted. Someone with nice hair," an envious in-law remembered decades later. But Fairy Mae was not the delicately featured, light-skinned beauty favored by many members of the black elite. As a symbol of the Madam Walker Company, however, her smooth cocoa complexion was an asset, an acknowledgment that Walker products were designed for brown and black women, rather than the near-white models often featured in newspaper ads. Fairy Mae's prominent nose, especially when viewed in profile, provided a physical reminder of the strong Native American genes that mingled with those of her African and European ancestors. Her penetrating almond eyes switched from warm to melancholy to intense. And when she smiled, the small gap between her upper front teeth appeared. Still, it was always her heavy, crinkly hair that made people stare, sometimes with admiration and sometimes with envy.

Mae had grown up in Noblesville, Indiana, with her seven siblings. In the summers and on holidays she often visited her grandmother, Samira Thomas Hammond, a washerwoman, who in 1911 had moved into rented rooms at the rear of 636 North West Street, two doors south of Madam Walker's factory. Samira—born in 1838 in Orange County, Indiana, and old enough to have been Madam Walker's mother—was the matriarch of a large extended family whose members regularly traveled the twenty miles via Interurban train between Noblesville and the Indiana Avenue neighborhood. Her daughter—and Fairy Mae's mother—Sarah Etta Hammond Bryant, was also a laundress who, like Madam Walker, had been born in 1867. Another of Samira's daughters, Della Hammond Ashley, and Della's husband, James Ashley, owned a small, popular Indiana Avenue cafe. "Aunt Del," who had no children of her own, doted on Fairy Mae and other visiting nieces and nephews.

Madam Walker had come to know Samira and Del as neighbors. And it is possible that she had met Sarah Etta, a Court of Calanthe sister, as early as March 1910, when she happened to have been in Noblesville during a revival at Sarah Etta's church. Because Bethel AME was the center of much black social activity in the town, Madam Walker could not have missed the handsome Bryant clan, a rainbow of complexions ranging from cream to chocolate, all three daughters with flowing, hip-length hair. That spring the other parishioners would have focused more attention than usual on Sarah Etta, who was still mourning the loss of her husband, Perry Bryant.

* * *

While Samira Hammond was by no means part of Indianapolis's colored elite, some of her ancestors had been among Indiana's earliest settlers of color. At the turn of the twentieth century, they were respected enough that their family illnesses and church activities warranted the occasional mention in the "Noblesville" column of the *Indianapolis Recorder*. "Little Miss Farrie [*sic*]Bryant, who has been visiting her grandmother and aunt in Indianapolis," the paper noted in August 1909, "returned home last Sunday evening." Although Samira's financial circumstances dictated a modest existence, she cherished her unusual family history. Unbeknown to most of her neighbors along North West Street, her great-grandfather, Ishmael Roberts, had been among a small group of freemen who had served in the Continental Army during the Revolutionary War. At the time of the first United States Census in 1790, Ishmael—who was born circa 1755 in Northampton County, North Carolina—and his Cherokee wife, Silvey, were among North Carolina's 5,041 free people of color. Between 1787 and 1826, he had purchased and sold more than 900 acres of land in Robeson and Chatham counties.

Descendants of the Roberts and Hammond families proudly claimed that their ancestors had never been slaves. But during the first three decades of the nineteenth century they had begun to lose some of their privileges because North Carolina plantation owners—fearful of slave revolts and abolitionists—had tightened laws affecting both slaves and freemen. With each successive term, "the Legislature stripped the free Negro of his personal liberties," so that by 1835 the state's lawmakers had clamped down on their migration into and out of the state, outlawed their freedom to preach, and rescinded their right to vote regardless of how much property they owned. In response, organized groups of free blacks fled the state, including dozens of Robertses, who had begun migrating to Indiana in the 1820s. By 1840, more than 150 people with the surname Roberts were living in nine southern and central Indiana counties.

The Hoosier State, however, was only relatively more welcoming than North Carolina had been, having passed a law in 1831 requiring all newly arrived Negro families to register with county authorities. In 1833, after settling in Orange County, Indiana, Ishmael and Silvey's son, Elias Roberts, and his wife, Nancy Archer Roberts, presented a certificate of freedom proving that "although persons of Couleur, [they] are free and entitled to all the rights and privileges of white persons."

Twenty years later, in August 1853, their daughter, Candiss, and her husband, Jordon Thomas, were compelled by Indiana law to enroll themselves and their children in the Orange County Register of Negroes and Mulattoes. Because the state legislature had adopted a provision in 1852 stating that "no negro or mulatto shall come into, or settle in the State" unless already a resident, those who wished to stay were required to register. One of those children was Samira, who was described on the ledger as a "mulatto 4 ft 11 1/2 in high." Six years later, when she turned twenty-one, she married Littleton Hammond, a Vigo County, Indiana, widower with a small son and another North Carolina transplant. Hammond's father, Elijah, was considered a "full blood Cherokee Indian." Sadly Littleton died in 1876, leaving Samira with eight children between infancy and fifteen years old, just as her mother, Candiss Roberts Thomas, had been widowed with eight minors.

In 1889, Samira's daughter Sarah Etta Hammond married Perry Bryant, one of the founders of Noblesville's colored Masonic lodge and an active member of the local Knights of Pythias chapter. By the time the couple's last child was born in 1907, they had settled in the town's Federal Hill area west of the White River. Perry, who worked as a fireman in one of the local factories, and Sarah Etta created a stable family whose close ties with Bethel AME Church made them well-regarded members of the town's African American community.

In late June 1909, however, the family's equilibrium was shattered when Perry Bryant died of cerebral meningitis and heart disease. The Grand Master of the Masons presided over as elaborate a funeral as any black man in Noblesville might receive. But despite the charitable hearts and hands of his fraternal brethren, as well as those of Sarah Etta's Eastern Star, Court of Calanthe and Bethel Needle Club sisters, Perry's personal assets and benevolent society benefits could not begin to support seven minor children, including an eighteen-month-old toddler, eight-year-old twin boys and Fairy Mae, the youngest of three daughters.

Having lost her own father when she was only nine years old, Sarah Etta Bryant had no illusions about the difficulties she faced. Just as her mother and grandmother had been widowed in their thirties, she now confronted the intimidating task of rearing a large brood on her own. So when Madam Walker first asked if Fairy Mae might serve as a model for Walker products, Sarah Etta welcomed the opportunity for her child. It may have been during Fairy Mae's trip to Harlem with Madam Walker and Lelia in early 1912 that the Walkers began to consider formally adopting her. The impressionable thirteen-year-old Fairy Mae, who had never been on a vacation, was mesmerized by a lavish Cinderella world of more food, clothes, privileges and indulgences than she had ever dreamed existed. The New York journey "turned her head," said a relative, so that when the Walker women offered to adopt her, Fairy Mae needed no convincing and "wanted to go."

Sarah Etta, on the other hand, was not so quickly or so easily persuaded. It was one thing to allow her child to travel and be exposed to a world she could only imagine. It was something else entirely to relinquish one's child to another woman. Yet the Walker women offered not only to continue Mae's education and to train her to run their business but to allow her to maintain contact with her family. Still, Sarah Etta remained torn. The unfathomable decision to surrender her child must have been made palatable only by degrees when she considered her own childhood and the fact that she, like Fairy Mae, had grown up as a fatherless child in the middle of a large group of siblings. "Mae was very special to the Bryant family, and her going to the Walkers was God-sent and deeply appreciated," said genealogist Coy D. Robbins, Jr., whose mother had known Mae as a child. "Etta did not see it as giving up, but rather as having a way economically and socially for Mae to acquire material things and life experiences that she, as a widow, could not provide."

Fairy Mae understandably was seduced by the opulence of Madam Walker's Indianapolis home with its twelve lavishly furnished rooms. For a child accustomed to living with several siblings in less than half the space, the calm and quiet of the rose-and-gold drawing room—with its brilliantly patterned Oriental rugs, gold-leaf curio cabinet and Tiffany chandelier— was like paradise. In the library, Fairy Mae could hold soft leather-bound books, run her fingers across the gleaming keys of the Chickering baby grand piano and admire the lovely oil paintings of young William Edouard Scott, the local colored artist who had studied in Paris. On a table covered with Battenberg lace, she watched Madam Walker's guests being served dinner on Havilland china with monogrammed silverware and sparkling crystal goblets. In Pittsburgh, at Lelia's home on Mignonette, the surroundings were much the same.

In late October 1912 a Pittsburgh judge approved Lelia's petition to adopt Fairy Mae Bryant with the consent of her mother, Sarah Etta Hammond Bryant, and with the understanding that her "welfare" would "be promoted by such adoption." Significantly, the decree granted Fairy Mae "all the rights of a child and heir of the said Mrs. Lelia Walker Robinson." It also legally changed her name from Fairy Mae Bryant to Mae Walker Robinson, though John Robinson would never have any significant involvement in her life. In fact, Lelia was not at all focused on Robinson, whom she would finally divorce nearly two years later.

Fascinated by business opportunities in New York and California, Lelia had persuaded her mother to buy property on both coasts. By early December she and Mae were house hunting in Los Angeles, hoping to find a base for her cousin Anjetta Breedlove to establish a West Coast Walker operation. As Lelia prepared to make the down payments on houses there and in Harlem, Ransom assured her that her mother was "very much impressed with the proposition." For his part, he praised her discerning eye and told her that she "would make an ideal real estate agent."

As the year ended, Madam Walker was unusually pleased with her daughter and with herself. While visiting friends in St. Louis for Christmas, she was ecstatic to learn of the *Freeman*'s eye-catching, full-page, holiday season layout declaring her "America's Foremost Colored Business Woman," and praising her wealth, her entrepreneurial acumen and her philanthropy. "The write-up in the *Freeman*," Ransom wrote to her on New Year's Day, "created quite an impression here." Madam Walker was delighted with the positive publicity, a fitting segue to another prosperous year.

CHAPTER 13

Sweet Satisfaction

Each morning's mail brought sacks of handwritten orders for Wonderful Hair Grower to Madam Walker's Indianapolis office. Crumpled dollar bills and crisp money orders accompanied appreciative testimonials and crudely scrawled requests for supplies of Glossine, Vegetable Shampoo, Temple Salve and Tetter Salve. In the Walker factory, neighborhood women hand-ladled the curative ointments into round tin containers, then boxed them for the shipping clerk's daily trip to Union Station and the post office.

In Florida, Georgia and Alabama during the spring of 1913, Madam Walker taught her beauty culture system to several dozen more agents, presenting them with diplomas and wiring their product orders to her secretaries in the North West Street office. In hamlets too small for a train depot, Madam Walker and her traveling assistants tossed packets of promotional booklets and fliers from passenger cars as locomotives crawled by to retrieve rural route mail pouches.

"Your business is increasing here every day," F. B. Ransom wrote from Indianapolis in one of their almost daily missives while she was on the road. Having tallied her receipts for April 1913—the third consecutive month exceeding $3,000—he marveled, "I think you are the money-making wonder of the age." Just four months into the year, she had already taken in more than $11,000, almost as much as her entire 1912 earnings and the equivalent of nearly $200,000 in today's dollars. "You will . . . have to keep a little mum on your annual income," Ransom cautioned, advising her of the soon-to-be-ratified Sixteenth Amendment, which would, for the first time, impose federal tax on all personal earnings greater than $3,000. With the average American breadwinner's annual wages amounting to less than $800, Madam Walker would soon become not only one of the few citizens subject to the levy but one of the even smaller number bound for the highest tax bracket.

"Madam is in a fair way to be the wealthiest colored person in America. I am ambitious that she be just that," Ransom revealed to Lelia. Subtly suggesting that Lelia curb some of her own extravagances he queried, "You will help me, won't you?"

Ransom quickly had learned that both mother and daughter loved to spend. And who could blame them after they had scrimped and sacrificed for so long? But while Madam Walker relied upon Ransom to manage such details as taxes and bank balances, she had not ignored the need to diversify her investments. "I am preparing myself so that when this hair business falls to the ground I will have an income and I won't have to come down," she said several months later as she noted the lengthening lineup of newly established hair preparations competitors. As a result, she had begun to buy real estate in several cities, including five lots in Indianapolis and twenty in Gary, Indiana, as well as the New York and Los Angeles properties that Lelia had discovered.

At the same time Madam Walker clearly relished the more ostentatious trappings that her good fortune afforded. In May, after her trip through the South, she treated herself to a sleek, seven-passenger Cole touring car, a limited-edition model comparable to the Cadillac. "Oh, it's the latest thing in autos," Ransom wrote Lelia. "So you see, you are quite an heiress."

Certainly Madam Walker did not discourage Lelia from indulging her own extravagant tastes in jewelry and clothes. And now that Lelia was renovating their Harlem town house and beauty salon, Madam Walker had no quarrel with her daughter's choice of the finest art and home furnishings their money would allow. Whether she articulated it or not, Madam Walker may have been attempting to compensate for the hungry, unstable John Davis years in St. Louis. But just as important, she was happy to reward her daughter's business instincts and her eagerness to assume responsibility for their East Coast operation. After pronouncing Lelia's tasteful New York office letterhead "perfectly beautiful," Ransom predicted "that daughter and mother are going to make a still more powerful business firm."

Ransom, however, made no secret that he thought the New York operation too costly. In fact, he rarely missed an opportunity to remind Lelia to limit her large expenditures. "I want you to join me in urging Madam . . . to bank a large portion of her money to the end that it be accumulating and drawing interest for possible rainy days," he counseled, referring as much to Lelia as to her mother.

As their business manager and attorney, Ransom was wise to monitor their freewheeling spending habits, but their decision to purchase the 136th Street property in New York—one of the first homes owned by an African American west of Lenox Avenue—was a sound one. With Harlem just on the cusp of becoming the vibrant nexus of black American political, intellectual and cultural activity, the Walker women's early foothold had poised them to assume an integral role in the development of this stimulating uptown Manhattan district.

As much as Indianapolis had continued to provide a solid base for the day-to-day functioning of Madam Walker's business, it was New York's electrified energy and heart-quickening vitality that she believed would catapult her work to the next level. She was comfortable in the Hoosier capital, but found herself beginning to outgrow it. Having tasted the power of the national recognition her YMCA gift had brought, Madam Walker fully understood how to use the larger platform for other purposes. The more her focus shifted to political causes and interests beyond her company—and the more her money became a means to an end—the more she wished for a presence in a city where she could amplify her voice.

As much public praise as Madam Walker had received, it rankled her that she still had not penetrated Booker T. Washington's inner circle. Despite his snubs, she had continued her campaign to enlist his support of her work. With her tenacity as persistent as his resistance, she took it upon herself to invite him to be her houseguest during his visit to Indianapolis for the July 1913 dedication of the new YMCA. When he accepted the offer, she was thrilled.

Anxious that he be shown "every courtesy," Madam Walker made her Cole and chauffeur available to the Tuskegee leader from the time of his 1:45 A.M. arrival at Union Station to his departure two days later. By late morning, "an army of newspaper people" from the white dailies and the three black weeklies had knocked on the door at 640 North West Street to call upon Washington. Among the reporters was the *Freeman*'s William Lewis, who interviewed Washington just before the ceremony "in the best of those splendid rooms of the Madam's mansion," a setting he judged unsurpassed for "elegance, comfort, convenience." As they completed their conversation, *Indianapolis World* publisher A. E. Manning—his competitor and a YMCA board member—rushed into the parlor. "Doctor, your time's up!" he announced to Washington as he whisked him off to the event.

At Senate Avenue and Michigan Street, more than 500 people crowded around the façade of the sturdy four-story brick Senate Avenue YMCA as Washington, Madam Walker and Manning made their way from her car to the sparkling glass entryway. Inside the building at least 1,200 black and white Indianapolis residents were crammed shoulder to shoulder, filling every available corner in the spacious gymnasium and the lobby as a midsummer thunderstorm scattered the group outdoors. Late into the evening, just before ten o'clock, former Vice President Charles Fairbanks introduced Washington. "This building should make our young men more industrious, more ambitious and more economical," Washington assured the audience. "Let this building result in putting a new spirit, a new ambition, into every young man of our race in Indianapolis."

He chose not to mention the disappointing news that more than half of the $20,600 pledged by the city's black community had not yet been collected. Less than $4,000 of the $59,000 pledged by whites remained outstanding. More a reflection of the limited resources of the community than any willful withholding, such a sobering and dissonant note might have soured the festivities. Instead, the man who frequently had slighted Madam Walker singled her out among the large donors as she beamed from her honored seat on the dais.

If she felt any residual resentment toward Washington, she refrained from revealing it. Instead, two weeks later, she assured him that it had been "a real pleasure . . . to be able to do my part toward making your stay here a pleasant one." Intent upon achieving her own goals, Madam Walker lathered on the compliments to a man whose ego required flattery. Of his house gift—a book he had authored—she wrote, "I shall read it with pleasure and cherish it as a token from one who is always proud of the success of another."

A few weeks later Madam Walker and Alice Kelly—the former Eckstein-Norton teacher who had recently joined her firm—were driven from Indianapolis to New York by Madam's chauffeur, Homer West. In Harlem, Lelia joined them for the road trip to Philadelphia for the fourteenth annual National Negro Business League convention. Arriving in her Cole, Madam Walker, Lelia and Miss Kelly must have caused a stir among the admiring male delegates, who marveled at the automobile's 40-horsepower 6-cylinder engine.

To Madam Walker's delight—and in contrast to her chilly reception the previous July—she was saluted by Washington as "a striking example of the possibilities of Negro womanhood in the business world." Known for calculating the impact of any gesture he made on his image and his school's bottom line, Washington apparently had discovered sufficient mutual benefit to embrace Madam Walker, just as she had measured the merits of his public approval. If nothing else, Washington must have begun to realize her moneymaking potential, as well as the symbolic and inspirational value of having a former washerwoman turned philanthropist support his school. She, in turn, fully understood the advantages of having a connection with the man who controlled the editorial policies and purse strings of dozens of black newspapers.

Because Washington had reserved a place for her on the program,

Madam Walker had the luxury of approaching the proceedings with more serenity than she had brought to the 1912 convention. Pleased to have Lelia by her side during the three-day conference, she proudly introduced her stylish daughter—the proprietor of her New York and Pittsburgh offices—to Washington and the other delegates.

Madam Walker also may have taken particular pleasure in seeing her old friends C. K. Robinson and Jessie Robinson. But, given the rivalry that still simmered between her and Annie Pope-Turnbo, she likely was less than thrilled to hear C.K. laud Pope-Turnbo, his fellow St. Louisan, as a "progressive business woman, who has built up . . . a large and magnificently appointed establishment devoted exclusively to hair culture." Confident, however, that she would take the stage within less than an hour, Madam Walker easily endured the fleeting focus on Pope-Turnbo, as well as the interminable local league reports that had frustrated her the previous year. Instead of having to muscle her way to the podium after a string of addresses on shoe polish manufacturing, catering and the florist business, she was ushered forward. "I now take pleasure in introducing to the convention one of the most progressive and successful business women of our race—Madam C. J. Walker, of Indianapolis, Indiana," Washington said generously.

As she moved toward the lectern, Madam Walker had every reason to be composed and in command. "Mr. President and members of the National Negro Business League," she began, "at Chicago last year, I said that my income per month was $1,500, and promised to double that amount by the time of this meeting." Each month since February, she told them, she had done just that. Now with a full week still remaining in August, she had already topped the $3,500 mark, for an income of more than $32,000, the equivalent of more than a half million dollars in today's money. "You can readily see that I have been able to make good my promise to you last year," she said to prolonged applause.

But heartened as she was by Washington's warm welcome, she did not shy away from noting his previous lack of receptivity. "Now in the so-called higher walks of life, many were prone to look down upon 'hair dressers' as they called us," she said frankly. "They didn't have a very high opinion of our calling, so I had to go down and dignify this work, so much so that many of the best women of our race are now engaged in this line of business, and many of them are now in my employ."

Among them was her traveling companion Alice Kelly, a Mobile, Alabama, native, who, along with Reverend Charles H. Parrish, had provided Madam Walker's first entree to Booker T. Washington. After Eckstein-Norton merged with another Kentucky school in 1912, Madam Walker persuaded Kelly to join the Walker Company as factory forelady. Proficient in Greek, Latin and French, Kelly had also become Madam

Walker's private tutor, supplementing her meager formal education by helping to polish her speech, grammar, penmanship and etiquette. Such efforts at self-improvement, as well as "honesty of purpose, determined effort, the real merit of my preparations and the fact that I am not and never have been 'close-fisted,'" Madam Walker advised the delegates, were the secrets to her success.

As the applause subsided, Washington moved to her side. "We thank her for her excellent address and for all she has done for our race," he said, provoking knowing laughter from those who believed her products had brought improvements to the grooming habits of her customers. "You talk about what the men are doing in a business way; why if we don't watch out, the women will excel us," he warned good-naturedly.

Under the refrain of "Blest be the tie that binds," Madam Walker could savor the sweet satisfaction that she had already bypassed most of the men in the room. Even sweeter was Washington's newly accommodating demeanor. Now, rather than approaching her with condescension, he treated her, if not as an equal, then with considerably more respect.

That fall Madam Walker wrote seeking his advice for her vision to establish an African school modeled on Tuskegee. "I know absolutely nothing about building a school," she admitted, "but am willing to furnish the means as far as I am able." Washington's answer, while not optimistic, lacked the dismissive tone of his earliest letters to her. "I wish I could offer some suggestion likely to prove helpful," he replied, but rather than suggest naiveté on her part, he confessed that his own efforts at a similar project had been unsuccessful.

"We ourselves have been considering several places for some two or three years," Washington confided, "but it is difficult for persons as far away as we are and unfamiliar with all of the circumstances." In fact, in 1900 he had sent three Tuskegee graduates and a faculty member to the West African nation of Togo with plows and a steam cotton gin to "interbreed" native and American cotton. Despite the promising enrollment of 200 African students in an agricultural school, the effort ultimately failed in 1909 when the director drowned in an accident and tsetse flies, locusts, drought and disease made the endeavor too costly.

In order to observe Tuskegee Institute's behind-the-scenes operations—and to learn more about running a school—Madam Walker spent part of February 1914 on campus. At Washington's request, she addressed the students after daily religious exercises. While there, she attended both the academic classes and the industrial training sessions. Impressed with the diligence of the student body—more than 1,500 young men and women from 32 states and 17 foreign countries—Madam Walker was persuaded by Washington to consider providing scholarships.

She followed her visit to Alabama with a small contribution, although Washington had requested much more. "Next year I hope to be able to help you in a larger way," she promised. But just as Washington had informed her a few years earlier that his work at Tuskegee required most of his attention and resources, she felt no qualms about telling him—albeit with more grace than he had shown her—that "while it is true I have a large business, yet with the increase in business comes the increase in expenses." Her intention to "build on all of my unimproved property here in Indianapolis," she said, demanded a large portion of her financial reserves.

Nevertheless, a few months later, at Washington's urging she pledged additional financial assistance for three male and two female students, including a young African man "whom I am educating for the purpose of founding and establishing a Negro Industrial School on the West Coast of Africa." Still Madam Walker reminded Washington that her resources were not limitless. "I am unlike your white friends who have waited until they were rich and then help," she scolded him. "But have in proportion to my success . . . reached out and am helping others, which may have been a mistake perhaps because I have been mistaken for a rich woman, which has caused scores of demands for help."

Certainly Washington had no illusions that her philanthropy could be on a par with that of multimillionaires Andrew Carnegie, John D. Rockefeller and Julius Rosenwald—some of Tuskegee's primary benefactors and among America's wealthiest men. Beginning in the 1890s Rockefeller annually had given the school at least $10,000, an amount that his son later increased. At first Carnegie had provided a similar amount, but after his admiration for Washington increased, he contributed $600,000 in U.S. Steel bonds for Tuskegee's endowment, a part of which was to be set aside as a private reserve to be used by Washington "for his wants and those of his family."

Having agreed to Washington's requests for scholarship support, Madam Walker felt comfortable in making an appeal of her own that he include her hairdressing course in Tuskegee's curriculum, teaching "it as you would any other industry." She offered to "build a little cottage for it," hoping that he would see the logic as well as the financial advantages to her proposal. "It would add quite a revenue to your school," she said persuasively, "as this work is an industry whereby [the students] can make more money than they could by sewing, or cooking or any other of these industries." Washington declined the offer, blaming the members of his executive committee, whom he said "are of the opinion that the time is not ripe for us to add this additional industry to our course." Nevertheless he softened his refusal by expressing his "very great pleasure" that she had enjoyed her recent campus visit.

As usual, Madam Walker was not deterred. Several weeks later she reminded Washington of her proposition "in regards to adopting my work as a part of the curriculum in your school." Just as he had been persistent in his request for scholarship funds, she was unwilling to let the matter drop. "I think I have demonstrated the fact to you that my business is a legitimate one as well as a lucrative one," she argued. "If successful it would mean thousands of dollars to both Tuskegee and myself . . . Then I could not only give hundreds of dollars to Tuskegee but thousands of dollars." Anticipating his refusal, she still hoped to extract some quid pro quo in exchange for her personal support of his institution. "If you can not see your way clear to adopt the work I do hope you will be willing to give me your endorsement in a public way," she added. Washington, however, remained firm in his rejection. "I have already written you frankly and fully with reference to putting your work in our course of study: our Trustees and Executive Committee do not see their way clear to follow your suggestion." It is unlikely, however, that the Tuskegee board would have overruled Washington had he truly favored the proposal. Having been so adamant in his early opposition to hairdressing for black women, he appears to have remained reluctant to sanction the occupation by including it as a course of study.

Still, at the August 1914 NNBL convention in Muskogee, Oklahoma, Washington once again gave Madam Walker and Lelia—who herself was now an NNBL life member—a friendly reception. On the second day of the proceedings, Washington surprised Madam Walker by summoning her to the platform. "She always says something we are glad to listen to," he said over enthusiastic applause. Referring to her ever-expanding philanthropy, he praised her as one who "not only makes money in business but gives liberally to many worthy enterprises. It is always encouraging to know that people are successful in business, but it is always more satisfactory to see them willing to distribute some of their profits among all good causes."

Calling the invitation an "unexpected pleasure," she used the opportunity to make a request of the delegates. "In coming before you I simply want to ask a favor of you in order that I, in turn, may be able to do more favors for our race."

Aware that most of the audience was familiar with her business, she used her time to discuss her dreams to create jobs for black women. "I am not merely satisfied in making money for myself, for I am endeavoring to provide employment for hundreds of the women of my race," she said. Her own struggles, she hoped, could provide a path for others.

"I had little or no opportunity when I started out in life . . . I had to make my own living and my own opportunity," she recounted to hearty applause. "But I made it. That is why I want to say to every Negro woman present, don't sit down and wait for the opportunities to come, but you have to get up and make them!"

Having excited them with her aspirations, she asked the delegates to pass a resolution endorsing her work because "it will help me to be of more practical service to the several worthy causes in which I am particularly interested" and "because it will help me in the struggle I am making to build up Negro womanhood." And lest some of the men balk at the idea of women working and advancing in business, she reminded them, "If the truth were known there are many women who are responsible for the success of you men." Their laughter and applause confirmed that they understood her meaning.

With Washington's approval, the resolution endorsing her as "the foremost business woman of our race" passed with no opposition.

At every convention Madam Walker attended during 1913 and 1914, she continued to campaign for this self-appointed title, no doubt to advance her goals for other women, but also to best her competitors. Both the Court of Calanthe at the Knights of Pythias convention in Baltimore and the women's auxiliary of the National Baptist Convention in Nashville in 1913 unanimously endorsed Madam Walker's hair preparations "as the best on the market" and proclaimed her "the foremost businesswoman of the race." During the NACW's 1914 biennial meeting, Victoria Clay Haley—one of Madam Walker's longtime St. Louis friends—presented a motion to "endorse the work of Madam C. J. Walker, who is doing so much for the elevation of the race."

Along with Alice Kelly and her chauffeur, Homer West, Madam Walker arrived in Washington, D.C., in early August 1913 to deliver a series of lectures entitled "The Negro Woman in Business" at ten area churches. By midmonth, she had become a "pronounced hit . . . speaking in all the churches and filling space in the dailies."

From the pulpits of the prestigious Metropolitan AME Church on M Street and the all-black First Baptist Church of Georgetown, she encouraged the "women of the race to rise above the laundry and kitchen . . . and to aspire to a place in the world of commerce and trade," Richard W. Thompson, the president of the National Negro Press Association—and her host for the week—reported in his nationally syndicated column.

"The girls and women of our race must not be afraid to take hold of business endeavor and, by patient industry, close economy, determined effort, and close application to business, wring success out of a number of business opportunities that lie at their very doors," she repeated all summer. Proud to announce that she was "employing hundreds of Negro girls and women all over this country as agents, clerks and otherwise," she told congregations and lodges, "I have made it possible for many colored women to abandon the wash-tub for more pleasant and profitable occupation." Even her latest ads emphasized training—"by mail or by personal instruction"—and job opportunities. "Learn to grow hair and make money," it promised. "A Diploma from Lelia College of Hair Culture is a Passport to Prosperity."

"Mme. Walker is essentially a businesswoman," wrote Thompson, a Washington disciple whose work was subsidized by the Tuskegee principal. "And no matter where she goes or on whatever errand, she talks business . . . She never loses an opportunity to emphasize to her sisters the importance of their getting into the world of business . . . making themselves financially independent and setting an example for all people of thrift, industry and practical application of their mental training."

As guests of Thompson and his wife near the District of Columbia's bustling U Street corridor, Madam Walker and Alice Kelly enjoyed theater and whist parties, as well as "motor parties to Baltimore, Alexandria and the suburbs." Madam Walker, of course, loved to socialize during all of her trips, but no business opportunity ever was overlooked.

Almost as soon as she returned to Indianapolis from the East Coast in September 1913, she began planning her first overseas trip to the Caribbean and Central America. After an October 31 farewell reception, she and her niece Anjetta Breedlove left for New York again in the custom-made Cole with Otho Patton, her new chauffeur. When they arrived in Harlem, soapbox orators on Lenox Avenue undoubtedly were still talking about the ten-day National Emancipation Exposition, a fiftieth anniversary commemoration of the signing of the Emancipation Proclamation. An unprecedented array of music and pageantry—ranging from the spectacular performance of bandleader James Reese Europe and his Clef Club to conductor Will Marion Cook's program of classical music and traditional spirituals—had been unveiled each day at the Armory near Columbus Circle. More than 30,000 people had attended the evening athletic events and the daytime political debates, as well as the ambitious historical extravaganza written and staged by Crisis editor W.E.B. Du Bois, with more than 300 elaborately costumed performers.

In New York, Madam Walker found herself with more social invitations than she could honor as she readied herself for a two-month journey to "introduce her hair preparations" to a large untapped market of women of African descent, including residents of overwhelmingly black Jamaica and Haiti, as well as Costa Rica, Cuba and the Panama Canal Zone, where as many as 40,000 West Indians now lived.

By design, she had coordinated her trip with Mme. Anita Patti Brown, a highly regarded coloratura soprano, whose globe-trotting had already taken her to the areas Madam Walker wished to cultivate. The two may have met in Chicago at the 1912 NNBL convention soon after Brown, a European-trained prima donna, had returned from "a triumphal tour" of Jamaica and the Central American states. But it is possible that they had encountered each other at an earlier time. Born in Atlanta, Brown had grown up in Indianapolis, where she had sung in a church choir, then worked as a maid until she moved to Chicago around 1900. Presumably, she maintained ties to the city where Madam Walker had moved in 1910.

Departing from New York on the steamer *Oruba* on November 8—with Brown's entourage, instruments and costumes, as well as Madam Walker's car, products and promotional literature—they arrived in Jamaica five days later. In Kingston, Madam Walker was greeted enthusiastically as "business men and high officials vied with one another in extending to her the hospitality of their country." Although still a British colony, Jamaica—as James Weldon Johnson would describe it just a few years later—had "black custom house officials, black soldiers, black policemen, black street car conductors, black clerks in the big shops, black girls in the telegraph office and at the news-stand of the fashionable Myrtle Bank Hotel." A few months later, W.E.B. Du Bois experienced "a strange sort of luxury" riding "on railways where engineers, firemen, conductors and brakemen were black." While he was enchanted with Kingston's Blue Mountains and Montego Bay's turquoise waters, he also discovered that "threaded through all this curious beauty . . . is tragedy of a poverty almost incomprehensible."

Nevertheless, the upper class of this predominantly black society provided a rich market for her products. "She was gratified to observe that it was only necessary to mention her business to secure more orders for goods than she could possibly supply," a reporter observed, noting that she "found more people willing to work than she could think of employing as agents." The trip was a happy mix of business and "gaiety." Her "chief delight," she said, was motoring through the countryside, where pastel orchids, crimson hibiscus and violet bougainvillea alternated with sugarcane fields and banana groves. "Long moonlight sails" with her hosts helped relieve the "intense heat" of the day.

From Kingston she and Anjetta traveled to Port-au-Prince, Haiti, with its picturesque bay, distant plum-colored mountains and boiling political turmoil. A country of stark contrasts and contradictions, its mostly mulatto elite looked down from their hilltop villas on thatched-roof peasant huts, their "outer walls . . . whitewashed or tinted blue, or pink, or yellow." Her stay, she said, was "a grand round of pleasure" as she was entertained by "many noted people, all of whom accorded her exceptional social courtesies." In a society that James Weldon Johnson found "on a level that for wealth and culture could not be matched by the colored people in any city in the United States," she was greeted by the "official family." A member of that family may have been President Michel Oreste, one of seven Haitian heads of state who were either deposed or dealt violent deaths between 1912 and 1915, when the United States sent military forces to occupy the island nation.

Madam Walker marveled at the opulence of the upper-class homes, but was perplexed by the crude and degrading Haitian prisons, where she discovered that "men and boys are, on the slightest pretext and least provocation, beaten and very often forgotten" and allowed to starve to death. The "real 'Chamber of Horrors,'" she said, was "the prison where the political offenders are confined" and "kept in irons and bound—hand and feet—in solitary confinement [with] no visitors but the guards." Learning that the cells were "bare with dirt floors" and contained no beds or mattresses, she was so distressed that she loaded her car with "18 chickens, one turkey, cakes and other things, and had a regular Christmas dinner prepared," though later she was led to believe that her gifts had never reached the prisoners.

Even so, in the city she found the Haitian men "polite" and the Haitian women "beautiful," just as James Weldon Johnson had observed. With "their baskets balanced on their colored-turbaned heads, the large, gold loops in their ears pendulating to their steps," Johnson wrote, "they strode along lithe and straight, almost haughtily, carrying themselves like so many Queens of Sheba."

After returning to Kingston for Christmas, Madam Walker traveled to Costa Rica, Panama and Cuba, where she trained more Walker hair culturists and made arrangements to ship her products through local customs agents. In late January she was back in New York with Lelia and quietly exploring a permanent move to the city, in part to become more involved in the city's political and cultural life, in part to spend more time with her daughter.

CHAPTER 14

New Horizons

—— e*ae ——

Madam Walker thrived on spoiling Lelia, giving her "baby" expensive presents and extravagant parties. And Lelia wanted nothing more than to please "Mother." But Madam's overindulgence and Lelia's inevitable dependence placed the two women on an emotional tightrope. The single-minded determination that had served Madam Walker so well in her business dealings frequently intruded on her personal relationship with her daughter. Even as Madam showered her with pricey gifts, Lelia could not help feeling that the largesse sometimes came with strings attached. On the one hand, Madam was proud of the sacrifices she had made on her daughter's behalf. On the other, Lelia struggled to remain in her mother's good graces and to display the requisite amount of dutiful gratitude.

"Fire and ice" was how one of Madam Walker's secretaries described their relationship. "They loved each dearly and they sometimes fought fiercely." But their estrangements were never prolonged because the glue of their past bound them in such an unusual way. No one they knew could comprehend their personal journey, a self-propelled ascent from utter destitution to bountiful luxury that few, if any, other mother-daughter pairs in America had experienced. Regardless of their periodic spats, they were more alike than different, plagued by an early sense of emotional abandonment and an attendant need to control and cling to those closest to them. On a healthier plane, they also shared a love of music, dancing and entertaining, and their generous spirits ultimately prevailed over the flare-ups that were ignited by their quick tempers.

During April 1914 Madam Walker hosted a spring dance and recital to celebrate Lelia's visit to Indianapolis. More than 200 guests assembled in the Pythian Hall amid palm fronds and baskets of fragrant white flowers, the ballroom festooned with gold streamers and ribbons. Even the Walker women's attire complemented the color scheme. Lelia, whose hair was draped with a double strand of pearls, donned a white Empire gown embroidered with gold thread. Madam Walker's diamonds sparkled above her intricately designed cream lace and white charmeuse dress. As the hostesses greeted their guests, an assistant distributed palm-sized, gold-tasseled dance programs embossed with "CJW 1914."

Men in cutaway coats and women in floor-length formal dresses reveled to an array of vocal numbers, violin selections and poetry recitations. Tenor Noble Sissle, an Indianapolis native who would later pen "I'm Just Wild about Harry," performed his signature song, "I Hear You Calling Me." Next, elocutionist Mary Ross Dorsey—dressed in diaphanous white chiffon—presented a poem by Paul Laurence Dunbar, whose humble and often humorous subjects Madam Walker especially enjoyed. Dorsey's rendition of "The Party"—a poem about a plantation shindig—offered an ironic mirror to the elaborately decorated hall and impeccably attired guests:

> Dey had a gread big pahty down to Tom's
> de othah night;
> Was I dah? You bet! I nevah in my life seen
> sich a sight . . .
> Evehbody dressed deir fines'—Heish yo' mouf
> an' git away,
> Ain't seen no sich fancy dressin' sense las'
> quah'tly meetin' day;
> Gals all dressed in silks an' satins, not a wrinkle
> ner a crease,
> Eyes a'battin', teeth a-shinin', haih breshed back
> ez slick ez grease.

The reference to hair surely made Madam Walker and the others laugh. And because Dunbar's rhythmic poems rarely failed to stimulate a crowd, by the time the band struck its first few notes, the dancers were more than ready to "make the scene a very brilliant one."

The following April, Lelia returned to Indianapolis for the second annual Walker spring musicale. This time the dance hall was adorned in luscious pink tones from floor to ceiling as a local photographer captured "the richly gowned women with their courteous escorts." Called "one of the most elaborate functions of many seasons," the event showcased singers and musicians from Chicago as well as Columbus and Springfield, Ohio.

During this visit, Lelia and Madam Walker shared two of their other favorite pastimes: sightseeing in Madam Walker's Cole and shopping. At H. P. Wassons, one of Indianapolis's first department stores, they purchased perfume, a hat, pumps, two suits, a camisole, an umbrella and towels. And no downtown excursion was complete unless Madam Walker called upon Julius Walk, the jeweler who had provided her monogrammed sterling silverware and treasured diamond earrings and necklace.

The following week, mother and daughter motored to Ohio, visiting Xenia, Wilberforce, Dayton and Springfield, where they "were the recipients of much social attention and many business engagements." Lelia loved riding in the touring car so much that her mother planned to surprise her at Christmas with her own automobile. Not long afterward Madam Walker informed Ransom that she had just purchased a Cadillac for Lelia. "I guess you think I am crazy," she wrote with a mild touch of self-consciousness. "I had a chance to get just what Lelia wanted in a car that had been used a little. It was worth $2,650 and I got it for $1,381.50 and since I was going to give her one for Xmas I thought I had better snatch this one as it would save me money." Accustomed to his boss's unpredictable splurges, Ransom replied, "No, I don't think you crazy, but think you very hard on your bank account. I take pleasure in the fact, that there can hardly be anything else for you to buy, ha, ha." Characteristic of their comfortable banter—and with faith that she was now making so much money that the purchase would have little impact on her budget—Madam parried, "I assure you I am not going to buy *another living thing.*" But when it came to her beloved only child, even she had to admit that such a promise would be impossible to keep.

Madam Walker's reputation as a generous woman had caused her to be inundated with requests for money from all over the country. What she had come to call "begging letters" arrived almost every day from prisoners, swindlers and scores of people down on their luck. Just within her own family she supported her sister-in-law, Lucy Breedlove, and four nieces in Denver, as well as her elder sister, Louvenia, who had recently moved to Indianapolis. Louvenia's son, Willie Powell, remained a disappointment despite Ransom's successful efforts at obtaining his release from Mississippi's Parchman Prison, where he had been serving time for manslaughter. "People know that he has been in prison and every step he makes will be watched," she said in refusing her sister's request to have him join her in Indianapolis. "The least thing he does will cast reflection on me."

Resentful, but duty-bound to care for her family members, Madam Walker had instructed Ransom to keep them on strict budgets, lest they become even more dependent upon her. "I am tired of fooling with those ungrateful Negroes," she wrote after falling out with her niece Anjetta. Following "another sassy letter" from Louvenia, she told Ransom, "I do not care to have any more communication with her . . . It seems the more I do for my people they are harder to please and I am going to quit trying to please them." But as with most unequal sibling relationships, she wavered, guilty that she had said "something too hard." Just two days later she wrote Ransom about the possibility of purchasing land for Louvenia in New Jersey: "I wish that you could get in touch with someone from whom I could get a little place about one or two acres so that she and Willie could live there and raise chickens, pigs and have a garden."

While her decisions to help her family involved a great degree of emotional angst, she was quite disposed to assist young men and women who showed a willingness to better themselves. "Mrs. Walker is grounded in the belief that every particle of talent in the colored race should be conserved; that no promising young person should be denied by fate the opportunity to reach his ideals," the *Recorder* reported.

She was so moved, in fact, by "the constant effort and untiring energy" of sixteen-year-old Frances Spencer that she called upon her friends in the white business community to help sponsor a Valentine's season benefit for Indianapolis's only black harpist. Spencer's plight particularly touched Madam Walker because, like herself, she was a "self-made girl, having started alone in the world at nine years." For the February 1915 concert, standing room was "at a premium" in the Pythian Hall in part because Noble Sissle was scheduled to perform along with P. L. Montani, the celebrated harpist, whose orchestra had offered to accompany his pupil, the "unusually talented" Spencer. At the end of the evening, Madam Walker presented Spencer with a $300 check for the down payment on an exquisite gold-leaf harp "in order that she might get her heart's desire." Madam Walker was extremely gratified by Spencer's obvious delight, but the young woman's request for additional aid unnerved her. "After the recital was over she came to my house and begged me to give her a home," Madam later said. "I told her that I had been so badly deceived in girls that I did not want to take her." Nevertheless, Spencer persisted until a wary Madam Walker allowed her to move into an extra room at 640 North West Street. "After remaining here for about two months and being treated like one of my own family and receiving a salary of $6 per week . . . she stole out everything which she had, including the harp," Madam Walker painfully told a reporter.

The incident had so soured her that she declared, "Now I want to say, and this is final, that I am through helping so-called people." Her temper erupting over Spencer's thievery, she continued, "There isn't a day that I am not besieged by people for help . . . and, near as I could, I have tried to help, or reach them in some way. In the future all appeals will be turned down and consigned to the waste basket." Her fit of pique proved to be temporary, but her skepticism for such personal appeals would become permanent.

"Madam loved going to the movies," remembered her longtime secretary, Violet Reynolds, who frequently accompanied her on afternoon trips to local theater houses for the silent romances, Westerns and comedies that were so popular at the time. As the movie industry was establishing itself in Hollywood and evolving from nickelodeon fare, the melodramas and crime stories provided an entertaining escape for Madam with their wealthy male and female characters, who inhabited a pampered fantasy world of mansions, chauffeurs and leisurely days. That these characters often had created their fortunes as entrepreneurs or financiers must have intrigued Madam Walker.

Less than a week after the Spencer recital Madam Walker arrived at the Isis Theatre in downtown Indianapolis prepared for a Saturday afternoon of fun. But when she presented her dime admission fee, the ticket agent refused to accept her money, informing her that "colored people" were now required to pay "twenty-five cents." In response to her demand for an explanation of the new policy, the young box office attendant replied that she had received "orders to charge colored persons twenty-five cents each for tickets." An irate Madam Walker insisted that Ransom take action against the theater. In his formal complaint to the Marion County Court, he demanded $100 in damages" for his "clean, sober, neat and orderly" client, who had faced racial discrimination in a public place. No document showing the disposition of the case exists in court records, but the incident surely added to Madam Walker's impatience with Indianapolis and increased her desire to move.

Without question, Madam Walker was known as Indianapolis's premier black hostess, her dinner invitations coveted, especially when she entertained prominent out-of-town African American visitors from across a spectrum of political ideologies. Fascinated as Madam Walker was by current events, the conversations always focused on the issues of the day, from the racial policies of President Woodrow Wilson and the sinking of the *Lusitania* to the rise in lynchings; from the escalating European war and the U.S. intervention in Haiti to the racism of D. W. Griffith's film *The Birth of a Nation*. But Madam's guests were just as happy for the chance to unwind in her well-appointed home, to hear recorded music on her gold-leaf Victrola—"the only one of [its] kind in Indianapolis"—and to experience the "unspeakable richness" of her grandfather clock as it chimed every quarter hour like the bells of Westminster Abbey.

In August 1914 after the National Association of Colored Women's biennial convention at nearby Wilberforce College, she hosted a Sunday afternoon reception for several hundred guests to honor her St. Louis NACW friends Victoria Clay Haley—a St. Paul's member and Royal Grand Matron of Missouri's Order of the Eastern Star—and Arsania Williams—president of St. Louis's Wheatley YWCA, who had taught at Dumas Elementary School while Lelia was a student there. A newer acquaintance, Mary Burnett Talbert, who was in line to become NACW president in 1916, also had accompanied her to Indianapolis for the festivities.

Two days later at an NACW "echo meeting"—where delegates gathered to discuss the convention proceedings—Talbert, an "unusually forceful speaker," encouraged local chapter members to become "a factor in the great affairs affecting the home, religion and politics." During the visit Madam Walker and Talbert began to forge a friendship and a strong political alliance as they chatted with Haley and Williams beneath the hand-carved alabaster chandelier in Madam's parlor. Despite the vast differences in their early life experiences—Talbert had graduated from Oberlin College in 1886 and married a successful Buffalo Realtor—the two women shared a dauntless dedication to improve the lives of black women.

The following spring, during April 1915, Madam Walker hosted a seven-course dinner for Robert Russa Moton, a Hampton Institute faculty member who was in town for three public appearances. Among the guests enjoying oyster cocktail, cream of popcorn soup, stuffed squab and asparagus salad in tomato aspic was Sidney Frissell, the son of Hampton president Hollis B. Frissell, as well as Madam Walker's closest local friends George Knox, Robert Brokenburr, Thomas E. Taylor, F. B. Ransom and their wives. During Moton's visit, Madam Walker surprised him with the promise of a $100 scholarship for his school, where he had served as commandant of male students since 1891.

Only one week later, William Monroe Trotter—the iconoclastic editor of the Boston *Guardian* and Harvard's first black Phi Beta Kappa graduate—was Madam Walker's houseguest during his second Midwestern speaking tour. As a founder of the Niagara Movement, an organization that had openly challenged Booker T. Washington's conciliatory political tactics as early as 1905, Trotter was at the opposite end of the political spectrum from Moton, a Bookerite and future Tuskegee Institute president. But Madam Walker, who remained open to almost all ideas that might "advance the race," had declined to criticize publicly either perspective, supporting what she could in both.

At the invitation of Ransom, who was president of the Good Citizens League, Trotter had been asked to speak at Bethel AME about President Woodrow Wilson's disappointing record concerning African Americans. A

Democrat and the first Southern-born President elected since the Civil War, Wilson recently had instituted the racial segregation of black civil servants in previously integrated federal buildings, excluding them from cafeterias in the post office and the Department of the Treasury. As a further blow to Trotter and the other blacks who had supported Wilson in his 1912 campaign, the number of African American federal appointees had dwindled markedly from thirty-one to eight during his first term in office.

Four months before Trotter's Indianapolis visit he had led a delegation to the White House to challenge Wilson's policies. After a heated exchange, the President expelled the smart but contentious Trotter from his office. The controversial publicity, however, had helped generate a large audience in Indianapolis, providing "the drawing card, for many," who, "out of curiosity, were anxious to see and meet the man who [had] 'sassed' the President." Having carried his message to Illinois, Minnesota, Nebraska and Missouri, Trotter considered his Indianapolis trip "one of the most beneficial of my . . . tour" both because he had "an intelligent and appreciative audience" and because he had organized a new chapter of his radical National Equal Rights League. "My home entertainment," Trotter wrote Mr. Ransom of his stay at 640 North West Street, "was royal."

One week later, while Daytona Normal and Industrial Institute founder Mary McLeod Bethune was in Indianapolis, Madam Walker presented her with a contribution for her Florida school. But one visitor Madam Walker did not personally entertain was Annie Pope-Turnbo, who had arrived for a week's stay in the city in late May 1915. Having married Aaron Malone, a former Bible salesman, in April 1914, she was now known as Annie Malone. To Madam Walker's annoyance, the new Mrs. Malone was featured on the front page of the *Recorder* in her seven-passenger Packard in a photograph very similar to Madam Walker's frequently used publicity shot at the wheel of her 1912 Ford Model T touring car. Details of Malone's social outings, including dinner with Mr. and Mrs. Elwood Knox—the son and daughter-in-law of the *Freeman*'s George Knox—as well as *Recorder* publisher George Stewart and Madam Walker's pastor, Dr. E. P. Roberts, were featured in the accompanying article.

In a thinly veiled slap at Madam, the *Recorder* piece reported that Malone "is known the country over for her charity work, and is always ready to help the deserving. She is the kind that gives and says nothing of it . . . [and] unlike many, [is] never heard to boast of what she has done." Earlier in the year, Stewart had run a front-page article calling Malone the "Race's Leading Business Woman" and "the queen of all Negro business women."

Although Stewart had carried similar articles praising Madam Walker, and although Madam Walker may have assumed that Malone had written the articles herself—just as Ransom had frequently supplied much of *her* copy to the country's black newspapers—she remained irked with Stewart that fall. "Now in regards to George Stewart and the Popes etc.," she fumed in a letter to Ransom. "I don't care a rap of my finger. I am no copy cat. They copy from me. I have naturally got the lead and there is nothing Stewart's paper can do for me. I bet they haven't 500 subscribers out of the city of Indpls."

Madam Walker's strategy to strengthen her business on the East and West Coasts kept her on the road for several months throughout 1914 and 1915. During September and October 1914, she gave twenty-five lectures to "full and appreciative houses" at the "leading churches" in Brockton, Boston and New Bedford, Massachusetts; Newport and Providence, Rhode Island; as well as New York City and Brooklyn.

In preparation for an extended trip to the West Coast during the summer and fall of 1915, she wrote to Booker T. Washington requesting his assistance. "Will you kindly give me a letter of introduction to Mr. Bob Owens and any other persons of influence that it would be well to meet or reside with in the states of California, Washington and Oregon?" she queried with the familiarity she had long hoped to have with Washington. "I hope to stop in all the large cities." His reply must have been a helpful one, because within a few weeks she sent him a $250 donation "in accordance with my promise to provide scholarships for certain worthy students, to the end, that I may, in a small way, help you in your great work." In what would become his final letter to her, he expressed his appreciation. "We shall see that the money is used in the way you desire, and thank you most sincerely for your very generous gift."

After stopping in St. Louis, Denver, Pueblo and Colorado Springs with Mae—who had come along to assist her—Madam Walker embarked on her long rail journey to California. En route Madam and her adopted granddaughter enjoyed the wonders of the West: the Mormon Temple in Salt Lake City, Yellowstone Park with its geysers, the "vast profound" Grand Canyon and what she described as its "gorgeous colored rocks as varied as the tints of the rainbow."

Within the first two weeks of leaving Indianapolis, Madam Walker had already begun to see a payoff. "My lecture Monday night was a grand success. The house was packed," she wrote Ransom. "The people applauded so I hardly had time to talk . . . I have been entertained two and three times a day ever since I've been here. Haven't had a day or evening to myself. Have had two cars put at my disposal."

Much of her popularity on this trip, she believed, was due to her "illustrated lectures," which described not only her hair care system but the accomplishments of African Americans in business and education since the Civil War. Presented on glass slides on a stereopticon projector manually operated by Mae, the lectures, Madam Walker said, were "taking fine," having proved to be a hit with audiences for whom movies were still a novelty. "Everybody gets enthused and wants to take the trade," she happily reported.

By the second week in September, Madam Walker and Mae had settled in Los Angeles into the bungalow Lelia had purchased at 1449 West Thirty-fifth Place. They were having such a productive trip that Madam Walker advised Ransom, "I fear I will not be able to reach home before the latter part of November, as there is a great demand for my work throughout the West." In fact, she said, interest was so high that she had been featured not only in the local black newspaper but in the Japanese, Italian and German papers as well.

As she traveled from one end of California to the other, Madam Walker marveled at the "indescribable beauty" of the "magnificent palms" and the "giant geraniums that entwined many of them to their very tops." But her main delight came from knowing that she had had more requests for speaking engagements than she could possibly accept. "I am sure that this trip is going to add at least two or three thousand per month to my income," Madam Walker wrote Ransom after a particularly productive meeting in Los Angeles. "I am succeeding in making agents everywhere I go. To my surprise, [I] had 12 [agents] present, and there are four others here whom I know did not get out to the meeting." In El Centro, near the Mexican border, she "aroused people to the highest pitch."

With her booming sales had come the inevitable imitators. "Now, Mr. Ransom, I find that a number of agents out here have adulterated my preparation," she wrote. "They are removing the [labels] and selling the goods without [them]. Will you advise me what to do?"

In one particular instance, a woman had ordered Madam Walker's metal product containers directly from the supplier, replacing the Walker name with her own. "Now, I think I do business enough with the American Can Company to ask them to refrain from selling her boxes or boxes to anyone else for hair goods," she complained to Ransom. "If the American Can Company can't refuse [to send] her boxes, then I will have to take my work from them and get an entirely new box made by a new company." A few weeks later Ransom assured Madam Walker that American Can, one of the nation's largest manufacturing companies, was "going to take steps concerning boxes."

For at least a week in October she and Mae trained agents and presented lectures in Oakland. While in the Bay Area they also visited San Francisco's Panama-Pacific International Exposition, a world's fair commemorating the recent opening of the Panama Canal, which had still been under construction during her winter 1914 visit to Central America. In late October the pair traveled farther north to Portland, Oregon. "Mr. Ransom, is it essential that I should be home by the first of December?" Madam Walker wrote, with hopes of extending her West Coast stay well beyond her scheduled return. "If not, I have a few other cities to make before reaching home." The months on the road, however, had made her long for friends and family. "I am truly homesick now," she wrote in reply to Ransom's letter telling her that his wife and two young sons missed her. "I am just as anxious to see Nettie and the babies as they are to see me." Still, her work took precedence. "This trip is and will mean so much to my business that I want to prolong it as [much as] possible."

The distance from her day-to-day operations had also given her time to think about new marketing plans, including ways to capitalize on the slide presentations. "Since I find that these pictures accompanied by lecture are creating such a wide interest among the people, I was thinking it would be a good idea to appoint some energetic capable women in certain territories, especially through the South and Middle West, where our people are in such great numbers," she proposed. Her plan, she told Ransom, was to pay them the handsome sum of $100 each month, plus "10 per cent or 25 per cent of all business they send over and above $100."

In early November, after stops in Seattle and Tacoma, Washington, she wired $10,000 to Ransom, who pronounced her deposit a "remarkable" accomplishment. "Yes, I say it is remarkable the way my bank account continues to increase and also remarkable how I continue to draw on it," she replied in anticipation of Ransom's ever-watchful eye. "While this has been the most expensive trip I have ever taken in America, I feel however that the returns will fully compensate."

A week later, while she was in Garrison, Montana, news of Booker T. Washington's death stunned her. "I have never lost anyone, not even one of my own family that I regret more than I do the loss of this great and good man for he is not only a loss to his immediate relations and friends but to the Race and the world," she lamented. "Even yet I can't picture him dead." Immediately she sent Margaret Murray Washington a telegram expressing her regrets at "the untimely passing away of Dr. Booker T. Washington, the greatest man America ever knew."

At the funeral three days later, Madam Walker was represented by Ransom, who had traveled from Indianapolis with the large, cross-shaped floral arrangement Madam had requested. Inscribed with the words "Thou who so bravely bore our cross, Thy place can ne'er be filled," it was placed alongside thousands of others as more than 8,000 mourners filed past his casket. "It gave me much pleasure to know, even though I was so far away, [that] I was represented so beautifully," she wrote to Ransom after the funeral.

"Indeed, I am glad it was thus, because his death touched me so forcibly that I am sure, or I fear, that I would have acted unwomanly at the funeral."

The jockeying for Washington's successor began even before his casket had closed. But while Stewart's *Recorder* and others speculated that Emmett Scott would step into the breach, it was Robert Russa Moton whom Tuskegee's predominantly white trustee board placed at the helm five weeks later.

Despite their differences—both personal and political—Madam Walker had sincerely admired Washington's accomplishments. And while she would prove to be much more radical than Washington in her approach to civil rights, her own background had helped her grasp the value of industrial training for the large numbers of African Americans who still remained illiterate and tied to the plantation way of life. Because she had chosen to denigrate neither Washington nor his critics, she was well positioned to cultivate her ties with Moton, Du Bois, Trotter and the roster of leading race men and women who would emerge during the next decade to fill the vacuum created by Washington's death.

As soon as Madam Walker returned to Indianapolis at the beginning of December, word spread of her contemplated move to New York. The next two months were filled with farewell parties, testimonials and dinners. In mid-December, the Senate Avenue YMCA hosted a banquet in her honor, presenting her with a leather-bound set of resolutions. In an attempt to persuade her to stay, they declared that this "benefactress in human uplift . . . has enshrined herself in the hearts of all of her fellow citizens." Praising "her marvelous business ability" and "immense wealth," their resolutions pled, "Be it resolved that we as citizens of Indianapolis generally, and members of the YMCA particularly, realizing the great loss her removal would be to the city and state, beg her to reconsider it and live always among us."

That Christmas, as had become her holiday season custom for the last six years, Madam Walker distributed dozens of food baskets to the neighborhood's needy families. And in her final gesture of generosity to the community, she sponsored a benefit to raise funds to pay off the mortgage of the Alpha Home, a black retirement residence that had been founded for pensionless former slaves. Her featured guest was Matilda Dunbar, the mother of the late poet Paul Laurence Dunbar, who "gloriously" recited his "Negro Soldiers." The young baritone Louis Depp, who had performed at one of Lelia's spring parties, had returned from Springfield, Ohio. Only the talented Noble Sissle, who recently had paired up with a promising ragtime pianist named Eubie Blake, was missing from Madam's lineup of favorites. Madam Walker fittingly capped the evening with one of the largest contributions the home had ever received.

"The citizens of Indianapolis, without regard to race, are one in their expressions of regret at the loss of Madam C. J. Walker as a resident of the city of Indianapolis," read the front-page *Freeman* article soon after she had departed. Her business enterprise, wrote reporter William Lewis, "is not only a credit to her and her race, but a monument to Negro thrift and industry throughout America." He proclaimed the Madam C. J. Walker Manufacturing Company "the largest of its kind in this country." Further, he said, "what is not generally known [is that] this company enjoys a large and growing white and foreign trade."

It was not her role as an entrepreneur that would be most missed, wrote Lewis, "but as the big-hearted race loving woman that she is." Her gifts, he believed, had been "so freely and so largely" given that the community had come to take them for granted. "When the needy poor and institutions are no longer cheered, inspired and helped by her timely assistance, then and not until then will we fully appreciate what she was to Indianapolis."

CHAPTER 15

Black Metropolis

— ☙❧ —

I t is just impossible for me to describe it to you," Madam Walker wrote
Ransom of Lelia's spectacularly renovated Harlem town house. The
first-floor hair salon, tastefully decorated in muted grays with royal blue
velvet and white marble accents, "beats anything I have seen anywhere
even in the best hair parlors of the whites," she gushed. "The decorators
said that of all the work they had done here in that line there is nothing
equal to it, not even on Fifth Avenue." And that apparently included the
posh midtown salons of Elizabeth Arden and Helena Rubinstein, the city's
premier skin care specialists who competed aggressively for New York's
elite white clientele.

Just after New Year's Day 1916, and a few weeks before Madam Walker's
permanent move to New York, Lelia celebrated the remodeling of the
Walker Hair Parlor and Lelia College with a festive open house. To the
rousing tunes of James Reese Europe's Tempo Club Ensemble—a favorite
of East Coast high society from Saratoga to Newport—hundreds of guests
glided along a deep-pile blue runner into Lelia's elegant lobby, past porcelain manicure tables, pristine operators' booths and sparkling display cases
of Walker products, then through beaded curtains into her Japanese-
themed tearoom. Even in the winter's chill, the backyard gazebo lured visitors into the garden.

Like her mother, Lelia loved staging social extravaganzas and providing
her guests with delicious food, appealing entertainment, inspired decorations and, above all, interesting people from the worlds of music, theater,
art, politics and business. And like her mother, she had a knack for engineering the events to create publicity for her business.

On this particular occasion, the *Indianapolis World* stringer lauded the
stylish hostess—a "most affable and courteous woman" whose personality
"permeates the atmosphere"—and anointed her "the presiding genius" of
this "exquisite beauty palace." So often overshadowed by Madam Walker's

prodigious accomplishments, Lelia relished the recognition. Even her mother had credited her with the idea of establishing a Walker presence in Harlem. The salon—with its refined ambience—would be her most enduring contribution to the expanding Walker enterprise.

"Now, Mr. Ransom, in regards to this house, you will agree with Lelia when she said that it would be a monument for us both," wrote the proud mother in late February 1916. And although they had initially planned to manufacture products in the basement, Madam Walker decided against marring the tranquil atmosphere. "Lelia and Mae are rejoicing over the fact that they will not have to make any more [hair] preparations," she told Ransom. "And I agree with you that this house is too fine to have a factory connected with it."

After having been irritated with Lelia for months over the excessive costs of the renovation, Madam Walker now had nothing but praise. "It was a surprise and I haven't a word to say against it," she said. Adept as Madam Walker could be at handling confrontation in her business affairs, she dreaded direct conflict with her daughter. Lelia, likewise, shrank from arguments with her mother. Still, they had their battles. Caught in the middle, Ransom frequently was required to serve as the go-between, buffering their impulsive tempers and diplomatically dispatching the criticisms and complaints that neither woman wanted to deliver to the other.

The clashes had begun only a few months into the first phase of the remodeling project at 108 West 136th Street as Lelia quickly ran through the $7,000 budget Madam had allotted. Fearing her mother's exasperation, she asked Ransom to convey the news of the contractor's cost overruns. "Am writing you to do a friendly turn for me. Am dodging behind you to keep the bullets from hitting me," she wrote, enclosing the "final" bill of $15,000, a sum which, she admitted, did "not include wall coverings or any of the hundred and one things that are taken in building."

Lelia anticipated Ransom's reprimand, but the closeness in their ages—Ransom was only three years her senior—made him a less intimidating judge. "Now I know, Mr. Ransom, Mother has been wonderful to me. She has been so good until I know it seems a rank imposition, and, so it is, for me to say money to her again. That is why I am getting behind you," she said both with diffidence and with a near-desperate hope that her mother would approve of her efforts. "You can trust me when I say the home is wonderful and if she was here she would back me in everything I am doing. There isn't one penny being wasted."

To soften the request, Lelia proposed a "loan from Mother in a businesslike way," rather than an outright gift for the additional funds. "I am willing to give Mother the same interest her bank gives her, even double.

I'll pay it, my word of honor as a woman, Mr. Ransom," she breathlessly bargained, pleading with him to intercede on her behalf. "Whatever you do, don't let her get sore at me and ball me out, for I certainly am one nervous child." So nervous, in fact, that she invoked the image of a recent high-seas rescue: "I realize I have certainly imposed some task on you, but you'll have to be to me what the *Carpathia* was to the *Titanic*."

To reassure Ransom, and ultimately her mother, she reminded him that she would more than make up for her costly renovations with expanded product sales, more Lelia College students and new customers. "My income now is $1,000 a month in poor seasons and in the summer time I know it will be $2,000 to $3,000 per month since I'll be able to take care of the increase in my trade." Like her mother, Lelia had nurtured a satisfied clientele, collecting testimonial letters that commended her work in New York and Pittsburgh. "Since you treated my hair, it has grown thicker and longer in 7 months than it has grown for 7 years," a happy customer from nearby Ninety-ninth Street wrote. Every six weeks Lelia and Mae instructed a class of twenty Walker hair culturists—many of them from other states, who then returned to their homes and trained others.

By January 1916, Lelia's monthly revenues indeed had reached the $2,000 mark. "The business has picked up wonderfully since she opened," Madam Walker told Ransom, vindicating Lelia's insistence on having an opulent setting for their New York operation. And although Lelia feared her mother's disapproval, her anxiety was as much self-imposed as real since her requests were almost always granted. "Lelia wants $3,000," Madam Walker had advised Ransom during the summer of 1915 as Lelia completed the purchase of 110, the building next door to 108 West 136th Street. "Am sending her a check today." Two months later, Madam Walker again instructed Ransom to honor Lelia's request for an additional $4,000. "Will you kindly go to the bank and see . . . if there is sufficient amount to cover the same? If not, you make arrangement so that they will honor my check."

At Lelia's direction, architect Vertner Tandy—a graduate of Tuskegee and Cornell and one of the first black licensed architects in New York State—combined 108 and 110 into a single stately building with a bowed red-brick-and-limestone Georgian façade. Scalloped pale gray chiffon curtains framed the stylized Venetian windows that spanned the street-level front wall. On the right, French doors opened onto the hair salon with its patterned metal ceiling and buffed parquet floor. To the left at 108, marble Doric columns guarded the entrance to the upstairs living quarters. On the third floor, Madam Walker's bedroom—with its intricately carved fireplace and English wall tapestries—was furnished in heavy mahogany. Down the hall Lelia's ivory Louis XVI suite was trimmed in gold, her dresser and mantel filled with framed photographs and statuettes, her floor scattered with hand-woven Persian rugs.

The women's love of music was evident on every level of the four-story house. In the bedroom hallway they shared a Victrola. A player organ reached from floor to ceiling in the main hall. But it was in the drawing room where music took center stage, whether from recordings on the gold Victrola, from the talents of professional musicians on the new gold-leaf-trimmed Aeolian grand piano or from Mae's hands as she practiced on the gold harp that had been retrieved from Frances Spencer.

As Madam Walker settled easily into her daughter's luxurious home, few outward traces of her earlier life remained. Some observed that her mannerisms, her grasp of public affairs and her cultural interests all meshed comfortably with her newly acquired status. Frances Garside, the first white reporter to pen an extensive profile of Madam Walker, noted in the Literary Digest that as she entered the drawing room in an "expensive pink-flowered lavender dressing-gown on a week-day morning," she carried herself "gracefully on high French heels . . . with a lack of self-consciousness few of us know when we get on our Sunday clothes."

Almost from the moment Lelia moved to New York in 1913, she had longed for her mother to join her, and with each trip to the city, Madam Walker became more and more receptive. In October 1914 an intimate Sunday evening dinner party that Lelia hosted in her honor may have sealed Madam Walker's decision to relocate. Amid decorations of orange and crimson autumn leaves and golden chrysanthemums, a few of Harlem's most influential residents dined upstairs at 108 while extolling the community's investment opportunities and rising real estate values. Among the guests seated beneath Lelia's dazzling crystal chandelier were New York Age publisher Fred Moore, Realtor Philip A. Payton, Jr., and composer and conductor James Reese Europe, all men whose accomplishments Madam Walker admired.

With his 125-member Clef Club Orchestra, the classically trained Europe had caused a cultural sensation in May 1912 when he introduced African American music and musicians to a racially mixed Carnegie Hall audience. As bandleader and music director for Vernon and Irene Castle—the celebrated husband-and-wife dance team—Europe had provided the rhythmic tunes that helped them popularize the turkey trot and the fox-trot among white American audiences during the 1910s. A dark-skinned man with a "statuesquely powerful build," Europe moved easily on the yachts and in the ballrooms of the Wanamakers, Goulds and Vanderbilts, who frequently booked his musicians for their private parties. With his recently formed Tempo Club Ensemble now headquartered in a row house at 119 West 136th Street, he and the Walkers had become neighbors.

Another guest, Philip Payton, was called "the Father of Colored Harlem" for his role in opening the area's housing to African Americans a decade earlier. While working as a janitor in a white-owned realty firm, the college-educated Payton had witnessed the profits to be made from lucrative real estate deals. To cash in on a surge of property speculation, Payton founded a small firm in 1900 when fewer than 5,000 of Manhattan's 36,000 black residents lived in Harlem. Four years later, under a new name—the Afro-American Realty Company—he began a concerted drive to rent apartments to blacks who were moving to Harlem from lower-Manhattan neighborhoods as well as from the American South and the Caribbean.

His biggest break surfaced, he often said, when a personal dispute between two white landlords on 134th Street caused the more creatively spiteful one to turn over an apartment house to Payton to "fill with colored tenants" in order that he might "get even." As a result, scores of the remaining white tenants fled, forcing other landlords in the neighborhood to hire Payton to fill their emptying buildings. It was a story that Fred Moore, another of the dinner guests—and an early officer and investor in the Afro-American Realty Company—knew well. Despite Payton's prescient coup, he had been forced to close his firm in 1908 after a series of legal and financial difficulties. Nevertheless, in 1914 he remained an astute investor and observer of the market.

Until the early 1870s Harlem had been a distant, rural village of mostly poor farmers on the northern end of Manhattan Island. The estates of its few wealthy residents were sparsely dispersed, isolated from the hustle and bustle of Wall Street and the gentility of the Astor, Carnegie and Vanderbilt mansions that later would stand like jeweled sentinels along Fifth Avenue. But by the end of that decade—when the launching of the city's first elevated train cut commuting time from lower Manhattan to the "el" station at 129th Street to less than half an hour—Harlem became the city's first suburb, a kind of "rural retreat of the aristocratic New Yorker."

Optimistic contractors and architects—including the acclaimed Stanford White—built block upon block of opulent brownstones and luxury apartment buildings. By the 1890s *Harlem Monthly Magazine* proclaimed the district "distinctly devoted to the mansions of the wealthy [and] the homes of the well-to-do." As the nineteenth century ended, subway construction sparked such feverish speculation that when the Interborough Rapid Transit line reached Lenox Avenue and 145th Street in 1904, risk-taking investors had transformed nearly all of Harlem's former farmland into residences. With this second wave, Irish and Jewish families joined the upper-class British and German residents who had begun arriving two decades earlier.

When the overheated real estate market finally collapsed in 1904 and 1905, West Harlem was saturated with vacant apartments. A shrewd Philip Payton capitalized on the situation, allegedly charging blacks higher rents than whites had paid, but also offering those middle-class blacks who could afford to leave the slums and tenements of the Tenderloin and San Juan Hill districts the first truly decent housing many of them had known. And while greater Harlem would remain predominantly white for many more years, the trickle of black migration began to turn into a torrent during the coming decade.

In 1908, around the time Madam Walker arrived in Pittsburgh, Payton was forced to close the Afro-American Realty Company. Two of his employees, John E. Nail and Henry Parker, filled the breach, combining their youthful ambition with Nail's considerable family connections. Nail's late father, John B. "Jack" Nail, had been a political boss who had owned a hotel and two popular taverns in the 400 block of Sixth Avenue in the Tenderloin district at the turn of the twentieth century. His investments in Harlem property and other real estate had made him one of the wealthiest black men in New York.

In 1911 when blacks were scattered between 128th Street on the south and 145th Street on the north between Fifth and Seventh avenues, the younger Nail joined with Reverend Hutchens C. Bishop—pastor of St. Philip's Episcopal Church's prosperous, all-Negro congregation—to engineer black New York's first million-dollar real estate transaction. The package—composed of land for a Vertner Tandy–designed church and rectory at 214 West 134th Street, as well as a row of ten apartment buildings along the north side of 135th Street between Lenox and Seventh that sold for $640,000—became the symbolic beachhead of an unstoppable black presence in Harlem.

The backlash from white Harlem residents—still very much in the majority—was swift. John G. Taylor, president of the Harlem Property Owners' Protective Association, called upon his members to "fight the common enemy." His solution for the new arrivals—regardless of their incomes or aspirations—was to "drive them out and send them to the slums where they belong." Just before St. Philip's 1911 purchase, a group of white homeowners on 136th Street had vowed to "neither sell nor rent to colored people." Taylor insisted that "no matter what happens, the residents on the south side of 136th Street will stick absolutely . . . by erecting a 24-foot fence in the back yards of the houses." Two years later, when Lelia persuaded Madam Walker to buy 108 West 136th Street in the block behind St. Philip's buildings—and on that very same "south side of 136th

Street"—no wall had been constructed and the owner was eager to sell. By October 1914, when Madam Walker dined with Payton, Europe and Moore, an estimated 50,000 blacks were living in Harlem.

Not long after their enjoyable meal, Madam Walker and the three men were joined by black Shakespearean actor Richard B. Harrison on an excursion to a nearby investment property. Convinced that "all she had to do was lay eyes on Bishop's Court"—the Flushing, Long Island, home of William B. Derrick, a recently deceased, and much revered, AME bishop—the men arranged a tour of the estate with his widow, Clara Derrick. "Naturally enough the New York folk felt that after New York came the end of the world," the *Freeman* jealously reported. Almost immediately Madam Walker made a deposit on the property.

Enchanted by the four-story, twenty-room house with its spiral staircase, frescoed ceilings, magnificent trees and customized Italian marble fireplace, Madam Walker admitted that she had been taken as much with its connection to the late bishop as with its actual market value, especially after she learned that the lovely mansion was surrounded by one of Flushing's poorest neighborhoods. Ransom could not help agreeing with Madam Walker that because of the bishop's status among African Americans, her association with his home—regardless of its location—would provide what she called "a big ad" for her and her business. But before Madam Walker could move into the house, Flushing's local governing board destroyed whatever fiscal value it had left by rezoning the district surrounding the estate from a residential to a business area. "The house is worth nothing . . . and the property as it stands altogether is worth no more than $17,000," S. A. Singerman, an attorney she had retained to handle her New York legal affairs, informed Ransom. "[It] is only good for the erection of cheap tenements." By late May—after black newspapers across the country had made much of the purchase—Madam Walker was seeking a discreet and graceful exit from the deal.

"Apparently your client has been fearfully imposed upon," Singerman continued, "and I would by all means suggest that an endeavor be made to obtain a return of the deposit." But because Madam Walker had signed a contract, the best Singerman and Ransom could do was to negotiate a lower price.

Whether Philip Payton played any role in misrepresenting the facts to Madam Walker is unknown since his business records no longer exist. But Ransom, who had little trust in the motivations of some of Madam Walker's New York acquaintances, could barely contain his annoyance. "As you know, Madam had gone into this before consulting me," the perturbed attorney wrote Lelia. "And even had she consulted me she would not have taken my advice for her heart was and is set on this property and on moving to New York." Fiercely opposed to the proposition, Ransom hoped to per-suade his client to delay her move for at least eighteen months until she had settled her current debts and "piled up a snug sum for rainy days." He also hoped to squelch entirely any plan to relocate the company headquar-ters to a city whose cost of living he considered astronomical. "I have advised Madam against moving her business to New York," he told Lelia. "She says she won't, but I take it that it will be only a question of time before she moves it to your city.

"There are those who say live while you are living," he cautioned Lelia. "But I can imagine no greater disgrace than to be known as your mother is known, and in the end give your enemies a chance to rejoice in the fact that you died poor."

Still, the disappointment over the Derrick house had not changed Madam Walker's mind in the least about moving. "As regards my coming back to Indianapolis, Mr. Ransom, that is clear out of the question," she declared. "Even if I don't build in New York, I will never come back to Indi-anapolis." And although she regretted leaving her friends, "among whom I class you, Nettie and Alice, the best, there is so much more joy living in New York where there are not so many narrow, mean people." Incidents such as the Isis Theatre episode had spoiled the appeal of Indianapolis; in contrast, she and Lelia had been greeted warmly by Italian tenor Enrico Caruso after a performance at New York's Metropolitan Opera.

Indianapolis had become too small, too confining, too conservative. And while she did not dispute the wisdom of maintaining her company headquarters in the Midwestern city, her unfolding political and cultural agenda required a larger canvas. New York simply had more of everything Madam Walker wanted: sophistication, wealth, culture and intellectual stimulation. That it also had more vice, corruption and poverty did not diminish its attraction. Unquestionably a city of extremes, precedents and immeasurable expansion, Manhattan held bragging rights to the world's tallest buildings, from the sixty-story Gothic terra-cotta Woolworth tower at Broadway and Park to the fifty-story Metropolitan Life Insurance Build-ing. By 1880 Manhattan had already become the first American city to exceed a million people. With its more than 25,000 factories, New York was the nation's indisputable center of manufacturing in 1890. A decade later it could claim the home offices of two-thirds of the largest 100 U.S. corpora-tions. By 1910 Manhattan's population topped the two-million mark, nearly ten times that of Indianapolis's 233,650. That same year, New York City was home to almost 92,000 blacks, more than four times the number of black Indianapolis residents.

Whereas the Hoosier capital city's leaders prided themselves on the dearth of immigrants, New York had dedicated the Statue of Liberty as a symbol of ethnic inclusion in 1886. And although the metropolis did not welcome all nationalities with equal enthusiasm, it had become home to a kaleidoscope of foreign arrivals. The large influx in the 1880s of Italians and Eastern European and Russian Jews, as well as smaller numbers of Greeks, Poles and Balkans, had begun pushing earlier groups of Germans and Irish farther north up Manhattan's avenues. And just as Southern and Eastern Europeans had flocked to the city—by 1910 there were at least a half million Italians and more than twice as many Jews—African Americans and black West Indians flowed into Harlem to form a cultural, political and intellectual mecca.

During the summer and on Sundays, the sidewalks of Lenox and Seventh avenues, at either end of 136th Street, were crowded with black Harlemites. Those attired "in loud-checked suits and flaming ties rub elbows with Negroes in most somber dress and mien. Much-beribboned women in cool, white dresses and carrying gay parasols make the avenues ring with their laughter and chatter, furnishing a contrast to almost as many who are soberly garbed," wrote one observer. "The visitor may see there all manner of style and dress just as he does down-town among New Yorkers of lighter hues."

While Harlem was not without its share of substandard housing, its west side was primarily a district of wide boulevards and grand homes that wealthy whites had begun to abandon in a frenzy. A National Urban League report concluded that "Negroes as a whole are . . . better housed [in Harlem] than in any other part of the country." The black populations in several large cities were exploding simultaneously, but it was "the character of Negro protest and thought" that rendered Harlem different from Chicago, Philadelphia, Baltimore and Washington, D.C. By 1916 Harlem was evolving into "the biggest and most elegant black community in the Western world . . . within the most urbane of American cities," wrote historian Nathan Irvin Huggins. As black leadership jockeyed to fill the void left by Booker T. Washington's death in late 1915, New York had become a magnet for many of the more militant thinkers, including some who had openly challenged the Tuskegee leader's gradualist politics and who had found his efforts at securing civil rights and suffrage for Southern African Americans inadequate. Among the most outspoken of these "New Negro" intellectuals was W.E.B. Du Bois, who, in 1910, had become the Director of Publicity and Research for the recently founded National Association for the Advancement of Colored People, with personal hopes of charting "a new course for racial assertiveness." By 1916, as Madam Walker herself was developing more assertive views on race, she was becoming eager to assume her place alongside Harlem's famous, influential and intriguing residents, including Reverend Adam Clayton Powell, Sr., of the Abyssinian Baptist

Church; Bert Williams, one of the era's most successful comedians; New York Colored Republican Club founder Charles W. Anderson; and James Weldon Johnson, former U.S. consul to Venezuela and Nicaragua.

Madam Walker's move to New York coincided with the huge influx of African Americans who were being pushed from the South by the floods of 1915 and the boll weevil infestations of 1915 and 1916, as well as the ongoing racial violence and untenable living circumstances. One Mississippi man told a commission investigating Southern working conditions that both men and women were forced to labor in the fields during harvest season. "After the summer crops were all in, any of the white people could send for a Negro woman to come and do the family washing at 75 cents to $1.00 a day," he contended. "If she sent word she could not come she had to send an excuse why . . . They were never allowed to stay at home as long as they were able to go." Consequently, women were as likely as men to leave, as many said, "to better their conditions." When they arrived Madam Walker was poised to offer just the opportunity they desired.

African Americans also were pulled to Northern cities by the factory jobs left open when the flood of European immigrants was stymied by the start of World War I in 1914. The steady deluge that had resulted in 25 million European arrivals between 1870 and 1915 dwindled to a trickle of just over 100,000 by 1918. Ready to fill the gap were an estimated half million African Americans who arrived from the South between 1916 and 1918 just as the nation's industries were escalating their wartime production. The chance to make as much as $8 a day in a factory in the North was a seductive incentive for farmhands who had been paid as little as 40 cents a day in the South.

Harlem attracted large numbers of black Southerners, especially new arrivals from towns and farms of the eastern seaboard states of Virginia, the Carolinas, Georgia and Florida. Churches, black newspapers, the YMCA, the YWCA and groups like the National League on Urban Conditions Among Negroes counseled the recent arrivals on the ways of the city and the expectations of "white employers [who] would judge their workers on the basis of general behavior, good manners, good conduct, and attention to dress and cleanliness, as well as efficient service." Urban League "block visitors" also advised the migrants—many of whom were barely literate and had come from areas where no black public schools existed—that "children should be scrubbed, their hair combed, and . . . kept in school as long as you are able."

Madam Walker tapped into the changing attitudes of women who longed to adopt a more urban, more sophisticated look, while also advocating personal grooming and the employment opportunities and financial independence offered by a Lelia College diploma. Most black women who arrived in the cities of the North went to work as maids, cooks and laundresses. The few who found jobs as unskilled laborers in munitions factories, meatpacking plants, rail yards and other industrial operations were placed in the "most dangerous departments" and given "the least desirable jobs at the worst pay." For women seeking something other than domestic work and the grime of factories, Madam Walker offered an alternative. Those who learned "Walker's Scientific Scalp Treatment," her ads promised, could earn "from $15.00 to $40.00 per week" in their own homes or salons. The focus of customer testimonials in Walker Company brochures continued to shift from "hair growing" to business development. "You have opened up a trade for hundreds of our colored women to make an honest and profitable living . . . where they can make as much in one week as a month's salary would bring from any other position a colored woman can secure," wrote Maggie Wilson, Madam Walker's top Pittsburgh agent. In a message designed to appeal to women tired of low-paying jobs, a Mrs. William James declared that with the Walker System she had made as much as $33 in one week. "It is a Godsend to unfortunate women who are walking in the rank and file that I had walked. It has helped us financially since 1910. We have been able to purchase a home and overmeet our obligations."

Their success had also become Madam Walker's success, pushing her annual sales above $100,000, the equivalent of more than $1.5 million in today's dollars. Ransom's midyear 1916 report only increased her excitement: "You don't know how it does my heart good to see the business come up. I am hoping for the million dollar mark in the six years you promised me." Within a decade of selling her first tin of Madam Walker's Wonderful Hair Grower, she confidently informed a reporter that she was "contemplating enlarging her present business into a million dollar corporation."

Harlem's black community welcomed Madam Walker with flattering headlines and offered a receptive and stimulating setting for her increasing involvement in national political issues. Within weeks of her February 1916 arrival, the *Colored American Review*—a magazine she would soon own—featured her on its cover surrounded by a collage of her homes, salon, factory and automobiles. Praising her ability to overcome "handicaps, restrictions and traditions that confront women, especially colored women," it elevated her to "a sphere unique when we consider the businesswoman of to-day." A *New York News* editorial—"Welcome to Madame Walker"—hailed her as a woman who "has risen to command the respect of tens of thousands of both races" and "an inspiring example to every colored girl and woman." In March the *New York Age* trumpeted her move to the city with an effusively complimentary article, drawing attention to her six-figure income and the 10,000 sales agents who sold her products on commission. Recounting the now familiar story of her early struggles, the widely read newspaper provided a ready platform for her self-help philosophy. "I first want to say that I did not succeed by traversing a path strewn with roses. I made great sacrifices, met with rebuff after rebuff, and had to fight hard to put my ideas into effect," Madam Walker proclaimed. "Having a good article for the market is one thing, and putting it properly before the public is another." Equally important to her was her ability to assist other women. "In Greater New York alone, two hundred agents are engaged in promoting 'The Walker System.' I feel that I have done something for the race by making it possible for so many colored women and girls to make money without working hard," she told the *Age* reporter, comparing the daily routines of self-employed Walker agents with the back-wrenching tasks required of field and household workers. Not long afterward, another publication—referring to her speeches on social issues and women's business pursuits—pronounced her "as famous for her lectures as she is for the wonderful preparations which she manufactures and which sell all over the country."

With such an introduction to the community—and with her already well-established reputation as a philanthropist—it is no wonder that the National Association for the Advancement of Colored People approached her for a contribution to the organization's first major antilynching campaign, part of its game plan to force mob violence onto the agenda of a Congress and a President reluctant to acknowledge its horrors. During February 1916, as Madam Walker was settling into her new home, Philip G. Peabody, a wealthy Boston attorney, and son of Judge Charles A. Peabody—pledged $1,000 to the seven-year-old group with the stipulation that it raise an additional $9,000 for the special fund. Peabody's conditional gift was also dependent upon his approval of the association's proposal for "an effective program to stamp out lynching." To Madam Walker's pleasure, her $100 contribution was acknowledged personally by *New York Evening Post* publisher Oswald Garrison Villard, the first NAACP board chairman and grandson of abolitionist William Lloyd Garrison.

It was Villard—spurred by a small group of white activists outraged over both the deadly August 1908 Springfield, Illinois, riot and the general deterioration in race relations—who had used his newspaper to print the February 12, 1909, "call" for the conference that led to the founding of the NAACP. Issued on the centennial of President Abraham Lincoln's birth, the document urged "all the believers in democracy to join in a national conference for the discussion of present evils, the voicing of protests, and the renewal of the struggle for civil and political liberty." More than fifty prominent men and women of both races signed on. Among them were W.E.B. Du Bois (a founder of the all-black Niagara Movement, whose goals paralleled those advocated in the call), journalist Lincoln Steffens, AME Zion bishop Alexander Walters and the iconoclastic William Monroe Trotter. One-third of the signatories were women, including white social reformers Jane Addams, the founder of Chicago's Hull-House, and Mary White Ovington, whose persistence had supplied the impetus for the conference's first planning meeting. Antilynching activist Ida B. Wells-Barnett and NACW founding president Mary Church Terrell were the only black women whose names appeared. All determined to combat lynching, disfranchisement and Jim Crow laws through litigation and political lobbying, the whites—many of whom were Socialists, liberal Jews and social workers—and the blacks—many of whom had backed the initiatives of the four-year-old Niagara Movement—joined forces in an unprecedented biracial coalition.

The previous summer's riot—in the hometown of Lincoln, the Great Emancipator—had "signaled that the race problem was no longer regional—a raw and bloody drama played out behind a magnolia curtain—but national," as characterized by Du Bois biographer David Levering Lewis. After a young black Springfield man was accused of raping a white woman, a large, unruly mob swarmed through the central Illinois town's black neighborhood with clubs and guns, some shouting, "Lincoln freed you, we'll show you where you belong." By the time the National Guard took control, two thousand blacks had been forced from their homes, scores were injured and at least eight people had been killed.

In the eight years since, there had been much to impel Madam Walker's donation to the NAACP's antilynching campaign. In 1915 alone the United States had recorded sixty-nine racially motivated killings. The April 1916 issue of *The Crisis* had "depicted in full-page ghoulishness . . . the group lynching of six black men in Lee County, Georgia." During the previous decade between 1906 and 1915, some 497 African Americans—almost one per week—had been drowned, dismembered, hanged, branded, shot or burned by white marauders. Whether the victims were surreptitiously strung from tree limbs in backwoods or defiantly displayed on main roads, the gruesome images of dangling, mutilated bodies haunted and angered black Americans and sympathetic whites. Having spent the first twenty years of her life in Louisiana and Mississippi—two of the South's deadliest lynching states—Madam Walker knew intimately the fear that gripped communities in the vise of what amounted to "state-sanctioned terrorism." Now as she revisited the region on sales trips, she knew from childhood conditioning that she could not relax her guard.

The decisive motivation for Madam Walker's check, however, may well have been a shocking July 1916 *Crisis* supplement—"The Waco Horror"—that detailed the unusually barbaric torture of Jesse Washington. The savage mid-May murder had galvanized African Americans across the country, providing "the opening wedge" for the association's antilynching fund campaign. Washington—a mentally retarded teenager and farmhand in Robinson, Texas—had confessed to brutally killing his employer's wife with a hammer after she "scolded him for beating the mules." He was so psychologically unbalanced that after the murder he finished his work in a nearby cotton field, then went home to the cabin he shared with his parents and siblings. After his arrest later that day, he was taken to the county jail in Waco, then transferred to Dallas for safekeeping. By Sunday he was back in Waco. The next morning, May 15, as the judge cracked his gavel, several hundred spectators crammed the courtroom while more than two thousand men, women and children congregated outside. Before noon, the jury—which included a convicted murderer—delivered the expected guilty verdict. Within seconds the crowd surged forward, pulling Washington from the courthouse to the street, where he was hitched to a car and dragged until the connecting chain snapped free. As the rabid crowd shredded his clothes, he was stabbed, castrated and clubbed until "his body was a solid color of red." In the meantime, a fire had been set at City Hall at the base of a tree beneath the mayor's office window. Chained to a sturdy limb, the naked Washington was "jerked into the air . . . as rapidly as possible" while "a shout from thousands of throats went up on the morning air," according to Elizabeth Freeman, a white investigator whose account supplied the material for Du Bois's eight-page extra edition. While Washington was lowered repeatedly into the fire, the mayor, the police chief and a horde that had swelled to an estimated 10,000 Texans craned to watch. Later Washington's decapitated corpse was strapped to a horse and paraded through downtown while his "limbs dropped off and . . . some little boys pulled out the teeth and sold them to some men for five dollars apiece." Nauseating photographs of Washington's "ghastly burnt cork husk" graphically exposed the depravity of the monstrous deed.

Intended to raise both money and consciousness, the *Crisis* supplement was mailed to 42,000 subscribers, as well as to all members of Congress, several hundred white newspapers, fifty Negro weeklies and 500 wealthy New Yorkers. From his *Evening Post* office, Villard made a personal appeal to thirty influential editors. Du Bois—influenced by a long tradition of protest journalism from Samuel Cornish and John B. Russwurm's *Freedom's Journal* to William Lloyd Garrison's *Liberator* and Frederick Douglass's *North Star*—knew an opportune moment when he saw one. But this was by no means his initial attempt to goad the public on the issue. Few editions of *The Crisis* had been without articles or items on the country's sorry response to vigilante law, from the magazine's inaugural issue—where Du Bois had written ironically of two murdered Italian-Americans having "the inalienable right of every free American citizen to be lynched"—to a routinely featured tabulation entitled "Colored Men Lynched without Trial." Accompanied by the verse "If blood be the price of liberty, Lord God, we have paid in full," the column tallied 2,732 lynchings—"the standard American industry"—from 1885 through 1914. Because Madam Walker received the magazine, she could well have seen items about eighteen-year-old Iver Peterson of Eufaula, Alabama, who was killed after having been charged with grabbing a white woman, or Will Porter of McLean County, Kentucky, who was seized on the stage of a local opera house, or the Honea Path, South Carolina, man whose lynching posse included a member of the state legislature.

In July—either just before or just after she had sent her donation to the NAACP—Madam Walker received an invitation to an extraordinary conference at Troutbeck, the Amenia, New York, estate of Joel Spingarn, the NAACP board chairman who had replaced Villard in late 1914. "I need not tell you how much we desire your cooperation in the work of the conference, which can hardly attain its real purpose without your presence," read Spingarn's letter of invitation. But previously scheduled travel plans forced Madam Walker to miss the gathering. "Much to my regret, I shall be in Kansas City on that date," she replied on August 13. "However, please accept my assurance that you have and shall have my most hearty cooperation in the spirit and purpose of the conference."

That Madam Walker was among the 200 invited guests signaled her inclusion in a select inner circle chosen to discuss nothing less than the "fundamental rights of the Negro" at the very moment that America's black leadership was realigning itself for a post–Booker T. Washington future. While the setting for the three-day conference was at Spingarn's Dutchess County, New York, estate, it was Du Bois who had engineered the concept and the agenda. He had also vetted the guest list, judiciously choosing men and women, black and white, from across the spectrum of "business, law, medicine, education, politics, scholarship, art" and other fields. "At last the time has come for a frank and free discussion on the part of the leaders of every school of thought, in an endeavor to ascertain the most advanced position that all can agree upon and hold as vantage ground from which to work for new conquests by colored Americans," Du Bois declared in the conference program.

With Washington dead less than a year, the *Crisis* editor wisely and strategically seized the moment to deescalate the suicidal sniping between the two camps, and very possibly to position his organization as first among equals. In a conciliatory gesture earlier that summer, he had prevailed in postponing the NAACP's annual meeting after learning that the date conflicted with a memorial service honoring Washington. As Du Bois assembled the participants for Troutbeck, he reached out to Washington disciples Robert Russa Moton, Emmett Scott and Fred Moore. On the final list was a mix of other conservative Bookerites, activist NAACP supporters and some who were, more or less, neutral, including St. Philip's Church's Hutchens Bishop, Morehouse College president John Hope, former diplomat James Weldon Johnson, Howard University scientist Ernest Just and former Assistant U.S. Attorney William H. Lewis. Among the eleven women who shared two tents on the shore of Spingarn's three-acre pond were Mary Church Terrell, Mary Burnett Talbert, YMCA organizer Addie Hunton and educators Lucy Laney and Nannie Helen Burroughs—women all known to Madam Walker from NACW conventions. Day visitors included Oswald Garrison Villard, New York congressman William S. Bennett, New York governor Charles A. Whitman, Realtor John E. Nail and architect Vertner Tandy. Helen Keller, Lincoln Steffens and Julius Rosenwald were among those invited guests who could not attend. Had Madam Walker been able to adjust her travel plans, she would have benefited as much from the formal addresses as from the camaraderie. In between serious discussions of "the thing which all of us call 'The Problem,'" Du Bois later wrote of the focus on overcoming Jim Crow laws and attitudes, the conferees "swam and rowed and hiked and lingered in the forests and sat upon the hillsides and picked flowers and sang."

"One can hardly realize today how difficult and intricate a matter it was to arrange such a conference, to say who should come and who should not, to gloss over hurts and enmities," Du Bois remembered. "The wall between the Washington camp and those who had opposed his policies was still there." James Weldon Johnson—at the time editor of the Booker T. Washington–allied *New York Age* and later secretary of the NAACP—viewed the gathering as pivotal. "The Amenia Conference came at an hour of exigency and opportunity . . . The great war in Europe, its recoil on America, the ferment in the United States, all conspired to break up the stereotyped conception of the Negro's place that had been increasing in fixity for forty years."

After the conference, Madam Walker was able to read about the group's seven resolutions, including one specifically addressing the partisanship that had long divided many of the conferees: "Antiquated subjects of controversy, ancient suspicions and factional alignments must be eliminated and forgotten if this organization of the race and this practical working understanding of its leaders are to be achieved." An optimistic Du Bois, buoyed by the confirmation that their differences were more "a matter of emphasis" than of objective, pronounced "the Negro race . . . more united and more ready to meet the problems of the world" as a result of the rustic assembly. "We all believed in thrift, we all wanted the Negro to vote, we all wanted the laws enforced, we all wanted assertion of our essential manhood; but how to get those things,—there of course was infinite divergence of opinion."

That the two factions had come together at all was considered a milestone, but "the legacy from Troutbeck was far less one of genuine understanding and real unity than of cosmetic harmony and pragmatic tolerance among the various factions," wrote David Levering Lewis. "It marked a definite shift in the balance of power within black America, a reflection of the increasingly industrial, northern, and national character of the American Dilemma. It affirmed the NAACP's primacy," and did little "in the way of converting veteran Bookerites to the activist goals of the NAACP." The fault lines were too fractured, the fissures too personal to expect more, and Du Bois's allies correctly calculated that the future belonged to them. At any rate, with Democrat Wilson's ascendancy to the White House, Booker T. Washington's political clout had begun to wane even before his death. And changing circumstances, as blacks began a decade-long Northern migration, had rendered many of his strategies out-of-date. Increasingly his approach to education began to seem "anachronistic," wrote historian Nathan Irvin Huggins, because "he encouraged training in obsolete crafts, based the Negro's economic future on a sick and dying southern agriculture [and] ignored the future urban role of Afro-Americans." While Washington's philosophy was rooted in a nineteenth-century agrarian reality, the NAACP, with its Northern roots, had begun to secure its position at the forefront of protest politics and was eager to challenge rather than accommodate and acquiesce.

Du Bois had become familiar with Madam Walker at least as early as the fall of 1911, when the national coverage of the Indianapolis YMCA fund drive had prompted him to include a small item in that December's *Crisis*. The next month Madam Walker's first *Crisis* advertisement—a half-page spread—appeared in the fifteenth issue of the ten-cent publication, which, in just one year, could boast a national circulation of 16,000. (In fact, its rapid growth so concerned Booker T. Washington that he urged Fred Moore to try to increase the *Age*'s circulation to 25,000 readers to keep rival Du Bois from gaining any political edge.) In the June 1914 *Crisis*, Madam Walker's proposal to "found an industrial school in West Pondoland, South Africa" drew a mention, though the project apparently never materialized. Later that year, she was featured in a quarter-page photograph in an article highlighting "large colored donors" to YMCA building funds.

There appears to be no existing correspondence between Du Bois, the Harvard intellectual, and Madam Walker, the self-educated businesswoman, until after 1916. Even then the trove is sparse. Without such letters, it is impossible to pinpoint the time, location or circumstances of their first meeting. But the occasion may have been during the summer of 1914 when both were featured speakers at the NACW's biennial gathering at Wilberforce College. Absent any documents, there also is no way to decipher how Du Bois initially viewed Madam Walker on the Bookerite/NAACP loyalty continuum. In 1916, of course, Madam Walker's contribution to the organization's antilynching drive surely gained his favor. But that same year Madam Walker also had committed her army of sales agents to a major fundraising role for the Washington memorial planned for Tuskegee's campus. "[I] don't want my agents to fall behind any body of women in this rally," she had advised Ransom that April, directing him to prepare a letter of appeal. "It will show to the world that the Walker agents are doing something else other than making money for themselves."

Madam Walker maintained cordial relations with both the conservative and militant circles, declining to pledge exclusive allegiance to either. By refusing to do so, she adopted a stance quite similar to that of many other politically informed black women of the time whose personal alliances through marriage and friendship frequently crisscrossed the ideological spectrum. As early as 1907 the NACW—itself already more than a decade old—had voiced support for the Niagara Movement, the black forerunner of the NAACP. But the fact that Margaret Murray Washington, the NACW president from 1912 to 1916, also happened to be Booker T. Washington's wife complicated the organization's internal politics. By 1910, four NACW members—including one past and two future presidents—had become part of the NAACP's leadership: Mary Church Terrell and Ida B. Wells-Barnett on its executive committee, and Mary Burnett Talbert and Elizabeth Carter on its general committee. In fact, Wells-Barnett and Frances Blascoer, the NAACP's first executive secretary, made a presentation at the NACW's Louisville convention in 1910, though the brilliant Wells-Barnett had been excluded from some early NACW activities because of her uncompromising, often argumentative personality. Members of both groups cooperated at the Hampton biennial in 1912 in their efforts to commute the sentence of Virginia Christian, the teenaged laundress who had killed her employer. By 1914 the NACW's Department for the Suppression of Lynchings had joined forces with the NAACP and others to make lynching "an American embarrassment," then allocated $100 for the NAACP's antilynching fund during the 1916 biennial in Baltimore. During the same session the women also voted to raise $1,000 for the Booker T. Washington memorial. While the men may have been inclined to draw staunch lines of demarcation, the women's barriers seemed more permeable and flexible, though no less principled.

Madam Walker greatly admired Mary Burnett Talbert, the NACW's sixth president and an early NAACP member in whose Buffalo, New York, home some of the radical Niagara Movement members had met during the time of their 1905 organizational meeting in Canada. As a leader of both groups, Talbert simultaneously organized activities and recruited members for the NACW and the NAACP as she traveled around the country on their behalf.

Madam Walker also deepened a personal friendship with Elizabeth Carter, another NACW president, when she visited Carter's New Bedford, Massachusetts, home during the fall of 1914. Both a teacher and the founding president of the racially integrated New Bedford Home for Aged People, Carter had displayed a militant streak during the summer of 1914. Responding to the widespread belief that President Wilson's wife, Ellen, had been a catalyst for racial segregation in federal facilities, Carter had objected to sending a letter of condolence from the NACW to the President when Mrs. Wilson coincidentally died during the organization's 1914 convention.

After Booker T. Washington's death, even the National Negro Business League showed signs of change. At the August 1916 convention, Madam Walker was just as comfortable paying tribute to Washington as she was hearing NAACP investigator Elizabeth Freeman's address on lynchings. As Madam Walker presented her stereopticon slides—now at the enthusiastic invitation of Emmett Scott—she fervently announced, "I never shall forget or cease to be grateful for the inspiration I received from the life and teaching of that grand hero of our Race, whose every thought and word and deed was for the uplift of the Negro—our own DR. BOOKER T. WASHING-TON!" Freeman's presence at the meeting showed that at least some of the barriers—by necessity and pragmatic expediency—were gradually coming down. "I am here in the interest of the NAACP to start a crusade against the modern barbarism of lynching human beings," said Freeman. "Your honored and lamented leader, Dr. Booker T. Washington, did much to awaken public sentiment against this new form of anarchy, termed 'lynching,'" she said, though some had argued that he had not protested forcefully enough. "But there yet remains much for us to do if we would curb this heinous disrespect of law and order and put an end to the dangerous practice of lynching human beings."

Like many other African Americans who straddled nineteenth- and twentieth-century America, Madam Walker was evolving with the times, adopting a more militant and politically assertive posture. During the Wilson administration, as domestic civil rights battles intensified and the international drama of war inched closer to the United States, Madam Walker would soon find herself among those in the forefront of the protest, lashing out against injustice and denouncing the mind-set that tolerated lynching. Her money and celebrity, as well as her ability to use both as tools for political activism, provided Madam Walker with an advantage that few other African American women—regardless of educational background or social status—could claim.

Southern Tour

— ❧ —

W ithin weeks of arriving in New York, Madam Walker conceived a brilliant plan: convene a national gathering of all Walker agents and beauty culturists to exchange business ideas, learn new hair care methods and compete for prizes and awards. By April 1916 she was busily organizing Lelia's 200 New York area agents into the first chapter of the Madam C. J. Walker Benevolent Association. Her mission was twofold: to show them how to increase their sales and to persuade them that contributing to charitable causes like the $2 million Booker T. Washington Memorial Fund was good for business. Through her memberships in the Court of Calanthe, the Mite Missionary Society and the National Association of Colored Women, Madam Walker had observed the power of women's collective action. Her agents—with few exceptions—were not the educated elite of the NACW or the wives of prominent men, but women who, nonetheless, had begun to savor economic success and independence. She believed they could be just as effective, if not more so, than other women's groups. Because they had been drawn together by the promise of financial rewards, she knew they were already highly motivated. Now she wanted to encourage them to harness their prosperity for improving their communities. What Madam Walker had gained in public recognition and admiration as an individual donor to Tuskegee and the YMCA, she wanted for her agents. With a national body of Walker representatives she could channel their combined muscle, buttressing the moral suasion and political rhetoric of groups like the NACW with the financial clout of businesswomen. Madam Walker envisioned what few had ever imagined: an enterprise on a grand scale controlled by black women with political and civic objectives.

Certainly other women had developed large companies and created fortunes before hers. Henrietta "Hetty" Green—called the "witch of Wall Street" because of her miserliness—would die later that year with an estate of $100 million. Annual sales of Lydia Pinkham's patent medicine tonic had reached $300,000 by the time of her death in 1883. Other direct-sales companies had preceded Madam Walker's. Avon, founded as the California Perfume Company in 1886, counted 10,000 door-to-door sales agents by 1903. The Fuller Brush Company, manufacturers of high-quality cleaning supplies, had been established in 1906—the same year as the Madam C. J. Walker Manufacturing Company. Its founder, Alfred C. Fuller, watched sales leap from $30,000 in 1910 to $250,000 in 1917 and $1 million in 1919. And of course Annie Pope-Turnbo Malone's Poro Company, Madam Walker's former employer, had been a pioneer of commission sales. All had their merits, but none had proposed what Madam Walker was now creating: a national sales force expressly organized around the principles of corporate responsibility, social betterment and racial justice.

Initially Ransom viewed her grand scheme with skepticism, believing that she planned to offer life insurance and burial policies for her saleswomen. "I think you misunderstood my meaning. I didn't mean to organize as a Fraternal Society," she corrected Ransom. "I meant to organize clubs all over the country, and at some time call a meeting of all the agents and form a National which would be similar to the Women's federated clubs." Uninterested in the entanglements of collecting local dues, she imagined a decentralized structure where "there would be no handling of money other than just to pay for literature and the like. Each club will handle its own money." Instead she meant to set up chapters in any town with "at least five agents" who would "come together and organize . . . for mutual protection and . . . charity work." As an incentive, she proposed annual prizes for state organizations with the most new agents, the highest sales and the most generous philanthropy. As well, she planned to hire a few carefully selected women whose exemplary leadership qualities had prepared them to "treat, teach, and organize." For the generous monthly salary of $125, she also expected them to deliver slide lectures on "The Negro Woman in Business" just as she was doing. At $1,500 a year, the pay was almost double the average annual wage for nonfarm workers, nearly $300 more than an executive-level federal employee and more than four times the average $337 paid that year to white public school teachers, who almost always took home more in their payroll envelopes than their black counterparts.

As Madam Walker prepared a spring sweep through the South, her central focus had become recruiting agents for her new association. Kicking off her tour in mid-April 1916, she reached the region as the dogwood trees were in full bloom. "An enthusiastic audience" greeted her at Salisbury, North Carolina's Livingstone College, one of the many campuses she had added to her itinerary. "I was very much flattered Sunday night at the splendid turn out to hear my lecture. Both white and colored came," she wrote with satisfaction. "They were all loud in their praise [and] frequently interrupted my lecture with loud and long applause."

Continuing her blitz across the Southeast, she arrived in Tuskegee later that week to visit the still-mourning Margaret Murray Washington. No longer an outsider among Tuskegee's leadership—having royally entertained Robert Russa Moton, its new president, in her Indianapolis home exactly a year earlier—she appeared before the students and faculty as an honored guest. Soon afterward she initiated a bold, behind-the-scenes campaign to gain appointment to the school's board of trustees. "I fear you might [think] me egotistical, [but] that has been the one desire of my life," she confided to Mr. Ransom, wishing for him to gauge Moton's receptivity on her behalf. "If Mr. Washington had lived I am sure it would come in time. I have been asked it by many smaller schools, but they will not mean as much to me." Still she knew such a suggestion would require powerful persuasion if she were to join the likes of Theodore Roosevelt, Julius Rosenwald and several wealthy white New York and Alabama businessmen, as well as President Moton and Tuskegee treasurer Warren Logan, two of the three black members. "Of course I know there are no women on the Board, but I believe if it is put up to them strong enough they will think kindly of it for I am now doing more for it than many who are on the Board," she wrote, confident that her contributions since 1912—as well as her efforts on behalf of the Washington Memorial Fund—had accumulated into a respectable sum. "After I build my home I mean to give them $1,000 per year. But I do think it is worth some recognition," she said without modesty.

That September, Madam Walker's $300 contribution to the school paved the way for Ransom's discreet query regarding the seat made vacant earlier that month by the death of board chairman Seth Low, a former Columbia University president and New York City mayor. "I am writing to suggest the name of a person, not to take Mr. Low's place, but one who is in every way worthy of a place on such a Board and the appointing of whom . . . would mean so much to your great institution," Ransom ventured a few days after receiving Emmett Scott's "grateful" acknowledgment of the scholarship gift. "The name that I would suggest is Madam C. J. Walker." Ever the circumspect lieutenant, he added, "You understand that I have made this suggestion without the knowledge of Madam Walker."

Moton delicately replied that while he and the school had "the highest respect for Madame Walker," he was "of the opinion that there is a certain custom to keep the balance on the Board of Trustees about as it has been hitherto, that is to say, filling the place of white men with white men." Even more to the point, he preferred "a man as near as possible to Mr. Low's type, a man of Mr. Low's spirit and wealth [and] business ability." In other words, a man capable of building the kind of magnificent, million-dollar library that Low had provided for Columbia University. "[T]hat is what Tuskegee needs just now. In the meantime I shall keep the Madame in mind, and I need not tell you it would give us a great deal of pleasure to have such a person on our board," he wrote, without commitment, but ever mindful of her past and potential contributions.

During April and May, Madam Walker barnstormed Alabama, Georgia, Tennessee, Kentucky and Indiana, juggling invitations to speak at black colleges, fraternal conferences, religious gatherings and prestigious churches, including "a packed house" at Reverend Peter James Bryant's renowned Wheat Street Baptist Church in Atlanta. After brief stays at her homes in Indianapolis and Harlem, she was off again in her touring car toward New England, stopping in New Haven during Yale's commencement week, then New London, Boston and Springfield as she cultivated local agents' clubs and signed up delegates for her forthcoming convention. At summer's end, Madam Walker crossed the Mason-Dixon Line again to make what she called "her last tour of the South" from Florida to Kentucky, from North Carolina to as far west as Texas and Oklahoma. In a carefully coordinated promotional drive, Ransom arranged for advertisements in local Negro papers the weeks before and during her arrival. Along the way Madam Walker tailored her message to appeal to women trapped in menial jobs and tied to communities suffering from the back-to-back boll weevil infestations of 1915 and 1916. Financial independence was her message for eager ears: "Open Your Own Shop. Secure Prosperity and Freedom. Many women of all ages who had despaired for years of acquiring success, confronted with the problem of earning a livelihood, have mastered the Walker System." For the new edition of her annual Walker Company brochure she advised Ransom to shift the emphasis from "hair work" to team building and community involvement: "We do not want to lay as much stress on the growing as we do on what the agents are doing." Regarding material promoting the national convention, she wrote, "In those circulars I wish you would use the words 'our' and 'we' instead of 'I' and 'my' . . . Address them as 'Dear Friend.'"

During mid-September, Madam Walker pronounced her National Baptist Convention speech—"From the Kitchen to the Mansion"—a "howling success in that I have been able to get before thousands of people." With nearly three million members—more than 60 percent of them women—the NBC was the largest black organization in the country by 1916, with more members than either of the two most prominent white Baptist groups, which had split apart prior to the Civil War. Madam Walker particularly relished the reception she received in Savannah from NBC president Reverend Elias Camp Morris and S. Willie Layten, president of the group's fiercely autonomous Women's Auxiliary. "All the big guns have shown me the greatest courtesies and kindness," she noted with glee. Madam Walker also had encountered "the Poro woman"—very possibly Annie Malone herself—in the convention hall. Noting that her competitor was "only in evidence by pinning tags on anyone who will allow them as they pass by," she allowed herself a moment of devilish gloating.

From Savannah, Madam Walker traveled to Augusta, then had a brief layover in the small farming community of Washington, Georgia. Although she reported "quite a deal of success here with the work," she "found so many poor people" who could not raise the $25 fee she now charged for her course that she "decided to let them have the trade for $10," supplying them with a "half dozen each of grower, Glossine, shampoo and comb. I put them on their honor to pay where they can."

She reached Atlanta in early October within days of Mae's arrival at Spelman Seminary, the all-female school founded in 1881 by two devoted white New England teachers. Initially called the Atlanta Baptist Female Seminary—the sister school to the Atlanta Baptist Seminary (later More-house College)—its "primary aim was to provide training for teachers, missionaries and church workers." In honor of the generosity of its first major benefactor—the religiously pious and astronomically wealthy Baptist John D. Rockefeller—the church boards that oversaw the school voted to change the name in 1884 to honor the parents of Rockefeller's wife, Laura Spelman Rockefeller. By 1916, Spelman had added to its ranks many daughters of the black elite during an era when only about 5 percent of Americans between the ages of eighteen and twenty-one were enrolled in a college, university or female seminary like Spelman. Among the 768 students was Laura Murray Washington, Margaret Murray Washington's niece, whom she and her husband had adopted in 1904 after the death of Laura's parents. It was Margaret Washington, in fact, who had suggested that Mae join Laura on the Georgia campus. Upon receiving Lelia's request to enroll Mae, Spelman's third president, Lucy Hale Tapley, solicited a reference from Margaret Washington in part because the seventeen-year-old Mae had not attended school for more than four years. Assured by Washington that she knew Mae "very well"—having just seen her during the summer—she added, "I know Mrs. Walker cares for and protects her. I am sure that she has good health while I do not know much about her disposition."

To enhance Mae's chances for acceptance, Madam Walker had prevailed upon Reverend James W. Brown, her pastor at Harlem's influential Mother AME Zion Church, to draft a recommendation on her granddaughter's behalf. "It gives me great pleasure to place in the hands of the bearer, Miss Mae Robinson, this letter of introduction, and at the same time to bear testimony of her good character," he wrote Tapley. "Fortune has favored her with a good home, and with the very best family and social connections. Mme. C. J. Walker, her grandmother, is a member in good standing in this church, and being her pastor, I have had an opportunity to come in close touch with the home life of every member of the family." AME Zion bishop Alexander Walters—an NAACP vice president and founder who was well known for his progressive attitudes toward women's rights—also lobbied on Mae's behalf. "Miss Robinson has a most amiable disposition, is modest, docile, ambitious and industrious, besides having had the advantage of training by her very worthy and capable grandmother and mother," he waxed with the requisite hyperbole reserved for such testimonials. "I am sure you will find her a most welcome addition to your body of students and that she will reflect credit on your school should she have the good fortune to study there."

On the application, Lelia called Mae both "honest and industrious" and in "perfect" health, though Mae may well have been experiencing some of the early diabetes symptoms that were to plague her throughout her adult life. At the time, however, Spelman officials likely were more concerned about tuberculosis and other communicable diseases. As explanation for Mae's lack of schooling since 1912, Lelia offered the commendable excuse that she had been "managing our business." Just a few weeks before Mae's eighteenth birthday, she entered the High School Department's academic English-Latin curriculum with plans to study music as well, finally fulfilling the Walkers' promise to Sarah Etta Bryant that her daughter would receive a formal education. By year's end, Dean Edith Brill praised Mae's "pleasing personality," as well as her academic performance. "We felt that she developed well for a first year. We are always anxious to give the best training possible for a life of usefulness, and to have students who desire that training and respond to our efforts," the earnest Brill wrote to Lelia. A classmate later recalled that Mae was "always very pleasant [and] she had a nice smile." Like many other young Spelman women, she eagerly anticipated campus concerts and the "social affairs" when "the Morehouse boys came over."

With Mae settled, Madam Walker headed west to Birmingham and Montgomery on her ambitious crusade to train hundreds more agents in time for her August 1917 assembly. In Mississippi she once again made her base in Jackson, where she was comfortably hosted by Ransom's father-in-law, Diamond Cox, a revered teacher and early member of the NAACP. From there, she and Louise Thompson, her recently hired traveling assistant, radiated across the state like General Sherman, charging forth to Meridian, Greenwood, Natchez, Clarksdale, Vicksburg and smaller towns in between during a hectic and exhausting four weeks. With long days of training sessions and late but enjoyable nights of speeches, receptions and dinners, Madam Walker and Louise averaged three or four days in each town. During some weeks, the pace quickened. "We are only making two day stops and have such little time to do our corresponding," she groused. But she could not complain about the large crowds who came to hear her lectures, which she often wisely scheduled on alternate nights at both the local Baptist and Methodist churches. "I truly made a hit in Natchez and am sure we'll get some good business from there," she wrote Ransom, elated over the welcome extended her by Henry and Albert Dumas, brothers who were both physicians and pharmacists. They "vied with each other in showing us every courtesy. [They] not only refused to take pay for our room and board, but carriage hire, medicine, professional services and even advertising. I never have met such people before in all my life [for them] to be strangers."

But it was her late-October side trip to Louisiana that surely touched her most deeply. "Went to my home in Delta yesterday and came back to Vicksburg and gave a lecture at Bethel Church to a very appreciative audience," she wrote Ransom the following day. Despite what must have been a nostalgic homecoming, she apparently was too rushed, as usual, to reflect upon the emotions she felt upon seeing her childhood cabin and the cotton fields where she and her parents had worked. In her letter to Ransom she mentioned no reunion with childhood friends and gave no introspective account of her memories. But the visit mattered enough that she preserved a clipping from the white Louisiana newspaper that had reported her return to the plantation of her birth. "World's Richest Negress in Delta," read the headline.

> Delta was honored Sunday by a visit of the richest negro woman in the world, C. J. Walker, proprietress of a hair straightener remedy. She was born Winnie Breedlove, a daughter of Owen Breedlove, a slave owned by Mr. Robert Burney. She came here to see the place of her nativity, and to call on Mrs. George M. Long, the only daughter of Mr. Burney living here. Mrs. Long has a childhood recollection of Owen Breedlove being one of the "lead hands" of her father. The visitor was very quiet and unassuming and a fine example to her race.

Apparently the meeting between old acquaintances was cordial, even pleasant, because Anna Burney Long's daughter visited Madam Walker two years later in New York. But she could not have been happy with the fact that the paper had called her a "Negress" rather than "Madam," misstated her birth name and insisted on not capitalizing the "N" in "Negro." Nor did she fail to notice the condescending tone that described her as "quiet and unassuming" and therefore "a fine example to her race." She was anything but "quiet and unassuming," and soon afterward told another newspaper, "The report that I advertise to take the kink out of Negro's hair is not true. I guarantee to make hair grow for them."

Within days of her triumphant Delta return, Ransom forwarded an unusual request: "I am enclosing a signature card from the Fletcher American Bank," he wrote. "They asked me to send same to you as you have improved so much in your penmanship since you signed the card they now have on file, until whenever a check comes in signed by you, they call me over to identify your signature before paying same." For someone who had been denied even the most rudimentary education, recognition of such identifiable personal improvement was all the more ironic because of its timing so close to the moment when she had just retraced the paths of her childhood.

But her euphoria was suddenly tempered by a near-tragedy. A few days before Thanksgiving, she and Louise Thompson almost lost their lives as they were being driven across a railroad intersection in northwestern Mississippi. "We had a narrow escape from death Tuesday in Clarksdale. As soon as the car we were in got on the track we heard a man yelling 'get out of the way,'" Madam recounted anxiously. "We looked around in time to see a freight train backing down on us, not a bell ringing or anything. The chauffeur in the nick of time put on more gas and shot forward. The train all but grazed the back of the car in which we were riding. I haven't been myself since."

Still shaken when she reached Memphis the next night, she was relieved to be met by her friend Bishop William T. Vernon, the former U.S. Treasury official whom she had met in Denver a decade earlier. "I arrived here sick Wednesday night and Dr. Vernon had a [doctor] for me right away. [H]e patched me up so I could give my lecture last night. I am feeling some[what] better to-day." But the physician was so concerned about a spike in her blood pressure that he insisted she cancel all remaining Tennessee commitments and "take not less than six weeks rest." Heeding his advice, she told Ransom, "I think instead of coming home I will go to Hot Springs where I can really get rest and quietude." Panicked at Madam Walker's fragile physical state, Louise inserted her own personal note before sealing the envelope: "Mme. really frightened me last night, Mr. Ransom. She was so very ill. I am so glad she has been persuaded to take this much needed rest."

Despite her fatigue, she labored through a second speech that Friday evening at Vernon's Avery Chapel AME. "I was so ill that I feared I couldn't make it, but made up my mind I would and did," wrote a determined Madam Walker. The next day Louise typed an alarming note beneath the message Madam Walker had dictated: "To-day the doctor told me she was on the verge of a nervous breakdown . . . You keep telling her after she gets to Hot Springs to remain there for six weeks." And although Madam Walker had vowed "to give my mind a real rest," she was too driven to curtail her activities. Even with the recent addition to her traveling staff of Alice Burnette—a highly capable former Jackson, Mississippi, schoolteacher—she fretted, "I don't know if they will be able to get along without me or not."

Two days later, Madam Walker checked into the Pythian Hotel and Bath House, the well-appointed two-year-old Hot Springs, Arkansas, hospital and spa owned by the black Knights of Pythias. Nestled among the densely wooded Ouachita Hills and Diamond Lakes of western Arkansas, the town drew patients and tourists eager to "take the waters" from its healing thermal springs, as well as gamblers and gangsters lured by its blackjack tables and racetrack. Like its white counterparts at the eight elegant European-style bathhouses along Central Avenue, the seventy-room, three-story Pythian on Malvern Avenue promised to administer care and cures for every ailment from rheumatism and gout, to arthritis and ulcers.

The "nervousness" that the Memphis doctor had noticed was brought on by overexertion from Madam Walker's ambitious and wearying recruitment trip, as well as the trauma and adrenaline rush of the train mishap. But she was also suffering from hypertension and the early but not yet diagnosed stages of kidney disease. Consistent with conventional medical practices of the time, Dr. Vernon's physician had prescribed a visit to Hot Springs in the belief that the heated baths would temporarily lower her blood pressure by dilating her blood vessels and eliminating toxins from her system. And although the baths had no lasting effect on her condition, she benefited from the pampering she received and the relaxing atmosphere. "I promise you I am going to let all business alone and look strictly after my health except little things which I am going to write to you about now. Ha. Ha," she joked with Ransom. Unable to extricate herself completely from her work, she continued to devise business schemes. "In reference to the salaries. While I fully appreciate what you say . . . I have decided long ago that I will not allow my help to dictate to me as to how I shall run my business, and how much I shall pay this or that one." Recalling a debate she had had with a former bookkeeper, she reminded Ransom of her philosophy toward rewarding "brain work" and manual labor. "I take the stand that laborious work such as [is] done in my factory is worth more than the office work. You would find many persons who have been trained for office [work] and could fill any one of their places much eas[ier] than you could Miss Kelly's, for everybody is looking for an easy job."

From her Pythian suite, she was also outlining plans to install her hair culture course in several black schools with vocational curricula, among them Pensacola's Normal Industrial and Agricultural College, Jacksonville's Florida Baptist Academy and Marshall, Texas's Wiley University. In exchange for $100 to furnish a training facility with running water, a basin and worktables, she proposed placing a Walker agent on the faculty. After the schools had paid for the teacher's course at Lelia College in New York and purchased a full line of products, Madam Walker suggested that the fee for "treatments be divided equally between the school and the agent."

Without hesitation, her friend Mary McLeod Bethune embraced the proposal for her Daytona Normal and Industrial Institute for Negro Girls. "For the past four years my girls and myself have been using your Wonderful Hair Grower . . . and would be very glad to place it in our school as a course of study," she wrote. Charlotte Hawkins Brown, whose fourteen-year-old Palmer Memorial Institute in Sedalia, North Carolina, was one of the state's only accredited black high schools, was interested as well. "I shall be glad to talk this matter over with you when I pass through N.Y. next week. I am sure that some of the requirements could not be met out here in the country, as there is no running water etc. I do think that some arrangements could be made, however," she wrote, always with an eye to raising extra funds to operate her struggling institution.

After an all too short visit from her friend and factory forelady Alice Kelly—"Alice is so dear and jovial that I think her visit with me did me as much good as the baths"—Madam Walker moved to the home of her local physician, Dr. James Webb Curtis, and his wife, Alice, for the Christmas holidays. Soon afterward, a local reporter learned of her recent purchase of four and a half acres in exclusive Irvington-on-Hudson, New York, twenty miles north of Manhattan in America's wealthiest residential community. Having abandoned her plans to occupy Bishop Derrick's former home, Madam Walker had already begun to review Vertner Tandy's specifications for a mansion to be built not far from John D. Rockefeller's Hudson River estate. "Negro Woman Gets in Society Addition," read the Hot Springs headline. "Will Build Herself $100,000 Home Next to America's Oil King—Hair Grower on Negro's Heads and Oil Magnate Will Be Neighbors If Plan Goes Through as Arranged." Blueprints awaited her in New York.

For the new year, Madam Walker looked forward to a special treat. Lelia's doctor, she informed Ransom, had "ordered her to Hot Springs. She will be here the first of January." What Ransom also knew was that mother and daughter had another dispute to resolve. In November, just prior to Madam Walker's close encounter with the train, she had proposed that Lelia forward all New York mail-order business to Indianapolis. With 700 agents in New York, Pennsylvania, Rhode Island and New Jersey—and the volume of sales that number represented—Lelia immediately panicked about how the lost revenue would affect her ability to meet her Harlem town house mortgage. Mother "may as well take [the house] now as to tell me to send the orders to Indianapolis to be filled, because as the people realize the preparation is coming from Indianapolis they will send directly there instead of sending to me." Her business, she complained, was slower in the winter than during the bumper summer months, fluctuating between $50 and $350 a week from season to season. And certainly while the weather legitimately affected her sales—because heat and humidity rendered the clients' hair more unmanageable than usual—Lelia lacked the hustle and hunger of her mother to make up the shortfall.

"I know mother is the best hearted person on earth," she replied to Ransom's consoling letter after her mother had threatened to transfer the mailorder operation. "All the same my feelings should be considered. Mother reminds me of the story of the cow who gives the good pail of milk and then kicks it over. If I am to be confronted with this house or threatened with the loss of it every time it pleases mother I cannot enjoy it and would rather not have it," Lelia ranted.

"Mother is just like an impulsive baby. I am no Breedlove. I am a McWilliams and that impulsiveness does not run in my blood," she grumbled. But of course both women could be equally impulsive. "Mother rules with an iron hand and forces her opinion upon me regardless of what I may think."

Because Lelia relied so heavily upon her mother, she had unwittingly relinquished much of her own autonomy. "I do not want to be dependent upon anyone," she confided to Ransom, who once again found himself thrust into the role of mediator. "Mother is willing to do anything for me, but I want to have enough independence to settle my own bills. Whenever I am entirely dependent upon mother as you say there will certainly be a clash."

In her frustration, Lelia proposed a solution that she thought would decrease the chance for conflict. "If mother and I should have any controversy I would far rather move away to some little Western town, Oakland, California, for instance, open a Hair Parlor there and buy my preparations from mother and have peace of mind and freedom," Lelia declared. "Contentment in a two room flat beats being pulled by the nape of my neck, whether it be sister, brother, husband or mother."

During their visit together, Lelia calmed down. With her mother on the road so much of the time, their communication—often conveyed through Ransom—was sporadic, disjointed and garbled. Madam Walker was so absorbed in her business that she overcompensated by spoiling Lelia with material substitutes, alternately tightening and loosening the purse strings. Inevitably, Ransom was caught in the cross fire. "You misunderstood me concerning Lelia, Mr. Ransom," she wrote in the midst of the mail-order flap. "I don't expect to have her give an account of the money she spends when I am giving it to her to do with as she wills. I shall let her keep her agents until I return." But access to her mother's bank account did not prevent Lelia from feeling isolated and abandoned. "With all of this big house and a nice income and above all a wonderful mother, I am so alone in the world," Lelia whined in a moment of depression and self-pity some months later.

But as mother and daughter said good-bye in Hot Springs, they had patched up their differences and agreed on Lelia's proposal to add southern Florida and Cuba to her territory. Eight weeks later, during March 1917, Lelia was in Havana, reveling in her newfound freedom. Cuba "is the most picturesque place on earth, I do believe," she wrote Ransom of her "wonderful trip." When she returned to Harlem later that month, she discovered two pieces of good news: sales were up and her mother had come to her rescue once again. "Mother is a brick to pay off that mortgage is all that I can say," she wrote of her loan on 108 and 110. She was overjoyed that her increased revenues would now allow her to do something nice for her mother in return. "If my business keeps up at this rate, I will be able to pay mother back in about one year and a half," she boasted proudly in a letter to Ransom. "You were right not to say anything to mother about what I was making, because when she comes home I want to surprise her. I want to be able to hand her a nice little sum." But within weeks Lelia felt her mother's interfering hand once again. "I am so afraid of having an argument, and I do not want mother to think I am obstinate, but Mr. Ransom, you realize my work is a separate business and it is very hard to work it as mother would have me do without messing everything up. Please try to make mother see it in the right light," she pleaded. "I am so afraid of 'getting in wrong' with mother."

After her recuperation in Hot Springs, Madam Walker resumed her Southern tour, blanketing several towns in Arkansas; New Orleans, Baton Rouge and Bogalusa in Louisiana; and Temple, Austin, San Marcos, Seguin, San Antonio, Houston, Beaumont and Orange in Texas, all during the first quarter of 1917. In April and May she returned to Tennessee, Kentucky and Indiana, then struck out for North Carolina and South Carolina before returning to New York in early June. "At the rate you are now going, we have now but five years before you will be rated as a millionaire, and I feel that every energy ought to be bent in that direction," Ransom wrote as she continued her dizzying crusade.

The more Madam Walker flourished, the more adversarial her rift with Annie Pope-Turnbo Malone grew. Not content simply to push her own products, Malone had begun to criticize Madam Walker's use of the metal hot comb, contending that the Poro System's disc-shaped hair pullers and pressing irons were the superior method for drying and straightening hair. In one Poro brochure, Malone had gone so far as to write, "Straightening Combs are not sold. Pressing Irons give best results." Despite her intention to discredit Madam Walker's system, Malone had inadvertently admitted that some of her customers were requesting the metal comb that Madam Walker believed left her customers' hair with a fuller, more natural and less flattened look.

Malone, whose company was growing as rapidly as Madam Walker's, deeply resented her rival's rise. In contrast, Madam Walker went out of her way, in public at least, to downplay their conflicts. When asked by a reporter about "the ill feeling" that had developed, Madam Walker declared that she wished "the banishment of the unpleasant feeling, that the past be forgotten whatever it held and that friendship should exist" between them. "We are succeeding and that should be sufficient," Madam Walker told the St. Louis Argus, Malone's hometown newspaper, after their squabbles had erupted in public during May when both women coincidentally appeared at Reverend Charles Parrish's church in Louisville and Madam Walker's Bethel AME in Indianapolis. "That the two women were not on the best terms was seen at the Indianapolis meeting," noted reporter William Lewis. Although Madam Walker offered to have her bookkeeper "preside at the piano" to assist Malone's program at Bethel, Malone dismissed her offer. To the audience Madam's gesture in her home church appeared gracious—"an olive branch of peace," said one observer—providing her with a public relations coup. Whether Madam Walker was truly as magnanimous as Lewis portrayed her, she was savvy enough to know that the snub had made Malone appear petty and unreasonable. "Mrs. Malone was very ugly and showed her hand, which killed her influence in Indianapolis forever and a day," Madam Walker later told Alice Burnette, her traveling agent.

Malone's bitterness was compounded by her private difficulties with Aaron Malone, the husband whose mental abuse would eventually lead to a costly divorce. Madam Walker, of course, had had her own troubles with men. But C. J. Walker—embarrassing and annoying as he had become— was her ex-husband, jettisoned before he could do serious damage to her company or her psyche. Aaron Malone, on the other hand, had begun to publicly humiliate his wife and interfere with her financial interests. Those who knew her well could see that it was exacting a personal toll.

For now, Madam Walker—who had been away from Harlem for most of the past year—had more important matters before her. She was eager to consult with Tandy about the contractor for her Westchester County home and to meet with Realtor John Nail to inspect the luxury Central Park West apartments he had purchased in Manhattan as an investment on her behalf. As well, she was anxious about the wartime restrictions that had been imposed on businesses like hers now that President Wilson had signed the resolution committing American troops to the battlefields of Europe. The summer of 1917 would also bring unexpected conflict on the domestic front—a deadly race riot that she and other African Americans had long feared.

CHAPTER 17

"We Should Protest"

— *◦✓ↀ◦* —

J ust as Madam Walker was returning to Harlem in mid-June 1917, Reverend Hutchens Bishop opened the doors of his elegant St. Philip's Church for a decidedly inelegant purpose: a mass meeting to decry "the frequency of lynching" in America. Even as tens of thousands of African Americans were enlisting in the Army "to do their bit to make the world safe for democracy" in the war against Germany, they were still subject to Jim Crow laws and vigilantism. Responding to what they called "the recent horror"—the murder of Eli Persons, who had been burned alive a month earlier in Memphis—the assembly vowed to stage a public protest so impressive that it would signal the "new spirit of the new Negro."

Less than two weeks later, on July 2, a race riot, far worse than the 1908 Springfield rampage, erupted in East St. Louis, Illinois, a polluted "industrial slum" still reeling from yearlong labor strikes and lockouts. Directly across the Mississippi River from St. Louis, where Madam Walker had lived for sixteen years, East St. Louis was a town whose streets and houses she knew well, a community in which she counted both friends and former laundry customers. The headline in the next morning's *New York Times*—hawked from street corners all over Manhattan—was ominous: "Race Rioters Fire East St. Louis and Shoot or Hang Many Negroes; Dead Estimated at from 20 to 75—Many Bodies in the Ruins." Because Madam Walker was so familiar with the area, she had no trouble imagining the horrible scene: smoldering buildings and the sickly sweet stench of incinerated flesh clinging to the smoky air. By the time the state militia restored order that night, the Illinois State's Attorney estimated the death toll at 250. And although that number turned out to have been wildly inflated, those initial reports fueled conspiracy theories that the attacks were part of a grand design to scare blacks away from Northern cities. In the end few could agree on the number of dead, but at least thirty-nine blacks and eight whites lay in the morgue after what one historian has called the "first American pogrom."

The seeds for calamity had been germinating for months. Home to the sprawling Swift and Armour meatpacking plants, as well as the Aluminum Ore Company, this southern Illinois river community had become snagged in a fight between union organizers and resistant plant managers just as wartime demand for their products swelled. Long a haven for graft and vice—with only sixty-three police officers to monitor a population of 75,000—East St. Louis's dives, pool halls and gambling dens operated unscathed. Because factory owners had manipulated zoning laws to avoid paying municipal taxes on their multimillion-dollar enterprises, the town had few sources of revenue other than licensing fees from its 376 saloons.

The shortage of workers—exacerbated by the precipitous drop in European immigration after the start of the war—had brought a rapid influx of black laborers to fill the vacuum. Like Pied Pipers, aggressive recruiters traveled through the South waving free tickets and signing up so many black men for the low-level but relatively well-paying jobs that Southern plantation owners and elected officials became as concerned about the departure of their workforce as Northern union bosses became about their arrival. For those who boarded Illinois-bound trains to take jobs "loading box cars, handling crates of meat and lard, and pushing trucks," the future looked infinitely more desirable than the drudgery of never-profitable peonage farming. That the new arrivals were filling some of the strikers' jobs only heightened the tension.

At the Aluminum Ore Company alone the number of black employees had risen dramatically from a dozen porters in 1914 to 470 industrial line workers—almost a quarter of the plant's total workforce—by the spring of 1917. But while the majority of the Aluminum Ore strikebreakers were white, the locked-out union workers focused their anger on the more easily identifiable blacks who had filled about 200 vacant slots. Union leaders goaded the strikers by fabricating stories that the company managers intended to turn East St. Louis into "a Negro town" by importing more than ten thousand black men and their families. By late June, after months of minor racial skirmishes—including a May confrontation that left three whites and three blacks wounded by gunfire and several black businesses ransacked—the city was primed for violence. Already riled by rumors of a July 4 race war, the townspeople found themselves too immersed in the deadly brew of hatred and retaliation to prevent it from boiling over.

Before midnight on July 1, a group of white men in a Model T–era Ford peppered several homes in a black neighborhood with gunfire. When the marauders sped through the block a second time, the residents fired back, striking the car as it raced off into the shadows beneath a moon "almost, if not quite full." Soon afterward, local police cruised by in a dark, unmarked Ford with dim headlights that closely resembled the attackers' car. In a case of mistaken identity, the men inside the houses delivered a barrage of fire, killing Samuel Coppedge and Frank Wadley, the two detectives most responsible for quelling the May clash. The next morning their "bullet-riddled," blood-soaked squad car—"like a flour sieve, all punctured full of holes"—was displayed outside police headquarters. Their murders so incensed some segments of the white community that by early afternoon dozens of blacks, "without regard to age or sex," were dragged from trolleys at the town's central transfer depot—where Madam Walker had often stood—and were "stoned, clubbed and kicked." Sympathetic whites who tried to intervene were intimidated and chased away. Chanting "Burn 'em out! Burn 'em out!" a white mob firebombed several houses, shooting at families as they fled the inferno. By midnight a sixteen-block area was engulfed in flames.

On the Missouri side of the river, Madam Walker's friends Jessie and C. K. Robinson were among those called upon to assist the refugees as they streamed across the Eads and Municipal bridges. At the Knights of Pythias Hall—where C.K. had long been an officer—the local NAACP chapter hurriedly convened, calling for militiamen to put down the violence, as well as for more aid for the 6,000 burned-out evacuees. Jessie, then in training with the city's first class of carefully chosen black women social workers, was pressed into service alongside white Red Cross relief workers at the Wheatley YWCA—where a dormitory for black women had been set up— and at the St. Louis Municipal Lodging House, which the mayor had opened to more than a thousand homeless people.

From an outraged black community, as well as some notably concerned white editors and members of Congress, the reaction was swift and indignant. At the White House, President Wilson refrained from public comment. Lacking any official statement from his leader, presidential secretary Joseph Patrick Tumulty echoed the sentiments of East St. Louis congressman W. A. Rodenburg when he called the uprising "so sickening" that he "had not been able to read much of the account of last night's rioting, murder and arson." While some members of Illinois's House delegation were said to have been "much humiliated" and concerned about their "state's fair name," its two senators—Democrat James Hamilton Lewis and Republican Lawrence Yates Sherman—made it clear that they opposed the intervention of federal troops, with one blaming "the great number of negroes" from the South for causing the "friction [that] has developed with white labor." Others blamed Wilson's refusal to denounce a rising tolerance of racism as one of the many sparks that ignited the July conflagration. "Ironically, Wilson helped create the climate for the first major wartime riot by accusing the Republicans of 'colonizing' black voters in East St. Louis," charged historian Kenneth O'Reilly about comments he made during the 1916 campaign year. "At the president's urging . . . the Justice Department and its Bureau of Investigation opened voting fraud cases, a decision that stirred up racial hatred in places that had problems enough."

Yet two weeks later when the sheriff of Bisbee, Arizona, helped herd striking copper workers onto cattle cars, then abandoned them in the uninhabited New Mexico desert, Wilson quickly and publicly repudiated the same kind of vigilantism he had declined to censure in East St. Louis. In support of the mostly white mine workers, he sent military investigators to the scene, appropriated federal money to assist the refugees and directed his Secretary of Labor to establish a mediation board to negotiate a settlement. "Waging war abroad, the President dared not divide the nation at home," wrote biographer August Heckscher of Wilson's decision to slight the situation in East St. Louis. Oswald Garrison Villard's *New York Evening Post*—a paper Madam Walker frequently read—considered Wilson's "failure to condemn the riot part of a pattern indicating an unsympathetic attitude toward Negroes."

Certainly the President had done little before the early July uprising to engender trust or confidence within the black community. In contrast, former President Theodore Roosevelt—during a Carnegie Hall rally celebrating the overthrow of the Russian czar—condemned the "appalling outbreak of savagery" in Illinois. "Before we speak of justice for others, it behooves us to do justice within our own household," he told the applauding crowd without the equivocation that had characterized Wilson's approach to the matter.

A now more militant black population, impatient with Wilson's neglect, resolved to register its own protest. At an executive committee meeting of the NAACP's Harlem branch even before the East St. Louis riot, James Weldon Johnson had suggested a "silent protest parade," an idea that first had been proposed by Villard at the 1916 Amenia Conference. In Washington, suffragettes had marched all spring and summer along Pennsylvania Avenue in front of the White House, successfully drawing attention to their cause, especially after members of the more militant National Women's Party were arrested and imprisoned in May.

Several Harlem leaders, including Madam Walker, joined a large committee whose "preparations were gone about with feverish enthusiasm," Johnson later remembered. Because the group agreed that the once effective Carnegie Hall rallies "now fail to possess any news value," they agreed with Johnson's notion that a march "in broad day light" would "be so striking and unusual a demonstration" that the Associated Press would be compelled to "flash" it "over this country and to the remotest parts of the civilized world."

With Du Bois in East St. Louis investigating the riot's aftermath, Johnson assumed responsibility for assembling the committee of prominent citizens and mobilizing the demonstrators. A "superb public speaker and organizer [and] an extremely tactful and diplomatic man," Johnson, the consummate gentleman, was ideal for the task. Barely two months earlier, just after visiting Madam Walker in Indianapolis, he had spent ten days in Memphis probing the lynching of Eli Persons, a retarded man who had been accused of murdering and decapitating a sixteen-year-old white girl.

Johnson's committee, which included Reverend Hutchens Bishop as president and Realtor John Nail as treasurer, raised more than $900 from a range of Harlem citizens of all stripes—West Indian aid societies, ministers, NAACP leaders and musicians—to pay for banners, handbills and other expenses. Among the donors were Lelia Walker Robinson, actor Bert Williams and James Weldon Johnson's brother, the composer J. Rosamond Johnson.

By noon on Saturday, July 28, hundreds of African Americans clutching signs with antilynching slogans assembled on Fifty-seventh, Fifty-eighth and Fifty-ninth streets east and west of Fifth Avenue as they waited for the parade to begin. "Treat Us So That We May Love Our Country," pleaded one banner. "Mr. President, Why Not Make America Safe for Democracy?" challenged another. An American flag was unfurled behind a large sign that accused: "Your Hands Are Full of Blood." No letter or newspaper accounts confirm Madam Walker's attendance, but barring illness, little else could have kept her away from this historic event.

More than 800 children, some as young as six, assembled at the front of the procession. Behind them, women dressed in white were followed by black men in dark suits—somewhere between 5,000 and 10,000 in all—who marched speechlessly and solemnly to the beat of muffled drums down the avenue toward Madison Square Park at Twenty-third Street. "Fully 20,000 negroes lined Fifth Avenue and gave silent approval of the demonstration," reported *The New York Times*, still refusing to capitalize the "N" in "Negro." As the marchers stepped deliberately past mansions and office buildings, black Boy Scouts dutifully pressed fliers into the hands of the somber sidewalk crowds. "We march because we want to make impossible a repetition of Waco, Memphis and East St. Louis, by rousing the conscience of the country and bringing the murderers of our brothers, sisters and innocent children to justice," declared their circular.

The following Wednesday, Madam Walker joined a small group of Harlem leaders on an early morning train to Washington to decry "the atrocious attacks . . . at East St. Louis and other industrial centers recently." Their destination: the White House. Their goal: linking African Americans' wartime loyalty and patriotism on the battlefields of Europe to their right to civil liberties at home. They also intended to appeal to President Wilson to "speak 'some public word' that would give hope and courage to the Negroes of the United States." Having been assured by Wilson political ally Robert S. Hudspath—the boss of Hudson County, New Jersey's Democratic political machine—that the President would meet with them, and having received Tumulty's invitation "to call at the White House at 12 o'clock," the delegation arrived at 1600 Pennsylvania Avenue late on the morning of August 1. As the noontime bells tolled across Lafayette Square, they were escorted into secretary Tumulty's office. Once inside, they were introduced by A. B. Cosey, the black New Jersey attorney who had engineered the pivotal 1912 meeting in which presidential candidate Wilson had pledged that blacks "may count upon me for absolute fair dealing, for everything by which I could assist in advancing the interest of their race in the United States." But just as that promise had been broken, the group was informed by Tumulty that Wilson was so absorbed in negotiations involving a "feed supply bill" that he "regretted that he would not be able to see the committee."

A former speaker of the New Jersey General Assembly, Tumulty served as Wilson's "political weather vane," buffering him from favor-seekers and protecting him from people and issues he preferred to avoid. Genial and hospitable as Tumulty proved to be, James Weldon Johnson—in his weekly *New York Age* column—dismissed Wilson's claims that an agricultural bill was worthy of taking precedence over murdered American citizens. "There is no doubt the President is extremely busy," Johnson editorialized, accusing Wilson of political expediency for avoiding a meeting with African Americans. "What we want from the President is some public utterance for fair play and justice to the American Negro." Asserting that Wilson had refused to meet with the delegation because he would have been unable to "escape making some statement as to his attitude on the Negro," Johnson then charged "that is something which Mr. Wilson seems bent on avoiding."

As spokesman for the group, Johnson, "in a few well chosen words," asserted that his delegation represented not only the Negro Silent Protest Parade Committee and "the colored people of Greater New York," but "the sentiments and aspirations and sorrows, too, of the entire Negro population of the United States." Noting that African Americans had answered the draft in disproportionate numbers—36 out of 100 eligible black men, compared with 25 of 100 eligible white men—the petition implored the President to "use his great powers" to assist lynching victims and to use "his great personal and moral influence in our behalf."

Completing his introductory remarks, Johnson presented to Tumulty the one-page, cream-colored petition, a document that noted that although many thousand lynchers had committed crimes "not a single one" had been convicted of murder for the death of "2,867 colored men and women" since 1885. With absolutely no faith in the individual states to uphold the law, the delegation proposed that "lynching and mob violence be made a national crime punishable by the laws of the United States." Tying their concerns to America's involvement in the European war, the petition declared, "No nation that seeks to fight the battles of civilization can afford to march in blood-smeared garments." Among the sixteen signatories were Madam Walker, James Weldon Johnson, John E. Nail, Fred Moore and W.E.B. Du Bois, as well as eight ministers, including Salem Methodist's Reverend Frederick A. Cullen, Abyssinian Baptist's Reverend A. Clayton Powell, Sr., and Mother AME Zion's Reverend James W. Brown.

After Johnson's presentation, Tumulty promised the visitors that "the matter would not be neglected" by the President, who, he claimed unconvincingly, "was in sympathy and was doing all he could for betterment" of the condition of black Americans. To assuage the disappointed delegation, Tumulty read excerpts from letters Wilson had written to his cabinet members in which he "ordered that everything be done to put a stop to the evils complained of." But the letters, Tumulty advised the group, "were not for publication."

After enduring a series of "general and platitudinous phrases," Fred Moore, who had been skeptical from the beginning about the planned visit to the White House, complained that "Negroes of influence and culture, men who stand for something, who respect themselves and demand respect in return, [can] receive no recognition whatsoever and their chances of getting a word with Mr. Wilson are very slim." Four weeks later—with the riots and parade no longer in the daily headlines—Wilson consented to a twenty-minute meeting with Tuskegee principal Robert Russa Moton. But Moore was not persuaded that the session was of any use since Wilson failed to "speak out against lynching and other injustices to which the Negro is subjected."

Denied an audience with the President on August 1, the committee members fanned out across Capitol Hill, calling upon several receptive members of Congress, among them Congressman George Lunn of New York and Senators Joseph L. Frelinghuysen of New Jersey and William M. Calder of New York, who volunteered to submit the appeals into the *Congressional Record* and "to urge an investigation" of the recent riots.

Two days after their return to New York, Reverend Cullen convened another public forum at Salem Church to describe the group's unsuccessful attempt to meet with Wilson. Although the group had failed to meet with the President, Madam Walker would manage to use the visit to advantage a few weeks later to motivate her agents to political action at the first annual Madam Walker Beauty Culturists Union convention in Philadelphia.

Madam Walker's whirlwind efforts to organize the Walker agents delivered just the reward she had envisioned as more than 200 delegates from "nearly every state" climbed the steps to Philadelphia's Union Baptist Church on August 31, 1917. Attentive to every detail, she had carefully selected the venue as much for its magnificent new 2,600-capacity sanctuary as for its influential pastor, Reverend Wesley G. Parks, vice-president-at-large of the powerful National Baptist Convention. That it was home to fifteen-year-old music prodigy and future internationally renowned operatic diva Marian Anderson may well have been an added attraction.

As Madam Walker surveyed the crowd during Philadelphia mayor Thomas B. Smith's welcoming remarks, she noticed that several women were wearing hats. Stylish as the head coverings were, they obscured the delegates' hair. And Madam Walker would have none of it, admonishing them good-naturedly that "in a session composed of graduates of the Walker system, who [are] experts in all things pertaining to the hair, it should not be necessary to request that the ladies remove their hats." With no further comment from Madam Walker, the minutes recorded that "every hat was then voluntarily removed," no doubt with a few embarrassed grimaces. Later, when the women gathered for a group photo in front of the stone church, fewer than a dozen donned hats. "A wonderful picture told the story of the unfolding and transformation of a race," the minutes noted. "The glory of woman lies in her hair."

Standing before the convention, Madam Walker herself continued to impress others with her own personal transformation. That June, *Freeman* reporter William Lewis had described her as "splendidly poised [wearing] her wealth and honors with ease as if she had [them] for all of the years . . . Madam Walker can hold her own in any gathering of women." Through her new organization she meant to help other women develop the same self-acquired confidence.

A Walker Company news release, probably written by Ransom, pronounced the four-day event "significant" because it had assembled "the business women of the race who [had] paid their way to tell about their success, see their great leader and get new ideas and inspiration." Gathered to exchange information and "transact business," the agents were also participating in one of the first national conventions strictly devoted to American women's entrepreneurial pursuits.

As the well-coiffed, fashionably dressed agents traveled throughout the city on streetcar sightseeing tours and automobile excursions, they were easily identified by their distinctive convention badges. Beneath a button-sized photograph of Madam Walker, a wide, deep-yellow satin ribbon announced the Madam C. J. Walker National Association of Hair Growers in black letters.

Setting aside the morning sessions for business, Madam Walker opened the afternoon and evening sessions to the public. Among her keynote speakers were her friends George Knox and S. Willie Layten, the National Baptist Convention's Women's Auxiliary president and an independent-minded divorcée who shared with Madam Walker an abiding concern for the thousands of young black women who were migrating to Northern cities. A resident of Philadelphia, Layten had founded the city's branch of the Association for the Protection of Colored Women, an organization designed to help these recent arrivals find jobs, adapt to city life and avoid unscrupulous employers. Reflecting Madam Walker's interest in movies and new technology, two pioneering black filmmakers—Clarence Wells of the Lincoln Motion Picture Company and Walter Sammons of the Monarch Talking Picture Company—discussed their innovative communications devices with the evening audience.

Throughout the sessions the agents shared their personal triumphs—new homes, increased monthly earnings, children's educational accomplishments—in proceedings similar to those of the National Association of Colored Women and the National Negro Business League. Women who had earned little more than a few dollars a week as domestic workers now took in two and three and ten times that much in one day. Margaret Thompson, president of the Philadelphia Union of Walker Hair Culturists, told her colleagues that she had been a $5-a-week servant when she met Madam Walker. "Her income [now] is $250 a week," reported the *Kansas City Star*. And there were scores more like Thompson because Madam Walker, Annie Pope-Turnbo Malone, Anthony Overton of Overton Hygienic and dozens of other black manufacturers had revolutionized the cosmetics industry by customizing products for black women. Each decade had seen steady growth in those who made their living as hairdressers, from only 514 black women who identified themselves as hairdressers in 1890 to 984 in 1900, then 3,093 in 1910. The most significant growth was to come in the decade between 1910 and 1920, when there would be 12,666 African American beauty culturists, according to the United States Census. And while it remains impossible to document the exact number of women who supplemented their incomes with part-time "hair work," the Walker Company alone claimed to have trained 20,000 agents by the end of the twentieth century's second decade.

For her own keynote message—"Woman's Duty to Woman"—Madam Walker reserved the final night. Emphasizing her "great interest" in her agents' "successes and their failures," she met head-on the grousing that had led to a brief boycott of her products by her Cincinnati agents in the spring. She also aimed to counter the complaint Ransom had discovered after visits with another group of agents who, he said, charged that "you were all for yourself." Assuring her that he considered the allegations neither "fair [nor] just," he wrote, "I have always resented it wherever I heard it, yet that is what one hears when one comes in contact with a bunch of your agents." Rather than become defensive, she vowed to position her enterprise "on a co-operative basis so that her agents will share in the profits." From Union Baptist's pulpit she reminded the women of her intention "to have this organization, its rules and regulations so strict, and perfect, until it will be utterly impossible for any one to handle our goods, unless such a one is a regular agent of the Company, and is a member of this National Organization." And she was extremely proud to announce that "the art of hair culture" was now being taught at black secondary schools and on college campuses, thus helping to raise the status of those who worked in the industry. She took special pleasure in presenting the prizes—$500 in all—to the members who had trained the most new agents, logged the highest sales figures and contributed the most to their local charities. In an early recycling program, necessitated by wartime restrictions on the use of metals, she awarded $25 to the agent who had returned the largest number of tin containers.

And while Madam Walker focused on business opportunities for her agents, she was determined that they be politically conscious citizens concerned about more than their own personal interests. In "a ringing message" she "spoke of the present war and advised her people to remain loyal to their homes, their country and their flag," the convention minutes reported. "After all, this is the greatest country under the sun. But we must not let our love of country, our patriotic loyalty cause us to abate one whit in our protest against wrong and injustice," she declared, undaunted by Woodrow Wilson's rebuff after the Silent Protest Parade. "We should protest until the American sense of justice is so aroused that such affairs as the East St. Louis riot be forever impossible." Moved by Madam Walker's speech—and emboldened by her visit to the White House—the Walker Union dispatched a telegram to President Wilson:

> We, the representatives of the National Convention of the Mme. C. J. Walker Agents, in convention assembled, and in a larger sense representing twelve million Negroes, have keenly felt the injustice done our race and country through the recent lynching at Memphis, Tennessee, and the horrible race riot at East St. Louis. Knowing that no people in all the world are more loyal and patriotic than the Col-

ored people of America, we respectfully submit to you this our protest against the continuation of such wrongs and injustices in this "land of the free, and home of the brave" and we further respectfully urge that you as President of these United States use your great influence that congress enact the necessary laws to prevent a recurrence of such disgraceful affairs.

With that gesture, the association had become what perhaps no other currently existing group could claim: American women entrepreneurs organized to use their money and their numbers to assert their political will.

As the convention closed with a church service in Union Baptist's semicircular sanctuary, Madam Walker was already thinking ahead to the next week's activities. After a brief stop in Cape May, New Jersey, where she was honored at a reception at the Hotel Dale—a popular destination for middle-class blacks who lived along the East Coast—she returned to New York to host the first trade association meeting of the country's black hair care products manufacturers.

That Wednesday night, more than a dozen company founders from St. Louis, Boston, New York and Chicago gathered in the Walker salon on 136th Street. Madam Walker told them she had brought them together because she believed it was "necessary and urgent" that they organize in the face of competition from a few well-funded white-owned companies that had begun to encroach upon their territory. Just as they had begun to overcome the exaggerated claims of businesses that pushed skin bleaches and caustic chemical concoctions, the black manufacturers—most still woefully undercapitalized—found themselves struggling to protect the market niche they had created. "[I]t has been so often the case that the white man who is not interested in Colored Women's Beauty only looks to further his own gains and puts on the market preparations that are absolutely of no aid whatsoever to the Skin, Scalp or Hair," read the minutes of the first session of the National Negro Cosmetics Manufacturers Association. In fact, they all were probably aware of a particularly insulting letter that had been exposed in the *Chicago Defender* a year earlier. Sent to white drugstore retailers by a distributor of Palmolive Soap products, its author had signed the correspondence: "Yours for Nigger Business."

Among those at the meeting were Alexander Johnson, the former president of the Boston NNBL, who, along with his wife, Mary L. Johnson, a scalp specialist and wig maker, had founded the Johnson Manufacturing Company in Boston in 1899. Noticeably absent was Annie Pope-Turnbo Malone, whom Madam Walker had chosen to exclude despite her prominent position in the industry. By assembling what she considered, "some of the best and most successful business men and women of the Race,"

Madam Walker hoped to create an organization to protect the members from "fraud and false representation . . . to encourage the development of Race enterprises and acquaint the public with the superior claims of high class goods."

That evening when the group assembled upstairs at 108 for dinner, the members discussed plans to reduce production costs by purchasing raw materials in bulk and ways to pool promotional resources by "devising some form of cooperative advertising." Madam Walker further proposed that they "fix a standard both in their prices and quality of their products," a plan that, had it been implemented, could have been in violation of federal antitrust laws prohibiting price fixing within an industry. But the motivation that triggered such a scheme—"unscrupulous persons who placed fake preparations on the market" and undercut prices with adulterated goods—was all too real and threatening.

With Madam Walker elected president, and with women holding half of the six executive committee positions, the members adjourned with renewed "enthusiasm and inspiration" to enhance their industry. Her goal, she reminded one of the officers, was to lay the groundwork for "the beginning of a powerful organization representing more working capital with more real results than any other among Colored Americans anywhere." The woman who had scrapped to have her words heard just five years earlier at Booker T. Washington's NNBL convention now intended to develop her own influential trade organization.

Two weeks later at Mother AME Zion Church in New York, Madam Walker joined nearly 200 men and women for the tenth annual convention of William Monroe Trotter's National Equal Rights League. As much as she had admired Washington, and as closely allied as she had become with the NAACP and its antilynching campaign, she did not shun the more pugnacious and zealous Trotter, who had become marginalized by the post-Washington-era black political establishment. Madam Walker's financial status granted her the independence she needed to be able to choose causes and issues rather than sides and personalities.

During its September 1917 conference, NERL delegates voted to demand "in precise terms" that President Wilson abolish segregation in federal offices and interstate travel, forbid disfranchisement of black voters, dismantle the peonage farming system and make lynching a federal crime. "Despite progress we are still surrounded by an adverse sentiment which makes our lives a living hell," their convention petition bluntly stated. By the end of the meeting, Madam Walker had been elected a vice-president-at-large. Antilynching activist Ida B. Wells-Barnett—who had joined the NERL in 1913 before entirely cutting her ties with the NAACP in 1915—now served as the group's Chicago delegate. Both she and Trotter remained wary of the NAACP's predominantly white leadership, preferring "an organization of the colored people and for the colored people and led by the colored people."

For Wells-Barnett the highlight of the NERL session proved to be a dinner at which Madam Walker "entertained the entire delegation royally." After the officers had been "ushered into the dining room, Madam sat at the head of her table in her décolleté gown, with her butler serving dinner under her direction," Wells-Barnett later wrote in her autobiography. "She had learned already how to bear herself as if to the manner born." Because that day's proceedings—like every day's proceedings—had focused on segregation in the federal government and concerns about lynching, the conversation around Madam Walker's large table must certainly have turned to East St. Louis. Having visited the devastated town just three days after the riot, Wells-Barnett had firsthand knowledge and graphic observations to share. Because she personally intended to carry the NERL's petition to Washington after the conference—and to attempt to persuade the Justice Department to "undertake an investigation of Negroes at East St. Louis"— Wells-Barnett and the others also would have been curious about Madam Walker's impressions of her White House visit in August.

Wells-Barnett, who had met Madam Walker around 1906, applauded her "hard work and persistent effort," as well as the "vision and ambition" that had allowed her to expand her business operations to New York. "I was indeed proud to see what a few short years of success had done for a woman who had been without education and training," Wells-Barnett, a brilliant but sometimes contentious woman, wrote with admiration. "I was one of the skeptics that paid little heed to her predictions as to what she was going to do . . . To see her phenomenal rise made me take pride anew in Negro womanhood."

Several times that week the two women motored to Irvington-on-Hudson to inspect the progress on Madam Walker's Hudson River home. "We drove out there almost every day, and I asked her on one occasion what on earth she would do with a thirty-room house," Wells-Barnett remembered. "She said, 'I want plenty of room in which to entertain my friends. I have worked so hard all of my life that I would like to rest.'"

Throughout the fall Madam Walker continued her frequent visits to Westchester County, quizzing the contractor, monitoring costs and reveling in the possibilities her new home promised. "Of late, Mme. Walker, in her high-powered motor car, has been a familiar visitor in Irvington," *The New York Times* reported. "On her first visits to inspect her property the villagers, noting her color, were frankly puzzled . . . 'Does she really intend to live there, or is she building it as a speculation?' the people have asked." When her wealthy neighbors learned that she did indeed intend to live among them, they were stunned. "'Impossible!' they exclaimed. 'No such woman of her race could afford such a place,'" the *Times* reporter wrote, noting a collective community "gasp of astonishment."

That same November 4, 1917, *New York Times Magazine* feature— "Wealthiest Negro Woman's Suburban Mansion"—placed Madam Walker's assets at "a cool million, or nearly that." The paper significantly overstated her net worth, giving rise to the belief that she had become the first American woman to make a million dollars on her own in business. And although she tried to correct the record, the claim stuck. "I am not a millionaire, but I hope to be some day," she told the reporter, "not because of the money, but because I could do so much more to help my race." When a reprint of the article appeared in the January 1918 issue of A. Philip Randolph's new publication, *The Messenger*, the story of Madam Walker's purported millionaire status caught hold among African Americans.

The news about her Irvington-on-Hudson residence brought white customers—some who also suffered from hair loss, scalp disease and kinky hair—as well as white admirers like Mrs. J. M. Minos of Rocky Ford, Colorado, who told Madam Walker of her "astonishment of your success in gaining the wealth you have. Not many have the brains to do this without financial help."

But while the construction on Madam Walker's house was progressing well, her health was deteriorating at a frightening pace. By mid-November 1917, Dr. George Sauer, a Chicago physician, had braced her for unwanted news. His diagnosis: nephritis, an acute, and often irreversible, inflammation of the kidneys exacerbated by her worsening hypertension. He advised that she check into Michigan's celebrated Battle Creek Sanitarium for "an indefinite stay." During her intake physical examination, a Dr. Judd measured her systolic blood pressure at 196, well over the 140 he considered healthy. In order to preserve her life, the sanitarium's doctors recommended that she cease working altogether. "This is necessary for all time and means she must give little or no attention again to business or heavy social activities," her traveling assistant, Louis George, wrote to Ransom.

A multiwinged, 1,000-bed hospital, Battle Creek catered to wealthy chronically ill patients, many of them wheelchair-bound invalids, desperate for relief and cure. Whereas Hot Springs had provided relaxation and respite from Madam Walker's grueling travel schedule, Battle Creek's "dictatorial" director, Dr. John Harvey Kellogg, prescribed a rigorous "regimen of fresh air, exercise and hydrotherapy." The bland, tasteless, vegetarian diet—so unlike Madam Walker's flavorful high-fat fare—banned all coffee, tea and alcohol, and offered such choices as bean and tapioca soup, buttered cauliflower, stewed raisins and granola.

Despite the pleasant surroundings—a rooftop dining room with hand-painted murals, a solarium filled with tropical palms and fruit trees and an imposing lobby as grand as that of any nineteenth-century European hotel—Madam Walker could not bring herself to stay longer than a few weeks. Unable to "tear herself away from the active conducting" of the Walker Company, she was also eager to celebrate her birthday and the holidays with Lelia. By mid-December she was back in New York, making regular trips with her architect, Vertner Tandy, to Irvington. "It is getting on fine," she was happy to report to Ransom of the now nearly completed mansion.

Two days after Christmas, as mother and daughter enjoyed each other's company, Lelia wrote Ransom from 108 to thank him for her gift. "You certainly touched my weak spot by sending a book," she wrote appreciatively. Grateful that her mother had recovered sufficiently to be at home, she added, "You know this was an especially merry xmas for me having mother with me." During the coming year both women would find themselves, like most Americans, immersed in the war effort.

CHAPTER 18

War Abroad, War at Home

— ✑ —

Protest and patriotism vied for headlines in the *New York Age* during the summer of 1917 as African American troops trained for the war abroad and Harlem leaders challenged mob violence at home. Even as black New Yorkers cautiously monitored congressional response to the East St. Louis riots, they were captivated by the military drills their khaki-clad sons, husbands and friends practiced outside the 132nd Street armory. That James Reese Europe—now a sergeant in the Harlem-based 15th Infantry Regiment of the New York Guard—had signed on to lead the regimental band only boosted their pride. With Noble Sissle strutting as his drum major, and a dozen handpicked Puerto Rican enlistees filling his reed section, Jim Europe's impromptu street parades did more for recruitment than any ten Selective Service offices.

On April 6, 1917, as President Woodrow Wilson placed his signature on the resolution declaring war on Germany, Madam Walker was in Louisiana busy with her own recruitment efforts to enlist more women into her growing army of Walker agents. But she was hardly oblivious to the conflict in Europe. Away from Harlem during most of the year, she stayed well informed through letters, telegrams and newspaper articles as her fellow African American leaders examined and debated their positions on black military involvement. Within weeks of America's entry into the war, Tin Pan Alley's biggest hit of 1916—"I Didn't Raise My Boy to Be a Soldier"—was quickly replaced by "Over There," an upbeat tune that assured the European Allies that "the Yanks are coming . . . And we won't be back till it's over over there."

Many African Americans caught the contagious flag-waving spirit, readying themselves to help "save the world for democracy." But in the months preceding America's intervention, a few Negro weeklies—incensed at proposed congressional legislation barring blacks from military service—had editorialized against black participation. "If war comes, the colored man is not wanted and it would be a white man's war between Germany and the U.S.," asserted the *Washington Bee* that March. Particularly indignant that President Wilson was "doing or saying nothing to stop lynching at home," the *Iowa Bystander* was even more direct: "Why need we go 3,000 miles to uphold the dignity and honor of our country and protect her citizens over in England and fail to uphold dignity at home?" In barbershops and on street corners, plainspoken sentiments conveyed similar meaning: "The Germans ain't done nothing to me, and if they have, I forgive 'em." Ultimately, however, the community's more patriotic voices prevailed. James Weldon Johnson—a former U.S. diplomat and now NAACP field secretary—had long advocated African American support of the war. As America mobilized, he proclaimed the black soldier willing to "take up the duty that comes to him and, as always, do his part." In turn, Johnson expected the nation to "do its duty to him." Later that summer W.E.B. Du Bois—the staunch antilynching crusader—set aside some of his own misgivings in what appeared to some to be an opportunistic statement of support just as he was being considered for an appointment to a captaincy in the Military Intelligence Division of the War Department. "Let us not hesitate," he urged in his July *Crisis* column. "Let us, while this war lasts, forget our special grievances and close our ranks shoulder to shoulder with our own white fellow citizens and the allied nations that are fighting for democracy."

Drawing upon a legacy of military participation in every conflict since the American Revolution, most African Americans swallowed their ambivalence and rallied. As always, they mustered their optimism, hoping loyalty, allegiance and blood would expedite long-overdue equal rights and equal opportunity, a kind of "civil rights through carnage," as David Levering Lewis has written. But this time the nation's black leadership also sought a precedent-setting quid pro quo. In exchange for contributing their "full quota to the federal army," they pressed for the establishment of a training camp for black officers. While many objected to a segregated facility, a sufficient number joined Du Bois in making the tortuous choice between "the insult of a separate camp and the irreparable injury of . . . putting no black men in positions of authority." A leading proponent of the effort was Joel Spingarn, then on leave from the NAACP board and serving in a reserve officers' training camp. At his urging the Howard University–based Central Committee of Negro College Men submitted more than 1,500 names of students—primarily from Howard, Lincoln, Fisk, Morehouse, Tuskegee, Hampton and Atlanta University—for officers' training. "Our country faces the greatest crisis in its history," opened their letter of petition seeking support from 300 congressmen. "The Negro, as ever loyal and patriotic, is anxious to do his full share in the defense and support of his country in its fight for democracy." In late May, when Secretary of War Newton Baker announced plans for a black officers' center at Fort Des Moines, the CCNCM claimed "victory," but spent little time basking. "The race is on trial," their circular warned. "If we fail, our enemies will dub us cowards for all time . . . But if we succeed, then eternal success."

With Madam Walker's architect, Vertner Tandy, now a major in the 15th Regiment—and the highest-ranking black officer in the New York Guard—she was all the more inclined to take a personal interest in the regiment's activities. When the American Red Cross initially excluded black women as volunteers and nurses, Madam Walker agreed without hesitation to join the advisory board of the Circle for Negro War Relief, a group of prominent black women who established a clearinghouse for money and supplies "to improve conditions among colored soldiers." Comprising more than fifty chapters around the country—with a dozen in New York alone— the Circle purchased an ambulance, provided several hundred hand-knitted pairs of socks and gloves and assisted the soldiers' families.

In early December 1917 as the men of the 15th—soon to be known as the 369th Hellfighters of the Provisional 93rd Division—prepared to leave for France, Madam Walker was still recovering at Battle Creek. But Lelia— whose party invitations were always in high demand—cohosted a farewell concert with James Weldon Johnson and J. Rosamond Johnson to aid the Circle's programs. On December 13, as the troops boarded European-bound transport ships in Hoboken, New Jersey, the Lelia College holiday greeting in *The Messenger* wished for the "speedy culmination of the war" and the "bravery and success of our boys in uniform."

In mid-January, with a fresh retinue of black trainees in the barracks at Long Island's Camp Upton—and with Madam Walker home from Michigan—the Walker women entertained the black officers of the 92nd Division at a military cotillion. Amid red, white and blue decorations in the music room upstairs at 108, the uniformed men and the "daintily dressed" women "made a pleasing sight." In addition to Major Vertner Tandy, other honored guests included two popular physicians—Captain Charles Garvin, who would soon become commanding officer of an ambulance company in France, and Lieutenant Colonel Louis Wright, a 1915 graduate of Harvard's Medical School. The Friday Evening Knitting Class—a group of Lelia's friends, including Edna Lewis, Madam Walker's social secretary, and Czarina Jackson, the manager of the Seventh Avenue Walker Salon— served as hostesses, dancing with the officers well beyond midnight to the tunes of the Harmony Quartet.

Relishing her role as society fund-raiser, Lelia next invited famed tenor Enrico Caruso to be her guest of honor at a Circle for Negro War Relief dance in early February. Like her mother, she embraced eclectic musical interests. Having spent her childhood enveloped in St. Louis ragtime, she also genuinely enjoyed opera. With Caruso at the peak of his career—"his voice is now at its richest, his acting is more polished with every performance," wrote one critic—Lelia knew his name would attract a large and diverse audience. And although he canceled "at the last minute . . . owing to a very important engagement for the next day," Lelia's disappointment was tempered by the tremendous turnout at the Manhattan Casino. "At any rate," she wrote Ransom, the invitation to Caruso had "served its purpose for the hall was crowded and it was a huge success."

Caruso, with whom Lelia enjoyed a cordial friendship, had "few intimate friends" and often was "bored" and "ill at ease at parties." So it is entirely possible that he bowed out of the commitment to avoid the crowd and the small talk. But he also was legitimately swamped that month and in the midst of a Metropolitan Opera season in which he sang a dozen different roles between February and April. After attending one of those performances (perhaps the February 12 special matinee of Giuseppe Verdi's *Aida*—the story of the star-crossed but courageous Ethiopian princess), Lelia sent a basket of flowers to Caruso's "luxurious" fourteen-room apartment at the Hotel Knickerbocker. Several months later when he visited her mother's Irvington-on-Hudson, New York, property, he found the setting and design so reminiscent of the estates of his native Italy that he christened the home "Villa Lewaro," creating an acronym from the first two letters of Lelia Walker Robinson. The name became permanent, gracing the Walker women's stationery during their lifetime and enduring into the twenty-first century.

Throughout early 1918, Lelia continued volunteering for a range of wartime committees. Whether serving lunch to the men of the 367th Infantry after a Fifth Avenue parade or helping form a black women's auxiliary to the American Red Cross, she was enjoying the sense of purpose the activities provided.

Having returned to Battle Creek in late January, Madam Walker missed much of Harlem's winter social season. Arriving at the sanitarium bundled against Michigan's frosty winter in her Hudson Seal cape, she complained of a pesky, persistent virus. "I am getting along fairly well, only my cold seems to be sticking by me," she wrote Ransom. But two weeks later—still surely in need of rest—she embarked upon a three-month Midwestern tour to Iowa, Kansas, Missouri, Illinois, Indiana, Ohio and Pennsylvania. Now, in addition to publicizing her business, she was visiting military camps and promoting the work of the Circle for Negro War Relief. At Fort Des Moines—where the 100 officers and 3,600 enlisted men of the 92nd Division's 366th Infantry awaited orders for European duty—Madam Walker was escorted by attorney George Woodson. Later the founding president of the National Bar Association, Woodson considered it his "good fortune and high honor to introduce her."

At the YMCA tent reserved for the "social, cultural and political" activities of black soldiers, Madam Walker praised the "boys," who were going "over there," for their bravery. "Now and then, but seldom, you hear one say, 'This is not my country. I have no right to fight for a flag that does not protect me,'" she told the men, as many strained to hear from outside the jam-packed canvas shelter. "But let me say to you that this [is] our home . . . All we have is here, and the time will come, and it is not far distant, until we must and will receive every protection guaranteed to every American citizen under the American Constitution."

Watching from the stage, Woodson was startled by Madam Walker's weakened condition. "The eloquent force which she put into that speech in spite of her nervous state, greatly alarmed me," he later wrote. During the reception following her remarks, Woodson's concern compelled him to request permission to measure her pulse. "I tried to get her away from the great mass of common people who crowded about her to admire and compliment her. But it was no use. She loved those common people and just would not leave them."

Later when Madam Walker arrived at the home of Sue Wilson Brown—her Des Moines hostess and the immediate past president of the Iowa Federation of Colored Women—she was greeted by a small group of admirers. Although Woodson "insisted that she go to bed and rest," Madam Walker lingered to talk with the visitors, as well as with her host, attorney S. Joe Brown. Valedictorian of his 1901 University of Iowa Law School class and a founder of Des Moines's NAACP chapter, Brown was considered "one of the seven or eight most important Negro lawyers in America" of the era. The next day, Woodson "begged the privilege of speaking plainly" to Madam Walker. "I told her that she was entirely too valuable to her Country and Race to be taking such desperate chances with her health and life," he later wrote.

But Madam Walker—only too aware of her progressing kidney disease—was all the more determined to resume her frenetic schedule. From Iowa, she traveled to Kansas City, St. Louis and Columbia, then on to Chicago. "The madam has developed into a magnetic platform speaker and is exceedingly witty and humorous," a *Chicago Defender* article later described her appearance at the city's Olivet Baptist Church. "The story of her success," declared the flattering account (in all probability penned by Ransom), was something that "every young woman in America should hear." Apparently Dora Larrie, C. J. Walker's second wife, had decided that she too needed to hear the message. "I understand that Mme. Walker No. 2 was out to my lecture last night. I know that she went away with a sick heart," Madam Walker "No. 1" gloated. "I had a crowded house and applause all through the lecture. I would have to wait nearly three minutes for them to get quiet before I could begin again."

That enthusiastic response, and Olivet's reputation as a haven for recently arrived Southern migrants, persuaded Madam Walker to select the church as the site for her second annual Walker agents convention. With nearly 1,000 newcomers streaming each month into Chicago's South Side from Mississippi Valley towns along the Illinois Central train line, Madam Walker easily envisioned ways to cultivate the untapped pool of thousands of potential Lelia College students, sales agents and customers. That young black women were being hired as tobacco strippers and hotel waitresses, chambermaids and kitchen helpers at $15 to $20 per week meant that a $1.75 Walker treatment was within their reach, even with the North's higher rents siphoning off much of their increased income. Julius Rosenwald's Sears, Roebuck and Company and Montgomery Ward had hired more than 1,500 black mail-order clerks, vastly increasing white-collar employment among African American women in the city. And although most remained in domestic service jobs, hundreds "deserted this grade of work for the factories" in order to guarantee evenings and Sundays off. Now part of a faster, more urbanized culture of consumerism, these working women were eager to spend a part of their incomes and free time on themselves. Having just rented a storefront for a Walker salon at 4656 South State Street—on the main commercial thoroughfare of Chicago's black community—Madam Walker was primed both to accommodate their desires and to provide an avenue to economic independence.

With the location of her August meeting settled, Madam Walker dashed ahead to more cities, adding nearby Gary and Fort Wayne, Indiana, to her itinerary. But en route to Indianapolis—where she intended to stay through late March—she wired Ransom, "Do not accept any social engagements. I want to rest." Not surprisingly, her break was brief. In Columbus, Ohio, during early April, she trained and organized enough women to create a new chapter of Walker agents. And her feisty spirit was in full force as she confronted a local woman known to have issued Walker diplomas under the false pretense that she was authorized to teach the Walker course. "She is as crooked as a black snake and I have cut her out entirely," Madam Walker informed Ransom. "And I announced it from the platform last night [while] she was present."

Forty miles south of Columbus in Chillicothe, Madam Walker was welcomed to the First Baptist Church—the town's largest and oldest black congregation—by Zella Ward, Dr. Joseph Ward's wife and Madam Walker's first Indianapolis hostess. Awaiting his assignment to a medical unit in France, Ward was now stationed at nearby Camp Sherman. With her dear friends as guides, Madam Walker learned of the discrimination the troops faced on the base and in the town. Although there were eleven Y buildings on the grounds, only one was not off-limits to the 2,000 black soldiers. In downtown Chillicothe the Ross County Courthouse posted a sign that advised: "Army Club No. 1 for White Soldiers' Friends and Relatives: Reading, Writing and Recreation Rooms." And throughout the country the backlash against black men in uniform had become more frequent and more demeaning. Scattered across seven training camps, the 92nd Division—in which almost all black troops were clustered—had been splintered intentionally to prevent any one encampment from being more than one-third black. General Charles Ballou, the division's white commanding officer, had even issued a directive ordering black troops to avoid situations and public places where their presence would be "resented," unfairly putting the burden on them to anticipate the racism of others. Only a few months earlier First Lieutenant Charles A. Tribbett, an electrical engineer and Yale graduate, had been arrested and forced from a train while en route with fellow servicemen from New York's Camp Upton to Fort Sill. Left behind in Chickasha, Oklahoma, he was jailed for "violating the separate coach laws of the state" because he had dared to occupy a Pullman car.

Despite these troubling incidents, Madam Walker encouraged the troops to persevere. "This is your country, your home," she reminded them. "What you have suffered in the past should not deter you from going forth to protect the homes and lives of your women and children." But she did not gloss over the very real discrimination and indignities they faced, vowing to use her influence on their behalf. Several months later, a member of Company D of the 317th Engineers wrote, "We all remember you, and . . . have often spoken of you, and of the words of consolation which you gave us at Camp Sherman, Ohio, on the eve of our departure. Those words have stayed with the boys longer than any spoken by any one that I have known or heard of." Her comments, he said, had even shored them up "one night while under shell-fire" on a French battlefield.

From Chillicothe Madam Walker made her way to Pittsburgh for a mid-April Madam C. J. Walker Benevolent Association event. "Her tribute to 'our boys' aroused her audience to unusual patriotic enthusiasm," the *Pittsburgh Courier* reported. "When the war began it was thought that 'our boys' would not be needed," she told the "packed house" of 600 people. "But we see that they are needed, and victory shall not have been won until the black boys of America shed their blood on the battlefield." And while Madam Walker's outreach on behalf of the Circle for Negro War Relief had become important, helping women better their economic circumstances remained her passionate priority. "What I have done you can do," she persuaded the Pittsburgh audience. "I am here to interest and inspire you, if possible. If I am not successful in helping you, remember I did the best I could."

When Madam Walker announced that she hoped to "meet every agent personally before I leave the city," she may well have been responding to a situation that required damage control. Much to her consternation, she had learned of a Mrs. Saunders, who not only had used her name on an unauthorized beauty salon sign but was saying that Lelia had "got drunk" and revealed the Wonderful Hair Grower formula. Saunders was "claiming," Madam Walker told Ransom, that "since I have gone to New York the goods are not made properly any more and . . . that I had gotten rich and gone to New York to sport." Incensed by the accusation, she sought retaliation. Aware that *Courier* publisher Robert Vann—who had been Lelia's attorney in her divorce from John Robinson—also represented Saunders, Madam Walker authorized Ransom to apply strategic pressure. "I think it will not be any trouble to get him to advise her to take down the sign since I am one of his heaviest advertisers," she said with confidence.

Madam Walker had also learned that some of her Pittsburgh agents were substituting "white vaseline and anything else that they can get cheap" for her more expensive Glossine, the moisturizing ointment she recommended they use in combination with the heated metal pressing comb. As well, several disgruntled agents were revolting over her recent decision to sell Glossine through retail outlets, complaining that the new policy had severely reduced their sales of the product. "They want me to take it out of the drug stores," Madam Walker wrote Ransom. Without question, she knew she would face the issue again during her August convention.

But she refused to let the momentary crises stymie her new initiatives. With plans for an expanded export operation, she was in search of a second interpreter to handle correspondence with her Spanish-speaking trade. And with intentions of organizing a cadre of national traveling agents, she was interviewing women—and a few men—in each city, searching for candidates with the proper blend of skill, personality and ambition to represent her and her company. "The pictures," she told a prospective saleswoman, referring to the stereopticon slides, are "the most important thing for it is that that arouses such keen interest." An entertaining presentation, she contended, was the most effective element in attracting new customers and trainees. "It isn't [just] a matter of going from town to town organizing clubs. That is a secondary matter. You can easily [organize them] after you get them together."

In order to establish a visible and permanent presence beyond her New York and Indianapolis offices, Madam Walker also had begun scouting locations for Walker schools and parlors. With the Chicago salon nearly remodeled, she now targeted St. Louis and Columbus for future Walker operations. Her vision: to create Walker franchises all over the country by financing the salon construction, then turning the operation over to the franchisee after she had been reimbursed—at 6 percent interest—for her initial outlay. Her long-term profit, she calculated, would come from increased sales volume. In explaining the arrangement to one potential shop owner, she wrote, "I don't think you quite understand me yet. I do not want you as a manager. I only want the public to think it is my business because of the prestige it will lend the place. All I want out of it is the money I loaned you until you can get on your feet." While assuring the prospective franchisee that "the parlor will be yours," she added a caveat designed to protect her investment and her reputation. "I want the parlor to remain in my name, and I reserve the right to make a change any time that I am not pleased with the way the business is run."

Urging the interested operator to bring in at least two additional rent-paying hair culturists to help cover "gas, electric and all that," she required that the franchisee display sufficient dynamism to sustain a self-sufficient, self-supporting business. "I don't think it a good idea to pay salaries," she wrote Ransom. "It is better to let them work up their own business." When her first choice to run the Columbus salon backed out, Madam Walker viewed her as "the most foolish woman I have ever seen, after asking me to help her then turning right around and demanding a salary." In the woman's place, Madam Walker sent Louise Thompson, her traveling assistant, to open the shop, deciding that it "will be better to have some one right from Lelia College to start them off."

When Ransom questioned the wisdom of developing satellite offices, Madam Walker begged to differ. "You said we should . . . have but one school of beauty culture and that in New York. I do not quite agree with you there, as in every section of the country you will find a Moler College or a Burnham College and they are known by that name everywhere. I think it lends dignity," she said, referring to two white cosmetology schools that had been founded in the late nineteenth century.

Having been away from New York since January, Madam Walker returned to her 136th Street home in late April 1918 eager to plunge into the daily office routine. But for Lelia, who had enjoyed the freedom of running the operation without interference, her mother's micromanagement was an annoyance. "Mother stews and frets and gets into everything and therefore she is always nervous and worked up," she had written Ransom earlier in the year. But with a massive log of back orders—caused both by wartime restrictions and by snafus in her Indianapolis factory—Madam Walker could hardly be blamed for being miffed. "We have been out of goods for a week," she wrote Ransom. "You should keep a supply on the road all the time and should we get overstocked we could let you know. To be out of goods has certainly upset everything with the agents here." Four days later the situation had worsened. "What is the trouble that we cannot get any preparations here?" she demanded of Ransom. "It is simply demoralizing the business . . . Please send us Tetter Salve and Grower by mail and keep some on the road until we get some on hand." At the end of May, still needing Grower "very badly," she complained again, "The situation here is getting terribly embarrassing." Equally frustrated by a shortage of tins, Lelia was also fending off angry customers and agents. "I started yesterday to make Grower. The Grower matter is certainly critical here. The folks are furious," she sputtered in a letter to Ransom. "Grower is in greater demand than any of the preparations, so when we send for preparation, please send more Grower than anything else." As long as the war continued, they would have to contend with a number of similar problems.

Since 1912, Madam Walker had rarely missed the summertime convention circuit—the Baptists, the AMEs and the AME Zions; the Knights of Pythias and the Court of Calanthe; the National Negro Business League and the National Association of Colored Women. At first she was more observer than participant, but during July of 1918 she was especially enthusiastic about making the rounds, knowing that she would be lauded at every stop. "Was surely received with honor in Denver," she wrote after registering for the NACW's eleventh biennial. "The only regret was that I could not remain with them longer that they might further demonstrate their appreciation for me," she joked with Ransom of her triumphant homecoming to the city where she had sold her first tin of Madam Walker's Wonderful Hair Grower.

Now, as one of the organization's most famous members, Madam Walker was invited to appear before the delegates several times during the proceedings. Leading a Tuesday afternoon panel on women in business, she "made an appeal for club women to get closer in touch with our women in the factory." That evening at another assembly she advocated racial solidarity and self-help in the struggle for "equality of opportunity," reminding the delegates that "none of us may live our own lives because we are all dependent on one another."

By far the highlight of her week unfolded in the sanctuary of Shorter AME, her former Denver church, as she and Mary Burnett Talbert presided over a mortgage-burning ceremony celebrating the successful two-year campaign to purchase Cedar Hill, the Washington, D.C., home where Frederick Douglass had lived from 1877 until his death in 1895. With Douglass's violin and personal library already donated by his widow, the women of the NACW sketched ambitious plans to convert the white brick Victorian house—with its panoramic view of the capital's grandest monuments—into an archive akin to a black Mount Vernon. "It will be beautiful and all relics, manuscripts and articles of historical value to the race will be accumulated therein for the benefit of the entire race, and will become a mecca to which the children will journey for information and inspiration," they promised.

As the women tingled with anticipation, Massachusetts teacher Elizabeth Carter read aloud from the mortgage, then handed it to NACW president Talbert, who had spearheaded the fund-raising drive. While the delegates sang "Hallelujah, 'Tis Done," Madam Walker—whose $500 gift made her the largest single donor—carefully held a slender lighted candle beneath the precious document, igniting its edges until the paper was consumed in flames. "I am glad to be able to show the world by this simple, visible act that the mortgage so long threatening this historic home has been reduced to ashes," she said with pride. Near Madam Walker's side was her Des Moines friend Mrs. S. Joe Brown, who had raised a total of $750 from individuals. Brown, who had been born in a sharecropper's shack and who had lived in an attic during her first few months in Denver, had helped rescue the hilltop home of one of America's most significant and accomplished figures.

Accompanied by Sue Brown, Madam Walker traveled by train to Des Moines for the second time that year. Before "a splendid mixed audience" in the city's "leading white church," and then at a local high school, she reviewed "the valor of our soldiers, from Crispus Attucks, who fell upon Boston Common, to the boys who used the bolo knife upon the Western front," referring to the recent heroic efforts of Privates Henry Johnson and Needham Roberts of New York's 369th. Though wounded by grenades, they alone had repelled two dozen German attackers with hand grenades, a rifle and a knife.

Before leaving Iowa, Madam Walker received the news that President Wilson had made his long-awaited statement on lynching. Under pressure from War Secretary Newton Baker, Wilson issued an open letter condemning mob violence on July 26. "My anxiety is growing at the situation in this country among the negroes," Baker had written Wilson after a July 1 meeting with Tuskegee president Robert Russa Moton. During the private session Moton had despaired over the unabated rise in lynchings since the start of the war, noting nineteen killings in May alone. Convinced that words from Wilson would have a "wholesome effect" on the nation, Baker also knew his President was vulnerable in the international arena as the Allies looked askance at America's entrenched racial dilemma. While the President "did not shrink from plotting for a new world," wrote historian Kenneth O'Reilly, he "claimed his own nation's racial landscape was beyond his ability." Nevertheless the reluctant President's statement was one of the only encouraging signals African Americans had seen from his administration. The "mob spirit," he admonished, "vitally affects the honor of the nation and the very character and integrity of our institutions. I say plainly that every American who takes part in the action of a mob or gives any sort of countenance is not a true son of this great democracy, but its betrayer." Wilson went as far as a steadfast states' righter might go, "earnestly and solemnly" imploring "the Governors of all the States, the law officers of every community, and, above all, the men and women of every community in the United States" to "cooperate—not passively merely, but actively and watchfully—to make an end of this disgraceful evil." In the end, however, he failed to mention the black victims who disproportionately endured the attacks and declined to offer any specific remedies for the racism that fueled the crimes.

What Madam Walker was thinking that day is not recorded. But her August 1917 visit to the White House had rendered her highly sensitive to the President's words and deeds, especially when they concerned matters of race. As she boarded the Chicago-bound train to attend the second annual Walker hair culturists convention, she had several hours to contemplate President Wilson's remarks and to prepare the message she and her delegates would soon send to him.

As she arrived in Chicago a few days early for her August 1–3 assembly, she knew the grumbling about drugstore sales of Glossine threatened to disrupt the proceedings. One group had gone so far as to submit a petition to Ransom: "We the undersigned agents of Mme. C. J. Walker do not feel that we have the proper protection from you by placing your goods in the drugstores. In this way our sale of goods has been greatly cut down."

A letter from Ransom outlining their concerns awaited Madam Walker at the home of her Chicago hosts. "Among the many objections which they set forth, the one to my mind having the most force is that when drug stores handle the preparations, persons who refuse to take the course and treatments go to a drug store, buy a cheap comb and Glossine and . . . hold themselves out as agents and thereby deceive a lot of people." In agreement with the agents, he urged Madam Walker to discontinue selling Glossine to retailers. "The real thing after all is making the agents feel that they enjoy some special privileges . . . and that these privileges are not in like manner extended to others who are not agents and who have not paid anything to take the course," he wrote, warning her to expect a floor fight. "One thing is sure. You will have to get your position clearly outlined and having once taken same you will have to stick to it."

On the first day of the convention, when the most outspoken agents mounted their challenge, Madam Walker remained resolute, insisting to the three hundred assembled delegates that selling Glossine in drugstores was a financial necessity in an increasingly competitive marketplace. Already Anthony Overton, a man whose business acumen she respected, had managed to become the first black cosmetics manufacturer to place his products in Woolworth's. White-owned companies continued to make inroads in black newspapers and corner stores with aggressive sales campaigns. And, truth be told, she believed that some of the very agents who opposed her policy were cutting corners by substituting cheap vaseline for Glossine.

"You doubtless are aware that these conventions are a great expense to me," she reminded the delegates in her opening remarks. "I have conducted my business this year almost at a loss owing to the unusual cost of material, heavy taxes, etc. I have not raised prices because I did not want my agents to suffer." Knowing full well that some of her agents were at that moment threatening to revolt, she pledged, "You have been loyal to me and by the help of God, I am trying to be loyal to you." With faith that the mutual loyalty shared by many of her agents would help thwart her opponents, she appealed to their better interests. "My friends, if out of these conventions I can . . . be of some real service to the Race, I say that if I can inspire such a spirit in the heart of one who has never thought along such lines, my money will have been well invested." And although she refrained from publicly castigating her detractors, she was prepared to part ways with those who could not grasp her message. "Never one to run away from a fight, Madam won out," her longtime secretary Violet Reynolds remembered decades later.

With the Glossine flap tamped down, Madam Walker was primed to move on to the real purpose of her meeting: educating the delegates about business, politics and foreign affairs, and exposing them to prominent "race men and women." In addition to hearing presentations from three of her NACW sisters, the agents were addressed by one of Chicago's first black aldermen, as well as by a former U.S. minister to Liberia. But the most riveting message was delivered by Robert Sengstacke Abbott, whose nationally distributed *Chicago Defender* could claim much credit for portraying the city as such a "promised land" that 50,000 Southern black migrants arrived between 1916 and 1918. The war, he often wrote, provided "opportunity" for blacks trapped by a sharecropping, Jim Crow society. "These same factories, mills and workshops that have been closed to us, through necessity are being opened to us," he editorialized in the paper he had founded in 1905. "We are to be given a chance, not through choice but because it is expedient. Slowly but surely all over the country we are gradually edging in first this and then that place, getting a foothold before making a place for our brother." Transported from city to city by Pullman porters and black entertainers, the *Defender*'s local and national circulation mushroomed from 10,000 to 93,000 between 1916 and 1918. By 1920, Abbott claimed to have "by far the largest circulation any black newspaper had ever achieved," with more than 280,000 readers, two-thirds of them outside Chicago.

On the second day at the convention as Madam Walker crossed the stage for her annual keynote address, she was greeted by a standing ovation. "We are here not only to transact the business of this convention, not only to inspire and receive inspiration, but to pledge anew our loyalty and patriotism . . . and to say to our President that the Colored women of America are ready and willing . . . to make any sacrifice necessary to bring our boys home victorious," she pronounced, aware that 7,000 black women had contributed $5 million to the most recent Liberty Loan drive.

Praising her agents as "some of the best women the Race has produced," she asserted that "nowhere will you find such a large number of successful business women as are among the delegates of this convention." For those in the audience seeking her formula for prosperity, she made clear that her achievements had depended upon effort and sacrifice. "I want you to know that whatever I have accomplished in life I have paid for it by much thought and hard work. If there is any easy way, I haven't found it," she counseled. "My advice to every one expecting to go into business is to hit often and hit hard; in other words, strike with all your might."

The emphasis she had placed on the "benevolent side" of her organization remained paramount. "I want my agents to feel that their first duty is to humanity." Concerned about the welfare of the black migrants, she exhorted the delegates "to do their bit to help and advance the best interests of the Race" by assuming responsibility for the needy in their communities. "I tell you that we have a duty to perform with reference to our brother and sister from the South. Shall we who call ourselves Christians sit still and allow them to be swallowed up and lost in the slums of these great cities?" she challenged fervently. "It is my duty, your duty, to go out in the back alleys and side streets and bring them into your home." Always conscious of her own struggles during her early years in St. Louis, she continued her eloquent appeal: "Bring them into your clubs and other organizations where they can feel the spirit and catch the inspiration of higher and better living. Yes, lend them the encouragement of your friendly interest, that the light of hope may continue to shine in their eyes and worthy ambition continue to throb in their hearts."

Beyond social work, Madam Walker intended to foster political and social activism among her agents. "I shall expect to find my agents taking the lead in every locality not only in operating a successful business, but in every movement in the interest of our colored citizenship," she said. Toward that end, the Walker delegates, "on behalf of 12,000,000 Negroes," dispatched a telegram commending President Wilson for his "strong and vigorous" condemnation of lynching. Wilson secretary Joseph Tumulty's reply was perfunctory, assuring them that their "patriotic sentiments are appreciated." Regardless of the dismissive response, the Walker agents knew their concerns had been duly registered with the highest office of the land.

Any sense of satisfaction they may have felt, however, was crushed by the horrifying *Defender* headline they faced on the final day of the convention. Two black women—Ethel Barrett and Ellen Brooks—had been "coated with tar and feathers" in Vicksburg, a town where Madam Walker still maintained ties. As if mocking Wilson's words, five vigilantes also had doused Brooks—the wife of an American soldier said to be "in the trenches in France"—in oily creosote and set her aflame. Although she was described as a "hardworking woman" by former white employers, her attackers felt justified in assaulting her because she appeared to have "no visible means of support." A woman's employment—or lack thereof—was certainly no crime. But it had become an issue of contention in the wartime South as local lawmakers perverted the federal Selective Service "work or fight" statutes that required all able-bodied men to be either gainfully employed or enlisted in the Army. Never intended to apply to women, the law in some jurisdictions had been twisted to force black women to perform the household work many had begun to abandon for factory jobs, self-employment or migration. Faced with complaints from local white housewives that there was a shortage of cooks and maids, Jackson, Mississippi, city council members passed legislation requiring all able-bodied black women—including the wives of black servicemen—to work. In Wetumpka, Alabama, in the case of Maria Parker, even a self-employed hairdresser was not exempt. Arrested because "her chosen occupation . . . did not meet the appropriate criteria of servility," both Parker and the washerwoman she employed were charged with "vagrancy" by an overzealous town marshal who "routinely monitored black women's labor output by counting the clothes hanging in their yards and arresting women who fell short of his quotas," according to historian Tera Hunter.

These attacks, charged the *Defender*, established a new kind of harassment "in that the spirit of [this] social unrest and disorder is determined to strike down the professional and independent men and women of our Race in the South." Such affronts only strengthened Madam Walker's desire to use her money and her power to "help my people" and to provide employment for them. As she closed her second annual convention, she was already preparing to open the doors of Villa Lewaro, her Westchester County mansion, for a late-August convention to discuss those very matters.

CHAPTER 19

Her Dream of Dreams

— ❧ —

Pronouncing Villa Lewaro a "wonder house" with a "degree of elegance and extravagance that a princess might envy," *The New York
Times* declared that Madam Walker "could hardly have chosen a more
attractive spot" for her home. Considering the affluence of her neighbors,
the *New York Herald* paid her no small compliment when it designated her
thirty-four-room mansion "one of the showplaces of the entire Hudson east
shore." Called "the wealthiest spot of ground in the world in proportion to
its population" during the early twentieth century, Irvington-on-Hudson
and Tarrytown—its neighboring village to the north—were home to some
of America's most prosperous capitalists. In the "zone of the metropolis's
millionaires" was Lyndhurst—railroad mogul Jay Gould's Gothic Revival
mansion—and Kykuit, John D. Rockefeller's 300-acre Pocantico Hills
estate. Tiffanys, Astors, Vanderbilts, Morgans and Rockefellers—some of
them from the founding families of the Ardsley Casino, arguably the
nation's most exclusive country club—were sprinkled among the county's
hills and vales.

Located less than twenty miles north of Manhattan, Villa Lewaro, with
its vermilion Spanish tile roof and milky stucco façade—a blend of white
sand and sparkling marble dust—was visible from North Broadway, the
well-traveled Westchester County thoroughfare that linked New York City
to the state capital in Albany. With Madam Walker's approval, Vertner
Tandy had situated his most ambitious architectural commission not along
the river for optimum seclusion, but near the main road in "the most exclusive part of Irvington," unabashedly heralding the presence of America's
premier black businesswoman. With imported Japanese prayer trees and
flowering shrubs and perennials timed to bloom continuously from early
spring until late fall, Madam Walker's Italian gardener intended to create a
setting as magnificent as that of any of the surrounding estates with their
formal gardens and impeccably tended grounds.

* * *

In June 1916, as soon as Ransom and S. A. Singerman, Madam Walker's New York attorney, had discreetly extricated her from any legal obligations to the Bishop Derrick property, Realtor John Nail began searching for an alternative venue. Quite knowledgeable about real estate in the metropolitan area beyond Harlem, he quickly began negotiations on the Irvington site. After some persuasion, Ransom, Madam Walker and Lelia concurred with Nail that "no better spot on earth could have been secured," though initially Ransom questioned the need for homes in Harlem and Westchester County. "Now in reference to having two mansions," Madam Walker informed Ransom from her office on 136th Street, "I will never be content to live in New York City. It does look like a shame after putting so much money in this place to build another." But because she wanted "comfort" more than anything else, she "could never be satisfied living in anybody else's home." And 108 was more her daughter's domain than her own. "For that reason I guess I am doomed to build the other house," she conceded. By the end of August 1916 she had signed the deed for the property at 67 North Broadway.

Irvington's elite—unable to ignore the daily progress of construction as they commuted to and from the train station at the foot of Main Street— did not warm to the idea of having Madam Walker in their midst, warily viewing her as a curiosity at best, an unwelcome intruder at worst. But as the house took shape, even the most resistant snobs could not deny its tastefulness. With the local speed limit set by the Village Board at twenty miles per hour, they motored slowly past the graceful Ionic columns that now framed the semicircular, two-story portico at the main entrance. By the time Madam Walker's interior decorators began arranging her furniture and artwork in the spring of 1918, she was too consumed with her own pleasure to care what the neighbors thought. Promising Ransom not to "overdo" herself during the move from Harlem, she admitted that "I am very anxious to get things straightened out" as she spent her first day in her "dream of dreams" on June 13.

From the curved balcony outside her sleeping porch Madam Walker could see the New Jersey Palisades looming above the Hudson River like a fortress, reminiscent of Vicksburg's towering bluffs. Her airy boudoir— which caught the early sun through French doors—was designed for pure indulgence with its twelve-piece Louis XVI chamber suite of ivory-enameled mahogany arrayed upon a nearly wall-to-wall hand-woven Aubusson carpet. On warm mornings her housekeeper served breakfast downstairs outside her first-floor dining room on the upper level of a two-tiered terrace. At night yachting parties were known to beam their searchlights across those terraces, illuminating the crochet-like balustrades that dramatically latticed the rear of the house.

Having spared no expense in her effort to create a breathtaking environment for herself, Lelia and Mae, Madam Walker later told a reporter, "I had a dream and that dream begot other dreams until now I am surrounded by all my dreams come true." At her direction, the walls of the main hall were lined with handcrafted tapestries selected to complement the soft shading of the elaborately carved medallions that were set in the room's coffered ceiling. In the center of that room a large oak table held a bronze Cartier sculpture of a jaguar attacking an equestrian and his rearing horse. Doorways on either side of the fireplace led to the music room, where a prized Estey organ—equipped with an automatic player mechanism—piped familiar harmonies and full symphonies to all floors of the house with the press of a button. Madam Walker's cozy dining room—with its recessed lighting and whimsical ceiling mural of sea sprites, mermaids and demons—opened from the center of the main hall onto a panoramic view of the river. With the guidance of a consultant from Brentano's, she had selected an impressive array of morocco-bound volumes for her paneled library. Poet Paul Laurence Dunbar—one of Madam Walker's favorites—shared shelves with Mark Twain, Honoré de Balzac, Nathaniel Hawthorne, Jean-Jacques Rousseau and Henry Wadsworth Longfellow. Two limited- edition collections stood out among all the others: a signed, hand-illustrated ten-volume set of the world's great operas with an introduction by Giuseppe Verdi and a fourteen-volume set of the rare wood- and pigskin-bound Hinckley Bible. Outside the library a broad marble staircase led to the second-floor landing, where Auguste Rodin's "La Vieille Courtisane" stood watch over the master bedroom and the lavishly furnished guest bedrooms.

As proud as many African Americans were of Madam Walker's good fortune, a grudging few accused her of "undue extravagance" and self-aggrandizement. She was quick to remind her detractors that "Villa Lewaro was not merely her home, but a Negro institution that only Negro money had bought." She had built the house, she said, to "convince members of [my] race of the wealth of business possibilities within the race, to point to young Negroes what a lone woman accomplished and to inspire them to do big things." Fully conscious of the symbolism Villa Lewaro evoked, she urged Ransom to deliver a clear message to newspaper reporters: "Do not fail to mention in the article for 'Negro History' that the Irvington home, after my death, will be left to some cause that will be beneficial to the race—a sort of monument." Ransom more than complied in a news release marked by his usual flourishes. "This residence will be all that the heart could wish, a monument to the brain, hustle and energy of this remarkable woman, and a milestone in the history of a race's advancement," he wrote. "We take a pardonable pride in stating the fact that a member of our race is now the owner of a valuable estate . . . within view of the famous Palisades." In a variation on Ransom's theme, *Freeman* columnist R. W. Thompson praised Madam Walker—his occasional Washington houseguest—for providing an "object lesson to her race as to what can be accomplished by thrift, industry and intelligent investment of money." Her abilities, he wrote with obvious pride, demonstrated that "all of the brains, executive ability and business acumen are [not] lodged in white craniums."

Less than a month after moving in, Madam Walker embarked on the summer tour that took her to Denver for the NACW biennial and Chicago for the Walker agents convention. But after five weeks away from Irvington, she was eager to return to the comfort and quiet of Villa Lewaro. By mid-August she was "busy as a bee" tending her backyard garden. "Every morning at six o'clock I am at work . . . pulling weeds, gathering berries, vegetables, etc. We are putting up fruit and vegetables by the wholesale," she wrote Ransom. "Tell Nettie she should see me now—am all dressed up in woman-alls, the feminine for overalls, and I am a full-fledged 'farmerette.'" To add to her delight, her Indianapolis housekeepers, James and Frances Bell, had arrived while she was away. "I think they are just the right folks for this place. Mrs. B. says this is a god-blessed place," she happily wrote, addressing her maid with the respect she had craved for herself during her days as a cook and washerwoman.

Relaxed and reinvigorated after two weeks in Irvington, Madam Walker traveled to Atlantic City on August 21 for the National Negro Business League's nineteenth annual convention. With less than a week before her first Villa Lewaro gala, she charged Lelia with overseeing the Bells, the gardeners and the interior decorators as they fussed with final preparations. Her guest of honor, Emmett Scott—the Special Assistant to the Secretary of War for Negro Affairs—also was the NNBL's featured speaker. Taking as his text "Winning the War," he reviewed the accomplishments of the 1,000 black captains and lieutenants in the United States Army and the Medical Reserve Corps, the forty black chaplains and the "more than 300,000 American Negro" draftees. "Two divisions of Negro troops are now in France with eight combat regiments to be trained in various cantonments in the country," he proudly announced to an audience eager to know the details of the latest battlefield activities of the 92nd Division and the 369th Regiment of the Provisional 93rd, now wearing French uniforms and attached to a French combat division.

That Friday, NNBL member Vertner Tandy—a physically imposing and charming man—effusively praised his most famous client, thanking her for contributing "more to architecture for Negroes than any person or group of persons in this country." Nodding in her direction, he peered through his round-rimmed glasses and urged his patron to step forward toward the podium so that he might address her personally. "I want to say to you, Madam Walker, in the presence of this august assembly that it has been through your unselfish loyalty to your race and to your achievements and successes that a Negro has been successful and has achieved success in architecture," Tandy announced. Calling her "the greatest woman this country has produced," he extolled her for sharing "with those of her race the glories that she has achieved." Tandy, it must be said, had profited handsomely from the arrangement, building commission fees into nearly every transaction, from the purchase of the organ to the acquisition of the roof tiles.

The NNBL audience was indeed, as the architect had suggested, "august," unquestionably the cream of black entrepreneurship and leadership. In the hall was George White, the former North Carolina congressman who had introduced the first federal antilynching bill in the House of Representatives, then developed a black town near Cape May, New Jersey. Maggie Lena Walker, founder of the St. Luke Penny Savings Bank and the first American woman bank president, sat not far from Atlanta Life Insurance Company founder Alonzo Herndon and Charles Clinton Spaulding, the general manager and soon to be president of the North Carolina Mutual Life Insurance Company. In addition to Madam Walker's competitors, Annie and Aaron Malone—who had just constructed an expensive and well-equipped factory and office building in St. Louis—were her friends John Nail and Charlotte Hawkins Brown.

Madam Walker had developed so much respect among this group of influential African Americans that when an Austin, Texas, physician was told by NNBL president James Carroll Napier that he had failed to follow protocol in his effort to introduce a resolution, she was able to successfully persuade the body to yield him the floor. Having herself faced a comparable dilemma six years earlier when Booker T. Washington refused her request to speak, she urged the group to support the doctor's motion to commend George W. Breckenridge, a white San Antonio newspaper publisher who had pledged $100,000 to help convict lynchers in his state. "I am very much in sympathy with what the gentleman has just stated. It was unfortunate he did not bring it to the attention of the Committee on Resolutions but since it didn't come up at that time, I do believe it can still go yet . . . and it will have the same effect," she appealed to Napier, just as George Knox had petitioned Booker T. Washington on her behalf in 1912. Impressed by a recent *New York Age* article about the generous fund,

Madam Walker herself had dispatched a telegram of support to Brecken-ridge the previous week. "I told [him] I represented 20,000 Negro busi-nessmen and women and that I spoke the sentiments of 12,000,000 loyal black Americans," she said, urging the NNBL to similarly display its appre-ciation. "I am in favor of this League sending a telegram or some kind of communication . . . I believe it will have much weight." Without further deliberation, Napier approved the proposal.

For the late-August Villa opening, Lelia and Edna Lewis Thomas—Madam Walker's social secretary and Lelia's close friend—selected engraved invi-tations with a small Walker crest fashioned from a "W" affixed to a cobalt-and-lavender shield. "Mme. C. J. Walker," read the elegantly scripted card, "requests the pleasure of your presence at an afternoon with Hon. Emmett J. Scott, Assistant Secretary of War, Sunday, August twenty-fifth from three until six at her residence, Villa Lewaro, Irvington-on-Hudson." Fully immersed in war-related matters—and intent upon positioning Villa Lewaro as a venue for both social enjoyment and political debate—Madam Walker had instructed Lelia to add the words "Conference of interest to the race" to the RSVP line. With Scott as honoree, she could be sure of lively conversation and high attendance.

Long past the stony condescension to which he had subjected Madam Walker during her first visit to Tuskegee, Scott apparently was pleased to accept her invitation. But when he received a preliminary guest list, he objected to some of the names. His personal secretary's subsequent letter to Lelia hurled her into a state of panic. "I have never in my life been so dis-turbed. I understand that one or two of those men are antagonistic to Mr. Scott," Lelia wrote Ransom. "I am awfully fearful about this thing wonder-ing how mother intends to bring these different factions together after they have scrapped all of these years. How she is going to bring them together is a mystery to me."

Afraid that Scott "might do one of two things, say that he is not coming, or let it go on as though he intends to be present and at the last minute, send a telegram regretting his inability to be present," Lelia continued to fret, perhaps reflecting upon Enrico Caruso's last-minute cancellation for her Circle for Negro War Relief concert. "In either case it would be a slam on mother." But because Madam Walker rarely allowed obstacles to impede her, she assumed that her good intentions, as well as the setting—in the spirit of Joel Spingarn's 1916 Amenia retreat—would provide a sufficient catalyst to loosen stalled dialogue and soothe old and irritated rivalries.

Certainly she knew that Scott had endured recent fire for adhering too closely to the accommodationist style of his mentor, Booker T. Washington. Among his critics were longtime adversaries Monroe Trotter and Ida B.

Wells-Barnett, both of whom could well have been included on Madam Walker's original guest list. Because Scott's letters to Madam Walker and Lelia are lost, and because his personal correspondence at Morgan State University is currently unavailable for review, there is no way to be certain of the complaints he may have lodged against specific guests. But if either Trotter or Wells-Barnett were invited, neither appears to have attended.

To them, as well as to some others, Scott had been too willing to rationalize and defend Secretary of War Baker's plan to assign more than half of the drafted African Americans to jobs as laborers and stevedores rather than to combat units and to staff their squadrons with mostly white officers. Soon after being appointed to his post in the fall of 1917, Scott had "proposed to popularize the war among 'the Colored people,'" as he wrote in a letter to Baker. But the secretary showed little reciprocal sentiment, informing Scott soon after that there "was no intention on the part of the War Dept. to undertake at this time a settlement of the so-called race problem." Despite Baker's rebuff—and perhaps because many of those who knew Scott understood his precarious and relatively powerless position—he continued to enjoy "widespread support," if only as a symbolic and token representative who could exercise occasional influence on behalf of the race to those in power.

Apparently Scott's initial reservations about the roster of invitees were sufficiently overcome by the time he prepared to leave the NNBL convention in Atlantic City. Traveling directly from New Jersey to Irvington, Scott and his wife, Eleanora Baker Scott, arrived the evening before the event, perhaps, like others, feeling that they had been "transported into a fairyland." Early the next afternoon "nearly 100 white and colored men and women, leaders in their respective races," entered the grounds, some chauffeured by Madam Walker's driver, others in automobiles from Manhattan, a few on foot from the Irvington train depot. Among the guests were Charlotte Hawkins Brown of Palmer Memorial Institute, NAACP Secretary John Shillady, Vertner Tandy and his wife, Sadie Dorsette Tandy, Massachusetts Realtor Watt Terry (whom Madam had first met during the 1912 NNBL convention), her longtime St. Louis friend Jessie Robinson, as well as several NACW members. Mae was home from her second year at Spelman and Lelia had added a handful of her closest friends to the guest list.

After an "appetizing" lunch on the rear terraces, with the river visible beyond the lush, leafy treetops, all adjourned to the music salon. Beneath two massive crystal chandeliers and gold-leaf-trimmed pilasters, the assembled party was treated to a concert arranged and hosted by J. Rosamond Johnson and featuring violinist Joseph Douglass and organist Melville Charlton. As much as anything her wealth afforded, Madam Walker enjoyed introducing emerging musicians and showcasing seasoned performers. Douglass, a grandson of abolitionist Frederick Douglass, had performed at the 1893 World's Columbian Exposition in Chicago and was the first black violinist to be featured on transcontinental tours. Charlton—the first African American admitted to the American Guild of Organists and chief organist at the Religious School of Temple Emanu-El (the wealthiest synagogue in America)—was masterful on the Estey.

Following the uplifting musical interlude, Ransom ceremoniously introduced Madam Walker, who, in outlining the purpose of the meeting, encouraged her guests to "confer" with Scott and "with each other regarding the part American Negroes were playing in the war." In the process, she hoped they would "forget all their differences [and] stand together for the higher principles involved in this war . . . to continue [to be] loyal to country [and] to the soldiers fighting for democracy."

Having visited several military camps earlier that year, Madam Walker had observed firsthand the treatment and living conditions of the troops. Like two of her guests—Mary White Ovington and James Weldon Johnson—she had spoken out in the most forceful terms about the bravery, the rights and the expectations of black soldiers. As the summer sun streamed through the fanlight windows and wide-open French doors, Madam Walker's remarks drew much agreement. Harlemites remained proud of Henry Johnson and Needham Roberts, the two men whose May heroics to thwart a nighttime German ambush had helped the 369th gain the nickname "Hellfighters" and caused the German soldiers to describe them as "blutlustige schwarze Männer" or "bloodthirsty black men."

Whether Madam Walker referred to it or not, her guests had not forgotten the December 1917 execution of more than a dozen black Camp Logan soldiers. Months of insults and assaults had pushed the base's troops—already at the flash point—to ignition. Angered after having been beaten and shot at by Houston police for insisting upon information about a fellow battalion member, Corporal Charles Baltimore—an experienced and popular noncommissioned officer—led close to 100 revenge-seeking black recruits from the camp into town. Before the resulting August 23, 1917, riot was halted, two black civilians and seventeen whites—including five policemen—lay dead. In response to the mortal confrontation, the Army court-martialed sixty-three members of the 24th Infantry, hanging thirteen of them at dawn on December 11.

Even fresher in their minds was the murder of a soldier at nearby Camp Merritt, New Jersey, exactly one week earlier. With tensions simmering on the evening of August 17, 1918—after two black soldiers had been ordered from a YMCA building because two white Mississippians "resented" their presence—a black soldier stabbed a white soldier. Soon after, black and white troops gathered in the streets and exchanged threats. While a commander attempted to disperse the crowd, armed guards—without orders—shot at the retreating black soldiers, wounding five and killing another with a bullet to the back. In his quick and defiant reaction, Reverend Francis Grimké, the attorney who had negotiated the NACW's purchase of the Douglass home, railed, "Every colored soldier who meets his death here before sailing for France because he resents the insults of southern white bullies . . . belongs on the honor roll of the noble dead."

Madam Walker could not have agreed more, yet she delivered a message of unity as she introduced Scott, signaling to her guests that any disagreements they may have harbored were best temporarily sacrificed for the greater good. Arising "amidst much applause," Scott paid his hostess "high tribute." Conscious of the criticism he faced, Scott used the occasion to trumpet small victories, suggesting that through his efforts some neighborhood Selective Service boards had been closed "because they treated Negro draftees unfairly." Then he proudly announced that "colored women would be sent overseas as Red Cross" volunteers after having been denied the privilege earlier in the war. As the afternoon progressed, Ransom presented several more speakers, each reflecting Madam Walker's interest in a range of political and educational issues: Mary Talbert and Fred Moore; former Assistant U.S. Attorney General William H. Lewis and Wilberforce president William S. Scarborough; the NAACP's John Shillady and Mary White Ovington, as well as William Jay Schieffelin, a longtime Tuskegee Institute board member. The speakers—whether white or black, Bookerites or NAACPers—all adopted Madam Walker's unity theme (at least for the afternoon) and "emphasized the necessity of the various elements in the race getting together," wrote the *New York Age*.

"It will be a very great pleasure during all the years to come that we were the first official guests entertained in Villa Lewaro," Scott wrote a few days later. "The wonderful gathering of friends who came to pay tribute to your great business ability and to congratulate you . . . was beyond compare." And although he had witnessed Booker T. Washington's many gatherings of esteemed philanthropists and prosperous industrialists at The Oaks on Tuskegee's campus, he deemed this event a most unusual one: "No such assemblage has ever gathered at the private home of any representative of our race, I am sure." Appreciative of the "manifestations of friendship" shown him and his wife, Scott assured Madam Walker of "my earnest willingness to serve you and any of your interests in any way possible, at any time."

With similar sentiments, George Lattimore, the field secretary of the Welfare League of the 367th Infantry, wrote that he was "transmitting . . . to our boys 'Somewhere in France' the message of assurance they are not forgotten." Noting that he had reminded them that Madam Walker stood "preeminently in the front ranks of the host of friends ready 'to do or die' over here," he then mused, "I imagine I can hear the boys now firing a salute in your honor."

Not all the guests, however, were pleased with Madam Walker's message. William Jay Schieffelin—a wealthy white New Yorker long involved in local political reform—soon was publicly criticizing Madam Walker and suggesting that her words about the rights and expectations of returning black soldiers were entirely too militant, even racially divisive. As president of Schieffelin Drugs—the family concern that had introduced Bayer aspirin to America in the 1890s—he moved in powerful circles. Nevertheless, Madam Walker did not hesitate to challenge him, disturbed that he was damaging her reputation by misrepresenting her position. Neither a verbatim account of Madam Walker's August 25 remarks nor a text of Schieffelin's comments exists, but her reply could not have been stronger. "It has given me no little annoyance that you have misinterpreted my meaning again and again in your talks," she wrote with great pique. "I feel it necessary to explain my position to you more fully that you will not again be in error in this particular respect."

Admonishing Schieffelin for his insensitivity, Madam Walker reminded him of the "hundreds of revolting, loathsome experiences which [my people] suffer from day to day." As the specially appointed colonel of New York's 15th National Guard, he doubtless knew the details of the racially motivated insults endured by her friend Noble Sissle and other members of the regiment during their training in South Carolina just prior to their departure for France. "The Negro in the south," she reminded him, "has been denied the use of firearms . . . and has been no match for the fiends and brutes who have taken advantage of his helplessness." Having "bravely, fearlessly bled and died" to help defend America's honor, she believed, the troops had every right to expect a patriot's reward. "Now they will soon be returning. To what? Does any reasonable person imagine to the old order of things? To submit to being strung up, riddled with bullets, burned at the stake? No! A thousand times No! And what good friend, even of humanity, would wish it so?" she exclaimed, with a not so subtle dig at his "claim to be a real friend to the Negro."

"They will come back to face like men, whatever is in store for them and like men defend themselves, their families, their homes," Madam Walker continued, refusing to soften her stance. "Please understand that this does not mean that I wish to encourage in any way a conflict between the two races. Such a thing is farthest from my mind," she insisted. "My message to my people is this: Go live and conduct yourself so that you will be above the reproach of any one. But should but one prejudiced, irrational boast infringe upon [your] rights as men—resent the insults like men . . . and if death be the result—so be it. An honorable death is far better than the miserable existence imposed upon most of our people in the south," she wrote, sadly noting her "resignation" to the situation. "I have tried so very hard to make you see the thing thru the eyes of a Negro, which I realize is next to impossible." Demanding that he refrain from further distorting her message, she scolded, "Your talks would do a far greater good if you would point out to the white people just what their duties to the Negro are and be assured if the advice is heeded, there will be no reason to find fault with the execution of the Negro's duty to the white man."

As the war dragged on—and African American leaders saw little official willingness to address domestic issues—such sentiments gathered momentum. Wholly disenchanted with the Wilson administration and the War Department, their diminishing patience left them less and less compelled to defer their complaints and displeasure. The following spring, in fact, when Du Bois returned from a postwar trip to France, he refused to contain his bitterness at the continued lynchings and the Army's Jim Crow policies. "By the God of heaven, we are cowards and jackasses if now that the war is over, we do not marshal every ounce of our brain and brawn to fight a sterner, longer, more unbending battle against the forces of hell in our own land," he wrote in so stinging an editorial that the New York Postmaster attempted to ban the May 1919 issue of *The Crisis* in which it appeared. With a defiance that nearly obliterated the collaborative tone of his earlier "Close Ranks" column, he wrote:

> We return.
> We return from fighting.
> We return fighting.
> Make way for Democracy! We saved it for France, and by the Great Jehovah, we will save it for the United States of America, or know the reason why.

Whereas Schieffelin may have expected the "old order of things," Moorfield Storey, the former president of both the American Bar Association and the NAACP, predicted, "Negroes will come back feeling like men and not disposed to accept the treatment to which they have been subjected."

While Madam Walker's personal spirit and public politics waxed ever more potent, her physical health waned, forcing her to stay close to home during the late summer and early fall. "Am still getting up to work in the garden every morning," she wrote Ransom from Villa Lewaro in mid-September, "but it's getting pretty cool here so am afraid I won't be able to do it much longer." In a note to her friend Jessie Robinson, Madam Walker joked that she and the Bells "are following the sun beams all over the house in an effort to keep warm." But the nippy weather failed to stifle her glee. "I wish my friends throughout the country would give me a chicken shower," she told Ransom, slipping comfortably into one of the more enjoyable memories of her rural Louisiana childhood. When an early October spell of Indian summer brought a welcomed respite from the morning frost, she was able to savor the autumn leaves as they engulfed the forest along the Palisades in flames of crimson, saffron and tangerine. "Am grateful for the warm weather as I don't want to start the fires any sooner than I can help," she wrote.

But her joy soon was jostled by an alarming notification from Ransom: her income taxes—dramatically inflated to more than $50,000 by a wartime surtax—were due "at once." Now the expense of firing her furnace had become the least of her worries. "After you take care of taxes, state, federal and income, you will hardly have any money for anything else than to look after general expenses," Ransom informed her. To add to the problems, the American Can Company remained under a strict mandate to fill government contracts first, leaving the Walker Company and other consumer manufacturers low in priority for their orders. And as the price of scarce metals increased, so too did the price of steel hot combs.

Still Madam Walker felt an obligation to contribute to the war bonds drive. "If I do not buy in Harlem, the colored people will not get the credit and there is a feeling in Washington that they have not measured up, so a letter from Mrs. Talbert tells me," she notified Ransom. When a small delegation of the Irvington Liberty Loan committee—apparently recovered from the village's initial shock at her presence—called upon Madam Walker to support its latest effort, she politely declined, informing them that she had made a commitment to Harlem's drive. "When I explained my intention of taking out bonds in N.Y. they readily understood and thought me justified in doing so," she wrote.

Try as she might to adhere to her doctor's advice, Madam Walker could not entirely confine herself to Irvington. On November 11, 1918, when the armistice ending the gunfire in Europe was signed, she was in Boston, where she spent a "delightful five days" as the city exploded into euphoric, round-the-clock bedlam. "Never has the old Puritan city seen such an outburst of spontaneous celebration," proclaimed the Boston Globe, as impromptu "parades, big and small, blocked every street" and thousands of revelers flocked to the expansive Boston Common to celebrate the surrender of Germany's Kaiser Wilhelm II. From dawn to dawn, the racket of factory whistles, car horns, jangling tin cans, booming drums, clanging frying pans, cheers and whoops filled the "bright, crisp" autumn air. The city's narrow downtown streets were deluged in a blizzard of confetti as streamers dangled from lampposts and telephone wires. Businessmen in pinstripes snake-danced past peddlers hawking American flags while automobiles and horse-drawn carts alike were trimmed in red, white and blue bunting. "It seems that the whole country went mad over the peace imminence," Madam Walker wrote to Ransom after returning to Irvington. "You were right to give the folks at the factory a half day."

Two weeks after Germany's surrender, Madam Walker and Lelia traveled to Washington for the Thanksgiving holiday. "Lelia and I had a very pleasant trip to Washington, altho it rained all day Thursday," she wrote, recalling an "especially good" recital that evening where they had "met lots of interesting folks." She also was delighted to have seen Emmett Scott, who, she wrote, "was especially courteous to us, sending us candy and flowers."

For her part, Lelia had a "splendid time," delighted with Scott's "lovely box of bon bons." But Lelia's primary focus was her new beau, Wiley Wilson, a pharmacist who was completing his medical studies at Howard University. A tall, "olive-brown," "commanding son of a gun," Wiley impressed Lelia, at least in part, because he was not in the least intimidated by her status or her money. Two years her senior, he was the youngest of three dashing, well-educated sons of a successful Arkansas farmer and cattle rancher. His elder brothers, John and Ed, had attended Lincoln University in Pennsylvania in the 1890s. Then, while Ed was enrolled at Union Theological Seminary, John returned to Pine Bluff, Arkansas, and became a sheriff. But after arresting a prominent white man, he was prohibited from apprehending whites. Incensed, he quit the force, purchased a saloon and openly operated two whorehouses. With some of his considerable earnings, he sent Wiley to Howard University's School of Pharmacy, then bankrolled a drugstore for his brother when he graduated. In 1911, when John was shot to death during a Mardi Gras quarrel with a former girlfriend, Ed and Wiley inherited his property and his cash.

The *New York Age* later reported that Lelia and the debonair Wiley had met in early 1918 in New York. But there were several other opportunities for their paths to have crossed long before that encounter. It is entirely possible that Lelia first saw him in Pine Bluff, where her Aunt Louvenia lived for at least a few years. They may also have met in Indianapolis during August 1911, when both attended the Knights of Pythias convention, as well as between 1911 and 1914, when Wiley and Ed operated Wilson Brothers Pharmacy in St. Louis and lived in the same block as one of Lelia's dearest friends.

What neither Madam Walker nor Lelia mentioned in their letters about their Washington visit was that Wiley had become an unspoken source of tension between mother and daughter. While Lelia was charmed by his self-confidence, Madam Walker, in her maternal protectiveness, sensed an arrogance that she suspected would wound her "baby." Lelia, however, was so smitten with a man as accustomed to the trappings of wealth as she that she was oblivious to his inadequate attentiveness. During the next several months, Madam Walker would struggle to keep her thoughts to herself.

Surrounded by a "shower" of birthday cards from friends and employees from across the country, Madam Walker celebrated her 51st birthday on December 23 amid the splendor of a festively decorated Villa Lewaro. That morning her former sister-in-law, Peggie Prosser, had arrived at the Irvington train station. In tow was little Frank Ransom, dressed in his new Christmas suit—"somewhat like the goods that soldiers are wearing in their overcoats"—that godmother Walker had bought for him. With Lelia in Washington—probably with Wiley—for the holiday, Madam Walker was ecstatic to have the rooms come alive with a child's laughter and wonderment.

The next afternoon on Christmas Eve the house began to fill with other friends. At dusk one of the final arrivals was Hallie Elvira Queen, a Spanish teacher at Dunbar High School, Washington, D.C.'s premier black public preparatory school, whose faculty included several Ivy League Ph.D. recipients, many of whom had been denied jobs in white institutions because of their race. Queen herself was a Dunbar graduate with an A.B. from Cornell and a master's degree from Stanford University. Fluent in Spanish, French and German, she had been honored for her work as an interpreter during the war. Because she was close to Lelia's age, Madam Walker may have looked upon her as a daughter—one with whom she found much in common because of Queen's work as chairman of Howard University's Red Cross chapter during the war and for the relief work she had done during the East St. Louis riots. What Madam Walker did not know was that Queen had been hired in May 1917 by the War Department's Military Intelligence Division as an informant and translator to monitor "Negro subversion," to "carry out surveillance activities among blacks" and to report on "'suspicious' activities including church meetings, conferences, streetcorner gatherings, and other such activities." Whether Queen was on official assignment during her Christmas visit to Villa Lewaro is not reflected in her confidential MID file because her reports to the War Department appear to have ended in November 1918. But by then, she had already determined that "no German propaganda [was] carried among colored families in Lower West Side & Upper Harlem between 125th & 142nd Streets," Madam and Lelia's Manhattan neighborhood.

Regardless of Queen's intentions, the keen powers of observation that had made her a competent spy also helped her capture the mood of Madam Walker's first Irvington Christmas. "The building and grounds, with all of their beauty, meant little to me except as 'a fitting temple for so great a Soul,'" Queen later remembered of her initial entry into the courtyard, "for the genius and achievement of the woman were far greater than buildings of marble and wood." Madam Walker, she wrote, was "gracious, cordial and unaffected by all the grandeur" as she introduced Queen to the other guests and joined them around the Victrola as they sang Christmas carols. Having "retired early," Madam Walker awakened everyone at midnight to wish them "Merry Christmas." Because Edna Lewis Thomas was away, she invited Queen to her room to help address gifts. "Well did they show the largesse of her heart!" Queen remembered. "It was significant that the most generous presents were made to people who could not return them, as the children of her chauffeur [and] her maids." While Madam Walker had received dozens of gifts from friends and employees, she was most proud of her daughter's presents. "With most loving care she showed bits of stationery and other gifts from Lelia, for these were indeed the most cherished of all," wrote Queen.

Early on Christmas morning, while some of her guests explored the grounds, Madam Walker sat snuggled before the "glowing fireplace" that Mr. Bell had prepared in the main hall. As the logs sizzled and crackled, everyone exchanged gifts until breakfast was served. "It was significant that in that beautiful state dining room, with its wonderful furnishing and rich indirect lighting and all the material good that life could expect," that "Madam insisted upon our kneeling while she returned to God thanks for the gift of the Christ child and for all other gifts that had come to her," Queen reverently reminisced. "The theme of her prayer was humility and awe in the presence of God."

Throughout the day additional dinner guests trickled in. May Howard Jackson, the sculptor, whose work had been exhibited at Washington, D.C.'s prestigious Corcoran Gallery, was accompanied by her husband, William Sherman Jackson, head of the mathematics department at Washington's M Street School, the city's oldest black public school. The accomplished couple was joined around the specially built Hepplewhite table by AME minister W. Sampson Brooks of Baltimore, who discussed his extensive European travels. Among the military men present were a Lieutenant Simmons, as well as a sailor from a torpedoed vessel and a wounded army officer, one of the members of the 369th who recently had received the Croix de Guerre, the French High Command's most coveted military honor. As Madam Walker contemplated a trip to France to observe the peace talks at Versailles, she was rapt as her dinner companions recounted stories of Europe and the war. "The personnel of that . . . party," wrote Queen, "may well be taken to show the diversity of interests shown by Madam Walker in selecting her friends."

After their early afternoon meal, the group explored the house as if it were a museum, moving from the music room, where they gathered to hear more carols on the Estey's automatic player, to the library, where they sampled the "magnificent selection of books." That evening Madam Walker's chauffeur, Louis Tyler, drove a small group into the city for a basketball game at the Manhattan Casino, the hall at 155th Street and Eighth Avenue where Lelia and James Weldon Johnson had hosted a farewell concert for the departing 369th earlier that year. "Mme's entrance was the signal for an ovation and she was at once requested to throw the ball from her box," wrote Queen. After the game, Tyler escorted the two women to Lelia's town house for the night.

Early the next morning Tyler drove Madam Walker to Pier A at the tip of Manhattan, where she joined New York City mayor John S. Hylan's committee to review the return of the Atlantic Fleet. At the mayor's personal invitation, she and other members of his welcoming party boarded the police boat *Patrol*. Although the first severe snowstorm of the season had turned the harbor into a "twilight gloom," the mood was festive as the police band played Christmas music beneath a twenty-foot tree fastened to the afterdeck. Among those on board observing the majestic procession of warships as they steamed through blowing snow past the Statue of Liberty were department store executive Rodman Wanamaker, newspaper publisher William Randolph Hearst, British Columbia governor Sir Frank Barnard, New York Police Commissioner Richard Enright and several city officials. On a nearby naval yacht, Secretary of the Navy Josephus Daniels and Secretary of War Newton Baker reviewed the passing ships as they received a nineteen-gun salute. While the Marine Band played "The Star-Spangled Banner"—its strains muffled by the misty fog—tens of thousands lined the shore from Battery Park at the southern tip of Manhattan to 173rd Street. That afternoon the sun broke through on cue, radiating brightly as 6,000 Marines and sailors stepped in time down Fifth Avenue.

Madam Walker greeted the new year with much anticipation and exhilaration as she reviewed Ransom's annual report. Her 1918 earnings had jumped to $275,937.88, an increase of $100,000 over the previous year, and an amount equivalent to more than $3 million today. "Your receipts exceeded over a quarter of a million and I have no doubt but that you can easily make it a half million in 1919," Ransom ecstatically predicted. "You should congratulate yourself on a remarkable business and when I say remarkable, I am putting it mildly."

Even with the wartime supply problems, her sales had more than doubled in September—her busiest month—and in December—usually one of her slowest months. And now with the war behind them, Grower tins and metal combs were back in stock. Just as she had expected, Chicago had turned into a lucrative market. "You will be surprised at the number of parlors that have been opened up since the Convention," Ransom wrote in mid-January after visiting the city. "Some really beautiful parlors. Chicago now reminds me of New York, a Walker Parlor on every corner." Even the conflicts with the agents over drugstore sales of Glossine had been resolved by a plan to open wholesale supply stations in several cities. And within weeks the Madam C. J. Walker Manufacturing Company would begin branching out from hair care into cosmetics, introducing a line of facial products that included cold cream, cleansing cream, witch hazel and four shades of face powder.

Still, potential money worries persisted. Madam Walker's 1918 expenditures—in large part due to the completion of Villa Lewaro—had ballooned to $329,016.85. "This makes an apparent deficit, which is, of course, offset by the loans, etc., all of which have been paid in full with the exception of the New York property," summarized the meticulous Ransom. "All Indianapolis property is absolutely clear, leaving you a balance in the bank to your credit of $5,228.27," which, both had to agree, left an uncomfortably tight margin. But after only one month into the new year, money was flowing in so quickly that Madam Walker found little reason to be pessimistic. "As for your business it is increasing in leaps and bounds, which is remarkable for January," Ransom gleefully announced. "For instance, your receipts for Monday, just one day, were over $2000.00. Your receipts for Wednesday were over $1400.00, so you can see where you are going. If nothing out of the ordinary happens, your receipts for this year will approximate a half a million if it does not go over." By month's end the company had taken in $26,477.43, exceeding January 1918 by $12,000.

To celebrate, Madam Walker visited Tiffany's showroom at Thirty-seventh Street and Fifth Avenue and treated herself to a few eye-catching treasures—a 3.38-carat solitaire diamond set in a platinum ring with "66 tiny diamonds" and a pair of matching earrings, "the pair weighing 7.28 carats." While there, she also arranged to have three one-carat diamonds from another ring placed into a new setting. Riding up Fifth Avenue after making her purchases, she had every reason to believe that 1919 would move her closer to the millionaire status that she and Ransom both expected her to achieve.

CHAPTER 20

Global Visions

———ⲉⲩⲣⲟ———

Africa—with its stunningly rich natural resources, its unrealized political potential and its overwhelming educational needs—had long fascinated Madam Walker. At least as early as 1912, she had dreamed, with a missionary's zeal, of establishing a girls' industrial training school on the continent. "By the help of God and the cooperation of my people in this country, I am going to build a Tuskegee Institute in Africa!" she had proclaimed during her first National Negro Business League conference. Soon afterward she arranged to pay the tuition for Edmund Kaninga, one of Tuskegee's small number of African students, whom she hoped to educate "for the purpose of founding and establishing a Negro Industrial School on the West Coast of Africa." Then in 1914 she contributed funds to a mission school in Pondoland, South Africa, and extended support to another African student at Hannon Industrial Institute in Greenville, Alabama. When it became clear that business demands would prevent her from personally developing her ambitious school project, she offered $1,000 to any one of the three major black denominations—the Baptists, the AMEs or the AMEZs—willing to "start a little Tuskegee Institute in Africa." And it was not only education that interested Madam Walker. Touched by a report that "seven African . . . girls were being held for ransom," she sent $100 to Liberia for their release in care of Baptist missionary Emma Bertha Delaney, a Spelman College graduate who would later found the Suehn Industrial Mission near Monrovia.

The roots of Madam Walker's curiosity about Africa may well have sprung from her childhood in Madison Parish, where an organized group of black Civil War veterans—swept up in the seductive Back to Africa movement of the 1870s—frequently met to discuss emigration to Liberia. But it probably was in the sanctuary of St. Paul AME Church in St. Louis where she first heard detailed descriptions of life on the faraway continent from visiting bishops and missionaries. As a member of the Mite Missionary

Society, she deposited pennies and nickels in the weekly offering basket to help pay the salaries of women missionaries in Africa. With churches in Liberia and Sierra Leone since the early nineteenth century, and in South Africa by the late 1800s, AME representatives—much to the consternation of colonial government officials—often mingled their religious messages with education and politics, militantly claiming "Africa for the Africans." Madam Walker's attraction to New York's Mother AME Zion Church was motivated, at least in part, by her admiration for Alexander Walters, the church's presiding bishop and a leading Africanist, who had been elected president of the Pan-African Association in London in 1900 and later traveled to West Africa on behalf of the church.

In late 1918 as plans for the Paris Peace Conference solidified, Madam Walker was among a group of politically conscious African Americans already discussing the status of Togo, Cameroon, German East Africa and German Southwest Africa—the four African colonies ruled by Germany since the Berlin Conference of 1884–85, when the European powers partitioned the continent among themselves. The colonies' future ownership loomed as a point of contention in any peace settlement. By 1900, Germany—along with Great Britain, France, Italy, Spain, Portugal and Belgium—had wrested control of nearly 90 percent of Africa's land in pursuit of the continent's mineral and agricultural abundance, including its gold, diamonds, cobalt, palm oil, rubber and cocoa.

In the November 1914 *Crisis*, which was mailed during the early months of the European conflict, W.E.B. Du Bois trained a racial prism on the war, denouncing it as a "wild quest for Imperial expansion," especially by Germany, England and France, into the resource-rich territories in Africa and Asia. "Today civilized nations are fighting like mad dogs over the right to own and exploit these darker peoples," he assailed. And although Madam Walker's thoughts about Du Bois's claims are not recorded, she doubtless saw, and probably read, his article, for her photograph accompanied a story about black YMCA donors in the same issue. Four years later, with Germany's defeat imminent, Du Bois's "Memorandum on the Future of Africa"—a document as ambitious as Woodrow Wilson's proposal for the League of Nations—laid out a plan for an "international Africa." Intended to encompass the almost one million square miles of land that made up the Belgian Congo, as well as the Portuguese and former German colonies, this proposed new territory was to be administered by a global commission comprised of white Europeans and Americans, as well as by representatives of what Du Bois called "the civilized Negro world": "black Americans and other people of African descent" from all hemispheres. U.S. Secretary of State Robert Lansing, upon receiving Du Bois's proposal, appears to have summarily dismissed it. In fact, any plan advocating sovereign "self-determination"—the right of a people to establish their own future political status—even when advanced by his own President, horrified him. "The more I think about the President's declaration as to the right of 'self-determination,' the more convinced I am of the danger of putting such ideas into the minds of certain races," he wrote soon afterward regarding one of Wilson's League of Nations principles. Certain that the phrase would "breed discontent, disorder and rebellion" among a range of disaffected peoples and become "the basis [for] impossible demands on the Peace Congress," he asked in his confidential memorandum, "What effect will it have on the Irish, the Indians, the Egyptians, and the nationalists among the Boers? Will not the Mohammedans of Syria and Palestine and possibly of Morocco and Tripoli rely on it?" Lansing did not even bother to mention black Americans, so unlikely were they to be able to wage any effective claims on the world stage.

As much as Du Bois attempted to redefine the issues of the European war to include African Americans, their concerns—whether domestic or foreign—were of little consequence to Woodrow Wilson, who considered the "disposition" of Germany's former African colonies as "not vital to the life of the world in any respect." Nevertheless, Du Bois, Madam Walker and others had begun to press the issue of black representation in the American peace delegation. In a late-November 1918 letter to Lansing, who still had not acknowledged his African memorandum, Du Bois requested approval of passports for six "carefully selected . . . representative American Negroes"—including himself—for travel to Paris to observe the conference proceedings. Claiming that "large numbers" of "the colored people of America, and indeed of the world," had written to him "concerning the Peace Conference," he declared, "It would be a calamity at the time of the transformation of the world to have two hundred million . . . human beings absolutely without voice." Already skittish about the notion that "certain races" might wish to have any voice at all in France, Lansing referred the matter to State Department Counselor Frank Polk, who recommended denying travel documents for the group. "I think your inclination not to grant passports is a wise one as racial questions of this nature ought not to be a subject to come before the Conference," Lansing cabled from Paris in late December, as he and President Wilson awaited the opening of the talks. Determined to minimize public dissent among the ranks of the American peace commission—and acutely aware that his own League of Nations plan had little support in Congress—Wilson already had excluded Republicans from the delegation. Needing all of his energy to negotiate with British Prime Minister David Lloyd George and French Premier Georges Clemenceau, the Democratic President had no desire to be distracted by black Americans who were intent upon raising embarrassing questions about domestic race relations and American foreign policy in Africa.

In early December, just four days after President Wilson sailed for Europe aboard the U.S.S. *George Washington*, however, Du Bois boarded the *Orizaba*, the authorized U.S. press boat. With his passport request languishing in the hands of Lansing and Polk, "only quick and adroit work on the part of myself and friends" allowed him to travel to France on official *Crisis* business. Also on board the otherwise all-white voyage to France were *New York Age* reporter Lester Walton, Tuskegee president Robert Russa Moton, and Moton's assistant, Nathan Hunt, with whom Du Bois shared a cabin. During the crossing Du Bois told a *New York Herald* reporter: "The leading Negroes of the U.S. will ask the peace conference to turn back to native control the German colonies in Africa for national organization by those there now and by other Negroes who may wish to live under a government of their own race in the old African land."

Like Du Bois, Madam Walker hoped to travel to Paris once the negotiations among the Allied nations—the United States, France, Great Britain, Italy, Japan and more than twenty other countries—commenced. During November and December, as several political groups approached her about representing them in France, she and Ransom debated the feasibility of black American efforts to influence the outcome of the peace talks. Always more conservative than she, Ransom scoffed at Monroe Trotter's plan to form his own overseas delegation. "I talked with Emmett Scott and he is in perfect accord with my opinion that there is no way that this can really be done," he wrote. "About all the American Negro could do is to send someone . . . to influence the Japanese and Liberian delegates to insist on the settling of the Race question at the Peace Conference." Because he was convinced that "domestic questions cannot and will not be thrashed out . . . in France," Ransom suggested that a more effective approach would be "a great Race Conference . . . to sit at Washington contemporaneously with Congress and the Peace Conference [so that] the Negro's position could be, by petition, properly placed before Congress and the United States President."

Despite Ransom's caveat, Madam Walker traveled to Washington in mid-December to attend Trotter's National Race Congress for World Democracy. Having been selected "by unanimous vote" to represent the National Equal Rights League's New York branch, she joined at least 250 delegates from all over the country at the venerable Metropolitan AME Church not far from the White House. If Madam Walker arrived expecting decorum and civility during the two-day conference, she was immensely disappointed by the tenor of the proceedings. "I wish you might have been at that conference," she wrote Ransom with annoyance. "A lot of old igno-ramus preachers—and every one wanted to be sent, or at least to have their particular friend sent."

On the one hand, she was flattered to learn that, in the selection of Paris representatives, she had polled more votes than all "the names submitted, even to the Bishops." On the other hand, she and Ida B. Wells-Barnett were offended when, despite their high tallies, the all-male nominating committee "decided that no women be sent except as alternates." As the council named its five-man delegation—while relegating the women to alternates required to pay their own expenses—Wells-Barnett remembered that such "a clamor arose" that "the committee's report was halted." Tak-ing the floor, she announced that she "regretted that the years spent in fighting the race's battles had made me financially unable to accept the honor which they had offered me." Madam Walker watched with pride as "Mrs. B. registered a strong protest and declined the empty honors which resulted in our being elected from the floor, as full and legal delegates."

Now with nine official National Race Congress delegates, Madam Walker told Ransom she doubted the organization "would be able to send two." With or without them, however, she was already planning her trip to Europe. "Since they have elected me, I shall go even if they cannot do everything for me in the way of expenses, tho I have not said as much to them," she wrote. "Of course Lelia will accompany me."

Ransom reluctantly congratulated Madam Walker on her election, but could not mask his misgivings about the organization. "Monroe Trotter may be all right, but he stands for practically nothing in America," warned Ransom, especially conscious of Trotter's past confrontations with Presi-dent Wilson, the head of the American delegation in Paris. "I hope you will be very careful in not identifying yourself too closely with the Trotter bunch, who may do something that will bring the whole delegation into ill-repute or offend the country. You must always bear in mind that you have a large business, whereas the others, who are going, have nothing. There are many ways in which your business can be circumscribed and hampered so as to practically put you out of business."

Whether Ransom was aware of it or not, the political pressure he feared for Madam Walker had already been applied to *Chicago Defender* publisher Robert Sengstacke Abbott, a man they both knew well. Earlier that year, Major Walter H. Loving, a black Military Intelligence Division agent, had personally visited Abbott to notify him that some of his articles and edito-rials—especially those about lynching and the rights of black soldiers—had given government officials the impression that he might be "unpatriotic." By the end of the visit the "chastened editor," sufficiently intimidated by the threat that his newspaper could be banned by government censors, was said to have "promised to print nothing offensive." During the summer of 1918—not long before Abbott attended Madam Walker's Chicago convention—representatives of the U.S. Post Office began scrutinizing each edition of the *Defender*, "convinced the paper promoted racial hatred and put misguided racial goals ahead of winning the war." By the fall of 1918, Abbott's trademark fiery criticisms, though not entirely absent, were accompanied by "professions of patriotism."

In addition to the War Department's MID operations and the Post Office censors, the State Department had stepped up its surveillance of private American citizens. Empowered by the Espionage Act of 1917 and the Sedition Act of 1918, federal agents now had the authority to punish even the "appearance of disloyalty," not only in the press but in any "writing or speech that *might* harm the country's war efforts, promote the cause of Germany, or discredit the American government, Constitution or flag." Near the end of the war anyone with ties to the Socialist Party or with sympathies for Russia's anticapitalist Bolshevik Revolution was especially vulnerable to accusations of disseminating "subversive" ideas. After the war, MID operatives continued to spy on such prominent Americans as Hull-House founder Jane Addams and former Stanford University president David Starr Jordan.

Even if Abbott failed to share the details of his visit from Major Loving with Ransom and Madam Walker, Ransom's apparently frequent contact with Emmett Scott, as well as his own wide-ranging reading habits, kept him well versed on Washington's political climate. "I am seriously of the opinion that you will not be able to get a passport," he predicted in a late-December letter to Madam Walker. At the time, of course, Ransom did not know just how close to the truth he might be, for Major Loving—not content to confine his surveillance activities to newspaper editors and publishers—had infiltrated the National Race Congress meetings just a week earlier. As a result, Madam Walker's name had been added to the Military Intelligence Division's files of "Negro Subversives." Along with Hallie Queen, the Christmas season visitor to Villa Lewaro whose spy work he supervised, Loving was "one of a half dozen" black MID operatives. His surveillance efforts within the black community, wrote David Levering Lewis, were "indefatigable." What particular strain of patriotism compelled this former music director of the Philippines Constabulary Band to engage in intra-race espionage remains unknown.

With Kaiser Wilhelm II and Germany no longer a threat, Communism and Bolshevism presented the MID and the White House with a postwar umbrella under which to place troublesome dissent of all stripes. Any aggressive protest in response to racial discrimination, lynching or the poor treatment of black soldiers—all issues that Madam Walker championed—

had become tantamount to radical and seditious behavior. In 1919 Attorney General A. Mitchell Palmer told Congress of "a well-concerted movement among a certain class of Negro leaders" to create "a radical opposition to the Government, and to the established rule of law and order." Many black publications, he charged, especially when reporting on lynchings, were filled with "defiance and insolently race-centered condemnation of the white race."

Apparently unable to fathom that African Americans might have legitimate concerns without ever looking beyond U.S. borders, Woodrow Wilson "confided the fear that black soldiers returning from Europe would be 'our greatest medium in conveying bolshevism to America.'" Wilson and Lansing, of course, wished to keep Madam Walker and other African Americans on the western shore of the Atlantic throughout the negotiations. As well, the three major European Allies were described as "puzzled by and cynical about the desire of a large number of black individuals and newly organized groups to attend the Paris conference." For entirely different reasons, some black Americans expressed doubts that the delegations could have any meaningful impact upon the proceedings. In late December 1918, after several groups had chosen delegates and held rallies, the *New York Age* editorialized: "This business of electing delegates to the peace conference at Versailles is being run into the ground . . . It might as well be understood that there is no sense or reason in this multiplying of so-called peace delegations that will never get as far down the harbor as the Statue of Liberty." Besides Trotter's National Race Congress, there were other eager contingents. In November, National Medical Association president George Cannon appealed to Wilson, "We feel that our unselfish devotion at home and our heroism and supreme sacrifice on the battle fields of Europe merit representation in the make-up of the Peace Conference." Within hours of the armistice announcement, Harlem's Palace Casino was packed with five thousand followers of Jamaican black nationalist Marcus Garvey, who himself boldly demanded that "the Allied Powers . . . hand over the ex-German colonies in Africa to black rule." By the end of Garvey's highly charged Universal Negro Improvement Association rally, Socialist labor leader A. Philip Randolph and Ida B. Wells-Barnett—herself now a delegate for at least two organizations—were selected to speak on behalf of the group's interests in France. A much smaller association, the Hamitic League, nominated as two of its representatives Puerto Rican bibliophile Arthur Schomburg and militant newspaper editor John Bruce, whose "Bruce Grit" column had been carried by several black publications since the 1880s. With no authorization from the United States government, the quixotic quest of all these groups still seemed likely to end, as the *Age* had predicted, in New York Harbor.

Nevertheless, in an effort to unite the various factions, Madam Walker joined forces with an eclectic group of activists—including Reverend A. Clayton Powell, Sr., Reverend Frederick Cullen (who had been part of the Silent Protest Parade delegation to the White House in 1917), A. Philip Randolph and Marcus Garvey—to form the International League of Darker Peoples. On January 2, 1919, as Madam Walker welcomed the coalition to Villa Lewaro, she announced her hopes for a permanent organization that would position itself to "engage world opinion even after the peace conference shall have ended." Randolph, the tall, chestnut-complexioned editor of *The Messenger*—a publication with decidedly leftist leanings—presented a set of "peace proposals" in the precise, Oxford-style English he had learned from a Shakespearean tutor. High on the list of demands was a call for "a more enlightened world politics" aimed at providing independence and autonomy for African nations. "Rapacious and unscrupulous 'world power' politics has raped Africa of over 100,000,000 souls and billions of wealth," Randolph, the League's secretary, asserted in his written statement. "No 'League of Nations' can long endure which ignores the just claims of Africa. The world cannot be 'made safe for democracy' while Africa is unsafe for the Africans," the sharply worded manifesto mocked President Wilson. Further, the ILDP document insisted upon an international agreement to abolish "all economic, political and social discriminations in all countries, based upon color." Under its plan, a "supernational" commission, composed of the world's "educated classes of Negroes," would develop and govern Germany's former colonies. Such a body, the group proposed with missionary-like presumption, would establish educational systems to teach "chemistry, physics, biology, horticulture, geology, mining, engineering and political science" and supervise the construction of transportation systems and communications networks. "If peace can be secured through a league of free nations," the ILDP declared, "so can the hydra-headed monster—race prejudice—be destroyed, by the darker peoples of the worlds . . . making common cause with each other, in one great world body."

As a document it was wildly idealistic and utopian. Nevertheless, it embodied a vision with which Madam Walker found little to disagree. And if some of the more excessive rhetoric seemed overblown, the proposed education programs meshed easily with her longtime dream for an African Tuskegee. Ransom, however, was not nearly so open-minded, labeling many of the ILDP goals "utterly impossible as well as impractical." As well, he found little to commend the League's membership roster. "It seems strange to me that so few prominent New Yorkers are connected with it, in fact, there seems to be practically none," he tartly observed. "Of course, they have your name and Mr. Powell's," he added a few days later. "People always seek to get the names of someone with standing to use as one would use vinegar to catch flies. You and Mr. Powell, however, owe it to yourselves to be very careful how you lend your names to every propagandist that comes along," he admonished.

Despite Ransom's reservations, Madam Walker continued to explore additional avenues to influence the peace talks. Aware that members of the Japanese peace delegation were in New York, the League—in the "spirit of race internationalism" and probably at Madam Walker's expense—sent them a floral arrangement "as a token of friendship and brotherhood." Five days after the ILDP's inaugural meeting—with hopes of persuading Japan's representatives to present the "race issue" before the Paris conference—Madam Walker hosted a gathering at the grand Waldorf-Astoria Hotel for a small League delegation and S. Kuriowa, a Japanese envoy and publisher of *Yorudo Choho*, a Tokyo newspaper. During the session, Kuriowa—whose Japanese American brethren had been prohibited from purchasing land in California because of their race—was said to have "assured the delegation of his unqualified and genuine approval of the darker peoples making common cause against the common enemy—race prejudice based upon color." In the only edition of *The World Forum*, the ILDP's newspaper, Kuriowa promised that "the race question will be raised at the peace table."

Having declared war on Germany in 1914 and deployed its navy in defense of British convoys in Far East waters throughout the conflict, Japan now was entitled to a seat in Paris with the other Allies. Harboring their own expansionist objectives, the country's leaders were intent upon continuing to occupy the Chinese territory they had invaded and assuming control over Germany's former Pacific islands north of the equator.

With Madam Walker already a target of the MID, her meeting with Kuriowa surely heightened Loving's suspicions. Just two months earlier, in fact, at a November 1918 rally, Marcus Garvey had attracted MID attention when he predicted—with a heavy dose of hyperbole—that "the next war would pit white nations against a black-Japanese alliance." More cautiously, the *Age* cited Japanese newspaper articles that urged Asian delegations to champion a peace agreement clause prohibiting worldwide racial discrimination. "If Japan and China raised this question at the peace table there would really be some chance at making it an issue," said the *Age*. But Ransom, ever the contrarian, saw little possibility for a genuine coalition with the Japanese. "There is no sympathy between Japan and the Negro, absolutely none between China and the Negro, or the Turk or any other of the Darker Peoples, and it cannot be brought about by a few theorists combined together," he advised Madam Walker in a rather testy foreign affairs lesson. Even Randolph—who was said to have arranged the Kuriowa meeting at Madam Walker's request—had discouraged any black-Japanese alliance seven months earlier in *The Messenger,* the publication he proudly called "the only radical Negro magazine in America." Branding Japan "imperialistic," "autocratic" and "reactionary" because of its threats to invade Siberia, Randolph and his coeditor, Chandler Owen, had written: "We admonish Negroes not to be appealed to on the ground of color . . . Japan oppresses shamefully her own Japanese people and she would oppress you likewise."

Quite aside from his skepticism about a partnership with the Japanese, Ransom told Madam Walker that he had "no faith in the management" of the ILDP and predicted "for it an inglorious failure." Madam Walker's appointment as treasurer was less an honor, he believed, than a transparent gesture to secure a sure source of funding. "You will have to watch your League for I very much suspect they will want you to finance most all of their little projects." He was, he said, "beginning to grow seriously apprehensive lest you will impair your usefulness by becoming identified with too many organizations fostered by highly questionable characters." Ransom specifically cautioned Madam Walker about Reverend R. D. Jonas, a Welshman and one of the League founders, whom he harshly blasted as a "nihilist, a fanatic [and] a petty grafter who seeks to gain his livelihood by appealing to the Negro on some phase of the Negro problem that will cause them to back him . . . in some impractical propaganda." Having been "run out of every City of size in the United States," including Indianapolis, Ransom counseled her that Jonas was "liable to mislead some well-meaning people," including—though he did not say so—Madam Walker herself.

Little did either of them know that, just as Major Loving had infiltrated the December National Race Congress, R. D. Jonas had become the ILDP's own homegrown informant, ferreting out information about his black "friends" for the United States government. For at least a year this undercover operative, who was sometimes known as Jonas the Prophet, had been gathering material, not only for the War Department's MID but for British military intelligence officials who had developed a particular interest in contacts between blacks and Japanese. After the January 2 session at Villa Lewaro and the January 7 meeting at the Waldorf-Astoria, Jonas also approached the Justice Department's Bureau of Investigation with hopes of being paid for information about the League. In a convoluted and illogical scheme, he told bureau officials that he was "recruiting black, Japanese, Hindu and Chinese socialists and Bolshevists to learn their plans and then secretly mobilize conservative black churchmen against them." Now, presumably, Madam Walker's name had been added to yet another surveillance file.

While Ransom was quite familiar with Jonas, he wrote Madam Walker that he knew "nothing about the man Randolph." But had he spent more time strolling the streets on his visits to Harlem, he surely would have heard the provocative, eloquent speeches that A. Philip Randolph regularly delivered from the corner of 135th and Lenox. The dignified and eloquent son of an AME minister, Randolph had arrived in New York in 1911 just a few years after graduating from Jacksonville, Florida's Cookman Institute, the first black high school in Florida. While taking night classes at New York's City College, he was exposed to the rhetoric of radical politics in the speeches of black Socialist Hubert Harrison, as well as Socialist Party founder Eugene Debs. Now one of Lenox Avenue's most able soapbox orators—in an era before most Americans had radios—Randolph with his rich baritone captivated passersby as he discussed topics as wide-ranging as the French Revolution and the history of slavery. "His delivery was . . . impeccable," a young admirer later remembered. "Instead of rabble rousing, he just talked."

Madam Walker and Randolph probably first met through his wife, Lucille Green Randolph, a Howard University graduate and former New York City schoolteacher, who had been one of the first graduates of Lelia College's Harlem branch. With her own salon on 135th Street, Lucille was one of the most successful Walker hair culturists in the city. She was a light-skinned woman of "medium height and build," whose "short-cropped, prematurely silver hair" rendered her striking rather than merely attractive. "Her customers ranged from the black elite in Harlem to well-to-do crinkly-haired whites from 'downtown,'" wrote her husband's biographer Jervis Anderson. Once a week she carried her satchel full of Walker products and curling irons to Atlantic City's "fashionable" Marlborough Blenheim Hotel, where she also counted a number of wealthy whites among her clients. Devoted to the same political causes as her husband, Lucille had run unsuccessfully for the New York state legislature on the Socialist slate in 1917. Her "considerable income," as well as her unhesitant willingness to share it with her husband, made it possible for him to pursue his "public ambitions." One acquaintance later said that he had never known Randolph to "work for a salary," yet he "never saw him without a starched collar, a carefully knotted tie, a white handkerchief in his breast pocket, and a blue serge suit that looked like he had just bought it from Brooks Brothers. It was his wife, of course." Randolph himself later said, "We were on an uncharted sea. Chandler and I had no job and no plan for the next meal. But I had a good wife. She carried us." While Madam Walker had been one of the first advertisers in *The Messenger*—a reprint of her November 1917 *New York Times* article appeared as a full-page ad in the magazine's second issue—it was Lucille Green Randolph who sustained the publication. "Without her money," Randolph often said, "we couldn't have started *The Messenger*."

That Lucille was a gregarious extrovert who thoroughly enjoyed Madam Walker's social gatherings seemed to create no conflict for Randolph, whom friends "never saw . . . at a dance or a party" because "he had bigger things in view." Lucille, they said, "sometimes invited him to Madam Walker's parties, but he always begged off, saying he had no time to waste with 'fly-by-night people.'" Apparently Randolph exempted Madam Walker herself from that unflattering category. "She was a woman of common sense and good business sense," he later remembered. But he also suggested that Madam Walker, who was almost entirely self-taught, still welcomed and needed assistance in preparing major speeches. "She was not a literate woman but she had money," he told an interviewer. "My wife would make trips" with her and would help "get her talks together."

Just as Madam Walker had not agreed with all of the political positions of Booker T. Washington, Monroe Trotter or Emmett Scott, she must surely have differed with Randolph in July 1918 when he countered Du Bois's controversial "Close Ranks" editorial with the position that "no intelligent Negro is willing to lay down his life for the United States as it now exists." Yet, as with others she liked personally, she did not sever contact with him over political disagreements. Had she known all the details of Randolph's August 1918 arrest for violating the Espionage Act, however, she would have had sufficient reason to be anxious about her relationship with him. While Randolph addressed a rally in Cleveland, a Justice Department intelligence agent confiscated copies of the July *Messenger*, citing Randolph and Chandler Owen for spreading subversive information. Undoubtedly, one section of the magazine that caught the agent's attention was an editorial that welcomed the "growth of socialism, which is the death of capitalism." After a two-day investigation and a brief trial, Randolph and Owen were released, but the newspaper, now in the possession of the Justice Department, included several references to Madam Walker. A concise biographical sketch praising her as "a factor in the economic, political [and] social life of the country" would have been of little consequence to the agent. More likely it was Madam Walker's prominent role as an advertiser that would have intrigued the bureau investigators, since her payments had helped fund the "seditious" contents. In addition to a full-page Walker Company ad on the magazine's back cover, Madam Walker was mentioned in two other full-page spreads, one purchased by Frank Smith, her interior decorator, the other by the Miller-Reed Company, the general contractors for Villa Lewaro, St. Philip's AME and Mother AME Zion. The link to Madam Walker, Smith and Miller-Reed was *The Messenger*'s advertising manager, Louis George. As an assistant to Madam Walker, he had accompanied her on her second trip to Battle Creek and often helped with marketing promotions in the 136th Street salon.

An earnest and enthusiastic young man, George and his wife, Czarina, were, along with Lloyd and Edna Thomas, Lelia's closest friends. But George, who had been named chairman of the ILDP's executive committee, was someone Ransom viewed with disdain, primarily because he had mismanaged both money and business transactions in the Walker Company's New York office. "I know you are fond of Louis George and I do not wish to hurt him in your estimation, but because you are fond of him does not make him fit to manage large affairs or lead the Race," Ransom huffed. "You certainly have seen enough to know he [is] utterly incompetent along business lines."

When Madam Walker suggested placing George in charge of her trust fund, Ransom was livid. "It evidently did not occur to you that Louis has not the capacity for such a position," he lectured. "People [who] know him know his limitations and will laugh at you thinking that you did not know any better."

As if Jonas's and George's affiliation with the League were not enough, Ransom could not have been pleased with the prominent coverage the two ILDP meetings received in the *Age*. "I, for one, am sorry that [Villa Lewaro] was the birthplace for such an organization," especially, he told her, because people would believe that she was "sponsor for the acts of fanatic and irrational beings." Concerned that the group might be "identified with the socialist element of our citizenship or radicals and agitators that are to be found among all Races," Ransom sounded another alarm. "Diplomatic, persistent agitation along conservative lines is alright, but anything that borders on Bolshevikism is to be avoided."

Unable to control Madam Walker's interactions with those he considered "irresponsible" zealots, or to curb what he implied might be his client's naiveté, Ransom once again urged her to consider her business and her reputation. "The only thing I am concerned with is the danger of your becoming identified with some person or persons whose acts will hurt your future in this country." To lessen Ransom's anxiety—and apparently because she too was having second thoughts—Madam Walker assured him that she would heed his advice and withdraw her support. "I am glad to note that you are not going to mix up into organizations and propositions in the future," Ransom wrote, reinforcing her responsibility to other African Americans. "You cannot be too careful in this respect. People who have developed great businesses, attained great wealth and influence, no longer belong to themselves but to the people and to posterity and they cannot be too careful as to entangling alliances, such as may bring them in ill-repute or in a way affect their business standing and integrity." Four days later, on February 5, Madam Walker resigned from the ILDP. "Owing to the fact that I do not expect to be in the city this winter and to the further fact that my physician has advised against my participation in public affairs, I herewith tender my resignation," she informed the group and the editors of the *Age*. Reverend Powell followed suit later that month, claiming that he had been selected as president without proper consent and asking that his name not be used in connection with the League. "While I believe in the objects and principles of the league and hope to remain a member, my limited time and ability will not allow me to serve as president." Without their backing, the International League of Darker Peoples collapsed. While most who knew Madam Walker found no fault with her short-lived flirtation with an organization that included a handful of Socialists, the damage to her reputation—at least among high government officials who could control her ability to travel to Europe—had been done.

As Madam Walker prepared her passport application in February 1919, she had no idea that her political and social activities had been monitored on at least four occasions by Walter Loving, Hallie Queen, R. D. Jonas and other government spies. Still, Ransom's warnings seem to have made her sufficiently sensitive to the government's preoccupation with political dissent that she applied for a commercial business passport, apparently to keep from attracting undue attention. She intended, she wrote on her affidavit, to travel to England, France and Italy to "buy and sell toilet preparations." Certainly her most recent advertisements—which touted her international sales with the words "We Belt the Globe"—indicated a legitimate aim to expand her overseas market. Nevertheless, Ransom cautioned her not to misrepresent the reasons for her trip, lest the State Department view her application as "merely subterfuge to get to the peace conference." The Wilson administration, he reminded her, was "quite determined" that no American be allowed to travel to "challenge" the government's position at the peace talks. "If you are not going to make a bonafide effort to represent your business over there, my advice would be not to go, because your actions will be observed," he wrote, alerting her that "secret service men are everywhere and the government does not intend to be deceived in granting passports." Less than two weeks later, Ransom told Madam Walker that Emmett Scott had informed him that she was included in a Military Intelligence Division file. "I was afraid that your name had been sent in," he wrote, advising her that she might now expect to have "trouble in getting passports" for herself, Lelia and the salesman she had hoped would accompany her.

Just as Ransom had predicted, Madam Walker's entanglements with Trotter and the International League of Darker Peoples had jeopardized her trip to France. On the recommendation of Loving, she and the other National Race Congress delegates, as well as the ILDP committee, had become targets of a Military Intelligence Division inquiry into the political activities of those whom the government considered "Negro subversives." Specifically naming Ida B. Wells-Barnett, Madam Walker and six men in his report, Loving wrote: "If passports are to be requested for the above named individuals I suggest that the record of each person be locked up before a passport is granted. I recommend this in the case of Mrs. Ida B. Wells-Barnett especially. This subject is a known race agitator." Three weeks after Loving's MID report, William E. Allen, the acting chief of the Bureau of Investigation, advised the State Department to refuse passports for all National Race Congress delegates in order to prevent them from mentioning "the negro question at the Peace Conference." Quoting Loving, Allen included Madam Walker among the group of people now considered "more or less agitators." In denying the passports, the State Department engaged in its "first major interference in African American politics," according to historian Theodore Kornweibel. Later the agency would contend that it had no "formal policy barring black travelers," yet clearly all but a few blacks who attempted to visit Paris in 1919 met with "deliberate bureaucratic delays." Although Madam Walker submitted her passport application in February 1919, State Department records at the National Archives today lead to a cold trail, perhaps because, as Loving had directed, they had been "locked up" beforehand as classified files.

In February, with Madam Walker's own prospects for going to Europe having vanished, she lent her support to Du Bois's efforts to convene a Pan-African Congress in Paris. As a member of the executive committee of the NAACP's New York chapter, Madam Walker sent a personal check for $25 to the parent organization after receiving James Weldon Johnson's February 11 letter asking that the committee approve a $100 expenditure from its treasury for the work of the congress. "We are hoping for some very tangible results from the efforts which Dr. Du Bois is making," Johnson wrote in his letter acknowledging her contribution. Having just received a cable from Paris, he was pleased to inform her that Blaise Diagne, a Senegalese member of the French Chamber of Deputies, had persuaded French Premier Clemenceau—against the wishes of President Wilson—to grant permission for Du Bois's conference to proceed. "In private advices from Dr. Du Bois," Johnson continued, "we learn that he has the support of all of the colored members of the French Chamber of Deputies," as well as the Liberian and Haitian delegates and members of the Aborigines Society of London, an organization Johnson described as similar to the NAACP. Du Bois's three-day Pan-African Congress opened on February 19 at Paris's Grand Hotel with a welcome address from Diagne to the fifty-eight delegates. Although "sixteen nations, protectorates and colonial entities" were represented, the number of participants would have been much higher had not the U.S. State Department, as well as other Allied governments, placed obstacles in the paths of most who wished to attend. Claiming falsely that the French government disapproved of the conference, the Wilson administration issued an announcement that it would be "unable to grant passports to persons desiring to proceed to Paris for the purpose of attending such a congress."

Before Du Bois left Paris, he had managed to personally present the assembly's resolutions to Colonel Edward M. House, President Wilson's close friend and political adviser. He also had "indirectly" dispatched the document to British Prime Minister David Lloyd George through an intermediary. Nevertheless, he returned to the United States "convinced that Allied officials had effectively sabotaged his attempts to appear before the Peace Conference."

Monroe Trotter, whose NERL had chosen Madam Walker as a delegate, had fared even worse. Denied a passport, he eventually posed as a cook and stowed away on a freighter, still hoping to arrive in time to lobby for a racial equality clause. But on the very day that he reached Paris, the Allies were sitting around a table at the Petit Trianon at Versailles presenting the German delegation with a draft of the treaty.

The final version of the Treaty of Versailles included no special provisions for the world's people of color. Germany's four colonies, not surprisingly, were parceled out between France and Great Britain with no mention of Du Bois's "international Africa" or Randolph's "supernational commission." And although the Japanese delegation had met with Colonel House to discuss a treaty amendment "terminating racial discrimination," the issue was entirely absent from the document. Throughout the process, Madam Walker and other black Americans had been relegated to the sidelines. Now the only battlefront left was the one at home.

CHAPTER 21

"I Want to Live to Help My Race"

—⦿—

A jubilant roar rippled through Manhattan from lower Fifth Avenue to the rooftops of Lenox Avenue as nearly a million New Yorkers greeted drum major Bill "Bojangles" Robinson and the men of the triumphant 369th. Now, on February 17, 1919, after having been in France for more than a year, Harlem's Hellfighters were home, stepping smartly to the military marches of Lieutenant James Reese Europe's battle-tested band. At Sixtieth Street, where Madam Walker had been invited to join other members of Mayor Hylan's welcoming committee, Sergeant Henry Johnson—the first American to receive the French Croix de Guerre—stood in a convertible waving red lilies while New York governor Alfred Smith, Emmett Scott and other assembled dignitaries applauded him. Extending for several blocks south of the reviewing stand, ambulances driven by members of the Colored Women's Motor Corps transported Johnson and the other wounded soldiers. As chair of the Corps's executive committee, Madam Walker had helped organize the convoy. With the Walker Hair Parlor closed for the celebration, few matters could have prevented Lelia—a Motor Corps captain and volunteer ambulance operator—from being at the wheel of her luxury Pathfinder.

Along the seven-mile route, exuberant parade watchers showered the 1,300 survivors with candy, cigarettes and coins. At Sixty-fifth Street and Fifth Avenue, Mrs. Vincent Astor and her friends waved American flags above rows of shiny bayonets and steel helmets, while eight blocks later, industrialist Henry C. Frick cheered from a window of his mansion. Then at the northern edge of Central Park, the troops turned west toward Harlem, quickening their steps as they swung north up Lenox Avenue. Enticed by a cloudless sky and springlike weather, families, friends and sweethearts jammed sidewalks, clung to fire escapes and leaned from windows to cheer their heroes. When Big Jim Europe's precise and patriotic tunes gave way to the syncopated rhythm of "Here Comes My Daddy Now," the crowd exploded with hysterical joy. Strutting and singing, with wives and girlfriends latched on to their arms, the soldiers abandoned any pretense of an ordered formation.

Harlemites had every reason to be proud. Claiming never to have "lost a prisoner, a trench or a foot of ground," the entire regiment had been awarded the Croix de Guerre by a grateful French government. Shunted away from combat by the American Expeditionary Forces, the unit had been attached to the French Army's 161st Division, with whom they had endured uninterrupted enemy fire for 191 days—longer, it was said, than any other American soldiers. "It was hell, but those boys faced the music," Colonel William Hayward had declared five days earlier as the division steamed past the Statue of Liberty into New York Harbor. "Every mother's son of them stood up and fought like a tiger." When the Armistice was signed, indebted French officers selected the unit to lead all Allied fighters across France to Germany's river Rhine. "We were received with enthusiasm in every town we entered," Hayward noted with pride.

That same spirit of acceptance and gratitude embraced the men all along the New York parade route. "That's one day that there wasn't the slightest bit of prejudice in New York," one soldier remembered. In the midst of nonstop concerts, parties and dinners in their honor, Madam Walker invited them to consider Villa Lewaro "as their own" during a two-week-long open house. Dozens of men and their families gladly made the trip to Irvington. Among Madam Walker's overnight houseguests that month was her physician Joseph Ward, who, as a colonel during his tour of duty in France, had become the U.S. Army's highest-ranking black medical officer as well as the first African American to command a base hospital. His wife, Zella, still grieving the loss of their son from the 1918 flu pandemic, had also joined him. With an interval of several months since their last visit in Chillicothe, Ward immediately noticed Madam Walker's deteriorating health. Her kidney disease—with its telltale bloating and lethargy—had advanced significantly, causing the doctor to insist that she curtail her speaking engagements. But, of course, Madam Walker found full compliance impossible, substituting home entertaining for public appearances. Barely a month later, while still suffering from "a severe cold," she happily welcomed her friend Mary Burnett Talbert to Villa Lewaro. Simultaneously serving as president of the NACW and a vice president of the NAACP, Talbert surely was brimming with tales of her recent efforts to organize NAACP chapters in Texas and Louisiana, areas already primed for her message because of the high incidence of lynchings. Familiar with the territory from her own campaigns to recruit sales agents, Madam Walker easily compared travel experiences. And with Lelia en route to Cuba, she craved the companionship that Talbert's visit provided.

Whether Madam Walker or Lelia could have admitted it at the time, Lelia's overseas trip was designed, in part, to mend the growing rift between them. Forced to reduce her own travels, Madam Walker had intensified her involvement in the New York operation, leading to inevitable conflict with her daughter. In her desperation to escape the daily scrutiny, Lelia had persuaded her mother to allow her to develop her own niche with the Caribbean, Central American and South American trade. Accompanied by Mae—on temporary leave from Spelman—and Antonio Davila, the Walker Company's Spanish-market sales representative, Lelia intended to remain abroad until August. Within days of Lelia's departure, the company announced that Madam Walker had "assumed entire control" of Lelia College and the Walker Hair Parlor in New York to allow her daughter "to travel in the interest of the company." The news release gave no hint of the tug-of-war between mother and daughter. Besides their philosophical disagreements over business matters, Wiley Wilson remained a major source of contention. Complicating the situation was Madam Walker's obvious preference for another of Lelia's suitors, Captain James Arthur Kennedy, an army surgeon and protégé of Joseph Ward. A native of tiny Cotton Plant, Arkansas, Kennedy had studied at Branch Normal Institute in Wiley Wilson's hometown of Pine Bluff, Arkansas, before enrolling at Meharry Medical School. Like Wilson, he was both a pharmacist and a physician. But "Gentleman Jack," as the lean and handsome Kennedy was affectionately known, had a decidedly more congenial and agreeable manner.

As much as Lelia resented Madam Walker's meddling in her personal life, she remained devoted to her mother. And just as Madam Walker fretted over Lelia's choice in men, Lelia worried with equal intensity about her mother's health. "Please see to it that Mother rests," she had begged Ransom on more than one occasion. Now, despite Dr. Ward's warnings and Lelia's concerns, Madam Walker began preparing in late March for a monthlong trip to the Midwest. Still recovering from her cold, she spent the first two weeks of April in Indianapolis, reviewing business matters with Ransom, seeing old friends and retracing the paths of some of her earliest successes.

While there she discussed the misconceptions that many people had developed about her products. "Right here let me correct the erroneous impression held by some that I claim to straighten hair," she told the *Indianapolis Recorder*. "I deplore such impression because I have always held myself out as a hair culturist. I grow hair." Sensitive to the critics who misunderstood the need for improved hygiene and grooming, especially in the rural areas she had visited, she continued, "I have absolute faith in my mission. I want the great masses of my people to take a greater pride in their appearance and to give their hair proper attention." She also added a new message that signaled her vision of an evolving beauty aesthetic for black women. "I dare say that in the next ten years it will be a rare thing to see a kinky head of hair and it will not be straight either."

Determined to introduce her new line of skin care products in St. Louis, the city where she had first learned beauty culture—and with hopes of spending Easter at St. Paul AME—Madam Walker pushed herself to travel to Missouri. But by Good Friday on April 25, she was in such "critical" condition that her hosts, Jessie and C. K. Robinson, insisted that she be examined by a specialist. From her bed, she confided to Jessie that she knew she had only a short time to live. Resigned to "God's will," she remained thankful for her blessings. "It was through His divine providence that I am what I am, for all good and perfect gifts come from above," she told her friend. Nevertheless, she wished for a longer life. "My desire now is to do more than ever for my race. I would love to live for them," she said. "I've caught the vision. I can see what they need."

Throughout the Easter weekend, the Robinsons and other old friends sang and prayed with her, as she had requested, hoping to boost her spirits before her Monday-morning departure for Villa Lewaro. In a flower-filled private Pullman car, William P. Curtis, her St. Louis physician, and his nurse, Antoinette Howard, monitored her condition as the train sped through the springtime farmlands of Illinois, Indiana, Ohio, Pennsylvania and New Jersey. When the conductor announced an unscheduled stop at Tarrytown, New York, curious passengers finally glimpsed the wealthy colored passenger. A uniformed Louis Tyler hovered with housekeeper Frances Bell and Lawyer Ransom as Madam Walker was placed in an ambulance for the short ride to Irvington. Dr. Ward, on temporary leave from Camp Upton, was soon at her bedside. Shortly afterward, he assured a *Chicago Defender* reporter that he was "optimistic over the prospects for her recovery." But his sunny public prognosis was at odds with the reality he knew so well. Convinced, in fact, that her remaining days were few, Madam Walker and Ransom drafted and signed a codicil to her will before the end of that day. Her plans to bequeath to Lelia all real estate and a third of the net profits of the Madam C. J. Walker Manufacturing Company remained unchanged. But the codicil stipulated that the remaining two-thirds of the company's net proceeds be divided equally between maintenance of her Irvington home and "the benefit of worthy charities." In addition to $10,000 bequests to granddaughter Mae, godsons Frank Breedlove Ransom and Hubert Barnes Ross, and longtime friend and factory forelady Alice Kelly, Madam Walker set aside smaller yet still generous gifts for more than a dozen employees, relatives and friends. She also named as beneficiaries her favorite charities and schools: Tuskegee Institute, Mary McLeod Bethune's Daytona Normal and Industrial Institute, Charlotte Hawkins Brown's Palmer Memorial Institute, Lucy Laney's Haines Industrial and Normal Institute, Jennie Dean's Manassas Industrial School, St. Paul's Mite Missionary Society, St. Louis's Colored Orphans' Home, Indianapolis's Alpha Home for the Aged and YMCAs and YWCAs in Louisville, St. Louis and New York. As well, she earmarked $10,000 for an endowment for an African mission school and instructed future trustees to designate part of her proposed trust fund to "help members of my Race to acquire modern homes." Under the revised will, Villa Lewaro, upon Lelia's death, was to be turned over to the NAACP or "such organization" judged by the trustees to be "doing the most for Racial uplift."

That same week Madam Walker purchased $4,000 worth of Victory Bonds and urged her agents and customers to display their "loyalty and patriotism" by helping to retire the nation's war debt. "Let us in this last campaign subscribe so promptly and liberally . . . that there will be no uncertainty as to where the Negro stands," she implored. "To my mind it cannot be too strongly emphasized that our boys have done their bit [and] brought home victory to our great cause . . . leaving it clearly up to the great army back home to make the victory complete."

Having tempered their outspokenness during the war, Madam Walker and other members of the NAACP were eager to resume plans for the antilynching conference they had first discussed in 1916. In late March, just a few days before Madam Walker's departure for Indianapolis, she had gladly responded to the organization's request to support an early May assembly. Already deeply committed to the NAACP's programs, she joined 118 other prominent Americans in signing the call to action against mob violence. Deliberately "nonpartisan and nonsectional," the roster of signatories included former Secretary of State Elihu Root, Missouri congressman Leonidas Dyer, U.S. Attorney General A. Mitchell Palmer, one current and one former Ivy League college president, and seven governors and ex-governors. Among the nine women were Mary Talbert, Mary White Ovington and National American Woman Suffrage Association president emerita Anna Howard Shaw. "It is time that we should wake to the need of action," the petition declared. "Public opinion, irresistible when aroused, should be enlisted against this barbarism in our midst." Shortly after Madam Walker agreed to endorse the document, NAACP president Moorfield Storey approached her with a request for financial backing, having been notified by Association Secretary John Shillady that she was a "prospect for [a] considerably sized contribution to [the] antilynching fund." To make the appeal more personal, Shillady advised Storey to use his own mono-grammed stationery rather than the NAACP letterhead. Madam Walker responded affirmatively and immediately to Storey's solicitation with a commitment to contribute $1,000 at the time of the conference. "There are no words by which I could express my appreciation for the splendid work being done by the Association and some day I hope to be able to prove this in a material way," she promised Storey.

But on May 5, when the mass meeting finally opened at Carnegie Hall, Madam Walker was confined to Villa Lewaro, too weak even to consider making the personal presentation she had planned. With more than 2,500 delegates—including NACW colleagues Nannie Helen Burroughs, Mag-gie Walker and Mrs. S. Joe Brown—the leadership vowed to organize state committees, rally public opinion and raise funds for an unprecedented advertising campaign "to awaken the national conscience" about lynching.

The first public relations strike—a carefully researched report entitled "Thirty Years of Lynching in the United States"—revealed the sobering sta-tistic that more than 3,200 people had been lynched in America between 1889 and 1918. To no one's surprise, most were black men and almost all were in the South. Texas and Louisiana—where Talbert had focused her organizing—along with Georgia and Mississippi were the nation's dead-liest states, each logging more than 300 victims during the three decades covered by the survey. In 1918 alone, sixty-three African Americans, includ-ing five women, as well as four white men, had been lynched. Now, in 1919, with the return of newly confident black war veterans, the vigilantes had found a fresh target for their rage and resentment. Among the most recent victims—just as Madam Walker had foreseen in her letter to William Jay Schieffelin—was a returning black soldier. Hounded and harassed for weeks in his southwestern Georgia hometown, Private William Little received anonymous letters "advising him to leave town if he wished to 'sport around in khaki.'" On April 3, he was discovered on the outskirts of Blakely, Georgia, beaten to death while still in uniform.

"You cannot dethrone justice in the South and let lynching go unpun-ished there and expect to be secure in this great metropolis of New York," said former Republican New York governor Charles Evans Hughes, one of the conference keynoters. "Duty begins at home. Little can be done in the cause of international justice unless nations establish strongly and securely the foundation of justice within their own borders," declared the future Chief Justice of the United States to a standing ovation. That same day James Weldon Johnson, always reluctant to inflame, chose his words care-fully when he proffered that "the race problem in the United States has resolved itself into a question of saving black men's bodies and white men's souls."

Forbidden by Dr. Ward to leave her home, Madam Walker entrusted Mary Talbert—who was soon to become the NAACP's antilynching campaign director—with her $1,000 check and a special message for the conference. Madam Walker, Talbert announced to electrified applause, was offering a pledge of $5,000 to the Association's fight against mob violence. Noting that her "most generous gift" was "the largest the Association has ever received," John Shillady informed Madam Walker that her donation had served as a catalyst for another $1,000 contribution from prosperous Arkansas farmer Scott Bond. Other conference delegates were similarly motivated, pledging an additional $3,400 at New York's Ethical Culture Hall the next night. Gratified that "the greater part of it [had come] from colored people," Shillady, an Irish-born former social worker, flattered Walker: "I know our branches and individuals subscribing and pledging were inspired to do so as much by your contribution as by the inspiration of the gathering itself." Mary White Ovington added her "deep appreciation" as well. "A gift like yours means a very real sacrifice," wrote the NAACP board chair, "but a sacrifice that you and I believe to [be] the most important cause today before the people of the United States." All regretted her absence and her illness, "knowing," Shillady wrote, "how much pleasure you would take in what proved to be a splendid Conference."

By the second week in May, Villa Lewaro was overflowing with floral arrangements and get-well wishes from all over the nation. "Our prayers have gone up for you," assured a "grateful" Mary McLeod Bethune, who had announced Madam Walker's "marvelously wonderful" $5,000 gift to Daytona Normal and Industrial Institute at her school's commencement the previous night. "Words fail me to express our appreciation for your generous contribution to our work . . . The Negroes and white people went wild with joy and appreciation." Bethune's letter closed with a plea that was echoed in much of the correspondence Madam Walker received that month: "God spare you to the race and humanity is the wish of your friends." On days when she was feeling relatively well, Madam Walker was heard to say, "I am not going to die, because I have so much work to do yet." But on May 15 she was too ill to answer Charlotte Hawkins Brown's acknowledgment of her $1,000 pledge to Palmer Memorial Institute. "Madam Walker is still very sick but we are happy to say that she is slowly improving," Ransom replied on her behalf.

The next day, to the household's delight, she was sufficiently alert to listen to Edna and Lou read Lelia's most recent letters. Buoyed by a particular piece of news she had longed to hear, Madam Walker rallied long enough to dictate her response. "My Darling Baby," her letter began. "You made me very happy to know that at last you have decided to marry Kennedy. Altho

I have never let you know this—it has been my wish ever since I met Wiley in Wash. I never thought he would make you happy, but I do believe Kennedy will." Racing ahead breathlessly, Madam Walker had already begun to orchestrate her daughter's engagement announcement and wedding ceremony.

My wish is for you to have a quiet wedding out here and leave shortly afterward for France. You may get your chateau and I will follow. Then I will take my contemplated trip around the world. Let Kennedy study abroad for a year. I will make France my headquarters. I never want you to leave me to go this far again . . . Nettie and the girls join me in love to you and Mae and I send my love, kisses and kisses and kisses.

Your devoted,
Mother

It was as if Lelia's news had temporarily suspended reality, allowing Madam Walker to forget her illness and its inevitable consequences. With her daughter's "future happiness . . . uppermost" in her mind, Madam Walker summoned Kennedy from his home in Chicago. When he reached her bedside she assured him he had her approval. "I want you to marry Lelia. Make her happy," Kennedy remembered her saying years later.

At the same time, Madam Walker hesitated to ask Lelia to return, reluctant to interfere with her efforts to establish her own footing. "If I must go I want to see my daughter, Lelia, but if the crisis passes I would not like to disturb her pleasure," she had said before leaving St. Louis. Other members of the household, however, had already wired Lelia of her mother's fragile state.

Three days later, on Monday, May 19, just before Madam Walker lost consciousness, Dr. Ward heard her say, "I want to live to help my race." That same day, Lelia cabled from Colón, Panama, that she had booked herself and Mae on the next ship. But with international maritime travel in the Southern Hemisphere subject more to freight requirements than passengers' needs, Lelia was at the mercy of unpredictable schedules. The specific reasons for her delayed departure are unknown, but it was to be nearly a week before she and Mae would leave Central America.

That Thursday a cold, gloomy rain only deepened the sad reality that a semiconscious Madam Walker could no longer speak or see. Near midnight on Saturday, when she slipped into an irreversible coma, Dr. Ward warned that "she could not last longer than Sunday." Throughout the night, Drs. Kennedy and Ward, along with Madam Walker's nurses and the other women of the household—Nettie, Edna, Lou, Peggie Prosser and three of her nieces—took turns monitoring her from around the four-poster bed. Then, on Sunday morning, May 25, shortly after the grandfather clock at the other end of the upstairs hallway chimed seven times, Dr. Ward broke the silence with the announcement all had feared. "It is over," he said quietly. In the end, Madam Walker's kidneys, long ravaged by the nephritis first diagnosed in 1916, had failed.

Now finally en route to New York, Lelia and Mae received word of Madam Walker's death in midocean. Still several hundred miles from New Orleans, the ship's officers radioed ahead to reserve a Pullman for their trip to New York.

Stunned black New Yorkers learned the details from dozens of Harlem and Tenderloin pulpits during hastily prepared memorial services. At Villa Lewaro, Edna and Lou began logging and organizing hundreds of resolutions, condolence letters and telegrams. By Sunday afternoon Ransom was fielding interviews with newspaper reporters and planning the funeral. Assuming that Lelia would arrive no later than midweek, he scheduled the services for Friday. But Wednesday, then Thursday came and went with no word from Lelia.

Early Friday morning the Irvington chief of police stationed himself on Broadway to direct the first of the thousand mourners as their slowly moving cars and buses stretched through the village. Inside Villa Lewaro, members of the Women's Motor Corps ushered early arrivals into the music room, where Madam Walker—dressed in a shroud of white satin with a spray of orchids at her breast—lay in a bronze casket. As Edna played "Communion in G" on the Estey, bereaved Walker agents from all over the country joined a Who's Who of black America in a solemn procession around the bier.

Just before eleven o'clock, family and close friends assembled in the second-floor hall. With Mother AME Zion pastor James W. Brown leading the way, they descended the marble stairwell, then walked through the front hall and into the music room behind the impressive lineup of pallbearers. First came composer J. Rosamond Johnson, then *New York Age* publisher Fred Moore, followed by architect Vertner W. Tandy, Realtor John Nail, Harlem YMCA secretary Thomas E. Taylor and finally Buffalo Realtor and city clerk William Talbert, whose wife, Mary, was in France on behalf of the Red Cross. The honorary pallbearers, carefully selected by Ransom to reflect the broad spectrum of Madam Walker's interests and political alliances—as well as his own ambitions—included Baptists and AMEs, Bookerites and NAACPers, entertainers and attorneys, journalists and physicians. There was Robert Russa Moton of Tuskegee, James Weldon Johnson of the NAACP, Emmett Scott of the War Department, James C. Napier of the National Negro Business League, Eugene Kinckle Jones of the National Urban League, George Knox of the *Freeman,* A. E. Manning of the *Indianapolis World* and comedian Bert Williams. Tragically absent was James Reese Europe, Madam Walker's friend and Harlem neighbor, who had been fatally stabbed by a deranged band member just three weeks earlier.

With the nieces—Anjetta, Mattie and Gladis—as well as the Ransoms, Alice Kelly, Jessie Robinson and Peggie Prosser seated near the open casket, the service began without Lelia and Mae. "The Lord is my Shepherd, I shall not want," intoned Reverend William H. Brooks of St. Mark's Methodist Episcopal Church, commencing an emotional recitation of Madam Walker's favorite psalm. Then, following a brief prayer by Reverend Brown, the lustrous baritone of Harry T. Burleigh—the man whose rendering of Negro spirituals had influenced Czech composer Antonin Dvořák—encompassed the room with "Safe in the Arms of Jesus." After Reverend A. Clayton Powell, Sr.'s obituary of Madam Walker, J. Rosamond Johnson's own fitting composition, "Since You Went Away," was so heartfelt that he "made all those present feel even more their loss," reported the *Chicago Defender.* At Madam Walker's request, Reverend W. Sampson Brooks of Baltimore's Bethel AME based his eulogy on the Twenty-third Psalm. The superbly eloquent minister recalled his last conversation with Madam Walker—perhaps during her visit to his home in November 1918—when they had read together from the Book of Revelation with its captivating descriptions of Heaven's golden altars and pearl-studded gates, or during Christmas Day dinner at Villa Lewaro. At the time, he remembered, "she had had a premonition of an early death."

Before the final prayer, a telegram from Lelia arrived with the news that she would reach Irvington that afternoon. But at two-thirty, as the hearse rounded Villa Lewaro's semicircular driveway en route to Woodlawn Cemetery, there was still no sign of Lelia and Mae. When their train finally pulled into Manhattan's Grand Central Station the next afternoon, Kennedy was there to comfort them. Profoundly distraught, Lelia put off until Monday a visit to the cemetery vault to view her mother's remains. Then on Tuesday, June 3, surrounded by a small group of intimates at one of Woodlawn's most peaceful sites, Lelia buried her mother in a private graveside ceremony, her final loving gesture a blanket of fragrant roses arrayed upon the casket.

Madam Walker's death was news all over the world, from Paris's *Le Figaro* and *La Liberté* to the *Chicago Defender,* from the *New York Herald* to the *Oklahoma City Black Dispatch.* A widely published Associated Press article called her "the wealthiest negro woman in the United States, if not the entire world . . . credited with having amassed a fortune of more than

$1,000,000 through the sale of a 'hair restorer.'" *The New York Times*, in an edited version of the same wire story, managed to transform the words into a singular insult: "Mrs. C. J. Walker, known as New York's wealthiest negress, having accumulated a fortune from the sale of so-called anti-kink hair tonic and from real estate investments, died yesterday." In contrast, the *St. Louis Republic*'s editorial—"A Negro Woman's Success"—applauded her, as did the *New York Post*: "The Negro race . . . gave itself a full stamp of Americanism by producing in 'Madam' Walker a woman who built up a great fortune."

Her highest praise, however, came from the black press in whose pages she had frequently appeared. "She owed her success not alone to the merit of her commodity. It was far more due to her ability as an organizer, her faith as well as talent, in advertising," wrote *The A.M.E. Church Review*. "Her largest legacy is the inspiring example she has left to ambitious souls to undertake the achievement of large affairs," wrote one observer. "The career of this self-made woman should be an incentive and an inspiration to all members of the race," said the *New York Age*, commending her for employing her "financial success" to "help the race on its upward stride."

Others focused on her pioneering efforts in the modern hair care industry. "It is given to few persons to transform a people in a generation. Yet this was done by the late Madam Walker," wrote Du Bois, crediting her with improving the hygiene practices of thousands of women who otherwise would have neglected their hair. Her use of the metal hot comb—"the least important or necessary" part of her method, he said—was widely misunderstood and ridiculed. The accusation that black women were straightening their hair "in order to imitate white folk," he continued, led her to modify her method to affect a more natural-looking texture, while still retaining the "essential" cleaning and brushing. "It is not too much to say that this revolutionized the personal habits and appearance of millions of human beings," Du Bois concluded, with praise for her philanthropic generosity. Nevertheless, through the next several decades Madam Walker's name became synonymous with hair straightening. Derisively dubbed the "de-kink queen," she had maintained until the end that she was a hair culturist, not a hair straightener. "She never claimed or advertised that she could straighten hair," Ransom told the *New York Sun* in an effort to correct the record soon after her death. "That statement is all a mistake. She asserted merely that she could grow hair on any head where the roots were not dead."

In their final assessments, several reporters focused on her contributions to the advancement of women's rights. "She was the herald of a new social order in which women will be independent and the oldest form of property will vanish forever," wrote journalist George Schuyler several years later, adding that Madam Walker "had given dignified employment to thousands of women who would otherwise have had to make their living in domestic service."

Many newspapers called her a millionaire, though in truth the value of her estate—her homes, factory, office, salons, apartment buildings, real estate, furnishings, cars, diamonds and furs—at the time of her death was probably closer to $600,000* with a large tax liability and $100,000 in outstanding bequests. But the speculation persisted, fueled by headlines and spurred by African Americans' yearning for a heroine whose financial success could rival any American rags-to-riches saga. Perhaps the primary purveyor of the million-dollar myth was Ransom himself: "Madam Walker's fortune of $1,000,000 or more was built up from the wide sale of a hair restorer strictly," he reportedly told one New York newspaper soon after her death. Accurately quoted or not, the claim attributed to him provided a welcome antidote to the perception of inferiority. Her career, the *Chicago Defender* proclaimed, was "a message to the world that the Negro can reach the American standard [and] that it is possible for a member of the Negro Race to overcome the handicaps of centuries in a single generation." Noting the dearth of "Negro . . . oil kings, movie magnates and magnificent stock exchange gamblers," the *New York Post* wrote: "Mrs. Walker demonstrated that [Negroes] may rise to the most distinctive heights of American achievement. Men who do nothing but sneer at what Coleridge-Taylor composed, Paul Laurence Dunbar wrote or Booker T. Washington built will be all respect when the Negroes have their full quota of millionaires."

It certainly had been Madam Walker's dream to become a millionaire, and a goal she and Ransom had envisioned for several years. Just months before her death, she told a reporter that she hoped to give "a million dollars to help my Race fight for its rights." Had she lived another decade she undoubtedly would have fulfilled her wish.

Ultimately, however, it was not the final figure in the ledger books that defined the measure of Madam Walker's life, but the promise she bequeathed to future generations that they might realize even greater successes and dream ever more elaborate dreams. The fact that several generations of African Americans have *believed* that she was a millionaire made such a goal seem possible.

In an affectionate parting remembrance, her friend Mary McLeod Bethune called her "the clearest demonstration I know of Negro woman's ability recorded in history. She has gone, but her work still lives and shall live as an inspiration to not only her race but to the world."

---

*$600,000 in 1919 is equivalent to approximately $6 million today.

A'Lelia Walker:
An Afterword

On June 6, 1919, just three days after she buried her mother, Lelia turned thirty-four years old. That same day, she also married Wiley Wilson.

Despondent at her loss and overwhelmed by the responsibilities now thrust upon her as president of the Madam C. J. Walker Manufacturing Company, Lelia was desperate for an emotional anchor. James Arthur Kennedy, the man she had promised her mother she would marry, was separated but not yet divorced from his first wife. Unwilling to wait even a few months, Lelia impulsively turned to Wiley. It was a decision she would soon regret.

Meanwhile in Indianapolis, F. B. Ransom was earnestly reassuring customers, vendors and creditors of the company's stability. At the same time he also was discovering that his boasts about the value of Madam Walker's estate had been wildly optimistic. In mid-June, when Lelia and Wiley stopped briefly in Indianapolis—en route to a two-month honeymoon in California and Hawaii—Ransom informed Lelia of the distressing financial news. That week they also learned that John Davis, Madam Walker's second husband—from whom she had not been legally divorced—was making claims against the estate, as were a few estranged family members who had not been included in the will. Lelia, who wanted no part of the confusion, headed west with Wiley, abdicating her responsibilities to Ransom in a way that her mother never would have done.

It always had been difficult enough for Lelia to measure up to her mother's private expectations, but now the comparisons were being discussed in public. Lelia, nearly everyone said, was neither the businesswoman nor the leader that Madam Walker had been.

Nevertheless, when Lelia returned to Harlem, she made every effort to focus on Lelia College and her New York and Pennsylvania sales agents.

278

But her marriage was already faltering and she was preoccupied with personal matters. That fall, hoping to regain Wiley's affection, she handed him the deed to a handsome four-story Seventh Avenue building for his new medical clinic. Instead of thanking her, he flaunted an affair with an old girlfriend, both humiliating her in public and daring her to protest. Just as Madam Walker had predicted, Wiley had broken her heart. By the fall of 1921, they were separated.

That November, Lelia Walker Wilson sailed alone for a five-month trip to Europe, Africa and the Middle East, turning heads as she strolled the decks of the *Paris* in her plumed hats and expensive jewels. Weary of the gossip in Harlem, she had decided to spend time abroad freeing herself from thoughts of Wiley. Still struggling with her mother's death, as well as her own role in the Walker enterprise, she also confided to a friend that she hoped to "find" herself.

Lelia's arrival in Paris was greeted with an "excellent write-up in the French papers." In fact, *La Liberté*'s coverage had been quite favorable. But a week later *L'Intransigeant* called her a *"négresse"* in a short article by a reporter who had been on board the *Paris* covering French Premier Aristide Briand's trip from America. "I am utterly surprised that a French paper would print an article, so unkindly phrased, concerning a person . . . that happens to be a black American," she wrote to the paper's editor from her suite at the Carlton Hotel on the Champs-Elysées. "From what the black soldiers of America told on their return after the war, I had expected more kindness from a French press."

The incident did little to dampen Lelia's pleasure throughout the holiday season as she shopped at Cartier and celebrated the new year in Paris, then traveled to Monaco, Nice and the South of France during January. In London she caused a sensation at Covent Garden as she was escorted to her box. "Her appearance," a friend later wrote, "was so spectacular that the singers were put completely out of countenance." In Rome, Lelia attended the coronation of Pope Pius XI, then sailed to the Middle East for a tour of Palestine. In Cairo she rode among the pyramids on camelback. Then, after steaming down the Suez Canal, she traveled the length of the Red Sea, disembarking at Djibouti for an overland sojourn to Ethiopia. In Addis Ababa, she became the first American to meet Empress Waizeru Zauditu, the daughter of Menelik II, the emperor who had distinguished himself among African leaders by defeating the invading Italian army in 1896.

For one of the few times since her mother's death, Lelia was having fun. She was also allowing herself to fall in love again, rekindling her relationship with Kennedy through a series of affectionate letters. Within days of reaching Paris, she had cabled her "Artie" of her safe arrival. In reply, he urged her to "have every pleasure that can be offered," just as he had done while in France during the final days of the war. "I think of the whole of Europe in terms of you," he wrote, with hopes that her "entire tour may be like . . . a beautiful long road strewn with fragrant crimson flowers, the end of which terminates within the circumference of my arms." By the time Lelia returned to New York in April 1922, they had decided to marry. Finally, after both their divorces were final, they had a quiet wedding ceremony in F. B. and Nettie Ransom's living room in Indianapolis on May 1, 1926. Lelia joined Kennedy in Chicago for a few months before returning to New York with the agreement that they would live in both cities. But one financial setback after another, and the day-to-day obligations of his medical practice, prevented Kennedy from traveling to New York as often as he had promised. Determined not to borrow money from Lelia, and not to take advantage of her in the way Wiley had, Kennedy accepted Dr. Joseph Ward's offer to become second-in-command at Tuskegee's new black veterans hospital, where Ward had been named chief medical officer. Lelia had been willing to commute between New York and Chicago. Tuskegee, however, would prove to be another matter entirely.

Despite Lelia's distractions, the Walker Company enjoyed unprecedented sales during the two years after Madam Walker's death: $486,762 in 1919—or the equivalent of $4.8 million today—and $595,353 in 1920— equal to more than $5 million today. In 1921, however, a brief postwar depression pushed sales below the $400,000 mark, and they continued to decline steadily during the next decade. Ransom, along with a cadre of very capable national sales representatives, made valiant efforts to carry on Madam Walker's work. By the end of 1920, the company could proudly claim to have trained 40,000 Walker agents since 1906. But without the benefit of their founder's charisma and vision, Ransom, Lelia and the others found themselves faced with fierce competition from Annie Pope-Turnbo Malone's Poro Company, Sarah Spencer Washington's Apex Company, Anthony Overton's Overton Hygienic Company and a score of other regional firms by the mid-1920s.

The eagerness to please her mother that Lelia had displayed when she ran the Denver and Pittsburgh offices, and when she first opened the Walker Salon in New York, was now gone. Out of a sense of obligation she continued to attend the annual conventions and to make occasional trips to represent the company. She sat on several boards—including the Harlem Child Welfare League, the Music School Settlement and the women's auxiliaries of the NAACP and National Urban League—and she contributed $25,000 to the Hampton-Tuskegee Endowment Fund, but her interests increasingly were elsewhere. In 1923, when Ransom solicited her suggestions for improving sales in the Harlem office, she had little to offer. "I do not know of anything that can be done to improve the New York sales," she wrote. "New York is a peculiar city; anything that is a nine days wonder takes, but just let it be ten days. Nothing excites blasé New York."

In fact, Harlem's corners were saturated with Walker, Apex and Poro salons. But whereas Lelia seemed willing to allow her competitors to make inroads, her mother would have been devising strategies to best them. "I feel we have exploited this field thoroughly and are getting as much right now out of this business as any concern is getting or can get," Lelia rationalized, convinced that the Walker Company's best days were long gone. "Everything has its day and lives its life. People are not as much interested in whether their hair grows or not, due probably to the short hair or bobbed hair style and there are numbers of similar preparations on the market that seem to grow hair as fast as ours."

Clearly Lelia lacked her mother's fortitude and perseverance. Nevertheless, she had inherited her flair for the dramatic. Whereas Madam Walker had influenced the commerce and politics of her era, Lelia would help create the social and cultural aura of hers. Sometime during 1922 she initiated her own personal transformation by changing her name. A few months after returning from her overseas trip, she added an "A" and an apostrophe to "Lelia," though exactly why she chose "A'Lelia" remains a mystery. With her new name—just as her mother had gone from "Sarah" to "Madam"—Lelia seemed to be lowering the curtain on one act of her life and lifting it on another. As if on cue, the lively, glamorous Harlem Renaissance was being ushered in by several cultural milestones, among them the debut of the all-black Broadway musical comedy *Shuffle Along*. A number of other notable literary events celebrating the "New Negro" and a talented generation of poets, novelists and artists were just on the horizon.

"It was the period when the Negro was in vogue," wrote poet Langston Hughes, one of Harlem's brightest lights, in 1925. The movement's "midwives"—Howard University's Alain Locke, *Opportunity* founder and editor Charles S. Johnson and *Crisis* literary editor Jessie Fauset—all hoped their cultural revolution of art, poetry and music would improve race relations in America in ways that six decades of post–Civil War protest, blood and politics had failed to do. But for all its high-flown cultural aspirations, the "renaissance," for many, was as much—or more—about the opening of Harlem's cabarets and speakeasies to downtown white revelers as it was about the creation of literature and sculpture. Harlem's nightlife, reported *Variety*, "now surpasses that of Broadway itself . . . from midnight until after dawn it is a seething cauldron of Nubian mirth and hilarity." Historian Nathan Huggins attributed the desire of a "generation of Americans to lose themselves in cabarets, rhythms, dances, and exotica" to a "postwar hangover." F. Scott Fitzgerald simply said that "America was going on the greatest, gaudiest spree in history." And A'Lelia Walker was poised to ride. "She wanted to miss nothing," remembered a friend. "She tried to miss nothing."

A'Lelia was the first to admit that she possessed no particular artistic talent, but she genuinely enjoyed the company of the free-spirited writers and had already developed longtime friendships with musicians Noble Sissle and Eubie Blake, as well as Flournoy Miller, one of the stars of *Shuffle Along*. Among this crowd, she was comfortable. As hostess to Harlem's cultural elite, A'Lelia had finally found her niche.

"She looked like a queen and frequently acted like a tyrant," wrote her friend Carl Van Vechten, the novelist and former arts critic who famously interpreted Harlem for other downtown whites. "She was tall and black and extremely handsome in her African manner. She often dressed in black. When she assumed more regal habiliments, rich brocades of gold or silver, her noble head bound in a turban, she was a magnificent spectacle." Her son-in-law, Marion Perry, remembered her as a woman with "royal instincts." Langston Hughes called her "a gorgeous dark Amazon." At five feet nine inches, with excellent posture and an evenly distributed 190 pounds, she was six feet tall when she dressed in her heels and turbans. "She had a superb figure, the type that artists like to draw," wrote one reporter who knew her well. W.E.B. Du Bois's assessment that she was "without beauty but of fine physique" may have said more about him than about her. Surely he found no agreement among Richmond Barthé, Augusta Savage, Berenice Abbott, R. E. Mercer and James Latimer Allen, a few of the many well-known artists and photographers for whom she sat during the 1920s.

A'Lelia "made no pretense of being intellectual," Langston Hughes later recalled, but she could be a charming and generous hostess, who "could engage you in conversation on most any topic and who gave you the impression of being well-informed on all of them." She had learned, she told the *Inter-State Tattler*, "the art of reading headlines, and the trick had served [her] well." And while one observer judged her attention span to be no longer than "seven minutes," at least one of her friends thought she was "one of the most subtly humorous women in Harlem."

A'Lelia's guest lists were quite diverse. "At her 'at homes' Negro poets and Negro numbers bankers mingled with downtown poets and seat-on-the-stock-exchange racketeers," Hughes remembered. Of course, her Harlem friends formed the core. Besides the young writers like Hughes, Countee Cullen and Bruce Nugent, regular visitors included Edna Lewis Thomas, Madam Walker's former social secretary, who was now an actress, and her husband, Lloyd; actor Paul Robeson and his wife and business manager, Eslanda (when they were in town); singer and vamp Nora Holt; *Pittsburgh Courier* columnist and New York School Board member Bessye Bearden and her husband, Howard; painter Aaron Douglas; entertainer Florence Mills; voice teacher Caska Bonds; *Inter-State Tattler* managing editor and *Pittsburgh Courier* columnist Geraldyn Dismond (later know as Gerri Major); Mayme White, A'Lelia's constant companion and social secretary; and McCleary Stinnett, a well-known bootlegger and A'Lelia's favorite dance partner. From downtown, Carl Van Vechten probably introduced poet Witter Bynner, writer and salon hostess Muriel Draper and novelist Max Ewing to A'Lelia's soirees.

A'Lelia's parties also had an international flavor and "were filled with guests whose names would turn any Nordic social climber green with envy." Among the European royalty and near-royalty were Princess Violette Murat of France, Osbert Sitwell and Peter Spencer Churchill of England, Prince Basil Mirski of Russia and a Rothschild or two. When A'Lelia was informed that a Scandinavian prince had not been able to maneuver the crowded hallway leading to her apartment, she "sent word back that she saw no way of getting His Highness in . . . nor could she herself get out through the crowd to greet him. But she offered to send refreshments downstairs to the Prince's car," Hughes recounted years later.

From time to time A'Lelia hosted celebrations at Villa Lewaro, on one occasion throwing a July Fourth extravaganza complete with fireworks for Liberian President C.D.B. King, on another, a lavish Christmas dinner in Kennedy's honor. But she did most of her entertaining at her 136th Street town house or at her much smaller pied-à-terre at 80 Edgecombe Avenue, where a large swath of rose and green taffeta draped sensuously from the living-room ceiling. There in Apartment 21, her collection of elephants— in "jade, velvet, metal, ivory and ebony"—were displayed everywhere, but especially on the built-in shelves of her custom-made mahogany studio couch. With accompaniment by the hot pianist of the moment, A'Lelia's Thursday visitors were likely to hear *Showboat* star Jules Bledsoe perform his signature "Ol' Man River" or see Al Moore and Fredi Washington teach the steps to their latest dance routine. After one of A'Lelia's parties, writer Max Ewing described the "extremely elegant" surroundings in a letter to his mother. "You have never seen such clothes as millionaire Negroes get into," he wrote. "They are more gorgeous than a Ziegfeld finale. They do not stop at fur coats made of merely one kind of fur. They add collars of ermine and gray fur, or black fur collars to ermine. Ropes of jewels and trailing silks of all bright colours."

In November 1923, A'Lelia turned her skills as an impresario to her daughter Mae's wedding, both orchestrating the event and choosing the groom.

That Mae was not particularly keen on Dr. Gordon Jackson, a Chicago surgeon who was thirteen years her senior, seemed to be a minor detail as far as A'Lelia was concerned. "I look upon this wedding as the very biggest advertisement we have ever had [except for] Villa Lewaro," A'Lelia wrote Ransom a week and a half before the ceremony, sure that the photographers and reporters would be out in full force to cover everything from the linen shower to the magnificent reception at Villa Lewaro. "This is the swellest wedding any colored folks have ever had or will have in the world. While its purpose certainly is not for the advertising, God knows we are getting $50,000 worth of publicity. Everything has its compensation." Although, in this case, it was at Mae's expense.

A'Lelia had sent out 9,000 invitations to friends and Walker agents in every state in the union, as well as to Nigeria, Liberia, England, France, Haiti and Panama. By midmorning, on November 24, despite a cold rain, thousands of people "white and colored, drawn out of curiosity," had gathered on 134th Street between Seventh and Eighth avenues in front of St. Philip's Protestant Episcopal Church. Inside the sanctuary, which was lavishly decorated with chrysanthemums, autumn leaves and palm trees, nearly two-thirds of the pews were filled a full hour before the ceremony was scheduled to begin.

The bridesmaids—mostly members of the Debutante Club that A'Lelia had started for Mae after her graduation from Spelman Seminary in 1920—wore silver dresses covered with cream Chantilly lace and trimmed with ropes of orange blossoms. The groomsmen, in formal morning attire, included five doctors and two attorneys, among them Henry Rucker, Jr., the grandson of nineteenth-century black Georgia Congressman Jefferson Long. The mother of the bride was stunning in her elegant gold metallic gown from Paris.

Although the bride was miserable, her breathtaking dress drew "gasps of admiration" as she moved slowly down the aisle. Luminescent sea pearls accented her train and created the frame of her headpiece, a crownlike ornament inspired by Egyptian artifacts from the recently opened King Tutankhamen tomb. In Mae's wedding photographs—taken later that day at Villa Lewaro and the day before her twenty-fifth birthday—she was noticeably melancholy. Gordon, on the other hand, looked stern and cocksure as he stood behind her. Predictably Mae's efforts to be the dutiful wife A'Lelia had advised her to be failed in the face of Gordon's volatile temper. In May 1926, when she was eight months pregnant, she moved from their Chicago home into her own apartment near Michigan Avenue. By early December, three years after the $46,000 wedding she had not wanted, Mae was divorced and back in New York with her six-month-old son, Gordon Walker Jackson.

The following August, she married attorney Marion R. Perry, Jr., who adopted young "Walker." Their daughter, A'Lelia Mae Perry, was born on July 22, 1928.

By early 1926 A'Lelia had begun to move as freely among her white down-town acquaintances as among her black Harlem pals. But few friends, white or black, were as close to her during the late 1920s as Carl Van Vechten. When James Arthur Kennedy, soon to be her husband, could not join her in New York for Easter 1926, she spent the holiday with Van Vechten and his Russian-born wife, Fania Marinoff, in their impressive apartment on West Fifty-fifth Street.

Van Vechten, who had been a well-known New York music critic until he was forty, had begun writing fiction in 1922. When he trained his sights on Harlem for the subject of his fifth novel, he was no stranger to African Americans. His father had helped support the Piney Branch School for Negro Children in Mississippi and he prided himself on his "fully inte-grated guest lists." But when Van Vechten's *Nigger Heaven* reached the bookstores in August 1926, its title alone scandalized many black New Yorkers. And while Van Vechten was careful to depict intellectually capa-ble and socially refined black characters, he seemed, to some critics, to be overly fascinated with the racy underworld of numbers bankers and pimps, as well as the sadomasochistic sexual encounters between two of the book's main characters.

Du Bois, in a scathing review in the December 1926 *Crisis*, called it "cheap melodrama" and "a caricature" of Harlem life. But James Weldon Johnson, with whom Van Vechten had developed a close friendship, called *Nigger Heaven* "a fine novel" and praised him for being an early champion of black culture by writing "frequent magazine articles and by his many per-sonal efforts in behalf of individual Negro writers and artists."

The character Adora Boniface was unmistakably based on A'Lelia. Although Adora was a former "music hall star" who lived on Striver's Row and had inherited her husband's real estate fortune, Van Vechten did not veer far from the truth in drawing her personality. "She was undeniably warm-hearted, amusing, in her outspoken way, and even beautiful, in a queenly African manner that set her apart from the other beauties of her race whose loveliness was more frequently of a Latin than an Ethiopian character." If she was nicer to Van Vechten after the book, as he later wrote a friend, perhaps it was because she appreciated his description of her "good heart" and "ready wit." Self-conscious about her size and her dark skin— Wiley had made it clear that he preferred light-skinned women—A'Lelia also appreciated the thoughts Van Vechten placed into the mind of Mary Love, the novel's prim librarian. "She was beautiful, of that there could be no question, beautiful and regal," Mary said of Adora. "Her skin was almost black; her nose broad, her lips thick . . . She was a type of pure African majesty."

A'Lelia may even have taken some perverse satisfaction in Van Vechten's fictional depiction of her relationship with some members of the city's black elite. "Frowned upon in many quarters, not actually accepted intimately in others—not accepted in any sense of the word, of course, by the old and exclusive Brooklyn set—Adora nevertheless was a figure not to be ignored," Van Vechten, the narrator, observed. "She was too rich, too important, too influential, for that."

With a first printing of 16,000 copies—and thirteen subsequent print-ings—*Nigger Heaven* became the most widely read of the Harlem Renais-sance–era novels. Translated into at least ten and possibly eleven languages, it made A'Lelia one of "the most discussed women" in New York and may have done as much to immortalize her role in Harlem's 1920s as did The Dark Tower, the salon she opened in 1927.

Although A'Lelia was never a patron in the sense of underwriting the living expenses of any of the young Harlem Renaissance writers and artists, she frequently opened her home and her kitchen, filling them up with her spicy spaghetti—the secret was cheese and wine—and staking them at poker games. During early 1927, at several gin-soaked brainstorming sessions, writer Bruce Nugent, painter Aaron Douglas and a few others talked with A'Lelia about creating a salon for poetry readings and art exhibits, some-thing "completely informal . . . homey [and] comfortable" where they could bring their friends. At Nugent's suggestion, they agreed to call it The Dark Tower, a nod to Countee Cullen's *Opportunity* column of the same name. But after the project was delayed by much procrastination—and appar-ently even more gin—A'Lelia moved forward without the original team of "consultants."

"We dedicate this tower to the aesthetes," announced the engraved invitations that began arriving in mid-October 1927. "That cultural group of young Negro writers, sculptors, painters, music artists, composers and their friends. A quiet place of particular charm. A rendezvous where they may feel at home."

But instead of a place of reverie and reflection, the opening-night recep-tion was like all of A'Lelia's other parties: crowded, bustling and well stocked with food, champagne and gin. Nugent, ever the tieless bohemian, almost was not admitted because of his casual dress. At any rate, he found the prices on the menu much too high for the struggling artists A'Lelia had initially intended to benefit. The "hall was a seething picture of well-dressed people," Nugent later wrote. "Colored faces were at a premium, the place filled to overflowing with whites from downtown who had come up expecting that this was a new and hot night club."

At one end of the room—which stretched across the back of A'Lelia's 136th Street town house—stood a customized bookcase. Designed by Paul Frankl in the shape of a skyscraper, it was filled with first-edition copies of books by Hughes, Cullen, Jessie Fauset, Jean Toomer and many of the other new Harlem writers. On the right side of the room Hughes's prize-winning poem "The Weary Blues" was carefully lettered on a buff-and-gold wall, its rhythmic words celebrating the black folk idiom:

> Droning a drowsy syncopated tune,
> Rocking back and forth to a mellow croon,
> I heard a Negro play.

Directly across from Hughes's blues was Countee Cullen's more formal sonnet "From the Dark Tower," which heralded the emerging voices of black writers.

> We shall not always plant while others reap
> The golden increment of bursting fruit
> Not always countenance, abject and mute,
> That lesser men should hold their brothers cheap.

Dark rose tables and chairs matched the wood of the piano and complemented rose-hued curtains and wine-colored candlesticks. A sky-blue Victrola was available whenever no live music was being played. A red graphic of The Dark Tower bookcase appeared atop all menus and stationery.

What had been conceived originally as a casual setting was now an upscale tearoom. But if A'Lelia hoped to make a profit from the enterprise, she soon was disappointed. Her friends were not accustomed to paying for her hospitality and the young artists couldn't afford the prices. Within a year the original Dark Tower was officially closed. "Having no talent or gift, but a love and keen appreciation for art, The Dark Tower was my contribution," A'Lelia announced on an engraved card that she mailed in October 1928. She blamed the "members" for not making use of the facility, but she had failed to mention that at least part of the reason the effort had lost money was that her hostess, Sari Price Patton, had embezzled some of the daily receipts. After November 1, A'Lelia continued to rent The Dark Tower for private parties, luncheons, teas, card parties, meetings and receptions.

In August 1928, during the twelfth annual Walker agents convention, A'Lelia and Ransom welcomed the delegates to the dedication ceremonies of the spectacular $350,000 headquarters and factory of the Madam C. J. Walker Manufacturing Company in Indianapolis. "It is the culmination of the dream of the late Madam C. J. Walker, who in her life planned for this very event . . . as [she] desired to give to the race the most modern plant for the manufacture of toilet preparations," wrote the *Amsterdam News* after the groundbreaking the previous year. "Like Villa Lewaro . . . it will contain the best that money can buy."

The building was indeed one of the most magnificent any African American company had ever built, but it could not have opened at a worse time. The next autumn, on October 24, 1929, the stock market crashed, sending the entire country into an economic tailspin. By then end-of-the-year company revenues had dipped to $213,327 and A'Lelia had been forced to rent the 136th Street town house to the New York City Health Department for a pediatric clinic. In 1930, when President Herbert Hoover asked Congress for $100 million to fund a public works program, soup kitchens had become a common sight and annual Walker Company revenues had fallen below $200,000 for the first time since 1917. By the end of that year, more than 1,300 banks had closed and 26,355 businesses had failed.

That fall the trustees of the Walker estate were so financially strapped that they arranged to auction Villa Lewaro's contents. On Thanksgiving weekend 1930, cars lined both sides of North Broadway in Irvington for a quarter of a mile in either direction. The more disrespectful buyers drove their cars through the front gate and parked on the grass.

Throughout the house cardboard tags hung from Madam Walker's treasures. Thousands of bargain hunters—some of them the very people who had sneered as they passed the house—trampled through her "dream of dreams," picking off the items she had so lovingly selected. "What am I bid for this beautiful Chickering concert grand piano?" said auctioneer Benjamin Wise of the gold-trimmed piano, as music played softly on the Estey organ at the other end of the music room. And so it went for three days on every floor of the house. Arthur Lawrence, the president of the Westchester County Parks Commission, bought one of the Aubusson tapestries from the drawing room for $1,150. Madam Walker's ten-piece Hepplewhite dining-room suite went for $1,100. The contents of the library—including the $15,000 ten-volume opera set by James Buel—sold for close to $1,800. In the end, the auctioneer estimated that he had received about twenty cents on the dollar. "Sale of Villa Lewaro Nets $58,500 in 3 Days as Millionaires Bid," read the *Pittsburgh Courier* headline.

Three weeks later A'Lelia and Ransom sent their annual Christmas telegram to all Walker Company employees. "Worry won't help matters. We must be cheerful as possible under existing conditions," A'Lelia wrote, though she was feeling anything but optimistic. "Worthwhile is the man who can smile when everything goes dead wrong."

Ransom's holiday message, however, minced no words. "Dear Co-worker. True there seems to be nothing to be particularly joyous about this Yuletide but when you know you have done your best you can at least enter the festivities with a clear conscience. Any number of you no doubt are thinking if the founder Madam C. J. Walker had lived things would have been different," he continued, anticipating their concerns. "If so you are wrong. No one could have foreseen the financial crisis that has gripped not only America but the world." He had only to look to Detroit—and to much larger corporations—to prove his point. The Ford Motor Company, which had employed 128,000 workers before the Crash, would be down to 37,000 by the following summer.

In 1931, Ransom's job only became more difficult as annual sales fell to just over $130,000. More than ever, he was pressuring A'Lelia to find a buyer for Villa Lewaro. At one point she even turned to Carl Van Vechten for help. "I have been holding on to this place through sentiment (my mother), but I've arrived at the conclusion it is foolish of me to maintain such a large and expensive home with no family ties." She was willing, she told him, to sell the house to him for $150,000, forty thousand dollars less than its assessed value. "There isn't a person I'd rather have Villa Lewaro than you," she closed. Van Vechten replied as gently as he could to his distressed friend, "But, dear A'Lelia, what would I do with a house? I am always away all summer. And where do you think I'd get all that money? A'Lelia behave!"

With Villa Lewaro's annual upkeep at $8,000, the fairy castle had become a white elephant, hungry for heating oil, maintenance and property taxes. Because the Indianapolis building produced revenue, Ransom concluded that the factory's mortgage should take priority over the maintenance of a house that was rarely used.

With Villa Lewaro on the market and 108 rented out, A'Lelia had still managed to hold on to her Lincoln, her baby grand piano, her sterling silver and enough trappings to keep herself comfortable. But she had pawned much of her jewelry and there were signs that she was depressed. Although she knew her blood pressure was hovering near the 200 mark, she refused to restrict her diet.

In March 1931, after five years of a long-distance marriage, she and Kennedy divorced. During the doctor's four and a half years in Tuskegee, A'Lelia had managed to visit only a few times. And demands of the veterans hospital prevented him from traveling to New York with any frequency. Kennedy filed for desertion, but they had both agreed several months earlier that a divorce was the best solution. "There was no place in A'Lelia's life for crickets, sandflies and firebugs, husband or no husband," a friend observed. "She could enjoy the country for a day, a week, perhaps a month, but not beyond that."

"In love and in marriage she was unsuccessful as was but natural," Carl Van Vechten wrote years later. "She was too spoiled, too selfish, too used to having her own way to make any kind of compromise."

In a letter dated August 12, 1931, Ransom delivered yet another blow: "We are merely taking in money enough to take care of the payroll, notwithstanding the fact that the payroll has been greatly reduced. We are able to do nothing about our outstanding bills," he wrote. "I am letting the factory people off every other week . . . I just want you to know how things are going." It is unclear whether A'Lelia ever received the letter, for three days later she and her close companion, Mayme White, drove to Long Branch, New Jersey, for their friend Mae Fain's weekend-long birthday party. On Sunday, after a day at the ocean and an indulgent dinner of lobster, champagne and chocolate cake, A'Lelia awakened with a headache so severe she could not see. At 5:03 the next morning she was pronounced dead of a cerebral hemorrhage. She was only forty-six years old.

A'Lelia "knocked herself out, because she wanted to be knocked out," her son-in-law, Marion Perry, said years later. With Walker Company sales at a trickle and no end to her personal financial woes, she saw nothing but poverty ahead.

Just as A'Lelia's parties had been grand, so was her funeral. More than 11,000 people filed past her casket at Howell's Funeral Home the following Friday. The mourners were "mostly women . . . young women, already stooped with the drudgery of work . . . old women, muttering indistinctly of the days when they knew 'Madam' . . . well-dressed women to whom the living woman's career had been a challenge," reported the *Philadelphia Tribune*. In the open casket, A'Lelia wore a gown of gold lace and tulle over lavender satin with a pale green velvet sash draped around her body. Her feet were covered in apple-green satin slippers. Around her neck were her cherished Chinese amber prayer beads. On her third finger was the silver-and-amber ring Mayme had given her. Three orchids, a gift from Bessye Bearden, had been placed in her hands. Above her head a spray of two dozen orchids decorated the inside of the casket.

By early Saturday morning nearly 1,000 people had gathered outside the mortuary for the invitation-only funeral. "But, just as for her parties, a great many more invitations had been issued than the small but exclusive Seventh Avenue funeral parlor could provide for," Langston Hughes remembered. For a few moments before the white-maned Reverend A. Clayton Powell, Sr., opened the service with the Ninetieth and Twenty-third psalms, he stood "motionless in the dim light" behind A'Lelia's silver casket. From the front row, Mae, Marion, Mayme and F. B. Ransom watched quietly. Among the dozens of Walker agents and longtime family friends who sat nearby were Jessie Robinson, Alice Burnette, Lucille Randolph and Edna Thomas. Even Wiley Wilson made an appearance, though Kennedy did not. The Van Vechtens and Countee Cullen were out of town.

Appropriately the service was filled with music performed by A'Lelia's friends. The Bon Bons, a female quartet, opened with "I Ain't Got Long to Stay, for My Lord Calls Me by the Thunder," then later sang "Steal Away to Jesus." Paul Bass, the tenor, who often had entertained at 80 Edgecombe, offered "I'll See You Again," A'Lelia's favorite melody from Noël Coward's 1929 play, *Bitter Sweet*.

Mary McLeod Bethune, speaking "in that great deep voice of hers," delivered the eulogy. "She recalled the poor mother of A'Lelia Walker in old clothes, who had labored to bring the gift of beauty to Negro womanhood, and had taught them the care of their skin and their hair, and had built up a great business and a great fortune to the pride and glory of the Negro race—and then had given it all to her daughter, A'Lelia," Hughes remembered. As friends and family sifted through the meaning of Mrs. Bethune's words, *Inter-State Tattler* columnist and music critic Edward Perry read "To A'Lelia," a poem that Langston Hughes had written two days after A'Lelia's death.

> So all who love laughter,
> And joy and light,
> Let your prayers be as roses
> For this queen of the night.

As Perry took his seat, several Walker agents lined up to place flowers on the closed casket.

At Woodlawn Cemetery, Mae, Marion, Mayme, Mrs. Bethune and a small group gathered around the flower-filled space that had been dug beside Madam Walker's grave. From above, Colonel Hubert Fauntleroy Julian, the world's first black licensed pilot, dropped two bouquets of gladiolas and dahlias from a small plane. "That was really the end of the gay times of the New Negro era in Harlem," Hughes later wrote. "The depression brought everybody down a peg or two. And the Negroes had but few pegs to fall."

In most of the obituaries, A'Lelia was inevitably compared with her mother. Almost always, she came up wanting. The *New York News & Harlem Home Journal* was harsh: "The happy, hapless life of A'Lelia Walker was a tragedy." Calling her "generous and free-handed to a fault," the best that Du Bois could manage was to say that "her memory, with all the things that mar it, is not altogether unlovely, and her life surely not quite in vain." But her closest friends, who understood her struggles and her disappointments, were more charitable. "A'Lelia's wealth had packed too many thrills into her life . . . It got to the point where her existence virtually depended upon a succession of swift and colorful events, like in a kaleidoscope," wrote the *Inter-State Tattler*'s Edgar Rouzeau. And in fact she once had told her son-in-law, Marion Perry, "I had everything I wanted in life. I just didn't have it long enough." But it may have been Carl Van Vechten who remembered her most enthusiastically. "You should have known A'Lelia Walker," he declared in a letter to author Chester Himes twenty-five years after her death. "Nothing in this age is quite as good as THAT. Her satellites were shocked and offended by her appearance in *Nigger Heaven*, but she was nicer to me after that, even than before. I miss her . . . What a woman!"

Epilogue

Today the Walker women's legacy is alive in two National Historic Landmarks: Villa Lewaro, their Irvington-on-Hudson, New York, mansion, and the Madam Walker Theatre Center in Indianapolis, Indiana. Home to the Madam C. J. Walker Manufacturing Company from 1927 until 1979, the Center now includes a small Walker museum room, sponsors a vibrant schedule of theater and musical performances, operates a cultural arts education program for Indianapolis youth and hosts the annual Madam Walker Spirit Awards for Entrepreneurs. Villa Lewaro, a private residence, was briefly opened to the public during the fall of 1998 when it was featured as a designer show house to benefit the United Negro College Fund. Although Madam Walker's will stipulated that the home was to be donated to the NAACP upon A'Lelia Walker's death, by mutual agreement—because of the high Depression-era taxes and upkeep—it was sold in 1932 to the Companions of the Forest, a women's benevolent organization that had no black members. In 1993 Villa Lewaro was purchased by Harold Doley, an African American investment banker, and his wife, Helena.

The original Madam C. J. Walker Manufacturing Company was sold by the Walker estate trustees in 1986. Today Madam Walker's role as a pioneer of the multibillion-dollar hair care and cosmetics industry is best exemplified by the successful member companies of the Chicago-based American Health and Beauty Aids Institute, who recently welcomed her into their hall of fame. In 1998 Madam Walker was honored as the twenty-first subject of the U.S. Postal Service's Black Heritage Series commemorative stamps. Madam Walker's papers and letters are archived at the Indiana Historical Society in Indianapolis.

Endnotes

ABBREVIATIONS

ARCHIVES, LIBRARIES AND COLLECTIONS
BTW/LOC—Booker T. Washington Papers/Library of Congress (Washington, DC)
CHS—Colorado Historical Society
CPL/VGHC—Chicago Public Library/Vivian G. Harsh Collection
CTS/MHS—Charles Turner Scrapbooks/Missouri Historical Society (St. Louis)
DPLWHD—Denver Public Library Western History Division
FWP/SCRBC—Federal Writers Program/Schomburg Center for Research in Black Culture (New York)
GSC/CU—Gumby Scrapbook Collection/Columbia University
IHS—Indiana Historical Society (Indianapolis)
LLCU—Low Library at Columbia University (New York)
LOC—Library of Congress (Washington, DC)
LPEC/MHS—Louisiana Purchase Exposition Collection/Missouri Historical Society (St. Louis)
MCML—Madison County, Mississippi, Library (Canton, MS)
MHS—Missouri Historical Society (St. Louis)
MPCH—Madison Parish, Louisiana, Court House (Tallulah, LA)
MSRC—Moorland Spingarn Research Center (Howard University, Washington, DC)
MSRC/YMCA—Moorland Spingarn Research Center/YMCA, Jesse Moorland Papers (Howard University)
MWC/IHS—Madam Walker Collection/Indiana Historical Society
MWFC/APB—Madam Walker Family Collection/A'Lelia Bundles (Alexandria, VA)
NARS—National Archives and Records Administration (Washington, DC)
OCHM—Old Court House Museum (Vicksburg, MS)
RACNP/LOC—Records of the American Commission to Negotiate Peace
RNACWC—Records of the National Association of Colored Women's Clubs
SCRBC—Schomburg Center for Research in Black Culture (New York)
TPL—Tallulah Public Library (Tallulah, LA)
UMSL—University of Missouri at St. Louis
UPHL—University of Pittsburgh Hillman Library

ORGANIZATIONS
NAACP—National Association for the Advancement of Colored People
NACW—National Association of Colored Women
NNBL—National Negro Business League

NAMES
MMB—Mary McLeod Bethune
RLB—Robert Lee Brokenburr
JWJ—James Weldon Johnson
JAK—James Arthur Kennedy
FBR—Freeman B. Ransom

LWR—Lelia Walker Robinson (A'Lelia Walker)
EJS—Emmett Jay Scott
CJW—Charles Joseph Walker
MW—Madam C. J. Walker
BTW—Booker T. Washington

CHAPTER 1 FREEDOM BABY

Page 26

born around 1828—Madison Parish Deed Book, COB: B pp. 289–90, "Caruther & Co. to Burney"; *Heirs of Burney v. John T. Ludeling,* Vol. 3, p. 490 (1895), Louisiana Supreme Court, 47 La. Ann. 1434, 17 SO. 877.

banner year—Stephen R. James, Jr., *Cultural Resources Investigations, Delta Mat Casting Field Additional Lands, Madison Parish, Louisiana* (Vicksburg: U.S. Army Corps of Engineers, Apr. 1993), submitted by Panamerican Consultants, Inc. (Tuscaloosa, AL), p. 13.

valued at $125,000—James Arthur Thomas, Jr., document with June 28, 1969, letter.

"growing up with weeds"—*Heirs of Burney,* p. 545.

in Morton, Mississippi—Matilda Thomas, Speech to the United Daughters of the Confederacy reprinted in *Kentucky New Era,* June 22, 1963.

Page 27

refugee camp—Freedmen's Bureau Record Group 105, Entry 1400, Morning Reports of the Assistant Surgeon at Birney Plantation, Jan. 1864–Feb. 1865, Louisiana Chief Medical Officer, Box No. 40; Southern Claims Commission Case No. 20441, *Estate of R. W. Burney v. the United States;* John Eaton, *Grant, Lincoln, and the Freedmen: Reminiscences of the Civil War with Special Reference to the Work for the Contrabands and Freedmen of the Mississippi Valley* (New York: Longmans, Green, 1907), p. 105.

"The refugees were crowded"—Eaton, *Grant,* p. 105.

burial ground—Inventory of remains, unpublished document, accompanying letters from Brig. Gen. H. M. Whittlesey, OCHM.

"shanties near the river"—*Heirs of Burney,* p. 545.

twenty-two years old—1860 U.S. Census lists his age as forty, which would make him twenty-two years old in 1842; Charles B. McKernan Affidavit, Receiver's Office, Ouachita, LA, Nov. 18, 1842, Receipt No. 7699, lists Burney's age as "about 24" in 1842.

$1.25 an acre—U.S. Department of the Interior, Bureau of Land Management, Eastern States Land Grant certificate #7699, General Land Office, Feb. 4, 1843.

160 acres—Madison Parish Deed Book, COB: B pp. 289–90.

Page 28

October 1846—James Arthur Thomas, Jr., unpublished family history: R. W. Burney and Mary Fredonia Williamson, Oct. 21, 1846, marriage, Christ Church, Vicksburg, MS (from Burney Long).

wealthy Mississippi landowner—Dunbar Rowland, *History of Mississippi: The Heart of the South,* Vol. I (Chicago and Jackson, MS: S. J. Clarke Publishing Company, 1925), p. 565; Janet Sharp Hermann, *The Pursuit of a Dream* (New York: Oxford University Press, 1981), p. 7.

fought as a teenager—John E. Hale, Jan. 21, 1995, "First Generation," unpublished memo, from MCML.

appointed Williamson surveyor general—C. Albert White, *A History of the Rectangular Survey System* (Washington, DC: GPO, U.S. Department of the Interior, Bureau of

Land Management, 1991), pp. 95 and 211; Senate Executive Journal, Jan. 30, 1998, phone conversation with Matt Fulgham (National Archives).

"Ownership was as American"—Robert V. Remini, *The Legacy of Andrew Jackson* (Baton Rouge: Louisiana State University Press, 1988), p. 89; Kenneth O'Reilly, *Nixon's Piano* (New York: The Free Press, 1995), p. 31.

at least a dozen slaves—R. W. Burney to Judge A. Snyder, Richmond, Louisiana, Apr. 1, 1850; *Mary F. Williamson et al. v. Eliza A. Dawson et al., No. 1205.*

Vicksburg investor—Gordon Cotton to A'Lelia Bundles, undated correspondence.

"negroes, Oxen, Corn"—*Heirs of Burney*, p. 489.

slaves Burney brought—Ibid., p. 490.

"to clear up"—Ibid., p. 489.

Page 29

"be invested in negroes"—Ibid., p. 491.

"any negro women"—Ibid., p. 495.

$10,000—1850 U.S. Census.

350,000 slaveholding families—Charles M. Christian, *Black Saga: The African American Experience* (Boston: Houghton Mifflin, 1985), p. 144.

"teaching them to read"—Howard A. White, *The Freedmen's Bureau in Louisiana* (Baton Rouge: Louisiana State University Press, 1970), p. 166, cites *The Consolidation and Revision of the Statutes of a General Nature* (New Orleans, 1852), p. 552.

"too much information"—Editorial, *Richmond Compiler*, Aug. 9, 1842, quoted in "Plantation Life," *Madison Journal*, Aug. 14, 1975.

unincorporated village—Thurston H. G. Hahn III, Allen R. Saltus, Jr., and Stephen R. James, Jr., *Delta Landing: Historical and Archaeological Investigations of Three Sunken Watercraft at Delta, Madison Parish, Louisiana* (Baton Rouge: Coastal Environments, and Vicksburg: U.S. Army Corps of Engineers, June 1994), pp. 15–16.

Page 30

"blackened like fire"—John Q. Anderson, *Brokenburn: The Journal of Kate Stone, 1861–1868* (Baton Rouge: Louisiana State University Press, 1972), p. 369.

700,000 black men—Eric Foner and Olivia Mahoney, *America's Reconstruction: People and Politics After the Civil War* (New York: HarperCollins, 1995), p. 81; John Hope Franklin, *Reconstruction After the Civil War* (Chicago: University of Chicago Press, 1994), p. 79.

127,639 registered voters—Charles Vincent, "Negro Leadership and Programs in the Louisiana Constitutional Convention of 1868," *Louisiana History*, Vol. 10, No. 4, (Fall 1969), p. 341, cites John Rose Ficklin, *History of Reconstruction in Louisiana (Through 1868)* (Baltimore, 1910), pp. 169–97; A. E. Perkins, "Some Negro Officers and Legislators in Louisiana," *Journal of Negro History*, Vol. 14 (Oct. 1929), pp. 523–28.

half the delegates—Vincent, *Louisiana History*, p. 341.

two were not Republicans—Joe Gray Taylor, *Louisiana Reconstructed 1863–1870* (Baton Rouge: Louisiana State University Press, 1974), p. 146.

"Congo Convention"—Vincent, *Louisiana History*, p. 344.

"Africanize"—Franklin, *Reconstruction*, p. 74.

"utterly so ignorant"—Ibid.

as much or more education—Charles Vincent, *Black Legislators in Louisiana During Reconstruction* (Baton Rouge: Louisiana State University Press, 1976), p. 58.

Johnson, a tailor—Paul F. Boller, Jr., *Presidential Anecdotes* (New York: Oxford University Press, 1996) p. 147.

Page 31

educated in France—Vincent, *Black Legislators*, pp. 52–53.

outlawing segregation on trains—Ibid., p. 62.

"government of white people"—W.E.B. Du Bois, *Black Reconstruction: An Essay Toward a History of the Part Which Black Folk Played in the Attempt to Reconstruct Democracy in America, 1860–1880* (New York: Harcourt, Brace, 1935), p. 454.

White Camellia—James G. Dauphine, "The Knights of the White Camellia and the Election of 1868: Louisiana's White Terrorists; a Benighting Legacy," *Louisiana History*, Vol. 30, No. 2 (Spring 1989), p. 173.

CHAPTER 2 MOTHERLESS CHILD

Page 32

one thousand murders—Dauphine, *Louisiana History*, pp. 175–76; Records of the Bureau of Refugees, Freedmen, and Abandoned Lands, Records of the Assistant Commissioner for the State of Louisiana, 1865–1869, Washington, DC, National Archives, Record Group 105, Microfilm 1027, roll 27, frames 16, 63, 262; roll 34, frames 206–308; *Report of the Joint Committee of the General Assembly of Louisiana on the Conduct of the Late Elections and the Condition of Peace and Order in the State*, Session of 1869 (New Orleans, 1869), p. 84; and *U.S. Miscellaneous Documents*, 41st Congress, 2nd Session, Serial 1435, No. 154, Part 1 (Washington, DC, 1879), pp. 298 and 555.

proximity to—Dauphine, *Louisiana History*, pp. 189–90.

widest margin—Ibid.

Page 33

"White Man's Government"—Eric Foner and Olivia Mahoney, *America's Reconstruction: People and Politics After the Civil War* (New York: HarperCollins, 1995), pp. 87–88.

"a black man, uncompromisingly"—Howard J. Jones, "Biographical Sketches of Members of the 1868 Louisiana State Senate," *Louisiana History*, Vol. 19, No. 1 (Winter 1978), p. 78, cites *New Orleans Louisianan*, Dec. 22, 1870, and *New Orleans Daily Picayune*, July 10, 1868.

championed Louisiana legislation—Charles Vincent, *Black Legislators in Louisiana During Reconstruction* (Baton Rouge: Louisiana State University Press, 1976), pp. 98–99.

blacksmith—"Human Interest Story: Madam Walker," unpublished essay from Tallulah Library, Madison Parish, Louisiana, p. 3; *Cholera Epidemic of 1873*, House Executive Document 95, 43rd Congress, 2nd Session (Washington, DC: GPO, 1875), p. 115.

"unmanageably large"—Louis C. Hunter, *Steamboats on the Western Rivers: An Economic and Technological History* (New York: Dover Publications, 1993), p. 176.

penny a pound—Ibid.

"improvements in dress"—Howard A. White, *The Freedmen's Bureau in Louisiana* (Baton Rouge: Louisiana State University Press, 1970), p. 130.

$100 marriage bond—Marriage bond (Nov. 20, 1869) and license (Dec. 6, 1869), Madison Parish, Louisiana, 13th District Court, Book B, p. 29, Madison Parish Court House.

"ordinary person"—"Human Interest Story," p. 3, TPL.

Page 34

"a-choppin' cotton"—Ibid.

"twisted and wropped with strings"—Ibid.

state legislature declined—Joe Gray Taylor, *Louisiana Reconstructed 1863–1877* (Baton Rouge: Louisiana State University Press, 1974), p. 462.

"hostility to schools"—John Richard Dennett, *The South As It Is, 1865-1866* (Baton Rouge: Louisiana State University Press, 1965), p. 353.

her father remarried—Marriage bond (Aug. 26, 1874) and license (Aug. 27, 1874), Madison Parish, Louisiana, 13th District Court, Book B, p. 378, Madison Parish Court House (Dick and Will Sevier).

"little or no opportunity"—*1914 NNBL Report.*

Page 35

1873 cholera epidemic—*Cholera Epidemic of 1873*, pp. 46 and 115.

"armed camp"—Vincent, *Black Legislators*, p. 183.

White League—The first White League was organized in Opelousas (St. Landry Parish) in late April 1874. Vincent, *Black Legislators*, p. 183.

"no security, no peace"—*Alexandria Caucasian*, Apr. 4, 1874, cited in Alice Bayne Windham, "Methods and Mechanisms Used to Restore White Supremacy in Louisiana, 1872–1876," unpublished M.A. thesis, Louisiana State University, 1948; Taylor, *Louisiana Reconstructed*, p. 282.

Page 36

removal of federal troops—C. Vann Woodward, *Reunion and Reaction: The Compromise of 1877 and the End of Reconstruction* (Boston: Little, Brown, 1951, and Garden City, NY: Doubleday Anchor, 1956), p. 239.

hollow log—"Through Tensas," *Chicago Tribune*, May 10, 1879, p. 16; Nell Irvin Painter, *Exodusters: Black Migration to Kansas after Reconstruction* (New York: Alfred A. Knopf, 1977), pp. 167–68 and 170; Frederick W. Williamson and George T. Goodman, *Eastern Louisiana: A History of the Watershed of the River and the Florida Parishes* (Shreveport: Historical Record Association, 1939), p. 171.

"hanging in the swamp"—Testimony of William Murrell in *Report and Testimony of the Select Committee of the United States Senate to Investigate the Causes of the Removal of the Negroes from the Southern States to the Northern States*, 46th Congress, 2nd Session, Report 693, Part II (Washington, DC: GPO, 1880), p. 520.

"excited the colored people"—Ibid.

"homeless, breadless"—Vernon Lane Wharton, *The Negro in Mississippi 1865-1890* (Chapel Hill: University of North Carolina Press, 1947), p. 112.

Page 37

a porter at C. L. Chambers—Gordon Cotton/OCHM to A'Lelia Bundles, June 5, 1988; A'Lelia Bundles to Gordon Cotton, Jan. 2, 1989, confirming 1988 letter re: 1877 *Vicksburg City Directory* listing for "Alex Breedlow"; Gordon Cotton to author, July 9, 1998; Khaled J. Bloom, *The Mississippi Valley's Great Yellow Fever Epidemic of 1878* (Baton Rouge: Louisiana State University Press, 1993), p. 107.

"craved for the beautiful"—"The Life Work of Mme. C. J. Walker," *Indpls. Freeman*, Dec. 26, 1914, p. 1.

re-created part of the floor plan—Author's conversations with Robert Burney Long and Anne Long Case.

"the province of black women"—Jacqueline Jones, *Labor of Love, Labor of Sorrow* (New York: Basic Books, 1985), p. 125.

"onerous"—Tera W. Hunter, *To 'Joy My Freedom* (Cambridge, MA: Oxford University Press, 1997), pp. 52 and 56.

"16 shooters"—Edward Leonard affidavit, *Select Committee of the United States Senate*, 1880, p. 61.

abridge their rights—Painter, *Exodusters*, p. 186.

Page 38

"Now is the time to go"—Benjamin "Pap" Singleton flier, Kansas Historical Society, Topeka.

railroad company circulars—R. C. Overton, *The First Ninety Years: An Historical Sketch of the Burlington Railroad 1850–1940* (Chicago: Chicago, Burlington & Quincy Railroad, 1940), pp. 22–23.

"plenty of coal"—Singleton flier.

"poor, battered"—Painter, *Exodusters*, p. 197.

clotted together at Vicksburg—Testimony of Charlton H. Tandy, *Select Committee of the United States Senate*, 1880, pp. 36–37.

"African hegira"—*Vicksburg Herald*, Feb. 28, 1879, cited in *St. Joseph North Louisiana Journal*, Mar. 8, 1879, and in Painter, *Exodusters*, p. 185.

"cut very bad"—Curtis Pollard Affidavit, *Select Committee of the United States Senate*, 1880, pp. 47–48.

nearly 700 refugees—Murrell Testimony, *Select Committee of the United States Senate*, 1880, pp. 512–13.

"every road"—Hinds County *Gazette*, Mar. 5, 1879, cited in Painter, *Exodusters*, p. 186.

"I was accused"—Pollard Affidavit, *Select Committee of the United States Senate*, 1880, p. 9.

Page 39

black Republican Club president—Murrell Testimony, *Select Committee of the United States Senate*, 1880, pp. 514–15.

1,600 Exodusters—Ibid., p. 513.

first job as a porter—*St. Louis City Directory*, 1881 and 1882.

CHAPTER 3 WIFE, MOTHER, WIDOW

Page 40

"I married at the age of fourteen"—*National Negro Business League Report of the Seventeenth Annual Session, Kansas City, Missouri, Aug. 16–18, 1916* (Washington, DC: William H. Davis, 1916), p. 135.

$200 Mississippi marriage bond—Gordon Cotton to author, Aug. 13, 1998.

Page 41

"exceptionally good"—Harry P. Owens, *Steamboats and the Cotton Economy: River Trade in the Yazoo-Mississippi Delta* (Jackson: University Press of Mississippi, 1990), p. 108.

churches and benevolent societies—W. E. Mollison, *The Leading Afro-Americans of Vicksburg, Mississippi* (Vicksburg: Biographia Publishing Co., 1908), pp. 73–78; Jonathan Beasley, "Blacks—Slave and Free—Vicksburg, 1850–1860," *Journal of Mississippi History*, Vol. 38, No. 1 (Feb. 1976), p. 12.

"Her father having been killed"—Konrad Bercovici, "The Black Blocks of Manhattan," *Harper's Monthly Magazine*, Vol. 40/41 (after 1923), GSC/CU.

Page 42

"I don't think"—David Levering Lewis, *When Harlem Was in Vogue* (New York: Alfred A. Knopf, 1981), p. 168, cites LWR to Walter White, Nov. 10, 1924 (Walter White Papers, LOC).

"reported killed in a race riot"—Marjorie Stewart Joyner, "The Saga of the First Woman Millionaire Manufacturer" (appears to be a convention booklet, possibly from Joyner's organization, circa 1946–48); on the basis of Marjorie Joyner's assertion that he had been lynched in this article and in personal conversations with Joyner during the 1980s, this author in *Madam C. J. Walker: Entrepreneur* (New York:

Chelsea House, 1991), a young adult biography of Madam Walker, stated that he was killed in an accident. But even the "accident" cannot be substantiated upon further investigation.

"Is Daddy coming back?"—Harry B. Webber, "Grim Awakening to Her Future Was Incentive to Mme. Walker," *Pittsburgh Courier*, Mar. 15, 1952, p. 12.

"bodies thrown into the river"—Ibid.

95 people whose lynchings—*NNBL Report 1916*, p. 176.

massacred in Carrollton—Christian, *Black Saga*, p. 267.

"impossible to make any estimate"—*Raymond Gazette*, July 18, 1885, cited in Wharton, *Negro in Mississippi*, p. 224.

Page 43

"several lynchings"—"Lynchings," Centennial Edition of the Madison *Journal*, Aug. 14, 1975, 8-VI, cites the *Times-Democrat*, July 24, 1889.

"no single instance"—Wharton, *Negro in Mississippi*, p. 224.

Mississippi lynching victims—E. M. Beck, "Listing of Lynching Victims: Mississippi, 1882–1930," unpublished, Feb. 26, 1996, pp. 1–6; Stewart E. Tolnay and E. M. Beck, *A Festival of Violence: An Analysis of Southern Lynchings, 1882–1930* (Urbana: University of Illinois Press, 1995), p. 41.

"5,000 Negroes Lynched"—Ralph Ginzburg, "A Partial Listing of Approximately 5,000 Negroes Lynched in the United States since 1859," in *100 Years of Lynching* (Baltimore: Black Classic Press, 1988), pp. 262–65.

aside from murder—A'Lelia Perry Bundles, *Madam C. J. Walker: Entrepreneur* (New York: Chelsea House, 1991), p. 27 (on the basis of interviews with Dr. Marjorie Stewart Joyner in the 1980s, the author was told that Moses McWilliams had died tragically, leading to the speculation in early editions of this young adult biography that he had "died in an accident").

Hundreds of young, single and widowed—Jacqueline Jones, *Labor of Love, Labor of Sorrow* (New York: Basic Books, 1985), pp. 155–56.

200,000 unmarried women—U.S. Bureau of the Census, *Eleventh Census of the United States: 1890* (Washington, DC: GPO, 1893), pp. 36–45; U.S. Bureau of the Census, *Negro Population 1790–1915*, pp. 509 and 526, cited in Beverly Washington Jones, *Quest for Equality: The Life and Writings of Mary Eliza Church Terrell, 1863–1954* (Brooklyn: Carlson Publishing, 1990), pp. 24 and 99 (fn. 29).

Anchor Line—Andrew Morrison and John H. C. Irwin, *The Industries of Saint Louis: Her Advantages, Resources, Facilities and Commercial Relations as a Center of Trade and Manufacture* (St. Louis: J. M. Elstner & Co., 1885), p. 29.

Page 44

"colored aristocracy"—Cyprian Clamorgan, *The Colored Aristocracy of St. Louis* (1858), Lawrence Oland Christensen, *Black St. Louis: A Study in Race Relations 1865–1916*, unpublished Ph.D. dissertation, University of Missouri, Dec. 1972, p. 82.

$20,000 worth of St. Louis real estate—Christensen, *Black St. Louis*, p. 105.

tonsorial palace—James Thomas, *From Tennessee Slave to St. Louis Entrepreneur: The Autobiography of James Thomas*, ed. Loren Schweninger (Columbia: University of Missouri Press, 1984), pp. 2 and 10–14.

Pelagie Rutgers—Christensen, *Black St. Louis*, p. 105.

nearly 300 black barbers—*Eleventh U.S. Census, Population, 1890, Part II*, pp. 724–25, cited in Christensen, *Black St. Louis*, p. 166.

best in the city—Lillian Brandt, "The Negroes of St. Louis," *American Statistical Association*, Vol. 8, No. 61 (Mar. 1903), p. 235.

laborers, servants—Ibid., Christensen, *Black St. Louis*, p. 166.

blacks had dominated the trade—*NNBL Report, 1916*, pp. 164–65.

"The colored barber"—"Black Barbers Must Go—The Whites Say That the Colored Shaver Is Falling Off in Popularity," *St. Louis Republic*, May 10, 1896, CTS/MHS.

Page 45

"We can no longer grow"—*The Smoke Nuisance; Report of the Smoke Abatement Committee of the Civic League* (St. Louis: Civic League of St. Louis, 1906), pp. 4–10, in Selwyn K. Troen and Glen E. Holt, *St. Louis* (New York: New Viewpoints, 1977), p. 115.

Italian, Jewish and black poor—Christensen, *Black St. Louis*, p. 149.

well known on the police blotter—"In Blood: Neil Furniss Left His Female Victim Weltering," unsourced St. Louis newspaper clipping from CTS/MHS.

"washing for families"—"Negro Woman, Rich Hair Tonic Maker, in City: Mrs. Sarah J. Walker, Former Laundress Here, Said to Be Worth Million or More," *St. Louis Post-Dispatch*, Mar. 4, 1918, p. 6.

Jennie Lias—Jennie Lias affidavit, Dec. 26, 1919; Ida B. Winchester affidavit, Dec. 26, 1919.

Like more than half—*Eleventh U.S. Census*, cited in Christensen, *Black St. Louis*, p. 174.

Page 46

two or three white families—Jones, *Labor of Love*, pp. 125–26; Tera W. Hunter, *To 'Joy My Freedom* (Cambridge, MA: Oxford University Press, 1997), pp. 56–57; "Bea, the Washerwoman" (Sarah Hull), *Federal Writers Project #3709*, Southern Historical Collection, Library of the University of North Carolina at Chapel Hill, March 13, 1939, p. 4 (FWP #3709, p. 2010).

"ten to twelve sheets"—"Bea, the Washerwoman," p. 4.

$4 to $12—Hunter, *To 'Joy My Freedom*, pp. 52–53.

"converted"—"America's Foremost Colored Woman," *Indpls Freeman*, Dec. 28, 1912, p. 16.

In September 1889—Typewritten copy of *Indpls. Freeman*, Mar. 7, 1891, article, UMSL Archives—"A Historical Sketch of the society founded half century ago by J.E.B.," p. 4.

Sarah Newton—"Panorama of Growth 1888–1963, How It Began, Mrs. Sarah Newton Cohron," page from untitled, undated brochure from the UMSL Archives; Gwendolyn Robinson, "Class, Race, and Gender: A Transcultural Theoretical and Sociohistorical Analysis of Cosmetic Institutions and Practices to 1920," unpublished Ph.D. dissertation, University of Illinois at Chicago, 1984 (Ann Arbor: University Microfilm International, 1984), p. 359.

religious instruction—*Report of the First National Conference of the National Federation of Afro-American Women*, Boston, Mass., July 29, 30 and 31, 1895, from *Records of the National Association of Colored Women's Clubs, 1895–1992, Part I: Minutes of National Conventions, Publications, and President's Office Correspondence* (Bethesda, MD: University Publications of America, 1993), p. 23.

"half-orphans"—Brandt, *American Statistical Association*, Mar. 1903, p. 260; Mrs. M. F. Pitts and Miss L. Carter, "St. Louis Colored Orphans' Home," in *Report of the Second National Conference of the National Federation of Afro-American Women*, RNACWC, p. 85.

escorted Lelia to Dessalines—Dessalines School Register, 1890, St. Louis Public Schools; Pitts, *National Federation of Afro-American Women*, 1896, RNACWC, 85; Brandt, *American Statistical Association*, Mar. 1903, p. 260.

Page 47
"kindnesses that were shown"—"America's Foremost Colored Woman," *Indpls. Freeman*, Dec. 28, 1912.

CHAPTER 4 ST. LOUIS WOMAN
Page 48
"I was at my washtubs" —"Wealthiest Negro Woman's Suburban Mansion," *The New York Times Magazine*, Nov. 4, 1917.

Page 49
Founded in 1841—Report of Lucy Jefferson, St. Paul AME Church, cited in J. W. Evans, "A Brief Sketch of the Development of Negro Education in St. Louis, Missouri," *Journal of Negro Education*, Vol. 7, No. 4 (Oct. 1938), p. 550; John A. Wright, *Discovering African-American St. Louis: A Guide to Historic Sites* (St. Louis: Missouri Historical Society Press, 1994), p. 68; Jervis Anderson, *A. Philip Randolph: A Biographical Portrait* (New York: Harvest Book/ Harcourt Brace Jovanovich, 1973), p. 28.
"constructed by and for Negroes"—Brandt, *American Statistical Association*, Mar. 1903, p. 257.
The largest organ built—*Indpls. Freeman*, Mar. 7, 1891, UMSL.
Mozart anthems—Ibid.
"Lamentation Day"—Lorenzo J. Greene, Gary R. Kremer, and Antonio F. Holland, *Missouri's Black Heritage* (rev. ed.; Columbia: University of Missouri Press, 1993), p. 109.

Page 50
"work in Africa"—"The A.M.E. Conference," *St. Louis Palladium*, Aug. 26, 1903; "The Conference—At St. Paul's Chapel Well Attended and Interesting," *St. Louis Palladium*, Oct. 10, 1903.
persecution of Russian Jews—"The Massacre of Jews Serves as a Text on Behalf of Negroes," *St. Louis Globe-Democrat*, June 1, 1903, and *St. Louis Palladium*, June 6, 1903.
predominantly white—"St. Paul A.M.E. Church—In the March of the Century," 1940, loose page, UMSL; "St. Paul A.M.E. Church Oldest A.M.E. Church West of Mississippi River," loose page, UMSL.
Having the rest of her family—*Gould's St. Louis City Directory*, 1891, p. 219.
Between 1891 and 1896—Sarah lived at 1407, 1615, 1517, and probably 1619 Linden according to *Gould's St. Louis City Directory*, 1891, 1894, 1895, and 1896; Application No. 57142 for License to Marry, State of Missouri, Aug. 11, 1894; Marriage License No. 57142, State of Missouri, Aug. 11, 1894.
In March 1892—"Colored Club," *Albuquerque Daily Citizen*, Mar. 16, 1892, p. 4.
convicted of manslaughter—F. B. Ransom to S. E. Garner, Dec. 6, 1911; FBR to J. H. Allen, Warden, Parchman State Prison, Dec. 4, 1911.
John Davis—Garner to FBR, Dec. 23, 1919, and Jan. 10, 1920; John H. Davis is also known as John L. Davis and John Lincoln Davis. John H. Davis died Dec. 22, 1929, at City Hospital #2 (Missouri State Board of Health Certificate of Death No. 386, filed Jan. 13, 1930).
moved in with Sarah—Garner to FBR, Jan. 10, 1920.
Saturday, August 11, 1894—Marriage License and Application, No. 57142, Aug. 11, 1894.
100 degrees—"Weather Conditions," *St. Louis Daily Globe-Democrat*, Aug. 12, 1894, p. 4.

Page 51

"Miss Sallie McWilliams"—Marriage Application No. 57142, Aug. 11, 1894.

German workers—Brandt, *American Statistical Association,* Mar. 1903, p. 238.

2 percent—Katharine T. Corbett and Mary E. Seematter, "Black St. Louis at the Turn of the Century," *Gateway Heritage,* Vol. 7, No. 1 (Summer 1986), pp. 43–44, with photo; Jones, *Labor of Love,* p. 124.

menial chores—Corbett and Seematter, "Black St. Louis," pp. 43–44; Jones, *Labor of Love,* p. 124.

tobacco factories—Brandt, *American Statistical Association,* Mar. 1903, p. 238.

26 percent—Cynthia Neverdon-Morton, *Afro-American Women and the Advancement of the Race, 1895–1925* (Knoxville: University of Tennessee Press, 1989), p. 68 cites R. R. Wright, Jr., "Negro in Unskilled Labor," *The Negro's Progress in Fifty Years: The Annals of the American Academy,* ed. Emory R. Johnson (Philadelphia: American Academy of Political and Social Science, 1913), pp. 25–26.

"were constantly in quarrels"—Jennie Gully Lias affidavit, Dec. 26, 1919, MWC/IHS.

"strike, beat and maltreat Sallie"—Lias affidavit; Ida B. Winchester affidavit, Dec. 26, 1919; Garner to FBR, Jan. 10, 1920, MWC/IHS.

"fussy, mean and dangerous"—Winchester affidavit; Garner to FBR, Jan. 10, 1920, MWC/IHS.

"before the courts"—Ibid.

a block away with her uncle James—Lucas Avenue had previously been named Christy, *Gould's St. Louis Directory for 1895* (St. Louis: Acme Printing Company, 1895), and *Gould's St. Louis Directory for 1896* (St. Louis: Acme Printing Company, 1896).

Page 52

"toughest neighborhood"—"Murderer Stack Lee Taken Out for a Drunk," newspaper clipping in CTS/MHS.

Bad Lands—"Sheriff's Men Are Gentle to the Criminals," *St. Louis Republic,* Feb. 20, 1896, CTS/MHS.

murders nearly doubled—*Annual Report of the Board of Police Commissioners, 1894–1895* (St. Louis, 1895), pp. 612–17; *Annual Report of the Board of Police Commissioners, 1895–1896* (St. Louis, 1896), p. 670.

"the most prolific murder center"—"Murderer Stack Lee Taken Out for a Drunk."

dives near Twelfth—"Butchered: Jessie Sims Carved to Death by Alexander Royle," *St. Louis Chronicle,* Nov. 29, 1895, CTS/MHS. Depending on the source, the surname is spelled either Royal or Royle.

"female denizens"—Ibid.

ten-cent bathhouses—"Snapshots of Daily Life on Lower Morgan Street—Once the Home of the 400 Club and of McAllister Bill Curtis," undated newspaper clipping, CTS/MHS.

"terror of the police"—Ibid.

a jealous boyfriend—"Conspiracy to Murder—Killing of James Freeman Said to Be the Result of a Plot," *St. Louis Globe-Democrat,* Dec. 5, 1895, CTS/MHS.

the day after Thanksgiving—*St. Louis Chronicle,* Nov. 29, 1895, CTS/MHS.

"two stab wounds"—"Butchered," *St. Louis Chronicle,* Nov. 29, 1895, CTS/MHS.

Page 53

multiple lacerations—"In Blood: Neil Furniss Left His Female Victim Weltering," newspaper clipping, CTS/MHS.

one neighbor fatally shot—"Shot and Killed—Henry Massey Receives Two Bullets from the Pistol of Nelson Casey," newspaper clipping (possibly *St. Louis Republic*), Dec. 11, 1895, CTS/MHS.

Shelton Lee—Depending on the source, the murderer is named Shelton Lee or Lee Shelton. The victim is sometimes called William Jones, at other times William Lyons. See "Murderer Stack Lee Taken Out for a Drunk."

"Stackalee shot Billy"—"Stackalee," a version collected by Onah L. Spencer, in Deirdre Mullane, ed., *Crossing the Danger Water: Three Hundred Years of African American Writing* (New York: Doubleday, Anchor, 1993), pp. 264–66.

Accompanied by two . . . deputy sheriffs—"Sheriff's Men Are Gentle to the Criminals," *St. Louis Republic*, Feb. 20, 1896, CTS/MHS.

"There is continual warfare"—Ibid.

Bad Lands murders continued—"Killed His Brother-in-Law—Taylor Jackson, Colored, Shot Twice by Louis Walton After a Quarrel," *St. Louis Republic*, Feb. 14, 1896, CTS/MHS.

since the 1850s—John A. Wright, *Discovering African-American St. Louis: A Guide to Historic Sites* (St. Louis: Missouri Historical Society Press, 1994), p. 23.

Bordered by Twentieth Street—Ibid.

"highroller Stetson"—W. C. Handy, *Father of the Blues: An Autobiography*, ed. Arna Bontemps (New York: Macmillan, 1941), p. 30, cited in Edward A. Berlin, *King of Ragtime: Scott Joplin and His Era* (New York: Oxford University Press, 1994), p. 90.

Page 54

2142 Walnut Street—*Gould's St. Louis Directory for 1898* for the year ending April 1, 1897 (St. Louis: Gould Directory Company); *Gould's 1899*; *L'Ouverture Elementary School Annual Register*, 1898, St. Louis Public Schools; *L'Ouverture Register*, 1899.

Following their pattern—Between 1896 and 1902 they lived at 2117, 2142, 2113 and 2231 Walnut. See *Gould's St. Louis Directory 1898* for the year ending April 1, 1897; *Gould's 1899*; *L'Ouverture Register*, 1898; *L'Ouverture Register*, 1899; *Gould's 1900*; 1900 Census.

Maria Harrison—"New Douglass Palm Garden," *St. Louis Palladium*, June 18, 1904.

L'Ouverture Elementary—Lelia attended Banneker Elementary School for at least one year in 1897 before transferring to L'Ouverture Elementary School in 1898. See *L'Ouverture Register*, 1898; "The Hudlin Family" PROUD Bicentennial II, 1976, p. 29, UMSL.

95 percent—Brandt, *American Statistical Association*, Mar. 1903, p. 239.

Girls with neatly parted hair—See circa 1900 photo of L'Ouverture School classroom in Wright, *Discovering*, p. 111.

proportion of black students—Brandt, *American Statistical Association*, Mar. 1903, p. 245.

Lelia missed only six days—*L'Ouverture Register*, 1898.

1899 school year—*L'Ouverture Register*, 1899.

She attended only twenty-three days—Ibid.

missed only thirteen days—*L'Ouverture Register*, 1900.

Page 55

Oberlin graduate—*100th Anniversary History of Charles Sumner High School*, 1975, p. 13, UMSL.

Twentieth Century Girls' Club—Nathan B. Young, *Your St. Louis and Mine* (St. Louis: N. B. Young, 1937), p. 23.

"open all day"—Rosebud Cafe ad, *St. Louis Palladium*, Jan. 2, 1904.

"uncrowned master"—Young, *Your St. Louis*, p. 62.

"I did washing"—*St. Louis Post-Dispatch*, Mar. 4, 1918.

gladly sent $7.85—*Knoxville College Catalogue 1901*, from Robert J. Booker, p. 9.

"sparingly granted"—Ibid.

Page 56

"normal school"—Ibid., pp. 6–7.

50,000 residents—Ibid., p. 7.

As one of twenty-four students—Robert J. Booker letter to author, Feb. 25, 1999.

$6 blue serge Norfolk jacket—*Knoxville College Catalogue 1901*, from Robert J. Booker, pp. 10–11.

In Elnathan Hall—Ibid., p. 8.

forty-year-old James—James Breedlove, Death Certificate No. 004364, City of St. Louis, Bureau of Vital Statistics, Division of Health.

Solomon succumbed—Solomon Breedlove, Death Certificate, City of St. Louis, Bureau of Vital Statistics, Division of Health.

In November 1903—Davis gave the date as November 1903 in his petition to claim one-third of the Walker estate drawn up Jan. 9, 1920; Petition of Executrix for Authority to Compromise Claim of John H. Davis, Filed Apr. 5, 1920, Marion County Probate Court, Sarah Walker Estate No. 56-14285; I believe Sarah left Davis as early as 1902, possibly around the time Lelia left for Knoxville, because Peggie Prosser met Lelia in Jan. 1903 in Knoxville. Davis himself claimed she deserted him in 1903.

fall of 1902—Peggie Prosser to FBR, Oct. 2 (no year: 1921 or 1922).

Page 57

three black newspapers—Brandt, *American Statistical Association*, Mar. 1903, p. 237.

as a barber and in a saloon—*Gould's St. Louis City Directory*, 1903.

He was a mix—Louise/Kansas City, MO, to Charles J. Walker, Jan. 11, 1912, MWC/IHS.

well-shined shoes—"C. J. Walker Says: 'As You Reap So Shall You Sow'—Former Husband of Well-Known Hair Manufacturer Regrets Past Life," *Indpls. Freeman*, Mar. 21, 1914.

"what you would call yellow"—Violet Davis Reynolds, Feb. 17, 1985.

lifelong confidante—Young, *Your St. Louis*, p. 15.

taught at Banneker—Sharon Huffman/St. Louis Public Records and Schools Archives to author, July 2, 1998, E-mail; *St. Louis Public Schools 1891–92 Annual Report*, Appendix, p. lviii.

French knots—photo in Young, *Your St. Louis*, p. 13.

Grand Chancellor—"Knights of Pythias—Eighth Biennial Session of the Colored Supreme Lodge," *St. Louis Republic*, Sept. 12, 1896, CTS/MHS.

Supreme Grand Secretary—Young, *Your St. Louis*, p. 11.

publisher of *The Clarion*—Julia Davis, "Saint Louis Public Schools Named for Negroes" (St. Louis: Banneker District St. Louis Public Schools, Nov. 1967), MHS; "Facts from *The Palladium* Scrap Book," *St. Louis Palladium*, May 12, 1906.

Page 58

"educated in night school"—Frank Lincoln Mather, *Who's Who of the Colored Race* (Chicago: Who's Who of the Colored Race, 1915), p. 274.

sixty-three washerwomen—*47th Annual Report of the Board of Education of the City of St. Louis, Mo., for the Year Ending June 30, 1901* (St. Louis: Nixon-Jones Printing Co., 1902), p. 100.

In 1903 students older than twenty—"Night School," *St. Louis Palladium*, Dec. 5, 1903.

including one at L'Ouverture—"Free Evening School," *St. Louis Palladium*, Oct. 8, 1904.

"forming female classes"—"Vashon's Female Classes," *St. Louis Palladium*, Nov. 5, 1904.

St. Paul's Mite Missionary Society—"150 Years of Service to God—St. Paul African Methodist Episcopal Church," souvenir brochure (1991); "St. Paul A.M.E. Church—In the March of the Century," 1940, loose page, UMSL.

"Membership within church clubs"—Darlene Clark Hine, *When the Truth Is Told* (Indianapolis: National Council of Negro Women/Indianapolis Section, 1981), pp. 26–27.

"She felt it was her duty"—A'Lelia Perry Bundles, *Madam C. J. Walker: Entrepreneur* (New York: Chelsea House, 1991), pp. 32–33.

Page 59

"I tried everything"—*The Walker Manufacturing Company* (Indianapolis: Walker Manufacturing Company, 1911), p. 3, BTW/LOC, MW file.

CHAPTER 5 ANSWERED PRAYERS

Page 60

"I was on the verge of becoming entirely bald"—*The Walker Manufacturing Company* (Indianapolis: Walker Manufacturing Company, 1911), p. 4, BTW/LOC, MW file.

"He answered my prayer"—"Queen of Gotham's Colored 400," *Literary Digest*, Vol. 55 (Oct. 13, 1917), p. 76, reprinted from Frances L. Garside, *Kansas City Star*.

"I made up my mind I would begin to sell it"—Ibid.

"When I made"—*The Walker Co.*, p. 4.

"an inspiration from God"—Ibid., p. 5.

"place in the reach"—"It Makes Short Hair Long and Cures Dandruff," Walker ad, *Indpls. Freeman*, Apr. 16, 1910, p. 2.

"Hair Feeder"—"Dr. W. D. Deshay's Hair Feeder," ad, *St. Louis Palladium*, May 12, 1906.

Page 61

all the other items—Product formulas of the Madam C. J. Walker Manufacturing Company in possession of the author.

only New York rivaled—Andrew Morrison and John H. C. Irwin, *The Industries of Saint Louis: Her Advantages, Resources, Facilities and Commercial Relations as a Center of Trade and Manufacture* (St. Louis: J. M. Elstner & Co., 1885), p. 51; *The Saint Louis of To-Day Illustrated: An Artistic Presentation of Her Business Interests* (St. Louis: Western Commercial Travelers' Association, 1888), pp. 28–29; "The Gilded Age," exhibit at the Missouri Historical Society Museum, Dec. 1997.

"part of my story may sound strange"—*New York Times Magazine*, Nov. 4, 1917.

"Judge in yourselves"—1 Corinthians 11:13–15.

"instead of well-set hair, baldness"—Isaiah 3:24.

Page 62

an antebellum elite—Willard Gatewood, *Aristocrats of Color: The Black Elite, 1880–1920* (Bloomington: Indiana University Press, 1990), pp. 149–81.

"Black men who clamor"—Alfred A. Moss, Jr., *The American Negro Academy: Voice of the Talented Tenth* (Baton Rouge: Louisiana State University Press, 1981), p. 55, cited in Paula Giddings, *When and Where I Enter: The Impact of Black Women on Race and Sex in America* (New York: William Morrow, 1984), p. 115.

Page 63

"apt to look to other races"—Fannie Barrier Williams, "The Colored Girl," *Voice of the Negro*, June 1905, p. 403, cited in Giddings, *When and Where*, p. 115.

"marry a woman for her color"—"Not Color But Character," Nannie Helen Burroughs, *Voice of the Negro*, July 1904, p. 277; Giddings, *When and Where*, p. 115.

"the Gibson Cure"—*This Fabulous Century*, Vol. 1: 1900–1910 (New York: Time-Life Books, 1985), p. 183.

"chic, haughty and graceful"—Ibid., pp. 181–83.

"one hundred thousand pounds"—C. Henri Leonard, *The Hair: Its Growth, Care, Diseases and Treatment* (Detroit: C. Henri Leonard, Medical Book Publishers, 1880), p. 9.

two dollars per ounce—Ibid., p. 10.

Page 64

"NAPPY HEADS!"—"Rip Saw Column of the *St. Louis Palladium*," *St. Louis Palladium*, May 26, 1906.

Pure Food and Drugs Act—*This Fabulous Century*, p. 173.

preparations manufactured by others—*The Walker Co.*, p. 3.

"personally" restored—Albert Anderson, "The Amazing Inside Story of the Malone Case," *The Light and "Heebie Jeebies,"* Vol. 3, No. 13 (Feb. 19, 1927), p. 15, Claude Barnett Papers, CPL/VGHC; Robinson, "Class, Race, and Gender," pp. 349–50; "Annie Turnbo-Malone," Jeanne Conway Mongold ms. copy Dec. 12, 1977, UMSL Archives.

An ambitious woman—*Second National Poro Convention Souvenir Program*, Chicago, July 24–26, 1949.

2223 Market Street—*"Poro" in Pictures with a Short History of Its Development* (St. Louis: Poro College, 1926); p. 5.

Page 65

free scalp treatments—Ibid., 5; *Second National Poro Convention*, 1949; Mongold, p. 1.

"South 16th Street"—Anderson, *The Light and "Heebie Jeebies,"* p. 15.

one of Pope-Turnbo's earliest sales agents—Mrs. C. J. Walker letter, *Colorado Statesman*, May 12, 1906, p. 5; handwritten notes from Willard Gatewood, Aug. 1992; "To the Ladies," *Denver Statesman*, May 18, 1906; George Ross to R. L. Brokenburr, Dec. 17, 1919, MWC/IHS; Anderson, *The Light and "Heebie Jeebies,"* p. 15; Robinson, "Class, Race, and Gender," pp. 349–50.

Tetter's tiny scales—*The Madam C. J. Walker Beauty Manual*, 2nd ed. (Indianapolis: Walker Manufacturing Company, 1940); pp. 102–3.

Hippocrates—Leonard, *The Hair*, pp. 172–73.

"Clean scalps mean clean bodies"—Anderson, *The Light and "Heebie Jeebies,"* p. 14.

unidentified illness—Annie Minerva Turnbo Pope Malone was born Aug. 9, 1869, the tenth of Robert and Isabella Cook Turnbo's eleven children. Annie Malone died May 10, 1957. *"Poro" in Pictures*, p. 4.

"with the return of her health"—Ibid.

"natural gift from childhood"—Mrs. A. M. Pope letter, *Colorado Statesman*, May 12, 1906; handwritten notes from Willard Gatewood, Aug. 1992.

Page 66

"weather-beaten building"—*Second National Poro Convention*.

Wonderful Hair Grower—*"Poro" in Pictures*, p. 4.

"I went around in the buggy"—Robinson, "Class, Race, and Gender," 1984, p. 348.

"stimulating washes"—Sir John Eric Erichsen, *Practical Treatise on the Diseases of the Scalp* (London: John Churchill, 1842), pp. 190–91.

"Shampoo with tar soap"—"Beauty Notes in General," *St. Louis Palladium*, Dec. 17, 1904.

"Princess Tonic Hair Restorer"—Fred L. Israel, ed., *1897 Sears, Roebuck Catalogue* (Philadelphia: Chelsea House, 1968), p. 31.

"Bathe the affected parts"—"Hair Growth" (Cuticura ad), *St. Louis Palladium*, July 18,

1903, p. 4; "WILD WITH ECZEMA," *St. Louis Palladium*, Apr. 8, 1905; "Seventy Years of Cuticura 1878–1948" (Malden, MA: Potter Drug & Chemical Company, 1948), n.p.

"only" and "most wonderful" —"Nelson's Straightine" ad, *St. Louis Palladium*, Oct. 10, 1903; "Kink-No-More," *Indpls. Freeman*, Feb. 18, 1911.

"members of the colored race"—"Ozono" ad, *St. Louis Palladium*, Jan. 10, 1903, p. 4, and "Ozono and Cedroline" ad, *St. Louis Palladium*, Mar. 21, 1903, p. 3.

Page 67

"Ozono will take the Kinks out"—*St. Louis Palladium*, Jan. 10, 1903, p. 4.

"the first preparation ever sold"—"Original Ozonized Ox Marrow" ad, *St. Louis Palladium*, Jan. 10, 1903, p. 4.

"peach-like complexion"—"A Wonderful Face Bleach—Crane and Company," May 7, 1904.

local distribution agent—*St. Louis Palladium*, Jan. 10, 1903.

"I am determined"—Fred R. Moore to Continental Chemical Company, Richmond, VA, May 29, 1905.

"Don't you think"—Moore to Continental Chemical Company, May 29, 1905. (Sent to author by Kenneth Hamilton. With the assistance of Booker T. Washington, Moore purchased the *New York Age* in 1907.)

secret financial benefactor—"Frederick Moore," John B. Wiseman in Rayford W. Logan and Michael R. Winston, *Dictionary of American Negro Biography* (New York: W. W. Norton, 1982), p. 447.

"uncompromisingly demanded equality"—Emma Lou Thornbrough, "T. Thomas Fortune," in Ibid., p. 236.

"such advertisements are improper in Negro journals"—"The Age-Times Debate," *Indpls. Recorder*, Sept. 4, 1909.

Page 68

"not the so-called hair straightening goods"—"The Best is always the Cheapest—Johnson Mfg. Company" ad, *St. Louis Palladium*, May 7, 1904; *National Negro Business League Annual Report of the Sixteenth Session and the Fifteenth Anniversary Convention, Aug. 18–20, 1915* (LOC Microfilm), pp. 237–39.

"NOT a STRAIGHTENER"—"Thomas' Magic Hair Grower," *Voice of the Negro*, Vol. 1, No. 7 (MSRC).

wild-haired caricatures—"The Best is always the Cheapest."

"the Great African Hair Unkinker"—"Hodgson, the Great African Hair Unkinker," *New York Times*, Feb. 9, 1859, cited in Middleton Harris, *The Black Book* (New York: Random House, 1974), p. 190.

"When I was a washerwoman"—*New York Times Magazine*, Nov. 4, 1917.

Page 69

Eliza Potter—Eliza Potter, *A Hairdresser's Experience in High Life* (Cincinnati, 1859), pp. 158–59, cited in Juliet E. K. Walker, *The History of Black Business in America: Capitalism, Race and Entrepreneurship* (New York: Macmillan Library Reference, USA, 1998), p. 141.

Mahan Sisters—"Fancy Hair-Dressers," *New York Citizen*, Aug. 5, 1865, cited in Harris, *The Black Book*, p. 190.

Harriet Wilson—Reginald Pitts to the author, Jan. 16 and 20, 1998, E-mail.

"hair-work seems to be pleasant"—Katherine D. Tillman, "Paying Professions for Colored Girls," *Voice of the Negro*, Jan. and Feb. 1907, p. 55 (LOC Microfilm Serial Set #5062).

"Some colored hair dressers earn"—Ibid.

CHAPTER 6 WORLD'S FAIR

Page 70

"the worst governed"—Jeffrey E. Smith, "A Mirror Held to St. Louis: William Marion Reed and the 1904 World's Fair," *Gateway Heritage*, Vol. 19, No. 1 (Summer 1998), p. 35.

Nudged in part—Ibid., pp. 36–37; Michael Lerner, "'Hoping for a Splendid Summer': African American St. Louis, Ragtime and the Louisiana Purchase Exposition," *Gateway Heritage*, Winter 1998–99, p. 31.

superficial sprucing-up—Ibid.

nearly twenty million people—"Meet Me at the Fair," *Humanities*, May–June 1996, p. 17.

100,000 African Americans—Lerner, "Hoping," p. 38.

Page 71

Engulfed in the blended aroma—Rydell, *All the World's*, p. 179, cites "Terrible Battles of the Bloody Boer War," *St. Louis World*, June 17, 1904, p. 5.

won twin bronze medals—John M. Hoberman, "The Olympic Movement," in Jack Salzman, David Lionel Smith and Cornel West, *Encyclopedia of African-American Culture and History*, Vol. 4 (New York: Macmillan Library Reference USA, 1996), pp. 2050, 2667 and 2868; Sue Ann Wood, "The 1904 World's Fair," *St. Louis Post-Dispatch Magazine* (reprint), June 16, 1996, p. 4.

Philippines Constabulary Band—Eileen Southern, *The Music of Black Americans: A History* (3rd ed.; New York: W. W. Norton, 1997), p. 307.

pianist Joe Jordan—"The Rose Bud Ball," Feb. 27, 1904, p. 1, reprinted in full in David A. Jasen and Trebor Jay Tichenor, *Rags and Ragtime* (New York: Seabury, 1978), pp. 102–3.

Three weeks later—"Grand Recital—Paul Laurence Dunbar," *St. Louis Palladium*, Mar. 19, 1904.

veteran of World's Fair orations—"Hon. Booker T. Washington," *St. Louis Palladium*, July 2, 1904.

"the wisest among my race"—Louis R. Harlan, *Booker T. Washington: The Making of a Black Leader, 1856–1901* (New York: Oxford University Press, 1972), p. 219.

Page 72

"the most intelligent people"—"Du Bois Without Fail," *St. Louis Palladium*, Sept. 24, 1904.

trolley-sized cars—Wood, "The 1904 World's Fair," p. 5.

"no discrimination"—*St. Louis Palladium*, Jan. 1904, quoted in Lerner, "Hoping," p. 31; Robertus Love, "To See the Fair," *St. Louis Palladium*, Apr. 23, 1904.

"the coming together"—William M. Farmer to Booker T. Washington, Apr. 8, 1904, BTW/LOC, Container 802; also LPEC/MHS, Folder 14.

unskilled service job—Lerner, "Hoping," p 37.

Those with entrepreneurial instincts—Ibid., p. 33.

job seekers from bordering states—Young, *Your St. Louis*, p. 33.

real estate valued at more than half a million—Lerner, "Hoping," p. 41.

Page 73

"Ragtime Millionaire"—Young, *Your St. Louis*, p. 34.

"The impression is fast"—BTW to Farmer, Apr. 22, 1904, BTW/LOC; LPEC/MHS, Folder 14.

few eating establishments—Ibid.

"The black man who desires"—Emmett J. Scott, "Louisiana Purchase Exposition," *Voice of the Negro*, Aug. 1904, p. 311 (LOC Microfilm Serial Set #5062).

"distinctively marked goblets"—"Proposes Bureau for Negro Race," St. Louis Globe-Democrat, June 2, 1904, p. 3, LPEC/MHS, Folder 14.

"now an element"—Susan Curtis, Dancing to a Black Man's Tune: A Life of Scott Joplin (Columbia: University of Missouri Press, 1994), p. 138, cites "The Negro and the World's Fair," World's Fair Bulletin 2 (Oct. 1901), p. 32.

they were largely omitted—"Bird's-Eye View of World's Fair," St. Louis Palladium, May 7, 1904; Indpls. Freeman, Mar. 16, 1901; Farmer to BTW, Apr. 8, 1904.

"showing Negro life"—Scott, "Louisiana Purchase," p. 310.

Page 74

Palladium's 1903 press run—Lerner, "Hoping," p. 38.

"to represent human progress"—"Anthropology," in Louisiana Purchase Centennial: Dedication Ceremonies, St. Louis, U.S.A., Apr. 30 and May 1–2, 1903 (no imprint), 41, in California State University, Fresno, Department of Special Collections, Expositions and Fairs Collection cited in Rydell, All the World's, p. 62.

"It is a matter"—W. J. McGee, "The Trend of Human Progress," American Anthropologist, n.s., Vol. 1 (July 1899), pp. 414 and 446, cited in Rydell, All the World's, p. 160.

The Japanese—Rydell, All the World's, pp. 180–81.

Beneath them McGee placed—"Hardcovers in Brief," Review of A World on Display: Photographs from the St. Louis World's Fair, 1904, Washington Post Book World, June 8, 1997, p. 13; Rydell, All the World's, p.163.

Forty-seven-acre reservation—Rydell, All the World's, pp. 163 and 171.

"white and strong"—W. J. McGee, "Trend," pp. 401–47, esp. 403, 410–11, 413, cited in Rydell, All the World's, p. 160.

Page 75

"general directive"—Max Barber, "In the Sanctum," Voice of the Negro, Vol. I (Nov. 1904), p. 562, cited in Christensen, Black St. Louis, p. 200.

Georgia troops had objected—St. Louis Post-Dispatch, July 16, 1904; Indpls. Freeman, July 16, 1904, cited in Christensen, Black St. Louis, pp. 200–1.

Now the 200 NACW delegates—Josephine B. Bruce, "The Afterglow of the Women's Convention," Voice of the Negro, Vol. 1 (Nov. 1904), p. 541.

Assembled in St. Paul's sanctuary—"NACW Program—Monday, July 11, 1904," Fourth Convention of the National Association of Colored Women (Jefferson City, MO: Hugh Stephens Printing Company, 1904): p. 3, RNACWC microfilm, 1895–1992, Reel I, Frames 0276–0297, LOC.

"Future success"—"Minutes: Tuesday, July 12, 1904—Evening Session," Ibid.

"progressive colored women"—Fannie Barrier Williams, "The Club Movement Among Colored Women of America," in A New Negro for a New Century, ed. John E. MacBrady (Chicago: American Publishing House, 1900), p. 418, quoted in Beverly Guy-Sheftall, Daughters of Sorrow: Attitudes Toward Black Women, 1880–1920 (Brooklyn: Carlson Publishing, 1990), p. 57.

15,000 women from thirty-one states—"Minutes, Tuesday, July 12, 1904," p. 9.

In 1896, six years after—Gerda Lerner, Black Women in White America: A Documentary History (New York: Vintage Books, 1973), p. 440; Guy-Sheftall, Daughters of Sorrow, pp. 21–22, 24 and 26.

Page 76

"The Negroes in this country"—Lerner, Black Women, p. 436.

"to withdraw the decision"—"Abandon Meeting at Fair—Mrs. Booker T. Washington Claims Colored Women Are Discriminated Against," St. Louis Globe-Democrat, July 13, 1904, quoted in St. Louis Palladium, July 16, 1904, p. 1.

"against Colored women"—*St. Louis Palladium*, July 16, 1904.

nearly 700 blacks—Stewart E. Tolnay and E. M. Beck, *Festival of Violence : An Analysis of Southern Lynchings, 1882–1930* (Urbana: University of Illinois Press, 1995), p. 271.

"We the representatives"—"Resolutions of N.A.C.W.," *Fourth NACW Convention*, p. 25.

Page 77

they urged a boycott—Ibid.

"rag time, coon songs"—"Colored Women—Interesting Proceedings of the National Association of Colored Women," *St. Louis Palladium*, July 16, 1904, p. 1; Young, *Your St. Louis*, p. 52; *Fourth NACW Convention*, p. 12.

"that the musical taste and talent"—*Fourth NACW Convention*, p. 12.

"the chief amusements"—Lerner, "Hoping," p. 35.

"One ever feels his two-ness"—W.E.B. Du Bois, *The Souls of Black Folk* (New York: Everyman's Library/Alfred A. Knopf, 1993; first published in 1903), p. 9.

"It is foolish"—Young, *Your St. Louis*, p. 52.

"What every woman who bleaches"—Nannie Helen Burroughs, "Not Color But Character," *Voice of the Negro*, July 1904, p. 278; Giddings, *When and Where*, p. 115.

CHAPTER 7 WESTWARD

Page 79

a few inches shorter—"Climate and Crops, Nebraska Section," Climate and Crop Service of the Weather Bureau, U.S. Department of Agriculture, Lincoln, Nebraska, Vol. 10, No. 7 (July 1905), p. 1.

stifling midnineties—"Another Hot Day Here Says Forecaster," *St. Louis Globe-Democrat*, July 19, 1905.

Page 80

$850 million bounty—*Denver of To-day* (no publisher listed, circa 1905), p. 1 (LOC).

"healthiest city"—Ibid., p. 5.

With the aid of irrigation—*Seeing Denver* (Denver: American Sight-seeing Car & Coach Company, 1904), p. 5.

nearly 540,000—U.S. Bureau of the Census, *Twelfth Census of the United States, 1900*, Vol. 1, *Population*, Part 1 (Washington, DC: U.S. Census Office, 1901), pp. 609–46, cited in Quintard Taylor, *In Search of the Racial Frontier: African Americans in the American West, 1528–1990* (New York: W. W. Norton, 1998), p. 143; Stephen J. Leonard and Thomas J. Neal, *Denver: Mining Camp to Metropolis* (Denver: University of Colorado Press, 1990), p. 117.

Denver was home—1900 Census, pp. 609–46; Leonard and Neal, *Denver*, pp. 180–81 and 481.

fewer than 4,000 Denverites were black—1900 Census, pp. 609–46, cited in Taylor, *In Search*, p. 143; Rosalyn Terborg-Penn, *African American Women in the Struggle for the Vote* (Bloomington: Indiana University Press, 1998), p. 138, cites Helen Laura Sumner Woodbury, *Equal Suffrage: The Results of an Investigation in Colorado, Made for the Collective Equal Suffrage League of New York State* (New York: Harper and Brothers, 1909), pp. 70, 114 and 117.

"the best appointed hotel"—"The Inter-Ocean," *Rocky Mountain News*, Oct. 22, 1873 (DPL).

used her nest egg—"Black Colorado: A Forgotten People Who Made History," *Denver Post Empire Magazine*, Nov. 16, 1969, p. 33.

mansion in downtown—Ibid.

$7,000 wedding dress—Leonard and Neal, *Denver,* pp. 103–4.

Colorado Equal Suffrage Association—Ibid., p. 100.

Page 81

1906 Carnival of Nations—Kristen Iversen, *Molly Brown: Unraveling the Myth* (Boulder: Johnson Books, 1999), p. 151.

"$1.50 in my pocket"—"Negro Woman, Rich Hair Tonic Maker, in City," *St. Louis Post-Dispatch,* Mar. 4, 1918. On occasion Madam Walker said she "began my business career on a capital of $1.25." See "Wealthiest Negro Woman's Suburban Mansion," *New York Times Magazine,* Nov. 4, 1917.

"I was convinced"—*St. Louis Post-Dispatch,* Mar. 4, 1918.

"alkali that was bad"—Ibid.

affected agricultural output—Leonard and Neal, *Denver,* p. 44.

"was working for Scholtz"—Zenobia "Peg" Fisher interview in Stanley Nelson, "Two Dollars and a Dream" (New York: Half Nelson Productions, 1987); Fisher, who was born circa 1896, was an employee of the Madam C. J. Walker Manufacturing Company from 1914 through the early 1930s.

home at 1351 Grant—Leonard and Neal, *Denver,* p. 43.

"roomer" at 1201 Humboldt—Jacqueline Lawson to author, July 22, 1989.

Page 82

"the most comprehensive line"—*Denver of To-day,* circa 1905, LOC; Mabel K. Hamlin, "Meet Me at Scholtz's," *Colorado Magazine,* Vol. 36, No. 4 (Oct. 1959), p. 289.

founders of the Colorado Pharmaceutical Society—"E. L. Scholtz, Retired Denver Drug Store Operator, Dies," *Rocky Mountain News,* Jan. 21, 1941.

"special attention to"—*Historical and Descriptive Review of Denver* (Denver: Jno. Lathem, circa 1902), p. 124 (CHS).

"She was making extra money"—Fisher in "Two Dollars and a Dream."

"in her spare time"—"Millionaire Negress, Once of Denver, Dies," *Denver Times,* May 26, 1919, p. 5.

"for three nights"—*St. Louis Post-Dispatch,* Mar. 4, 1918.

resign her kitchen job—*Denver Times,* May 26, 1919.

"I hired a little attic"—*St. Louis Post-Dispatch,* Mar. 4, 1918.

at 1923 Clarkson—*Denver Statesman,* Dec. 1, 1905.

"two days a week"—*DenverTimes,* May 26, 1919.

"I made house-to-house canvasses"—*New York Times Magazine,* Nov. 4, 1917.

Five Points area—Leonard and Neal, *Denver,* p. 193; Lyle W. Dorsett, *The Queen City: A History of Denver* (Boulder: Pruett Publishing Company, 1977), p. 172.

Page 83

became a member of the missionary society—Justina Grizzard (Shorter Chapel AME, Denver) to Natasha Mitchell, Oct. 1999; Natasha Mitchell to author, Oct. 4, 1999.

Colorado's second black church—Harrison F. Smith, "History of Shorter A.M.E. Church," in Souvenir and Official Program of the Annual Sessions of the Bishops' Council, 1929, p. 26, DPLWHD.

annual Sunday-school picnic—"Shorter A.M.E." ad, *Denver Statesman,* July 21, 1905.

"I sold her her first batch"—George Ross to R. L. Brokenburr, Dec. 17, 1919, MWC/IHS.

"I spent 25 cents"—*St. Louis Post-Dispatch,* Mar. 4, 1918.

claimed readership in—Armistead S. Pride and Clint C. Wilson II, *A History of the Black Press* (Washington, DC: Howard University Press, 1997), p. 102.

she placed a small announcement—*Denver Statesman,* Dec. 1, 1905.

"Mrs. McWilliams, formerly"—Ibid.

"As fast as she earned"—"Queen of Gotham's Colored 400," *Literary Digest*, Vol. 55 (Oct. 13, 1917), p. 76.

"splendid personality"—Anderson, *The Light and "Heebie Jeebies,"* Feb. 19, 1927, p. 15.

Page 84

Along Arapahoe—"Our Showing Along Business Lines," *Denver Statesman*, Jan. 13, 1905, and Feb. 2, 1906; "Pastime Club" ad, *Denver Statesman*, Feb. 16, 1906; "Fraternities," *Denver Statesman*, July 21, 1905.

Within walking distance—Leonard and Neal, *Denver*, 96.

"newcomers to Denver"—"Denver Doings," *Denver Statesman*, Dec. 8, 1905.

J. C. Harris Orchestra—"Harris Orchestra," "Moorish Drill" and "Masons" ads, *Denver Statesman*, Dec. 1, 1905, and Dec. 8, 1905.

a quiet marriage ceremony—Affidavit verifying Jan. 4, 1906, marriage signed by Delilah Givens, July 6, 1918. According to *The Walker Manufacturing Co.*, 1911, p. 12, the marriage took place on Jan. 3, 1906, but both of these references may be unreliable.

Denver's first near-in suburbs—Thomas J. Noel, *Denver Landmarks & Historic Districts: A Pictorial Guide* (Denver: University Press of Colorado, 1996), p. 83.

Created in 1871—Ibid.

detached brick homes—Ibid.

"There is no divorce record"—Garner to FBR, Jan. 10, 1920.

"positively unable to find"—Thomas Campbell to Robert Lee Brokenburr, Jan. 9, 1920, MWC/IHS.

Page 85

Washington had been invited—"Woman's Week in Denver," *Denver Statesman*, Jan. 19, 1906; "Mrs. Booker T. Washington," *Colorado Statesman*, Jan. 20, 1906.

"white and colored . . . filled"—*Denver Statesman*, Jan. 19, 1906; "Mrs. Booker T. Washington—Lectures to Large Audience at Shorter AME Church," *Colorado Statesman*, Jan. 20, 1906; "Mrs. Booker T. Washington," ibid.

News of her teas—*Denver Statesman*, Jan. 19, 1906; *Denver Statesman*, Jan. 13, 1905.

well-kept rooming house—"Our Showing Along Business Lines"; *Denver Statesman*, Feb. 16, 1906; "Denver Locals," *Denver Statesman*, Apr. 27, 1906; *The Walker Manufacturing Co.*, 1911, p. 13; "Madam C. J. Walker," *Indpls. Freeman*, Nov. 11, 1911.

"fifteen cents and up"—"Denver Locals," *Denver Statesman*, Apr. 27, 1906, p. 7.

"Mrs. C. J. Walker"—"Local Notes," *Denver Statesman*, Apr. 6, 1906.

Industrial Real Estate Loans—"The Fields Investment Co.," *Denver Statesman*, Aug. 31, 1906; Jacqueline Lawson to author, July 22, 1989.

"a number of houses to rent"—"Personal Briefs: B. W. Fields, C. J. Walker" ad, *Denver Statesman*, Apr. 27, 1906.

Page 86

Bert Williams and George Walker—"Personal Briefs," *Denver Statesman*, Apr. 20, 1906.

"Grand May Festival"—*Denver Statesman*, Apr. 27, 1906.

"The lady receiving the largest"—Ibid.

"high class trade"—*Denver of To-day*, p. 7.

eye-catching photograph—Real Estate Want Ads, *Denver Statesman*, Feb. 16, 1906; "Mrs. Walker's Offer," *Denver Statesman*, May 11, 1906.

Page 87

"A grand old-fashioned time"—"Denver Doings," *Denver Statesman*, May 4, 1906.

"the only first-class hotel"—*Nothing Is Long Ago: A Documentary History of Colorado 1776/1976* (Denver: Denver Public Library, 1976), p. 105.

"WHERE ARE YOU GOING"—"Local Notes," *Denver Statesman*, May 25, 1906.

"Two years ago"—"Mrs. C. J. Walker" ad, *Denver Statesman*, May 18, 1906.

"a pulpiteer"—"Career and Work of W. T. Vernon," *Indpls. Recorder*, Feb. 19, 1910.

recently been nominated—"William Tecumseh Vernon," in Joseph J. Boris, ed., *Who's Who in Colored America*, Vol. 1 (New York: Who's Who in Colored America Corp., 1927), p. 208; "Reverend William T. Vernon," *Colorado Statesman*, Jan. 1, 1906, p. 1. His term as "Register," the title then used by the Department of the Treasury, was June 12, 1906, through Oct. 30, 1909. (Jim Marshall, Bureau of Engraving Department of Public Affairs, conversation with author, May 3, 2000.)

occupant's signature appeared—Boris, *Who's Who*, p. 208; "Career and Work of W. T. Vernon," *Indpls. Recorder*, Feb. 19, 1910, p. 1; "New Register of the Treasury," *Indpls. Recorder*, Oct. 22, 1910; "Socrates a Negro, Vernon Declares," *St. Louis Republic*, Jan. 12, 1912 (CTS/MHS)

"the highest place held"—*Indpls. Recorder*, Feb. 19, 1910.

Page 88

Booker T. Washington disciple—Dorsett, *The Queen City*, p. 172.

"Now as to the oil"— MW letter from Mrs. A. M. Pope, *Colorado Statesman*, May 12, 1906 (note from Willard Gatewood, Aug. 26, 1992).

"Shops are failing every day"—*Colorado Statesman*, May 12, 1906.

"I wish to say"—Ibid.

"I represent the preparation"—"To the Ladies," *Denver Statesman*, May 18, 1906.

she had emerged as "Madam C. J. Walker"—Walker ad, *Denver Statesman*, July 27, 1906.

"spent two successful weeks"—*Denver Statesman*, July 27, 1906.

"an urgent appeal"—Ibid.; "Various Cities—Trinidad Items," *Franklin's Paper The Statesman*, Aug. 17, 1906.

"was very successful"—*Denver Statesman*, July 27, 1906; *Franklin's Paper The Statesman*, Friday, Aug. 17, 1906.

Page 89

classes "at a very reasonable price"—Mrs. C. J. Walker ad, *Denver Statesman*, May 5, 1906 (note from Willard Gatewood, Aug. 26, 1992).

"one of the prettiest receptions"—*Franklin's Paper The Statesman*, Aug. 17, 1906.

brief stopover in Colorado Springs—*Denver Statesman*, July 27, 1906; "Mme. Walker, the hair grower," *Franklin's Paper The Statesman*, Aug. 17, 1906.

Lelia had taken a hair-growing course—"Mme. C. J. Walker," *Denver Statesman*, Aug. 24, 1906; *Denver Statesman*, Sept. 7, 1906.

"After locating in her new quarters"—"Mme. C. J. Walker," *Denver Statesman*, Aug. 31, 1906.

With Lelia now "in charge"—*St. Louis Post-Dispatch*, Mar. 4, 1918.

leaving on September 15, 1906 —"Mr. and Mme. C. J. Walker," *Denver Statesman*, Sept. 7, 1906, p. 8; "City News," *Colorado Statesman*, Sept. 15, 1906.

"The proof of the value"—"Poro" ad, *Denver Statesman*, May 3, 1907.

"never claimed her preparation"—"No Misrepresentation," *Colorado Statesman*, Sept. 28, 1906.

Page 90

"Mme. Walker's Wonderful Hair Grower"—"Mme. Walker, the hair grower."

"It is somewhat trying to me"—CJW to FBR, Oct. 17, 1922.

"could see nothing ahead"—*Denver Statesman*, Sept. 7, 1906.

"She was discouraged"—*The Walker Manufacturing Co.*, 1911, p. 13; *The Walker Manufacturing Co.*, 1919, p. 4.

packaged the "pressing oil"—"Retiring from Business," *Denver Statesman*, May 17, 1907.

"If you want long"—*Denver Statesman*, Sept. 28, 1906.

"LADIES ATTENTION"—*Denver Statesman*, May 17, 1907.

"Madam C. J. Walker and Miss McWilliams"—Ibid.

CHAPTER 8 ON THE ROAD

Page 92

an income greater than—*Report of the 13th Annual Convention of the NNBL held at Chicago, Illinois*, Aug. 21–23, 1912, p. 54; Scott Derks, ed., *The Value of a Dollar: Prices and Incomes in the United States* (Detroit: Gale Research, 1994), pp. 91–92.

took in $3,652—*NNBL Annual Report*, 1912, p. 154.

"for sores of any description"—*The Walker Manufacturing Co.*, 1911, p. 6.

Throughout Oklahoma, Texas—"America's Foremost Colored Woman," *Indpls Freeman*, Dec. 28, 1912, p. 16; 1919 Walker Company Booklet, p. 4.

Page 93

"My hair was the talk"—*The Walker Manufacturing Co.*, 1911, p. 10.

"old bald-headed lady"—Ibid., pp. 8–9.

After visits to New York—"America's Foremost Colored Woman"; 1919 Walker Company Booklet, p. 4.

sixteen rail lines—John Bodnar, Roger Simon and Michael P. Weber, *Lives of Their Own: Blacks, Italians and Poles of Pittsburgh 1900–1960* (Urbana: University of Illinois Press, 1982), p. 21.

temporary headquarters—*The Walker Manufacturing Co.*, 1911, p. 13.

August 1907—*The Walker Manufacturing Co.* (Indianapolis: Walker Manfacturing Co., undated). She "remained in Pittsburgh for two years and six months."

March 1908—*The Walker Manufacturing Co.*, 1919, p. 15. She "traveled for about a year and a half."

Page 94

"Hell with the lid off"—Liz Seymour, "Non-stop Pittsburgh," *U.S. Airways Magazine*, May 1997, p. 52.

unquestionable leader—Bodnar et al., *Lives of Their Own*, p. 15.

11 million tons—Ibid., p. 21.

In the triangular wedge—Ibid., p. 22

"the congestion"—Arthur Shadewell, *Industrial Efficiency: A Comparative Study of Industrial Life in England, Germany and America*, Vol. I (London, 1906), p. 325, cited in Bodnar et al., *Lives of Their Own*, p. 22.

Underground Railroad—Abraham Epstein, *The Negro Migrant in Pittsburgh* (Pittsburgh: University of Pittsburgh School of Economics, 1918), p. 19.

grew from 20,355 to 25,623—*Negroes in the United States 1920–1932* (Washington, DC: GPO, U.S. Department of Commerce, Bureau of the Census, 1935), p. 55; Bodnar et al., *Lives of Their Own*, p. 20.

ranked fifth—*Negroes in the U.S.*, p. 55; Bodnar et al., *Lives of Their Own*, p. 20.

New York was first—*Negroes in the U.S.*, p. 55.

During the autumn of 1907—John R. Commons and William M. Leiserson, "Wage-

Earners of Pittsburgh," in Paul Underwood Kellogg, *Wage-Earning Pittsburgh: The Pittsburgh Survey* (6 vols.; New York: Russell Sage Foundation/Survey Associates, Inc., 1914), p. 118.

Knickerbocker Bank—Lorraine Glennon, ed., *Our Times: The Illustrated History of the 20th Century* (Atlanta: Turner Publishing, 1995), p. 57.

"Hardly another city"—Commons and Leiserson, "Wage-Earners of Pittsburgh," p. 118. By April 1908—Ibid.

Page 95

"well-equipped" hair parlor—*Pennsylvania Negro Business Directory: Industrial and Material Growth of the Negroes of Pennsylvania, 1910* (Harrisburg: Jas. H. W. Howard & Son, 1910), p. 31.

Once a favored residential area—Bodnar et al., *Lives of Their Own*, p. 70.

Between 1890 and 1900—Jacqueline Wolfe, "The Changing Pattern of Residence of the Negro in Pittsburgh," unpublished MS thesis, University of Pittsburgh, 1964 (University of Pittsburgh, Hillman Library), p. 21.

Blacks, who would come—Alonzo Moron, "Distribution of the Negro Population in Pittsburgh, 1910–1930," unpublished MA thesis, University of Pittsburgh, 1933 (University of Pittsburgh, Hillman Library), p. 29; Helen A. Tucker, "The Negroes of Pittsburgh (1907–08)" in Kellogg, *Wage-Earning Pittsburgh*, p. 426 (originally published in *Charities and The Commons*, Jan. 3, 1909); Bodnar et al., *Lives of Their Own*, p. 71.

their enterprises were sprinkled—Bodnar et al., *Lives of Their Own*, p. 79.

five lawyers—*Pennsylvania Negro Business Directory*, p. 31.

"manufactory of hair-growing preparations"—Tucker, "The Negroes of Pittsburgh," p. 429; Bodnar et al., *Lives of Their Own*, pp. 79–80.

no weekly black newspaper—Pride and Wilson, *A History of the Black Press*, p. 138.

prominent blacks—Richard R. Wright, *The Negro in Pennsylvania: A Study in Economic History* (Philadelphia: AME Book Concern Printers, 1909), p. 66, quoted in Wolfe, "The Changing Pattern," p. 22.

Pittsburgh's East End—*Pennsylvania Negro Business Directory*, p. 36.

"speak easies, cocaine joints"—Tucker, "The Negroes of Pittsburgh," p. 426.

Page 96

twenty-five chapters—Ibid., p. 433.

"We, the undersigned"—*The Walker Manufacturing Co.*, 1911, p. 5.

earned $6,672—*1912 NNBL Annual Convention*, p. 154.

earned $8,782—Ibid.

just over $150,000—Estimate based on Bureau of Labor statistics using 1913 and 2000 CPI indexes.

"one of the most successful"—*Pennsylvania Negro Business Directory*, p. 36. (The directory was published in 1910, but was compiled in 1909.)

about a hundred dressmakers—Tucker, "The Negroes of Pittsburgh," p. 431.

more than 90 percent—Ibid.

Page 97

men's wages—Ibid.

half of the city's teamsters—Bodnar et al., *Lives of Their Own*, p. 19.

municipal jobs—Tucker, "The Negroes of Pittsburgh," p. 429; *Pennsylvania Negro Business Directory*, p. 30.

assets of $1,804,000,000—*This Fabulous Century, Vol. 1: 1900–1910* (New York: Time-Life Books, 1985), p. 9.

$1.20-a-week—"Mr. Carnegie's Address at the Dedication of the Carnegie Library of Pittsburgh, Nov 5, 1895," www.clpgh.org/exhibit/neighborhoods/oakland/oak_n77, downloaded Aug. 8, 1998; "Andrew Carnegie and His Philanthropies," www.carnegie.org/philanth, downloaded Aug. 10, 1998; Michael Klepper and Robert Gunther, *The Wealthy 100: From Benjamin Franklin to Bill Gates* (Secaucus, NJ: Carol Publishing Group, 1996), pp. 31–32 and 102.

established a bridge-building business—"Andrew Carnegie," www.carnegie.org.

An antebellum-era abolitionist—Joseph Frazier Wall, *Andrew Carnegie* (Pittsburgh: University of Pittsburgh Press, 1989), pp. 147 and 972.

hired blacks as early as the 1880s—R. R. Wright, Jr., "One Hundred Steel Workers," in Kellogg, *Wage-Earning Pittsburgh*, p. 97.

Homestead Strike—Tucker, "The Negroes of Pittsburgh," p. 429.

nearly 350—Ibid.

least-skilled—*Pennsylvania Negro Business Directory*, p. 30.

$400 million—Klepper and Gunther, *The Wealthy 100*, pp. 31–32 and 102; Wall, *Andrew Carnegie*, p. 1042, cited at Carnegie Library Web site at www.clpgh.org/exhibit/carnegie (downloaded Aug. 5, 1998); the exact figure Carnegie had contributed at the time of his death in 1919 is said to be $350,695,653.

$600,000 to Booker T. Washington's—Wall, *Andrew Carnegie*, pp. 972–73.

"The man who dies"—"Andrew Carnegie, City of Edinburgh, July 8, 1887," www.ebs.hw.ac.uk/hisc/digest/carnl.

Page 98

"Do you realize"—*The Walker Manufacturing Co.*, 1911, p. 6.

"Soil that will grow"—Ibid.

"years of experience"—Ibid.

Having trained dozens—Ibid., p. 13.

treated fifty-one—Ibid., pp. 5–6.

Another Ohio woman—Mrs. W. A. Snead to MW, Mar. 1, 1910.

"I have not the knowledge"—*The Walker Manufacturing Co.*, 1911, p. 6; "Mrs. W. A. Snead Pays a High Tribute to Madam Walker," *Indpls. Recorder*, Mar. 19, 1910, p. 2; Mrs. W. A. Snead to MW, Mar. 1, 1910.

At the end of October—Lelia to Mme. C. J. Walker, photo postcard, Oct. 31, 1908.

blacks had had a strong presence—Stuart McGehee, Craft Memorial Library, Bluefield, WV, phone conversation with author, Aug. 11, 1998.

Page 99

As Bluefield grew—Stuart McGehee, "The History of Bluefield, West Virginia," http://ci.bluefield.wv.us/history/stewart, downloaded Aug. 11, 1998; Michael A. Fletcher, "A College Fades to White," *Washington Post*, Dec. 8, 1997; Bluefield Colored Institute is now Bluefield State College.

married John Robinson—John B. Robison [sic] and Lelia McWilliams, Washington County, PA, Marriage License Application #18667, Oct. 18, 1909; Washington County, PA, Marriage Certificate #18667, Clerk of Courts. On this marriage license application Lelia McWilliams claims that a previous marriage was "dissolved by death." If this previous marriage occurred, there is currently no record available and she never mentioned it in any other documents or in public interviews. Shortly before her death she said she had been married three times.

"hotel telephone operator"—Edgar Rouzeau, *Interstate Tattler*, Sept. 3, 1931. (There is no Fort Smith Hotel in Pittsburgh city directories during the years Lelia McWilliams lived in Pittsburgh.)

possible that they met—*Lelia Robinson v. John Robinson*, No. 1740, October Term 1913, *Testimony before Master*, Court of Common Pleas of Allegheny County, July 16, 1914, p. 4.

Italian Renaissance courthouse—*Historic Washington and Greene Counties* brochure, n.d. (pre–1982); *Washington County, Pennsylvania, Courthouse History* brochure, n.d. (pre–1982).

train ride—*Arden Trolley Museum* brochure (Washington, PA), n.d. (pre–1982).

well-furnished home—*Robinson v. Robinson*, p. 2.

CHAPTER 9 BOLD MOVES

Page 100

"Now what I would like"—Madam Walker to Booker T. Washington, Jan. 19, 1910 (BTW/LOC, Special Correspondence, Madam Walker file).

"I know I can not do"—Ibid.

bids from "white firms"—Ibid.

Page 101

"My time and attention"—BTW to MW, Jan. 26, 1910 (BTW/LOC).

"My heart went out to her"—Agnes "Peggie" Prosser to FBR, Oct. 2, 1922 (MWC/IHS); Prosser was probably born around 1875 or 1876, based on information in her Oct. 2, 1922, letter to Ransom.

"meeting the postman"—Ibid.

Page 102

"so favorably impressed"—"Over 10,000 in Her Employ," *New York Age*, undated clipping. (While the official Walker Company history always said that Madam Walker arrived in Indianapolis on Feb. 10, 1910, it appears that she had visited the city at least once during 1909 and had actually moved to the city either in late January or earlier in February.) Also see "Mme Walker announcement," *Indpls Recorder*, Feb. 12, 1910, p. 2, and *The Walker Manufacturing Co.*, 1911, p. 13.

the first president—"Second Annual Session of the Indiana Association of Negro Physicians, Dentists and Pharmacists," *Indpls. Recorder*, Aug. 28, 1909; "Negroes Close Sessions," *Indpls. Recorder*, Sept. 11, 1909.

training school for black nurses—Ray Boomhower, "Joseph H. Ward," in David J. Bodenhamer and Robert G. Barrows, eds., *Encyclopedia of Indianapolis* (Bloomington: Indiana University Press, 1994), p. 1411.

officer of the Knights of Pythias—Ibid.; Emma Lou Thornbrough, *The Negro in Indiana Before 1900: A Study of a Minority* (Indianapolis: Indiana Historical Bureau, 1985; Bloomington: Indiana University Press edition, 1993), p. 377.

"THE NOTED HAIR CULTURIST"—"Mme. Walker ad," *Indpls. Recorder*, Feb. 12, 1910, p. 4; Mme Walker announcement, ibid.

her photograph—Ibid.

revival services—"Lodge News," ibid.

hosted a masked ball—"Personal Mention" column, ibid., p. 4.

Republican downtown men's club—Robert L. Gildea, "Columbia Club" in Bodenhamer and Barrows, *Encyclopedia*, p. 459.

Douglass Memorial parade—"YMCA Notes," *Indpls. Recorder*, Feb. 12, 1910.

Hallie Q. Brown—"The Churches" column, ibid.

Page 103

Having just elected—"Business League Officer," ibid.

"Don't fail to call"—"Mme. Walker ad," ibid.

"consultation"—Ibid.

relatively expensive $1—"Mme. Walker ad," *Indpls. Recorder,* Mar. 12, 1910.

A month later—"Is Your Hair Short?" Walker Ad, *Indpls. Recorder,* Apr. 16, 1910.

"the patronage of every woman"—"Madam Walker" announcement, *Indpls. Recorder,* Mar. 19, 1910.

offering "3 months treatment"—"Mme. Walker Ad," *Indpls. Recorder,* Feb. 26, 1910.

five-room rental flat—"FOR RENT," *Indpls. Recorder,* Dec. 31, 1910.

advertising budget—"It Makes Short Hair Long and Cures Dandruff," Walker ad, *Indpls. Freeman,* Apr. 16, 1910. national circulation—Willard B. Gatewood, *Slave and Freeman: The Autobiography of George L. Knox* (Lexington: University Press of Kentucky, 1979), pp. 31–32.

one of the most widely read—Louis R. Harlan, *Booker T. Washington: The Wizard of Tuskegee, 1901–1915* (New York: Oxford University Press, 1983), p. 98, quotes R. W. Thompson to Emmett Scott, June 21, 1906.

traveling to small towns— "In Society," *Indpls. Recorder,* Apr. 30, 1910.

"Before the entrance of Mme Walker"—Ida Webb Bryant, "Glimpses of the Negro in Indianapolis—1863–1963," unpublished manuscript, IHS.

Page 104

233,000 people in 1910—Bodenhamer and Barrows, *Encyclopedia,* p. 29; Polk's *1910 Indpls. Directory,* p. 6.

within thirty-five miles—Polk's *1910 Indpls. Directory,* p. 6; "Steelville: Where U.S. Population Strikes a Balance," *Washington Post,* Sept. 26, 1991, p. A3.

thousands of freight cars—Polk's *1910 Indpls. Directory,* p. 5.

100 electric—Edward A. Leary, *Indianapolis: Story of a City* (Indianapolis: Bobbs-Merrill, 1971), p. 173.

Auto-parts producers—James H. Madison, "Economy," in Bodenhamer and Barrows, *Encyclopedia,* pp. 64–66; Polk's *1910 Indpls. Directory,* p. 6.

By 1913 it ranked second—Leary, *Indianapolis,* p. 168.

21,816 in 1910—Bodenhamer and Barrows, *Encyclopedia,* p. 55; Z. R. Pettet and Charles E. Hall, eds., *Negroes in the United States, 1920–32* (Washington, DC: GPO, 1935), p. 55.

After an 1821 malaria outbreak—Clyde Nickerson Bolden, "Indiana Avenue: Black Entertainment Boulevard," MCP thesis, Boston University School of Planning, 1983, p. 7.

"many saloons and gambling dens"—"J. E. Moorland, Secretary to YMCA International Committee, New York City," Feb. 6, 1900 (MSRC/YMCA).

9 percent of the city's total—Bodenhamer and Barrows, *Encyclopedia,* p. 55.

At the turn of the century—"Moorland," Feb. 6, 1900.

Page 105

"Indianapolis had more Negro business"—"Ralph W. Tyler in City," *Indpls. Freeman,* Nov. 8, 1913.

One of its most notable—H. L. Sanders ad, *Indpls. Recorder,* Feb. 12, 1910, p. 4; "H. L. Sanders Anniversary," *Indpls. Recorder,* Oct. 22, 1910.

$10,000 . . . home—Based on the Bureau of Labor Statistics, U.S. Commerce Department.

By December—"Local News," *Indpls. Recorder,* Dec. 24, 1910.

an investment property—Audrey Gadzekpo, "Infield Housing Area Is Rich in History and Heritage," *Indpls. Recorder,* May 11, 1991.

That month she reviewed—*The Walker Manfacturing Co.,* 1911, p. 13.

"Room to Let"—*Indpls. Recorder,* Dec. 10, 1910.

"You understand she was struggling"—FBR to Edgar T. Rouzeau, Sept. 25, 1931 (MWC/IHS).

Within the next few weeks—"In Society," *Indpls. Recorder*, Aug. 6, 1910; "Local News," *Indpls. Recorder*, Sept. 3, 1910.

With more than 3.6 million—*The Negro Population in the United States 1790–1915*, pp. 517–21.

Page 106

Ransom, born in Grenada, Mississippi—LWR's Madam Walker agents convention speech, 1920, p. 1.

one of sixteen children—A'Lelia Ransom Nelson interview, Dec. 10, 1982, p. 8.

valedictorian of both classes—LWR, 1920 speech, p. 1.

"read law for nearly two years"—Ibid.

"It was in the Fall"—FBR to Rouzeau, Sept. 25, 1931 (MWC/IHS).

"He always said"—Nelson, Dec. 10, 1982, p. 33.

"He was very disciplined"—Ibid.

third black YMCA college chapter—Rayford W. Logan, "William Alphaeus Hunton," in Logan and Winston, *Dictionary of American Negro Biography*, p. 339.

"In those days"—Nelson, Dec. 10, 1982, p. 8.

A native of Phoebus—LWR, 1920 speech, p 1.

Page 107

"honesty and efficiency"—"Att'y Brokenburr—Efficient Young Attorney Gains Enviable Reputation at Bar," *Indpls. Recorder*, Feb. 4, 1911.

"He will not tell"—*Indpls. Recorder*, Feb. 4, 1911.

At least for a short period—LWR, 1920 speech, p. 1.

equivalent of almost $200,000—Bureau of Labor Statistics, Consumer Price Index Conversion Table.

for several months—"Society Gossip," *Indpls. Recorder*, Jan. 21, 1911, p. 4.

"We had a quarrel"—*Robinson v. Robinson*, p. 2.

"We had a talk"—Ibid.

because "she supports herself"—Ibid., p. 7.

In August 1911—"City and Vicinity," *Indpls. Freeman*, Aug. 12, 1911.

Among them was Alice Kelly—Ibid.

Page 108

welcome her St. Louis friends—"City and Vicinity," ibid.; "YMCA Notes," *Indpls. Freeman*, Aug. 5, 1911.

Supreme Keeper of Records—"Supreme Lodge K. of P. Sixteenth Biennial Session in Indianapolis," *Indpls. Freeman*, Sept. 2, 1911.

he was expected to reach the city—"City and Vicinity," *Indpls. Freeman*, Aug. 5, 1911.

"the finest building"—"The Pythian Temple," *Indpls. Recorder*, Dec. 3, 1910.

publicity and decorations committee—"The K. of P. Meeting," *Indpls. Freeman*, Aug. 26, 1911, p. 1.

Supreme Medical Register "The K. of P. Parade a Monster Demonstration," *Indpls. Freeman*, Sept. 2, 1911.

"I thought to again remind you"—MW to BTW, July 18, 1911 (BTW/LOC).

"I hope to have the privilege"—BTW to MW, July 21, 1911 (BTW/LOC).

That same evening—William M. Lewis, "The K. of P. Meeting," *Indpls. Freeman*, Aug. 26, 1911.

Page 109

"No man of any race"—Ibid.

most popular vaudeville house—Bodenhamer and Barrows, *Encyclopedia*, pp. 149–50.

classically trained black diva—Eileen Southern, *The Music of Black Americans—A History* (3rd ed.; New York: W. W. Norton, 1997), pp. 246 and 302; Willia E. Daughtry, "Sissieretta Jones," in Darlene Clark Hine et al., *Black Women in America—An Historical Encyclopedia* (Brooklyn: Carlson Publishing, 1993), p. 654; "Park Theatre" ad for Black Patti, *Indpls. Freeman*, Aug. 19, 1911; "Black Patti—Musical Comedy Company Makes Good at the Park Theatre, Indianapolis," *Indpls. Freeman*, Aug. 26, 1911.

"When women get together"—"Calanthe Court Hears Speeches by Members of Supreme Lodge," *Indpls. Freeman*, Sept. 2, 1911.

52,000 members—"Supreme Lodge K. of P. Sixteenth Biennial Session."

who now claimed 950 Walker sales agents—*Articles of Incorporation of the Madam C. J. Walker Manufacturing Company of Indiana*, Sept. 11, 1911, State of Indiana, Office of the Secretary of State.

"sell a hairgrowing"—Ibid.

She named herself—Ibid.

Page 110

"the two Negro towns"—"Returns Home," *Indpls. Freeman*, Apr. 13, 1912.

CHAPTER 10 "THE SALVATION OF YOUR BOYS AND GIRLS"

Page 111

"the Lord prospers her"—"America's Foremost Colored Woman," *Indpls. Freeman*, Dec. 28, 1912, p. 16.

working-class Germans—Frances Stout phone conversation with author, Nov. 6, 1999.

coal-oil lamps—L. M. Campbell Adams, "An Investigation of Housing and Living Conditions in Three Districts of Indianapolis," *Indiana University Bulletin, Indiana University Studies*, Vol. 8, No. 8 (Sept. 1910), pp. 125–26; Frances Stout, Nov. 6, 1999.

wood-frame flats—Carolyn Brady, "Indianapolis and the Great Migration, 1900–1920," *Black History News & Notes*, Aug. 1996, No. 65, p. 5.

one-story frame tenements—Ray Stannard Baker, *Following the Color Line* (New York: Doubleday, 1908), p. 112.

"Quite a number own"—"J. E. Moorland, Secretary to YMCA International Committee, New York City," Feb. 6, 1900 (MSRC/YMCA).

"People had a lot of pride"—Stout, Nov. 6, 1999.

"Practically everybody had flowers"—Ibid.

Page 112

"nothing but gambling places"—"Judge Recalls Police Court Cases Showing Needs of Colored YMCA," undated clipping (MSRC/YMCA).

an adjacent coal shed—"New Building Sought for America's Largest Colored YMCA," *Indpls. Star*, Nov. 8, 1911 (MSRC/YMCA).

"It is utterly impossible"—"YMCA Notes," *Indpls. Freeman*, Sept. 2, 1911.

Since that January—*The Crisis*, Nov. 1914, Vol. 9, No. 1. (By November 1914 buildings were completed in Washington, Chicago, Indianapolis and Philadelphia. Several more black YMCAs were completed during the next decade.)

"We must get busy"—"YMCA Notes," *Indpls. Freeman*, Sept. 2, 1911.

As president—"YMCA Notes," *Indpls. Freeman*, Oct. 14, 1911.

helped to raise nearly $275,000—George C. Mercer, *One Hundred Years of Service 1854–1954* (Indianapolis: YMCA, circa 1954), p. 91.

His best-known customer—Gatewood, *Slave and Freeman*, p. 20.

policies he had trumpeted—Darrel E. Bigham, "George L. Knox," in Bodenhamer and Barrows, *Encyclopedia, p. 875.*

"harem of an Eastern caliph"—Gatewood, *Slave and Freeman*, p. 18.

Page 113

most powerful black politician—Ibid., pp. 24–25.

"hair restorative" to rid the scalp—Ibid., p. 11.

Chicago's enormously successful—Michael R. Winston, "Jesse Edward Moorland," in Logan and Winston, *Dictionary of American Negro Biography*, pp. 448–49.

conditional $25,000 contributions—Untitled editorial, *Indpls. Recorder*, Jan. 21, 1911.

$67,000 in just ten days—"News from Round About: Chicago, Illinois," *Indpls. Recorder*, Jan. 14, 1911.

Moorland's proposition—Nina Mjagkij, *Light in the Darkness: African Americans and the YMCA, 1852–1946* (Lexington: University Press of Kentucky, 1994), p. 76; Winston, "Jesse Edward Moorland," in Logan and Winston, *DANB*, p. 449.

was "so favorably impressed"—Ibid.

"would eventually help reduce"—Mjagkij, *Light in the Darkness*, p. 77.

"establishing an Association"—"Moorland," Feb. 6, 1900.

Page 114

"four to five thousand"—Ibid.

grown to 15,931— Thornbrough, *The Negro in Indiana*, p. 228.

large number from Kentucky—*The Indianapolis Study/Flanner House* (Indianapolis: Flanner House, 1939), p. 10; Thornbrough, *The Negro in Indiana*, p. 224. The 1880 Indianapolis population was 6,500 per Gatewood, *Slave and Freeman*, p. 16; black population of Indianapolis: 1880—6,500; 1890—9,154; 1900—15,931; 1910—21,816 (Flanner House).

"Vice is on the increase"—"Moorland," Feb. 6, 1900.

"It is apparent"—Ibid.

organized a "Young Men's Prayer Band"—"The Indianapolis Y," *The Crisis*, Mar. 1924, p. 205.

1905 arrival—Stanley Warren correspondence with author, Dec. 24, 1999.

membership grew to 400—*The Crisis*, Mar. 1924, p. 206; "New Building Sought for America's Largest Colored YMCA," *Indpls. Star*, Nov. 8, 1911 (MSRC/YMCA).

one of the largest Y's—Several articles of the time call it the "largest" black YMCA (see "New Building Sought for America's Largest Colored YMCA," but Mjagkij (*Light in the Darkness*, pp. 69 and 73) says the Washington, DC, branch had 600 members in 1905 and 1,000 members in 1909.

"several men sleep"—"Judge Recalls Police Court Cases Showing Needs of Colored YMCA" (MSRC/YMCA).

communicable diseases "rampant"—Ibid.

His investigation of 1910—Ibid.

Taylor's "encouraging" rehabilitation and "What the young negro"—Ibid.

"The presence in any city"—"A Commendable Proceeding," *Indpls. Star*, Nov. 30, 1910 (MSRC/YMCA).

"an almost inconceivably narrow"—Ibid.

Page 115

"teach him how to"—"New Building Sought."

"100 percent American town"—James J. Davita, "Demography and Ethnicity," in Bodenhamer and Barrows, *Encyclopedia*, p. 55.

"the foreign floating element"—Ibid.

Page 116
"It is to our selfish interest"—"New YMCA Gets $15,000 Start" (MSRC/YMCA).
"agreed to bear the greater burden"—"The Colored YMCA," *Indpls. Freeman,* Oct. 13, 1911.
"It is the responsibility"—"YMCA Notes," *Indpls. Freeman,* Oct. 14, 1911.
scheduled "monster rallies"—Winston, "Jesse Edward Moorland," pp. 449–50.
"A new building for your association" and "You are belittled"—"Urges Colored Folk to Support YMCA," *Indpls. Star,* Oct. 16, 1911 (MSRC/YMCA); Moorland's cousin, Sarah Newton Cohron, was one of the founders of the St. Louis Colored Orphans' Home, where Lelia had stayed for a short time during the late 1880s.
pioneered refrigerated railroad cars—Kevin Corn, "Arthur Jordan," in Bodenhamer and Barrows, *Encyclopedia,* p. 852.
Madam Walker confidently pledged $1,000—"Colored Folk Pledge $2,900 to YMCA," Oct. 23, 1911 (MSRC/YMCA).

Page 117
"If the association can save our boys"—"Mme. C. J. Walker Who Subscribed $1,000 to the Y.M.C.A. Building Fund," *Indpls. Freeman,* Oct. 28, 1911.
"The Young Men's Christian Association"—Ibid.
$500 from Mrs. L. E. McNairdee— "Colored Folk Pledge $2,900 to YMCA."
"the first colored woman"—"Mme. C. J. Walker Who Subscribed"; James H. Tilghman, a retired messenger for the Chicago Telephone Company, became the first black man to subscribe $1,000, his life's savings. (See Mjagkij, *Light in the Darkness,* p. 78.)
"an income of $1,000 per month"—"Madam C. J. Walker," *Indpls. Freeman,* Nov. 11, 1911.
Skeptics wondered—"America's Foremost Colored Woman," *Indpls Freeman,* Dec. 28, 1912, p. 16.
450 canvassers—"YMCA Canvassers to Tour City in Auto," undated clipping; "Colored Folk Pledge $2,900 to YMCA"; and "New YMCA Gets $15,000 Start" (MSRC/YMCA).
"By the rules of the campaign"—"Colored Men Rally for New Home" (MSRC/YMCA).

Page 118
"I am greatly delighted"—"Second Day Brings Fund to $56,343.62" (MSRC/YMCA).
aggregate to $8,019.64—"Colored Teams Add $1,845.52," *Indpls. Freeman,* Oct. 28, 1911.
first $250 installment—Ibid.
more than $64,000—Ibid.
"are just getting warmed up"—Ibid.
Poet James Whitcomb Riley—"Day's Pledges Raise Fund to $75,037.34" (MSRC/YMCA).
childhood in Greenfield—Gatewood, *Slave and Freeman,* p. 88–93.
colored porters of the Eli Lilly—"$73,422.71 Subscribed for Colored YMCA," *Indpls. News,* Oct. 27, 1911 (MSRC/YMCA).
more than $2,000—"Many Small Pledges for Colored YMCA," *Indpls. News,* Oct. 30, 1911 (MSRC/YMCA).
By the end of the day—"$18,705.06 Required in YMCA Campaign," *Indpls. Star,* Oct. 29, 1911 (MSRC/YMCA).
"Unless there is a more generous"—"$18,705.06 Required," *Indpls. Star,* Oct. 29, 1911.
a rousing 200-voice male chorus—"$79,240.34 Subscribed but More Help Needed," *Indpls. News,* Oct. 28, 1911 (MSRC/YMCA).

"We're going to build"—"Many Small Pledges."

"it is the greatest thing"—"Urge YMCA Teams to Redouble Efforts," undated clipping (MSRC/YMCA).

canvassers hit a snag—"Many Small Pledges."

Page 119

"A chain is no stronger"—"$15,000 Mark Passed by Colored Workers," *Indpls. Star,* Oct. 31, 1911 (MSRC/YMCA).

exceeded their $15,000 goal—"Colored YMCA Is Now Nearly Assured," Nov. 1, 1911, clipping (MSRC/YMCA); "$15,000 Mark Passed by Colored Workers."

"Here's our opportunity"—"$15,000 Mark Passed by Colored Workers."

total topped $93,000—"Ask Voluntary Gifts for Colored YMCA" and "General Call Issued for Aid to YMCA," undated clippings (MSRC/YMCA).

"gave three cheers"—"Ask Voluntary Gifts."

"Effort Ends Today"—*Indpls. Freeman,* Nov. 4, 1911 (MSRC/YMCA).

mount a "supreme effort"—"4,458.66 Is Needed, Progress of Campaign," *Indpls. Freeman,* Nov. 4, 1911.

Electric railway entrepreneur—"$104,226.18 Is Raised for Colored YMCA," undated clipping (MSRC/YMCA).

"This movement"—Ibid.

"the biggest and most enthusiastic"—"4,458.66 Is Needed." The articles describing the 6:15 P.M. Central YMCA rally mentions the men not mention Madam Walker. But throughout the campaign, women who were involved were largely ignored in the newspaper coverage. In view of her financial commitment, it is hard to imagine that she did not participate in all of the final day's festivities.

an unexpected $104,000—"104,226.18 Is Raised." There is a discrepancy of $510.70 from different sources. On the basis of Jesse Moorland's final tally of $20,610.73 and "Work to Be Rushed on New YMCA Home" (undated clipping in MSRC/YMCA), which gives the Central Y total of $59,126.15, the final total would be $104,736.88 ($20,610.73+$59,126.15+$25,000=$104,736.88).

more than 1,500 African American—"Subscriptions to Building Fund, Indianapolis" (MSRC/YMCA). Other sources show the final tally as $20,556.35. See "YMCA Notes," *Indpls. Freeman,* Nov. 11, 1911; "The Great YMCA Campaign Closed," ibid. "Work to Be Rushed" gave the figure as $20,100.03 (MSRC/YMCA).

The Central YMCA—"Work to Be Rushed."

"The colored people"—"The Colored YMCA Movement," *Indpls. Freeman,* Nov. 18, 1911.

Page 120

"a sign of the best possible condition"—Untitled column, *Indpls. Freeman,* Nov. 4, 1911.

A "skilled debater"—Gatewood, *Slave and Freeman,* p. 11.

"Best Known Hair Culturist"—"Madam C. J. Walker," *Indpls. Freeman,* Nov. 11, 1911.

"Hurrah for the $100,000 YMCA"—Untitled column, *Indpls. Freeman,* Nov. 4, 1911.

"Mr. Rosenwald's gift"—Winston, "Jesse Edward Moorland," in Logan and Winston, *DANB,* p. 450.

CHAPTER 11 "I PROMOTED MYSELF . . ."

Page 121

"to ask if you"—MW to BTW, Dec. 2, 1911 (BTW/LOC); Louis Harlan and Raymond W. Smock, ed., *The Booker T. Washington Papers,* Vol. 11: *1911–1912* (Urbana: University of Illinois Press, 1972), p. 384.

sixteen-page booklet "which will"—MW to BTW, Dec. 2, 1911; Harlan and Smock, *The BTW Papers*, p. 384; "The Walker Manufacturing Co." (16-page booklet) (BTW/LOC).

Because advance publicity—"The Tuskegee Negro Farmers' Conference," *Indpls. Freeman*, Nov. 25, 1911.

purchased a second building—"Wonderful Success of Mme. C. J. Walker," *The Colored American Review*, Mar. 1916 (GSC/CU, Vol. 41).

Page 122

Her annual earnings—*Report of the 13th Annual Convention of the NNBL held at Chicago, Illinois, Aug. 21–23, 1912*, p. 154.

"if it is necessary to remain"—Louis R. Harlan, "Booker T. Washington," *Humanities*, May–June 1997.

"I fear you misunderstand"—BTW to MW, Dec. 6, 1911 (BTW/LOC); Harlan and Smock, *The BTW Papers*, p. 398.

"the Negro farmer often passes"—Booker T. Washington, *The Negro in Business* (Wichita, KS: DeVore & Sons, 1992, reprint of Hertel, Jenkins & Co., 1907), p. 18.

"a meeting of poor farmers"—BTW to MW, Dec. 6, 1911, Harlan and Smock, *The BTW Papers*, p. 398.

"well acquainted"—Ibid.

but it appears that Emmett J. Scott—E-mail from Scott biographer Maceo Crenshaw Dailey, Jr., to author, Oct. 15, 1998.

Washington's authorized ghostwriter—Ibid.; "I think I am right about the signature. Having pored so long over the documents, I noticed many curious habits"—Dailey E-mail, Oct. 16, 1998.

he may or may not have consulted Washington—Dailey E-mail, Oct. 15, 1998.

Washington's Iago—Harlan, *Booker T. Washington*, pp. xi–xii.

"it was almost impossible to tell"—Louis R. Harlan, "Booker T. Washington," in Logan and Winston, *DANB*, p. 550.

Washington "first opposed"—Harlan and Smock, *The BTW Papers*, p. 385.

"paint and powder" were undesirable artifice—Mary F. Armstrong, *On Habits and Manners* (Hampton, VA: Normal School Press, 1888), p. 31, cited in Kathy Peiss, *Hope in a Jar: The Making of America's Beauty Culture* (New York: Metropolitan Books, Henry Holt, 1998), p. 25.

he "deliberately left out"—Louis R. Harlan phone conversation with author, Sept. 11, 1989; Washington, *The Negro in Business*, p. 105.

The two black women hairdressers—*Report of the Second Annual Convention of the National Negro Business League at Chicago, Illinois, Aug. 21–23, 1901* (Chicago: R. S. Abbott Publishing Company, 1901), p. 29; Carrie W. Clifford, "The Story of the Business Career of Mrs. M. E. Williams," in *Report of the Sixth Annual Convention of the National Negro Business League held in New York City, Aug. 16th–18th, 1905*, pp. 119–20.

Page 123

"view with alarm"—BTW, Dec. 18, 1911, to Fred R. Moore, in Harlan and Smock, *The BTW Papers*, Vol. 11, p. 420. (Special thanks to Kenneth Hamilton for identifying this letter.)

"clandestinely advanced money"—Thornbrough, "Booker T. Washington," in Logan and Winston, *DANB*, p. 635.

"You ought to very seriously"—BTW to Moore, Dec. 18, 1911.

"no identifiable 'cosmetics industry'"—Peiss, *Hope in a Jar*, p. 19.

"an emergent class"—Ibid., p. 97.

"devised a national system"—Ibid.

made "cosmetics affordable"—Ibid., p. 99.

"It is pleasant to note"—FBR to LWR, Dec. 6, 1911 (MWC/IHS).

had begun calling herself—"City and Vicinity," *Indpls. Freeman*, Dec. 23, 1911.

Page 124

"sweet and kind letter"—"Louise" to Charles J. Walker, Jan. 11, 1912 (MWC/IHS).

letter of introduction—The Taylor letter does not appear to be extant in the BTW/LOC papers. There is no correspondence listed between Taylor and Washington.

"She came knocking"—Louis Harlan phone conversation with author, Sept. 11, 1989; Harlan believed he had heard the story from Washington's daughter, Portia Washington Pittman, though, at the time of Madam Walker's January 1912 visit, Portia was likely in Washington, DC, with her husband, Sidney Pittman, whom she had married in October 1907. (See Harlan, *Booker T. Washington*, p. 119, for the marriage.)

"be kind enough to introduce me"—MW to BTW, Jan. 17, 1912 (BTW/LOC).

"I want them to know"—Ibid.

"It is possible Scott may have taken some liberties"—Dailey E-mail, Oct. 15, 1998. "This is conjectural, but worth pursuing—I sense something 'afoul,'" wrote Dailey.

Page 125

"I have talked with Mr. Washington"—Emmett Scott to MW, Jan. 17, 1912 (BTW/LOC).

That evening in chapel—MW to BTW, Jan. 17, 1912.

She urged them—Ibid.

Scott was its editor—Dailey to author, Jan. 2000.

"The folklore is"—Harlan phone conversation with author, Sept. 11, 1989.

"84 demonstrative treatments"—"Mme. C. J. Walker at Tuskegee," *Indpls. World*, undated, but probably Jan 27, 1912 (BTW/LOC).

As president of the Mothers' Council—"My Visit to Tuskegee Industrial Institute," *Indpls. Freeman*, undated clipping, probably Dec. 16 or 23, 1911.

"no end to her praises"—"Mme. C. J. Walker at Tuskegee."

kindness "shown both myself"—MW to BTW, Mar. 29, 1912 (BTW/LOC, Box 726, Donations 1912).

Her $5 contribution—Ibid.

Page 126

Washington thanked her "heartily"—BTW to MW, Apr. 16, 1912 (BTW/LOC, Box 726, Donations 1912).

For her local representative—"Mme. C. J. Walker at Tuskegee"; FBR to Dora Larrie, Sept. 26, 1913 (MWC/IHS). The agent's name has many spelling variations in the newspaper articles where she is mentioned, including Cora Larry, Dora Larrie and Dora Larry; FBR's letter is addressed to Dora Larrie.

headed south again—"Mme. C. J. Walker at Tuskegee."

In late March they reunited—FBR to MW, Mar. 26, 1912 (MWC/IHS).

"laid our plans"—"C. J. Walker Says: 'As You Reap So Shall You Sow'—Former Husband of Well-Known Hair Manufacturer Regrets Past Life," *Indpls. Freeman*, Mar. 21, 1914.

"be master of the situation"—Ibid.

Page 127

"She realized that everything"—Violet Reynolds Interview with author, July 1982.

trip "cut short"—"Returns Home," *Indpls. Freeman,* Apr. 13, 1912.

"the moral and social"—"Locals and Personals—Madam C. J. Walker," *Indpls. Recorder,* July 13, 1912. The article says Lynch is from South Carolina, but other sources give her location as North Carolina.

was "poorly ventilated"—Harlan, *Booker T. Washington,* pp. 417 and 420.

"No matter how many colored women"—Ibid., p. 417, cites Booker T. Washington, "Is the Negro Having a Fair Chance?" *Century,* Nov. 1912.

Fortunately for Madam Walker—Madam Walker's treatment on Pullman cars is based on the author's family oral history.

400 purposeful black women—"Women Hold Big Convention," *New York Age,* Aug. 1, 1912, p. 1.

Page 128

250 students—Bernice Reagon, "Mary McLeod Bethune," in Logan and Winston, *DANB,* pp. 41–42.

By 1912—Elaine M. Smith, "Mary McLeod Bethune," in Hine et al., *Black Women in America,* p. 115.

"No matter how deep my hurt"—Reagon, "Mary McLeod Bethune," pp. 41–42.

"declared in favor of full woman suffrage"—"The Meeting of the NACW at Hampton, Virginia," Chicago *Broad Ax,* Aug. 10, 1912.

seventeen-year-old Virginia Christian—"Christian Virginia vs. Virginia Christian," *The Crisis,* Sept. 1912, p. 237.

"In a blind rage"—Ibid., pp. 237–38.

"irresponsible being"—"Women Hold Big Convention."

declared mentally incompetent—*New York Age,* Aug. 1, 1912.

Page 129

"Owing to all the circumstances"—*Minutes of the Eighth Biennial Convention of the NACW,* July 23–27, 1912, Hampton Normal and Industrial Institute, p. 21.

declined to "show clemency"—Ibid., p. 36.

donation to cover all travel costs—Ibid., p. 40.

"rising vote of thanks"—Ibid.

"a great deal to improve"—Ibid., p. 20.

"captivated the vast audience"—*Walker Company Booklet,* 1919, p. 15.

At noon they docked—*1912 NACW Biennial Minutes,* p. 70; "Women Hold Big Convention."

essential "instrument" for achieving—Harlan, *Booker T. Washington,* p. 269.

Page 130

W.E.B. Du Bois recommended "the organization"—Harlan, *Booker T. Washington,* p. 266, cites W.E.B. Du Bois, ed., *The Negro in Business: Report of a Social Study made under the Direction of Atlanta University; Together with the Proceedings of the Fourth Conference for the Study of the Negro Problems, held at Atlanta University, May 30–31, 1899* (Atlanta University Publications, No. 4, 1899), pp. 12 and 50. In 1896 a group of men and women from thirteen states formed the Invincible Sons and Daughters of Commerce, "a national incorporated secret society of Colored merchants and buyers," preceding the NNBL by four years. See "The Invincible Sons and Daughters of Commerce, 1899," in Herbert Aptheker, *A Documentary History of the Negro People in the United States,* Vol. 2: *From Reconstruction to the Founding of the N.A.A.C.P.* (New York: Citadel Press, 1990), pp. 774–75.

black "economic salvation"—E. Franklin Frazier, *Black Bourgeoisie* (New York: Collier Books, 1962), p. 130.

economic nationalism as a defense—Du Bois, *The Negro in Business,* cited in Frazier, *Black Bourgeoisie,* p. 130.

"Business seems to be not only simply"—Ibid.

"The policy of avoiding entrance"—Abram L. Harris, *The Negro as Capitalist: A Study of Banking and Business among American Negroes* (Chicago: Urban Research, 1992 reprint), p. 64, cites Du Bois, *The Negro in Business,* p. 59.

"During America's greatest industrial"—Juliet E. K. Walker, *The History of Black Business in America: Capitalism, Race, Entrepreneurship* (New York: Macmillan Library Reference, USA, 1998), p. 182.

"the total wealth"—Ibid. The fifteenth annual report of the National Negro Business League contradicts the year, citing $700 million as the worth of black America's wealth in 1914. See *1913 NNBL Report* (Nashville: Sunday School Union, 1914), p. 18.

Du Bois's postconference study—David Levering Lewis, *W.E.B. Du Bois: Biography of a Race 1868–1919* (New York: Henry Holt, 1993), p. 220.

Page 131

eliminated his meager postage budget—Harlan, *Booker T. Washington,* pp. 266–67.

Washington set about contacting—Ibid., p. 266.

Wells publicly accused Washington—Ibid., p. 267.

"the business league idea was born"—Ibid., p. 266

"the myth of Negro business"—Frazier, *Black Bourgeoisie,* p. 135.

"an organized body of loyal"—Harlan, *Booker T. Washington,* p. 266.

"These discriminations are only blessings"—*Report of the Fourth Annual Convention of the National Negro Business League* (Wilberforce, OH, 1903), p. 24, cited in August Meier, *Negro Thought in America, 1880–1915* (Ann Arbor: University of Michigan Press, 1998), p. 125.

To some degree—August Meier and David Levering Lewis, "History of the Negro Upper Class in Atlanta, Georgia, 1890–1958," in *Journal of Negro Education,* Vol. 28 (Spring 1959), p. 128.

Page 132

"No race that has anything to contribute"—"The Atlanta Exposition Address," in Booker T. Washington, *Up From Slavery* (New York: Penguin Books, 1986), p. 223.

he had chosen to ignore—"Side Lights on the Meeting of the National Negro Business League," Chicago *Broad Ax,* Aug. 31, 1912.

Nearly 2,000 visitors—R. W. Thompson, "Recent League Meet!" Aug. 31, 1918.

$500,000 holdings in Brockton—*Report of the 13th Annual Convention of the NNBL held at Chicago, Illinois, Aug. 21–23, 1912,* pp. 34–39.

Page 133

Endowment fund of more than $1.2 million—*Colored American Review,* Nov. 1915.

"If we do not do our duty now"—*1912 NNBL Convention,* p. 50.

That evening Mrs. Julia H. P. Coleman—Ibid., p. 66.

"Every year the styles"—Ibid., p. 64.

"By force of circumstance"—Ibid., p. 65.

"manufactured by our colored women"—Ibid., p. 65.

Instead Washington complimented Coleman—Ibid., p. 66.

Page 134

"the largest Colored manufacturing enterprise"—"The 13th Annual Meeting of the NNBL," Chicago *Broad Ax,* Aug. 24, 1912, pp. 1 and 9.

"for the most beautiful colored woman"—*1912 NNBL Convention,* pp. 99–100.

"I arise to ask"—Ibid., p. 100.

Sidney Pittman, had designed—"Success in Architecture," *Indpls. Recorder,* Mar. 27, 1909.

"But, Mr. Knox, we are"—*1912 NNBL Convention,* p. 101.

Page 135

uniform manufacturer—"Colored Man Takes High Rank," *Indpls. Freeman,* Dec. 16, 1911.

contributed only $250 to the building fund—Ibid.

Then, as Washington thanked—*1912 NNBL Convention,* pp. 145–53.

"Surely you are not going to shut the door"—Ibid., p. 154.

"I went into a business that is despised"—Ibid.

"I have been trying to get before you"—Ibid.

Page 136

"I am not ashamed of my past"—Ibid.

"Everybody told me"—Ibid.

"I have built my own factory"—Ibid.

"Please don't applaud"—Ibid.

"Now my object in life"—Ibid., p. 155.

"My ambition is to build"—Ibid.

"I arise to attest"—Ibid.

"The next banker to address us"—Ibid.

the "big hits" of the conference—*Indpls. Freeman,* Sept. 14, 1912.

CHAPTER 12 BREAKING TIES, MAKING TIES

Page 137

F. B. Ransom filed papers—*Sarah Walker v. Charles J. Walker,* Cause No. 87943, Marion County Superior Court Docket, Sept. 5, 1912.

October 5, after C.J. had failed to appear—*Walker v. Walker,* Divorce Decree, Cause No. 87943, Marion County Superior Court.

"no money" was paid—*Walker v. Walker*

C.J. placed two advertisements—"For Long and Beautiful Hair," Walker-Prosser Co., *Indpls. Freeman,* Sept. 14, 1912; "C. J. Walker (Walker-Prosser Co.)," *Indpls. Freeman,* Sept. 14, 1912.

"We did not do so well"—"C. J. Walker Says: 'As You Reap So Shall You Sow'—Former Husband of Well-Known Hair Manufacturer Regrets Past Life," *Indpls. Freeman,* Mar. 21, 1914.

Page 138

"We were not married long"—Ibid.

"All I got was ten cents"—Ibid.

"When we began to make ten dollars"—"10,000 in Her Employ," *New York Age,* undated, but probably early 1916.

But of course their philosophical differences—Ibid.

"let drink and this designing evil woman"—"C. J. Walker Says"; FBR to CJW, July 6, 1914 (MWC/IHS).

"still love better than life"—"C. J. Walker Says."

"Madam does not understand"—FBR to CJW, July 6, 1914.

"keep sober"—Ibid.

"worse than" Dora Larrie—Agnes "Peggie" Prosser to MW, undated letter (MWC/IHS).

"Say Mme, How would you like"—CJW to MW, undated letter (MWC/IHS).

"My heart is changed"—Ibid.

Page 139

whined about his rheumatism—CJW to MW, Mar. 11, 1917 (MWC/IHS).

selling her formula—FBR to CJW, undated letter (MWC/IHS). C.J. denied revealing the formula ("I refused absolutely to give" the formula to others) in "C. J. Walker Says."

"would spend every penny that she ever had"—FBR to CJW, undated letter.

Lelia legally adopted thirteen-year-old Mae—Adoption of Fairy Mae Bryant by Mrs. Lelia Walker Robinson, Decree of Court, Court of Common Pleas of Allegheny County, Pennsylvania, No. 505, January Term, 1913, Docket "A"; Janice M. McNamara, Court of Common Pleas of Allegheny County, Orphans' Court Division to author, Aug. 31, 1998. (The adoption occurred on Oct. 22, 1912.)

Fairy Mae as she ran errands—Marion R. Perry, phone interview, circa 1982.

"young girl solicitor"—"Madam Walker" announcement, *Indpls. Recorder*, Mar. 19, 1910; "Is Your Hair Short?" Walker ad, *Indpls. Recorder*, Apr. 16, 1910.

"good commission"—Ibid.

Page 140

"Mae had beautiful hair"—Margaret Bryant interview with author and Stanley Nelson, Sept. 22, 1982.

rented rooms at the rear of 636 North West Street—1912 *Indianapolis City Directory*. Samira Hammond is listed at 611 West North Street in the 1911 city directory and at 640 North West Street in the 1912 city directory. Since data was gathered for city directories in the year before publication, it is reasonable to assume that she was living at 640 North West Street before the end of 1911.

born in 1867—1880 *Tenth Annual U.S. Census*, Noblesville Township, Hamilton County, Indiana, Microfilm T-9, Roll No. 281; Sarah Etta Hammond Bryant, Marion County Health Department Death Certificate filed April 1927. Date of death: April 27, 1927. (Birth date on death certificate—Jan. 10, 1874—is incorrect.)

Indiana Avenue cafe—1912 *Indianapolis City Directory*.

Page 141

"Little Miss Farrie [sic] Bryant"—"Noblesville," *Indpls. Recorder*, Aug. 7, 1909.

served in the Continental Army—Paul Heinegg, *Free African Americans of North Carolina and Virginia* (3rd ed.; Baltimore: Clearfield Company, 1997), p. 600, and Paul Heinegg, *Free African Americans of Virginia, North Carolina, South Carolina, MD and Delaware* (www.freeafricanamericans.com/Roberts_Skip.htm, March 1999), p. 6; Jeffrey J. Crow, Paul D. Escott and Flora J. Hatley, *A History of African Americans in North Carolina* (Raleigh: North Carolina Division of Archives and History, 1994), p. 36. The author is deeply indebted to historian and genealogist Coy D. Robbins, Jr., for revealing this important piece of my family history. Without his diligent scholarship and research, I may never have discovered this on my own.

born circa 1755—Paul Heinegg, *Free African Americans* (Internet site), p. 6. (Ishmael Roberts lived circa 1755–1826.)

Cherokee wife, Silvey—Coy D. Robbins, Jr., *Forgotten Hoosiers: African Heritage in Orange County, Indiana* (Bowie, MD: Heritage Books, 1994), p. 136, says there were 639 free black families in North Carolina in 1790. (Research on Silvey's Native American ancestry is incomplete at this time, but family oral history and Cherokee Claims applications identify her as Cherokee.)

North Carolina's 5,041 free people of color—John Hope Franklin, *The Free Negro in*

Endnotes

North Carolina 1790–1860 (Chapel Hill: University of North Carolina Press, 1995, originally published 1943), p. 14, cites John Cummings, Negro Population in the United States, 1790–1915 (Washington, DC, 1918), p. 57.

900 acres of land—Paul Heinegg, Free African Americans (3rd ed.), p. 600.

ancestors had never been slaves—Della Hammond Ashley, Eastern Cherokee Application No. 25682, National Archives, Reel 213, M1104 Cabinet 094–01.

"stripped the free Negro"—Guion Griffis Johnson, Ante-bellum North Carolina: A Social History (Chapel Hill: University of North Carolina Press, 1937), cited in Crow et al., A History of African Americans, p. 48.

by 1835 the state's lawmakers—Franklin, The Free Negro, pp. 58–74; Crow et al., A History, p. 48.

By 1840, more than 150 people with the surname Roberts—Robbins, Forgotten Hoosiers, p. 136, cites Carter G. Woodson, Free Negro Heads of Families in the United States in 1830 (Washington, DC: Association for the Study of Negro Life and History, 1925), pp. 225–26.

Elias Roberts—Roberts was born in 1793 and died in 1866. See Paul Heinegg, Free African Americans of Virginia, p. 10.

Nancy Archer Roberts—The daughter of Thomas Archer, a Revolutionary War soldier, she lived from 1800 to 1876.

"although persons of Couleur"—Certificate of Freedom, Chatham County, NC, Feb. 10, 1823 (Coy D. Robbins, Jr., to author, Feb. 2, 2000); Robbins, Forgotten Hoosiers, p. 37, and Robbins, Indiana Negro Registers 1852–1856 (Bowie, MD: Heritage Books, 1994); I do not know when Elias and Nancy Archie/Archer Roberts arrived in Orange County, though there is an Elias Roberts listed in the 1830 (Fifth) U.S. Census. See Robbins, Forgotten Hoosiers, p 153.

Page 142

"no negro or mulatto"—Article XIII of the 1851 Indiana State Constitution went into effect in 1853; see Robbins, Forgotten Hoosiers, pp. 41–49; Thornbrough, The Negro in Indiana Before 1900, pp. 67–68. Only six of the nine Thomas children appear on the rolls. Candiss Roberts Thomas may have been pregnant with her last child when they registered on Aug. 27, 1853.

One of those children was Samira—"Register of Negroes and Mulattoes in Orange County, Indiana, 1853" (IHS); Robbins, Forgotten Hoosiers, pp. 45 and 49.

Vigo County, Indiana, widower—Robbins to author, Feb. 2, 2000.

"full blood Cherokee Indian"—Della Hammond Ashley, Cherokee Claims affidavit. Application denied in 1908.

Sadly Littleton died in 1876—Littleton-Samira THOMAS Hammond, Orange County, Indiana Family Group Record A:\ROBERTSI.G21 from Coy D. Robbins, Jr.; Samira later married a man named Joseph K. Scott (1833–1916) on Jan. 28, 1894, in Hamilton County, Indiana.

Federal Hill area—Robbins, Forgotten Hoosiers, p. 139.

Perry Bryant died . . . Grand Master of the Masons presided—"Perry Bryant," Indpls. Recorder, July 3, 1909.

It may have been during Fairy Mae's trip to Harlem—Margaret Bryant interview with author and Stanley Nelson, Sept. 22, 1982.

"turned her head"—Ibid.

was not so quickly or so easily persuaded—Ibid.

Page 143

"Mae was very special"—Robbins E-mail to author, Nov. 4, 1997.

332

"Etta did not see it as giving up"—Ibid.

rose-and-gold drawing room—"America's Foremost Colored Woman," *Indpls. Freeman,* Dec. 28, 1912.

In the library—Ibid.

On a table covered with Battenberg—Ibid.

would never have any significant involvement—*Robinson v. Robinson,* pp. 1–3.

buy property on both coasts—FBR to LWR, Dec. 10, 1912 (MWC/IHS).

house hunting in Los Angeles—Ibid.

Page 144

she "would make an ideal real estate agent"—Ibid.

"The write-up in the *Freeman*"—FBR to MW, Jan. 1, 1913 (MWC/IHS).

CHAPTER 13 SWEET SATISFACTION

Page 145

tossed packets—Violet Reynolds to author, undated phone conversation and Dec. 1975 interview.

"Your business is increasing"—FBR to MW, May 2, 1913 (MWC/IHS).

more than $11,000—*Report of the 14th Annual Convention of the National Negro Business League, Philadelphia, August 20, 21, 22, 1913* (Washington, DC: William H. Davis, Official Stenographer), p. 210.

"You will . . . have to keep a little mum"—FBR to MW, May 2, 1913.

greater than $3,000—Lorraine Glennon, ed., *Our Times: The Illustrated History of the 20th Century* (Atlanta: Turner Publishing, 1995), p. 69.

less than $800—Scott Derks, ed., *The Value of a Dollar* (Detroit: Gale Research, 1994), p. 123.

highest tax bracket—Glennon, *Our Times,* p. 69.

Page 146

"Madam is in a fair way to be"—FBR to LWR, May 27, 1913, and June 30, 1913 (MWC/IHS); Lelia and Mae were living at 592 Lenox Avenue, Apt. 12, in late May 1913 while awaiting renovations on 108 W. 136th Street, where they moved in June 1913.

"I am preparing myself"—*Report of the 15th Annual Convention of the National Negro Business League, Muskogee, Oklahoma, August 19–21, 1914* (Nashville: AME Sunday School Union, 1914), p. 151.

she had begun to buy real estate—*1914 NNBL Report,* p. 152; FBR to LWR, May 27, 1913.

"Oh, it's the latest thing in autos"—FBR to LWR, May 27, 1913; comparable to a Cadillac—Frank N. Ownings, Jr., "Cole Motor Car Company," in Bodenhamer and Barrows, *Encyclopedia,* p. 456; Beverley Rae Kimes and Henry Austin Clark, Jr., *Standard Catalog of American Cars: 1805–1942* (3rd ed., Iola, WI: Kraus Publications, 1996), pp. 350–51.

Madam Walker had no quarrel with her daughter's choice—FBR to MW, June 30, 1913 (MWC/IHS).

"perfectly beautiful"—Ibid.

"I want you to join me"—FBR to LWR, May 27, 1913.

Page 147

Anxious that he be shown "every courtesy"—"Dr. Booker T. Washington," *Indpls. Freeman,* July 12, 1913.

"an army of newspaper people"—Ibid.

"in the best of those splendid rooms"—Ibid.; MW to BTW, July 28, 1913 (BTW/NNBL Microfilm Reel 3, Correspondence, T-Y/Dec. 1912; June–Nov. 1913).

"Doctor, your time's up!"—*Indpls. Freeman,* July 12, 1913.

filling every available space—"New YMCA Opened," Ibid.

Page 148

Fairbanks introduced Washington—"Dedication Program—Dr. Booker T. Washington Speaker at New YMCA," *Indpls. Recorder,* July 12, 1913, and "New YMCA Opened."

"This building should make our young men"—*Indpls. Freeman,* July 12, 1913.

"Let this building"—Ibid.

He chose not to mention—Ibid.

singled her out—Ibid.

"a real pleasure"—MW to BTW, July 28, 1913. BTW's note to MW has not yet been found in the BTW or Walker papers.

"I shall read it with pleasure"—Ibid.

In Harlem, Lelia joined them—*1913 NNBL Report,* p. 311 (Lelia was listed among the registrants).

Arriving in her Cole—R. W. Thompson, "The Negro Women in Business," *Indpls. Freeman,* Sept. 20, 1913.

"a striking example"—*1913 NNBL Report,* p. 18.

Page 149

she proudly introduced her daughter—Ibid.

"progressive business woman"—*1913 NNBL Report,* p. 185; C. K. and Jessie Robinson are listed in the 1913 membership directory.

"I now take pleasure in introducing"—Ibid. p. 210.

"Mr. President and members"—Ibid.

Now with a full week still remaining—Ibid., p. 211.

"You can readily see"—Ibid.

Proficient in Greek—A'Lelia Walker, 1920 Walker Agents Convention speech, p. 3.

Page 150

"honesty of purpose"—*1913 NNBL Report,* p. 212.

"We thank her for her excellent address"—Ibid.

"You talk about what the men are doing"—Ibid.

Under the refrain—Ibid.

"I know absolutely nothing"—MW to BTW, Sept. 27, 1913 (BTW/LOC).

"I wish I could offer"—BTW to MW, Oct. 4, 1913 (BTW/LOC).

"We ourselves have been"—Ibid.

sent three Tuskegee graduates—Harlan, *Booker T. Washington,* pp. 267–68.

Despite the promising enrollment—p. 268.

At Washington's request—"Personal Mention," *Indpls. Recorder,* Feb. 21, 1914; Scott to MW, Feb. 24, 1914 (MWC/IHS).

more than 1,500 young men and women—"Tuskegee Institute's Work Given in Report," *Indpls. Recorder,* Oct. 31, 1914.

Page 151

"Next year I hope"—MW to BTW, Mar. 13, 1914 (BTW /LOC, Box 746, 1914 Donation File).

"while it is true I have a large business"—MW to BTW, May 5, 1914 (BTW/LOC).

Her intention to "build"—MW to BTW, Mar. 13, 1914.

"whom I am educating"—*1914 NNBL Report*, p. 152; MW to BTW, Mar. 13, 1914; MW to BTW, May 5, 1914.

"I am unlike your white friends"—MW to BTW, May 5, 1914.

Beginning in the 1890s—Harlan, *Booker T. Washington*, p. 130.

At first Carnegie—Ibid., pp. 134–35.

teaching "it as you would any other industry"—MW to BTW, Mar. 13, 1914.

"It would add quite a revenue"—Ibid.

Washington declined the offer—BTW to MW, Mar. 24, 1914 (BTW/LOC).

his "very great pleasure"—Ibid.

Page 152

"in regards to adopting my work"—MW to BTW, May 5, 1914.

"I think I have demonstrated"—Ibid.

"If you can not see your way clear"—Ibid.

"I have already written you frankly"—BTW to MW, May 22, 1914.

It is unlikely—BTW was "barely running Tuskegee by then," according to Maceo Crenshaw Dailey, Jr. (undated correspondence with author).

a friendly reception—MW to BTW, Aug. 27, 1914, *Records of the NNBL, Part 2: Correspondence and Business Records, 1900–1923*, Microfilm Reel 5, Correspondence "U" to "Y," Jan.–Dec. 1914 (University Publications of America, Bethesda, MD); *1914 NNBL Report*, p. 12.

"She always says something"—Ibid., p. 150

"not only makes money"—Ibid.

"unexpected pleasure"—Ibid.

"In coming before you"—Ibid.

"I am not merely satisfied"—Ibid.

"I had little or no opportunity"—Ibid.

Page 153

"it will help me to be of more practical service"—Ibid., p. 152

"If the truth were known"—Ibid.

"the foremost business woman of our race"—Ibid., pp. 152–53.

Both the Court of Calanthe—*Walker Company Booklet*, 1919, p. 12; R. W. Thompson, "The Negro Women in Business," *Indpls. Freeman*, Sept. 20, 1913.

"as the best on the market"—Minutes, *National Association of Colored Women 1914 Convention*, Wilberforce, OH, p. 32.

lectures entitled "The Negro Woman in Business"—*Indpls. Freeman*, Sept. 20, 1913.

"pronounced hit"—"Mme. C. J. Walker's Return Home," *Indpls. Freeman*, Feb. 7, 1914.

she encouraged the "women of the race"—*Indpls. Freeman*, Sept. 20, 1913.

president of the National Negro Press Association—Pride and Wilson, *A History of the Black Press*, pp. 175–76.

"The girls and women of our race"—*1913 NNBL Report*, p. 210.

"employing hundreds of Negro girls"—Ibid., p. 211.

Page 154

Even her latest ads emphasized training—"Learn to Grow Hair," Walker ad, *Indpls. Freeman*, Apr. 12, 1913.

Washington disciple—Harlan, *Booker T. Washington*, p. 95.

"And no matter where she goes"—*Indpls. Freeman*, Sept. 20, 1913.

"motor parties to Baltimore"—Ibid.

After an October 31 farewell—"Good News from Madam Walker," Chicago *Broad Ax*, Jan. 24, 1914.

ten-day National Emancipation Exposition—Reid Badger, *A Life in Ragtime: A Biography of James Reese Europe* (New York: Oxford University Press, 1995), pp. 74–75; Howard Dodson, Christopher Moore and Roberta Yancy, *The Black New Yorkers: The Schomburg Illustrated Chronology* (New York: John Wiley & Sons, 2000), pp. 94–95.

In New York—"Madam Walker Sails for Cuba," *Chicago Defender*, Nov. 29, 1913.

40,000 West Indians now lived—"Items of Race Interest," *Indpls. Freeman*, Nov. 25, 1911.

Mme. Anita Patti Brown—"Famous Clef Club Gives Concert, Mme. Anita Patti Brown Visits the Capital," *Indpls. Freeman*, Nov. 22, 1913; Southern, *The Music of Black Americans*, p. 282.

Page 155

"a triumphal tour" of Jamaica—"Summary of the News," *Chicago Daily News*, Aug. 20, 1912.

Born in Atlanta—*The Crisis*, Vol. 10, No. 4, Aug. 1915, p. 169.

Oruba on November 8—*Indpls. Freeman*, Nov. 22, 1913; "City and Vicinity," *Indpls. Freeman*, Nov. 8, 1913; "Madam Walker Sails for Cuba," *Chicago Defender*, Nov. 29, 1913; "Mme. C. J. Walker's Return Home," *Indpls. Freeman*, Feb. 7, 1914; "News in a Nutshell," *Indpls. Freeman*, Feb. 7, 1914; "Good News from Madam Walker," Chicago *Broad Ax*, Jan. 24, 1914.

In Kingston—Chicago *Broad Ax*, Jan. 24, 1914; *Indpls. Freeman*, Feb. 7, 1914.

"black custom house officials"—James Weldon Johnson, *Along This Way: The Autobiography of James Weldon Johnson* (New York: Penguin Books, 1990), p. 267.

"a strange sort of luxury"—"An Amazing Island," *The Crisis*, June 1915, p. 80.

"She was gratified"—*Indpls. Freeman*, Feb. 7, 1914.

"Long moonlight sails"—Chicago *Broad Ax*, Jan. 24, 1914; *Indpls. Freeman*, Jan. 17, 1914.

their "outer walls . . . whitewashed"—Johnson, *Along This Way*, p. 349.

"a grand round of pleasure"—R. W. Thompson, "Short Flights," *Indpls. Freeman*, Jan. 3, 1914.

"on a level that for wealth and culture"—Johnson, *Along This Way*, p. 349.

Page 156

"official family"—Chicago *Broad Ax*, Jan. 24, 1914.

violent deaths between 1912 and 1915—"May Have Killed President," *Baltimore Afro-American Ledger*, Aug. 24, 1912.

"men and boys are, on the slightest pretext"—"Madam C. J. Walker, of Indianapolis, Seeing the Islands of the Southern Seas," *Indpls. Freeman*, Jan. 17, 1914.

cells were "bare with dirt floors"—Ibid.

"18 chickens, one turkey"—Ibid.

The "real 'Chamber of Horrors'"—Ibid.

With "their baskets balanced"—Johnson, *Along This Way*, p. 350.

In late January—"Mme. C. J. Walker's Return Home" and "City and Vicinity," *Indpls. Freeman*, Feb. 7, 1914.

CHAPTER 14 NEW HORIZONS

Page 157

"Fire and ice"—Violet Reynolds, conversation with author, Dec. 1975.

More than 200 guests—"Mme. C. J. Walker Entertains in Honor of Her Daughter, Mrs. Lelia Robinson, of New York," *Indpls. Recorder*, Apr. 25, 1914.

Even the Walker women's attire—Ibid.

Page 158

gold-tasseled dance programs—Original dance program, author's Walker Family Collection.

Men in cutaway coats—*Indpls. Recorder*, Apr. 25, 1914.

Tenor Noble Sissle—Dance program; "Personal Mention," *Indpls. Recorder*, Apr. 11, 1914; *Indpls. Recorder*, Apr. 25, 1914; "Personal Mention," *Indpls. Recorder*, Apr. 25, 1914; Bodenhamer and Barrows, *Encyclopedia*, p. 1264.

"The Party"—"The Party" by Paul Laurence Dunbar.

"make the scene a very brilliant one"—*Indpls. Recorder*, Apr. 25, 1914.

"the richly gowned women"—"Locals and Personals," *Indpls. Recorder*, Apr. 17, 1915; "Mme. C. J. Walker's Musicale for Mrs. Lelia Robinson," *Indpls. Recorder*, Apr. 24, 1915.

Called "one of the most elaborate functions"—"To Entertain at Recital," Indpls. Recorder, Mar 27, 1915; "Mme. C. J. Walker's Musicale."

At H. P. Wassons—H. P. Wasson May–July 1915 bill (MWC/IHS).

Page 159

the jeweler who had provided—William M. Lewis, "The Life and Work of Mme. C. J. Walker," Indpls. Freeman, Dec. 26, 1914.

"were the recipients of much social attention"—"Business Woman to Make Lengthy Far West Tour," Indpls. Recorder, June 19, 1915, p. 1.

"I guess you think I am crazy"—MW to FBR, July 31, 1915 (MWC/IHS).

"No, I don't think you crazy"—FBR to MW, Aug. 2, 1915 (MWC/IHS).

"I assure you I am not going to buy"—MW to FBR , undated, but probably Aug. 1915 (MWC/IHS).

"People know that he has been in prison"—MW to FBR, June 26, 1916 (MWC/IHS).

"I am tired of fooling with"—MW to FBR, June 3, 1916 (MWC/IHS).

"another sassy letter" and "I do not care to have any more communication"—MW to FBR, Mar. 20, 1916; MW to FBR, Feb. 16, 1916 (MWC/IHS).

Page 160

said "something too hard"—MW to FBR, June 3, 1916.

"I wish that you could get in touch"—Ibid.

"Mrs. Walker is grounded in the belief"—"The Frances Spencer Benefit," *Indpls. Recorder*, Feb. 6, 1915.

"the constant effort"—"Musicale and Dance," *Indpls. Recorder*, Dec. 19, 1914.

white business community—"The Frances Spencer Benefit," *Indpls. Recorder*, Feb. 20, 1915.

only black harpist—"Personal Mention," *Indpls. Recorder*, Dec. 12, 1914.

"at a premium"—*Indpls. Recorder*, Feb. 20, 1915.

"unusually talented" Spencer—*Indpls. Recorder*, Dec. 19, 1914.

$300 check and "in order that she might get"—"Mme. C. J. Walker Says Harpist Is Ungrateful," *Chicago Defender*, May 8, 1915; "A Tribute," *Indpls. Recorder*, Feb. 27, 1915. (Special thanks to Paula Giddings for first making me aware of the Spencer incident.)

"After the recital"—*Chicago Defender*, May 8, 1915.

"After remaining here for about two months"—Ibid.

"Now I want to say, and this is final"—Ibid.

Page 161

"Madam loved going to the movies"—Violet Reynolds, conversations with author between 1975 and 1983.

As the movie industry was establishing itself—Robert Sklar, *Movie-Made America: A Cultural History of American Movies* (New York: Vintage Books, 1994), p. 89.

But when she presented her dime—*Sarah Walker v. The Central Amusement Company*, State of Indiana, Marion J.P. Court, undated.

he demanded $100 in damages—Ibid.

"the only one of [its] kind in Indianapolis"—*Indpls. Freeman,* Dec. 26, 1914.

Page 162

she hosted a Sunday afternoon reception—"Distinguished Guests at Mme. C. J. Walker's," *Indpls. Freeman,* Aug. 15, 1914.

in line to become NACW president—Rayford Logan, "Mary Burnett Talbert," in Logan and Winston, *DANB,* p. 576.

"a factor in the great affairs"—"In Club Circles—Echo Meeting," *Indpls. Recorder,* Aug. 15, 1914.

During the visit—*Indpls. Recorder,* Aug. 15, 1914; "City and Vicinity," *Indpls. Freeman,* Aug. 15, 1914.

Talbert had graduated from Oberlin College—Lillian S. Williams, "And Still I Rise: Black Women and Reform, Buffalo, New York, 1900–1940," in Darlene Clark Hine, Wilma King and Linda Reed, eds., *"We Specialize in the Wholly Impossible": A Reader in Black Women's History* (Brooklyn: Carlson Publishing, 1995), p. 523; Rayford Logan, "Mary Burnett Talbert," *DANB,* p. 576.

hosted a seven-course dinner—"Madam C. J. Walker Entertains in Honor of Major R. R. Moton," *Indpls. Recorder,* Apr. 3, 1915, and *Indpls. Freeman,* Apr. 3, 1915.

three public appearances—"YMCA Notes," *Indpls. Recorder,* Mar. 27, 1915, and "Hampton Institute," *Indpls. Recorder,* Mar 27, 1915.

Among the guests—*Indpls. Recorder,* Apr. 3, 1915, and *Indpls. Freeman,* Apr. 3, 1915.

$100 scholarship—*Indpls. Recorder,* Mar. 27, 1915.

William Monroe Trotter—"Locals and Personals," *Indpls. Recorder,* Apr. 3, 1915; Trotter to LWR, June 28, 1919 (author's Walker Family Collection).

At the invitation of Ransom—"W. Monroe Trotter," *Indpls. Recorder,* Mar. 27, 1915

Page 163

excluding them from cafeterias—David Levering Lewis, *W.E.B. Du Bois: Biography of a Race 1868–1919* (New York: Henry Holt, 1993), p. 510.

dwindled markedly from thirty-one to eight—Ibid.

The controversial publicity—"Equal Rights or Segregation," *Indpls. Recorder,* Apr. 3, 1915.

"one of the most beneficial"—Trotter to FBR, Apr. 6, 1915 (MWC/IHS).

contribution for her Florida school—Mary McLeod Bethune to MW, Apr. 5, 1917 (MWC/IHS); "Mrs. Mary Bethune, a Noted Race Woman, to Be in the City Tuesday," *Indpls. Recorder,* May 15, 1915.

But one visitor Madam Walker did not entertain—"Mme. A. M. Pope Turnbo Malone's Visit to the Hoosier Metropolis," *Indpls. Recorder,* May 29, 1915.

Having married Aaron Malone—"Malone-Pope-Turnbo Nuptials!" *Indpls. Freeman,* Apr. 25, 1914.

the new Mrs. Malone was featured—"Mme. A.M. Pope Turnbo Malone's Visit."

Malone "is known the country over"—Ibid.

"the queen of all Negro business women"—*Indpls. Freeman,* Apr. 25, 1914.

Page 164

"Now in regards to George Stewart"—MW to FBR, Oct. 20, 1915 (MWC/IHS).

she gave twenty-five lectures—"Madam C. J. Walker Buys Splendid Eastern Home," *Indpls. Recorder,* Oct. 31, 1914; "Mme. C. J. Walker Home from the East—Will Make Her Future Home in Flushing, NY," *Indpls. Freeman,* Oct. 31, 1914.

"Will you kindly give me a letter of introduction"—MW to BTW, July 9, 1915 (BTW/LOC).

$250 donation "in accordance with my promise"—MW to BTW (BTW/LOC, Box 759 TA-WE, 1915 Donation File).

"We shall see that the money"—BTW to MW (BTW/LOC, Box 759 TA-WE, 1915 Donation File).

"gorgeous colored rocks"—"Mme. C. J. Walker's Travelogue a Success," *Indpls. Freeman*, Jan. 22, 1916.

"My lecture Monday night"—MW to FBR, undated but probably mid to late July 1915 (MWC/IHS).

Page 165
"Everybody gets enthused"—MW to FBR, July 31, 1915 (MWC/IHS).

"I fear I will not be able to reach home"—MW to FBR, Sept. 9, 1915 (MWC/IHS).

Japanese, Italian and German papers—Ibid.

As she traveled—*Indpls. Freeman*, Jan. 22, 1916.

"I am sure that this trip"—MW to FBR, Sept. 9, 1915.

she "aroused people to the highest"—MW to FBR, Oct. 5, 1915 (MWC/IHS).

"Now, Mr. Ransom, I find that a number of agents"—MW to FBR, Sept. 9, 1915.

"Now, I think I do business enough"—MW to FBR, Oct. 5, 1915.

"going to take steps"—MW to FBR, Oct. 23, 1915 (MWC/IHS).

presented lectures in Oakland—MW to FBR, Sept. 18, 1915 (MWC/IHS).

While in the Bay Area—"Business Woman to Make Lengthy Far West Tour," *Indpls. Recorder*, June 19, 1915.

visited San Francisco's Panama-Pacific Exposition—MW to FBR, Sept. 18, 1915.

Page 166
farther north to Portland—MW to FBR, Oct. 23, 1915.

"Mr. Ransom, is it essential"—MW to FBR, Oct. 20, 1915 (MWC/IHS).

"I am truly homesick now"—MW to FBR, Oct. 23, 1915.

"This trip is and will mean so much"—Ibid.

"Since I find that these pictures"—Ibid.

she wired $10,000 to Ransom—MW to FBR, Oct. 23, 1915, Oct. 29, 1915, and Nov. 6, 1915 (MWC/IHS).

"Yes, I say it is remarkable the way my bank account"—MW to FBR, Nov. 6, 1915 (MWC/IHS).

"I have never lost anyone"—MW to FBR, undated, but probably Nov. 19, 1915 (MWC/IHS).

Immediately she sent Margaret Murray Washington—MW to Margaret Murray Washington (BTW/LOC).

cross-shaped floral arrangement—"Madam C. J. Walker," *Indpls. Recorder*, Nov. 20, 1915.

8,000 mourners—"8,000 Attend Funeral of B. T. Washington," *Indpls. Recorder*, Nov. 20, 1915; N. Barnett Dodson, "B. T. Washington Dies at Tuskegee," *Indpls. Recorder*, Nov. 27, 1915.

"It gave me much pleasure"—MW to FBR, undated, but probably Nov. 19, 1915 (MWC/IHS).

Page 167
it was Robert Russa Moton—"Major Moton Succeeds Booker T. Washington," *Indpls. Recorder*, Dec. 25, 1915.

As soon as Madam Walker returned—MW to Emmett J. Scott, Dec. 1, 1915 (BTW/LOC).

"Be it resolved"—"Membership Banquet in Honor of Madam C. J. Walker, Friend and Benefactress," *Indpls. Recorder*, Dec. 18, 1915.

That Christmas—"Locals and Personals—Persons Desiring Christmas Baskets," *Indpls. Recorder*, Dec. 18, 1915.

Her featured guest—William Lewis, "Mme. C. J. Walker's Travelogue a Success," *Indpls. Freeman*, Jan. 22, 1916.

Only the talented Noble Sissle—Badger, *A Life in Ragtime*, pp. 131–32.

Page 168

"The citizens of Indianapolis"—"Madame C. J. Walker Leaves Scene of Her Labor and Success," *Indpls. Freeman*, Feb. 12, 1916.

"is not only a credit"—Ibid.

"but as the big-hearted"—Ibid.

CHAPTER 15 BLACK METROPOLIS

Page 169

"It is just impossible"—MW to FBR, Feb. 22, 1916 (MWC/IHS).

To the rousing tunes of James Reese Europe—"Mrs. Lelia Walker Robinson Opens Beauty Parlor," *Indpls. World*, Jan. 22, 1916.

East Coast high society—Badger, *A Life in Ragtime*, p. 139.

Lelia's elegant lobby—*Literary Digest*, Oct. 13, 1917.

"most affable and courteous woman"—*Indpls, World*, Jan. 22, 1916.

Page 170

Even her mother had credited her—"Walker Presence in Harlem—Wonderful Success of Mme. C. J. Walker," *The Colored American Review*, Mar. 1916 (GSC/CU,Vol. 41).

"Now, Mr. Ransom, in regards to this house"—MW to FBR, Feb. 22, 1916 (MWC/IHS).

"Lelia and Mae are rejoicing"—Ibid.

"It was a surprise"—Ibid.

"Am writing you to do a friendly turn"—LWR to FBR, Dec. 7, 1913 (MWC/IHS).

"Now I know, Mr. Ransom, Mother has been wonderful"—Ibid.

To soften the request, Lelia proposed—Ibid.

Page 171

"I realize I have certainly imposed"—Ibid.

"My income is now $1,000 a month"—Ibid.

"Since you treated my hair"—"Walker's Hair Parlor and Lelia College," pamphlet, circa 1915, p. 10 (MWFC/APB).

Every six weeks—*Literary Digest*, Oct. 13, 1917, pp. 75–76.

"The business has picked up"—MW to FBR, Feb. 22, 1916 (MWC/IHS).

"Lelia wants $3,000"—MW to FBR, undated but probably mid to late July 1915.

completed the purchase of 110—LWR to FBR, July 30, 1915 (MWC/IHS). (Blanche L. Rosenthal of 46 West 96th Street held the mortgage on 110 W. 136th Street.)

"Will you kindly go to the bank"—MW to FBR, Sept. 9, 1915 (MWC/IHS).

Page 172

Lelia's ivory Louis XVI—*Literary Digest*, Oct. 13, 1917, p. 76.

mantel filled with framed photographs—Photograph of LWR's bedroom, Byron Collection, Museum of the City of New York. (Special thanks to Michael Henry Adams for making me aware of this photograph.)

A player organ—*Literary Digest*, Oct. 13, 1917, p. 76.

an "expensive pink-flowered lavender"—Ibid.

Among the guests seated—"Mme. C. J. Walker Honored," *Indpls. Recorder*, Nov. 7, 1914.

With his 125-member Clef Club and music director for Vernon and Irene Castle—Badger, *A Life in Ragtime*, pp. 66 and 77.

"statuesquely powerful build"—Ibid., p. 67.

Page 173

recently formed Tempo Club Ensemble now headquartered in a row house—Ibid., pp. 88 and 138, cites *New York Age*, July 6, 1916. (The Tempo Club was founded in Jan. 1914 after Europe left the Clef Club Orchestra.)

Another guest, Philip Payton—*Indpls. Recorder*, Nov. 7, 1914.

Four years later, under a new name—Dodson et al., *The Black New Yorkers*, p. 120.

As a result, scores of the remaining white tenants—"The New York Negro as a Tenant," Philip A. Payton ad, *The Crisis*, Vol. 1, No. 1 (Nov. 1910), p. 20; Gilbert Osofsky, *Harlem: The Making of a Ghetto* (2nd ed.; New York: Harper Torchbooks, 1971), p. 94, cites the *New York Age*, Dec. 5, 1912.

an early officer and investor—John B. Wiseman, "Fred(erick Randolph) Moore," in Logan and Winston, *DANB*, p. 447.

he had been forced to close—Thaddeus Russell, "Philip A. Payton, Jr.," in Jack Salzman et al., *Encyclopedia of Africa-American Culture and History* (New York: Macmillan Library Reference USA, 1996), p. 2116.

The estates of its few wealthy residents—Jeff Kisseloff, *You Must Remember This: An Oral History of Manhattan from the 1890s to World War II* (New York: Harcourt Brace Jovanovich, 1989), p. 87; Osofsky, *Harlem*, p. 71.

Harlem became the city's first suburb—Osofsky, *Harlem*, p. 71.

"rural retreat"—Ann Douglas, *Terrible Honesty: Mongrel Manhattan in the 1920s* (New York: Farrar, Straus and Giroux, 1995), pp. 309–10.

"distinctly devoted to the mansions"—Osofsky, *Harlem*, p. 2.

Page 174

When the overheated real estate market—Ibid., p. 80.

the trickle of black migration—Charles E. Hall and Z. R. Pettet, *Negroes in the United States: 1920–32* (Washington, DC: GPO, 1935), p. 55.

Nail's late father—"Passing of Jack Nail," *Indpls. Recorder*, Jan. 29, 1910.

His investments in Harlem—James Weldon Johnson, *Black Manhattan* (New York: Da Capo Press, 1991; originally published by Knopf, 1930), p. 149, and Maceo Crenshaw Dailey, Jr., "John (Jack) E. Nail," in Logan and Winston, *DANB*, pp. 469–70.

In 1911 when blacks were scattered—Jervis Anderson, *A. Philip Randolph: A Biographical Portrait* (New York: Harcourt Brace Jovanovich, 1972), p. 54.

black New York's first million-dollar real estate transaction—Osofsky, *Harlem*, p. 117; Dailey, "John (Jack) E. Nail."

"fight the common enemy"—Osofsky, *Harlem*, p. 107. (Some sources call the organization the Harlem Property Owners' Improvement Corporation.)

"drive them out and send them to the slums"—Ibid.

Just before St. Philip's 1911 purchase—"Nail and Parker 'Pull Off' Big Deal," *New York Age*, Mar. 30, 1911, in Allon Schoener, ed., *Harlem on My Mind: Cultural Capital of Black America 1900–1978* (New York: Delta, Dell Publishing, 1979), pp. 23–24.

"no matter what happens"—"Loans to White Renegades Who Back Negroes Cut Off," *Harlem Home News*, Apr. 7, 1911, in Schoener, *Harlem on My Mind*, p. 25.

Page 175

no wall had been constructed—LWR to FBR, Dec. 7, 1913 (MWC/IHS).

50,000 blacks—Osofsky, *Harlem*, p. 105.

Richard B. Harrison and convinced that "all she had to do"—Will M. Lewis, "The Life Work of Mme. C. J. Walker," *Indpls. Freeman,* Dec. 26, 1914.

"Naturally enough the New York folk"—S. A. Singerman to FBR, Nov. 30, 1914 (MWC/IHS); "Walker vs. Derrick," Nov. 28, 1914, in Singerman to FBR, Nov. 28, 1914 (MWC/IHS). The property was located at Prince and State streets in Flushing, Queens, on Long Island.

Enchanted by the four-story, twenty-room house—Singerman to FBR, Nov. 5, 1914 (MWC/IHS).

But before Madam Walker could move—Untitled, undated manuscript about Villa Lewaro, pp. 2–3 (MWC/IHS).

Madam Walker was seeking a discreet . . . exit—MW to FBR, May 25, 1916 (MWC/IHS).

"Apparently your client has been fearfully imposed upon"—Singerman to FBR, Nov. 5, 1914.

But because Madam Walker had signed a contract—"Walker vs. Derrick."

"As you know, Madam had gone into this"—FBR to LWR, Nov. 30, 1914 (MWC/IHS).

Page 176

"piled up a snug sum"—Ibid.

"I have advised Madam against"—Ibid.

"There are those who say live"—Ibid.

"As regards my coming back to Indianapolis"—MW to FBR, June 3, 1916 (MWC/IHS).

the sixty-story Gothic terra-cotta Woolworth tower—George L. Lankevich, *American Metropolis: A History of New York City* (New York: New York University Press, 1998), p. 150; Edward Robb Ellis, *The Epic of New York City: A Narrative History* (New York: Kodansha International, 1997, originally published 1966), pp. 495–96.

fifty-story Metropolitan Life Insurance Building—Lankevich, *American Metropolis,* pp. 149–50; Ellis, *The Epic of New York City,* p. 495.

to exceed a million people—Osofsky, *Harlem,* p. 75, cites Walter Laidlaw, *Population of the City of New York, 1890–1930* (New York, 1932), p. 51.

more than 25,000 factories—Lankevich, *American Metropolis,* p. 126.

two-thirds of the largest 100 U.S. corporations—Ibid.

topped the two-million mark—Ibid., p. 148.

Page 177

The large influx in the 1880s—Ibid., p. 122.

a half million Italians—Ibid., pp. 122–23.

African Americans and black West Indians flowed into Harlem—Nathan Irvin Huggins, *Harlem Renaissance* (London: Oxford University Press, 1971), p. 18.

Those attired "in loud-checked suits"—*Literary Digest,* Oct. 13, 1917, quotes an undated report from the National League on Urban Conditions Among Negroes.

While Harlem was not without its share—Osofsky, *Harlem,* p. 111.

"Negroes as a whole are . . . better housed"—National League on Urban Conditions Among Negroes, *Housing Conditions Among Negroes in Harlem, New York City* (New York, 1915), p. 8.

"the character of Negro protest and thought"—Huggins, *Harlem Renaissance,* p. 18.

"the biggest and most elegant"—Ibid., p. 14.

charting "a new course for racial assertiveness"—Lewis, *Du Bois,* p. 387.

alongside Harlem's famous, influential and intriguing—Osofsky, *Harlem,* p. 112.

Page 178

"After the summer crops were all in"—Chicago Commission on Race Relations, *The*

Negro in Chicago (Chicago: University of Chicago Press, 1922), p. 386, cited in Jones, *Labor of Love*, p. 157.

African Americans also were pulled—Florette Henri, *Black Migration: Movement North 1900–1920* (Garden City, NY: Doubleday, Anchor, 1975), p. 52.

25 million Europeans—Gerald Rosenbaum, *Immigrant Workers* (New York: Basic Books, 1973), p. 70, and Stephen Steinberg, *The Ethnic Myth* (Boston: Beacon Press, 1981), pp. 35 and 40, cited in Carole Marks, *Farewell—We're Good and Gone* (Bloomington: Indiana University Press, 1989), p. 81.

100,000 by 1918—Henri, *Black Migration*, p. 52.

an estimated half million—Gerald Patton, *War and Race: The Black Officer in the American Military, 1915–1941* (Westport, CT: Greenwood Press, 1981), p. 27, cites George Edmund Haynes, "Negroes Move North," Part I, *Survey* (May 4, 1918), pp. 115–22; Chicago Commission: *The Negro in Chicago*, p. 79.

as much as $8 a day—Chicago Commission: *The Negro in Chicago*, pp. 80 and 84.

of the eastern seaboard states—Osofsky, *Harlem*, p. 18.

"white employers [who] would judge"—William M. Tuttle, Jr., *Race Riot: Chicago in the Red Summer of 1919* (Urbana: University of Illinois Press, 1970), p. 100.

"children should be scrubbed"—T. Arnold Hill to Arthur T. Aldis, July 5, 1917, cited in ibid., p. 100.

Page 179

"most dangerous departments"—Jones, *Labor of Love*, pp. 166–67.

"least desirable jobs"—Marks, *Farewell*, p. 131.

"You have opened up a trade"—Maggie Wilson to MW, Oct. 1, 1913, in "Walker's Hair Parlor and Lelia College," brochure, circa 1914, p. 4 (MWFC/APB).

pushing her annual sales above $100,000—"Over 10,000 in Her Employ," *New York Age*, no date, 1916, Hampton Institute Archives.

"You don't know how it does my heart good"—MW to FBR, June 3, 1916 (MWC/IHS).

"contemplating enlarging her present business"—*The Colored American Review*, July–Aug. 1916 (GSC/CU, Vol. 41).

a magazine she would soon own—MW to FBR, June 18, 1916, Letter #2 (MWC/IHS).

"handicaps, restrictions"—*The Colored American Review*, Mar. 1916 (GSC/CU).

"has risen to command the respect"—"Welcome to Madame Walker," *New York News*, Mar. 4, 1916.

Page 180

"I first want to say that I did not succeed"—*New York Age*, undated, Hampton Institute Archives, Madam Walker file.

"as famous for her lectures"—*The Colored American Review*, July–Aug. 1916 (GSC/CU).

Philip G. Peabody—a wealthy Boston attorney—"P. G. Peabody Dies," *New York Times*, Feb. 26, 1934, p. 37.

pledged $1,000—*The Crisis*, Nov. 1918, p. 18.

"an effective program to stamp out lynching"—Charles Flint Kellogg, *NAACP: The National Association for the Advancement of Colored People* (Baltimore: Johns Hopkins Press, 1967), pp. 216–18, cites NAACP Board Minutes on May 31, 1916, June 12, 1916, Oct. 9, 1916, and Jan. 2, 1917.

her $100 contribution was acknowledged—Oswald Garrison Villard, receipt for $100 contribution, Aug. 4, 1916 (MWC/IHS).

It was Villard—Lewis, *Du Bois*, pp. 390–91.

"all the believers in democracy"—Dorothy Salem, *To Better Our World: Black Women in Organized Reform, 1890–1920*, Vol. 14 of *Black Women in United States History: From Colonial Times to the Present* (Brooklyn: Carlson Publishing, 1990), p. 148; Kellogg, NAACP, p. 298.

Page 181

One-third of the signatories were women—Ibid.

only black women whose names appeared—Ibid., p. 148.

"signaled that the race problem"—Lewis, *Du Bois*, p. 387.

"Lincoln freed you"—Ibid., p. 388.

By the time the National Guard—Ibid.

In 1915 alone—"Lynchings and Race Riots," cited in Kellogg, NAACP, p. 256.

"depicted in full-page ghoulishness"—Lewis, *Du Bois*, p. 514.

"state-sanctioned terrorism"—Stewart E. Tolnay and Beck, *A Festival of Violence: An Analysis of Southern Lynchings, 1882–1930* (Urbana: University of Illinois Press, 1995), pp. 19 and 50.

Page 182

"the opening wedge"—Kellogg, NAACP, p. 218, cites *Washington Bee*, July 8, 1916, and NAACP Board Minutes, June 12, 1916, and July 10, 1916.

"scolded him for beating the mules"—"The Waco Horror," Supplement to *The Crisis*, July 1916.

He was so psychologically unbalanced—Ibid.

After his arrest—Ibid. (See also Kellogg, NAACP, p. 218, which cites *New York Times*, May 16, 1916; "The Will to Lynch," *New Republic*, Oct. 14, 1916, p. 261; and NAACP Board Minutes, June 12, 1916.

"ghastly burnt cork husk"—Lewis, *Du Bois*, pp. 514–15.

the *Crisis* supplement was mailed—Kellogg, NAACP, p. 218.

knew an opportune moment—David Levering Lewis, "Du Bois and the Challenge of the Black Press," *The Crisis*, July 1997, p. 43.

Page 183

"the inalienable right of every free American"—Du Bois, "Editorial—Agitation," *The Crisis*, Nov. 1911, p. 11.

Eufaula, Alabama—"Along the Color Line—Crime," *The Crisis*, Mar. 1911, p. 10.

"McLean County, Kentucky"—"Along the Color Line—Crime," *The Crisis*, June 1911, p. 53.

"Honea Path"—"Opinion—Lynchers Triumphant" and "Opinion—South Carolina Protest," *The Crisis*, Dec. 1911, p. 60.

"I need not tell you how much"—Dr. Joel E. Spingarn, undated invitation to Amenia Conference, Joel Spingarn Papers, Box 95–13 (MSRC).

"Much to my regret"—MW to J. E. Spingarn, Spingarn Papers, Box 95–13 (MSRC).

"fundamental rights of the Negro"—Johnson, *Along This Way*, pp. 308–9.

He had also vetted the guest list—"The Amenia Conference," Spingarn Papers, Box 95–13, Folder 519 (MSRC).

"At last the time has come"—"W. E. Burghardt Du Bois, "The Amenia Conference: An Historic Negro Gathering" (Amenia, NY: Troutbeck Leaflets No. 8, 1925), p. 10, Joel Spingarn Papers, Box 95–13, Folder 525 (MSRC).

Page 184

As Du Bois assembled the participants—"The Amenia Conference," program with schedules and list of participants, Spingarn Papers, Box 95–13, Folder 525 (MSRC).

Among the eleven women—Ibid.

Day visitors included—Ibid.

Helen Keller, Lincoln Steffens—"First List Invited for Day Only," Spingarn Papers, Box 95–13, Folder 522 (MSRC).

"the thing which all of us call 'The Problem'"—Du Bois, "The Amenia Conference," p. 13.

"One can hardly realize today"—Ibid.

"The wall between the Washington camp"—Ibid.

"The Amenia Conference"—Johnson, *Along This Way*, pp. 308–9.

"Antiquated subjects of controversy"—"Second draft Amenia, NY, August 26, 1916," Spingarn Papers, Box 95–13 (MSRC).

Page 185

more "a matter of emphasis"—Lewis, *Du Bois*, p. 521.

"We all believed in thrift"—Du Bois, "The Amenia Conference," p. 12.

"the legacy from Troutbeck was far less one"—Lewis, *Du Bois*, p. 521.

"It marked a definite shift"—Ibid.

"anachronistic" and "he encouraged training"—Huggins, *Harlem Renaissance*, p. 20.

Du Bois had become familiar—"Along the Color Line," *The Crisis*, Vol. 3, No. 2 (Dec. 1911), p. 51.

Madam Walker's first *Crisis* advertisement—"Madame Walker's Preparations," *The Crisis*, Vol. 3, No. 3 (Jan. 1912), p. 130, and Vol. 3, No. 4 (Feb. 1912), p. 174 (Madam Walker's second *Crisis* ad appeared in Feb. 1912).

circulation of 16,000—"Publishers' Chat with Readers," *The Crisis*, Apr. 1912, p. 222.

In fact, its rapid growth—Harlan, *Booker T. Washington*, p. 365.

proposal to "found an industrial school"—"Along the Color Line—Education," *The Crisis*, Vol. 8, No. 2, p. 59. (There are no documents in Walker's papers regarding this school.)

Page 186

she was featured in a quarter-page photograph—C[hanning] H. Tobias, "The Colored Y.M.C.A.," *The Crisis*, Nov. 1914, p. 34.

There appears to be no existing correspondence—There are no letters in the author's personal Walker Collection or in the Walker Collection at the Indiana Historical Society between Madam Walker and Du Bois before 1916. In Jan. 2000, Linda Seidman, curator of the Du Bois Collection at the University of Massachusetts–Amherst, could locate no Walker/Du Bois correspondence.

Madam Walker also had committed—*The Colored American Review*, July–Aug. 1916 (GSC/CU, Vol. 41).

"[I] don't want my agents to fall behind"—MW to FBR, Apr. 1916 (undated but after April 16 and before Easter 1916) (MWC/IHS).

voiced support for the Niagara Movement—"Negro Women Greet the Niagara Movement," 1907 Du Bois MSS, reprinted in Herbert Aptheker, ed., *A Documentary History of the Negro People in the United States*, Vol. 2: *From Reconstruction to the Founding of the NAACP* (New York: Citadel Press/Carol Publishing Group, 1990; originally published in 1951), p. 913.

By 1910, four NACW members—"The N.A.A.C.P.," *The Crisis*, Vol. 1, No. 1 (Nov. 1910), p. 12; Salem, *To Better Our World*, p. 155.

Members of both groups cooperated—Salem, *To Better Our World*, p. 114.

Page 187

make lynching "an American embarrassment"—Ibid., pp. 114–15.

allocated $100—*Minutes of the Tenth Biennial Convention of the National Association of Colored Women, August 7–10, 1916* (NACW, 1916), p. 69.

Mary Burnett Talbert—Lillian S. Williams, "And Still I Rise: Black Women and Reform, Buffalo, New York, 1900–1940," in Hine et al., eds., *"We Specialize in the Wholly Impossible,"* p. 522.

Both a teacher and the founding president—"Madam C. J. Walker Buys Splendid Home," *Indpls. Recorder,* Oct. 31, 1914, p. 1.

Carter had objected to sending a letter—*Minutes of the Ninth Biennial Convention of the National Association of Colored Women,* 1914 (Library of Congress microfilm), p. 36.

"I shall never forget"—*Report of the 17th Annual Convention of the National Negro Business League, Kansas City, Missouri, Aug. 16–18, 1916* (Washington, DC: William H. Davis, 1916), p. 134.

"I am here in the interest of the NAACP"—Ibid., p. 176.

CHAPTER 16 SOUTHERN TOUR

Page 189

first chapter of the Madam C. J. Walker Benevolent Association—MW to FBR, Apr. 10, 1916 (MWC/IHS).

Booker T. Washington Memorial Fund—"Appeal to be addressed to the Negro People of the United States in behalf of the Booker T. Washington Memorial Fund of $2,000,000.00," no date, Library of Congress R#613 (from Kenneth Hamilton).

Henrietta "Hetty" Green—"Henrietta Howland Green," in *Webster's Dictionary of American Women* (New York: Smithmark Publishers, 1996), pp. 248–49; Norris McWhirter, *Guinness Book of World Records, 1980 Super Edition* (New York: Bantam Books, 1979), p. 494.

Page 190

Annual sales of Lydia Pinkham's patent medicine—Caroline Bird, *Enterprising Women* (New York: W. W. Norton, 1976), p. 126.

Other direct-sales companies—Peiss, *Hope in a Jar, p. 72.*

watched sales leap from $30,000—Alfred C. Fuller, *A Foot in the Door* (New York: McGraw-Hill, 1960), p. 114.

Initially Ransom viewed her grand scheme—MW to FBR, Apr. 10, 1916.

"I think you misunderstood my meaning"—MW to FBR, undated (after Apr. 16, before Easter), 1916 (MWC/IHS).

Instead she meant to set up—Ibid.

As an incentive, she proposed annual prizes—Ibid.

For the generous monthly salary of $125—MW to FBR, undated (after Apr. 16, before Easter), 1916.

"An enthusiastic audience"—MW to FBR, Apr. 10, 1916.

"I was very much flattered"—MW to FBR, undated (after Apr. 16, before Easter), 1916.

Page 191

"I fear you might [think] me egotistical"—MW to FBR, handwritten letter, no date (MWC/IHS).

"Of course I know there are no women"—Ibid.

That September, Madam Walker's $300 contribution—Tuskegee Normal and Industrial Institute receipt, Warren Logan to Madam Walker, Sept. 22, 1916 (MWC/IHS). (Seth Low died Sept. 17, 1916.)

"I am writing to suggest the name"—FBR to R. R. Moton, Sept. 27, 1916 (Robert Russa Moton Papers, LOC, Box GC-5, f.27) (sent by John A. Vernon).

the school had "the highest respect"—R. R. Moton to FBR, Oct. 4, 1916 (Robert Russa Moton Papers, LOC, Box GC-5, f.27) (sent by John A. Vernon).

Page 192

religious gatherings—AMEZ "General Conference"—MW/NY to FBR/Indpls., Feb. 22, 1916 (MWC/IHS).

"a packed house" at Reverend Peter James Bryant's and "her last tour of the South"— "Mme. C. J. Walker's Lecture Tour," *The Colored American Review,* July–Aug. 1916, (GSC/CU, Vol. 41).

At summer's end—MW to FBR, Oct. 5, 1916 (MWC/IHS).

"Open Your Own Shop"—"Mme. C. J. Walker's Preparations for the Hair/Supreme in Reputation," ad in *The Messenger,* Vol. 2, No. 1 (Jan. 1918).

"In those circulars I wish you would"—MW to FBR, Oct. 30, 1916.

"Address them as 'Dear Friend'"—MW to FBR, undated (after Apr. 16, before Easter), 1916.

"From the Kitchen to the Mansion"—Evelyn Brooks Higginbotham, *Righteous Discontent: The Women's Movement in the Black Baptist Church, 1880–1920* (Cambridge, MA: Harvard University Press, 1993), p. 169.

"howling success" and "All the big guns"—MW to FBR, Sept. 10, 12 and 14, 1916 (MWC/IHS); "Mme. C. J. Walker's Lecture Tour"; "Madame C. J. Walker Visiting the City," *Atlanta Independent,* Oct. 7, 1916, p. 1. Usually referred to as S. Willie Layten, she was born in Memphis in 1863 to a Baptist minister and his wife. During the 1880s, while living in California with her husband, she became active in religious and secular groups. By 1894 she had moved to Philadelphia with her daughter and without her husband, soon assuming a leadership role among Baptist women; Higginbotham, *Righteous Discontent,* p. 157.

Nearly three million and two most prominent white Baptist groups—Higginbotham, *Righteous Discontent,* p. 166.

Page 193

"only in evidence by pinning tags on anyone"—MW to FBR, Sept. 10, 1916.

"found so many poor people"—MW to FBR, Sept. 26, 1916 (MWC/IHS).

She reached Atlanta in early October—"Madame C. J. Walker Visiting the City," *Atlanta Independent,* Oct. 7, 1916 (thanks to Herman "Skip" Mason, Jr. for this article).

Mae's arrival at Spelman Seminary—LWR to FBR, Sept. 28, 1916 (MWC/IHS).

founded in 1881—Beverly Guy-Sheftall and Jo Moore Stewart, *Spelman: A Centennial Celebration* (Atlanta: Spelman College, 1981), p. 12.

its "primary aim"—Ibid., p. 27.

to honor the parents of Rockefeller's wife—Ibid., pp. 22 and 24.

only about 5 percent of Americans—Kristen Iversen, *Molly Brown: Unraveling the Myth* (Boulder: Johnson Books, 1991), p. 129.

Among the 768 students—"Annual Report to the Trustees of Spelman Seminary, 1916–1917," *Spelman Messenger* (from Taronda Spencer, College Archivist, Spelman College).

adopted in 1904 after the death of Laura's parents—Harlan, *Booker T. Washington,* p. 124.

Upon receiving Lelia's request—Lucy Hale Tapley to LWR, Sept. 14, 1916 (Spelman College Alumnae Office).

"I know Mrs. Walker cares for and protects her"—Margaret Murray Washington to Tapley, Sept. 16, 1916 (Spelman College).

"It gives me great pleasure"—Reverend James W. Brown to Tapley, Sept. 20, 1916 (Spelman College).

Page 194

"Miss Robinson has a most amiable disposition"—Bishop Alexander Walters to Tapley, Sept. 20, 1916 (Spelman College).

On the application—Spelman Application and Registration, Sept. 11, 1916.

English-Latin curriculum—Ibid.; Spelman Assistant Registrar Selonia Smith to Willard B. Ransom, Aug. 7, 1950 (Spelman College).

study music—Tapley to LWR, Sept. 14, 1916 (Spelman College).

Mae's "pleasing personality"—Dean Edith V. Brill to LWR, Sept. 14, 1917 (Spelman College).

Mae was "always very pleasant"—Juanita Martin interview with author, 1982.

early member of the NAACP—"Along the Color Line," *The Crisis*, Vol. 35, No. 9 (Sept. 1928), p. 304.

charging forth to Meridian, Greenwood—MW to FBR, Oct. 27, 1916 (MWC/IHS).

Page 195

"We are only making two-day stops"—MW to FBR, Nov. 8, 1916 (MWC/IHS).

"I truly made a hit in Natchez"—Ibid.

"Went to my home in Delta"—MW to FBR, Oct. 30, 1916 (MWC/IHS).

"World's Richest Negress"—"World's Richest Negress in Delta," Oct. 30, 1916, clipping with no newspaper name shown (MWFC/APB).

Page 196

"The report that I advertise to take the kink out"—"Negro Woman Gets in Society Addition," undated clipping, but appears to be Hot Springs, Arkansas, newspaper in Jan. 1917 (MWFC/APB).

"I am enclosing a signature card"—FBR to MW, Nov. 4, 1916 (MWFC/APB).

"We had a narrow escape"—MW to FBR, Nov. 24, 1916 (MWC/IHS).

"I arrived here sick"—Ibid.

"I think instead of coming home"—Ibid.

"Mme. really frightened me"—Ibid.

"I was so ill"—MW to FBR, Nov. 25, 1916 (MWC/IHS).

Page 197

"To-day the doctor told me she was on the verge"—MW to FBR, Nov. 24, 1916 (MWC/IHS).

"to give my mind a real rest"—MW to FBR, Nov. 27, 1916 (MWC/IHS).

a highly capable former Jackson schoolteacher—LWR's 1920 Walker agents convention speech, p. 3 (undated manuscript).

"I don't know if they will be able"—MW to FBR, Nov. 24, 1916.

Madam Walker checked into the Pythian—MW to FBR, Dec. 1, 1916 (MWC/IHS).

two-year-old Hot Springs, Arkansas, hospital—Linda McDowell to author, Jan. 22, 2000, E-mail.

seventy-room—Ibid.

eight elegant European-style—Shirley Abbott, "Hot Springs, Ark., Fondly Recalled as a Paradise Lost," *Smithsonian*, Vol. 22, No. 4 (July 1991), p. 106.

adrenaline rush—Marvin Moser, "What You May Not Know about High Blood Pressure," *Bottom Line Personal*, Nov. 30, 1993, p. 13.

temporarily lower her blood pressure—David Brown, review of Robert and Michele Root-Bernstein, *Honey, Mud, Maggots, and Other Medical Marvels*, in *Washington Post Book World*, Jan. 11, 1998, p. 6.

"I promise you I am going to let all business alone"—MW to FBR, Dec. 1, 1916 (MWC/IHS).

"I take the stand that laborious work"—Ibid.

outlining plans to install her hair culture course—MW to Pensacola Normal Industrial and Agricultural College, Mar 27, 1917; M. W. Dogan/Marshall, TX, to MW, Mar 6, 1917; M. W. Dogan to MW, Mar 26, 1917; W. H. Holtzclaw/Utica to MW, Mar 15, 1917; N. W. Collier/Jacksonville, FL, to MW, Mar 22, 1917 (all MWC/IHS).

Page 198

fee for "treatments be divided equally"—MW to FBR, Dec. 15, 1916 (MWC/IHS).

"For the past four years my girls"—Mary McLeod Bethune to MW, Apr. 5, 1917 (MWC/IHS).

"I shall be glad to talk this matter over"—Charlotte Hawkins Brown to MW, May 23, 1917 (MWC/IHS).

"Alice is so dear"—MW to FBR, Dec. 15, 1916.

Dr. James Webb Curtis—1910 Census, Garland County, Hot Springs, Twp ED #63, Sheet 6, Line 54, from Linda McDowell, Butler Collection, Little Rock Public Library.

a local reporter learned of her recent purchase—"Negro Woman Gets in Society Addition."

"ordered her to Hot Springs"—MW to FBR, Dec. 1, 1916.

700 agents—Louis George to MW, no date (first page missing); Lelia immediately panicked—LWR to FBR, Nov. 6, 1916 (MWC/IHS).

Page 199

Mother "may as well take"—Ibid.

fluctuating between $50 and $350—Ibid.

"I know mother is the best hearted person"—Ibid.

"Mother is just like an impulsive baby."—Ibid.

"Mother rules with an iron hand"—Ibid.

"I do not want to be dependent upon anyone"—Ibid.

"Mother is willing"—Ibid.

"If mother and I should have any controversy"—Ibid.

"You misunderstood me concerning Lelia"—MW to FBR, Nov. 24, 1916 (MWC/IHS).

Page 200

"With all of this big house"—LWR to FBR, May 4, 1917 (MWC/IHS).

Cuba "is the most picturesque place"—LWR to FBR, Mar. 26, 1917 (MWC/IHS).

"Mother is a brick"—Ibid.

"I am so afraid of having an argument"—LWR to FBR, undated, but probably June 1917 (MWFC/APB).

"At the rate you are now going"—FBR to MW, Feb. 14, 1917 (MWFC/APB).

Page 201

When asked by a reporter about "the ill feeling"—William Lewis, "Madam Walker Visits Former Indiana Home," *St. Louis Argus,* June 8, 1917.

"Mrs. Malone was very ugly"—MW to Alice Burnette, June 9, 1917 (MWFC/APB).

CHAPTER 17 "WE SHOULD PROTEST"

Page 203

a mass meeting to decry "the frequency"—Herbert Aptheker, ed., *A Documentary History of the Negro People in the United States, 1910–1932,* Vol. 3 (New York: Citadel Press, 1973, reprint 1993), p. 181.

"to do their bit to make the world safe"—Johnson, *Along This Way,* p. 319.

the murder of Eli Persons—William D. Miller, *Memphis During the Progressive Era* (Memphis: Memphis State University, 1957), pp. 191–95.

"industrial slum"—Elliott Rudwick, *Race Riot at East St. Louis, July 2, 1917* (Urbana: University of Illinois Press, 1982, originally published by Southern Illinois University Press, 1964), p. 5.

former laundry customers—Violet Reynolds, "The Story of a Remarkable Woman" (Indianapolis: Madam C. J. Walker Manufacturing Co., 1973), p. 4.

The headline in the next morning's—"Race Rioters Fire East St. Louis," *New York Times,* July 3, 1917, p. 1.

those initial reports fueled conspiracy theories—Rudwick, *Race Riot,* pp. 63–64.

Page 204

"first American pogrom"—Lewis, *Du Bois,* p. 536.

fight between union organizers—Richard L. Stokes, "East St. Louis Riot Appalling to Nation," *St. Louis Globe-Democrat,* July 8, 1917 (CTS/MHS).

with only sixty-three police officers—Ibid.

licensing fees from its 376 saloons—Lindsey Cooper, "The Congressional Investigation of East St. Louis," *The Crisis,* Vol. 15, No. 3 (Jan. 1918).

Like Pied Pipers . . . waving free tickets—Horace R. Cayton and St. Clair Drake, *Black Metropolis* (London: Jonathan Cape, 1946), p. 58.

"loading box cars, handling crates"—*St. Louis Post-Dispatch,* July 3, 1917, quoted in Selwyn K. Troen and Glen E. Holt, *St. Louis* (New York: New Viewpoints, 1977), p. 154; *St. Louis Globe-Democrat,* July 8, 1917.

new arrivals were filling—Cooper, "Congressional Investigation."

a dozen porters in 1914 to 470—Rudwick, *Race Riot,* pp. 16–17.

200 vacant slots—Ibid., pp. 17 and 19.

"a Negro town"—Ibid.

a May confrontation—Ibid., pp. 29–33.

July 4 race war—Ibid., p. 37.

"almost, if not quite full"—Cooper, "Congressional Investigation."

Page 205

In a case of mistaken identity—Rudwick, *Race Riot,* p. 38.

"bullet-riddled"—Ibid., p. 40.

"stoned, clubbed and kicked"—Ibid., pp. 43–44.

Sympathetic whites—Ibid., p. 45

Chanting "Burn 'em out!"—Ibid., p. 48.

At the Knights of Pythias Hall—"St. Louis Negroes Plan to Care for Refugees," *St. Louis Globe-Democrat,* July 4, 1917, p. 2.

Jessie, then in training—Young, *Your St. Louis and Mine,* p. 16.

relief workers at the Wheatley YWCA—Mongold, "Vespers and Vacant Lots," unpublished manuscript, p. 26 (UMSL).

"so sickening" that he "had not been able"—"Outrage, Say Congressmen of Race Riot," *St. Louis Globe-Democrat,* July 4, 1917.

"much humiliated" and "state's fair name"—Ibid.

"Ironically, Wilson helped create"—Kenneth O'Reilly, *Nixon's Piano: Presidents and Racial Politics from Washington to Clinton* (New York: The Free Press, 1995), p. 91.

Page 206

In support of the mostly white mine workers—August Heckscher, *Woodrow Wilson: A Biography* (New York: Collier Books, 1991), p. 451.

"Waging war abroad"—Ibid., p. 451–52.

"failure to condemn the riot"—Rudwick, *Race Riot*, p. 133; see *The Crisis*, Vol. 14 (1917), p. 305.

"appalling outbreak of savagery"—"Roosevelt and Gompers Row at Russian Meeting," *New York Times*, July 7, 1917; Rudwick, *Race Riot*, p. 134.

"Before we speak of justice"—*New York Times*, July 7, 1917.

suggested a "silent protest parade"—Johnson, *Along This Way*, p. 308. (JWJ wrote: "During the conference I had a talk with Oswald Garrison Villard, in which he said that one of the most effective steps the Negro in New York could take would be to march down Fifth Avenue in a parade of silent protest.")

In Washington, suffragettes—Michael D. Shear, "Local Leaders Pay Tribute to Women," *Washington Post*, Aug. 26, 1995.

arrested and imprisoned—Ellen Carol Dubois, "Suffrage Movement," in Wilma Mankiller, Gwendolyn Mink, Maysa Navarro, Barbara Smith and Gloria Steinem, eds., *The Reader's Companion to U.S. Women's History* (Boston: Houghton Mifflin, 1998), p. 580.

"preparations were gone about with feverish"—Johnson, *Along This Way*, p. 320.

"so striking and unusual a demonstration"—Aptheker, *A Documentary History*, p. 182.

Page 207

With Du Bois in East St. Louis—Lewis, *Du Bois*, p. 539.

A "superb public speaker"—Bruce Kellner, *The Harlem Renaissance: A Historical Dictionary for the Era* (Westport, CT: Greenwood Press, 1984), p. 199.

Barely two months earlier—Johnson, *Along This Way*, p. 317.

just after visiting Madam Walker—Dr. Sondra Kathryn Wilson to author, Feb. 26, 2000, E-mail re: timing of Johnson's Indianapolis visit.

a retarded man—Miller, *Memphis*, pp. 191–95.

Johnson's committee and Reverend Hutchens Bishop as president—Aptheker, *A Documentary History*, p. 181.

raised more than $900—"Raise $918.17 for the Silent Protest Fund," *New York Age*, Aug. 9, 1917.

Among the donors—Ibid.

By noon on Saturday—"Silent Parade Notice," *New York Age*, July 26, 1917; "Nearly Ten Thousand Take Part in Big Silent Protest Parade Down Fifth Avenue," *New York Age*, Aug. 2, 1917.

More than 800 children—"Negroes in Protest March in Fifth Av," *New York Times*, July 29, 1917.

Behind them, women dressed in white—Aptheker, *A Documentary History*, p. 181.

"Fully 20,000 negroes"—*New York Times*, July 29, 1917.

"We march because"—Johnson, *Along This Way*, p. 321.

Madam Walker joined a small group—*New York Times Magazine*, Nov. 4, 1917.

to decry "the atrocious attacks"—"President Wilson Asked to Speak," *Colorado Statesman*, Aug. 18, 1917, from *New York Evening Post*, Aug. 1, 1917.

Page 208

to "speak 'some public word'"—*Colorado Statesman*, Aug. 18, 1917.

boss of Hudson County—Heckscher, *Woodrow Wilson*, p. 202.

"to call at the White House"—Fred R. Moore, "New York Delegation Goes to Washington to See President; Greeted by Secretary Tumulty," *New York Age*, Aug. 9, 1917.

"may count upon me for absolute fair dealing"—"Wilson Tells Where He Stands on Race Question," *Indpls. Recorder*, Aug. 17, 1921; John Hope Franklin, *From Slavery to Freedom* (5th ed.; New York: Alfred A. Knopf, 1980), p. 324.

"feed supply bill"—*New York Age*, Aug. 9, 1917.

"regretted that he would not"—"Silent Protest Parade Committee Report," Ibid.

Wilson's "political weather vane"—Arthur Walworth, *Woodrow Wilson* (New York: W. W. Norton, 1978), p. 277.

"There is no doubt"—James Weldon Johnson, "News and Reviews"/"We Want the Public Word," *New York Age*, Aug. 9, 1917.

Asserting that Wilson—Ibid.

"in a few well chosen words"—*Colorado Statesman*, Aug. 18, 1917.

36 out of 100 eligible black men—Rudwick, *Race Riot*, p. 133; *The Crisis*, Vol. 14 (1917), p. 305.

the petition implored the President—*Colorado Statesman*, Aug. 18, 1917.

Page 209

"not a single one" had been convicted—Petition from the Negro Silent Protest Parade committee ("To the President and Congress of the United States"), original petition (MWFC/APB).

"No nation that seeks to fight" and among the sixteen signatories—Ibid.

"the matter would not be neglected"—*Colorado Statesman*, Aug. 18, 1917.

"was in sympathy"—"Silent Protest Parade Committee Report," *New York Age*, Aug. 9, 1917.

But the letters . . . "were not for publication"—Moore, "New York Delegation Goes to Washington."

"general and platitudinous phrases"—Rudwick, *Race Riot*, p. 135.

"Negroes of influence and culture"—Moore, "New York Delegation."

Wilson failed to "speak out"—"Dr. Moton Has Talk with President Wilson," *New York Age*, Sept. 6, 1917.

the committee members fanned out—Moore, "New York Delegation."

Reverend Cullen convened another public forum—*New York Age*, Aug. 9, 1917.

Page 210

Reverend Wesley G. Parks—"Union Baptist Church History" (Philadelphia: Union Baptist Church, 1992), p. 22.

Marian Anderson—Charles L. Blockson, "Philadelphia Guide to African American State Historical Markers" (Philadelphia: Charles Blockson Collection, 1992), p. 9.

As Madam Walker surveyed the crowd—"Hair Culturists' First Convention," *New York Age*, Sept. 6, 1917; *Minutes of the First National Convention of the Mme. C. J. Walker Hair Culturists' Union of America, Philadelphia, Pennsylvania, Aug. 30–31, 1917*, p. 1.

"in a session composed of graduates"—*Walker Hair Culturists' Union Minutes, 1917*, p. 1.

"every hat was then voluntarily removed"—Ibid.

"A wonderful picture told the story"—Ibid.

"splendidly poised"—William Lewis, "Madam Walker Visits Former Indiana Home," *St. Louis Argus*, June 8, 1917.

"the business women of the race"—*Walker Hair Culturists' Union Minutes, 1917*, p. 1.

Page 211

distinctive convention badges—MW to FBR, June 11, 1917 (MWFC/APB).

Setting aside the morning sessions—*Walker Hair Culturists' Union Minutes, 1917*, p. 1.

Layten had founded the city's branch—Lisa Clayton Robinson, "National League for the Protection of Colored Women," in Kwame Anthony Appiah and Henry Louis Gates, Jr., eds., *Africana: The Encyclopedia of the African and African American Experience* (New York: Basic Civitas Books, 1999), p. 1395.

two pioneering black filmmakers—*New York Age*, Sept. 6, 1917.

"Her income [now] is $250 a week"—*Literary Digest*, Oct. 13, 1917, p. 76.

Each decade had seen steady growth—*Negro Population 1790–1925* (Washington, DC: GPO/Department of Commerce, Bureau of the Census, 1918). In 1930 there were more than 12,800 black female hairdressers; see *Negroes in the United States, 1920–1932* (Washington, DC: GPO/Department of Commerce, Bureau of the Census, 1935), pp. 526 and 332.

The most significant growth—*Fourteenth Census of the United States, 1920*, Vol. 4, pp. 358–59; Nathan E. Jacobs, ed., *NHCA's Golden Years* (National Hairdressers and Cosmetologists Association/Western Publishing Company, 1970), p. 15.

Page 212

reserved the final night—MW to FBR, June 11, 1917 (MWFC/APB).

"I have always resented"—FBR to MW, Feb. 14, 1917 (MWFC/APB).

"on a co-operative basis"—"Notice to the Agents of the Madam C. J. Walker Manufacturing Company," undated (MWC/IHS).

"to have this organization, its rules"—Ibid.

"the art of hair culture" was now being taught—MW to FBR, Mar 23, 1917 (MWC/IHS).

the prizes—$500 in all—"To the Agents of the Madam C. J. Walker Manufacturing Company," undated (MWC/IHS).

"a ringing message"—*Walker Hair Culturists' Union Minutes, 1917*, p. 2.

"We, the representatives"—Ibid., p. 3

Page 213

After a brief stop in Cape May—"Flashes and Sparks," *Philadelphia Tribune*, Sept. 8, 1917.

more than a dozen company founders—*Minutes of the National Negro Cosmetic Manufacturers Association*, Sept. 5, 1917, New York (MWC/IHS).

"necessary and urgent"—National Negro Cosmetic Manufacturers Association news release, undated (MWC/IHS).

"[I]t has been so often the case"—*Minutes of the NNCMA*.

"Yours for Nigger Business"—Shane White and Graham White, *Stylin'—African American Expressive Culture from Its Beginnings to the Zoot Suit* (Ithaca, NY: Cornell University Press, 1998), p. 185, cites *Chicago Defender*, Aug. 5, 1916.

had founded the Johnson Manufacturing Company—*National Negro Business League Annual Report of the Sixteenth Session and the Fifteenth Anniversary Convention, Aug. 18–20, 1915* (LOC microfilm), p. 237.

"some of the best and most successful"—NNCMA news release.

Page 214

"devising some form of cooperative advertising"—*Minutes of the NNCMA*.

"fix a standard both in their prices"—Ibid.

"unscrupulous persons"—NNCMA news release.

Madam Walker elected president—*Minutes of the NNCMA*.

"enthusiasm and inspiration"—MW to W. A. Johnson, Sept. 12, 1917 (MWC/IHS).

"the beginning of a powerful organization"—Ibid.

Madam Walker joined nearly 200 men and women—"National Equal Rights League Tenth Annual Meeting," *Colorado Statesman*, Oct. 6, 1917.

NERL delegates voted to demand—Ibid.

"Despite progress we are still surrounded"—"Woman Leader of Negroes Will Battle 'Lynch Law,'" *Colorado Statesman*, Oct. 6, 1917.

elected a vice-president-at-large—"NERL Tenth Annual Meeting."

Page 215

preferring "an organization of the colored people"—Linda O. McMurry, *To Keep the Waters Troubled: The Life of Ida B. Wells* (New York: Oxford University Press, 1998), pp. 302–3.

Madam Walker "entertained the entire delegation"—Alfreda M. Duster, ed., *Crusade for Justice: The Autobiography of Ida B. Wells* (Chicago: University of Chicago, 1970), p. 378.

"ushered into the dining room"—Ibid.

Having visited the devastated town—Mildred I. Thompson, *Ida B. Wells-Barnett: An Exploratory Study of an American Black Woman, 1893–1930* (Brooklyn: Carlson Publishing, 1990), p. 119.

to "undertake an investigation"—"Woman Leader of Negroes Will Battle 'Lynch Law,'" *Colorado Statesman*, Oct. 6, 1917.

applauded her "hard work"—Duster, *Crusade for Justice*, p. 378.

"I was indeed proud"—Ibid.

"I was one of the skeptics"—Ibid.

"We drove out there almost every day"—Ibid.

"Of late, Mme. Walker, in her high-powered motor car"—*New York Times Magazine*, Nov. 4, 1917.

"'Impossible!' they exclaimed"—Ibid.

Page 216

" a cool million, or nearly that"—Ibid.

"I am not a millionaire"—Ibid.

When a reprint—Louis George to FBR, Nov. 16, 1917 (MWC/IHS).

brought white customers—Ibid.

"astonishment of your success"—Mrs. H. M. Minos/Rocky Ford, CO, to MW/NY, Dec. 10, 1917 (MWC/IHS).

His diagnosis: nephritis—"Famous Beauty Culturist Succumbs to an Attack of Bright's Disease," *Chicago Defender*, May 31, 1919. (This article identifies Sauer as a Chicago physician.)

"an indefinite stay"—Ibid.

"This is necessary for all time"—Louis George to FBR, Nov. 16, 1917.

Battle Creek's "dictatorial" director and "regimen of fresh air"—Nancy Rubin, *The Life and Times of Marjorie Merriweather Post* (New York: Villard Books, 1995), p. 4.

The bland, tasteless, vegetarian diet—Mary Butler, Frances Thornton and Garth "Duff" Stoltz, *The Battle Creek Idea: Dr. John Harvey Kellogg and the Battle Creek Sanitarium* (Battle Creek, MI: Heritage Publications, 1998), p. 32.

Despite the pleasant surroundings—Ibid.

Page 217

Unable to "tear herself away"—*Chicago Defender*, May 31, 1919.

"It is getting on fine"—MW to FBR, Dec. 20, 1917 (MWC/IHS).

"You certainly touched my weak spot"—LWR to FBR, Dec. 27, 1917 (MWC/IHS).

CHAPTER 18 WAR ABROAD, WAR AT HOME

Page 218

captivated by the military drills—Badger, *A Life in Ragtime*, p. 152.

With Noble Sissle strutting as his drum major—"A Pageant," *New York Age*, June 21, 1917.

Madam Walker was in Louisiana—MW to FBR, Apr. 11, 1917 (MWC/IHS).

"If war comes"—*Washington Bee*, Mar. 25, 1916.

Page 219

"Why need we go 3,000 miles"—*Iowa Bystander*, Feb. 9, 1917, cited in Gerald W. Patton, *War and Race: The Black Officer in the American Military, 1915–1941* (Westport, CT: Greenwood Press, 1981), p. 37.

"The Germans ain't done nothing"—Ira D. Reid, "A Critical Summary: The Negro on the Home Front in WWI and II," Journal of Negro Education, Vol. 12 (Summer 1943), p. 514, cited in Patton, *War and Race*, p. 36.

"take up the duty that comes to him"—James Weldon Johnson, "View and Reviews," *New York Age*, Apr. 5, 1917.

"Let us not hesitate"—"Close Ranks," *The Crisis*, July 1918.

"civil rights through carnage"—Lewis, *Du Bois*, p. 530.

"full quota to the federal army"—Patton, *War and Race*, p. 40.

"insult of a separate camp"—Lewis, *Du Bois*, p. 530.

A leading proponent of the effort—Patton, *War and Race*, p. 40.

"Our country faces the greatest crisis"—Ibid.

Page 220

CCNCM claimed "victory"—Ibid., p. 43.

"The race is on trial"—Emmett J. Scott, *The American Negro in the World War* (New York, 1919), p. 87, cited in Patton, *War and Race*, p. 46.

join the advisory board of the Circle for Negro War Relief—"Show Interest in War Relief," *New York Age*, Jan. 19, 1918.

"to improve conditions"—Adele Logan Alexander, *Homelands and Waterways: The American Journey of the Bond Family, 1846–1926* (New York: Pantheon Books, 1999), p. 367, cites *The Circle for Negro Relief, Inc., Annual Report, 1919*.

Lelia . . . co-hosted a farewell concert"—"Tandy Made Major of 15th Battalion," *New York Age*, Nov. 29, 1917.

Lelia College holiday greeting—"Mme. C. J. Walker's Preparations for the Hair," ad in *The Messenger*, Jan. 1918.

"daintily dressed" women—"News of Greater New York: Mrs. Robinson's Military Cotillion," *New York Age*, Jan. 26, 1918.

commanding officer of an ambulance company—Russell H. Davis, "Charles Herbert Garvin," in Logan and Winston, *DANB*, p. 256.

1915 graduate of Harvard's Medical School—Rayford W. Logan, "Louis Tompkins Wright," in Logan and Winston, *DANB*, p. 670.

The Friday Evening Knitting Class—*New York Age*, Jan. 26, 1918.

Lelia next invited famed tenor Enrico Caruso—"Caruso to Appear at War Relief Benefit," *New York Age*, Feb. 9, 1918.

Page 221

"his voice is now at its richest"—Howard S. Greenfield, *Caruso: An Illustrated Life* (North Pomfret, VT: Trafalgar Square Publishing, 1991), pp. 138–39.

canceled "at the last minute"—LWR to FBR, Feb. 12, 1918 (MWC/IHS).

"few intimate friends"—Greenfield, *Caruso*, pp. 144–46.

he sang a dozen different roles—Ibid., pp. 138–39.

special matinee of Giuseppe Verdi's *Aida*—"Caruso Sings in 'Aida,'" *New York Times*, Feb. 13, 1919.

basket of flowers—Enrico Caruso to LWR, Feb. 18, 1918 (MWC/IHS).

"luxurious"—Greenfield, *Caruso*, pp. 144–46.

Whether serving lunch—"Battalion of 367th Infantry Makes Big Hit in Parade of Camp Upton Men in New York," *New York Age*, Mar. 2, 1918.

helping form a black women's auxiliary—"From Auxiliary to Red Cross in Harlem," *New York Age,* Mar. 23, 1918.

Hudson Seal cape—Selig Dry Good Co., No. 1811, Storage Receipt, Apr. 20, 1918 (MWC/IHS).

"cold seems to be sticking"—MW to FBR, Jan. 14, 1918 (MWC/IHS).

100 officers and 3,600 enlisted men—Patton, *War and Race,* p. 184.

escorted by attorney George Woodson—George H. Woodson to FBR, May 30, 1919 (MWC/IHS).

Later the founding president of the National Bar Association—J. Clay Smith, Jr., *Emancipation: The Making of the Black Lawyer 1844–1944* (Philadelphia: University of Pennsylvania Press, 1993), p. 469.

Page 222

"good fortune and high honor"—George H. Woodson to FBR, May 30, 1919.

"social, cultural and political"—Patton, *War and Race,* p. 59.

"Now and then, but seldom"—"Mme. C. J. Walker Holds Second Annual Convention," *Chicago Defender,* Aug. 10, 1918, p. 12.

"The eloquent force"—Woodson to FBR, May 30, 1919.

"I tried to get her away from the great mass"—Ibid.

Later when Madam Walker arrived at the home—Ibid.

Although Woodson "insisted"—Ibid.

Valedictorian of his 1901—Joseph J. Boris, *Who's Who in Colored America,* Vol. 1 (New York: Who's Who in Colored America Corp., 1927), p. 28.

"one of the seven or eight"—L. N. Bergmann, "The Negro in Iowa," *Iowa Journal of History and Politics,* Vol. 56, No. 3 (Jan. 1948), p. 82, cited in Smith, Jr., *Emancipation,* p. 454.

"begged the privilege"—Woodson to FBR, May 30, 1919.

"The madam has developed into"—"Mme. C. J. Walker to Speak Next Sunday," *Chicago Defender,* July 27, 1918.

"I understand that Mme. Walker No. 2"—MW to FBR, Feb. 20, 1918 (MWC/IHS).

Page 223

With nearly 1,000 newcomers—Chicago Commission on Race Relations, *The Negro in Chicago* (Chicago: University of Chicago Press, 1922), pp. 79 and 357; Horace Cayton and St. Clair Drake, *Black Metropolis* (London: Jonathan Cape, 1946), p. 8.

tobacco strippers and hotel waitresses—Chicago Commission, *The Negro in Chicago,* pp. 367 and 368.

1,500 black mail-order clerks—Ibid., pp. 379–81.

"deserted this grade of work"—Ibid., p. 371.

4656 South State Street—Samuel G. Grodson to FBR, Mar. 28, 1918 (MWC/IHS). In Aug. 1918 there was a Walker salon at 3115 South Prairie across from what is now Dunbar Park. See LWR to FBR, July 19, 1918 (MWC/IHS).

"Do not accept any social engagements"—MW to FBR, Mar 15, 1918 (MWC/IHS).

"She is as crooked as a black snake"—MW to FBR, Apr. 6, 1918 (MWC/IHS).

Madam Walker was welcomed—Zella Ward to FBR, Feb. 26, 1918 (MWC/IHS).

oldest black congregation—Reverend Jonathan McReynolds, phone conversation with author, Feb. 20, 2000.

Page 224

Although there were eleven Y buildings—G. Richard Peck, *The Rise and Fall of Camp Sherman* (Chillicothe: U.S. National Park Service, 1972), YWCA Hostess House photo in photo section.

"Army Club No. 1 for White Soldiers'"—Ibid., Ross Court House photo in photo section.

issued a directive ordering black troops—"What the N.A.A.C.P. Has Done for the Colored Soldier," in Aptheker, A *Documentary History*, p. 208.

jailed for "violating the separate coach laws"—"Harassment of Afro-American Soldiers in the United States," in Aptheker, A *Documentary History*, pp. 203–4, cites "Negro Lieutenant Ejected from Pullman . . . ," *Savannah Tribune*, Mar. 30, 1918.

"This is your country"—"Madam C. J. Walker Tells of Her Success," *Pittsburgh Courier*, Apr. 19, 1918 (GSC/CU, Vol. 41).

"We all remember you"—William E. St. to MW, Nov. 21, 1918 (MWC/IHS).

"one night while under shell-fire"—Ibid.

From Chillicothe—*Pittsburgh Courier*, Apr. 19, 1918.

"Her tribute to 'our boys'"—Ibid.

"packed house"—MW to R. L. Brokenburr, Apr. 12, 1918 (MWC/IHS).

"But we see that they are needed"—*Pittsburgh Courier*, Apr. 19, 1918.

"What I have done you can do"—Ibid.

Page 225

hoped to "meet every agent"—Ibid.

"since I have gone to New York"—MW to FBR, Apr. 15, 1918 (MWC/IHS).

"I think it will not be any trouble"—Ibid.

substituting "white vaseline"—MW to FBR, Apr. 19, 1918 (MWC/IHS).

"They want me to take it out"—Ibid.

in search of a second interpreter—Hallie E. Queen to FBR, June 17, 1918 (MWC/IHS).

"The pictures . . . the most important"—MW to Miss Lynch, June 10 or 11, 1918 (MWC/IHS).

Page 226

"I don't think you quite understand"—MW to Mrs. N. J. Skelton, Apr. 12, 1918 (MWC/IHS).

"I don't think it a good idea to pay salaries"—MW to FBR, Apr. 18, 1918 (MWC/IHS).

"the most foolish woman"—MW to FBR, Apr. 25, 1918 (MWC/IHS).

"will be better to have some one"—Ibid.

"You said we should . . . have but one"—Ibid.

"Mother stews and frets"—LWR to FBR, Feb. 20, 1918 (MWC/IHS).

"We have been out of goods for a week"—MW to FBR, May 3, 1918 (MWC/IHS).

Page 227

"What is the trouble?"—MW to FBR, May 7, 1918 (MWC/IHS).

"The situation here is getting terribly embarrassing"—MW to FBR, May 29, 1918 (MWC/IHS).

"I started yesterday to make Grower"—LWR to FBR, May 24, 1918 (MWC/IHS).

"Grower is in greater demand"—LWR to FBR, May 28, 1918 (MWC/IHS).

"Was surely received with honor in Denver"—MW to FBR, July 21, 1918 (MWC/IHS).

"made an appeal for club women"—*Minutes of the Eleventh Biennial Convention of the NACW, July 8 to 13, 1918* (Washington, DC: NACW, 1918), microfilm LOC, p. 38.

"none of us may live our own lives"—"Colored Women Ask Opportunity Be Made Equal—Will Make Good If Given Change, Says Speaker at Convention," *Denver Post*, July 11, 1918.

With Douglass's violin—"The National Association of Colored Women Hold Meeting," *Colorado Statesman,* July 13, 1918; Mary B. Talbert, "The Frederick Douglass Home," *The Crisis,* Feb. 1917, p. 174.

"It will be beautiful and all relics"—"As Reported by Press Agent," *Denver Star,* July 13, 1918.

Page 228

"I am glad to be able"—Rose Atwood, "Frederick Douglass Memorial," *The Competitor,* Vol. 1, No. 2 (Feb. 1920); *1918 NACW Biennial Minutes,* p. 24.

$750 from individuals—*1918 NACW Biennial Minutes,* p. 7.

helped rescue the hilltop home—Today the Frederick Douglass Home in Anacostia in Washington, DC, is a National Historic Landmark maintained by the National Park Service.

"a splendid mixed audience"—MW to FBR, July 21, 1918 (MWC/IHS).

she reviewed "the valor"—"N.Y. Woman Addresses High School Graduates," *Chicago Defender,* July 27, 1918.

"My anxiety is growing"—Baker to Wilson, July 1, 1918, Series 4, No. 152, Wilson Papers; Trotter to Wilson, Mar. 5, 1918, Series 4, No. 543, Wilson Papers, cited in O'Reilly, *Nixon's Piano,* p. 93.

Moton had despaired—Stephen R. Fox, *The Guardian of Boston: William Monroe Trotter* (New York: Atheneum, 1970), p. 221.

"wholesome effect"—Baker to Wilson, July 1, 1918, Wilson Papers; Trotter to Wilson, Mar. 5, 1918, Series 4, No. 543, Wilson Papers, cited in O'Reilly, *Nixon's Piano,* p. 93.

"did not shrink"—President Woodrow Wilson to Oswald Garrison Villard, July 23, Aug. 15 and 21, Sept. 22 and Oct. 2, 1913, Series 4, No. 152A, Wilson Papers, cited in O'Reilly, *Nixon's Piano,* p. 87.

Page 229

"The mob spirit . . . vitally affects the honor"—"President Wilson Declares Against Mob Rule," *Chicago Defender,* Aug. 3, 1918; "President Denounces Mob Spirit," *New York Age,* Aug. 13, 1918.

imploring "the Governors of all the States"—Ibid.

"We the undersigned agents"—Walker Agents/Chicago to FBR, Apr. 22, 1918 (MWC/IHS).

"Among the many objections"—FBR to MW, July 26, 1918 (MWC/IHS).

"The real thing after all is making the agents feel"—Ibid.

"One thing is sure"—Ibid.

Page 230

his products in Woolworth's—White and White, *Stylin',* p. 185.

"You doubtless are aware that these conventions"—"Mme. C. J. Walker Holds Second Annual Convention," *Chicago Defender,* Aug. 10, 1918.

"My friends, if out of these conventions"—Ibid.

"Never one to run away from a fight"—Violet Reynolds, "The Story of a Remarkable Woman" (Indianapolis: The Mme. C. J. Walker Manufacturing Co., 1973), p. 8.

"These same factories, mills and workshops"—Cayton and Drake, *Black Metropolis,* p. 60.

from 10,000 to 93,000 between 1916 and 1918—Henri, *Black Migration,* p. 63.

Page 231

"by far the largest circulation"—Ibid., p. 65.

"We are here not only to"—*Chicago Defender,* Aug. 10, 1918.

contributed $5 million—"Denver Entertains National Assn. of Colored Women," *Denver Star,* July 13, 1918.

"some of the best women the Race has produced"—*Chicago Defender,* Aug. 10, 1918.
"I want you to know that whatever I have accomplished"—Ibid.
"I want my agents to feel"—Ibid.
"to do their bit to help"—Ibid.
"I tell you that we have a duty"—Ibid.
"Bring them into your clubs"—Ibid.
"I shall expect to find my agents"—Ibid.
the Walker delegates . . . dispatched a telegram—Ibid.

Page 232

"patriotic sentiments are appreciated"—Joseph Tumulty to MW, Aug. 5, 1918 (MWC/IHS).
"coated with tar and feathers"—"Dr. Foote and Harrison Barred from Vicksburg," *Chicago Defender,* Aug. 10, 1918; "Professional Men Tarred and Feathered in Mississippi," *Chicago Defender,* Aug. 3, 1918.
soldier said to be "in the trenches"—Ibid.
local lawmakers perverted the federal Selective Service—Hunter, *To 'Joy My Freedom,* pp. 227–28, cites Walter F. White, "'Work or Fight' in the South," *The New Republic* Vol. 18 (Mar. 1, 1919), pp. 144–46; Cynthia Neverdon-Morton, *Afro-American Women and the Advancement of the Race, 1895–1925* (Knoxville: University of Tennessee Press, 1989), p. 73.
Jackson, Mississippi, city council members passed—"Washington Officials Deny Report Women Can Be Made to Work," *New York Age,* Nov. 16, 1918; Neverdon-Morton, *Afro-American Women,* p. 73, cites "Report of Conditions Found in Investigations of 'Work or Fight' Laws in Southern States," NAACP Administrative Files, Box 417, Aug. 19 and Oct. 26, 1918, Manuscript Division, LOC.
the case of Maria Parker—Hunter, *To 'Joy My Freedom,* p. 229, cites White, "'Work or Fight' in the South."
"in that the spirit of [this] social unrest"—*Chicago Defender,* Aug. 3, 1918.

CHAPTER 19 HER DREAM OF DREAMS

Page 233

"a wonder house" with a "degree of elegance"—"Wealthiest Negro Woman's Suburban Mansion," *New York Times Magazine,* Nov. 4, 1917; also quoted verbatim in "Madame Sarah J. Walker Dies; Was Wealthiest Negress and Gave Freely to Help Her Race," *New York Herald,* May 25, 1919.
"one of the showplaces"—*New York Herald,* May 25, 1919.
Called "the wealthiest spot of ground"—Polly Anne Graff and Stewart Graff, *Wolfert's Roost: Portrait of a Village* (Irvington-on-Hudson, NY: Washington Irving Press, 1971), p. 116.
In the "zone of the metropolis's millionaires"—R. W. Thompson, "Short Flights," *Indpls. Freeman,* undated, probably Jan. 6 or 13, 1917 (MWC/IHS).
founding families of the Ardsley Casino—Elizabeth Cushman, "Ardsley Club Founded as 'Casino' by Swells," *Tarrytown Daily News,* Sept. 14, 1931, reprinted in *The Roost* (Irvington Historical Society), p. 77; Graff and Graff, *Wolfert's Roost,* p. 117.
"the most exclusive part of Irvington"—Untitled, undated manuscript describing Villa Lewaro (MWC/IHS).
timed to bloom continuously—*New York Times Magazine,* Nov. 4, 1917; untitled, undated manuscript describing Villa Lewaro (MWC/IHS).

Page 234

Nail began searching for an alternative—MW to FBR, June 3, 1916 (MWC/IHS).

"no better spot on earth"—John E. Nail to FBR, Jan. 12, 1918 (MWC/IHS).

"Now in reference to having two mansions"—MW to FBR, May 25, 1916 (MWC/IHS).

By the end of August 1916 she had signed—Westchester County Record of Deeds, Book 2124, pp. 135 and 143, Sept. 2, 1916 (deed transferred Aug. 31, 1916, and recorded Sept. 2, 1916, for $20,000).

"I am very anxious"—MW to FBR, June 13, 1916 (MWC/IHS).

twelve-piece Louis XVI chamber suite—"Special Police Called Out to Handle Traffic," *Baltimore Afro-American*, Dec. 6, 1930.

At night yachting parties were known—*New York Times Magazine*, Nov. 4, 1917.

Page 235

"I had a dream and that dream begot"—"Mme. Walker's Objets d'Art on Block/ Ex-Laundress' Art Works on Sale," Harlem-Bronx Section of the *New York Evening Journal*, Nov. 25, 1930.

"undue extravagance"—*New York World*, Dec. 2, 1923.

"convince members of [my] race"—Ibid.

"Do not fail to mention"—MW to FBR, Sept. 14, 1918 (MWC/IHS).

"This residence will be"—Untitled, undated manuscript about Villa Lewaro (MWC/IHS).

Page 236

"object lesson to her race"—*Indpls. Freeman*, undated, probably Jan. 6 or 13, 1917.

"Every morning at six o'clock"—MW to FBR, Aug. 14, 1918 (MWC/IHS).

"Two divisions of Negro troops"—"311,308 Race Men in Khaki," *New York Age*, Aug. 31, 1918.

physically imposing and charming man—Carson A. Anderson, "The Architectural Practice of Vertner W. Tandy: An Evaluation of the Professional and Social Position of a Black Architect," master's thesis, University of Virginia School of Architecture, 1982, p. 47.

Page 237

contributing "more to architecture for Negroes"—*Report of the Eighteenth and Nineteenth Annual Sessions of the National Negro Business League, Chattanooga, Tenn., 1917, and Atlantic City, N.J., 1918* (Washington, DC: William H. Davis, 1918), p. 314.

"I want to say to you, Madam"—*1918 NNBL Report*, p. 314.

had introduced the first federal antilynching bill—George W. Reid, "George Henry White," in Logan and Winston, *DANB*, p. 645.

Maggie Lena Walker, founder of the St. Luke Penny—"Membership Enrollment at Atlanta [sic] City, N.J.," *1918 NNBL Report*, unnumbered page at end of report.

she urged the group to support the doctor's motion—Ibid., p. 315.

"I am very much in sympathy"—Ibid.

Impressed by a recent *New York Age* article—"$100,000 Fund to Combat Lynching in United States, *New York Age*, Aug. 17, 1918.

Page 238

"I told [him] I represented 20,000 Negro businessmen—*1918 NNBL Report*, p. 315.

Without further deliberation—Ibid.

"Mme. C. J. Walker . . . requests the pleasure"—Invitation to Villa Lewaro, Aug. 25, 1918, George Stewart Collection/IHS.

Madam Walker had instructed Lelia—LWR to FBR, Aug. 2, 1918 (MWC/IHS).

he objected to some of the names—LWR to FBR, July 24, 1918 (MWC/IHS).

"I have never in my life been so disturbed"—Ibid.

"I am awfully fearful"—Ibid.

Afraid that Scott "might do one of two things"—Ibid.

Among his critics were longtime adversaries—Linda O. McMurry, *To Keep the Waters Troubled: The Life of Ida B. Wells* (New York: Oxford University Press, 1998), p. 271.

Page 239

Scott had been too willing to rationalize—Lewis, *Du Bois*, p. 542.

Scott had "proposed to popularize"—Patton, *War and Race*, p. 66, cites Memorandum from Emmett J. Scott to Newton D. Baker, Secretary of War (Oct. 8, 1917), RG165, E. J. Scott Papers, National Archives.

there "was no intention on the part of the War Dept."—Baker to Scott, Nov. 21, 1917, Scott Papers, National Archives, cited in Patton, *War and Race*, pp. 83–84.

continued to enjoy "widespread support"—Patton, *War and Race*, p. 66.

"transported into a fairyland"—Bessye Bearden, "Valuables Bought by Those Who Opposed Mansion on Hudson," *Baltimore Afro-American*, Dec. 6, 1930.

"nearly 100 white and colored"—"Emmett Scott and Other Notables Dedicate Madam Walker's Villa," *Pittsburgh Courier*, Sept. 6, 1918.

violinist Joseph Douglass—Ibid.

J. Rosamond Johnson—"Conference at Villa Lewaro," *New York Age*, Aug. 31, 1918.

Page 240

performed at the World's Columbian Exposition—Southern, *The Music of Black Americans*, pp. 256, 283–84.

featured on transcontinental tours—Ibid., p. 286; Boris, *Who's Who in Colored America*, Vol. 1, p. 40.

Temple Emanu-El—"Men of the Month," *The Crisis*, Feb. 1912, p. 147.

"forget all their differences [and] stand together"—*Pittsburgh Courier*, Sept. 6, 1918.

"bloodthirsty black men"—Badger, *A Life in Ragtime*, p. 186.

December 1917 execution—Aptheker, *A Documentary History*, pp. 184–85.

hanging thirteen of them—Johnson, *Along This Way*, pp. 321–23.

Even fresher in their minds—"Shooting Black Soldiers," in Aptheker, *A Documentary History*, p. 226.

Page 241

"Every colored soldier who meets his death"—Ibid., p. 225

Arising "amidst much applause"—*Pittsburgh Courier*, Sept. 6, 1918.

"because they treated Negro draftees unfairly"—Ibid.

"colored women would be sent overseas"—Ibid.

Ransom presented several more speakers—"Conference at Villa Lewaro," *New York Age*, Aug. 31, 1918.

"emphasized the necessity of the various elements"—Ibid.

"No such assemblage has ever gathered"—Emmett Scott to MW, Aug. 28, 1918 (MWC/IHS).

Appreciative of the "manifestations of friendship"—Ibid.

field secretary of the Welfare League—George Lattimore to MW, Aug. 29, 1918 (MWC/IHS).

"transmitting . . . to our boys"—Lattimore to MW, Aug. 29, 1918 (MWC/IHS).

Page 242

"It has given me no little annoyance"—MW to Col. Wm. Jay Schieffelin, Jan. 13, 1919 (MWC/IHS).

"I feel it necessary"—Ibid.

"The Negro in the south . . . has been denied the use of firearms"—Ibid.

"Now they will soon be returning. To what?"—Ibid.

"They will come back to face like men"—Ibid.

"Please understand that this does not mean that I wish"—Ibid.

Page 243

"I have tried so very hard to make you see the thing"—Ibid.

"By the God of heaven"—W.E.B. Du Bois, "Returning Soldiers," *The Crisis*, Vol. 18 (May 1919), pp. 13–14, in Herbert Aptheker, ed., *Selections from The Crisis*, Vol. 1, pp. 196–97; Theodore Kornweibel, Jr., *Seeing Red: Federal Campaign Against Black Militancy: 1919–1925* (Bloomington: Indiana University Press, 1998), p. 57; Lewis, *Du Bois*, p. 578.

We return—W.E.B. Du Bois, "Returning Soldiers," *The Crisis*, Vol. 18 (May 1919), pp. 13–14, in Aptheker, *Selections from The Crisis*, Vol. 1, pp. 196–97.

"Negroes will come back feeling like men"—Moorfield Storey quoted in David Levering Lewis, *When Harlem Was in Vogue* (New York: Alfred A. Knopf, 1981), p. 15.

"Am still getting up to work in the garden"—MW to FBR, undated (perhaps Sept. 17, 1918) (MWC/IHS).

Page 244

"are following the sun beams"—MW to Jessie Robinson, Sept. 22, 1918 (MWC/IHS).

"Am grateful for the warm weather"—MW or Villa to FBR, Oct. 3, 1918 (MWC/IHS).

her income taxes . . . were due "at once"—MW to Righter & Kolb, undated (possibly Sept. 1918) (MWC/IHS).

"After you take care of taxes"—FBR to MW, Sept. 13, 1918 (MWC/IHS).

"If I do not buy in Harlem"—MW to FBR, Sept. 27, 1918 (MWC/IHS).

"When I explained my intention"—MW to FBR, Oct. 8, 1918 (MWC/IHS).

"Never has the old Puritan city seen"—"Boston Lifts the Lid Today" and "Seen in Newspaper Row," *Boston Evening Globe*, Nov. 11, 1918, pp. 1 and 2.

Page 245

Businessmen in pinstripes—Ibid.

"It seems that the whole country"—MW to FBR, Nov. 14, 1918 (MWC/IHS).

"Lelia and I had a very pleasant trip"—MW to FBR, Dec. 1, 1918 (MWC/IHS).

"was especially courteous to us"—MW or Irvington to FBR, Dec. 4, 1918 (MWC/IHS).

a "splendid time"—LWR to FBR, Nov. 30, 1918 (MWC/IHS).

A tall, "olive-brown"—Dorothy Butler phone interview with author, Apr. 9, 2000.

"commanding son of a gun"—Marion R. Perry, Jr., interview with author, June 17, 1982.

New York Age later reported—"Weds Three Days After Burial of Her Mother," *New York Age*, June 14, 1919.

It is entirely possible—Marion R. Perry interview with author, Oct. 7, 1982.

They may also have met—*Gould's St. Louis Directory*, 1914.

Page 246

a "shower" of birthday cards—FBR to MW, Dec. 19, 1918 (MWC/IHS).

Peggie Prosser, had arrived—MW to FBR, Dec. 20, 1918 (MWC/IHS); FBR to MW, Dec. 21, 1918 (MWC/IHS).

"somewhat like the goods that soldiers"—MW to FBR, Dec. 19, 1918.

Spanish teacher at Dunbar—"Miss H. E. Queen, Dunbar Teacher's Funeral Arranged,"

Washington Tribune, Oct. 12, 1940; "Miss Hallie Queen, Dunbar Teacher, Buried in Harmony," *Washington Post*, Oct. 13, 1940, clippings (from Charles Cooney).

master's degree from Stanford—Boris, *Who's Who in Colored America*, Vol. 1, p. 164; *Washington Tribune*, Oct. 12, 1940.

A.B. from Cornell—*Washington Tribune*, Oct. 12, 1940; *Washington Post*, Oct. 13, 1940.

Fluent in Spanish, French and German—Hallie Queen File on microfilm in RG 165, Records of the War Department and Special Staffs; Name Index to Correspondence of the Military Intelligence Division of the War Department Staff, 1917–1941, M1194.

chairman of Howard University's Red Cross and relief work done during the East St. Louis riots—*Washington Tribune*, Oct. 12, 1940.

"Negro subversion"—Lewis, *Du Bois*, p. 559.

to "carry out surveillance"—Patton, *War and Race*, p. 76 n. 73, cites RG 165, 10218 MID, 1917–1941, NARS.

reports to the War Department . . . ended in November 1918—Hallie Queen File on microfilm in RG 165, Records of the War Department.

"no German propaganda [was] carried"—Ibid.

"The building and grounds"—Hallie E. Queen, "The Last Christmas Day," undated (MWC/IHS).

Page 247

was "gracious, cordial and unaffected"—Ibid.

"Well did they show the largesse"—Ibid.

"It was significant that in that beautiful state dining room"—Ibid.

sculptor, whose work had been exhibited—"Men of the Month," *The Crisis*, Vol. 4, No. 2 (June 1912), p. 67.

"The personnel of that . . . party"—Queen, "The Last Christmas Day."

Page 248

"magnificent selection of books"—Ibid.

Early the next morning—Ibid.

At the mayor's personal invitation—Grover A. Whalen (Secretary to Mayor John S. Hylan) to MW, Dec. 7, 1918 (MWC/IHS); Queen, "The Last Christmas Day."

Although the first severe snowstorm and "twilight gloom"— "Ovation to Sea Fighters," "Ships Pass in Review" and "Mayor's Fleet of Welcome," *New York Times*, Dec. 27, 1918; "Thick Weather Dims View of Dreadnaughts," *New York Evening Post*, Dec. 26, 1918.

Her 1918 earnings had jumped to $275,937.88—FBR to MW, Jan. 6, 1919 (MWC/IHS).

"Your receipts exceeded over a quarter of a million"—Ibid.

"You should congratulate yourself"—FBR to MW, Jan. 23, 1919 (MWC/IHS).

Even with the wartime supply problems—FBR to MW, Dec. 16, 1918 (second of two letters on Dec. 16) (MWC/IHS).

Page 249

"You will be surprised at the number of parlors"—FBR to MW, Jan. 23, 1919 (MWC/IHS).

Even the conflicts with the agents—FBR to MW, Jan. 1919, undated partial letter (MWC/IHS).

introducing a line of facial products—FBR to MW, Jan. 14, 1919 (MWC/IHS).

"This makes an apparent deficit"—FBR to MW, Jan. 6, 1919 (incorrectly dated as Jan. 6, 1918) (MWC/IHS).

"For instance, your receipts for Monday . . . were over $2,000"—FBR to MW, Jan. 1919, undated partial letter (MWC/IHS).

By month's end the company had taken in $26,477.43—FBR to MW, Feb. 3, 1919, #2 (MWC/IHS).

a 3.38-carat solitaire—Tiffany & Co. to MW, Mar. 8, 1919 (MWFC/APB).

CHAPTER 20 GLOBAL VISIONS

Page 250

"By the help of God"—*Report of the Thirteenth Annual Convention of the National Negro Business League, held at Chicago, Illinois, Aug. 21–23, 1912,* p. 155.

"for the purpose of founding"—*Report of the Fifteenth Annual Convention of the National Negro Business League, held at Muskogee, Oklahoma, August 19–21, 1914* (Nashville: AME Sunday School Union, 1914), p. 52.

Then in 1914 she contributed funds—FBR to Ella Croker, Nov. 19, 1914 (MWC/IHS).

she offered $1,000 and "start a little Tuskegee Institute in Africa"—*Report of the Seventeenth Annual Convention of the National Negro Business League, held at Kansas City, Missouri, Aug. 16–18, 1916* (Washington, DC: William H. Davis, 1916), p. 135. (The school that Madam Walker envisioned was never built.)

"seven African . . . girls"—*Indpls. Freeman,* Dec. 28, 1912.

Emma Bertha Delaney—Sylvia Jacobs, "Emma Bertha Delaney," in Hine et al., *Black Women in America,* p. 316.

black Civil War veterans . . . frequently met—Painter, *Exodusters,* p. 141.

Page 251

to help pay the salaries—Sylvia Jacobs phone conversation with author, Apr. 4, 2000.

"Africa for the Africans"—C. Eric Lincoln and Lawrence H. Mamiya, *The Black Church in the African American Experience* (Durham: Duke University Press, 1990), p. 74.

president of the Pan-African Association—John E. Fleming, "Alexander Walters," in Logan and Winston, *DANB,* p. 631.

German East Africa is now Tanzania. German Southwest Africa is now Namibia, ruled by Germany since the Berlin Conference—Belinda Cooper, "Germany," in Appiah and Gates, *Africana,* p. 827.

control of nearly 90 percent—Elizabeth Heath, "Berlin Conference of 1884–85," in Appiah and Gates, *Africana,* p. 226.

"wild quest for Imperial expansion"—W.E.B. Du Bois, "World War and the Color Line," *The Crisis,* Nov. 1914, p. 28.

what Du Bois called "the civilized Negro world"—Elliott P. Skinner, *African Americans and the U.S. Policy Toward Africa, 1850–1924* (Washington, DC: Howard University Press, 1992), p. 390.

Page 252

"The more I think about the President's declaration"—Robert Lansing, "Self-Determination and the Dangers," Lansing Papers, Private Memorandum, 1915–1922, Container 63 (reel 1), Manuscript Division, LOC.

"not vital to the life of the world in any respect"—William Roger Lewis, "The United States and the African Peace Settlement: The Pilgrimage of George Louis Beer," *Journal of African History,* Vol. 4 (1963), pp. 413–33, cited in Skinner, *African Americans,* p. 408.

passports for six "carefully selected"—Du Bois to Robert Lansing, Nov. 27, 1918, Du Bois Papers (Amherst), Reel 7, Frame 87, LOC.

"It would be a calamity"—Ibid.

recommended denying travel documents—Frank Polk to Robert Lansing, Dec. 20, 1918, RG 256, RACNP/LOC, File 138–12 (Microfilm M820, Reel 48).

"I think your inclination not to grant passports"—Lansing to Polk, Dec. 21, 1918, Ibid.

Wilson already had excluded Republicans—Laurence Urdang, ed., *The Timetables of American History* (New York: Simon and Schuster, 1981), pp. 295–96.

Page 253

black Americans . . . intent upon raising embarrassing questions—Skinner, *African Americans*, pp. 393–94, cites Clarence G. Contee, "Du Bois, the NAACP, and the Pan-African Congress of 1919," *Journal of Negro History*, Vol. 57 (Jan. 1972), pp. 13–28.

"only quick and adroit work"—W.E.B. Du Bois, *Dusk of Dawn* (New York: Schocken Books, 1968), pp. 260–61, cited in Skinner, *African Americans*, p. 396.

"The leading Negroes of the U.S. will ask"—*New York Herald*, Dec. 12, 1918, cited in Skinner, *African Americans*, p. 397.

"I talked with Emmett Scott"—FBR to MW, Nov. 27, 1918 (MWC/IHS).

"domestic questions cannot and will not be thrashed out"—FBR to MW, Jan. 6, 1919 (incorrectly dated as Jan. 6, 1918) (MWC/IHS).

traveled to Washington to attend Trotter's National Race Congress—Walter H. Loving report to Director of Military Intelligence on National Race Congress, Dec. 20, 1918, RG 165, File 10218-302, Records of the War Dept. General and Special Staffs, Correspondence of the Military Intelligence Division Relating to "Negro Subversion," Microfilm M1440.

"by unanimous vote"—W. Stephenson Holder to MW, Dec. 12, 1918 (MWC/IHS).

"I wish you might have been at that conference"—MW to FBR, Dec. 19, 1918 (MWC/IHS).

Page 254

all "the names submitted, even to the Bishops"—Ibid.

such "a clamor arose"—Duster, ed., *Crusade for Justice*, p. 380.

she "regretted that the years spent in fighting"—Ibid.

"Mrs. B. registered a strong protest"—MW to FBR, Dec. 19, 1918.

"Since they have elected me"—Ibid.

"Monroe Trotter may be all right"—FBR to MW, Jan. 11, 1919 (MWC/IHS).

"I hope you will be very careful"—FBR to MW, Dec. 24, 1918 (MWC/IHS).

Major Walter H. Loving . . . had personally visited Abbott—Theodore Kornweibel, Jr., *"Seeing Red"—Federal Campaigns Against Black Militancy 1919–1925* (Bloomington: Indiana University Press, 1998), p. 39.

Page 255

"convinced the paper promoted racial hatred"—Ibid.

"professions of patriotism"—Ibid.

State Department had stepped up its surveillance—Ibid., p. 4.

"appearance of disloyalty"—Ibid., p. 5.

Near the end of the war—Ibid., p. 3.

After the war, MID operatives continued to spy—Ibid., p. 12.

"I am seriously of the opinion"—FBR to MW, Dec. 24, 1918.

"one of a half dozen" and "indefatigable"—Lewis, *Du Bois*, p. 559.

former music director—Southern, *The Music of Black Americans*, p. 307.

Any aggressive protest—Kornweibel, *"Seeing Red,"* p. 9.

Page 256

"a well-concerted movement"—U.S. Senate, *Investigation Activities of the Department of*

Justice, 66th Congress, 1st Session, Senate Document 153 (Washington, DC, 1919), pp. 172–73, cited in ibid.

filled with "defiance and insolently race-centered"—Kornweibel, *"Seeing Red,"* p. 9.

"confided the fear that black soldiers"—Diary of Dr. Cary T. Grayson, Mar. 10, 1919, *Woodrow Wilson Papers*, Vol. 55, p. 471, cited in ibid., p. 37.

"puzzled by and cynical about the desire"—Skinner, *African Americans*, p. 395.

"This business of electing delegates"—*New York Age*, Dec. 21, 1918, p. 4, cited in Fox, *The Guardian of Boston*, pp. 223–24.

"We feel that our unselfish devotion"—George R. Cannon, "Representation at Race Conference Asked," *New York Age*, Nov. 7, 1918.

"the Allied Powers . . . hand over ex-German colonies"—Tony Martin, *Race First: The Ideological and Organizational Struggles of Marcus Garvey and the Universal Negro Improvement Association* (Dover, MA: The Majority Press, 1976), p. 11.

the Hamitic League—Skinner, *African Americans*, p. 395.

"Bruce Grit" column—Ernest Kaiser, "John Edward [Bruce Grit] Bruce," in Logan and Winston, *DANB*, p. 76. (Bruce also wrote a column for Marcus Garvey's *Negro World*.)

Page 257

"engage world opinion"—"Villa Lewaro-on-the-Hudson, Birthplace of International League of Darker Peoples," *The World Forum*, Jan. 1919 (from RG 165, File 10218-296, Records of the War Dept. General and Special Staffs, Correspondence of the Military Intelligence Division Relating to "Negro Subversion," M1440, Reel 5).

Oxford-style English he had learned—Paula F. Pfeffer, *A. Philip Randolph: Pioneer of the Civil Rights Movement* (Baton Rouge: Louisiana State University Press, 1990), p. 8.

"Rapacious and unscrupulous 'world power' politics"—The World Forum, Jan. 1919.

Under its plan, a "supernational"—Ibid.

teach "chemistry, physics, biology"—Ibid.

"If peace can be secured"—Ibid.

"utterly impossible as well as impractical"—FBR to MW, Jan. 25, 1919, #3 (MWC/IHS).

"It seems strange to me"—FBR to MW, Jan. 17, 1919 (MWC/IHS).

"Of course, they have your name"—FBR to MW, Jan. 25, 1919, #1 (MWC/IHS).

Page 258

in the "spirit of race internationalism"—*The World Forum*, Jan. 1919.

"assured the delegation of his unqualified and genuine approval"—Ibid.

Harboring their own expansionist objectives—Heckscher, *Woodrow Wilson*, pp. 520 and 566.

"the next war would pit white nations"—Kornweibel, "Seeing Red," p. 101.

"If Japan and China raised"—"The Race Issue at the Peace Table," *New York Age*, Nov. 30, 1918.

"There is no sympathy between Japan"—FBR to MW, Jan. 25, 1919, #3.

who was said to have arranged the Kuriowa meeting—Robert A. Hill, ed., *The Marcus Garvey and Universal Negro Improvement Association Papers*, Vol. 1: 1826–August 1919 (Berkeley: University of California Press, 1983), p. 345.

Page 259

"We admonish Negroes not to be appealed to"—A. Philip Randolph and Chandler Owen, "Japan and the Far East" *The Messenger*, July 1918, p. 23.

had "no faith in the management"—FBR to MW, Jan. 25, 1919, #1 (MWC/IHS)

"You will have to watch your League"—FBR to MW, Jan. 17, 1919.

"beginning to grow seriously apprehensive"—FBR to MW, Jan. 25, 1919, #1.

For at least a year this undercover operative—Kornweibel, *"Seeing Red,"* p. 80.

Jonas also approached the Justice Department's Bureau of Investigation—Ibid. (The Bureau of Investigation became the Federal Bureau of Investigation in 1936.)

"recruiting black, Japanese, Hindu and Chinese"—Ibid.

Now, presumably, Madam Walker's name had been added—A Freedom of Information Act request for FBI files on Madam Walker yielded no information. (J. Kevin O'Brien, Chief, Freedom of Information Privacy Acts Section, Federal Bureau of Investigation, U.S. Department of Justice, letter to author, Dec. 3, 1993, regarding Request No. 376915 and 376916/C. J. Walker and A'Lelia Walker.)

"nothing about the man Randolph"—FBR to MW, Jan 25, 1919, #1. As founder of the Brotherhood of Sleeping Car Porters and as an organizer of the 1963 March on Washington, Randolph would become one of the most important black political leaders of the twentieth century.

Page 260
The dignified and eloquent son—Anderson, A. *Philip Randolph,* p. 44.

While taking night classes—Pfeffer, A. *Philip Randolph,* p. 8.

Randolph with his rich baritone—Anderson, *Randolph,* p. 77.

"His delivery was . . . impeccable"—Ibid., p. 78.

Madam Walker and Randolph probably first met—Ibid., p. 70.

With her own salon on 135th Street—Ibid.

a light-skinned woman—Ibid.

Lucille had run . . . for the New York state legislature—Kornweibel, *"Seeing Red,"* p. 77.

Her "considerable income"—Anderson, *Randolph,* pp. 71 and 75.

"work for a salary"—Ibid., p.78.

"We were on an uncharted sea"—Ibid.

the magazine's second issue—Kornweibel, *"Seeing Red,"* p. 77.

"Without her money"—Anderson, *Randolph,* p. 82.

Page 261
"never saw . . . at a dance or a party"—Ibid., p. 72.

"sometimes invited him to Madam Walker's parties"—Ibid.

"She was a woman of common sense"—"The Reminiscences of A. Philip Randolph," transcript of interview by Wendell Wray, 1972, pp. 124, 128–29 and 137, Oral History Research, Columbia University.

"She was not a literate woman"—Ibid.

"no intelligent Negro is willing"—Anderson, *Randolph,* p. 104, cites *The Messenger,* July 1918.

"growth of socialism, which is the death of capitalism"—Randolph and Owen, "Japan and the Far East," p. 22; "Who's Who: Mme. C. J. Walker," *The Messenger,* July 1918, p. 30.

"a factor in the economic, political"—FBR to MW, Jan. 25, 1919, Letter #1.

Page 262
"I know you are fond of Louis George" Ibid.

"It evidently did not occur"—FBR to MW, Jan. 27, 1919 (MWC/IHS).

"I, for one, am sorry"—FBR to MW, Jan. 25, 1919, #3.

"identified with the socialist element" and "Diplomatic, persistent"—FBR to MW, Jan 6, 1919 (incorrectly dated as Jan. 6, 1918).

"The only thing I am concerned"—FBR to MW, Jan. 11, 1919.

"I am glad to note that you are not"—FBR to MW, Feb. 1, 1919, #2 (MWC/IHS).

"Owing to the fact"—FBR to MW, Feb. 3, 1919, #1 (MWC/IHS); "Mme. C. J. Walker Quits Newly Formed League," *New York Age*, Feb. 8, 1919.

Page 263

"While I believe in the objects"—"Dr. Powell Resigns As Head of League," *New York Age*, Mar. 15, 1919.

Without their backing, the International League of Darker People collapsed—Hill, *Marcus Garvey Papers*, Vol. 1, p. 345.

"buy and sell toilet preparations"—"Affidavit in support of application for a passport to go abroad on commercial business," Feb. 5, 1919.

Certainly her most recent advertisements—"A Million Eyes Turned Upon It Daily," Walker ad, *New York Age*, Feb. 18, 1919.

"merely subterfuge to get to the peace conference"—FBR to MW, Feb. 5, 1919 (MWC/IHS).

The Wilson administration . . . was "quite determined"—Ibid.

"If you are not going to make a bonafide effort"—Ibid.

"I was afraid that your name had been sent in"—FBR to MW, Feb. 17, 1919 (MWC/IHS).

Page 264

"If passports are to be requested for the above"—W. H. Loving report on National Race Congress, Dec. 20, 1918.

refuse passports for all National Race Congress delegates—Acting Chief, FBI, to R. W. Flournoy, State Dept., from RG 65, Records of the Federal Bureau of Investigation, File OG 336880 (Microfilm M1085). The Acting Chief, not formally appointed until Feb. 10, 1919, was William E. Allen (per Maureen Grenke, FBI Research Office, phone conversation with author, Apr. 5, 2000).

"more or less agitators"—Ibid.

"first major interference in African American politics"—Kornweibel, "*Seeing Red,*" p. 15.

no "formal policy barring black travelers"—Ibid.

Madam Walker sent a personal check for $25—MW to James Weldon Johnson, Feb. 15, 1919, NAACP Papers, Part I (1909–1959), Administrative File, Subject File, Pan African Congress, LOC; Johnson to Executive Committee of NAACP New York Branch, Feb. 11, 1919, NAACP Papers, LOC.

Having just received a cable from Paris—Johnson to MW, Feb. 19, 1919, NAACP Papers, LOC.

"In private advices from Dr. Du Bois"—Ibid.

"sixteen nations, protectorates and colonial entities"—Lewis, *Du Bois*, p. 574.

Page 265

"unable to grant passports"—"Cannot Attend Conference to Be Held in Paris in Feb'y," *New York Age*, Feb. 8, 1919.

"convinced that Allied officials had effectively sabotaged"—Skinner, *African Americans*, pp. 407–8.

But on the very day he reached Paris—Fox, *The Guardian of Boston*, p. 226.

still hoping to . . . lobby for a racial equality clause—Stephen R. Fox, "William Monroe Trotter," in Logan and Winston, *DANB*, p. 605; Heckscher, *Woodrow Wilson*, p. 567.

And although the Japanese delegation had met with Colonel House—"Japanese Again Bring Up the Race Question," *New York Age*, undated clipping (1919).

A'LELIA WALKER: AN AFTERWORD

Page 279

she hoped to "find" herself—JAK to LWR, Feb. 2, 1922 (MWFC/APB).

"excellent write-up in the French papers"—JAK to LWR, Dec. 30, 1921 (MWFC/APB).

"*négresse*"—LWR to the editor of *L'Intransigeant*, MSRC, OG Folder, #276, 1921.

"I am utterly surprised"—Ibid.

"Her appearance . . . was so spectacular"—Bruce Kellner, ed., *"Keep a-Inchin' Along": Selected Writings of Carl Van Vechten about Black Art and Letters* (Westport, CT: Greenwood Press, 1979), p. 154.

In Addis Ababa, she became the first American—"Mrs. Lelia Wilson Guest of Abyssinian Empress," *Chicago Defender*, Mar. 25, 1922.

Page 280

"I think of the whole of Europe"—JAK to LWR, Dec. 8, 1921 (MWFC/APB).

$486,762 in 1919—Sale of Products, undated document, circa 1936 (MWFC/APB).

Page 281

"I do not know of anything that can be done"—LWR to FBR, Dec. 8, 1923 (MWC/IHS).

"I feel we have exploited this field" and "Everything has its day"—LWR to FBR, Nov. 13, 1923 (MWC/IHS).

"the Negro was in vogue"—Langston Hughes, *The Big Sea* (New York: Hill and Wang, 1981; originally published 1930), pp. 223–28.

all hoped their cultural revolution—Arnold Rampersad, "Introduction" in Alain Locke, ed., *The New Negro: Voices of the Harlem Renaissance* (New York: Macmillan, 1992; originally published by Albert & Charles Boni, 1925), p. xvi.

"now surpasses that of Broadway"—*Variety*, Oct. 16, 1929.

desire of "a generation of Americans to lose themselves" and "postwar hangover"—Huggins, *Harlem Renaissance*, p. 289.

Page 282

"America was going on the greatest, gaudiest spree"—F. Scott Fitzgerald, *This Side of Paradise* (New York: Charles Scribner & Sons, 1920).

"She wanted to miss nothing"—Edgar Rouzeau, "The Walkers: A Condensed History of the Lives of A'Lelia and Her Mother," Part V, *Inter-State Tattler*, Sept. 10, 1931.

"She looked like a queen"—Kellner, *"Keep a-Inchin' Along,"* p. 154.

"a gorgeous dark Amazon"—Hughes, *The Big Sea*, p. 245.

190 pounds—Rouzeau, "The Walkers."

"She had a superb figure"—Ibid.

"without beauty but of fine physique"—W.E.B. Du Bois, "A'Lelia Walker," *The Crisis*, Oct. 1931, p. 351.

A'Lelia "made no pretense of being intellectual"—Hughes, *The Big Sea*, p. 244.

"could engage you in conversation"—*Inter-State Tattler*, Aug. 27, 1931.

"the art of reading headlines"—Ibid., cited in Carole Marks and Diana Edkins, *The Power of Pride: Stylemakers and Rulebreakers of the Harlem Renaissance* (New York: Crown, 1999), p. 71.

"seven minutes"—Lewis, *When Harlem Was in Vogue*, p. 166.

"one of the most subtly humorous"—Edward G. Perry, "Impressions," *Inter-State Tattler*, undated, p. 8 (MWFC/APB).

"At her 'at homes'"—Hughes, *The Big Sea*, p. 244.

Page 283

voice teacher Casca Bonds—Perry, "Impressions."

well-known bootlegger—Bruce Kellner, ed., *The Harlem Renaissance: A Historical Dictionary for the Era* (Westport, CT: Greenwood Press, 1984), p. 343.

"were filled with guests whose names"—Hughes, *The Big Sea,* pp. 223–28.

she "sent word back that she saw no way"—Ibid., pp. 244–45.

a large swath of rose and green taffeta—Max Ewing to his parents, Apr. 29, 1929, Beinecke Collection, Yale University.

"jade, velvet, metal, ivory and ebony"—"Walker Heiress Dies Suddenly Sunday Night," *Baltimore Afro-American,* Aug. 22, 1931.

Jules Bledsoe—Edward G. Perry, "Royalty and Blue-blooded Gentry Entertained by A'Lelia Walker at Lewaro and Townhouse," *Amsterdam News,* Aug. 26, 1931.

"You have never seen such clothes"—Max Ewing to parents, Apr. 29, 1929.

Page 284

"I look upon this wedding"—LWR to FBR, Nov. 13, 1923 (MWC/IHS).

"This is the swellest wedding"—LWR to FBR, Nov. 17, 1923 (MWC/IHS).

"white and colored, drawn out of curiosity"—*St. Louis Argus,* Nov. 30, 1912.

Inside the sanctuary—*New York Age,* Dec. 1, 1923.

The bridesmaids—*St. Louis Argus,* Nov. 30, 1912.

"gasps of admiration"—*St. Louis Post-Dispatch,* Nov. 27, 1923.

Page 285

helped support the Piney Branch—Kellner, *"Keep a-Inchin' Along,"* p. 5.

"fully integrated guest lists"—Ibid., p. 8.

"cheap melodrama"—W.E.B. Du Bois review, *The Crisis,* Dec. 1926, reprinted in Carl Van Vechten, *Nigger Heaven* (New York: Harper Colophon Books, 1971; originally published by Alfred A. Knopf, 1926), pp. vii–ix.

"a fine novel"—Johnson, *Along This Way,* p. 382.

by writing "frequent magazine articles"—Ibid.

"She was undeniably warm-hearted"—Van Vechten, *Nigger Heaven,* p. 21.

her "good heart"—Ibid.

"She was beautiful"—Ibid., p. 28.

Page 286

"Frowned upon in many quarters"—Ibid., p. 21.

With a first printing of 16,000 copies—Kellner, *"Keep a-Inchin' Along,"* p. 77.

"the most discussed women"—Perry, "Impressions."

something "completely informal . . . homey"—Richard Bruce Nugent, "On the Dark Tower," FWP/SCRBC; Perry, "Royalty and Blue-blooded Gentry."

"We dedicate this tower"—Invitation to The Dark Tower (MWFC/APB).

"Colored faces were at a premium"—Nugent, "On the Dark Tower."

Page 287

Dark rose tables—William Pickens, "The Dark Tower," undated, unpublished (MWFC/APB).

"Having no talent or gift"—"Dear Members"/Dark Tower Closing (MWFC/APB).

$350,000 headquarters—FBR to LWR, Apr. 13, 1931 (MWFC/APB).

"It is the culmination of the dream"—*Amsterdam News,* June 15, 1927.

Page 288

revenues had dipped to $213,327—Sale of Products, undated document, circa 1936 (MWFC/APB).

forced to rent the 136th Street town house—"Mme. Walker's Palace Finery Sold at Auction," *New York Herald,* Nov. 11, 1929.

26,355 businesses had failed—T. H. Watkins, *The Great Depression: America in the 1930s* (Boston: Little, Brown, 1993), p. 55.

That fall the trustees of the Walker estate—"Sightseers Hamper Villa Lewaro Sale," *New York Times*, Nov. 28, 1930.

cardboard tags hung—*New York Herald*, Nov. 11, 1929.

"What am I bid"—Ibid.

Arthur Lawrence, the president—"Sale of Villa Lewaro Nets $58,500," *Pittsburgh Courier*, undated.

twenty cents on the dollar—"Buyers Throng Mme. Walker's Mansion at Sale," *New York Herald Tribune*, Nov. 30, 1930.

"Worry won't help matters"—LWR to Walker Employees, Western Union Holiday Greeting, Dec. 22, 1930.

"Dear Co-worker"—FBR to "Co-workers," Western Union Holiday Greeting, Dec. 22, 1930.

Page 289

employed 128,000 workers before the Crash—Howard Zinn, *A People's History of the United States, 1492–Present* (New York: HarperCollins, 1995), p. 378.

"I have been holding on to this place"—Jervis Anderson, *This Was Harlem 1900–1950* (New York: Farrar, Straus and Giroux, 1981), p. 229.

"But, dear A'Lelia, what would I do"—Carl Van Vechten to LWR, Aug. 10, 1930 (MWFC/APB).

annual upkeep of $8,000—"Estimated Cost of Upkeep of Villa Lewaro for 1931," Mar. 25, 1931 (MWFC/APB).

the factory's mortgage—FBR to LWR, Apr. 13, 1931.

"There was no place in A'Lelia's life"—Rouzeau, "The Walkers."

Page 290

"In love and in marriage"—Kellner, *"Keep a-Inchin' Along,"* p. 154.

"We are merely taking in money enough"—FBR to LWR, Aug. 12, 1931 (MWFC/APB).

At 5:03 the next morning she was pronounced dead—A'Lelia Walker Death Certificate, City of Long Branch, Long Branch, New Jersey, Aug. 17, 1931.

The mourners were "mostly women"—"11,000 Persons View Body of A'Lelia Walker," *Philadelphia Tribune*, undated (MSRC).

silver-and-amber ring—"Throngs of Morbidly Curious Crowd Street," *New York Age*, Aug. 29, 1931.

Three orchids—Ibid.

two dozen orchids—"A'Lelia Walker Buried in $3,500 Bronze Casket," *Baltimore Afro-American*, Aug. 29, 1931.

"But, just as for her parties"—Hughes, *The Big Sea*, p. 246.

"motionless in the dim light"—Ibid.

Mae, Marion, Mayme—*Baltimore Afro-American*, Aug. 29, 1931.

Page 291

The Van Vechtens—Ibid.

The Bon Bons, a female quartet, opened—"11,000 Persons View Body."

"I'll See You Again"—*Baltimore Afro-American*, Aug. 29, 1931.

speaking "in that great deep voice of hers"—Hughes, *The Big Sea*, p. 246.

several Walker agents lined up to place flowers—Ibid., pp. 246–47.

the flower-filled space—*Philadelphia Tribune*, undated (MSRC).

Julian . . . dropped two bouquets—"A'Lelia Walker Buried in $5,000 Air Tight Casket," ANP clipping (MSRC).

"That was really the end of the gay times"—Hughes, *The Big Sea*, p. 247.

"The happy, hapless life"—"The Death of A'Lelia Walker," *New York News & Harlem Home Journal,* Aug. 22, 1931.

Calling her "generous and free-handed"—W.E.B. Du Bois, "A'Lelia Walker," *The Crisis,* Oct. 1931, p. 351.

Page 292

"A'Lelia's wealth had packed too many thrills"—Rouzeau, "The Walkers."

"I had everything I wanted"—Marion R. Perry, Jr., to author, undated, family oral history.

"You should have known A'Lelia Walker"—Kellner, *The Harlem Renaissance,* p. 282.

Selected Bibliography

Books

Adele Logan Alexander, *Homelands and Waterways: The American Journey of the Bond Family, 1846–1926* (New York: Pantheon Books, 1999).

James D. Anderson, *The Education of Blacks in the South, 1860–1935* (Chapel Hill, NC: University of North Carolina Press, 1988).

Jervis Anderson, *A. Philip Randolph: A Biographical Portrait* (New York: Harvest Books/Harcourt Brace Jovanovich, 1973).

———, *This Was Harlem 1900–1950* (New York: Farrar, Straus and Giroux, 1981).

John Q. Anderson, *Brokenburn: The Journal of Kate Stone, 1861–1868* (Baton Rouge: Louisiana State University Press, 1972).

Kwame Anthony Appiah and Henry Louis Gates, Jr., eds., *Africana: The Encyclopedia of the African and African American Experience* (New York: Basic Civitas Books, 1999).

Herbert Aptheker, ed., *A Documentary History of the Negro People in the United States, Vol. 2: From Reconstruction to the Founding of the N.A.A.C.P.* (New York: Citadel Press, 1990).

———, *A Documentary History of the Negro People in the United States, 1910–1932, Vol. 3* (New York: Citadel Press, 1973, reprint 1993).

Reid Badger, *A Life in Ragtime: A Biography of James Reese Europe* (New York: Oxford University Press, 1995).

Ray Stannard Baker, *Following the Color Line* (New York: Doubleday, 1908).

Edward A. Berlin, *King of Ragtime: Scott Joplin and His Era* (New York: Oxford University Press, 1994).

Caroline Bird, *Enterprising Women* (New York: W. W. Norton, 1976).

Khaled J. Bloom, *The Mississippi Valley's Great Yellow Fever Epidemic of 1878* (Baton Rouge: Louisiana State University Press, 1993).

David J. Bodenhamer and Robert G. Barrows, eds., *Encyclopedia of Indianapolis* (Bloomington: Indiana University Press, 1994).

John Bodnar, Roger Simon and Michael P. Weber, *Lives of Their Own: Blacks, Italians and Poles of Pittsburgh 1900–1960* (Urbana: University of Illinois Press, 1982).

Paul F. Boller, Jr., *Presidential Anecdotes* (New York: Oxford University Press, 1996).

Joseph J. Boris, ed., *Who's Who in Colored America, Vol. 1* (New York: Who's Who in Colored America Corp., 1927).

Eric Breitbart, *A World on Display: Photographs from the St. Louis World's Fair 1904* (Albuquerque: University of New Mexico Press, 1997).

A'Lelia Perry Bundles, *Madam C. J. Walker: Entrepreneur* (New York: Chelsea House, 1991).

Mary Butler, Frances Thornton and Garth "Duff" Stoltz, *The Battle Creek Idea: Dr. John Harvey Kellogg and the Battle Creek Sanitarium* (Battle Creek, MI: Heritage Publications, 1998).

Horace R. Cayton and St. Clair Drake, *Black Metropolis* (London: Jonathan Cape, 1946).

The Chicago Commission on Race Relations, *The Negro in Chicago* (Chicago: University of Chicago Press, 1922).

Charles M. Christian, *Black Saga: The African American Experience* (Boston: Houghton Mifflin, 1985).

Cyprian Clamorgan, *The Colored Aristocracy of St. Louis* (1858).

Katharine T. Corbett and Howard S. Miller, *Saint Louis in the Gilded Age* (St. Louis: Missouri Historical Society Press, 1993).

Jeffrey J. Crow, Paul D. Escott and Flora J. Hatley, *A History of African Americans in North Carolina* (Raleigh, NC: North Carolina Division of Archives and History, 1994).

Susan Curtis, *Dancing to a Black Man's Tune: A Life of Scott Joplin* (Columbia: University of Missouri Press, 1994).

John Richard Dennett, *The South As It Is, 1865–1866* (Baton Rouge: Louisiana State University Press, 1965).

Scott Derks, ed., *The Value of a Dollar: Prices and Incomes in the United States* (Detroit: Gale Research, 1994).

Howard Dodson, Christopher Moore and Roberta Yancy, *The Black New Yorkers: The Schomburg Illustrated Chronology* (New York: John Wiley & Sons, 2000).

Lyle W. Dorsett, *The Queen City: A History of Denver* (Boulder, CO: Pruett Publishing Company, 1977).

Ann Douglas, *Terrible Honesty: Mongrel Manhattan in the 1920s* (New York: Farrar, Straus and Giroux, 1995).

W.E.B. Du Bois, *Black Reconstruction: An Essay Toward a History of the Part Which Black Folk Played in the Attempt to Reconstruct Democracy in America, 1860–1880* (New York: Harcourt, Brace, 1935).

———, *The Souls of Black Folk* (New York: Everyman's Library/Alfred A. Knopf, 1993; originally published 1903).

Alfreda M. Duster, ed., *Crusade for Justice: The Autobiography of Ida B. Wells* (Chicago: University of Chicago Press, 1970).

John Eaton, *Grant, Lincoln, and the Freedmen: Reminiscences of the Civil War with Special Reference to the Work for the Contrabands and Freedmen of the Mississippi Valley* (New York: Longmans, Green, 1907).

Edward Robb Ellis, *The Epic of New York City: A Narrative History* (New York: Kodansha International, 1997; originally published 1966).

Abraham Epstein, *The Negro Migrant in Pittsburgh* (Pittsburgh, University of Pittsburgh School of Economics, 1918).

Sir John Eric Erichsen, *Practical Treatise on the Diseases of the Scalp* (London: John Churchill, 1842).

Henri Florette, *Black Migration: Movement North 1900–1920* (Garden City, NY: Anchor Press/Doubleday, 1975).

Eric Foner, *Freedom's Lawmakers* (Baton Rouge: Louisiana State University Press, 1996).

———, and Olivia Mahoney, *America's Reconstruction: People and Politics after the Civil War* (New York: HarperCollins, 1995).

Stephen R. Fox, *The Guardian of Boston: William Monroe Trotter* (New York: Atheneum, 1970).

John Hope Franklin, *From Slavery to Freedom* (5th ed.; New York: Alfred A. Knopf, 1980).

———, *Reconstruction After the Civil War* (Chicago: University of Chicago Press, 1994).

———, *The Free Negro in North Carolina 1790–1860* (Chapel Hill: University of North Carolina Press, 1995; originally published 1943).

E. Franklin Frazier, *Black Bourgeoisie* (New York: Collier Books, 1962).

Alfred C. Fuller, *A Foot in the Door* (New York: McGraw-Hill, 1960).

Willard Gatewood, *Aristocrats of Color: The Black Elite, 1880–1920* (Bloomington: Indiana University Press, 1990).

———, *Slave and Freeman: The Autobiography of George L. Knox* (Lexington, KY: University Press of Kentucky, 1979).

Paula Giddings, *When and Where I Enter: The Impact of Black Women on Race and Sex in America* (New York: William Morrow, 1984).

Ralph Ginzburg, *100 Years of Lynching* (Baltimore: Black Classic Press, 1988).

Polly Anne Graff and Stewart Graff, *Wolfert's Roost: Portrait of a Village* (Irvington-on-Hudson, NY: Washington Irving Press, 1971).

Lorenzo J. Greene, Gary R. Kremer and Antonio F. Holland, *Missouri's Black Heritage* (rev. ed.; Columbia: University of Missouri Press, 1993).

Howard S. Greenfield, *Caruso: An Illustrated Life* (North Pomfret, VT: Trafalgar Square Publishing, 1991).

Beverly Guy-Sheftall, *Daughters of Sorrow: Attitudes Toward Black Women, 1880–1920* (Brooklyn, NY: Carlson Publishing, 1990).

———, and Jo Moore Stewart, *Spelman: A Centennial Celebration* (Atlanta: Spelman College, 1981).

Thurston H. G. Hahn III, Allen R. Saltus, Jr., and Stephen R. James, Jr., *Delta Landing: Historical and Archaeological Investigations of Three Sunken Watercraft at Delta, Madison Parish, Louisiana* (Baton Rouge: Coastal Environments and Vicksburg, U.S. Army Corps of Engineers, June 1994).

Charles E. Hall and Z. R. Pettet, *Negroes in the United States: 1920–32* (Washington, DC: GPO, 1935).

Louis R. Harlan, *Booker T. Washington: The Making of a Black Leader, 1856–1901* (New York: Oxford University Press, 1972).

———, *Booker T. Washington: The Wizard of Tuskegee, 1901–1915* (New York: Oxford University Press, 1983).

Abram L. Harris, *The Negro as Capitalist: A Study of Banking and Business Among American Negroes* (Chicago: Urban Research, 1992 reprint).

Middleton Harris, *The Black Book* (New York: Random House, 1974).

Alferdteen Harrison, ed., *Black Exodus: The Great Migration from the American South* (Jackson: University of Mississippi Press, 1991).

August Heckscher, *Woodrow Wilson* (New York: Collier Books, 1991).

Paul Heinegg, *Free African Americans of North Carolina and Virginia* (3rd ed.; Baltimore: Clearfield Company, 1997).

———, *Free African Americans of Virginia, North Carolina, South Carolina, MD and Delaware* (www.freeafricanamericans.com/Roberts_Skip.htm, March 1999).

Janet Sharp Hermann, *The Pursuit of a Dream* (New York: Oxford University Press, 1981).

Evelyn Brooks Higginbotham, *Righteous Discontent: The Women's Movement in the Black Baptist Church, 1880–1920* (Cambridge, MA: Harvard University Press, 1993).

Robert A. Hill, ed., *The Marcus Garvey and Universal Negro Improvement Association Papers, Vol. I: 1826–August 1919* (Berkeley: University of California Press, 1983).

Darlene Clark Hine, *When the Truth Is Told* (Indianapolis: National Council of Negro Women, Indianapolis Section, 1981).

———, Wilma King and Linda Reed, eds., *We Specialize in the Wholly Impossible* (Brooklyn, NY: Carlson Publishing, 1995).

———, Elsa Barkley Brown and Rosalyn Terborg-Penn, eds., *Black Women in America: An Historical Encyclopedia* (Brooklyn: Carlson Publishing, 1993).

Nathan Irvin Huggins, *Harlem Renaissance* (London: Oxford University Press, 1971).

Langston Hughes, *The Big Sea* (New York: Hill and Wang, 1981; originally published 1930).

Louis C. Hunter, *Steamboats on the Western Rivers: An Economic and Technological History* (New York: Dover Publications, 1993).

Tera W. Hunter, *To 'Joy My Freedom* (Cambridge, MA: Oxford University Press, 1997).

Fred L. Israel, ed., *1897 Sears, Roebuck Catalogue* (Philadelphia: Chelsea House, 1968).

Kristen Iversen, *Molly Brown: Unraveling the Myth* (Boulder, CO: Johnson Books, 1999).

Nathan E. Jacobs, ed., *NHCA's Golden Years* (National Hairdressers and Cosmetologists Association/Western Publishing, 1970).

Stephen R. James, Jr., *Cultural Resources Investigations, Delta Mat Casting Field, Additional Lands, Madison Parish, Louisiana* (Vicksburg, MS: U.S. Army Corps of Engineers, April 1993), submitted by Panamerican Consultants, Inc. (Tuscaloosa, AL).

David A. Jasen and Trebor Jay Tichenor, *Rags and Ragtime* (New York: Seabury, 1978).

James Weldon Johnson, *Along This Way: The Autobiography of James Weldon Johnson* (New York: Penguin Books, 1990).

———, *Black Manhattan* (New York: Alfred A. Knopf, 1930; reprinted New York: Atheneum, 1968).

Beverly Washington Jones, *Quest for Equality: The Life and Writings of Mary Eliza Church Terrell, 1863–1954* (Brooklyn, NY: Carlson Publishing, 1990).

Jacqueline Jones, *Labor of Love, Labor of Sorrow* (New York: Basic Books, 1985).

Bruce Kellner, *The Harlem Renaissance: A Historical Dictionary for the Era* (Westport, CT: Greenwood Press, 1984).

———, ed., *"Keep a-Inchin' Along": Selected Writings of Carl Van Vechten About Black Art and Letters* (Westport, CT: Greenwood Press, 1979).

Charles Flint Kellogg, *NAACP: The National Association for the Advancement of Colored People* (Baltimore: Johns Hopkins University Press, 1967).

Paul Underwood Kellogg, *Wage-Earning Pittsburgh: The Pittsburgh Survey* (6 vols.; New York: Russell Sage Foundation/Survey Associates, Inc., 1914).

Beverley Rae Kimes and Henry Austin Clark, Jr., *Standard Catalog of American Cars: 1805–1942* (3rd ed.; Iola, WI: Krause Publications, 1996).

Jeff Kisseloff, *You Must Remember This: An Oral History of Manhattan from the 1890s to World War II* (San Diego and New York: Harcourt Brace Jovanovich, 1989).

Theodore Kornweibel, Jr., *"Seeing Red": Federal Campaign Against Black Militancy: 1919–1925* (Bloomington: Indiana University Press, 1998).

George L. Lankevich, *American Metropolis: A History of New York City* (New York: New York University Press, 1998).

C. Henri Leonard, *The Hair: Its Growth, Care, Diseases and Treatment* (Detroit: C. Henri Leonard, Medical Book Publishers, 1880).

Stephen J. Leonard and Thomas J. Neal, *Denver: Mining Camp to Metropolis* (Denver: University of Colorado Press, 1990).

Gerda Lerner, *Black Women in White America: A Documentary History* (New York: Vintage Books, 1973).

David Levering Lewis, *When Harlem Was in Vogue* (New York: Alfred A. Knopf, 1981).

———, *W.E.B. Du Bois: Biography of a Race 1868–1919* (New York: Henry Holt, 1993).

C. Eric Lincoln and Lawrence H. Mamiya, *The Black Church in the African American Experience* (Durham: Duke University Press, 1990).

Alain Locke, ed., *The New Negro: Voices of the Harlem Renaissance* (New York: Macmillan, 1992; originally published by Albert & Charles Boni, 1925).

Rayford W. Logan and Michael R. Winston, *Dictionary of American Negro Biography* (New York: W. W. Norton, 1982).

Gordon McKibben, *Cutting Edge: Gillette's Journey to Global Leadership* (Boston: Harvard Business School Press, 1998).

Linda O. McMurry, *To Keep the Waters Troubled: The Life of Ida B. Wells* (New York: Oxford University Press, 1998).

Norris McWhirter, *Guinness Book of World Records, 1980 Super Edition* (New York: Bantam Books, 1979).

The Madam C. J. Walker Beauty Manual (2nd ed., Indianapolis: The Madam C. J. Walker Manufacturing Company, 1940).

Wilma Mankiller, Gwendolyn Mink, Maysa Navarro, Barbara Smith and Gloria Steinem, eds., *The Reader's Companion to U.S. Women's History* (Boston: Houghton Mifflin, 1998).

Carole Marks, *Farewell—We're Good and Gone* (Bloomington: Indiana University Press, 1989).

————, and Diana Edkins, *The Power of Pride: Stylemakers and Rulebreakers of the Harlem Renaissance* (New York: Crown, 1999).

Tony Martin, *Race First: The Ideological and Organizational Struggles of Marcus Garvey and the Universal Negro Improvement Association* (Dover, MA: Majority Press, 1976).

Frank Lincoln Mather, *Who's Who of the Colored Race* (Chicago: Who's Who of the Colored Race, 1915).

William D. Miller, *Memphis During the Progressive Era* (Memphis: Memphis State University, 1957).

Nina Mjagkij, *Light in the Darkness: African Americans and the YMCA, 1852–1946* (Lexington: University Press of Kentucky, 1994).

W. E. Mollison, *The Leading Afro-Americans of Vicksburg, Miss.* (Vicksburg: Biographia Publishing Co., 1908).

Andrew Morrison and John H. C. Irwin, *The Industries of Saint Louis: Her Advantages, Resources, Facilities and Commercial Relations as a Center of Trade and Manufacture* (St. Louis: J. M. Elstner & Co., 1885).

Deirdre Mullane, ed., *Crossing the Danger Water: Three Hundred Years of African American Writing* (New York: Anchor Press/Doubleday, 1993).

William M. Murphy, *Notes from the History of Madison Parish, Louisiana* (1927).

Cynthia Neverdon-Morton, *Afro-American Women and the Advancement of the Race, 1895–1925* (Knoxville: University of Tennessee Press, 1989).

Thomas J. Noel, *Denver Landmarks & Historic Districts: A Pictorial Guide* (Denver: University of Colorado Press, 1996).

Kenneth O'Reilly, *Nixon's Piano* (New York: The Free Press, 1995).

Gilbert Osofsky, *Harlem: The Making of a Ghetto* (2nd ed.; New York: Harper Torchbooks, 1971).

Harry P. Owens, *Steamboats and the Cotton Economy: River Trade in the Yazoo-Mississippi Delta* (Jackson: University Press of Mississippi, 1990).

Nell Irvin Painter, *Exodusters: Black Migration to Kansas After Reconstruction* (New York: Alfred A. Knopf, 1977).

Gerald W. Patton, *War and Race: The Black Officer in the American Military, 1915–1941* (Westport, CT: Greenwood Press, 1981).

Kathy Peiss, *Hope in a Jar: The Making of America's Beauty Culture* (New York: Metropolitan Books/Henry Holt, 1998).

Paula F. Pfeffer, *A. Philip Randolph: Pioneer of the Civil Rights Movement* (Baton Rouge: Louisiana State University Press, 1990).

Eliza Potter, *A Hairdresser's Experience in High Life* (Cincinnati, 1859).

Armistead S. Pride and Clint C. Wilson II, *A History of the Black Press* (Washington, DC: Howard University Press, 1997).

Robert V. Remini, *The Legacy of Andrew Jackson* (Baton Rouge: Louisiana State University Press, 1988).

John William Reps, *St. Louis Illustrated* (Columbia: University of Missouri Press, 1989).

Coy D. Robbins, Jr., *Forgotten Hoosiers: African Heritage in Orange County, Indiana* (Bowie, MD: Heritage Books, 1994).

Dunbar Rowland, *History of Mississippi: The Heart of the South*, Vol. 1 (Chicago and Jackson, MS: S. J. Clarke Publishing Company, 1925).

Nancy Rubin, *The Life and Times of Marjorie Merriweather Post* (New York: Villard Books, 1995).

Elliott Rudwick, *Race Riot at East St. Louis, July 2, 1917* (Urbana: University of Illinois Press, 1982; originally published Carbondale: Southern Illinois University Press, 1964).

Robert W. Rydell, *All the World's a Fair* (Chicago: University of Chicago Press, 1984).

Dorothy Salem, *To Better Our World: Black Women in Organized Reform, 1890–1920*, Vol. 14 of *Black Women in United States History: From Colonial Times to the Present* (Brooklyn, NY: Carlson Publishing, 1990).

Jack Salzman, David Lionel Smith and Cornel West, *Encyclopedia of African-American Culture and History* (New York: Macmillan Library Reference, 1998).

Allon Schoener, ed., *Harlem on My Mind: Cultural Capital of Black America 1900–1978* (New York: Delta/Dell Publishing, 1979).

Elliott P. Skinner, *African Americans and the U.S. Policy Toward Africa, 1850–1924* (Washington, DC: Howard University Press, 1992).

Robert Sklar, *Movie-Made America: A Cultural History of American Movies* (New York: Vintage Books, 1994).

J. Clay Smith, Jr., *Emancipation: The Making of the Black Lawyer 1844–1944* (Philadelphia: University of Pennsylvania Press, 1993).

Eileen Southern, *The Music of Black Americans: A History* (3rd ed.; New York: W. W. Norton, 1997).

Joe Gray Taylor, *Louisiana Reconstructed 1863–1870* (Baton Rouge: Louisiana State University Press, 1974).

Quintard Taylor, *In Search of the Racial Frontier: African Americans in the American West, 1528–1990* (New York: W. W. Norton, 1998).

Rosalyn Terborg-Penn, *African American Women in the Struggle for the Vote* (Bloomington: Indiana University Press, 1998).

James Thomas, *From Tennessee Slave to St. Louis Entrepreneur: The Autobiography of James Thomas*, edited with an introduction by Loren Schweninger (Columbia: University of Missouri Press, 1984).

Mildred I. Thompson, *Ida B. Wells-Barnett: An Exploratory Study of an American Black Woman, 1893–1930* (Brooklyn, NY: Carlson Publishing, 1990).

Emma Lou Thornbrough, *The Negro in Indiana Before 1900: A Study of a Minority* (Indianapolis: Indiana Historical Bureau, 1985; Bloomington: Indiana University Press, 1993).

Stewart E. Tolnay and E. M. Beck, *A Festival of Violence: An Analysis of Southern Lynchings, 1882–1930* (Urbana: University of Illinois Press, 1995).

Selwyn K. Troen and Glen E. Holt, *St. Louis* (New York: New Viewpoints, 1977).

Ted Tunnell, *Crucible of Reconstruction: War, Radicalism, and Race in Louisiana, 1862–1877* (Baton Rouge: Louisiana State University Press, 1984).

William M. Tuttle, Jr., *Race Riot: Chicago in the Red Summer of 1919* (Urbana: University of Illinois Press, 1970).

Carl Van Vechten, *Nigger Heaven* (New York: Alfred A. Knopf, 1926; reprinted Colophon Books, 1971, and Urbana: University of Illinois Press, 2000, with an introduction by Kathleen Pfeiffer).

Charles Vincent, *Black Legislators in Louisiana During Reconstruction* (Baton Rouge: Louisiana State University Press, 1976).

Juliet E. K. Walker, *The History of Black Business in America: Capitalism, Race and Entrepreneurship* (New York: Macmillan Library Reference, 1998).

Joseph Frazier Wall, *Andrew Carnegie* (Pittsburgh: University of Pittsburgh Press, 1989).

Booker T. Washington, *The Negro in Business* (Wichita, KS: DeVore & Sons, 1992; reprint of Hertel, Jenkins & Co., 1907).

———, *Up From Slavery* (New York: Penguin Books, 1986).

T. H. Watkins, *The Great Depression: America in the 1930s* (Boston: Little, Brown, 1993).

Vernon Lane Wharton, *The Negro in Mississippi 1865–1890* (Chapel Hill: University of North Carolina Press, 1947).

C. Albert White, *A History of the Rectangular Survey System* (Washington, DC: GPO, U.S. Department of the Interior, Bureau of Land Management, 1991).

Howard A. White, *The Freedmen's Bureau in Louisiana* (Baton Rouge: Louisiana State University Press, 1970).

Shane White and Graham White, *Stylin'—African American Expressive Culture from Its Beginnings to the Zoot Suit* (Ithaca, NY: Cornell University Press, 1998).

Walter White, *A Man Called White: The Autobiography of Walter White* (Bloomington: Indiana University Press, 1948).

Frederick W. Williamson and George T. Goodman, *Eastern Louisiana: A History of the Watershed of the River and the Florida Parishes* (Shreveport: The Historical Record Association, 1939).

C. Vann Woodward, *Reunion and Reaction: The Compromise of 1877 and the End of Reconstruction* (Boston: Little, Brown, 1951, and Garden City, NY: Doubleday Anchor, 1956).

John A. Wright, *Discovering African-American St. Louis: A Guide to Historic Sites* (St. Louis: Missouri Historical Society Press, 1994).

Nathan B. Young, *Your St. Louis and Mine* (St. Louis: N. B. Young, 1937).

Robert L. Zangrando, *The NAACP Crusade Against Lynching, 1909–1950* (Philadelphia: Temple University Press, 1980).

Howard Zinn, *A People's History of the United States, 1492–Present* (New York: HarperCollins, 1995).

Government and Legal Documents

Della Hammond Ashley, Eastern Cherokee Application No. 25682, National Archives, Reel 213, M1104 Cabinet 094-01.

Owen Breedlove and Minerva Anderson, Marriage bond (Nov. 20, 1869) and license (Dec. 6, 1869), Madison Parish, Louisiana, 13th District Court, Book B page 29, MPCH.

Owen Breedlove and Mary Lewis, Marriage bond (Aug. 26, 1874) and license (Aug. 27, 1874), Madison Parish, Louisiana, 13th District Court, Book B page 378, MPCH.

Adoption of Fairy Mae Bryant by Mrs. Lelia Walker Robinson, Decree of Court, Court of Common Pleas of Allegheny County, Pennsylvania, No. 505 January Term, 1913, Docket "A."

Cholera Epidemic of 1873, House Executive Document 95, 43rd Congress, Second Session (Washington, DC: GPO, 1875).

"Climate and Crops, Nebraska Section," Climate and Crop Service of the Weather Bureau, U.S. Department of Agriculture, Lincoln, Nebraska, Vol. 10, No. 7, July 1905.

The Consolidation and Revision of the Statutes of a General Nature (New Orleans, 1852).

Heirs of Burney v. John T. Ludeling, Vol. 3 (1895), Louisiana Supreme Court, 47 La. Ann. 1434, 17 SO. 877.

Jennie Lias—Jennie Lias affidavit, Dec. 26, 1919.

Walter H. Loving report to Director of Military Intelligence on National Race Congress, Dec. 20, 1918, RG 165, File 10218-302, Records of the War Dept. General and Special Staffs, Correspondence of the Military Intelligence Division, Correspondence relating to "Negro Subversion," Microfilm M1440.

Charles B. McKernan Affidavit, Receiver's Office, Ouachita, LA, Nov. 18, 1842, Receipt No 7699.

Madison Parish Deed Book COB: B page 289–290, "Caruther & Co. to Burney," MPCH.

Records of the Bureau of Refugees, Freedmen, and Abandoned Lands, Records of the Assistant Commissioner for the State of Louisiana, 1865–1869, Washington, DC, National Archives, Record Group 105, Microfilm 1027, roll 27, frames 16, 63, 262; roll 34, frames 206–308, National Archives.

Records of the Bureau of Refugees, Freedmen, and Abandoned Lands, Record Group 105, Entry 1400 Morning Reports of the Assistant Surgeon at Birney Plantation January 1864–February 1865, Louisiana Chief Medical Officer, Box No 40, National Archives.

Report of the Joint Committee of the General Assembly of Louisiana on the Conduct of the Late Elections and the Condition of Peace and Order in the State, Session of 1869 (New Orleans, 1869).

Report and Testimony of the Select Committee of the United States Senate to Investigate the Causes of the Removal of the Negroes from the Southern States to the Northern States, 46th Congress, 2d Session, Report 693, Parts I, II and III (Washington, DC: GPO, 1880).

Lelia Robinson v. John Robinson, No. 1740 October Term 1913, Testimony Before Master, Court of Common Pleas of Allegheny County, July 16, 1914.

John B. Robison (sic) and Lelia McWilliams, Washington County, PA, Marriage License Application #18667, Oct. 18, 1909; Washington County, PA, Marriage Certificate #18667 Clerk of Courts.

Southern Claims Commission, Case No 20441, Estate of R. W. Burney v. the United States, Testimony of Congressman Greenburg Fort, Mar. 5, 1874.

U.S. Bureau of the Census, *Seventh Census of the United States: 1850* (Washington, DC: GPO).

———, *Eighth Census of the United States: 1860* (Washington, DC: GPO).

———, *Eleventh Census of the United States: 1890* (Washington, DC: GPO, 1893).

U.S. Department of Interior, Bureau of Land Management, Eastern States Land Grant Certificate #7699, General Land Office, Feb. 4, 1843.

Sarah Walker v. Charles J. Walker, Cause No. 87943, Marion County Superior Court Docket, Sept. 5, 1912.

Ida B. Winchester affidavit, Dec. 26, 1919.

Convention Proceedings

Madam Walker Hair Culturists' Union

Minutes of the First National Convention of the Mme. C. J. Walker Hair Culturists' Union of America, Philadelphia, Pennsylvania, Aug. 30–31, 1917.

National Association of Colored Women

Report of the First National Conference of the National Federation of Afro-American Women, Boston, Mass., July 29, 30 and 31, 1895, in Records of the National Association of Colored Women's Clubs, 1895–1992, Part I: Minutes of National Conventions, Publications, and President's Office Correspondence (Bethesda, MD: University Publications of America, 1993).

Mrs. M. F. Pitts and Miss L. Carter, "St. Louis Colored Orphan's Home," in Report of the Second National Conference of the National Federation of Afro-American Women, Washington, DC, July 20–22, 1896, from Records of the National Association of Colored Women's Clubs, 1895–1992, Part I: Minutes of National Conventions, Publications, and President's Office Correspondence (Bethesda, MD: University Publications of America, 1993).

Fourth Convention of the National Association of Colored Women (Jefferson City, MO: Hugh Stephens Printing Company, 1904): p. 3, RNACWC microfilm, 1895–1992, reel I, frames 0276–0297, LOC.

Minutes of the Eighth Biennial Convention of the NACW, July 23–27, 1912, Hampton Normal and Industrial Institute, LOC.

Minutes of the Ninth Biennial Convention of the NACW, Aug. 4–6, 1914, Wilberforce, OH, LOC.

Minutes of the Tenth Biennial Convention of the NACW, Aug. 7–10, 1916, Baltimore, MD, LOC.

Minutes of the Eleventh Biennial Convention of the NACW, July 8 to 13, 1918 (Washington, DC: NACW, 1918), LOC Microfilm.

National Negro Business League

Report of the Second Annual Convention of the National Negro Business League at Chicago, Illinois, Aug. 21–23, 1901 (Chicago: R. S. Abbott Publishing Company, 1901).

Report of the Fourth Annual Convention of the National Negro Business League (Wilberforce, OH, 1903).

Report of the Sixth Annual Convention of the National Negro Business League held in New York City, Aug. 16th–18th, 1905.

Report of the 13th Annual Convention of the NNBL held at Chicago, Illinois, Aug. 21–23, 1912.

Report of the 14th Annual Convention of the National Negro Business League, Philadelphia, Aug. 20, 21, 22, 1913 (Washington, DC: William H. Davis, Official Stenographer).

Annual Report of the 15th Annual Convention of the National Negro Business League, Muskogee, Oklahoma, Aug. 19–21, 1914 (Nashville: AME Sunday School Union, 1914).

National Negro Business League Annual Report of the Sixteenth Session and the Fifteenth Anniversary Convention, Aug. 18–20, 1915, LOC Microfilm.

National Negro Business League Report of the Seventeenth Annual Session, Kansas City, Missouri, Aug. 16–18, 1916 (Washington, DC: William H. Davis, 1916).

National Negro Business League Report of the Eighteenth and Nineteenth Annual Sessions, Chattanooga, Tenn., 1917, and Atlantic City, NJ, 1918 (Washington, DC: William H. Davis, 1918).

National Negro Cosmetic Manufacturers Association
Minutes of the National Negro Cosmetic Manufacturers Association, Sept. 5, 1917, New York, MWC/IHS.
Poro Company
"Poro" in Pictures with a Short History of Its Development (St. Louis: Poro College, 1926).
Second National Poro Convention Souvenir Program (Chicago: July 24–26, 1949).

Periodicals, Articles, Essays and Reports
L. M. Campbell Adams, "An Investigation of Housing and Living Conditions in Three Districts of Indianapolis," *Indiana University Bulletin, Indiana University Studies,* Vol. 8, No. 8 (Sept. 1910).
Albert Anderson, "The Amazing Inside Story of the Malone Case," *The Light and "Heebie Jeebies,"* Vol. 3, No. 13, Chicago, Feb. 19, 1927.
Rose Atwood, "Frederick Douglass Memorial," *The Competitor,* Vol. 1, No. 2 (Feb. 1920).
Jonathan Beasley, "Blacks—Slave and Free—Vicksburg, 1850–1860," *Journal of Mississippi History,* Vol. 38, No. 1 (Feb. 1976).
Konrad Bercovici, "The Black Blocks of Manhattan," *Harper's Monthly Magazine,* nd (after 1923), Gumby Scrapbooks, Vol. 40/41, LLCU.
Carolyn Brady, "Indianapolis and the Great Migration, 1900–1920," *Black History News & Notes,* No. 65 (Aug. 1996).
Josephine B. Bruce, "The Afterglow of the Women's Convention," *Voice of the Negro,* Nov. 1904.
Nannie Helen Burroughs, "Not Color But Character," *Voice of the Negro,* July 1904.
Civic League of St. Louis, "The Smoke Nuisance; Report of the Smoke Abatement Committee of the Civic League" (St. Louis: The Civic League of St. Louis, 1906), in Selwyn K. Troen and Glen E. Holt, *St. Louis* (New York: New Viewpoints, 1977).
Katharine T. Corbett and Mary E. Seematter, "Black St. Louis at the Turn of the Century," *Gateway Heritage,* Vol. 7, No. 1 (Summer 1986).
James G. Dauphine, "The Knights of the White Camellia and the Election of 1868: Louisiana's White Terrorists; a Benighting Legacy," *Louisiana History,* Vol. 30, No. 2 (Spring 1989)
Frances Garside, "Queen of Gotham's Colored 400," *Literary Digest,* Vol. 55 (Oct. 13, 1917).
Mabel K. Hamlin, "Meet Me at Scholtz's," *Colorado Magazine,* Vol. 36, No. 4 (Oct. 1959).
The Indianapolis Study/Flanner House (Indianapolis: Flanner House, 1939).
Howard J. Jones, "Biographical Sketches of Members of the 1868 Louisiana State Senate," *Louisiana History,* Vol. 19, No. 1 (Winter 1978).
Michael Lerner, "'Hoping for a Splendid Summer': African American St. Louis, Ragtime and the Louisiana Purchase Exposition," *Gateway Heritage,* Winter 1998–99.
August Meier and David Levering Lewis, "History of the Negro Upper Class in Atlanta, Georgia, 1890–1958," *Journal of Negro Education,* Vol. 28 (Spring 1959).
National League on Urban Conditions Among Negroes, *Housing Conditions Among Negroes in Harlem, New York City* (New York, 1915).
Pennsylvania Negro Business Directory: Industrial and Material Growth of the Negroes of Pennsylvania, 1910 (Harrisburg, PA: Jas. H. W. Howard & Son, 1910).
A. E. Perkins, "Some Negro Officers and Legislators in Louisiana," *Journal of Negro History,* Vol. 14 (Oct. 1929).

Emmett J. Scott, "Louisiana Purchase Exposition," *Voice of the Negro*, Aug. 1904.

Jeffrey E. Smith, "A Mirror Held to St. Louis: William Marion Reedy and the 1904 World's Fair," *Gateway Heritage*, Vol. 19, No. 1 (Summer 1998).

Matilda Thomas, Speech to the United Daughters of the Confederacy, reprinted in Kentucky *New Era*, June 22, 1963.

Katherine D. Tillman, "Paying Professions for Colored Girls" *Voice of the Negro*, Jan. and Feb. 1907.

Charles Vincent, "Negro Leadership and Programs in the Louisiana Constitutional Convention of 1868," *Louisiana History*, Vol. 10, No. 4 (Fall 1969).

Harry B. Webber, "Grim Awakening to Her Future Was Incentive to Mme. Walker," *Pittsburgh Courier*, Mar. 15, 1952.

Fannie Barrier Williams, "The Colored Girl," *Voice of the Negro*, June 1905.

Lillian S. Williams, "And Still I Rise: Black Women and Reform, Buffalo, New York, 1900–1940," in Darlene Clark Hine, Wilma King and Linda Reed, eds., *We Specialize in the Wholly Impossible* (Brooklyn, NY: Carlson Publishing, 1995).

Sue Ann Wood, "The 1904 World's Fair," *St. Louis Post-Dispatch Magazine* (reprint), June 16, 1996.

Newspapers

Chicago Bee
Chicago Defender
Denver Statesman
Indianapolis Freeman
Indianapolis Recorder
Indianapolis World
Inter-State Tattler
Madison Journal
New York Age
Pittsburgh Courier
Richmond Compiler
St. Louis Post-Dispatch
St. Louis Republic
Washington Afro-American

Pamphlets

Historical and Descriptive Review of Denver (Denver: Jno. Lathem, circa 1902).

Marjorie Stewart Joyner, "The Saga of the First Woman Millionaire Manufacturer" (convention booklet circa 1946–48).

R. C. Overton, *The First Ninety Years: An Historical Sketch of the Burlington Railroad 1850–1940* (Chicago: Chicago, Burlington & Quincy Railroad, 1940).

G. Richard Peck, *The Rise and Fall of Camp Sherman* (Chillicothe: U.S. National Park Service, 1972).

Violet Reynolds, "The Story of a Remarkable Woman" (Indianapolis: The Madam C. J. Walker Mfg. Co., 1973).

The Saint Louis of To-Day Illustrated: An Artistic Presentation of Her Business Interests (St. Louis: The Western Commercial Travelers' Association, 1888).

Seeing Denver (Denver: American Sight-seeing Car & Coach Company, 1904).

City Directories
Denver City Directories, 1890–1920
Indianapolis City Directories, 1909–1920
St. Louis City Directories, 1879–1908
Vicksburg City Directory, 1877

Unpublished Master's Papers and Doctoral Dissertations
Carson A. Anderson, "The Architectural Practice of Vertner W. Tandy: An Evaluation of the Professional and Social Position of a Black Architect," master's thesis, University of Virginia School of Architecture, 1982.

Clyde Nickerson Bolden, "Indiana Avenue: Black Entertainment Boulevard," MCP thesis, Boston University School of Planning, 1983.

Lawrence Oland Christensen, "Black St. Louis: A Study in Race Relations 1865–1916," unpublished Ph.D. dissertation, University of Missouri, Dec. 1972.

Alonzo Moron, "Distribution of the Negro Population in Pittsburgh, 1910–1930," MA thesis, University of Pittsburgh, 1933 (University of Pittsburgh, Hillman Library, microfilm).

Gwendolyn Robinson, "Class, Race, and Gender: A Transcultural Theoretical and Sociohistorical Analysis of Cosmetic Institutions and Practices to 1920," unpublished Ph.D. dissertation, University of Illinois at Chicago, 1984 (Ann Arbor: University Microfilm International, 1984).

Jacqueline Wolfe, "The Changing Pattern of Residence of the Negro in Pittsburgh," unpublished MS thesis, University of Pittsburgh, 1964 (University of Pittsburgh, Hillman Library).

Unpublished Sources
E. M. Beck, "Listing of Lynching Victims: Mississippi, 1882–1930," Feb. 26, 1996.

John E. Hale, Jan. 21, 1995, memo, "First Generation," Canton, MS, Madison County Library Files.

Sarah Hull, "Bea, the Washerwoman," *Federal Writers Project #3709*, Southern Historical Collection, Library of the University of North Carolina at Chapel Hill, Mar. 13, 1939.

"Human Interest Story: Madam Walker," unpublished essay from Madison Parish Library.

James Arthur Thomas, Jr., Burney and Williamson Family Papers.

Charles Turner Scrapbooks Collection, MHS.

Ida Webb Bryant, "Glimpses of the Negro in Indianapolis—1863–1963," unpublished manuscript, IHS.

"Inventory of Remains" (from Madison Parish) and accompanying letters from Brig. Gen. H. M. Whittlesey, OCHM.

"The Reminiscences of A. Philip Randolph," transcript of interview by Wendell Wray, 1972, Oral History Research, Columbia University.

Audio Interviews
Regina and William Andrews—July 8, 1982
Richmond Barthé—Feb. 2, 1983
Margaret Bryant—Sept. 9, 1982
Dick Campbell—Nov. 17, 1982

Jimmie Daniels—July 6, 1982
Marion Moore Day—Nov. 14, 1982
Geraldyn Dismond (Gerri Major)—June 21, 1982
Zenobia "Peg" Fisher—Mar. 20, 1983
Mildred Randolph Foster—Aug. 2, 1982
Revella Hughes—Nov. 19, 1982
Marjorie Stewart Joyner—1981 and Aug. 1, 1982
Vivian Kaufman—Nov. 30, 1982
A'Lelia Ransom Nelson—Dec. 1982
Bruce Nugent—Nov. 11, 1982
Marion R. Perry, Jr.— Jan. 12, 1976, and July 11, 1982
Violet Davis Reynolds—Dec. 26, 1975
Alberta Williams and Lucy Davis—Aug. 7, 1982
Judge Nathan Young—Aug. 5, 1982

Permissions

Acknowledgments

Most of all, *On Her Own Ground* has been a labor of love. That labor, of course, has been made much sweeter by the participation of scores of people who have contributed with their personal memories, scholarly research, suggestions, questions, moral support and encouragement. Even at the most difficult moments—and there always are some—I was fortified by the knowledge that so many friends were waiting for the book parties and so many scholars were waiting for the footnotes.

Of course, I owe a tremendous debt of gratitude to several historians and biographers who have been generous with both their time and their scholarship. Just as it has been my good fortune that my family inheritance from Madam Walker was the gift of a phenomenal story, so have I also had the advantage of conducting my research during the last three decades of the twentieth century when the history of African Americans and of women has flourished as never before both at the university and in popular culture. With the caveat that I know I have forgotten someone essential, I must single out a few who, in some instances, have been a part of this journey almost as long as I have been on it.

First I must give special thanks to historian Adele Logan Alexander, whose friendship and eagerness to share research I have valued ever since we discovered nearly twenty years ago that our grandmothers had known each other. To Gordon Cotton of the Old Court House Museum in Vicksburg, who has never failed to go out of his way to answer my most obscure questions. To Phyllis Garland, my adviser at Columbia University Graduate School of Journalism, who guided me through my first serious attempt at telling this story. To Willard Gatewood, whose books, *Aristocrats of Color* and *Slave and Freeman: The Autobiography of George Knox*, served as important sources, and who has been extremely generous in sharing precious gems of information. To archivist Wilma Gibbs, whose stewardship of the Madam Walker Collection at the Indiana Historical Society provides me with the assurance that the papers are in excellent hands, and whose early reading of the manuscript kept me on the right track. To Paula Giddings, whose *When and Where I Enter* helped pave the way for much of today's scholarship on black women and whose discovery of harpist Frances Spencer's story found its way into these pages. To the late Nathan Irvin Huggins, who willingly gave advice when I was a graduate student, then arranged for me to write *Madam C. J. Walker: Entrepreneur*, my young adult biography, while he was a senior consulting editor at Chelsea House Publishers. To Carl Van Vechten's biographer Bruce Kellner, whose book *The Harlem Renaissance: A Historical Dictionary for the Era* remained next to my Webster's and Roget's and whose tough and thoughtful questions pushed me. To David Levering Lewis, whose beautifully crafted books—*When Harlem Was in Vogue* and *W.E.B. Du Bois: Biography of a Race*—set a high bar and who kindly introduced me to one of his longtime researchers. To Nell Irvin Painter, whose seminal scholarship in *The Exodusters* illuminated late-nineteenth-century Louisiana and Mississippi, and who provided an intellectual role model for me when I was still a college student. To Arnold Rampersad, whose devotion to the art of biography inspires me and who took my work seriously long before I had anything on paper. To Kathy Peiss, whose work on women in the cosmetics and hair care industries has given it credibility as an area worthy of scholarly pursuit. To Coy D. Robbins, Jr., a gifted and meticulous genealogist whose vast knowledge of African Americans in Indiana introduced me to another amazing branch of my family tree—with roots in the Revolutionary War, no less—about whom I knew almost nothing. To Juliet E. K. Walker, whose exhaustive scholarship on the history of black entrepreneurs has been invaluable.

In 1980 as I was moving from Houston to Atlanta, I first learned of R. W. Burney—the man on whose plantation this story began—when I made a fortuitous detour to Delta, Louisiana. A few years later some of his descendants and I began to develop a friendship that continues to this day. I am especially indebted to Captain R. Burney Long, Anna Long Case and their cousin, the late James A. Thomas, who provided access to Burney family papers and helped me understand their own very interesting family.

Researching a biography of this scope requires many hands. I am fortunate to have had, at various times during the last three years, the assistance of four tireless researchers: James Harper; Charles D. Johnson, who never complained about some of my more obscure requests; Charles Cooney, who is a master at ferreting out lost documents and who persisted until he discovered the Military Intelligence Division records I had wanted for so long; and Natasha Mitchell, whose determination and fresh eye uncovered details about the life of one of Madam Walker's surprisingly peripatetic brothers. As well, I am grateful to William R. Sevier and Richard P. Sevier, who combed through documents and ledgers in Louisiana and Mississippi for long-forgotten marriage licenses and property deeds.

It truly requires uncommon commitment to be willing to read downloaded computer files and unbound manuscripts. Thankfully there were many who were willing to do so. I am indebted to Helen Baker, who enthusiastically read each chapter as soon as it was written and who raised perspectives I had not considered. To Avarita Hanson, who has been an enthusiastic advocate of my various Walker "projects" since the mid-1970s and whose insightful questions I hope I have answered adequately in the final manuscript. To Susan McHenry, who edited my first published magazine article about Madam Walker and who cares about this story as much as I do. To Ishmael Reed for long ago helping me believe that I really was a writer. I know I benefited immensely from the helpful suggestions of others who read all or part of the manuscript, including Teri Agins, Desne Crossley, George Curry, Maceo Crenshaw Dailey, Jr., David Evans, Sam Fullwood, Henry Louis Gates, Jr., Kenneth Hamilton, Julianne Malveaux, Jill Nelson, Claudia Polley, Cokie Roberts, Lynn Sherr, Bernie Sofronski, Stanley Warren, Cheryl West, Jack E. White, Lillian Williams and Thomas Wirth.

When I first began to research Madam Walker's life, several Walker Company employees and their families welcomed me into their homes and freely shared their memories. Special thanks to Mary Pendegraph, Alice and William T. Ray, Russell White, Tony and Lucy Reynolds and A'Lelia Ransom Nelson. Although they are gone, I still must express my gratitude to the late Marie Overstreet and Willard B. Ransom, as well as Myrtis Griffin, Marjorie Stewart Joyner, Vivian Kaufman and Violet Reynolds, who were particularly adept at describing the early years of the Walker Company.

During the last three decades, there have been scores of people who have provided their professional expertise, helped me locate essential puzzle pieces, offered wise counsel and, in many instances, were willing to speak with me although we had never met. My thanks to Dr. William Alexander, Carson Anthony Anderson, Reid Badger, Etta Moten Barnett, E. M. Beck, Edward F. Bergman, Timuel Black, Charles Blockson of the Blockson Collection, Robert J. Booker of Knoxville College, Gaynell Theodore Catherine, Paul Coates, Robert DeForrest, Vincent DeForrest, AME Church historiographer Dennis Dickerson, Richard Dozier, Michael Flug of the Vivian G. Harsh Research Collection at the Chicago Public Library, Mildred Franklin, Donald Gallup of the Beinecke Collection at Yale University, Bettye Gardner, James Gascho, Earl Graves, Donna Griffin, Beverly Guy-Sheftall, Louis R. Harlan, Evelyn Brooks Higginbotham, Robert Hill, Beth Howse and Jean Carney Smith of Special Collections at the Fisk University Library, Dante James, John H. Johnson, Geri Duncan Jones of the American Health and Beauty Aids Institute, John Jordan, Randall Kennedy, Gwendolyn Kenney and her daughters, Linda and Diane Kenney, Susan Krampe of the Fuller Brush Company, Patricia La Pointe of the Memphis Shelby County Public Library, Larry Lester, Jack Lufkin of the State Historical Society of Iowa, Herman "Skip" Mason, Jr., Linda McDowell of the Butler Collection at the Little Rock Public Library, Susan McElrath of the National Archives for Black Women's History, C. Stuart McGehee of Bluefield, West Virginia's Craft Memorial Library, Carole Merritt of the Herndon Home, Grace Moore of Philadelphia's Union Baptist Church, Yvette Moyo, Sally Nichols of the Ross-Chillicothe Convention and Visitors Bureau, Marc Pachter, Raymond Petrie, Basil Phillip, Rick Rennert, Noliwe Rooks, Loren Schweninger, Taronda Spencer of Spelman College, Ruth Ann Stewart, Fred Sweets, Sister Francesca Thompson, Bridget Warren, Steven Watson, Donald West, Daniel Williams of Tuskegee University, Deborah Willis, Diana Willis of the Jamaican Tourist Board and Dr. Sondra Kathryn Wilson.

Several organizations and their members have been instrumental as well. Among them are the Association of Black Women Historians, especially Elizabeth Clarke-Lewis, Bettye Collier-Thomas, Gloria Dickinson, Carolyn Dorsey, Sharon Harley, Sylvia Jacobs, Rosalyn Terborg-Penn and Lillian Williams, who welcomed me into their sisterhood; the Afro American Historical and Genealogical Society and its president, Barbara Dodson Walker; and the Association for the Study of Afro American Life and History.

Since 1975 I have traveled to more than a dozen cities in pursuit of the Walker women's story. In each city there were several friends who opened their doors. For their kindness, I am especially grateful to Gladys Lipkin and the late Nathan Lipkin, who provided the keys to their New York apartment in 1997, surely allowing me to stretch my travel and research budget by several more weeks. To Julia Branton Jones, who made me feel welcome in Pine Bluff, Arkansas, even though I spent most of my visit in the library. To Gordon Lewis, who was my host in Los Angeles for a few days when I was completing my first book about Madam Walker. And to Helena and Harold Doley, the current residents of Villa Lewaro, who gave me unlimited access to my great-great-grandmother's former home on my visits to Irvington during 1997 and 1998.

In Madison Parish, Louisiana, I am grateful to Hazel Ellerbee of the Madison Parish Courthouse, James Griffin, James and Eudora Hill, Rosalind Hodges, Mayor Theodore Lindsey, Charlie Mitchell, Judge Alwine Ragland, Codie Ray, Phyllis Scurria, Henry Clay Sevier, Clara Blondelle Surles, Martha Wade, Martin Williams, Zelma Wyche, Gay Yerger, the members of Women Together, the Madam C. J. Walker Temple No. 648 of The Elks and the Madison Parish Historical Society. In Vicksburg I must give special thanks to Lenore Barkley of the Vicksburg Convention and Visitors Bureau, Irene Beach, Josephine Calloway, Patty K. Elliott at the U. S. Army Corps of Engineers, Honorable George Flaggs, Jr., Kelly Franco, Hobbs Freeman, Janie Gardner, Laura Jones, former mayor Joseph Loviza, Zelmarine Anderson Murphy, Thelma Rush, Doris Sanders, Patricia Anderson Segrest, Blanche Terry, Dorothy and Tillman Whitley, and Emma Lee Wilson.

Acknowledgments

In Missouri my research benefited from the expertise of Charles E. Brown of the St. Louis Mercantile Library; Ernestine Hardge, Dennis Northcott, Debbie Schraut, Jason Stratman, Carol Verble and Dina Young of the Missouri Historical Society; Jean E. Meeh Gosebrink, Noel Holobeck, Cynthia Millar, Kathleen Smith and the microfilm-room staff of the St. Louis Public Library; Kenn Thomas, Ann Morris and William Fischetti of the Western History Collection at the University of Missouri at St. Louis; Joan Wibbenmeyer and Ann Rogers of the State Historical Society of Missouri; Recorder of Deeds Sharon Quigley Carpenter and archivist Tom Gruenenfelder; St. Louis Public Schools archivist Sharon Huffman; St. Louis Police Department librarian Barbara Miksicek; *St. Louis American* publisher Donald Suggs and James Vincent of River Tours. I also appreciate the help of Elise Davis, Melba Sweets, Geraldine Ambrose Wells, Ernestine White, Jean Neal and Joan Williams of the Annie Malone Children's Home and Monica Peterson and Reverend Felix Dancy of St. Paul AME Church.

In Denver my thanks go to Justina Grizzard of St. Paul AME, Jacqueline Lawson, Wallace Yvonne McNair of the Black America West Museum, and Gwendolyn Crenshaw, Eleanor M. Gehres, James Jeffrey and Kay Wisnia of the Western History/Genealogy Department of the Denver Public Library. In Pittsburgh, I am grateful to Reverend Elsie Neal and Pearl Woolridge and Kevin Burrell of the University of Pittsburgh's Hillman Library.

In Indianapolis I am particularly indebted to Frances Stout, Claudia Polley and Jean Spears, as well as to Bruce Johnson, Peter Harstad and Susan Sutton of the Indiana Historical Society and John Selch at the Indiana State Museum. Special gratitude must go the staff and board of the Madame Walker Theatre Center, especially Karen Ann Lloyd, Mildred Ball and Charles Blair, who are among those dedicated many who keep Madam Walker's legacy alive. In Pine Bluff, Arkansas, my thanks go to Brenda Tatum of the Pine Bluff Public Library and to James Leslie.

In New York I must acknowledge the assistance of Howard Dodson, Diana Lachatenere, Troy Belle, Lela Sewall and Allison Quammie at the Schomburg Center for Research in Black Culture, as well as Michael Adams, Ruth Ellington, Bobby Short, Stanley Nelson (whose film *Two Dollars and a Dream* first brought Madam Walker's story to a national television audience) and Anne Easterling and Marguerite Lavin of the Museum of the City of New York. In Irvington-on-Hudson and Westchester Country, New York, I am grateful to Elizabeth Fuller and Katherine Hite of the Westchester County Historical Society; Tema Harnik; Anne Herman; Kevin Ruane and Diana Maull of the Westchester County Office of County Clerk; Larry Schopfer; Elaine Massena of the Westchester Country Archives and especially to Peter Oley, Karen Schatzel, Douglas Wilson and Betsy Griggs of the Irvington Historical Society; and Agnes Sinko and Lenora Munigle of the Irvington Public Library.

In Washington thanks go to Ardie Myers, Sheridan Harvey and Jeffrey Flannery at the Library of Congress. To Thomas Battle, Joellen El-Bashir and Janet Sims-Wood at the Moorland-Spingarn Research Center at Howard University. To John A. Vernon, Matthew Fulgham and especially Reggie Washington at the National Archives. And to Edwin Bearrs at the National Park Service.

I am grateful for the understanding of my Radcliffe College Alumnae Association colleagues, especially Mary Carty, Judith Stanton and Jane Tewksbury, and for the support of my ABC News colleagues Robin Sproul, Jane Brooks Aylor and Glennwood Branche.

My mother's Pine Bluff, Palmer Memorial Institute and Howard University friends—including Sterling Branton, Erness Bright Brody, Roselyn Payne Epps, Jewell

Means Greer, Lu Juana Hunter and Blanche Currie Stephens—have provided important information and encouragement.

My personal network has sustained me even when I was in my "writer's cocoon." I thank them all for tolerating my inattentiveness. Reverend Annette Barnes, Beverly Branton Lamberson, Linda Chastang, Cassandra Clayton, Deborah Gentry Davis, Reverend June Gatlin, Gwen Russell Green, Sandra Gregg, Gwen Ifill, Marie Johns, Susan LaSalla, Rebecca Lipkin, Dianne Martin, Arona McNeill-Vann, Cheryl McQueen, Michel Martin, Gloria Murray, Njambi, Henri Norris, Dennis Powell, Judy Ransom, Reverend Marilynn Sasportas Robinson, Carole Simpson, Jane E. Smith, Diana Wallette, Gladys Watkins, Brenda Young, and Bill and Antoinette White.

While they were alive, the following people provided important insights and hospitality: Romare Bearden, Jimmie Daniels, Julia Davis, Lucy Davis, Zenobia "Peg" Fisher, Alex Haley, Alberta Hunter, Jean Blackwell Hutson, Geraldyn Dismond Major, Bruce Nugent, Alyeene Perry, David Rice, Alberta Williams, and Judge Nathan Young.

There are no words adequate enough to thank my family: my father, S. Henry Bundles, who has always been my enthusiastic advocate; my late mother, A'Lelia Mae Perry Bundles, who remains my inspiration; my brother, Lance, whose encouragement is a blessing; my brother, Mark, who I hope will benefit from the knowledge in these pages; and my late grandfather, Marion R. Perry, who preserved the treasures of my childhood.

This book, of course, would not have been possible without my editor, Lisa Drew, who had faith in it from the very beginning. I could not have asked for more consistent or caring support. My thanks also go to her assistant, Jake Klisivitch, who suggested the title. As well I am grateful to my agent Gail Ross and my attorney Ken Kaufman, who have helped advise me throughout this process.

And finally, but not least, I happily thank Frederick Cooke, my heart and my balance.

Index